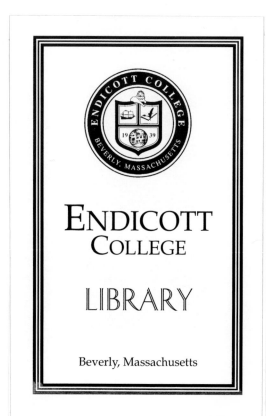

New York Shakespeare Festival.
Avery Brooks, Reyno and
Latanya Richardson in *Spell #7*.
Photo: Martha Swope.

A Resource Book of
Nonprofit Professional Theatres
in the United States

David J. Skal, Editor
Michael Finnegan, Associate Editor
Bob Callahan, Design Consultant

Introduction by John Houseman

Published by Theatre Communications Group, Inc.
New York

Dedication

To the memory of Jules Irving (1925-1979), whose work, beginning in 1952 when he founded the Actors Workshop with Herbert Blau, helped us all in extending our vision of the nonprofit professional theatre, and who was a major force in the establishment of TCG.

Photo: Martha Swope.

Theatre Communications Group, Inc.

Peter Zeisler
Director

Lindy Zesch
Arthur Bartow
Associate Directors

Board of Directors

Gordon Davidson
President

W. Duncan Ross
Vice President

Robert Moss
Secretary/Treasurer

Jane Alexander
Albert Andrews, Jr.
Lee Breuer
James Clark
Zelda Fichandler
Richard Foreman
Stuart Gordon

John Hirsch
Jon Jory
Marjorie Kellogg
Ming Cho Lee
Lynne Meadow
Sara O'Connor
Lloyd Richards
Alan Schneider
Rosemarie Tichler
Robert Tolan
Luis Valdez
Douglas Turner Ward
Paul Weidner
Lanford Wilson
Peter Zeisler

TCG gratefully acknowledges the support of the William H. Donner Foundation, Exxon Corporation, the Ford Foundation, the National Endowment for the Arts, the New York State Council on the Arts, and the Andrew W. Mellon Foundation.

The editor wishes to thank the following people for their support, advice and special assistance during the lengthy editorial process: Kate Barefield, Kirsten Beck, Lance Brilliantine, Peter Burbage, Paul Casadonte, Cynthia Crumlish, Marsue Cumming, Suzanne Ford, Gerry Goodstein, Daniel Hincks, Caryn Katkin, Mike Marciano, Stephen Murray, and Judy Wilson.

Manufactured by Lithographics, Inc., Canton, CT

LC 76-641618   Volume 4
ISBN 0-930452-07-0   Price: $12.95

Contents

Introduction
John Houseman

Actors Theatre of Louisville.
Denny Dillon in *Getting Out*.
Photo: David S. Talbott.

With its 39,000 performances this past year in more than 160 theatres in 85 cities and towns, America's nonprofit professional theatre needs no introduction (though one could still wish for a less prosaic name for the rich and variegated thing it has become). Indeed, as I sit down to write the foreword to this fourth volume of *Theatre Profiles,* I feel rather like the last speaker at a banquet at which my predecessors—with more knowledge and greater eloquence than I possess— have dealt conclusively with most of the subjects to which I was prepared to address myself. Not only was *Theatre Profiles 3* a beautiful book, astonishing in the scope and variety of the theatrical activities it described: it was preceded by two pieces that admirably defined the nature and function of those new institutions that "have succeeded not only in reconstituting the geography of the theatre in America, but also in stimulating a redefinition of the theatre as a humanistic and unifying force."

In his introduction, Gordon Davidson spoke with the double authority of president of the Theatre Communications Group and head of one of the leading theatres in this country when he boldly assumed certain broad artistic and social responsibilities not normally associated with the entertainment business and accepted on behalf of the nonprofit professional theatre "a role in society that goes far beyond the sum of individual productions or the development of a subscription audience."

TCG director Peter Zeisler reinforced Davidson's claim when he observed that "a major reason these theatres have developed such large and diverse audiences is that they are not just performance facilities or pieces of real estate operated for commercial advantage. They are institutions that have devised ways of reaching out to their own special audiences by preparing and delivering an astounding number of programs and services for their communities."

In the two years that have passed since *Profiles 3* was published, there has been further growth. The number of theatres and the size of their audiences have continued to rise; even more important, there are two significantly creative areas in which development has been incessant and accelerating.

The first relates to the problem of performance. In their unceasing search for actors capable of fulfilling the demanding assignments required by the scope and variety of their current programs, institutional theatres are attaching ever-increasing importance to the background and training of the actors they include in their companies. This, is turn, emphasizes the urgent need for more general and expert actor-training. Under pressure from the regional theatres, reinforced by their capacity to furnish work at a living wage to young actors, a number of our liberal arts colleges are finally accepting the necessity of giving the students in their theatre arts departments the essential elements of professional training.

The second development relates to the creation and performance of new plays. Zeisler has observed that up to a few years ago, "what professional theatre the American public saw was what had been deemed 'successful' in New York or London ... the national perception of theatre was determined by the taste of an audience comprising a very small percentage of the population of one single, atypical, enormously complex city in the Northeast. Today, as much is going *to* New York as is coming *from* it. Hundreds of new plays are being developed and performed in theatres all over the United States."

This did not happen easily or automatically. Until quite recently most of our institutional theatres were still fighting a losing battle in that field. Their urge to present original plays was consistently frustrated by the combined timidity of their artistic directors and their boards of trustees, all of whom lived in understandable terror of jeopardizing their hard-won stability and the goodwill of their newly acquired audiences through the inevitable risks incurred in putting on untried productions. (Even the actors seemed to prefer the security of established roles to the hazards of a virgin text.) Today it seems to be generally recognized that a theatre without new plays is a mausoleum and will not long survive.

For some years now American playwrights have been receiving subsidies and encouragement from various sources—with dubious results. Good plays are rarely written in solitude; even "residencies" have proved of limited value compared to the harsh but salutary experience of having a play performed professionally before sympathetic but critical audiences of habitual theatregoers—audiences that are not corrupted by the "hit" or "flop" syndrome that threatens to destroy the commercial theatre. This is what our institutional theatres have been doing lately in increasing numbers. That is what Zeisler and Davidson (himself a pioneer in this field) are referring to when they speak of the new "humanistic" force of theatre in America and "its ability to reach out to its own participating audience" in all parts of the country.

If this inclusion of the audience has tended to temper the more extreme experimentation of some of our new playwrights, it is in the age-old tradition of vital theatre that recognizes and welcomes the audience as part of the creative process.

This brings me to a final and somewhat metaphysical area—one in which I believe that our nonprofit theatres are fulfilling an essential and healthy function in our national cultural life. Restricted by the physical limitations of its playhouses and the need to keep faith with its new audiences, the institutional theatre has remained comparatively free from the anxiety and greed that currently dominate almost every branch of the entertainment business, including the commercial theatre—a state of mind induced by the haunting possibility of "hitting the jackpot" with that enormous, faceless, indeterminate audience of tens of millions which the Nielsen ratings and its equivalents have projected into such an overpowering position of importance in our lives.

If our institutional theatres had done nothing else they would have justified their existence through their abstention from the general madness that pervades and corrupts our society—the rule of *numbers.* They remain isolated and eloquent proof that quantity does not necessarily equate with quality and that the cultural impact on a few hundred people reacting directly and personally on a high level of emotion to a dramatic experience may ultimately be no less potent or significant than the effects of a television show viewed by tens or even hundreds of millions. It is the obligation of the nonprofit theatre to see that its work is central to the lives of individuals.

Theatre Profiles 4, in which each theatrical company receives equal mention, regardless of its size or success, offers eloquent proof of the degree to which this obligation is being fulfilled. It is a valuable documentation of one of the most remarkable and encouraging cultural phenomena of our time. Besides which, it is full of rewarding and stimulating reading.

Center Stage. Michael Moriarty and Mark Jenkins in *G. R. Point.* Photo: Richard Anderson.

Editor's Note

First published in 1973, *Theatre Profiles* is a unique reference series on the nonprofit professional theatre in the United States, offering a range of information available nowhere else. This fourth edition expands and improves on the work begun in earlier volumes; a handsome, streamlined new format has been adopted and the organization of material has been refined in several ways that will increase the overall usefulness of the book to theatre professionals, students, researchers and others concerned with the revolutionary impact of institutional theatre on dramatic art in this country.

New features in this edition include an enlarged dramatist/director/designer section, comprehensive tables of programs and services, a quick reference guide to touring theatres and a chronology of the resident theatre movement.

All theatres included are constituents of Theatre Communications Group, Inc., the national service organization for nonprofit professional theatre. Information was requested in the spring and summer of 1979 from approximately 170 theatres, 165 of which submitted materials and are represented in this volume.

The following notes are provided as a guide to the use of this book:

Directors

The artistic and administrative directors of each theatre are listed. The information is current as of summer 1979 and does not necessarily reflect the theatres' leadership during the 1977-78 and 1978-79 seasons.

Founding

The founding date represents the beginning of public performances or in a few cases, the conceptual or legal establishment of the institution.

Season

The months listed indicate the beginning and closing dates of the theatre's major performing season. "Year-round" indicates that the company performs throughout the year, often without formal opening and closing dates. "Variable" indicates a changeable or unstructured season. In such cases, current season information can be obtained directly from the theatre.

Schedule

Evening and matinee performance days are listed for theatres which have established regular performing schedules for the run of each production. Wherever possible, this edition also includes variable performance days (e.g., "Selected Saturdays"). Again, specific information on variable schedules should be requested directly from the theatre.

Facilities

Seating capacities and types of stages are included only for those theatres that own, rent or regularly use a specific performing space or spaces. Theatre facility names and addresses are included when they differ from the institutional name and/or business address. The information is current as of August 1979 and does not necessarily reflect the two seasons highlighted in the book.

For the sake of clarity in this edition, a common terminology for types of stages has been adopted, eliminating idiosyncratic nomenclature in favor of the following general designations:

Proscenium:
The traditional, picture-window stage, which the audience views from a single "fourth wall" perspective.

Modified Thrust:
Might also be called a "modified proscenium," utilizing a jutting or fan-shaped apron on which much of the action is played. The audience still maintains a basic "fourth wall" relationship, however.

Thrust:
All types of stage arrangements in which the audience sits on three sides of the playing area.

Arena:
The audience completely surrounds the playing space.

Flexible:
All types of stages and spaces which can be altered or converted from one category to another (e.g., proscenium to thrust, thrust to arena, etc.). Also included in this designation are "environmental" spaces or stages created to meet the demands of individual productions.

Cabaret:
A simple performance platform.

Finances

Financial figures reflect the most recently completed fiscal year for each theatre. For this edition, all figures (operating expenses, earned and unearned income) have been rounded to the nearest thousand. While most are based on precise, audited figures, their purpose in this book is to provide a sense of the *general* relationship between expenses and income.

Audience

The paid percent of capacity, as represented by subscribers and single-ticket holders, is provided for the most recently completed season, in addition to the total number of subscribers and estimated total annual attendance for all theatre events.

Touring contact

For the convenience of potential sponsoring organizations, specific names are listed for theatres offering major touring and residency programs.

Booked-in events

Many theatres regularly sponsor arts events or rent their facilities to other performing groups and individual artists. Interests in specific types of events are indicated to assist companies seeking performance spaces or bookings.

Actors' Equity Association

Information on Actors' Equity Association (AEA) is included for theatres operating under union contracts. Please note that COST indicates the Council of Stock Theatres contract, CORST denotes the Council of Resident Stock Theatres contract and LORT signifies the League of Resident Theatres contract, which has four categories: A, B, C and D. Other AEA abbreviations include BAT for the Bay Area (San Francisco) Theatre contract, COLT for the Chicago Off-Loop Theatre contract and HAT for the Hollywood (California) Area Theatre contract. For more specific information on these and other contracts listed, contact Actors' Equity Association, 1500 Broadway, New York, N.Y. 10036.

Artistic statements

All theatres were invited to submit an artistic statement of any length up to 300 words reflecting the current philosophy and goals, community impact, etc. While most have been edited for style, every attempt has been made to retain the individuality and unique flavor of these personal statements.

Programs and services

Because of the increasing importance of theatres not only as producing units but also as local cultural resources, a listing of theatre activities outside of regular production is included. Additionally, an appendix of programs and services beginning on page 242 offers an "at-a-glance" overview of the diverse outreach programs offered by resident theatres.

Manhattan Theatre Club. Sloane
Shelton in *Play*.
Photo: Gerry Goodstein.

Production lists
Productions of the 1977-78 and 1978-79
seasons (1978 and 1979 for summer
operations) are listed with authors, translators,
adaptors, composers and lyricists, along with
source materials of literary adaptations, as
provided by the theatres. In the case of revivals,
only the title of the production is repeated in the
second listing.

Photographs
Photographs were selected to convey the range
and diversity of production activity. In general,
individual performers are identified when
appearing in groups of five or less.

Dramatists/Directors/Designers Index
One of the most popular appendices to the last
edition, the directors and designers index has
been expanded to include dramatists (including
composers and lyricists for musicals),
translators and adaptors. No entry appears
when design work was not attributed by the
theatre to a particular person, or in a few cases,
when the information was unavailable at press
time.

Theatre on Tour
A new feature for this edition, *Theatre on Tour*
provides another handy "at-a-glance" reference
guide for touring sponsors, indicating regional
availability and types of programming. It
complements the *Touring contact* listing in each
profile.

Regional Index
To readily identify theatres located in individual
states, a geographical index begins on page
256.

Theatre Chronology
Another new feature, this "time line" history of
the nonprofit professional theatre movement is
intended to demonstrate the amazing growth
and decentralization of the American theatre,
especially in the last 10 years.

Index of Names and Titles
All playwrights, play titles, artistic and
administrative directors and theatre founders
appearing in this edition are listed in the index
starting on page 258. The index is particularly
useful in determining which theatres have
produced a specific play or the work of a
particular playwright, and the frequency of
production.

Theatre Profiles will continue as a fluid, ever-
evolving resource tool responsive to the needs
of its users. Reader comments have been and
will continue to be useful in charting the future
direction of the series. On behalf of TCG, I
would like to thank the theatres included for
their overwhelming eagerness to be part of the
volume—a testimonial to the book's impact and
importance in its field.

David J. Skal

PAF Playhouse *An Angel Comes to Babylon.*
Photo: Gerry Goodstein.

Theatre Profiles

A Contemporary Theatre

Gregory A. Falls
Artistic Director

Andrew M. Witt
General Manager

100 West Roy St.
Seattle, WA 98119
(206) 285-3220 (business)
(206) 285-5110 (box office)

Founded 1965
Gregory A. Falls

Season
May–October

Schedule
Evenings
Tuesday–Sunday
Matinees
Wednesday, Saturday

Facilities
709 First Ave. West
Seating capacity: 422
Stage: thrust

Finances
Jan. 1, 1978–Dec. 31, 1978
$887,000 operating expenses
$646,000 earned income
$215,000 unearned income

Audience
Paid capacity: 93%
Subscribers: 7,831
Annual attendance: 143,525

Touring contact
Jody Harris

Booked-in events
Performing arts

AEA LORT (C) and Theatre for Young Audiences contracts

Shaun Austin-Olsen and Si Osborne in *Ballymurphy*. Photo: Chris Bennion.

One of several thriving professional theatres in Seattle, A Contemporary Theatre has produced more than 90 new or nearly new contemporary plays for Pacific Northwest audiences. The theatre continues to encourage new play development, especially musical theatre.

In addition to six mainstage productions last season, ACT produced *A Christmas Carol*, adapted by Gregory A. Falls, for the third year, using ACT's children's theatre company as the principal cast. This cast, called the Young ACT Company, toured six western states in 1978 and recently took its production of *The Odyssey* to the Kennedy Center in Washington, D.C. That production, along with another YAC production, *The Forgotten Door*, also played to more than 60,000 Washington state students through the Washington State Cultural Enrichment Program.

As part of ACT's educational outreach philosophy, theatre audiences air their thoughts and feelings about the mainstage plays during post-performance discussions, sponsored in part by the Washington Commission for the Humanities. ACT continues its creative dramatics program for younger children during matinee performances and, with the help of the Seattle Central Community College's Drama and Deaf Project, recently sponsored a specially interpreted performance of *The Sea Horse* for the hearing-impaired. ACT also solicits the support of local businesses to buy theatre tickets for international students.

Broadening the scope of the theatre itself, in 1978 ACT began a continuing relationship with theatres in Australia—first by hosting the Salamanca Theatre Company, Tasmania's leading Theatre in Education; then by producing the American premiere of Alexander Buzo's *Makassar Reef*, with the playwright in residence.

Programs and services
Administrative and technical/production internships, student performances, programs-in-schools, creative dramatics program with the University of Washington, humanities seminar series, student and senior citizen ticket discounts, free ticket distribution, national children's theatre touring, newsletter, magazine, theatre rentals.

Productions 1978
Henry IV, Part I, William Shakespeare
The Shadow Box, Michael Cristofer
Ballymurphy, Michael Neville; music: Stan Keen
The Sea Horse, Edward J. Moore
Makassar Reef, Alexander Buzo
Anything Goes, book: Guy Bolton, P.G. Wodehouse, Howard Lindsay and Russel Crouse; music and lyrics: Cole Porter
A Christmas Carol, adapt: Gregory A. Falls
The Odyssey, adapt: Gregory A. Falls and Kurt Beattie
The Forgotten Door, Gregory A. Falls, from Alexander Key's novel

Productions 1979
Man and Superman, George Bernard Shaw
Fanshen, David Hare
Otherwise Engaged, Simon Gray
Holy Ghosts, Romulus Linney
The Water Engine, David Mamet
The Fantasticks, book and lyrics: Tom Jones; music: Harvey Schmidt
A Christmas Carol, adapt: Gregory A. Falls

John Gilbert and James W. Monitor in *A Christmas Carol*. Photo: Chris Bennion.

Academy Festival Theatre

Vivian Matalon
Artistic Director

Michael O'Rand
Managing Director

Box 88
Lake Forest, IL 60045
(312) 295-6650 (business)
(312) 234-6750 (box office)

Founded 1967
Marshall Migatz

Season
June–September

Schedule
Evenings
Tuesday–Sunday
Matinees
Wednesday, Saturday

Facilities
Drake Theatre
Barat College
Seating capacity: 669
Stage: thrust

Finances
Dec. 1, 1978–Nov. 30, 1979
$621,000 operating expenses
$300,000 earned income
$321,000 unearned income

Audience
Paid capacity: 60%
Subscribers: 6,000
Annual attendance: 50,000

Booked-in events
Theatre

AEA Non-Resident Stock contract

The Academy Festival Theatre has had a richly varied history and a sizeable impact upon both the national and local theatre scene. Founded as a small summer stock theatre, the Academy Playhouse (as it was then named) quickly became a favorite among audiences throughout metropolitan Chicago.

In 1973, William Gardner assumed the position of producer and focused national attention on AFT as a theatre originating productions which found audiences and won awards not only in Chicago, but also in New York, Washington, Boston, Philadelphia and Los Angeles. Highlights of Gardner's work included O'Neill's *A Moon for the Misbegotten,* produced in 1973, starring Colleen Dewhurst and Jason Robards and directed by Jose Quintero. The production later moved to Broadway, toured the United States and was taped as a television special.

The 1975 season featured Tennessee Williams' *Sweet Bird of Youth* with Irene Worth and Christopher Walken, later presented at the Kennedy Center in Washington, D.C., and on Broadway. In 1977, a revival of Shaw's *Too True to be Good* with Jean Marsh traveled to both Boston and Philadelphia, and the world premiere of John Guare's *The Landscape of the Body* with Shirley Knight went on to a subsequent production at the New York Shakespeare Festival.

Now under the artistic leadership of Vivian Matalon, AFT continues to present a four-play summer season featuring a mix of classics, revivals and new plays. There is now a new emphasis on making the theatre a lively and integral part of its immediate community. By working closely with the women's board and guild organizations of the theatre, Matalon is endeavoring to increase the involvement of his audience in the artistic process of their theatre.

In its 1980 and 1981 seasons, AFT plans to expand its programming to encompass a second stage series directed toward the production of newer works and to develop an extensive training program for apprentices and interns in administrative, technical design and production areas.

Programs and services
Student performances, study materials, student and senior citizen ticket discounts, post-performance discussions, newsletter, speakers bureau, volunteer auxiliary.

Productions 1978
Twelfth Night, William Shakespeare
After the Season, Corinne Jacker
What the Butler Saw, Joe Orton
Serenading Louie, Lanford Wilson

Productions 1979
Charley's Aunt, Brandon Thomas
Morning's at Seven, Paul Osborn
Uncle Vanya, Anton Chekhov; trans: David Magarshack
The Interview, Thom Thomas

The Academy Festival Theatre suspended operations in the fall of 1979.

Charles Cioffi and Irene Worth in *After the Season.* Photo: Lisa Ebright.

Tony Roberts and Lindsay Crouse in *Serenading Louie.* Photo: Lisa Ebright.

Academy Theatre

Frank Wittow
Artistic Director

Nancy Hager
General Manager

Box 77070
Atlanta, GA 30309
(404) 755-2753 (business)
(404) 892-0880 (box office)

Founded 1956
Frank Wittow

Season
October–June

Schedule
Evenings
Wednesday–Sunday
Matinees
Saturday, Sunday

Facilities
Seating capacity: 500
Stage: thrust

Finances
July 1977–July 1978
$337,000 operating expenses
$188,000 earned income
$149,000 unearned income

Audience
Paid capacity: 82%
Subscribers: 2,015
Annual attendance: 113,000

Touring contract
Linda Loety

Booked-in events
Theatre, dance, music,
experimental performing groups

Gay Griggs, John Stephens,
Chris Curran and Edward Lee in
Waiting for Godot. Photo: Marty
King.

Frank Wittow founded the Academy Theatre in 1956 so that skilled theatre artists could build distinguished and versatile professional careers centered in the life of the Atlanta region. Over the years the Academy has sought artistic excellence in classic, contemporary and company-developed plays, as well as innovative community outreach and teaching programs.

The Academy's mainstage season includes a subscription series of four classic and contemporary plays, a new program of free performances in an Atlanta park, and a seven-state tour of the Southeast sponsored by the Southern Arts Federation and the Georgia Council for the Arts and Humanities, including extensive teaching residences. The Academy Theatre for Youth program produces a season of two or three original plays on its mainstage and a statewide artists-in-schools residency program of two or three original scripts, usually company-developed, accompanied by improvisational theatre workshops. The theatre maintains close ties with the Atlanta University Center, through the education department at Clark College, with resources for teacher training courses and residencies at the Academy for the Governor's Intern Program. It

also regularly hosts interns from other high schools and colleges in the region. The Academy Playwrights' Unit and Guest Artist series host new and innovative works throughout the season, ranging from staged readings and critiques to full productions. The Academy's School of Performing Arts serves as the bridge from beginning student to professional, with an Apprentice Program for pre-company level actors, through which actors phase into various paid positions. The school also has its own Lab Theatre which regularly produces 10 to 15 new scripts and lesser-known classics each season.

New programs emerge organically from ongoing Academy services. For example, a new two-year project is beginning with six south Georgia rural communities to create a full-length original play based on folklore and traditions of this unique "Wiregrass" region of the South.

Programs and services
Professional training in acting, directing, design, production and administration; classes for nonprofessionals and children; artistic, administrative and technical/production internships; Actors' Apprentice Company, student performances, programs-in-schools, study materials, ticket discounts for students and the disadvantaged, free ticket distribution, regional touring, post-performance discussions, workshop productions and staged readings, souvenir book, script publication, volunteer auxiliary, theatre rentals.

Productions 1977-78
Waiting for Godot, Samuel Beckett
The Hostage, Brendan Behan
The Lady's Not for Burning, Christopher Fry
The Blood Knot, Athol Fugard
Long Day's Journey into Night, Eugene O'Neill
Clerambard, Marcel Ayme
Dream Nibbler, John Stephens and company
Batteries Not Included, John Stephens and
    company
Crocodile Casserole, company developed
Masks, company developed
Up Close, company developed

Productions 1978-79
Death of a Salesman, Arthur Miller
Tartuffe, Moliere; trans: Richard Wilbur
Streamers, David Rabe
Heavenly Shades of Night Are Falling, Jim Peck
Good Night, Mr. Potato, John Stephens and
    company
The Wind in the Willows, John Stephens and
    company, from Kenneth Grahame's novel
The Flexible Fireman, Ethel McFarland and
    Frank Wittow
Families, company developed

Marat/Sade. Photo: Marty King.

The Acting Company

John Houseman
Producing Artistic Director

Michael Kahn
Alan Schneider
Artistic Directors

Margot Harley
Executive Producer

Howard Crampton-Smith
General Manager

420 West 42nd St.
New York, NY 10036
(212) 564-3510

Founded 1972
John Houseman, Margot Harley

Season
July–May

Finances
June 1, 1978–May 31, 1979
$1,047,000 operating expenses
$ 580,000 earned income
$ 381,000 unearned income

Audience
Annual attendance: 130,000

Touring contact
Rob Hill

AEA LORT (C) contract

The Acting Company tours a repertoire of classical and modern plays from coast to coast, and offers teaching demonstrations and workshops. The only permanent American company combining all of these features, the troupe is dedicated to ensemble production of stylistically varied works. Now in its eighth season, the company has performed 34 plays in 165 cities in 39 states, traveling more than 75,000 miles.

In 1972, John Houseman, then head of the Theater Center of the Juilliard School in New York, saw in his first graduating class a group of actors so talented that he felt they should not be disbanded. Houseman and executive producer Margot Harley formed them into a professional company, which debuted as the dramatic arm of the Saratoga, N.Y., Performing Arts Festival. The group became known as the City Center Acting Company, under the auspices of New York's City Center of Music and Drama. When this affiliation ceased in 1975, its name became simply "The Acting Company."

The 1979-80 season featured a traditional month-long stand in Saratoga, subsequent national tour, and a six-week tour of Australia under the auspices of the Australian Elizabethan Theatre Trust, with productions staged by Michael Kahn, Liviu Ciulei and Gerald Gutierrez.

Programs and services
Administrative and technical/production internships, programs-in-schools, international touring and residencies, post-performance discussions, workshop productions and staged readings, guest lecturers, newsletter, speakers bureau.

Productions 1977-78
King Lear, William Shakespeare
Mother Courage and Her Children, Bertolt Brecht; trans: Ralph Manheim
The Duck Variations, David Mamet
The Other Half, Elinor Jones
Chapeau, book and lyrics: Alfred Uhry; music: Robert Waldman

Productions 1978-79
Antigone, Jean Anouilh; adapt: Lewis Galantiere
Broadway, George Abbott and Philip Dunning
Romeo and Juliet, William Shakespeare
A Voice of My Own, Elinor Jones; music: Kathrin King Segal

Leslie Geraci and Charles Shaw-Robinson in *Romeo and Juliet.*
Photo: Gerry Goodstein

Charles Shaw-Robinson, Richard Ooms and Matthew Kimbrough in *Broadway.* Photo: Susan Cook.

Actors Theatre of Louisville

Jon Jory
Producing Director

Alexander Speer
Administrative Director

Trish Pugh
Associate Director

316-320 West Main St.
Louisville, KY 40202
(502) 584-1265 (business)
(502) 584-1205 (box office)

Founded 1964
Richard Block, Ewel Cornett

Season
October–May

Schedule
Evenings
Tuesday–Sunday
Matinees
Variable

Facilities
Pamela Brown Auditorium
Seating capacity: 641
Stage: thrust
Victor Jory Theatre
Seating capacity: 161
Stage: thrust

Finances
June 1, 1978–May 31, 1979
$1,551,000 operating expenses
$1,090,000 earned income
$ 499,000 unearned income

Audience
Paid capacity: 95%
Subscribers: 18,200
Annual attendance: 175,000

Booked-in events
Theatre

Touring contact
Alexander Speer

AEA LORT (B) contract

Leo Burmester and Patrick Tovatt in *Lone Star*. Photo: David S. Talbott.

Joe Morton and John Hancock in *Third and Oak*. Photo: David S. Talbott.

It began in a converted loft, formerly an Egyptian tea room, with a seating capacity of only 100. The following year, sold-out houses necessitated a move to larger headquarters in a converted railway station. Now ensconced since 1972 in a $1.7 million theatre complex (a former bank building), Actors Theatre of Louisville continues to grow, having mounted 17 productions in two theatres for the 1978-79 season. That slate included eight world premieres of American plays and two American premieres of foreign works.

ATL offers a seven-play season in the Pamela Brown Auditorium and a three-play season in the smaller Victor Jory Theatre. It was in the latter space that the Pulitzer Prize-winning *The Gin Game* had its professional premiere in 1977. Since 1977 ATL's three Festivals of New American Plays have propelled the company into the national spotlight. The 1979 festival drew visitors from 23 states and three foreign countries.

In 1978, ATL and Jory received the Margo Jones Award and the following year the Shubert Foundation's James N. Vaughan Award, both prizes given to regional theatres outstanding for their development of new works. ATL was officially designated the State Theatre of Kentucky in 1973.

Jon Jory became ATL's producing director in 1969. Since then, subscriptions have increased fivefold, substantially expanding ATL's support base into neighboring states. ATL has also participated in production exchange with Cincinnati Playhouse in the Park.

Jory's emphasis on producing new American works has led to the commissioning of 21 playwrights, all of whose creations have been staged in either the regular subscription series or in workshop form. ATL serves its hometown region through tours to area schools and colleges, poetry programs in private homes, assistance to local businesses through the development of industrial shows and a consulting service for high school and community theatres. The company annually tours a fully-mounted production across the state for three weeks in the spring.

Programs and services
Professional training in acting, directing, design, production and administration; classes for children; artistic, administrative and technical/production internships; student performances, programs-in-schools, study materials, student and senior citizen ticket discounts, statewide touring, post-performance discussions, workshop productions and staged readings, guest lecturers, restaurant, auction, newsletter, speakers bureau, volunteer auxiliary, theatre rentals.

Productions 1977-78
Living Together, Alan Ayckbourn
Getting Out, Marsha Norman
Does Anybody Here Do the Peabody?, Enid Rudd
Andronicus, book: Jon Jory, from William Shakespeare's *Titus Andronicus;* music and lyrics: Jerry Blatt
The Front Page, Ben Hecht and Charles MacArthur
Lu Ann Hampton Laverty Oberlander, Preston Jones
The Mousetrap, Agatha Christie
Peg o' My Heart, J. Hartley Manners
Daddies, Douglas Gower
The Bridgehead, Frederick Bailey
Sizwe Bansi Is Dead, Athol Fugard, John Kani and Winston Ntshona
Third and Oak, Marsha Norman
Round and Round the Garden, Alan Ayckbourn
A Christmas Carol, adapt: Barbara Field
An Independent Woman, Daniel Stein
The Louisville Zoo, various writers
The Lion in Winter, James Goldman

Productions 1978-79
Whose Life Is It Anyway?, Brian Clark
The Splits, Erika Ritter
The Runner Stumbles, Milan Stitt
The Play's the Thing, Ferenc Molnar; adapt: P. G. Wodehouse
A Christmas Carol
What Every Woman Knows, J. M. Barrie
Circus Valentine, Marsha Norman
Matrimonium, Peter Ekstrom
Find Me, Olwen Wymark
Crimes of the Heart, Beth Henley
Lone Star, James McLure
Holidays, various writers
The Gin Game, D. L. Coburn
The Shadow Box, Michael Cristofer
Gold Dust, book: Jon Jory; music and lyrics: Jim Wann

Actors Theatre of St. Paul

Michael Andrew Miner
Artistic Director

Jan Miner
Managing Director

2115 Summit Ave.
St. Paul, MN 55105
(612) 698-5559

Founded 1977
Michael Andrew Miner

Season
October–April

Schedule
Evenings
Thursday–Sunday
Matinees
Saturday, selected Thursdays

Facilities
Foley Theatre
Seating capacity: 260
Stage:proscenium

Finances
July 1, 1978–June 30, 1979
$175,000 operating expenses
$ 60,000 earned income
$129,000 unearned income

Audience
Paid capacity: 43%
Subscribers: 460
Annual attendance: 18,170

Touring contact
Richie Christy

Booked-in events
Dance

AEA LORT (D) contract

Actors Theatre of St. Paul is committed to the development of a cohesive ensemble approach to a stylistically varied repertoire of contemporary and classical plays. At the heart of its aesthetic is the development of a resident professional acting company capable of and responsive to the unique demands of ensemble acting. Every aspect of the theatre's program is formulated, organized, measured and modified in light of that goal.

The recently founded company has thus far produced two seasons of plays and engaged in a variety of ancillary projects. Both seasons were eclectic, including such diverse scripts as Shaw's *Arms and the Man* and James Nicholson's *Down by the Gravois (Under the Anheuser-Busch).* ATSP's emphasis on developing an ensemble has manifested itself in a focus on "character plays." Although they vary radically in form, literary genre and period, all of the plays share a concern with character development, character self-revelation, character interaction or character assertion over social circumstances as their author's chief purpose.

The company eagerly embraces the current national concern for developing new playwrights and has consistently endeavored to assist writers through production, readings and residencies.

Ancillary educational and outreach programs at ATSP include touring, specially subsidized student performances, in-school workshops, and an internship program of significant scope for theatre students at a growing number of colleges.

Plans for the 1979-80 season include a continued emphasis on the development of the acting ensemble, the expansion of rehearsal periods for more complex works, the engagement of a literary manager to oversee the theatre's growing activity with new scripts, and a Shakespearean workshop.

Programs and services

Artistic, administrative and technical/production internships; student performances, programs-in-schools, study materials, student and senior citizen ticket discounts, voucher program, regional touring, post-performance discussions, children's theatre, newsletter, speakers bureau, volunteer auxiliary.

Productions 1977-78
Scenes from American Life, A.R. Gurney, Jr.
The Farm, David Storey
Down by the Gravois (Under the Anheuser-Busch), James Nicholson
Arms and the Man, George Bernard Shaw

Productions 1978-79
The Waltz of the Toreadors, Jean Anouilh; trans: Lucienne Hill
The Mandrake, Niccolo Machiavelli; adapt: Camille Gifford
Androcles and the Lion, Aurand Harris
The Iron Harp, Joseph O'Connor
Custer, Robert E. Ingham
U.S.A., John Dos Passos
Two for the Seesaw, William Gibson

Custer. Photo: Richie Christy.

Nancy Bagshaw in *Androcles and the Lion.* Photo: Richie Christy.

Alabama Shakespeare Festival

Martin L. Platt
Artistic Director

Josephine E. Ayers
Executive Producer

Anne F. Zimmerman
Managing Director

Box 141
Anniston, AL 36202
(205) 236-7503 (business)
(205) 237-2332 (box office)

Founded 1972
Martin L. Platt

Season
July–August
Touring
September–November

Schedule
Evenings
Tuesday–Sunday
Matinees
Wednesday, Saturday, Sunday

Facilities
Festival Theatre
12th and Woodstock Sts.
Seating capacity: 950
Stage: thrust

Finances
Jan. 1, 1978–Dec. 31, 1978
$252,000 operating expenses
$187,000 earned income
$ 66,000 unearned income

Audience
Paid capacity: 60%
Subscribers: 2,411
Annual attendance: 55,000

Touring contact
Alexine Saunders

AEA Actor/Teacher contract

Charles Antalosky in *The Merchant of Venice*. Photo: Jerry Harris.

The objective of the Alabama Shakespeare Festival, which has provided professional classical repertory theatre for Alabama and the southeastern United States since 1972, is to challenge its audience and company by mounting productions directly serving the ideas and philosophies of the dramatists represented.

Operating in Anniston, a city of 300,000 located in northeastern Alabama, almost equidistant from Birmingham and Atlanta, the festival has explored the canons of many other playwrights besides its 25 productions of Shakespeare and two non-subscription productions, ASF mounts a three-month southeastern tour each fall. In 1978, touring brought the festival's audience base of 23,000 an additional 30,000 spectators.

When ASF first opened, founder Martin L. Platt produced the season in a 400-seat proscenium house in an abandoned school facility. In its next season, ASF moved into its current home, a beautiful 950-seat thrust theatre in Anniston's new Educational Park Complex. Throughout its first eight seasons, the festival has assembled a strongly based "home company" of actors and a resident design staff, which are flexible and attentive to the needs of guest directors and help plan future repertory seasons.

The key to ASF's rapid growth has been the "Shakespeare magnet." The Bard has proved exciting to audiences, with response to the lesser-known works such as *Measure for Measure* and *Love's Labour's Lost* equalling and, in some cases, exceeding the more often seen *Hamlet* and *Othello*. The festival never loses sight of the fact that Shakespeare was a people's playwright, writing to the common audience, entertaining, exciting, moving and uplifting them and becoming a part of their life experience.

Programs and services
Professional acting and administrative training, administrative internships, programs-in-schools, study materials, laboratory courses in association with the University of Alabama/Tuscaloosa, free ticket distribution, student and military ticket discounts, regional touring, post-performance discussions, workshop productions and staged readings, film series, guest lecturers, newsletter, souvenir book, speakers bureau, volunteer auxiliary, theatre rentals.

Productions 1978
Othello, William Shakespeare
The Merchant of Venice, William Shakespeare
Private Lives, Noel Coward
Measure for Measure, William Shakespeare
Clarence Darrow, David W. Rintels
A Lover's Complaint, adapt: Martin L. Platt, from verse by William Shakespeare, et al.
The Taming of the Shrew, William Shakespeare

Productions 1979
As You Like It, William Shakespeare
Macbeth, William Shakespeare
The Comedy of Errors, William Shakespeare
The Country Wife, William Wycherley
Clarence Darrow
Oh, William!, adapt: Martin L. Platt, from musicals based on Shakespeare
Twelfth Night, William Shakespeare

Peter Jack, Jane Moore and William McHale in *Measure for Measure*. Photo: Martin L. Platt.

Alaska Repertory Theatre

Robert J. Farley
Artistic Director

Paul V. Brown
Producing Director

523 West Eighth Ave., Suite 110
Anchorage, AK 99501
(907) 276-2327 (business)
(907) 276-5500 (box office)

Founded 1976
Alaska State Council on the Arts

Season
December–May
July–August

Schedule
Evenings
Tuesday–Saturday
Matinees
Sunday

Facilities
Sydney Laurence Auditorium
Sixth Ave. and F St., Anchorage
Seating capacity: 646
Stage: proscenium
University of Alaska Fine Arts Theatre
Fairbanks
Seating capacity: 481
Stage: proscenium

Finances
July 1, 1978–June 30, 1979
$1,358,000 operating expenses
$ 468,000 earned income
$1,036,000 unearned income

Audience
Paid capacity: 81%
Subscribers: 5,544
Annual attendance: 62,520

Touring contact
Paul V. Brown

Booked-in events
Regional and children's theatre, music

AEA LORT (B) contract

Alaska's first professional performing arts organization, Alaska Repertory Theatre serves a population of roughly 425,000 scattered across a land mass one-fifth the size of the contiguous 48 states. The theatre is committed to high artistic standards, diverse and challenging programming, and a broad range of statewide services.

In 1975, the Alaska State Council on the Arts, with support from the National Endowment for the Arts, contracted Paul V. Brown to conduct a research project into the feasibility of a statewide professional theatre company. This research, along with the advice and encouragement of the Foundation for the Extension and Development of the American Professional Theatre (FEDAPT), led to the incorporation of Alaska Repertory Theatre in 1976 with Robert J. Farley as artistic director and Brown as producing director.

Alaska Repertory Theatre has two "home bases"; year-round offices are maintained in Anchorage and Fairbanks. The theatre is committed to producing distinctive classic, contemporary and original works and to making productions and ancillary services available to large and small communities throughout the state. In three seasons, 12 productions have attracted a total audience of more than 135,000 in Anchorage, Fairbanks and (on the first statewide tour in 1978) seven other Alaskan communities. Nineteen communities, from Arctic Eskimo villages to the state capital in Juneau, have booked the second statewide tour, planned for the winter and spring of 1980.

Community outreach programs, including such services as workshops and school performances, are part of each Alaska Repertory Theatre residency. The theatre's Professional Training Program provides an opportunity for young people interested in theatre as a career to develop their skills, working toward the professional level. Artistic, technical and administrative consultations and equipment loans make Alaska Repertory Theatre a unique resource for educational institutions and arts organizations throughout Alaska.

Programs and services
Professional training in acting, production and administration; student performances, programs-in-schools, study materials, student and senior citizen ticket discounts, free ticket distribution, statewide touring, children's theatre, newsletter, souvenir book, speakers bureau, volunteer auxiliary; statewide artistic, technical and administrative workshops and consultations.

Productions 1977-78
Sherlock Holmes (and The Curse of the Sign of the Four or *The Mark of the Timber Toe),* Dennis Rosa, from Arthur Conan Doyle's novel
The Fourposter, Jan de Hartog
The Eccentricities of a Nightingale, Tennessee Williams
Diamond Studs, book: Jim Wann; music and lyrics: Bland Simpson and J. Wann

Productions 1978-79
The Fourposter
A Christmas Carol, adapt: Martin L. Platt
Terra Nova, Ted Tally
The Taming of the Shrew, William Shakespeare
Slow Dance on the Killing Ground, William Hanley
Deathtrap, Ira Levin
Diamond Studs

Philip Pleasants and Marshall Borden in *Terra Nova.* Photo: Jim Lavrakas.

John-Fredrick Jones and Shannon Eubanks in *The Taming of the Shrew.* Photo: Jim Lavrakas.

Alliance Theatre Company/Atlanta Children's Theatre

Fred Chappell
Artistic Director

Wallace Chappell
Associate Director

Bernard Havard
Managing Director

1280 Peachtree St., NE
Atlanta, GA 30309
(404) 892-7529 (business)
(404) 892-2414 (box office)

Founded 1969
Atlanta Arts Alliance, Inc.

Season
October–May

Schedule
Evenings
Tuesday–Sunday
Matinees
Saturday, Sunday

Facilities
Alliance Theatre
Seating capacity: 784
Stage: proscenium
Studio Theatre
Seating capacity: 200
Stage: flexible

Finances
Aug. 1, 1977–July 31, 1978
$1,078,000 operating expenses
$ 588,000 earned income
$ 319,000 unearned income

Audience
Paid capacity: 86%
Subscribers: 8,776
Annual attendance: 301,015

Touring contact
Bernard Havard

Booked-in events
Dance, music, theatre

*AEA LORT (B) and (D) and
Theatre for Young Audiences
contracts*

Richard Dreyfuss and Paul
Winfield in *Othello.* Photo:
Charles M. Rafshoon.

The Alliance Theatre/Atlanta Children's Theatre is a merging of two previously independent theatre companies housed in the Atlanta Memorial Arts Center, which is also home to the Atlanta Symphony Orchestra, the High Museum of Art and the Atlanta College of Art.

The Alliance Theatre presents a six-play mainstage season with an emphasis on diversity. Plays reflect an eclecticism comprising a range of classical and contemporary works relevant to the region. The Atlanta Children's Theatre produces two or three in-house mainstage productions each season. Scripts are chosen or developed to stimulate the imaginations of young theatre audiences, as well as adults.

In the belief that the development of new playwrights and new scripts is vital to the growth of theatre in this country, the Alliance Theatre has helped to spearhead the Atlanta New Play Project, a two-week series of new works by regional playwrights presented by each of Atlanta's theatre companies. Current programming in Alliance's 200-seat Studio Theatre emphasizes new plays by American playwrights.

Adaptations by the Atlanta Children's Theatre, the outreach program of the theatre, are an important aspect of the operation. The Umbrella Players, a touring team for youth, plays to more than 60,000 young people annually, with a three-play repertoire for lower, middle and high school students. A six-week adult tour for the southeastern region was slated for the fall of 1979.

In the summer of 1979, the Alliance Theatre School opened a professional training center for young actors, and the Alliance has sponsored such visiting companies as the National Theatre of the Deaf, the Barter Theatre and Stage South for special performances. In cooperation with the Atlanta Area School for the Deaf, the Alliance has formulated an innovative program for the hearing-impaired community. The National Endowment for the Arts has awarded a special projects grant to document the program for the use of other theatres across the country.

Programs and services
Technical/production internships, student performances, programs-in-schools, study materials, student and senior citizen ticket discounts, free ticket distribution, regional touring of mainstage productions and children's theatre, post-performance discussions, workshop productions and staged readings, guest lecturers, newsletter, volunteer auxiliary, theatre rentals.

Productions 1977-78
Vanities, Jack Heifner
Cole, music and lyrics: Cole Porter; adapt: Benny Green and Alan Strachan
A Christmas Carol, adapt: Martin L. Platt
Tiger Tail, Tennessee Williams
The Diary of Anne Frank, Frances Goodrich and Albert Hackett
Lu Ann Hampton Laverty Oberlander, Preston Jones
The Taming of the Shrew, William Shakespeare
Beauty and the Beast, adapt: Bix Doughty
Robin Hood, Sharon O'Brien

Productions 1978-79
The Shadow Box, Michael Cristofer
Peter Pan, J. M. Barrie
The Little Foxes, Lillian Hellman
Absurd Person Singular, Alan Ayckbourn
The Robber Bridegroom, book and lyrics: Alfred Uhry; music: Robert Waldman
Othello, William Shakespeare
The Halloween Tree, Wallace Chappell, from Ray Bradbury's story
Tales from the Brothers Grimm, adapt: Wallace Chappell

Valerie Charles and Penny Fuller
in *Peter Pan.* Photo: Charles M.
Rafshoon.

AMAS Repertory Theatre

Rosetta LeNoire
Artistic Director

Marshall B. Purdy
Administrative Director

1 East 104th St.
New York, NY 10029
(212) 369-8000

Founded 1969
Rosetta LeNoire, Gerta Grunen,
Mara Kim

Season
October–May

Schedule
Evenings
Thursday–Saturday
Matinees
Sunday

Facilities
Experimental Theatre
Seating capacity: 99
Stage: proscenium

Finances
May 1, 1978–April 30, 1979
$167,000 operating expenses
$ 54,000 earned income
$ 89,000 unearned income

Audience
Paid capacity: 80%
Annual attendance: 8,300

Touring contact
Rosetta LeNoire

AEA Showcase Code

The AMAS Repertory Theatre, Inc., is a multiracial performing arts organization devoted exclusively to the development of musical theatre. Entering its 10th season under the artistic direction of its founder Rosetta LeNoire, the theatre is a pioneer in racial integration among theatre artists and their audiences.

The primary component of AMAS' extensive programming is its professional showcase theatre. In developing new musical theatre works, the organization's artistic policy places emphasis on the creation of a library of musical biographies. Past seasons have included new musicals based on the lives of important black artists such as Bill "Bojangles" Robinson, Langston Hughes, Scott Joplin, Eubie Blake and Noble Sissle, and Ethel Waters. In 1978 AMAS was selected as one of six national recipients of a special Kennedy Center Black Playwrights Award. This recognition of AMAS' ability to provide a laboratory for new playwrights helped to produce *Sparrow in Flight*, a musical based on the life of Ethel Waters, written by Charles Fuller and based on a concept by Rosetta LeNoire. Other noted theatre artists such as Lucia Victor, Bernard Johnson, Henry LeTang and Micki Grant have been active collaborators in the theatre's 1978-79 season. *Bubbling Brown Sugar*, originally developed and produced by AMAS Repertory Theatre, has enjoyed successful runs on Broadway and in London, and continues national and international touring.

The subsidiary programs of the AMAS Repertory Theatre provide professional training and performance experience for children and adults. The Eubie Blake Children's Theatre offers comprehensive, disciplined training in music, dance and drama for children between the ages of 5 and 16. Many students continue to study at AMAS for several consecutive years and eventually enter the professional arena. Adult workshops in acting and voice offer instruction for the experienced professional, as well as the interested beginner. A summer touring program presents an original musical revue at community centers and public sites and is designed to bring quality, multiracial musical theatre productions to a broad-based public audience free of charge.

Programs and services
Professional acting and voice training, classes for nonprofessionals and children, technical/production internships, student performances, student and senior citizen ticket discounts, free ticket distribution, statewide touring, children's theatre.

Productions 1977-78
Helen, book: Lucia Victor; music and lyrics: Johnny Brandon
Beowulf, book and lyrics: Betty Jane Wylie; music: Victor Davies
Come Laugh and Cry with Langston Hughes, adapt: Rosetta LeNoire
Boston Boston, book: William Michael Maher; music: Bill Brohn; lyrics: B. Brohn and W. M. Maher

Productions 1978-79
Sparrow in Flight, Charles Fuller and Rosetta LeNoire
Helen, book: Lucia Victor; music and lyrics: Johnny Brandon
It's So Nice to Be Civilized, book, music and lyrics: Micki Grant
Suddenly the Music Starts, book, music and lyrics: Johnny Brandon

It's So Nice to Be Civilized. Photo: Don Paul.

Sparrow in Flight. Photo: Michael Meadows.

American Conservatory Theatre

William Ball
General Director

James B. McKenzie
Executive Producer

450 Geary St.
San Francisco, CA 94102
(415) 771-3880 (business)
(415) 673-6440 (box office)

Founded 1965
William Ball

Season
October–May

Schedule
Evenings
Monday–Saturday
Matinees
Wednesday, Saturday

Facilities
Geary Theatre
415 Geary St.
Seating capacity: 1,049
Stage: proscenium
Marines' Memorial Theatre
Mason and Sutter Sts.
Seating capacity: 640
Stage: proscenium
Playroom
Seating capacity: 50
Stage: flexible

Finances
June 1, 1978–May 31, 1979
$5,746,000 operating expenses
$4,651,000 earned income
$1,025,000 unearned income

Audience
Paid capacity: 73%
Subscribers: 20,216
Annual attendance: 500,000

Touring contact
James B. McKenzie

Booked-in events
Dance, theatre

AEA LORT (A) contract

Michael Winters, Raye Birk and Elizabeth Huddle in *Hotel Paradiso*. Photo: William Ganslen.

Marrian Walters, David Hudson, Elizabeth Huddle, Sydney Walker and William Paterson in *The Circle*. Photo: Hank Kranzler.

The American Conservatory Theatre is one of the largest and most active of the nation's resident professional companies. One of only a handful playing in true rotating repertory, ACT is the only company whose annual seasons of public performances are concurrent with, and inseparable from, a continuing program of conservatory training for professional actors and students.

The company employs more than 250 professionals annually, including actors, directors, teachers, designers, administrators, craftsmen and technicians, supported by more than 11,000 hours of volunteers' time. Every year ACT presents a 33-week season at San Francisco's historic Geary Theatre, offering more than 300 performances of 10 plays in repertory. ACT also sponsors commercial engagements of non-repertory productions at the smaller Marines' Memorial Theatre and at the Geary when the resident company is not performing. Since settling in San Francisco in 1967, ACT has presented more than 165 productions, seen by more than 500,000 playgoers in its two theatres. ACT draws its repertoire from the classics of dramatic literature and outstanding modern works. The concurrent Plays-In-Progress series presents five previously unproduced works by new American writers.

From its inception, the company has maintained its dual objectives as a producing organization and a full-time professional conservatory. Seeking to create an energetic atmosphere which would support and encourage theatre artists, William Ball has built a company in which actors teach, teachers act, directors act and actors direct, while students learn professional techniques and discipline through close association with experienced theatre artists. ACT conducts five actor-training programs, including the three-year, full-time Advanced Training Program that offers a Master of Fine Arts degree.

Two ACT productions, *Cyrano de Bergerac* and *The Taming of the Shrew,* have aired on the PBS *Theater in America* series. Regional, national and international touring complements the company's San Francisco activities. In 1976, ACT celebrated the nation's Bicentennial with a State Department-sponsored tour of the Soviet Union. In 1978, the company was the first American resident theatre to tour Japan. In 1979, ACT received the United States Institute for Theatre Technology Award for Excellence and an Antoinette Perry ("Tony") Award for sustained theatrical excellence and commitment to the development of American theatre artists.

Programs and services
Professional acting conservatory, classes for nonprofessionals and children; administrative and technical/production internships, black actors workshop, special performances for students, senior citizens and the disadvantaged; study materials, student and senior citizen ticket discounts, free ticket distribution, international touring, post-performance discussions, workshop productions and staged readings, guest lecturers, souvenir book, newsletter, speakers bureau, volunteer auxiliary, theatre rentals.

Productions 1977-78
Travesties, Tom Stoppard
Hotel Paradiso, Georges Feydeau and Maurice Desvallieres; trans: Peter Glenville
Absurd Person Singular, Alan Ayckbourn
The National Health, Peter Nichols
Julius Caesar, William Shakespeare
All the Way Home, Tad Mosel, from James Agee's novel *A Death in the Family*
The Master Builder, Henrik Ibsen; trans: Allen Fletcher
The Circle, W. Somerset Maugham
A Christmas Carol, adapt: Dennis Powers and Laird Williamson

Productions 1978-79
Hay Fever, Noel Coward
The Visit, Friedrich Dürrenmatt; adapt: Maurice Valency
A Month in the Country, Ivan Turgenev; adapt: Willis Bell
The Circle
The Winter's Tale, William Shakespeare
Hotel Paradiso
Ah, Wilderness!, Eugene O'Neill
A Christmas Carol
Heartbreak House, George Bernard Shaw
The 5th of July, Lanford Wilson

American Place Theatre

Wynn Handman
Director

Julia Miles
Associate Director

111 West 46th St.
New York, NY 10036
(212) 246-3730 (business)
(212) 246-0393 (box office)

Founded 1964
Wynn Handman, Michael Tolan,
Sidney Lanier, Myrna Loy

Season
September–June

Schedule
Evenings
Tuesday–Sunday
Matinees
Wednesday, Saturday

Facilities
Mainstage
Seating capacity: 299
Stage: flexible
Sub-Plot Cafe
Seating capacity: 100
Stage: flexible
Basement Space
Seating capacity: 100
Stage: flexible

Finances
July 1, 1978–June 30, 1979
$641,000 operating expenses
$184,000 earned income
$424,000 unearned income

Audience
Paid capacity: 75%
Subscribers: 4,061
Annual attendance: 26,000

Booked-in events
Theatre, dance

AEA Special contract

The American Place Theatre was founded as a forum for living American writers at New York's St. Clement's Church in 1964. With its move to a new building in 1971, the theatre has continued to provide a place for emerging playwrights. The selection of writers and plays is eclectic, reflected in the more than 60 plays which have been given full productions in the theatre's 15-year history, including William Alfred's *Hogan's Goat* and Robert Lowell's *The Old Glory;* plays by Sam Shepard, Ronald Tavel and Maria Irene Fornes; and the first plays of Ronald Ribman, Steve Tesich and Jonathan Reynolds. Works by black playwrights Ed Bullins, Phillip Hayes Dean, Elaine Jackson, Ron Milner and Charlie Russell, by Asian-American Frank Chin and by distinguished writers in other media, such as Robert Coover, Anne Sexton, Joyce Carol Oates and Bruce Jay Friedman, have also been presented.

A total program is sustained in a creative environment free of commercial pressure, providing optimum conditions for the growth and realization of each writer's work. In addition to four fully mounted productions, the season includes numerous works-in-progress—from rehearsed readings to fully staged productions without scenery. The Basement Space Series, begun in 1975, presents plays (generally by young writers experimenting with theatre language and form) that will work well in an informal space. The American Humorist Series presents cabaret entertainment in the theatre's Sub-Plot Cafe. The Women's Project, begun in 1978, expands the opportunities for the development of women writers and directors through a pilot program funded by the Ford Foundation. In 1978-79, 20 staged readings and four studio productions were presented.

In recent years the American Place has expanded its efforts to draw audiences from various sectors of the community, with emphasis on attracting college students, the potential audiences of the future. The theatre hopes to cultivate a concerned and knowledgeable audience, reflective of the theatre's diverse community, that will participate in the overall process of contemporary theatre to the mutual benefit of both artist and audience member alike.

Programs and services
Professional training for directors, designers, technicians and administrators; artistic, administrative and technical/production internships; student performances, study materials, student and senior citizen ticket discounts, post-performance discussions, workshop productions and staged readings, cabaret, newsletter, theatre rentals.

Productions 1977-78
Cockfight, Elaine Jackson
Passing Game, Steve Tesich
Fefu and Her Friends, Maria Irene Fornes
Conjuring an Event, Richard Nelson

Productions 1978-79
The Grinding Machine, Annalita Marsili Alexander
Touching Bottom, Steve Tesich
Seduced, Sam Shepard
Tunnel Fever or the Sheep Is Out, Jonathan Reynolds

Loren Brown and Joanna Merlin in *The Grinding Machine.* Photo: Martha Holmes.

Rip Torn in *Seduced.* Photo: Martha Holmes.

American Stage Festival

Harold DeFelice
Artistic Director

Marilyn S. Kenison
Managing Director

Box 225
Milford, NH 03055
(603) 673-3143 (business)
(603) 673-7517 (box office)

Founded 1975
Terry C. Lorden and local citizens

Season
June–September

Schedule
Evenings
Tuesday–Sunday
Matinees
Wednesday

Facilities
Seating capacity: 500
Stage: proscenium

Finances
Nov. 1, 1977–Oct. 31, 1978
$245,000 operating expenses
$137,000 earned income
$108,000 unearned income

Audience
Paid capacity: 75%
Subscribers: 2,500
Annual attendance: 45,000

Booked-in events
Theatre, music, dance, arts, crafts

AEA Stock (Z) contract

Laura Hicks and Michael Gross in *Dracula*. Photo: The Camera Centre.

Jeffrey Jones and Elizabeth Franz in *The Royal Family*. Photo: The Camera Centre.

The American Stage Festival's home, which stands on a nine-acre peninsula of woods and fields on New Hampshire's Souhegan River, is a modern 500-seat theatre featuring a 40-foot proscenium stage and removable thrust. Now in its sixth year, ASF has grown impressively from origins in community and semi-professional theatre to burgeoning professional summer stock activity to its present status as the state's largest professional arts organization. The impetus for ASF's development has been the unwavering support of surrounding communities in the primarily residential southern New Hampshire and northern Massachusetts area. ASF's audience comes from more than 100 New Hampshire towns, and more than 90 communities in Massachusetts and other northeastern states.

Over the past seasons, ASF has developed a repertoire that mixes enduring American classics, each explored with a fresh poetic sensibility, with new plays and world premiere productions commissioned by ASF. Previous presentations include the premiere of Israel Horovitz's *Alfred Dies*, three world premiere musicals in three successive seasons, a new *Dracula* adaptation and the first theatrical adaptation of *The Hunchback of Notre Dame*. The works of O'Neill, Williams, Wilder, Kaufman and Steinbeck have dotted ASF's calendar, and the productions have consistently aimed for striking visual and design elements, which emerge from an imaginative and contemporary approach to dramatic literature.

The "festival" concept of ASF has been important from the very beginning. Although the season's major thrust is its six mainstage productions, the company also sponsors a children's workshop featuring guest artists and original presentations, weekly art gallery exhibits, a special events series including such groups as the New Hampshire Symphony and the Hartford Ballet, play discussion seminars, a twice-weekly farmers market and an annual arts and crafts fair.

Recognizing its commitment to training young theatre artists, ASF has established an apprentice program for performers and an intern program for students in management and production.

Programs and services
Professional training in acting, directing, design, production and administration, classes for nonprofessionals and children; artistic, administrative and technical/production internships; student performances, workshops, demonstrations, lectures; student, senior citizen and corporate ticket discounts; post-performance discussions, children's theatre, farmers market, arts and crafts fair, art exhibits, newsletter, speakers bureau, theatre rentals.

Productions 1978
The Royal Family, George S. Kaufman and
  Edna Ferber
The Glass Menagerie, Tennessee Williams
Bandstand, company developed; music and
  lyrics: various
A Moon for the Misbegotten, Eugene O'Neill
Peg o' My Heart, J. Hartley Manners
Dracula, adapt: Tom Haas

Productions 1979
Troupers!, music and lyrics: various; adapt:
  Harold DeFelice
Of Mice and Men, John Steinbeck
Tartuffe, Moliere; trans: Richard Wilbur
Artichoke, Joanna Glass
Our Town, Thornton Wilder
The Hunchback of Notre Dame, Ron Whyte,
  from Victor Hugo's novel
American Pie, Lawrence Smith
Tall Tales, Lawrence Smith

American Theatre Company

Jerald D. Pope
Artistic Director

Kitty Roberts
Managing Director

Box 1265
Tulsa, OK 74101
(918) 582-5353 (business)
(918) 581-5271 (box office)

Founded 1970
Kitty Roberts

Season
October–May

Schedule
Evenings
Thursday–Sunday
Matinees
Sunday

Facilities
Performing Arts Center
Second and Cincinnati Sts.
John H. Williams Theatre
Seating capacity: 429
Stage: proscenium
Studio One Theatre
Seating capacity: 288
Stage: flexible
Brook Theatre
3405 South Peoria St.
Seating capacity: 500
Stage: proscenium

Finances
Jan. 1, 1979–Dec. 31, 1979
$181,000 operating expenses
$ 48,000 earned income
$133,000 unearned income

Audience
Paid capacity: 60%
Subscribers: 1,000
Annual attendance: 36,000

Touring contact
Robert L. Odle

Booked-in events
Theatre, dance, music

During its recent 10th season, the American Theatre Company arrived at two milestones, becoming a resident company of Tulsa's new Performing Arts Center and securing permanent offices and a second stage in a renovated movie house.

The company was founded to provide the Tulsa area with exciting, quality theatrical experiences, from original productions to classics; to establish a salaried professional company; and to provide Tulsa's artists with an alternative to leaving Oklahoma. Buoyed by an active board of directors, ATC has achieved these goals. It has staged several original works, including *O Tulsa!*, which won a special award from the National Conference of Christians and Jews. Several productions, among them *O Tulsa!* and a popular musical adaptation of *A Christmas Carol*, have featured original scores composed by music director Richard Averill.

Other projects include an extensive education program under James E. Runyan's direction, and a major youth program, headed by Kerry Hauger. In 1979, for the fifth consecutive summer, ATC toured Oklahoma's parks with an original melodrama.

The recent move into the former Brook Theatre adds another dimension to previous accomplishments: an improvisational cabaret theatre bringing new forms of entertainment to Tulsans and providing a training ground for local talent. The 500-seat house is used for experimental plays, improvisational comedy, music, classic films and children's shows. It also provides permanent office space and generates auxiliary income.

The major season is divided between two stages in the Performing Arts Center. After being named the multi-stage facility's resident company in March 1979, ATC generated its most successful season ticket campaign ever. ATC is forming a Tulsa theatre communications group among several smaller player troupes to facilitate cooperation and the success of the city's theatrical environment.

Programs and services
Professional and nonprofessional training in acting, directing, design, production and administration; classes for children; programs-in-schools, free ticket distribution, student and senior citizen ticket discounts, regional touring, children's theatre, post-performance discussions, guest lecturers, cabaret, mime, commedia dell'arte, magazine; speakers bureau, volunteer auxiliary.

Productions 1977-78
The Ruling Class, Peter Barnes
Long Day's Journey into Night, Eugene O'Neill
A Christmas Carol, book: Robert L. Odle; music and lyrics: Richard Averill
The Miser, Moliere
Lu Ann Hampton Laverty Oberlander, Preston Jones
Vanities, Jack Heifner

Productions 1978-79
Dracula, adapt: Robert L. Odle
The Real Inspector Hound, Tom Stoppard
A Christmas Carol
The Merry Wives of Windsor, William Shakespeare
Ms. Raccoon's Profession, book and lyrics company developed; music: Richard Averill, et al.
The Glass Menagerie, Tennessee Williams

Vic Tolman, Richard Crawford, Gregory Roach and Bob Bethell in *Dracula*. Photo: Dennis Fry.

Robert L. Odle and Kerry Hauger in *The Miser*. Photo: Dennis Fry.

Arena Stage

Zelda Fichandler
Producing Director

Thomas C. Fichandler
Executive Director

David Chambers
Associate Producing Director

Sixth and Maine Aves., SW
Washington, DC 20024
(202) 554-9066 (business)
(202) 488-3300 (box office)

Founded 1950
Zelda Fichandler, Edward
Mangum, Thomas C. Fichandler

Season
October–June

Schedule
Evenings
Tuesday–Sunday
Matinees
Saturday

Facilities
Arena Stage
Seating capacity: 827
Stage: arena
Kreeger Theater
Seating capacity: 514
Stage: modified thrust
Old Vat Room
Seating capacity: 160
Stage: cabaret

Finances
July 1, 1978–June 30, 1979
$2,871,000 operating expenses
$1,829,000 earned income
$ 874,000 unearned income

Audience
Paid capacity: 91%
Subscribers: 16,300
Annual attendance: 250,000

Touring contact
Robert Alexander,
Living Stage

AEA LORT (B) contract

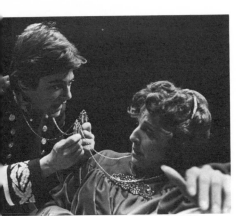

Kristoffer Tabori and Elizabeth
Franz in *Hamlet*. Photo: Joe B.
Mann.

Stanley Anderson in *Curse of the
Starving Class*. Photo: Joe B.
Mann.

The story of Arena Stage parallels that of the American resident theatre. One of the very few American theatre institutions that has enjoyed continuity of leadership, Arena's artistic and philosophical viewpoint has been molded since the beginning by its co-founder and producing director, Zelda Fichandler, a resident theatre pioneer.

New American plays, premieres of important European plays, classics reborn in vivid modern interpretations, new musical works, recent plays that proved financially unsuccessful in the commerical theatre but can be given new life in a nonprofit setting—all are presented in Arena's triplex of modern, intimate playhouses. A resident acting company is supplemented by actors from around the country engaged for one or more plays each season.

The Arena began in the Hippodrome, an old Washington movie house. Soon the potential income from a 247-seat house proved too small to support production costs, and a new home was found at an old brewery, which became known as the Old Vat. The theatre had 500 seats and 40 productions were presented there from 1955 through 1960. When the Old Vat was slated for demolition, architect Harry Weese was selected to work with Zelda and Thomas Fichandler on designing a new theatre based on the direct experience of an existing theatre company. It is the only dramatic playhouse in the country to be built as a total arena. The new Arena theatre opened in 1961, and a second stage, the contrasting fan-shaped Kreeger, also designed by Weese, opened in 1971. In 1976, an intimate 180-seat cabaret theatre, dubbed the Old Vat Room after Arena's previous home, was opened in the Kreeger's basement.

In 1973, Arena Stage was selected by the United States Department of State to be the first American theatre company to tour the Soviet Union, presenting *Our Town* and *Inherit the Wind*. The 1975 production of *Zalmen or the Madness of God* aired on the PBS *Theater in America* series. In 1976, Arena became the first theatre outside New York to receive an Antoinette Perry ("Tony") Award for theatrical excellence. In 1978, Arena was invited to present excerpts from its production of *The 1940s Radio Hour* at the White House. Since 1965, Arena Stage has housed and supported Living Stage, an improvisational community outreach company (see separate entry).

Arena's 1978-79 and 1979-80 seasons were produced by David Chambers, while Zelda Fichandler took a two-year leave of absence.

Programs and services
Artistic, administration and technical/production internships; student performances, student and senior citizen ticket discounts, free ticket distribution, national touring company (Living Stage), post-performance discussions, workshop productions and staged readings, newsletter, volunteer auxiliary, souvenir book, theatre rentals.

Productions 1977-78
The National Health, Peter Nichols
Nightclub Cantata, Elizabeth Swados
Starting Here, Starting Now, music: David
  Shire; lyrics: Richard Maltby, Jr.
The Caucasian Chalk Circle, Bertolt Brecht;
  trans: John Holstrom
A Streetcar Named Desire, Tennessee Williams
Comedians, Trevor Griffiths
Hamlet, William Shakespeare
Gemini, Albert Innaurato
Duck Hunting, Alexander Vampilov; trans: Alma
  H. Law

Productions 1978-79
Tales from the Vienna Woods, Odon von
  Horvath; trans: Christopher Hampton
Curse of the Starving Class, Sam Shepard
The 1940s Radio Hour, Walton Jones
Ah, Wilderness! Eugene O'Neill
Loose Ends, Michael Weller
Don Juan, Moliere; trans: Richard Nelson
Nevis Mountain Dew, Steve Carter
Idiot's Delight, Robert Sherwood
Tintypes: A Ragtime Revue, music and lyrics:
  various; adapt: Mary Kyte, Mel Marvin and
  Gary Pearle

Arizona Theatre Company

Sandy Rosenthal
Artistic Director

Mark Lamos
Acting Artistic Director

David Hawkanson
Managing Director

120 West Broadway
Tucson, AZ 85701
(602) 884-8210 (business)
(602) 622-2823 (box office)

Founded 1966
Sandy Rosenthal

Season
Tucson
November–April
Scottsdale
March

Schedule
Evenings
Tuesday–Sunday
Matinees
Variable

Facilities
Tucson Community Center Little Theatre
Seating capacity: 526
Stage: proscenium
Doubletree Inn Cabaret Theatre
Seating capacity: 210
Stage: cabaret
Scottsdale Center for the Arts
Seating capacity: 750
Stage: proscenium

Finances
July 1, 1978–June 30, 1979
$710,000 operating expenses
$435,000 earned income
$275,000 unearned income

Audience
Paid capacity: 63%
Subscribers: 3,775
Annual attendance: 64,000

Booked-in events
Theatre

AEA LORT (C) contract

The fall of 1979 marked the start of the 13th season of the Arizona Theatre Company (formerly the Arizona Civic Theatre). Under the guidance of founder and artistic director Sandy Rosenthal, the company serves an ever-increasing audience in one of the fastest growing cities in the country.

ATC strives to excite and inspire the mind, imagination and conscience of the people of the Southwest. The prime artistic focus is on ensemble excellence and in the past two seasons, ATC has operated with a resident acting company.

ATC's growth has been commensurate with that of its region. In the past six seasons ATC's operating budget has increased eightfold. Increased fiscal activity has affected programming and the company has constantly stretched its resources to keep abreast of the demands of the growing audience. Six productions are offered during the mainstage season at the Tucson Community Center Little Theatre. Concurrent with that season, two productions out of the six are also presented to Phoenix area audiences during a four-week residency at the Scottsdale Center for the Arts. During summer months ATC offers light entertainment at its cabaret theatre in the Doubletree Inn, one of Tucson's resort hotels.

ATC's theatre arts training program, Encompass, is viewed as a place for discovery and as a community cultural resource for all age groups. Since the school's inception in 1977, it has enjoyed an annual enrollment exceeding 500 in classes taught by acting company members. Operating from its own facility in Tucson's historic district downtown, Encompass generates the creative energy and provides a performance outlet for future innovative programming.

Israel Hicks serves as acting artistic director for the 1979-80 season, while Rosenthal takes a year-long observership sabbatical.

Programs and services
Classes for nonprofessionals and children; artistic, administrative and technical/production internships; student performances, programs-in-schools, workshops for high school counselors and drug rehabilitation staffs, student and senior citizen ticket discounts, free ticket distribution, statewide touring, post-performance discussions, guest lecturers, cabaret, newsletter, speakers bureau, volunteer auxiliary.

Productions 1977-78
Pygmalion, George Bernard Shaw
Slow Dance on the Killing Ground, William Hanley
Equus, Peter Shaffer
Black Comedy, Peter Shaffer
The Shadow Box, Michael Cristofer
Rodgers and Hart, music: Richard Rodgers; lyrics: Lorenz Hart; adapt: Richard Lewine and John Fearnley

Productions 1978-79
Cold Storage, Ronald Ribman
A Christmas Carol, adapt: Keith Fowler
Tartuffe, Moliere; trans: Richard Wilbur
The Royal Hunt of the Sun, Peter Shaffer
Boesman and Lena, Athol Fugard
The Show-Off, George Kelly

John McMurtry and Dee Maaske in *Tartuffe.* Photo: Tim Fuller.

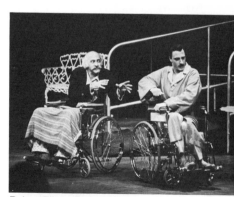

Robert Ellenstein and Robert F. LuPone in *Cold Storage.* Photo: Tim Fuller.

Arkansas Repertory Theatre

Cliff F. Baker
Director

Jane Mooney
General Manager

712 East 11th St.
Little Rock, AR 72202
(501) 378-0405

Founded 1976
Cliff F. Baker

Season
September–June

Schedule
Evenings
Thursday–Saturday
Matinees
Sunday

Facilities
Seating capacity: 120-165
Stage: flexible

Finances
July 1, 1978–June 30, 1979
$201,000 operating expenses
$146,000 earned income
$ 55,000 unearned income

Audience
Paid capacity: 84%
Subscribers: 600
Annual attendance: 36,480

Touring contact
Jane Mooney

Craig Fuller and Jean Lind in *The Glass Menagerie*. Photo: Tom Gordon.

Jeannine LeMay in *Vanities*. Photo: Ken Klingenmeier.

The Arkansas Repertory Theatre, the only professional theatre in its state, is committed to creative performance and innovative program development. Now in its fourth season, ART exemplifies the phenomenal growth and success which a resident theatre can enjoy with a responsive public, an emphasis on artistic quality and sound management.

ART presents a six-production mainstage season, balancing contemporary works, classics, experimental and original pieces. Each year, several productions are selected for statewide touring. A successful guest director program augments the mainstage season, and a recently inaugurated workshop theatre series called Act II promises to become a forum for new works by regional playwrights.

Both ART and its founding director Cliff Baker are committed to the development of programs serving people not traditionally considered "culture consumers." The largest of these is an artists-in-schools program, which yearly provides hundreds of performances and workshops to Arkansas students and teachers. Included is a theatre enrichment program for gifted high school students, one of the first such programs in the state. A theatre workshop program in the Arkansas prison system has attracted national attention, and ART has also developed a pilot workshop program reaching senior citizens throughout the state.

The 10 actors and actresses who compose the resident company bring a variety of talents and experience to ART and have been drawn from across the nation. In order to increase the opportunities for professional training in Arkansas, an internship/apprentice program is being established. ART is also planning the renovation of its current quarters, an architecturally and historically distinguished church in downtown Little Rock.

Programs and services
Classes for nonprofessionals, technical/production internships, student performances, programs-in-schools, study materials, student ticket discounts, statewide touring, post-performance discussions, workshop productions and staged readings, newsletter, volunteer auxiliary, theatre rentals.

Productions 1977-78
Jacques Brel Is Alive and Well and Living in Paris, music and lyrics: Jacques Brel; adapt: Eric Blau and Mort Shuman
Kennedy's Children, Robert Patrick
Happy Birthday, Wanda June, Kurt Vonnegut
Fitting for Ladies, Georges Feydeau; trans: Peter Meyer
An Evening of Gershwin, music: George Gershwin; lyrics: Ira Gershwin, et al.; adapt: Cliff F. Baker and Sharon Douglas
The Glass Menagerie, Tennessee Williams

Productions 1978-79
Sweet Charity, book: Neil Simon; music: Cy Coleman; lyrics: Dorothy Fields
Celebration, book and lyrics: Tom Jones; music: Harvey Schmidt
An Evening of Gershwin
The Boys in the Band, Mart Crowley
Vanities, Jack Heifner
The Runner Stumbles, Milan Stitt
Twelfth Night, William Shakespeare
Who's Afraid of Virginia Woolf?, Edward Albee
Lola-Lola, book: Cliff F. Baker; music and lyrics: Sharon Douglas

Asolo State Theater

Richard G. Fallon
Executive Director

Robert Strane
Artistic Director

Howard J. Millman
Managing Director

Drawer E
Sarasota, FL 33578
(813) 355-7115 (business)
(813) 355-2771 (box office)

Founded 1960
Arthur Dorlag, Richard G. Fallon,
L. Eberle Thomas, Robert Strane

Season
February–September

Schedule
Evenings
Tuesday–Sunday
Matinees
Tuesday, Wednesday, Saturday

Facilities
Asolo Theater
Ringling Museums
5401 Bayshore Road
Seating capacity: 320
Stage: proscenium
Asolo Stage Two
1247 First St.
Seating capacity: 185
Stage: thrust

Finances
Oct. 1, 1977–Sept. 30, 1978
$949,000 operating expenses
$508,000 earned income
$443,000 unearned income

Audience
Paid capacity: 94%
Subscribers: 3,500
Annual attendance: 174,904

Touring contact
Linda M. DiGabriele

AEA LORT (C) contract

Firmly committed to the challenges and rewards of European-style rotating repertory, the Asolo State Theater remains first and foremost an actor's theatre. Here the actor's presence, scope and versatility can flourish in a wide variety of roles throughout a season including both classic and contemporary plays. In Asolo's rotating schedule an actor confronts a range of stylistic challenges available at relatively few other theatres. Casting exigencies are primary in the choice of repertoire. Shows must "cast out" correctly not only in terms of budgetary allowances for actors but, more importantly, in terms of productive utilization of the assembled company. Actors are auditioned for a series of roles rather than a single assignment, and each actor hired knows his entire character repertoire for the season when he signs his contract. Rehearsals begin in mid-January and the season closes Labor Day weekend.

Since tourism is a major industry, Asolo audiences comprise people expecting to see as many as five plays during a short stay in Sarasota. Every effort is made to ensure a vital theatrical diversity in the season lineup, including importation of as many as five guest directors and designers, all chosen for their highly individualized contributions to specific plays. The plays comprising the typical Asolo season are selected with a mind to the greatest eclecticism, and with these convictions: that (as Peter Hall, head of the National Theatre of Great Britain, has said) audiences come to the theatre *primarily* to watch actors at work; and that plays with the best roles, those infinite in their capacity to nurture their performers, make the best theatre.

Programs and services
Professional training in acting, directing, design, production and administration in association with Florida State University; artistic; administrative and technical/production internships, student performances, programs-in-schools, study materials, student ticket discounts, regional touring of children's theatre, post-performance discussions, workshop productions and staged readings, newsletter, souvenir book, volunteer auxiliary.

Productions 1977-78
The Royal Family, George S. Kaufman and Edna Ferber
Juno and the Paycock, Sean O'Casey
She Stoops to Conquer, Oliver Goldsmith
The School for Wives, Moliere; trans: L. Eberle Thomas
Travesties, Tom Stoppard
Richard III, William Shakespeare
The Man Who Came to Dinner, George S. Kaufman and Moss Hart
The Inspector General, Nikolai Gogol; trans: Thomas Edward West
Catsplay, Istvan Orkeny; trans: Clara Gyorgyey
Archy and Friends, book company developed from Don Marquis' stories; music and lyrics: John Franceschina

Productions 1978-79
Design for Living, Noel Coward
The Shadow Box, Michael Cristofer
Volpone, Ben Jonson
Let's Get a Divorce, Victorien Sardou and Emile de Najac; trans: Brian Kelly
Long Day's Journey into Night, Eugene O'Neill
A History of the American Film, book and lyrics: Christopher Durang; music: Mel Marvin and John Franceschina
Othello, William Shakespeare
Stag at Bay, Charles MacArthur and Nunnally Johnson
The Cherry Orchard, Anton Chekhov; trans: Jean-Claude van Itallie
Merlin, book company developed; music and lyrics: John Franceschina

Robert Beseda and Robert Murch in *Volpone.* Photo: Gary W. Sweetman.

Isa Thomas, Elizabeth Horowitz, David S. Howard and Bradford Wallace in *Juno and the Paycock.* Photo: Gary W. Sweetman.

BAM Theater Company

David Jones
Artistic Director

Arthur Penn
Associate Director

Charles Dillingham
Managing Director

Brooklyn Academy of Music
30 Lafayette Ave.
Brooklyn, NY 11217
(212) 636-4135 (business)
(212) 636-4100 (box office)

Founded 1976
Frank Dunlop
Harvey Lichtenstein

Season
January–June

Schedule
Evenings
Tuesday–Sunday
Matinees
Saturday, Sunday

Facilities
Helen Owen Carey Playhouse
Seating capacity: 1,078
Stage: proscenium
Lepercq Space
Seating capacity: 300-450
Stage: flexible
Opera House
Seating capacity: 2,100
Stage: proscenium

Booked-in events
Dance, music, theatre

AEA Production contract

Keith Gordon and Richard Backus in *Gimme Shelter*. Photo: Paul Kolnik.

The aim of the newly reorganized Brooklyn Academy of Music (BAM) Theater Company is to provide New York with a permanent classical repertory company, having a committed group of actors prepared to work over a period of time to develop their skills, and to explore and define a specifically American approach to the presentation of classical drama.

The company's individual interpretation of the classics must be worked out on the rehearsal room floor and not to be molded to fit a preconceived theory. Its intent is to establish a feasible rotating repertory of two or three different productions available to theatregoers at any given time.

A successful classical company cannot be formed overnight. It took the Royal Shakespeare Company three years before it was properly free from the West End tyranny of the star names and instant success. BAM believes that the success of a company's overall work shouldn't rest with the judgement of an individual production. The test must be whether the company has established an identity and a reputation exciting and welcoming enough to make regular visits to Brooklyn an essential part of the New York experience.

BAM has budgeted for a company of about 25 actors, a medium-sized troupe in which each player can be afforded a proper scope of casting and as much detailed attention and training as possible. The four-month spring 1980 season will include four productions, and subsequent seasons will feature six productions.

BAM members aim to be discoverers wherever possible, reviving lively or entertaining plays that have slipped out of the mainstream and, in the spirit of adventure, staging the more established classics in ways fresh and relevant to the moment.

The Dodger Theater, a special BAM project which bowed in 1978, serves as BAM Theater Company's contemporary counterpart. In striving to show new work to as good advantage as its fellow troupe's classical productions, Dodger hopes to become a developmental theatre that goes beyond a preliminary presentation of a script and produces on a level that is in itself final and complete.

Programs and services
Student performances, programs-in-schools, student and senior citizen ticket discounts, voucher program, lobby buffet, newsletter, theatre rentals.

Productions 1977-78
The Devil's Disciple, George Bernard Shaw
The Play's the Thing, Ferenc Molnar; adapt:
P.G. Wodehouse
Julius Caesar, William Shakespeare
Waiting for Godot, Samuel Beckett

Productions 1978-1979
Gimme Shelter, Barrie Keeffe
On Mount Chimborazo, Tankred Dorst; adapt:
Peter Sander

Richard Dreyfuss, Ken Letner, George McDaniel, Rene Auberjonois, Thomas Hulce and Austin Pendleton in *Julius Caesar*. Photo: Jack Mitchell.

Barter Theatre

Rex Partington
Artistic Director and Producer

Box 867
Abingdon, VA 24210
(703) 628-2281 (business)
(703) 628-3991 (box office)

Founded 1933
Robert Porterfield

Season
April–October

Schedule
Evenings
Tuesday–Sunday
Matinees
Wednesday, Saturday

Facilities
Theatre
Seating capacity: 380
Stage: proscenium
Playhouse
Seating capacity: 125
Stage: thrust

Finances
Nov. 1, 1977–Oct. 31, 1978
$545,000 operating expenses
$332,000 earned income
$ 85,000 unearned income

Audience
Theatre paid capacity: 59%
Playhouse paid capacity: 64%
Subscribers: 2,777
Total annual attendance: 75,332

Touring contact
Pearl Hayter

AEA LORT (C) contract

Located in a town of fewer than 5,000 inhabitants, the Barter Theatre was founded at the height of the Depression by Robert Porterfield, an enterprising young actor. Faced with the darkened marquees of Broadway, Porterfield and 22 other actors arrived in Abingdon, Va., in the spring of 1933 and advertised that their plays could be seen for "30 cents or the equivalent in produce." In 1972, following Porterfield's death, Rex Partington was selected as artistic director/producer. Placing a primary emphasis on artistic achievement, he guides Barter's growth as an ensemble repertory company in producing drama in a wide range of theatrical styles.

Barter is a true regional theatre, serving the five-state area of Virginia, Tennessee, North Carolina, West Virginia and Kentucky.

With a resident company augmented by guest performers, directors and designers, Barter performs in Abingdon from April through October, producing 11 plays in two performance spaces. At least one new play is included in the mainstage repertoire, and a "Works-in-Progress" program gives new playwrights an opportunity to see and revise their work.

In addition to producing plays in Abingdon, the Barter provides many other services. Touring has always been and remains an important part of Barter's program. In 1949, the Barter production of *Hamlet* was chosen to represent the United States in performance at Kronborg Castle in Elsinore, Denmark. Each spring one or two productions tour regionally, and if feasible, nationally. The Artists-in-Schools residencies and tours provide plays and workshops to educational institutions.

Admission to the Barter Playhouse, located across the street from the theatre, is still by donation of cash or produce, thus keeping alive the "barter" tradition.

Programs and services
Professional training; artistic, administrative and technical/production internships; student performances, programs-in-schools, study materials, apprentice program, student ticket discounts, national touring, post-performance discussions, workshop productions and staged readings, film series, children's theatre, newsletter, speakers bureau, volunteer auxiliary.

Productions 1978
Two Gentlemen of Verona, William Shakespeare
The Mousetrap, Agatha Christie
Born Yesterday, Garson Kanin
The Corn Is Green, Emlyn Williams
Tartuffe, Moliere
The Apple Tree, book: Jerry Bock and Sheldon Harnick; music: J. Bock; lyrics: S. Harnick
Hay Fever, Noel Coward
The Second Man, S. N. Behrman
How the Other Half Loves, Alan Ayckbourn
I Do! I Do!, book and lyrics:Tom Jones; music: Harvey Schmidt
The Owl and the Pussycat, Bill Manhoff
Oh, Coward!, music and lyrics: Noel Coward; adapt: Roderick Cook

Productions 1979
I Do! I Do!
The Wonderful Ones!, one-act plays by Tennessee Williams and Anton Chekhov
A Doll's House, Henrik Ibsen
Same Time, Next Year, Bernard Slade
Misalliance, George Bernard Shaw
Dames at Sea, book and lyrics: George Haimsohn and Robin Miller; music: Jim Wise
Absurd Person Singular, Alan Ayckbourn
Hay Fever, Noel Coward
Side by Side by Sondheim, music and lyrics: Stephen Sondheim, et al.; adapt: Ned Sherrin
Luv, Murray Schisgal
The Fantasticks, book and lyrics: Tom Jones; music: Harvey Schmidt

Cleo Holladay in *The Corn Is Green.* Photo: Bill Blanton.

John Morrow, Cleo Holladay, Sam Blackwell and Beverly Jensen in *The Second Man.* Photo: Bill Blanton.

Berkeley Repertory Theatre

Michael W. Leibert
Producing Director

Mitzi K. Sales
General Manager

2980 College Ave.
Berkeley, CA 94705
(415) 841-6108 (business)
(415) 845-4700 (box office)

Founded 1968
Michael W. Leibert

Season
September–August

Schedule
Evenings
Tuesday–Sunday
Matinees
Sunday

Facilities
Seating capacity: 153
Stage: thrust

Finances
Sept. 1, 1978–Aug. 31, 1979
$268,000 operating expenses
$196,000 earned income
$ 58,000 unearned income

Audience
Paid capacity: 73%
Subscribers: 4,000
Annual attendance: 37,536

AEA BAT contract

Nicole Baptiste and Don West in
He Who Gets Slapped. Photo:
Michael Porter.

The Berkeley Repertory Theatre has developed a unique style generated by an intimate relationship between performer and audience. In the belief that the San Francisco East Bay area needed its own resident acting company, a handful of actors from the University of California/Berkeley moved to a rented 85-seat theatre a mile from the campus in 1968. As audience demand increased, the theatre was expanded to its current 153-seat capacity in 1972. Attention from the press and a strong subscriber base helped stabilize the theatre during its first decade.

The close of the 1970s saw exciting developmental and artistic challenges. A new 400-seat theatre began construction in 1979 in downtown Berkeley, the first all-new construction of a professional theatre facility in northern California. Company members collaborated with architects Angell, Lockwood & Associates of Oakland in designing the new complex. An unprecedented Urban Development Action Grant from the United States Department of Housing and Urban Development (HUD) provided the theatre with the funding required to begin construction, and the theatre's relocation has spearheaded a downtown revitalization effort commanding national attention.

No longer drawing its repertoire solely from classical material, Berkeley Rep now presents new works on a regular basis. The new theatre will allow the development of a year-round apprentice/internship program. A second stage area will provide the opportunity for children's theatre, new works and a continuing lecture series. A stronger and more active board of directors has also contributed substantially to the Rep's success. The Backstagers, the theatre's volunteer group, has presented highly successful fund-raising events and helped increase the theatre's community visibility.

Programs and services
Artistic, administrative and technical/production internships; programs-in-schools, student and senior citizen ticket discounts, post-performance discussions, speakers bureau, volunteer auxiliary, newsletter, theatre rentals.

Productions 1977-78
A Flea in Her Ear, Georges Feydeau; trans: John Mortimer
Rep!, Stanley R. Greenberg
Major Barbara, George Bernard Shaw
Mad Oscar, Sheldon Feldner
The Servant of Two Masters, Carlo Goldoni; adapt: Joan Liepman, Joe Spano and Albert Kutchins
A Moon for the Misbegotten, Eugene O'Neill
Wait Until Dark, Frederick Knott
Arms and the Man, George Bernard Shaw
As You Like It, William Shakespeare
They Knew What They Wanted, Sidney Howard
Misalliance, George Bernard Shaw

Productions 1978-79
The Skin of Our Teeth, Thornton Wilder
She Stoops to Conquer, Oliver Goldsmith
The Tavern, George M. Cohan
He Who Gets Slapped, Leonid Andreyev; adapt: Michael W. Leibert
The Last of the Marx Brothers' Writers, Louis Phillips
Room Service, John Murray and Allen Boretz

Paul Laramore, Alice Rorvik and
Dale Elliott in *Arms and the Man*.
Photo: Michael Porter.

Berkeley Stage Company

Robert W. Goldsby
Angela Paton
Artistic Directors

Anthony Taccone
General Manager

Box 2327
Berkeley, CA 94702
(415) 548-4728

Founded 1974
Robert W. Goldsby,
Angela Paton, Drury Pifer

Season
October–June

Schedule
Evenings
Wednesday–Sunday

Facilities
1111 Addison St.
Seating capacity: 99
Stage: flexible

Finances
Jan. 1, 1978–Sept. 30,1978
$84,000 operating expenses
$28,000 earned income
$45,000 unearned income

Audience
Paid capacity: 77%
Subscribers: 734
Annual attendance: 15,000

AEA 99-seat waiver

The Berkeley Stage Company's primary mission is the production of new scripts. Thus far, more than 50 original works have been presented, the majority with playwrights in residence at the company's home, a converted garage. The versatile space has been used with actors surrounding the audience; with the audience encircling the actors; with the audience on all three sides, two sides, the conventional one side; or with no audience/actor separation at all.

The choice of plays is influenced by the company's interest in the process of the individual writer and his or her interpreters, rather than a predetermined aesthetic or ideology. All theatrical forms have been presented, from naturalism to "image-ism," from nonverbal experiments to plays centered on the complexities of language, from the remembrance of Old West wagon trains to visions of eastern phantasmagoria. As touchstones of excellence, Berkeley Stage has also produced each year one or two major works by the most innovative writers in the contemporary theatre—Beckett, Bond, Brecht, Handke, Rabe and others.

Illustrating the growth of Berkeley Stage as a theatre devoted to new writers and the continued exposure of work, its production of Rena Down's *The People vs. Inez Garcia* was broadcast nationwide on PBS, and Patrick Meyers' *Feedlot,* discovered in Berkeley Stage's playwrights workshop and later performed there as a major production, was later seen by New York audiences during the Circle Repertory Company's 1977-78 season. The company's 1978 production of Albert Innaurato's *Earthworms,* presented in association with the New York Shakespeare Festival, received four Bay Area Theatre Critics Circle Awards, including outstanding dramatic production. International crosscurrents have enabled the theatre to perform David Rabe's *Sticks and Bones* in Italy at the Venice Biennale and to present for its home audiences the American premieres of Japanese playwright Kobo Abe's *The Man Who Turned into a Stick* and East German writer Heiner Müller's *Cement,* the latter with the author in residence.

Programs and services
Technical/production internships, student performances, programs-in-schools; ticket discounts for students, senior citizens and the unemployed; vouchers, post-performance discussions, workshop productions and staged readings, newsletter, weekly one-act play series.

Productions 1977-78
Feedlot, Patrick Meyers
Womansong, various writers
The Sea, Edward Bond
The IX John Paul, Rick Foster
Three Sons, Richard Lortz
The Caucasian Chalk Circle, Bertolt Brecht; trans: Eric Bentley
Safe House, Nicholas Kazan
Earthworms, Albert Innaurato
Leading Off and Playing Shortstop, Philip Bosakowski
Ashes, David Rudkin
Artichoke, Joanna Glass
The Dancing Bear Routine, William Harrar

Productions 1978-79
Mackerel, Israel Horovitz
The Man Who Turned into a Stick, Kobo Abe; trans: Donald Keene
Centralia 1919, book and lyrics: Barry Pritchard; music: Robert MacDougall
Cement, Heiner Muller; trans: Helen Fehevary, Sue-Ellen Case and Marc D. Silberman
The Tennis Game, George W.S. Trow
Curse of the Starving Class, Sam Shepard

Roderick Prindle and Dana G. Evans in *Safe House*. Photo: Jerry Morse.

Angela Paton in *Earthworms*. Photo: Jerry Morse.

BoarsHead Theater

Richard Thomsen
John Peakes
Artistic Directors

Carol Conn
Managing Director

Center for the Arts
425 South Grand Ave.
Lansing, MI 48933
(517) 484-7800 (business)
(517) 484-7805 (box office)

Founded 1970
Richard Thomsen, John Peakes

Season
October–September

Schedule
Evenings
Thursday–Sunday

Facilities
Center for the Arts
Seating capacity: 250
Stage: thrust
Ledges Playhouse
Fitzgerald Park, Grand Ledge
Seating capacity: 350
Stage: thrust

Finances
Oct. 1, 1978–Sept. 30, 1979
$262,000 operating expenses
$173,000 earned income
$ 89,000 unearned income

Audience
Paid capacity: 66%
Subscribers: 1,741
Annual attendance: 36,000

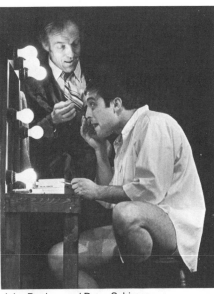

John Peakes and Doug Schirner in *A Life in the Theatre*. Photo: Rick Brown.

The BoarsHead Theater is dedicated to a regional but not a parochial voice: that of American plays and developing American playwrights. Under the artistic direction of Richard Thomsen and John Peakes, the BoarsHead began from a set of related ideas: that an indigenous theatre must grow from within the community it serves, that a working theatre must be perceived as a natural part of the working life of the city, and that the repertoire should reflect as clearly as possible the lives of the audience it serves.

Its theatre now established, the BoarsHead company is growing in stength. Its repertoire is shaped by new works and new writers. Milan Stitt, author of *The Runner Stumbles*, functions as the theatre's dramaturg. In the 1978-79 season Gus Kaikkonen's *Time Steps* premiered, and in future seasons up to half the schedule will be given over to new works.

The BoarsHead is committed to plays of a distinctly theatrical nature. The performing space, a small auditorium in a converted downtown garage, is best suited for plays that can be presented in an "open" manner. More importantly, the BoarsHead audience has demonstrated through the years that it prefers events not available to it elsewhere.

The BoarsHead involves its community in two major ways. The theatre itself is the only major downtown arts activity, and it administers theatre courses through programs coordinated by Lansing Community College and the Lansing School District. The college subsidizes a ticket program which enables a broad segment of the student body to attend performances on a regular basis.

Programs and services
Professional training in acting and directing; artistic, administrative and technical/production internships; student and senior citizen ticket discounts, free ticket distribution, subsidized college ticket program, post-performance discussions, workshop productions and staged readings, newsletter, speakers bureau, teaching program with Lansing Communxt College.

Productions 1977-78
Last of the Red Hot Lovers, Neil Simon
Living Together, Alan Ayckbourn
Who's Afraid of Virginia Woolf?, Edward Albee
Private Lives, Noel Coward
Equus, Peter Shaffer
Stop the World—I Want to Get Off, book, music and lyrics: Leslie Bricusse and Anthony Newley
The Runner Stumbles, Milan Stitt
Vanities, Jack Heifner
The Sunshine Boys, Neil Simon
Cabaret, book: Joe Masteroff; music: John Kander; lyrics: Fred Ebb
Fiddler on the Roof, book: Joseph Stein; music: Jerry Bock; lyrics: Sheldon Harnick
The Male Animal, James Thurber and Elliott Nugent

Productions 1978-79
The Last Meeting of the Knights of the White Magnolia, Preston Jones
The Underpants, Carl Sternheim
Dandelion Wine, Peter John Bailey, from Ray Bradbury's novel
A Life in the Theatre, David Mamet
Uncle Vanya, Anton Chekhov
Steambath, Bruce Jay Friedman
Time Steps, Gus Kaikkonen
The House of Blue Leaves, John Guare
Harvey, Mary Chase
Man of La Mancha, book: Dale Wasserman; music: Mitch Leigh; lyrics: Joe Darion
George M!, book: Michael Stewart, John and Fran Pascal; music and lyrics: George M. Cohan
Same Time, Next Year, Bernard Slade

Time Steps. Photo: Rick Brown.

Body Politic Theatre

Dale McFadden
Artistic Director

Sharon Phillips
Managing Director

2261 North Lincoln Ave.
Chicago, IL 60614
(312) 525-1052 (business)
(312) 871-3000 (box office)

Founded 1969
Community Arts Foundation

Season
September–August

Schedule
Evenings
Wednesday–Sunday
Matinees
Sunday

Facilities
Upstairs Theatre
Seating capacity: 150
Stage: flexible
Center Theatre
Seating capacity: 150
Stage: thrust
Little Theatre
Seating capacity: 70
Stage: proscenium

Finances
Jan. 1, 1978–Dec. 31, 1978
$344,000 operating expenses
$301,000 earned income
$ 22,000 unearned income

Audience
Paid capacity: 35%
Subscribers: 722
Annual attendance: 20,000

Booked-in events
Mime, puppet and experimental
theatre, music, dance

AEA COLT contract

In 1969, Chicago's Community Arts Foundation purchased a building on the city's Lincoln Avenue in order to establish and expand a relationship between artists, their work and the community. The facility, called the Body Politic, includes three theatres, as well as rehearsal space. With a major emphasis on theatre, the Body Politic has played an important role in the emergence of a diverse alternative theatre community in Chicago. Its wide range of activity has influenced the careers of many performers, directors and playwrights. As a place "where the arts are," the Body Politic also shelters and supports muralists, dancers, poets and teachers.

In 1978, the Body Politic launched its first subscription season, comprising recent works of modern American and European classics, with an emphasis on stretching the expectations of both the actor and the audience. The New Playwrights Series encourages new plays, primarily those by midwestern writers. The Mixed Events Series sponsors production of works that are experimental in form and content with much of the work done by groups imported from around the country. The company's Bible Story Theatre performs for Sunday schools, and the Theatre-in-Museums project develops theatre pieces based on museum exhibits, performing in museums, hospitals and homes for the handicapped.

As part of a vital neighborhood with a high percentage of people involved in education, communication and culture, the Body Politic is active in festivals, benefits and other affairs consistent with its equal commitment to the community and the arts.

Programs and services
Professional training in acting and directing; classes for nonprofessionals and children; student performances, programs-in-schools, student and senior citizen ticket discounts, free ticket distribution, regional touring, guest lecturers, poetry readings, children's theatre, theatre rentals.

Productions 1977-78
Lunching, Alan Gross
Samuel: The First Book of the Kings, company developed from the King James Version of the Bible
The Baron Must Die, Frank Shiras
Let It Play, James Barry, John Green, Dale McFadden and Eric McGill
Bingo: Game of the Gods, book: Virginia Smiley and company; music: Melissa Shiflett; lyrics: Karyne G. Pritikin
Slapstick and Sawdust, T.J. Tatters

Productions 1978-79
Red Rover, Red Rover, Oliver Hailey
Angel City, Sam Shepard
Spring's Awakening, Frank Wedekind
Statements After an Arrest Under the Immorality Act, Athol Fugard
Scenes from Soweto, Steve Wilmer
Eyes of Wonder, company developed
Hide and Seek, Frank Shiras
Dead of Night, John Ostrander
Station J, Richard France

Robert Jackson and Joette Waters in *Statements After an Arrest Under the Immorality Act.* Photo: Stuart Markson.

Annemarie Daniels and Mark Atkinson in *Eyes of Wonder.* Photo: Richard Maize.

Boston Arts Group

Van McLeod
Interim Artistic Director

Virginia Land
General Manager

367 Boylston St.
Boston, MA 02116
(617) 267-7196 (business)
(617) 267-8518 (box office)

Founded 1975
Bart McCarthy, Virginia Land,
Pam Enion, Roger Curtis

Season
September–June

Schedule
Evenings
Thursday–Saturday
Matinees
Sunday

Facilities
Mainstage
Seating capacity: 110
Stage: flexible
Stage Two
Seating capacity: 70
Stage: flexible

Finances
July 1, 1978–June 30, 1979
$109,000 operating expenses
$ 49,000 earned income
$ 60,000 unearned income

Audience
Paid capacity: 60%
Annual attendance: 22,000

Touring contact
Deborah Brown

Booked-in events
Dance, music, theatre

Rob Donaldson and Diane
Edgecomb in *A Martian Trilogy.*
Photo: Roger Ide.

The objectives of the Boston Arts Group are to develop, produce and showcase innovative works and new dramatic forms and simultaneously create new audiences for them. Though BAG presents a wide variety of productions in its two theatres, its output conveys a humanistic outlook and often employs nontraditional dramatic structures and staging, emphasizing ensemble and improvisational techniques, as well as integrating music, dance and other media.

BAG also reaches beyond avant-garde audiences. Its Senior Citizen Series and Boston Lunchtime Theatre have served special audiences which can more easily attend theatre in the afternoon than in the evening. The Children's Tour Program has performed to thousands of youngsters. Two Beckett plays numbered among the productions toured throughout New England for older audiences. The company also performs a play outdoors in the summer along the historic Freedom Trail.

BAG's Women's Theatre Series has showcased the works of four women's theatre companies this past year and has produced two new plays by and about women. A training program for disadvantaged youth in both acting and technical theatre gives aspiring actors and designers a chance to work alongside professionals, and the company's internship program familiarizes area college students with all aspects of theatre arts and management.

The company also works for theatre and audience development by teaching theatre arts in area public schools, by giving acting and stagecraft lessons in its own school, and by providing rehearsal and performance spaces to other small-scale performing arts troupes.

Programs and services
Professional training in acting, directing and production; artistic and technical/production internships, student performances, programs-in-schools, study materials, student and senior citizen ticket discounts, free ticket distribution, Arts Boston subsidized ticket program, regional touring of children's theatre, post-performance discussions, guest lecturers, theatre rentals.

Productions 1977-78
The Hot l Baltimore, Lanford Wilson
Kansas City K.R.O.W., Bart McCarthy and
   Arthur Crowley
The Dumb Waiter and *The Lover,* Harold Pinter
Passions, Dreams and Revelations, David
   Zucker and Kate Bentley
A Martian Trilogy, Bart McCarthy, from stories
   by Ray Bradbury and H.G. Wells
The Snark Was a Boojum, Pam Enion, from
   stories by Lewis Carroll

Productions 1978-79
Radio, company developed
Macbett, Eugene Ionesco
Yellow Wallpaper, Ann Titolo
I Can Feel the Air, Lis Adams
History of Western Civilization, Roger Curtis
Waiting for Godot, Samuel Beckett
Lincoln Log, Bart McCarthy
Savages, Christopher Hampton

Boston Shakespeare Company

Bill Cain
Artistic Director

B.J. Krintzman
Managing Director

300 Massachusetts Ave.
Boston, MA 02115
(617) 267-5630 (business)
(617) 267-5600 (box office)

Founded 1975
Bill Cain, Janet Buchwald,
Norman Frisch

Season
September–June

Schedule
Evenings
Wednesday–Saturday

Facilities
Mainstage
Seating capacity: 320
Stage: modified thrust
New England Life Hall
Seating capacity: 685
Stage: proscenium

Finances
July 1, 1978–June 30, 1979
$215,000 operating expenses
$185,000 earned income
$ 30,000 unearned income

Audience
Paid capacity: 76%
Subscribers: 1,253
Annual attendance: 97,500

Touring contact
B.J. Krintzman

The Boston Shakespeare Company is a classical rotating repertory company devoted to the concept of mounting lively, exciting, moving productions of the world's greatest plays, especially the works of Shakespeare, for a wide audience. The company's deep interest in Shakespeare is not antiquarian, and BSC offers its work as a reflection of the present. The company is devoted to the development of a broad-based audience composed not simply of scholars or academics, but of people from a great variety of backgrounds, professions and income levels. The company also has an enduring commitment to sharing its work with area students.

BSC's work is divided into three major areas: resident mainstage productions, a special student matinee program and a touring program. The company's mainstage production schedule runs 38 weeks each season, four or five performances a week, and always in repertory. In September 1978, BSC opened a new playhouse in historic Horticultural Hall, directly opposite Boston's Symphony Hall. In addition to an intimate, 320-seat, open-stage theatre, the new complex houses dressing room space, administrative offices, shops and a box office. During the 1978-79 season, BSC's first in the new theatre, more than 40,000 people attended mainstage performances.

BSC's educational programs serve a wide and diverse audience. A student matinee program begun in 1977 offers specially mounted 90-minute adaptations of Shakespeare. A touring program offers two shows—*An Invitation to Theatre* and *Shakespeare's World*—which have been performed more than 300 times during the past four seasons.

Under the leadership of artistic director Bill Cain and with a dedicated resident acting company, BSC continues to explore new production concepts and new directions for its repertoire, from Moliere's *The Miser* to Saroyan's *The Time of Your Life,* to occasional original scripts based on classical material.

Programs and services
Technical/production internships, student performances, programs-in-schools, study materials, student and senior citizen ticket discounts, post-performance discussions, newsletter, theatre rentals.

Productions 1977-78
Twelfth Night, William Shakespeare
The Taming of the Shrew, William Shakespeare
Henry IV, Part I, William Shakespeare
Much Ado About Nothing, William Shakespeare
Antigone, Jean Anouilh; trans: Lewis Galantiere
As You Like It, William Shakespeare

Productions 1978-79
Hamlet, William Shakespeare
As You Like It
The Miser, Moliere; trans: Sylvan Barnet, Morton Berman and William Burto
Twelfth Night
Measure for Measure, William Shakespeare
Two Gentlemen of Verona, William Shakespeare
Romeo and Juliet, William Shakespeare

Grey Cattell Johnson and Will Lebow in *The Miser.* Photo: Dan Coven.

Measure for Measure. Photo: Dan Coven.

California Actors Theatre

Sheldon Kleinman
Producing Director

Francine E. Gordon
General Manager

Box 1355
50 University Ave.
Los Gatos, CA 95030
(408) 354-3939 (business)
(408) 354-6057 (box office)

Founded 1974
Sheldon Kleinman

Season
October–August

Schedule
Evenings
Fall: Tuesday–Sunday
Summer: Monday–Saturday
Matinees
Fall: Wednesday, Saturday,
Sunday

Facilities
Old Town Theatre
50 University Ave.
Seating capacity: 418
Stage: modified thrust
Fox Theatre
2215 Broadway
Redwood City, CA 94063
Seating capacity: 850
Stage: modified thrust

Finances
Sept. 1, 1978–Aug. 31, 1979
$812,000 operating expenses
$705,000 earned income
$107,000 unearned income

Audience
Paid capacity: 85%
Subscribers: 12,500
Annual attendance: 130,000

Touring contact
Karl R. Schuck

AEA LORT (C) contract

John H. Fields, Patricia Boyette
and Maury Cooper in *Twelfth
Night.* Photo: John Naretto.

In order to develop new audiences in one of the country's fastest growing communities, California Actors Theatre emphasizes the concept of a thriving multi-faceted performance company rather than any particular type of play. Located in the northern California city of Los Gatos, a suburb of San Jose, CAT draws its audience from the entire South Bay and Mid-Peninsula areas. Experimentation with programming has been important in the development of CAT and the average season combines new plays (a world premiere each year), contemporary works and classics. Many seasons have included American and West Coast premieres as well, programming which attracts leading actors, directors and designers to an area where no other professional theatre exists.

In the summer of 1979, a five-play "summer stock" series was presented in the Napa Valley as well as in Los Gatos. Production costs were shared by CAT and the Napa Valley Association for the Performing Arts in Yountville. Thus, a shared services model was created to bring professional theatre to communities unable to support a full-time company. Another recent innovation is the opening of each production for a one-week run at a second, larger facility, the Sequoia Fox Theatre in Redwood City, located midway between Los Gatos and San Francisco. A repertory cinema utilizes that theatre between productions. Within two seasons, CAT expects to be operating both theatres full-time, and the expanded financial base will permit increased experimentation in programming. Another recent venture was a joint production with the San Jose Symphony of *A Midsummer Night's Dream* with the full Mendelssohn score.

CAT maintains intern programs with several local colleges and universities, providing work-study opportunities with college credit for students. An Equity children's theatre performs in residence at the theatre and also travels extensively in northern California.

Program and services
Artistic, administrative and technical/production internships; student performances, programs-in-schools, study materials, student and senior citizen ticket discounts, statewide touring of children's theatre, post-performance discussions, workshop productions and staged readings, film series, newsletter, speakers bureau, volunteer auxiliary, theatre rentals.

Productions 1977-78
Henry IV, Parts I and II, William Shakespeare
Save Grand Central, William Hamilton
Scapino, adapt: Frank Dunlop and Jim Dale
    from *Moliere*
The Price, Arthur Miller
You Can't Take It with You, George S. Kaufman
    and Moss Hart
Steambath, Bruce Jay Friedman
Wild Oats, John O'Keeffe

Productions 1978-79
Plymouth Rock, William Hamilton
The Marriage Proposal and *Swan Song*, Anton
    Chekhov; trans: Theodore Hoffman
The Brute, Anton Chekhov; trans: Eric Bentley
Bus Stop, William Inge
Playing with Fire, August Strindberg; trans:
    Edwin Bjorkman
The Collection, Harold Pinter
Holiday, Philip Barry
The Play's the Thing, Ferenc Molnar; adapt:
    P. G. Wodehouse
Twelfth Night, William Shakespeare
Crimes of the Heart, Beth Henley

Save Grand Central.
Photo: John Naretto.

The Cambridge Ensemble

Joann Green
Artistic Director

Barbara Bregstein
General Manager

c/o 6 Arlington St.
Cambridge, MA 02140

Founded 1973
Joann Green, Barbara Bregstein

Season
September–June

Schedule
Evenings
Thursday–Saturday

Facilities
Seating capacity: 120
Stage: flexible

Finances
Sept. 1, 1977–Oct. 31, 1978
$64,000 operating expenses
$39,000 earned income
$25,000 unearned income

Audience
Paid capacity: 85%
Annual attendance: 20,000

Touring contact
Barbara Bregstein

Booked-in events
Theatre

AEA letter of agreement

Now in its seventh season, the Cambridge Ensemble is a developmental theatre, dedicated to presenting new and rarely performed plays, and the adaptation of narrative works for the stage. The flexible and intimate space of the Ensemble's theatre provides a minimum of technical appurtenances and requires maximum reliance on the actor. Casts are generally small, and the emphasis is placed on ensemble work. Plays are chosen for their theatrical potential and possibilities for investigative interpretation. The theatre produces three to five plays per season. Included in a representative year are an American premiere, such as Ionesco's *A Hell of a Mess*, and an original adaptation, such as Joann Green's dramatization of Gogol's *The Diary of a Madman*.

The Ensemble's hospital program, featuring free performances in hospitals throughout Massachusetts, is now four years old. It and other community-oriented programs have resulted in the Ensemble's first formal neighborhood project, funded and organized by the city of Cambridge. The Ensemble performs specially designed shows in low income areas, with workshops and discussions following performances.

Plans for the 1979-80 season include a concerted effort at financial expansion and the adaptation of a novel by a major modern writer and philosopher.

Programs and services
Professional training in acting; classes for nonprofessionals and children; artistic and administrative internships, student performances, programs-in-schools, free ticket distribution, voucher program, national touring, post-performance discussions, workshop productions and staged readings, performances in hospitals and low-income neighborhoods.

Productions 1977-78
The Oresteia, Aeschylus; adapt: Joann Green
Puntila and Matti, His Hired Man, Bertolt Brecht;
    trans: Ralph Manheim
A Hell of a Mess, Eugene Ionesco; trans: Helen
    Gary Bishop
Tales of Chelm, company developed

Productions 1978-79
A Sorrow Beyond Dreams, Peter Handke;
    trans: Ralph Manheim
Gulliver's Travels, company developed from
    Jonathan Swift's novel
Tales of Chelm
The Diary of a Madman, Joann Green, from
    Nikolai Gogol's story

Noya Lancet and Randall Richard
in *A Sorrow Beyond Dreams.*
Photo: Eric Levenson.

Tim McDonough and John Wright
in *A Hell of a Mess*. Photo: Eric
Levenson.

Center Stage

Stanley Wojewodski, Jr.
Artistic Director

Peter W. Culman
Managing Director

700 North Calvert St.
Baltimore, MD 21202
(301) 685-3200 (business)
(301) 332-0033 (box office)

Founded 1963
Community Arts Committee

Season
October–May

Schedule
Evenings
Tuesday–Sunday
Matinees
Wednesday, Saturday, Sunday

Facilities
Seating capacity: 500
Stage: modified thrust

Finances
July 1, 1978–June 30, 1979
$1,124,000 operating expenses
$ 668,000 earned income
$ 517,000 unearned income

Audience
Paid capacity: 88%
Subscribers: 12,909
Annual attendance: 213,056

Booked-in-events
Film, music

Touring contact
Jean Doyle

AEA LORT (B) contract

Herb Rice, Lori Tan Chinn,
Michael Moriarty, Michael Jeter
and Howard E. Rollins, Jr., in *G.R.
Point*. Photo: Richard Anderson.

Terry O'Quinn and Tana Hicken in
Measure for Measure. Photo:
Richard Anderson.

Center Stage recognizes the need to bring to Baltimore audiences well-balanced theatre seasons, including masterworks (both classic and contemporary) and recent works, as well as other programs which provide theatre to audiences who might otherwise be excluded. It also provides opportunities, through intern programs and creative workshops, for the development of emerging artists.

Plans for the 1979-80 season include the inauguration of a new program, First Stage, comprising a series of new scripts performed "in process" in advance of a full production. Study has also begun for the construction of a second theatre. This space will eventually provide a home for the First Stage series as well as an arena for extended investigation of performance styles.

Recently designated the official state theatre of Maryland, Center Stage is enjoying renaissance under artistic director Stanley Wojewodski, Jr., and managing director Peter W. Culman, under whose guidance the institution moved to its present downtown location after a mid-season fire in 1974. The Center Stage facility, a gift from the Jesuit Province of Maryland, was renovated at a cost of $1.7 million and received an American Institute of Architects award for restoration.

The subscription series includes six mainstage productions. The specially commissioned adaptation of Charles Dickens' *A Christmas Carol* by Israel Horovitz is presented annually outside this series. Easy access to New York City makes it possible to supplement a small resident group of actors with others specifically suited to particular productions. Close association with a small pool of designers stimulates full and varied utilization of the modified thrust mainstage.

Center Stage's Young People's Theatre tours annually to elementary and high schools throughout Maryland's 23 counties, bringing specially commissioned theatre pieces and individual classroom performances to more than 100,000 students. An internship program for secondary school students and an artists-in-schools residency program highlights the unique accessibility of a community-based arts resource to the secondary school curriculum.

Center Stage's programming provides a varied schedule for its Maryland audiences and diverse production challenges for its artists and administrators.

Programs and services
Classes for nonprofessionals and children; artistic, administrative and technical/production internships; student performances, programs-in-schools, study materials, student ticket discounts, free ticket distribution, statewide touring, post-performance discussions, summer film series, restaurant/cafe, speakers bureau, volunteer auxiliary.

Productions 1977-78
The Goodbye People, Herb Gardner
The Rivals, Richard Brinsley Sheridan
The Runner Stumbles, Milan Stitt
Ashes, David Rudkin
The Night of the Iguana, Tennessee Williams
Blithe Spirit, Noel Coward

Productions 1978-79
The Shadow Box, Michael Cristofer
Born Yesterday, Garson Kanin
A Christmas Carol: Scrooge and Marley, adapt: Israel Horovitz
G.R. Point, David Berry
You Can't Take It with You, George S. Kaufman and Moss Hart
Measure for Measure, William Shakespeare
Bonjour, là, Bonjour, Michel Tremblay; trans: John Van Burek and Bill Glassco

The Changing Scene

Alfred Brooks
President

1527½ Champa St.
Denver, CO 80202
(303) 893-5775

Founded 1968
Alfred Brooks
Maxine Munt

Season
October–September

Schedule
Evenings
Thursday–Sunday

Facilities
Seating capacity: 76
Stage: flexible

Finances
Jan. 1, 1978–Dec. 31, 1978
$79,000 operating expenses
$14,000 earned income
$62,000 unearned income

Audience
Paid capacity: 24%
Subscribers: 47
Annual attendance: 25,000

Touring contact
Alfred Brooks

Booked-in events
Dance, experimental theatre,
film, mime, music, poetry, video,
visual arts exhibits

The Changing Scene presents new work in all the arts under an operating philosophy that the theatre is the natural meeting place for all creative media. Sculptors, painters, photographers, filmmakers and video artists not only have solo shows in the Changing Scene gallery but frequently discover that the larger involvement in theatre productions is greatly satisfying. This discovery in turn leads to unique artistic collaborations.

Only new plays are produced and are chosen by an affiliated director, with the playwright in residence and intimately involved in artistic decisions.

Several of the Changing Scene's premieres have played in New York recently, including Israel Horovitz and Bob Breuler's *The Longest Way Home* (the company's 18th play to be subsequently produced in New York).

The 1978-79 season was augmented by 75 additional performances given in community centers, senior citizen centers, schools, drug and alcohol rehabilitation centers and hospitals throughout the city.

The Changing Scene also conducts an outreach educational program in public elementary schools, offering two classes per week as part of the regular school curriculum.

A newly enlarged board of trustees, representing a broad spectrum of both ethnic and occupational diversity, has demonstrated abundant energy in initiating projects in audience development and analysis, community awareness and fund-raising.

Programs and services
Professional training in acting, student performances, programs-in-schools, student ticket discounts, free ticket distribution, statewide touring, workshop productions and staged readings, film series, poetry readings, newsletter, volunteer auxiliary.

Productions 1977-78
Mencken, James Crowell
Day upon Day, Andrea Shepard
Custer, Robert E. Ingham
Batteries Not Included, William Smith and company
Short Plays for a Man on the Moon and *the Teachings of John Brown in Florida,* Michael Meyers
Repast, David Lang
Apparent Discrepancies, Eric Charles Baldwin
The Mantis Flies Alone, David Lang
The First Interplanetary Voyage of J. Alfred Carnelian, Eric Charles Baldwin

Productions 1978-79
L'Ecole des Veuves, Jean Cocteau
Le Petit Prince, Jacques Ardouin, from Antoine de Saint Exupery's novel
Two Small Bodies, Neal Bell
Coke Dreams and *Bride Doll,* Teresa Marffie-Evangelista
The Man Who Knew John Dillinger, Janet McReynolds
Spit, Bob Breuler
Parade of Arms, Don Katzman

Charlotte Liethen, Anne Bradley and Kathi Schneider in *The Man Who Knew John Dillinger.* Photo: Fred Schultz.

Jack Henri and Kimimela Garrett in *Bride Doll.* Photo: Zorba.

Chelsea Theater Center

Robert Kalfin
Producing Director

Harrison Cromer
Managing Director

407 West 43rd St.
New York, NY 10036
(212) 541-8616 (business)
(212) 541-8394 (box office)

Founded 1965
Robert Kalfin
George Bari

Season
October–June

Schedule
Evenings
Tuesday–Saturday
Matinees
Wednesday, Saturday, Sunday

Facilities
Westside Theatre Mainstage
Seating capacity: 221
Stage: modified thrust
Second Stage
Seating capacity: 196
Stage: thrust
Chelsea Encore Cabaret
Seating capacity: 75
Stage: flexible

Finances
July 1, 1978–June 30, 1979
$621,000 operating expenses
$252,000 earned income
$369,000 unearned income

Audience
Paid capacity: 65%
Subscribers: 810

Booked-in events
Theatre

AEA LORT (D) contract

Lou Ferguson and Leon Morenzie
in *Rum an Coca Cola*. Photo:
Martha Swope.

The Chelsea Theater Center considers itself first and foremost a *creative* producing organization. It is dedicated to providing an environment in which artists can take risks in their attempt to produce work that will ultimately contribute to international dramatic literature. The theatre's staff works with directors in developing physical concepts for production that will amplify and elucidate the text. Chelsea often brings together various individuals with the specific aim of stretching their artistic gifts through interaction toward a common goal. Individual plays determine the theatre's approach, affecting everything from rehearsal methods to the redefining of the physical relationship of the audience to the performance.

The theatre seeks works of universal and lasting value. Chelsea concentrates on new plays by American playwrights, new theatre works created from other sources, foreign works by major contemporary playwrights and major works of international dramatic literature that are previously unknown or rarely performed for American audiences, such as *Strider: The Story of a Horse*, a musical adaptation of a Tolstoy story.

As a nonprofit institution, the Chelsea's role is that of a service organization for the New York, national and international theatre community. In order to keep the American theatre abreast of what is theatrically possible elsewhere, the Chelsea feels an obligation to offer work in New York which is neglected by others, and which can have an impact on the American theatre, as well as on individual artists.

Programs and services
Artistic, administrative and technical/production internships; student performances, programs-in-schools, study materials, dramaturgical library, student and senior citizen ticket discounts, free ticket distribution to schools, voucher program, post-performance discussions, workshop productions and staged readings, guest lecturers, poetry readings, cabaret, newsletter, support group, theatre rentals.

Productions 1977-78
Rum an Coca Cola, Mustapha Matura
Green Pond, book and lyrics: Robert
    Montgomery; music: Mel Marvin
Old Man Joseph and His Family, Romulus
    Linney

Productions 1979
Biography: A Game, Max Frisch; trans: Michael
    Bullock
Strider: The Story of a Horse, book: Mark
    Rozovsky; lyrics: Uri Riashentsev and Steve
    Brown; adapt: Robert Kalfin and S. Brown;
    music: M. Rozovsky, S. Vetkin and Norman
    L. Berman

Strider: The Story of a Horse.
Photo: Peter Krupenye.

The Children's Theatre Company

John Clark Donahue
Artistic Director

Jay Bush
Administrative Director

2400 Third Ave. South
Minneapolis, MN 55404
(612) 874-0500 (business)
(612) 874-0400 (box office)

Founded 1961
Beth Linnerson

Season
September–July

Schedule
Evenings
Thursday–Saturday
Matinees
Wednesday–Sunday

Facilities
Seating capacity: 736
Stage: proscenium

Finances
July 1, 1978–June 30, 1979
$1,306,000 operating expenses
$ 696,000 earned income
$ 626,000 unearned income

Audience
Paid capacity: 57%
Annual attendance: 120,810

Touring contact
Tony Steblay

Booked-in events
Dance, music

"If we've done anything to bring children's theatre closer to the center of theatrical energy and creation and focus, it's because adults as well as children have been moved and impressed with the total effect of certain works that they have seen," says John Clark Donahue, artistic director of the Children's Theatre Company of Minneapolis.

Housed within its $4.5 million theatre/classroom facility which opened in the fall of 1974, the Children's Theatre Company and School offers some 250 performances each season to nearly 160,000 young people and adults. The Company began in the early 1960's, and has evolved into the largest professional theatre for young people in the nation. The troupe employs a resident staff of 65 artists, educators, technicians and administrators.

Donahue and his company believe that the arts are important, powerful tools for the communication of human insights and understanding. Through CTC's annual presentation of eight or nine plays of widely varying content and approach, young audiences develop an early appreciation for the infinite possibilities of the performing arts.

Education is a primary operational principle at the Children's Theatre, through performing arts training for young people and adults, as well as through the experience of live theatre performance. The Children's Theatre School, a decade old, offers some 90 high school students the opportunity to receive daily training from the theatre's professional staff in both performing and technical theatre disciplines. A newly developed community school provides classes in dramatics and dance to the public, and an expanded outreach training/residency program allows additional opportunity for the exploration of individual creative potential.

The Children's Theatre Company and School's commitment to all of its constituencies is found through its continuing pursuit of performing and educational excellence—a pursuit which has brought the organization national and international acclaim.

Programs and services
Classes for nonprofessionals and children; artistic, administrative, and technical/production internships; dance school for children and adults, student performances, programs-in-schools, study materials, student and senior citizen ticket discounts, post-performance discussions, speakers bureau, volunteer auxiliary, theatre rentals.

Productions 1977-78
Aladdin and the Wonderful Lamp, adapt: Timothy Mason
Thieves' Carnival, Jean Anouilh; trans: I.A. Humm
The Little Match Girl, John Clark Donahue, from Hans Christian Andersen's story
Beauty and the Beast, adapt: Timothy Mason
A Circle Is the Sun, book and lyrics: Frederick Gaines and John Clark Donahue; music: Frank Wharton
The Pied Piper of Hamelin, book and lyrics: Thomas W. Olson, from Robert Browning's tale; music: Richard A. Dworsky
The Rivals, Richard Brinsley Sheridan
Punch and Judy and the Three Sillies, adapt: Timothy Mason

Productions 1978-79
The Legend of Sleepy Hollow, book and lyrics: Frederick Gaines, from Washington Irving's story; music: Roberta Carlson
Hansel and Gretel, adapt: Timothy Mason
A Christmas Carol, adapt: Frederick Gaines
The Little Mermaid, Timothy Mason, from Hans Christian Andersen's story
Good Morning, Mr. Tillie, John Clark Donahue
Pinocchio, Timothy Mason, from Carlo Collodi's story
The Green Beetle Dance, book and lyrics: John Clark Donahue; music: Steven M. Rydberg
The Sitwells at Sea, Gar Hildenbrand, from Edith Sitwell's poetry and journals

Bain Boehlke in *Good Morning, Mr. Tillie.*

A Circle Is the Sun. Photo: George Heinrich.

Cincinnati Playhouse in the Park

Michael Murray
Producing Director

Robert W. Tolan
Managing Director

Box 6537
Cincinnati, OH 45206
(513) 559-9500 (business)
(512) 421-3888 (box office)

Founded 1960
Community members

Season
October–September

Schedule
Evenings
Tuesday–Sunday
Matinees
Sunday, selected Wednesdays

Facilities
962 Mt. Adams Circle
Robert S. Marx Theatre
Seating capacity: 627
Stage: thrust
Shelterhouse
Seating capacity: 227
Stage: thrust

Finances
Sept. 1, 1978–Aug. 31, 1979
$1,073,000 operating expenses
$ 733,000 earned income
$ 391,000 unearned income

Audience
Paid capacity: 85%
Subscribers: 13,284
Annual attendance: 150,000

AEA LORT (B) contract

Nancy Donohue and Tania Myren
in *Benefit of a Doubt.* Photo:
Sandy Underwood.

The professional theatre for a three-state region of the Ohio River Valley, Cincinnati Playhouse in the Park produces a wide variety of theatrical offerings. The Playhouse has attracted a record number of season subscribers and reaches new audiences through a greatly expanded student season (which presents an average of four shows each season to student audiences), regional touring of mainstage productions, and special programs as diverse as a three-week residency by New York's Big Apple Circus, a visit by Cleveland's Karamu House company in *Sizwe Bansi Is Dead,* and a unique transformation of the Playhouse's Marx Theatre stage into a cabaret for summer productions of intimate musical revues.

The Playhouse has recently renewed its commitment to the development of new American plays with mainstage premieres of Edward Clinton's *Benefit of a Doubt* and Jonathan Marc Feldman's *The Buddy System.*

The theatre's first home was the 100-year-old Shelterhouse, a Victorian fieldstone structure in a hilltop park overlooking downtown Cincinnati. The innovative 627-seat Robert S. Marx Theatre was built in 1968 to complement the 227-seat Shelterhouse facility. A National Endowment for the Arts Challenge Grant has spurred a current fund drive to support construction to renovate the theatre's offices, enclose the plaza between the buildings and completely refurbish the Shelterhouse, leading to expanded programming on the theatre's "second stage."

Simply stated, the primary artistic concern is for quality and the full realization of each play presented. Productions are cast separately, although many artists frequently return, forming a "floating company." Through its relationships with the League of Professional Theatre Training Programs, the University of Cincinnati and Cincinnati's Public School for the Creative and Performing Arts, the Playhouse has become an important training resource for artists from the Cincinnati area and around the country. Since its inception, the Playhouse has presented 168 productions, including 13 world premieres and four American premieres.

Programs and services
Student performances, programs-in-schools, study materials, student and senior citizen ticket discounts, statewide touring, post-performance discussions, workshop productions and staged readings, dessert bar, cabaret, newsletter, speakers bureau, volunteer auxiliary, theatre rentals.

Productions 1977-78
The Threepenny Opera, book and lyrics: Bertolt Brecht: trans: Marc Blitzstein; music: Kurt Weill
The Imaginary Invalid, Moliere: adapt: R.G. Davis
Benefit of a Doubt, Edward Clinton
Of Mice and Men, John Steinbeck
The House of Bernarda Alba, Federico Garcia Lorca
The Royal Family, George S. Kaufman and Edna Ferber

Productions 1978-79
Romeo and Juliet, William Shakespeare
Otherwise Engaged, Simon Gray
Room Service, John Murray and Allen Boretz
Hedda Gabler, Henrik Ibsen
The Buddy System, Jonathan Marc Feldman
Man of La Mancha, book: Dale Wasserman; music: Mitch Leigh; lyrics: Joe Darion
Magic to Do, music and lyrics: Stephen Schwartz; adapt: Ernie Zulia and Frank Bartolucci

The Threepenny Opera. Photo:
Sandy Underwood.

Circle in the Square

Theodore Mann
Artistic Director

Paul Libin
Managing Director

1633 Broadway
New York, NY 10019
(212) 581-3270 (business)
(212) 581-0720 (box office)

Founded 1951
Theodore Mann, Aileen Cramer,
Edward Mann, Jose Quintero,
Emily Stevens, Jason Wingreen

Season
Year-round

Schedule
Evenings
Tuesday–Saturday
Matinees
Wednesday, Saturday, Sunday

Facilities
Circle in the Square Uptown
Seating capacity: 681
Stage: arena
Circle in the Square Downtown
159 Bleecker St.
Seating capacity: 299
Stage: thrust

Finances
July 1, 1978–June 30, 1979
$2,753,000 operating expenses
$2,134,000 earned income
$ 619,000 unearned income

Audience
Paid capacity: 78%
Subscribers: 21,280
Annual attendance: 275,671

*AEA Production and Off
Broadway contracts*

In 28 years, Circle in the Square has presented many of the world's finest actors in challenging productions of new and established plays. By producing four plays a year, Circle's directors have made it possible for audiences to see the work of actors who would otherwise be unable to commit themselves to an extended-run Broadway play. Because of Circle's arena staging, its audiences also experience a uniquely intimate relationship with these performers, which no other Broadway house can provide. Circle's original home in Greenwich Village, now called Circle in the Square Downtown, continues to be operated as an Off Broadway theatre.

Especially noted for bringing the work of distinguished American playwrights to the stage, Circle is also dedicated to bringing new theatrical life to great works from the British, European and classical repertoire. In recent years the company has included important new plays intended to stand alongside the work of O'Neill, Williams, Ibsen, Shaw or Moliere.

Other plays are developed in Circle in the Square's new plays-in-progress program, New Spheres, through which 30 new plays a year are given public readings on Monday nights by professional actors. Promising scripts are then selected for development in full-scale Equity showcase productions at Off-Off Broadway houses, while exceptional plays are considered for mainstage production at Circle.

Circle also participates in an outreach program funded by Citicorp called "Circle in the Schools." To make theatre accessible to children who have never attended a theatrical production, study materials, scripts, theatre tours, school visits by actors and discussions before and after performances are extended to students in the public school system. Post-performance discussions—142 last season—and theatre tours are available to other groups as well.

The Circle in the Square Theatre School and Workshop, founded in 1961, offers a training program with a staff of professional actors and directors. Another program, affiliated with New York University, provides students with a four-year theatre training program at Circle, in conjuction with academic classes at NYU.

Programs and services
Professional acting training, administrative internships, programs-in-schools, study materials, theatre tours; ticket discounts for students, senior citizens and the handicapped; free ticket distribution, voucher program, post-performance discussions, workshop productions and staged readings, newsletter.

Productions 1977-78
Tartuffe, Moliere; trans: Richard Wilbur
Saint Joan, George Bernard Shaw
13 Rue de l'Amour, Georges Feydeau; adapt:
  Mawby Green and Ed Feilbert
Once in a Lifetime, Moss Hart and George S.
  Kaufman

Productions 1978-79
The Inspector General, Nikolai Gogol; trans:
  Betsy Hulick
Man and Superman, George Bernard Shaw
Spokesong, Stewart Parker; music: Jimmy
  Kennedy
Loose Ends, Michael Weller

George Grizzard and Ann Sachs
in *Man and Superman.* Photo:
Martha Swope.

Tammy Grimes, John Wood and
Stefan Gierasch in *Tartuffe.*
Photo: Martha Swope.

Circle Repertory Company

Marshall W. Mason
Artistic Director

Porter Van Zandt, Jr.
Managing Director

111 Eighth Ave.
New York, NY 10011
(212) 691-3210 (business)
(212) 924-7100 (box office)

Founded 1969
Marshall W. Mason,
Robert Thirkield, Lanford Wilson,
Tanya Berezin

Season
October–July

Schedule
Evenings
Tuesday–Saturday
Matinees
Sunday

Facilities
Sheridan Square Playhouse
99 Seventh Ave. South
Seating capacity: 150
Stage: flexible

Finances
Oct. 1, 1978–Sept. 30, 1979
$520,000 operating expenses
$165,000 earned income
$355,000 unearned income

Audience
Paid capacity: 65%
Subscribers: 750
Annual attendance: 40,900

Booked-in events
Music

AEA Off Broadway contract

Joyce Reehling and William Hurt
in *The Runner Stumbles*. Photo:
Ken Howard.

Judd Hirsch and Trish Hawkins in
Talley's Folly. Photo: Gerry
Goodstein.

For a decade Circle Repertory Company has occupied a unique position as the only permanent company of artists devoted to creating new American drama. The resident ensemble of 35 actors, many of whom have worked together for the full 10 years, as well as resident designers John Lee Beatty, Dennis Parichy, Laura Crow and Chuck London, have tuned their collective talents to the creation of new works by resident playwrights Lanford Wilson, Milan Stitt, John Bishop, Julie Bovasso, Albert Innaurato and others. Together they have established their style of lyrical realism as a native voice of American theatre. Original productions have included such contemporary classics as Wilson's *The Hot l Baltimore*, Mark Medoff's *When You Comin' Back, Red Ryder?*, Edward J. Moore's *The Sea Horse*, Jules Feiffer's *Knock Knock*, Innaurato's *Gemini* and Corinne Jacker's *Harry Outside*.

Circle Rep spent its first five years in a loft at 83rd Street and Broadway on Manhattan's upper west side before moving to Greenwich Village's old Sheridan Square Playhouse. The acting company meets for physical, vocal and ensemble training 15 hours each week, and each Friday reads a new play written for it by the resident writers or recommended by the dramaturgical staff. Plays deemed worthy graduate to staged readings with three weeks of rehearsal in the Projects in Progress series, which includes post-performance discussions with the audience. Further revisions may then bring the script to a full major production at Circle Rep or in some cases, at other theatres. One-act plays have their own forum in the Late Show series, following each major production at 11 p.m.

In 1978, Porter Van Zandt became the producing director and president of the board, and Stitt became dramturg, joining Mason, Wilson and casting director Robert Thirkield in designing artistic policy. Among Circle Rep's 77 world premieres are Wilson's *The Mound Builders, The 5th of July* and *Talley's Folly;* Megan Terry's *Hothouse;* and Bishop's *Winter Signs*. New York premieres include Sam Shepard's *Suicide in B Flat*, Tennessee Williams' *Battle of Angels*, David Storey's *The Farm*, Dylan Thomas' *The Doctor and the Devils* and Wilson's *Serenanding Louie*.

Programs and services
Artistic, administrative and technical/production internships; student performances, student and senior citizen ticket discounts, voucher program, post-performance discussions, workshop productions and staged readings, newsletter.

Productions 1977-78
Feedlot, Patrick Meyers
Ulysses in Traction, Albert Innaurato
Lulu, Frank Wedekind
Brontosaurus, Lanford Wilson
Cabin 12, John Bishop
The 5th of July, Lanford Wilson

Productions 1978-79
Glorious Morning, Patrick Meyers
In the Recovery Lounge, James Farrell
The Runner Stumbles, Milan Stitt
Winter Signs, John Bishop
Talley's Folly, Lanford Wilson
Gertrude Stein Gertrude Stein Gertrude Stein, Marty Martin
Buried Child, Sam Shepard

Cleveland Play House

Richard Oberlin
Director

Nelson Isekeit
Business Manager

Box 1989
Cleveland, OH 44106
(216) 795-7000

Founded 1915
Raymond O'Neil

Season
October–April

Schedule
Evenings
Wednesday–Saturday
Matinees
Thursday, Sunday

Facilities
2040 East 86th St.
Francis E. Drury Theatre
Seating capacity: 515
Stage: proscenium
Charles S. Brooks Theatre
Seating capacity: 160
Stage: proscenium
Euclid–77th St. Theatre
Seating capacity: 560
Stage: thrust

Finances
July 1, 1978–June 30, 1979
$1,195,000 operating expenses
$ 762,000 earned income
$ 477,000 unearned income

Audience
Paid capacity: 82%
Subscribers: 9,525
Annual attendance: 150,000

Booked-in events
Theatre

AEA LORT (C) contract

The Cleveland Play House, America's oldest resident professional theatre, regards artistic growth as its first priority. Its basic tenet is to provide quality productions selected from the classics, well-crafted plays relevant to the times, and new works, presented by a skilled resident company supplemented by visiting directors and performing artists.

Begun in 1915 with just three full-time staff members and a handful of spectators, the Play House now employs nearly 100 full-time employees and plays to more than 150,000 people each year. The Play House operated in private homes, barns and attics until its 1917 move to a renovated church. In 1929, the Play House moved into a new building with two theatres, the land being donated by Mr. and Mrs. Francis Drury, after whom the largest theatre is named. At the present time, a new theatre complex is being designed by the noted architect Philip Johnson. Scheduled for completion in the early 1980s, it will be located adjacent to the current Drury/Brooks Theatre site.

Audiences are offered varied fare, and the staff benefits from a wide range of theatrical challenges. Among the more than 71 world and American premieres that have been staged are Tennessee Williams and Donald Windham's *You Touched Me,* Donald Freed's *The United States vs. Julius and Ethel Rosenberg (Inquest),* Paul Zindel's *The Effect of Gamma Rays on Man-in-the-Moon Marigolds* and Lawrence and Lee's *First Monday in October.*

In 1979, the Play House performed its 50th summer season, staffed by Play House personnel, at the renowned Chautauqua Institution in Chautauqua, N.Y. The annual residency is a nine-week series comprising productions from the previous Cleveland season. A six-week, college-accredited theatre training school for students coincides with the summer production season.

The Play House provides Cleveland area students with a multitude of educational services that include programs-in-schools and a youth theatre (begun in 1933), as well as the regularly scheduled student matinees of all productions, and frequent symposia and theatre enrichment programs.

Programs and services

Professional training in acting and administration; classes for children; administrative and technical/production internships, student performances, programs-in-schools, study materials, student and senior citizen ticket discounts, free ticket distribution, regional touring, summer residency at Chautauqua Institution, post-performance discussions, workshop productions and staged readings, guest lecturers, restaurant, newsletter, souvenir books, speakers bureau, volunteer auxiliary, theatre rentals.

Productions 1977-78

Living Together, Alan Ayckbourn
The Learned Ladies, Moliere; trans: Richard Wilbur
Round and Round the Garden, Alan Ayckbourn
Great Expectations, Paul Lee, from Charles Dickens' novel
The Prague Spring, book and lyrics: Lee Kalcheim; music: Joseph G. Raposo
The Little Foxes, Lillian Hellman
Knock Knock, Jules Feiffer
The Romantics, Maxim Gorky; trans: William Stancil
The Club, music and lyrics adapt: Eve Merriam

Productions 1978-79

Night Must Fall, Emlyn Williams
The Shadow Box, Michael Cristofer
The Importance of Being Earnest, Oscar Wilde
Gemini, Albert Innaurato
Equus, Peter Shaffer
Threads, Jonathan Bolt
The Last of the Marx Brothers' Writers, Louis Phillips
The Odyssey, adapt: Gregory A. Falls and Kurt Beattie
Something's Afoot, book, music and lyrics: James McDonald, David Vos and Robert Gerlach

James Richards and Margaret Hamilton in *Night Must Fall.* Photo: Mike Edwards.

Harper Jane MacAdoo, Sharon Bicknell, June Gibbons and Providence Hollander in *Something's Afoot.* Photo: Mike Edwards.

Cohoes Music Hall

Louis J. Ambrosio
Producing Director

Kristine A. Koba
Administrative Director

58 Remsen St.
Cohoes, NY 12047
(518) 237-7700 (business)
(518) 237-7045 (box office)

Founded 1974
James D. O'Reilly,
Louis J. Ambrosio,
City of Cohoes

Season
October–March

Schedule
Evenings
Tuesday–Sunday
Matinees
Saturday, Sunday

Facilities
Seating capacity: 444
Stage: proscenium

Finances
July 1, 1978–June 30, 1979
$381,000 operating expenses
$262,000 earned income
$119,000 unearned income

Audience
Paid capacity: 63%
Subscribers: 4,100
Annual attendance: 42,000

AEA LORT (C) contract

Janet Zarish, John Milligan and
Mary Pat Gleason in *Tartuffe.*
Photo: Bill Demichele.

Reconstructed interior of the
historic Cohoes Music Hall.

Believing that every theatre has a responsibility to its community, the Cohoes Music Hall has, from its inception, involved its constituency in all phases of its operation. The CMH audience is one whose theatrical experience is limited as geographic and economic barriers have prevented many from experiencing professional theatre. For them, a visit to CMH is an introduction to a totally new art form. In the first few seasons of the theatre's existence, the selection of plays emphasized entertainment values but through a slow introduction of more sophisticated material, CMH is now able to present a varied repertoire. CMH's audiences have responded favorably and now eagerly participate in a Thursday evening seminar series, in which subscribers have the opportunity to talk with the actors about a wide range of theatrical offerings.

The second objective of CMH is the creation of a supportive environment for its staff. Communication among directors, actors, designers and technicians is of paramount importance. The theatre, striving for artistic quality and expression, also believes in giving its artists the freedom to explore and experiment, the premise on which regional theatre was founded. By providing sufficient rehearsal time and a pleasant environment, and by fostering mutual consideration and respect among the entire staff, CMH works to accomplish its goals.

Programs and services:
Professional training in acting and directing; classes for children; artistic and technical/production internships, programs-in-schools, student and senior citizen ticket discounts, post-performance discussions, workshop productions and staged readings, newsletter, volunteer auxiliary, theatre rentals.

Productions 1977-78
The Glass Menagerie, Tennessee Williams
Vanities, Jack Heifner
A Moon for the Misbegotten, Eugene O'Neill
The Unexpected Guest, Agatha Christie
Private Lives, Noel Coward

Productions 1978-79
Tartuffe, Moliere; trans: Richard Wilbur
The Runner Stumbles, Milan Stitt
Angel Street, Patrick Hamilton
Long Day's Journey into Night, Eugene O'Neill
Oh, Coward!, music and lyrics: Noel Coward;
    adapt: Roderick Cook
Look Back in Anger, John Osborne

Colonnades Theatre Lab

Michael Lessac
Artistic Director

Robert N. Lear
Executive Producer

Steve Simon
Administrative Director

428 Lafayette St.
New York, NY 10003
(212) 228-6640 (business)
(212) 673-2222 (box office)

Founded 1974
Michael Lessac

Season
September–June

Schedule
Evenings
Wednesday–Saturday
Matinees
Saturday, Sunday

Facilities
Seating capacity: 75-99
Stage: flexible

Finances
July 1, 1978-June 30, 1979
$331,000 operating expenses
$ 59,000 earned income
$272,000 unearned income

Audience
Paid capacity: 78%
Annual attendance: 8,750

Touring contact
Sara Tornay

AEA Mini contract

The Colonnades Theatre Lab was founded to provide a permanent home for a resident acting company where a cohesive, flexible style could be developed to meet the demands of both the classical repertoire and new theatre forms.

Essentially a "regional" theatre in the middle of New York City, CTL faces many of the problems of survival confronting most institutional theatres in the U.S. today. But unlike many, it is firmly committed to the waning, expensive concepts of a resident company and rotating repertory, maintained on a semi-permanent basis.

With several critical successes in the past four seasons, including the award-winning *Moliere in Spite of Himself,* Colonnades seems to have made a fine beginning. Its work is maturing, and more effective ways to achieve the ensemble ideal are being developed. Innovative uses of sound, space and movement are being applied to an increasing diversity of styles and theatre spaces, as the company prepares for its first national tour in the spring of 1980. In short, CTL has laid the groundwork for a lasting theatre.

However, it will take another five or 10 years to transform the company into a permanent, year-round troupe, performing and developing a full repertoire of classics and new works. During the next five years, several steps will be taken to effect this transformation: the start of a musical theatre ensemble; the beginning of a repertory film production unit working out of a resident professional theatre; an active search for a larger, equally flexible but more economically viable second space; and the

building of a broader confederation of theatre artists who share the desire and the need to preserve the ensemble tradition and have the stamina to create a lasting institution around it.

Programs and services
Professional training in acting, production and administration; classes for children; administrative and technical/production internships, ensemble training for corporate executives, programs-in-schools, study materials, student and senior citizen ticket discounts, national touring, workshop productions and staged readings, improvisational theatre, musical theatre lab, newsletter, script publication, volunteer auxiliary, theatre rentals.

Productions 1977-78
Moliere in Spite of Himself, Mikhail Bulgakov; adapt: Michael Lessac and David Morgan
Anatomy of an Ensemble, concept: Michael Lessac

Productions 1978-79
The Ballroom in St. Patrick's Cathedral, Louis Phillips
Moliere in Spite of Himself

Peter Kingsley, Marcia Hyde and Tom V. V. Tammi in *Moliere in Spite of Himself.* Photo: Diane Gorodnitzki.

Louis Giambalvo and Jackie Cassel in *The Ballroom in St. Patrick's Cathedral.* Photo: Gerry Goodstein.

The Cricket Theatre

Louis Salerni
Artistic Director

William H. Semans
Producing Director

Hennepin Center for the Arts
528 Hennepin Ave.
Minneapolis, MN 55403
(612) 333-5241 (business)
(612) 333-2401 (box office)

Founded 1971
William H. Semans

Season
October–June

Schedule
Evenings
Wednesday–Sunday
Matinees
Saturdays

Facilities
Seating capacity: 400
Stage: thrust

Finances
Aug. 1, 1978–June 30, 1979
$429,000 operating expenses
$104,000 earned income
$302,000 unearned income

Audience
Paid capacity: 74%
Subscribers: 1,608
Annual attendance: 31,000

AEA LORT (D) contract

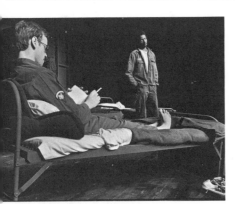

Bill Schoppert and David Harris in
Streamers. Photo: Craig
Litherland.

The Cricket Theatre was founded in 1971 and is dedicated to producing plays by contemporary American playwrights, its principal goal being to discover, nurture and produce the work of living writers in a creative and innovative environment.

Since its inception, the Cricket has produced 74 plays of which 32 have been world premieres and 38 regional premieres. During the 1979-80 season, the Cricket will produce seven plays on its mainstage and another seven in its Works-in-Progress Series. In addition, the Cricket will inaugurate its ninth season in a new 400-seat theatre atop the Hennepin Center for the Arts in downtown Minneapolis. The theatre has been specially designed to meet the Cricket's needs and will be its permanent home. Listed as a landmark building in the National Historic Register, the Hennepin Center has been restored as a cultural center to house both the Cricket and Minnesota Dance Theatre.

The Cricket believes that the future of theatre in America lies in the emergence of new writers of excellence and in the ability of theatres to creatively contribute to the writer's unique vision. In keeping with this philosophy, the Cricket established a Works-in-Progress Series in the fall of 1977, consisting of a series of staged readings of scripts by promising writers. For the first two years, Works-in-Progress limited itself to producing 10-hour workshops, culminating in a public reading of the script by professional actors with the playwright in residence. However, in 1979-80 Works-in-Progress will be expanded to include three 30-hour workshops with limited productions.

In an effort to expand the thrust of the theatre's production program, the Cricket has recently initiated a National Playwright Commission policy, for which the theatre will award three $5,000 grants to authors and provide production of the winning scripts.

Programs and services
Artistic, administrative and technical/production internships; student performances, student and senior citizen ticket discounts, free ticket distribution, post-performance discussions, workshop productions and staged readings, newsletter, speakers bureau, volunteer auxiliary, theatre rentals.

Productions 1977-78
The Trip Back Down, John Bishop
Red Rover, Red Rover, Oliver Hailey
The Club, music and lyrics adapt: Eve Merriam
The Shadow Box, Michael Cristofer
Indulgences in the Louisville Harem, John Orlock
And If That Mockingbird Don't Sing, William Whitehead
Streamers, David Rabe

Productions 1978-79
Mourning Pictures, Honor Moore
Sort of a Love Song, Glenn Allen Smith
The 5th of July, Lanford Wilson
Aleola, Gaetan Charlebois
The D.B. Cooper Project, book, music and lyrics: John Orlock
A Life in the Theatre, David Mamet

Bill Schoppert and Allen Hamilton
in *A Life in the Theatre*. Photo:
Craig Litherland.

CSC Repertory

Christopher Martin
Artistic Director

Dennis Turner
Executive Director

Alberto Tore
General Manager

136 East 13th St.
New York, NY 10003
(212) 477-5808 (business)
(212) 677-4210 (box office)

Founded 1967
Christopher Martin

Season
September–May

Schedule
Evenings
Tuesday–Sunday
Matinees
Sunday

Facilities
Seating capacity: 200
Stage: thrust

Finances
July 1, 1978–June 30, 1979
$215,000 operating expenses
$ 99,000 earned income
$ 96,000 unearned income

Audience
Paid capacity: 58%
Subscribers: 1,300
Annual attendance: 24,350

AEA Off Broadway contract

"Classics in the present tense" is the artistic imperative of Christopher Martin, CSC Repertory's founder and artistic director. CSC productions are intended to convey the author's intent and have an effect on the contemporary audience comparable to that of the play's original impact. In bridging the playwright's world and today's society, CSC upholds an obligation to carefully assemble a compelling repertoire, while commissioning new translations or adaptations.

Emphasis in the 1979-80 season remains on staging rarely performed classics and new plays by foreign authors. Over 12 seasons, CSC has mounted more than 80 productions, balancing as many as five productions in rotating repertory.

Three forces govern the final production: the author and his words, the company and its technique, and the audience and its collective impulse. Therefore, CSC actors must conform to a regimen of frequent physical and verbal workshops, with special sessions geared to productions demanding specialized skills.

Since its inception, CSC has strived to maintain a dialogue with major European theatres, its permanent ensemble endeavoring to define the universal aspects of Western civilization.

Programs and services
Artistic, administrative and technical/production internships; student performances, free ticket distribution, student and senior citizen ticket discounts, voucher program, post-performance seminars, workshop productions and staged readings, subscriber newsletter, volunteer auxiliary, theatre rentals.

Productions 1977-78
A Midsummer Night's Dream, William Shakespeare
Rosmersholm, Henrik Ibsen; trans: Christopher Martin
Serjeant Musgrave's Dance, John Arden
The Maids, Jean Genet; trans: Bernard Frechtman
The Running of the Deer, Karen Sunde
The Madwoman of Chaillot, Jean Giraudoux; adapt: Maurice Valency

Productions 1978-79
Richard II, William Shakespeare
Henry IV, Part I, William Shakespeare
Henry IV, Part II, William Shakespeare
Wild Oats, John O'Keeffe
The Marquis of Keith, Frank Wedekind; trans: Christopher Martin

Noble Shropshire and Karen Sunde in *The Marquis of Keith.* Photo: Kirsten Beck.

Wild Oats. Photo: Gerry Goodstein.

Dallas Theater Center

Paul Baker
Managing Director

Mark Beardsley
Business Manager

3636 Turtle Creek Blvd.
Dallas, TX 75219
(214) 526-8210 (business)
(214) 526-8857 (box office)

Founded 1959
Robert D. Stecker, Sr.,
Beatrice Handel, Paul Baker,
Dallas citizens

Season
October–August

Schedule
Evenings
Tuesday–Saturday
Matinees
Wednesday, Saturday

Facilities
Kalita Humphreys Theater
Seating capacity: 516
Stage: thrust
Down Center Stage
Seating capacity: 56
Stage proscenium

Finances
Sept. 1, 1977–Aug. 31, 1978
$1,279,000 operating expenses
$ 761,000 earned income
$ 519,000 unearned income

Audience
Kalita Humphreys Theater
Paid capacity: 84%
Subscribers: 10,518
Down Center Stage
Paid capacity: 73%
Subscribers: 329
Total annual attendance; 172,000

Dallas Theater Center. Dick
Trousdell and Rebecca Logan in
The Imaginary Invalid.
Photo: Linda Blase.

Tim Haynes, Jim Marvin, Bill
Wheat, Alan Scarfe and Chris
Hendrie in *The Devil's General.*
Photo: Linda Blase.

Completing its 20th anniversary season in 1979, the Dallas Theater Center was opened in 1959 as a nonprofit civic institution for the development and presentation of theatre arts. Located on a wooded site four miles from downtown Dallas, the Theater Center building is the only public theatre facility designed by Frank Lloyd Wright. The artistic policy of the center, as set forth by managing director Paul Baker, is to develop a source of creative energy for a wide range of theatrical activities.

The theatre aims to develop audience excitement and enthusiasm for a very broad selection of plays directed, designed and performed by a resident company of about 30 artists. DTC is also committed to the development of playwrights and the production of new plays. The past two seasons have seen the world premieres of 16 new scripts, including *Remember* by Preston Jones, *Years in the Making* by Glenn Allen Smith, *Lady Bug, Lady Bug, Fly Away Home* by Mary Rohde, *Firekeeper* by Mark Medoff, and *Door Play* by Sallie Laurie. In May 1979, DTC sponsored a "Playmarket" in which nine new plays were presented for an invited group of critics, agents, producers, writers and diretors.

The theatre also operates a graduate theatre program in conjunction with Trinity University in San Antonio for the training of theatre artists, as well as a children's theatre school devoted to helping children discover their own unique talents. Performing and teaching in schools through an artists-in-schools program, DTC artists conduct special classes and workshops for students in such subjects as Shakespeare, techniques of play production and mime.

DTC tours to schools and communities throughout Texas with children's plays and full-length mime shows. For the past three summers, Mime-Act, in association with the Dallas Park and Recreation Department, has toured the city's 16 city parks with free shows for children.

In 1973, the center's board of directors presented the theatre complex, debt-free, as a gift to the city of Dallas, which maintains the property as a major civic asset.

Programs and services
Professional training in acting, directing, design, production and administration; classes for children; artistic, administrative and technical/production internships; student performances, programs-in-schools, study materials, student and senior citizen ticket discounts, free ticket distribution, national touring, post-performance discussions, workshop productions and staged readings, film series, guest lecturers, children's theatre, newsletter, souvenir books, speakers bureau, volunteer auxiliary.

Productions 1977-78
The Imaginary Invalid, Moliere; trans: Alec Stockwell
Vanities, Jack Heifner
The Night of the Iguana, Tennessee Williams
Three Men on a Horse, John Cecil Holm and George Abbott
Firekeeper, Mark Medoff
The Royal Family, George S. Kaufman and Edna Ferber
Door Play, Sallie Laurie
The Cigarette Man, David Blomquist
The Night Visit, Roy Hudson
Lady Bug, Lady Bug, Fly Away Home, Mary Rohde
Inside the White Room, Paul R. Bassett
InterWeave, company developed
Equepoise, book and lyrics: Phil Penningroth; music: Howard Quilling
Snow White, book company developed; music and lyrics: Alex Winslow and Mark Momberger
The Tiger in Traction, book and lyrics: Gifford Wingate; music: Robert R. Smith, Jr.
The Adventures of Tom Sawyer, book, music and lyrics: Sam L. Rosen, from Mark Twain's novel

Productions 1978-79
A Midsummer Night's Dream, William Shakespeare
A Texas Trilogy, Preston Jones
　Lu Ann Hampton Laverty Oberlander
　The Last Meeting of the Knights of the White Magnolia
　The Oldest Living Graduate
The Devil's General, Carl Zuckmayer; trans: Ingrid Komar
As You Like It, William Shakespeare
Blood Money, book and lyrics: M.G. Johnston; music: Jim Abbott
To Kill a Mockingbird, dramatized from Harper Lee's novel
Attic Aphrodite, Sally Netzel
A Disposable Woman, Frederic Hunter
Remember, Preston Jones
Years in the Making, Glenn Allen Smith
Jack and the Beanstalk, adapt: Sally Netzel
Heidi, Lucille Miller, from Johanna Spyri's novel
The New Adventures of Raggedy Ann and Andy, company developed from Johnny Gruelle's stories
The Squires and the Golden Kings, book and lyrics: Paul Munger; music: Maria Figueroa

Dell'Arte

Carlo Mazzone-Clementi
Artistic Director

Joan Schirle
Administrative Director

Box 816
Blue Lake, CA 95525
(707) 668-5411

Founded 1971
Carlo and
Jane Mazzone-Clementi

Season
May–September
Touring
January–April

Schedule
Evenings
Tuesday–Saturday
Matinees
Saturday, Sunday

Finances
Oct. 1, 1978–Sept. 30, 1979
$123,000 operating expenses
$ 43,000 earned income
$ 79,000 unearned income

Audience
Annual attendance: 10,000

Touring contact
Joan Schirle

The location of a *commedia dell'arte*–inspired theatre company and school in the heart of northern California redwood country suggests the uniqueness of Dell'Arte, named for the popular European tradition incorporating pantomime and improvisation to portray archetypal comic characters. Dell'Arte's home of Blue Lake, Calif., is a town founded at a Gold Rush crossroads within a region still rich in native American culture as well as the ways of pioneers, miners, fishermen and lumberjacks. For Dell'Arte to locate there was, in many ways, as improbable a leap as Columbus' journey to North America. But like Columbus' discovery, the juxtaposition of European forms and American content provided a productive cross-fertilization of human cultures.

Dell'Arte's goals correspond to its situation. The company's productions are designed to bring quality theatre to a non-urban region. The actors develop new audiences by bringing shows to remote rural towns, schools, hospitals and senior citizen centers—places usually deprived of artistic benefits. Besides performing existing works, Dell'Arte creates new plays of particular interest to specific audiences, dramatizing such subjects as herbicide spraying, the Salmon War, and the search for Bigfoot. These shows—which draw characters from local history, popular culture and Indian tales—contribute to the culture of the Northwest, a culture which makes connections between the diversity of peoples who live here. The company tours its plays regionally five months each year.

However zany its productions, Dell'Arte remains historically oriented and concerned about sane living in the present tense. The company aspires to a future in which these values will be shared equally with its audiences.

A major aspect of Dell'Arte's task is the education of theatre professionals. A full-time year-long training program is offered in which students study with Dell'Arte founder Carlo Mazzone-Clementi, members of the professional acting company and special instructors in clowning, juggling, acrobatics and other performance skills. At the culmination of their training, Dell'Arte students create, perform and tour two plays—an invaluable experience for actors. In this way, Dell'Arte hopes its works in northern California may generate similar projects throughout North America.

Programs and services
Professional training in acting, acrobatics, juggling, mime, dance, *commedia dell'arte* and clowning, programs-in-schools, study materials, regional touring, children's theatre.

Productions 1977-79
Infancy, Thornton Wilder
The Greenfields, George Courteline; adapt: Jael Weisman
The Gloaming, Oh My Darling, Megan Terry
Birds of a Feather, Stan Laurel
Bittersweet Blues, Joan Schirle
Save Me a Place at Forest Lawn, Lorees Yerby
The Amazing Zoroasters, Jael Weisman
Cash Valley, Jon' Paul Cook
Underwater Worlds, Jon' Paul Cook
Tintypes: A Revue, company developed

Michael Fields and Donald Forrest in *Birds of a Feather.* Photo: Tom Copi.

Joan Schirle and Peter Kors in *The Loon's Rays.* Photo: Marion Goldsmith.

Downtown Cabaret Theatre

Claude McNeal
Artistic Director

Joseph Migliaro
Managing Director

263 Golden Hill St.
Bridgeport, CT 06604
(203) 576-1634 (business)
(203) 576-1636 (box office)

Founded 1975
Claude McNeal

Season
January–December

Schedule
Evenings
Thursday–Sunday
Matinees
Saturday

Facilities
Seating capacity: 300
Stage: proscenium

Finances
July 1, 1978–June 30, 1979
$458,000 operating expenses
$346,000 earned income
$ 48,000 unearned income

Audience
Paid capacity: 65%
Annual attendance: 74,969

Booked-in events
Jazz, folk and ethnic music,
international artists

The Thirties. Photo: Joseph Sia.

The Downtown Cabaret Theatre is planning to expand both its facilities and artistic direction to accommodate, entertain and enlighten its ever-growing audience.

Programs and services
Artistic, administrative and technical/production interships; apprentice program, programs-in-schools, student and senior citizen ticket discounts, free ticket distribution, children's theatre, newsletter, speakers bureau, audio-visual presentation, volunteer auxiliary.

Productions 1977-78
The Sixties
Lead Ins ...
The Fabulous Fifties
The Late Great Billion Dollar Movie
The Thirties

Productions 1978-79
The Sixties
The Thirties
The Forties—Songs of Love and War
The Fabulous Fifties
The Rise and Fall of the Andrews Sisters
The Seventies—The Way We Are
Comedie Cabaret

All productions are musical revues conceived and written by Claude McNeal, blending popular tunes with new songs by composer Stanley Wietrzychowski and lyricist McNeal.

Tink Matzek, Patricia Hemenway, Judy Lisi and Paul Luskin in *The Rise and Fall of the Andrews Sisters.* Photo: Joseph Sia.

The Downtown Cabaret Theatre is unique in its exclusive presentation of original cabaret revues on a year-round basis. It also presents a year-round children's theatre company made up of advanced theatre students from area high schools, who are part of free-of-charge work-exchange apprentice program. The children's shows, also original, are directed and guided by theatre professionals.

The principal artistic work of the theatre is, of course, its cabaret shows, usually musical satires on America's past, present and future. The shows are generally presented in a two-act multimedia structure and have social themes that concentrate on a specific time in recent American history. They attempt to unite distinctly popular appeals with the more deeply philosophical undercurrents of American society. For example, a show called *The Seventies—The Way We Are* brings music, vignettes and visual projections together in a way that entertains and also demonstrates the tremendous changes occurring between the volatile '60s and '70s: the Watergate debacle, emerging cults, disco fever, and the overwhelming influence of television and gluttonous abuse of natural resources.

East West Players

Mako Iwamatsu
Artistic Director

Rae Creevey
Executive Producer

Rick Momii
Administrator

4424 Santa Monica Blvd.
Los Angeles, CA 90029
(213) 660-0366

Founded 1965
Beulah Quo, Mako, Pat Li, Guy
Lee, James Hong, June Kim

Season
September–August

Schedule
Evenings
Friday–Sunday

Facilities
Seating capacity: 91
Stage: flexible

Finances
July 1, 1978–June 30, 1979
$133,000 operating expenses
$ 92,000 earned income
$ 42,000 unearned income

Audience
Paid capacity: 80%
Subscribers: 332
Annual attendance: 45,000

Touring contact
Rick Momii

AEA 99-seat waiver

The East West Players, the first Asian-American theatre in the United States, has taken the development of orginal work for the stage as its primary thrust, giving depth, dimension and definition to this ever strengthening voice of a one-time "silent minority."

A theatrical language and a literature are emerging as well—distinct, individual and peculiar to the needs of the Asian-American community, but breaching the walls that have traditionally separated the Asian-American from his neighbors.

EWP's 1978-79 season consisted of two original Asian-American works, a Greek revival, a family Christmas musical, a production of the musical *Pacific Overtures*, 100 performances of a Theatre for Youth tour, and two staged readings.

The present season reaffirms EWP's commitment to the production of new works. The creative voice of the Asian-American is growing stronger, and nowhere is this to be seen more dramatically than at the East West Players.

Programs and services
Professional training in acting, directing, design, production and administration; classes for nonprofessionals; technical/production internships, programs-in-schools, student and senior citizen ticket discounts, free ticket distribution, regional touring, workshop productions and staged readings, children's theatre, newsletter, speakers bureau.

Productions 1977-78
Points of Departure, Paul Stephen Lim
Bunnyhop, Jeffrey Paul Chan
Once upon in America, various writers
O-Men: An American Kabuki, Karen Yamashita

Productions 1978-79
Voices in the Shadow, Edward Sakamoto
The Frogs, Aristophanes; trans: Richmond Lattimore
Princess Charley, book: Jim Ploss and Norman Cohen; music: Roger Perry; lyrics: J. Ploss
The Avocado Kid, Philip Gotanda
Pacific Overtures, book: John Weidman; music and lyrics: Stephen Sondheim

Soon-Teck Oh and Sab Shimono in *Pacific Overtures*. Photo: Karen Juie.

Dana Lee and Shizuko Hoshi in *Princess Charley*. Photo: Rick Momii.

El Teatro Campesino

Luis Valdez
Artistic Director

Jose Delgado
Administrative Director

Box 1278
312 Fourth St.
San Juan Bautista, CA 95045
(408) 623-4505

Founded 1965
Luis Valdez

Season
Year-round

Finances
Jan. 1, 1978–Dec. 31, 1978
$264,000 operating expenses
$222,000 earned income
$ 49,000 unearned income

Audience
Paid capacity: 85%
Annual attendance: 50,000

Touring contact
Jose Delgado

Booked-in events
Dance, theatre

Socorro Valdez Cruz in *La Gran Carpa de los Rasquachis*. Photo: Berlincioni-Pacifico.

Ana Aguirre and Pedro Martinez in *La Gran Carpa de los Rasquachis*. Photo: Berlincioni-Pacifico.

Born out of the social struggle of the United Farm Workers in California, the work of El Teatro Campesino is part of an international movement of cultural activists struggling to recapture the power of self-determination and to establish anew the humanity and dignity of Chicano reality through the popular arts. If Chicanos remain a mystery to the rest of America, it is a mystery whose story can only be accurately expressed in Chicano words.

The artistic aims of El Teatro have basically remained the same: to replace the lingering negative stereotype of the Mexican in the United States with a new, positive image created through Chicano art, and to dramatize the social despair of Chicanos living in an Anglo-dominated society. As a theatre company and cultural organization, El Teatro strives to express Chicano reality to other Americans who are unfamiliar with what Chicanos represent as a people or a cause. El Teatro's cultural responsibility commits it to the inspiration and development of actors, actresses, directors and playwrights, giving them the opportunity to work locally, nationally and internationally in television, motion pictures and professional theatre. El Teatro is presently involved in the development of a training program able to accommodate more visiting artists interested in working with the company, as well as other theatre and media experts seeking professional exchange. In short, El Teatro is committed to the involvement of the Chicano *teatro* in the mainstream of American theatrical arts.

El Teatro presents new portrayals of early California history through adaptations of traditional plays, as well as original works based on historical characters or events.

Programs and services
Professional acting training, classes for children; programs-in-schools, study materials, senior citizen ticket discounts, free ticket distribution, national touring, workshop productions and staged readings, film series, poetry readings, children's theatre, cabaret, newsletter.

Productions 1977-79
El Fin del Mundo III, company developed
Las Cuatro Apariciones de la Virgen de Guadalupe, company developed
La Pastorela, company developed; music: Daniel Valdez and David Silva
La Gran Carpa de Los Rasquachis VI, company developed; music: Daniel Valdez
El Fin del Mundo IV, Luis Valdez; music: Daniel Valdez and David Silva

The Empty Space Theatre

M. Burke Walker
Artistic Director

Daniel Caine
Managing Director

919 East Pike St.
Seattle, WA 98122
(206) 325-4444 (business)
(206) 325-4443 (box office)

Founded 1971
M. Burke Walker,
Julian Schembri,
Charles Younger, James Royce

Season
October–September

Schedule
Evenings
Tuesday–Sunday
Matinees
Sunday

Facilities
Seating capacity: 99
Stage: flexible

Finances
Oct. 1, 1978–Sept. 30, 1979
$209,000 operating expenses
$ 85,000 earned income
$121,000 unearned income

Audience
Paid capacity: 94%
Subscribers: 1,250
Annual attendance: 25,000

Touring contact
Daniel Caine

Booked-in events
Experimental theatre

AEA letter of agreement

Serving as a crucible for new works in the Pacific Northwest since 1970, Seattle's Empty Space Theatre employs professional actors, playwrights, directors, designers and technicians for a 10-play season in an intimate, 99-seat space.

In the first two seasons, 18 productions were presented, ranging from first Seattle productions for Sam Shepard and Peter Handke to *The Tempest* and *Happy Days.* The theatre's programming philosophy was immediately established: major emphasis on new plays by contemporary authors, offset by selected scripts from the classical and modern repertoires.

The older, more established plays are an integral part of the schedule. In addition to their intrinsic worth, they propel actors and designers in new directions and also provide important touchstones against which to weigh the new play production. The Space's "Midnight Theatre" and summer productions are an important third component: burlesque, vaudeville, melodrama, improvisation and slapstick combine to create a production signature that is physical, presentational and unabashedly theatrical.

The heart of the theater's programming, however, has always been new plays by new authors. Numerous works by new playwrights were premiered in Seattle from 1957 to 1977, including three specially commissioned world premieres. The next two seasons saw the beginnings of three specially commissioned world premieres. The next two seasons saw the beginnings of the New Playwrights Forum, a program of staged readings and workshop productions of plays-in-progress. The Forum dovetails with the mainstage work, helping to fulfill two major goals: the creation of a regional center for the professional production of new plays and new playwrights, and the projected 1981 opening of a new 280-seat theatre to house that center.

Programs and services
Artistic, administrative and technical/production internships, student and senior citizen ticket discounts, half-price and free tickets, statewide touring, post-performance discussions, workshop productions and staged readings, guest lecturers, midnight shows, newsletter, volunteer auxiliary.

Productions 1977-78
Ashes, David Rudkin
The Misanthrope, Moliere; trans: Tony Harrison
Gossip, George F. Walker
Landscape of the Body, John Guare
Angel City, Sam Shepard
Oregon Gothic, Kurt Beattie
The Pulse of New York, John Kauffman and company

Productions 1978-79
Illuminatus!, Parts I, II and III, Ken Campbell and Chris Langham, from novels by Robert Shea and Robert Anton Wilson; music: John Engerman and Steve Amadek
A Prayer for My Daughter, Thomas Babe
Psychosis Unclassified, Ken Campbell, from Theodore Sturgeon's story
Bonjour, là, Bonjour, Michel Tremblay; trans: John Van Burek and Bill Glassco
Zastrozzi, George F. Walker
Skungpoomery, Ken Campbell
The Voice of the Mountain, John Kauffman and company
Hooters, Ted Tally

Clockwise from top: Dana Cox, Steve Tomkins, Michael Longfield and Nancy Lane in *Illuminatus!*
Photo: Nick Gunderson.

Robert Wright, Vicki Carver, John Norwalk and John Procaccino in *Angel City.* Photo: Nick Gunderson.

Ensemble Studio Theatre

Curt Dempster
Artistic Director

Marian Godfrey
Associate Director

549 West 52nd St.
New York, NY 10019
(212) 247-4982

Founded 1971
Curt Dempster

Season
October–June

Schedule
Evenings
Wednesday–Sunday

Facilities
Mainstage
Seating capacity: 99
Stage: flexible
Workshop
Seating capacity: 50
Stage: flexible

Finances
Oct. 1, 1978–Sept. 30, 1979
$210,000 operating expenses
$ 35,000 earned income
$184,000 unearned income

Audience
Paid capacity: 61%
Annual attendance: 11,000

AEA letter of agreement

Stefan Gierasch and David
Margulies in *The Old Tune*.
Photo: Gerry Goodstein.

Socorro Santiago and Shawn
Elliot in *Eulogy for a Small-Time
Thief*. Photo: Gerry Goodstein.

The Ensemble Studio Theatre was founded in 1971 as a membership organization of theatre professionals. Presently its membership comprises more than 200 playwrights, actors, directors, designers and technicians. The theatre is located in a warehouse owned by the City of New York. Its facilities on two floors include a flexible 99-seat theatre space, a smaller 50-seat workshop space, offices, dressing rooms and rehearsal areas.

The Ensemble Studio Theatre is dedicated to preserving and developing the resources of the professional theatre by developing new works for the stage, and by providing artistic and financial support for the individual theatre artist. The theatre nurtures and protects the creative impulse of theatre artists by providing a permanent home base where they can work among their peers, free of commercial pressures. Principal programs each season are: the Major Production Series of five productions of new American plays; the Workshop and Experimental Projects Series of 10 to 15 workshop productions and 40 to 50 play readings; the Playwrights' Unit, in which 25 participating writers meet regularly to present works-in-progress and discuss craft problems; the Theatre Bank, providing financial support to playwrights, directors and actors in the form of stipends for production-related expenses, commissions, emergency grants and loans; the Summer Theatre Colony at the Barlow School in upstate New York; and the Ensemble Studio Theatre Institute for Professional Training.

One of the theatre's primary artistic concerns during the past two seasons has been the revitalization of the one-act form. The annual spring Marathon of one-act plays acknowledges the debt both new and established writers owe to the one-act form in developing their craft.

Programs and services
Professional training in acting, directing and playwriting; artistic, administrative and technical/production internships; student and senior citizen ticket discounts, free ticket distribution, post-performance discussions, workshop productions and staged readings, music series, script library.

Productions 1977-78
Reflections of a China Doll, Susan Merson
Eulogy for a Small-Time Thief, Miguel Piñero
Mama Sang the Blues, Katherine Cortez
Innocent Pleasures, Arthur Giron
Marathon '78, 19 new one-act plays by
    American writers

Productions 1978-79
End of the War, Vincent Canby
Three:
    Bicycle Boys, Peter Maloney
    Playing Dolls, Susan Nanus
    Buddy Pals, Neil Cuthbert
A Special Evening:
    The Man with the Flower in His Mouth, Luigi
    Pirandello
    The Old Tune, Robert Pinget; adapt: Samuel
    Beckett
Welfare, Marcia Haufrecht
Marathon '79, 13 new one-act plays by
    American writers

Equinox Theatre

Bruce Bowen
Artistic Director

Jodie Olbrych
Executive Director

3617 Washington Ave.
Houston, TX 77007
(713) 868-4546 (business)
(713) 868-5829 (box office)

Founded 1976
Bruce Bowen
Jodie Olbrych

Season
October–August

Schedule
Evenings
Thursday–Saturday

Facilities
Seating capacity: 99
Stage: flexible

Finances
July 1, 1978–June 30, 1979
$77,000 operating expenses
$22,000 earned income
$35,000 unearned income

Audience
Paid capacity: 67%
Subscribers: 100
Annual attendance: 12,000

Touring contact
Jodie Olbrych

Equinox Theatre aims to entertain through public performance from a broad range of the performing arts. The company also provides facilities for classes and workshops, and works with the existing institutions (theatres, schools, media and museums) and supports and encourages directors, choreographers, composers, playwrights, designers, technicians and performers in the exploration and synthesis of the old and the new in their respective fields.

Equinox's artistic offerings for mid-1979 reflect its recognition of the versatility of contemporary performing arts. Its ever-expanding audience was exposed to dance-drama through the world premier of *The Saga of Jean Lafitte,* "choreo-poetry" in *For Colored Girls who have Considered Suicide/When The Rainbow is Enuf,* and innovative contemporary theatre in the Houston premiere of Julian Barry's *Lenny.* Performances were also scheduled by Spectrum Deaf Theatre for both hearing and non-hearing audiences.

Equinox is committed to nurturing new performers, writers and directors. Its continuing educational activities include workshops, staged readings and directors' laboratory productions. Through an innovative seminar series, Equinox has provided the opportunity for aspiring playwrights, performers and directors to participate in intimate dialogues with several of America's leading playwrights, including Christopher Durang, Robert Anderson and Ntozake Shange.

Under the leadership of its co-founders, executive producer Jodie Olbrych and artistic director Bruce Bowen, and an active board of directors, Equinox is expanding its audience through a major subscription campaign, with plans for a move to larger production facilities underway.

Programs and services
Professional training in acting, directing, production and administration; classes for nonprofessionals; artistic, administrative and technical/production internships; playwright seminars, student performances, programs-in-schools, free ticket distribution, statewide touring, post-performance discussions, workshop productions and staged readings, guest lecturers, poetry readings, newsletter, souvenir books, speakers bureau, theatre rentals.

Productions 1977-78
In the Boom Boom Room, David Rabe
Fortune and Men's Eyes, John Herbert
Charlie's Ear, Gary Chason
The Basic Training of Pavlo Hummel, David Rabe
Hair, book and lyrics: Gerome Ragni and James Rado; music: Galt MacDermot
American Buffalo, David Mamet
Denizens, Gary Chason
Sexual Perversity in Chicago and *The Duck Variations,* David Mamet
Nightlife, Jeff and Mary Galligan
Sticks and Bones, David Rabe
Solitaire/Double Solitaire, Robert Anderson
The Rocky Horror Show, book, music and lyrics: Richard O'Brien

Productions 1978-79
The Idiots Karamazov, Christopher Durang and Albert Innaurato
The Water Engine and *Mr. Happiness,* David Mamet
The Saga of Jean Lafitte, James Clouser
For Colored Girls who have Considered Suicide/When The Rainbow is Enuf, Ntozake Shange
Lenny, Julian Barry

Jeri Carvajal-Dabne and Edward Muth in *The Rocky Horror Show.* Photo: Alecia Alexander.

Stan Mathews and Big Skinny Brown in *The Duck Variations.*

The First All Children's Theatre Company

Meridee Stein
Producer/Artistic Director

37 West 65th St.
New York, NY 10023
(212) 873-6400

Founded 1969
Meridee Stein

Season
October–May
Summer touring
June, July

Schedule
Evenings
Variable
Matinees
Saturday, Sunday

Facilities
Seating capacity: 100-200
Stage: thrust

Finances
Sept. 1, 1978–Aug. 31, 1979
$197,000 operating expenses
$ 72,000 earned income
$121,000 unearned income

Audience
Paid capacity: 90%
Annual attendance: 14,000

Touring contact
Lee DeWeerdt

Booked-in events
Dance, theatre

The Incredible Feeling Show.
Photo: Carol Rosegg.

*Clever Jack and the Magic
Beanstalk.* Photo: Carol Rosegg.

Recently celebrating its 10th anniversary, the First All Children's Theatre (First ACT) Company is dedicated to producing professional theatre with and for young people. Comprising two interracial companies, the Meri Mini Players (ages 6-13) and the Teen Company (ages 14-17), First ACT has developed a unique repertory style, involving young people in the creative process, as well as promoting excellence in the writing and production of theatre for young people by trained theatre professionals. Through its special approach to children's theatre, First ACT seeks to inspire and cultivate in a youthful audience an awareness of theatre's ability to excite, reveal and challenge.

Each season five original musicals are produced over a 40-week period, including one piece by a major playwright. Most recently, Elizabeth Swados' *The Incredible Feeling Show* was developed and produced by First ACT under a special New York State Council on the Arts subsidy. Since its inception, First ACT has produced 16 original plays and musical scores, an anthology of which will soon be published for nationwide distibution by Bantam Books. Other artistic credits include performances at the New York Shakespeare Festival, the Ontario Summer Festival of the Arts, the Eugene O'Neill Theater Center, the Berkshire Theatre Festival, the Paul Robeson Performing Arts Center, the John Drew Theatre, appearances on all three major television networks, including an ABC television special, and a "Benefit on Broadway" at New York's Shubert Theatre.

First ACT's 10th anniversary celebration saw the renovation of its theatre complex across from Lincoln Center and the rapid emergence of the company as a national resource for child arts. In this capacity First ACT was recently selected to represent the United States on the satellite telecast that officially launched the United Nations' International Year of the Child (IYC), and the company has subsequently participated in numerous other IYC presentations.

Artistic achievement in theatrical production has been and shall remain First ACT's primary objective. But its commitment to the growth of young people has brought about a host of complementary program activities. These community outreach programs have grown to include: teacher training seminars and workshop, free and discounted tickets for handicapped and disadvantaged youngsters, "Education Through the Performing Arts" programs in inner-city classrooms in conjunction with the Fordham University Learning Center, and the creation of a mural and filmstrip honoring IYC that are available to educators across the nation.

Programs and services
Professional training in acting, production and administration; artistic, administrative, and technical/production internships; student performances, programs-in-schools, study materials, teacher training seminars, free ticket distribution, voucher program, national touring, post-performance discussions, souvenir book.

Productions 1977-78
Who's Next?, book: David Damstra; music: Matthew Kaplowitz; lyrics: D. Damstra and M. Kaplowitz
A Whinny and a Whistle, book: Cheryl Scammon and Mary Steenburgen; music and lyrics: Matthew Kaplowitz
Clever Jack and the Magic Beanstalk, book: Ian Elliot and Meridee Stein; music and lyrics: Judie Thomas and John Forster
The Pushcart Fables, book: Betsy Shevey; music and lyrics: Judith Thomashefsky
Three Tales at a Time, book, music and lyrics: various writers

Productions 1978-79
Three Tales at a Time
Alice Through the Looking Glass, book: Susan Dias and Meridee Stein, from Lewis Carroll's story; music: Philip Namanworth; lyrics: S. Dias
The Incredible Feeling Show, book, music and lyrics: Elizabeth Swados
Clever Jack and the Magic Beanstalk
The Pushcart Fables

Florida Studio Theatre

Jon Spelman
Artistic Director

Robert Miller
General Manager

4619 Bay Shore Road
Sarasota, FL 33580
(813) 355-4096

Founded 1973
John Spelman

Season
October–May

Facilities
1241 North Palm Ave.
Seating capacity: 75
Stage: flexible

Finances
Jan. 1, 1978–Dec. 31, 1978
$114,000 operating expenses
$ 18,000 earned income
$ 87,000 unearned income

Audience
Paid capacity: 89%
Subscribers: 200
Annual attendance: 35,000

Touring contact
Jay Julian

Booked-in events
Dance, mime, music,
experimental and children's
theatre

Florida Studio Theatre is dedicated to exciting professional productions of exceptional plays. FST focuses on new scripts as well as the most significant work of the past, bringing these productions to a wide variety of audiences, particularly those lacking access to the magic of live theatre. The theatre often performs in non-theatrical environments and also conducts residencies, seminars and workshops.

FST has produced plays by Handke, Beckett, Pinter and Orton, new American works and adaptations from the medieval and Elizabethan periods. It has also commissioned original plays and is currently developing scripts in collaboration with a playwright-in-residence. The company plans to enrich its work with cabaret and outdoor Shakespearean presentations.

Florida Studio Theaatre is headquartered in an historic building in downtown Sarasota, one block from a bayfront park. The building contains offices and a flexible 75-seat theatre where the company rehearses and offers its plays in a subscription series to the general public. Most FST productions tour throughout Florida, usually two or three at a time in repertory. The company has also toured the Southeast and traveled to Washington, D.C., and Baltimore's New Theatre Festival. Tour performances are scheduled at colleges, schools, other theatres, prisons, community centers and churches. In addition to single touring performances, the company offers workshops, community residencies and post-performance discussions.

FST is a founding member of Alternate ROOTS, an organization of southeastern theatre companies, and hosted ROOTS' first performance festival. The company has also been represented at the Bergamo Conference organized by UNESCO and the International Theatre Institute.

Programs and services
Classes for nonprofessionals and children; artistic, administrative and technical/production internships; college residencies, programs-in-schools, study materials, student and senior citizen ticket discounts, free ticket distribution, national touring, post-performance discussions, guest lecturers, poetry readings, cabaret, newsletter, script publication, speakers bureau, theatre rentals.

Productions 1977-78
Second Shepherds' Play, adapt: Jon Spelman
The Promise, Aleksei Arbuzov; trans: Ariadne Nicolaeff
Extremities, company developed

Productions 1978-79
Lunatics and Lovers, adapt: Jon Spelman, from William Shakespeare's *A Midsummer Night's Dream*
Echoes, N. Richard Nash
Cabin Fever, Joan Schenkar
When I'm 64 ..., Carol F. Duval
The Dumb Waiter, Harold Pinter

Tina Johnson and Nancy Buttenheim in *When I'm 64 ...*
Photo: Free Lance Associates.

Tina Johnson, Jon Spelman and Norman Ussery in *Cabin Fever.*
Photo: Free Lance Associates.

Folger Theatre Group

Louis W. Scheeder
Producer

Michael Sheehan
Associate Producer

201 East Capitol St., SE
Washington, DC 20003
(202) 547-3230 (business)
(202) 546-4000 (box office)

Founded 1970
O.B. Hardison
Richmond Crinkley

Season
October–July

Schedule
Evenings
Tuesday–Sunday
Matinees
Saturday, Sunday

Facilities
Seating capacity: 214
Stage: thrust

Finances
July 1, 1978–June 30, 1979
$719,000 operating expenses
$391,000 earned income
$328,000 unearned income

Audience
Paid capacity: 103%
Subscribers: 7,910
Annual attendance: 65,000

Touring contact
Michael Sheehan

Booked-in events
Music

AEA LORT (D) contract

Michael Tolaydo and David Butler
in *Hamlet.* Photo: Joan E. Biren.

The Folger Theatre Group is a division of the internationally noted Folger Shakespeare Library. Capitalizing on its facility, a replica of an Elizabethan stage, as well as the scholastic wealth of the library, the Folger Theatre Group has embraced Shakespeare as its "playwright in residence." After nine seasons of producing nearly half the Bard's works, the Theatre Group has developed a distinctly American approach to Shakespeare. Relying heavily on the text, the Folger's regularly returning actors, directors and designers continually "go back to the words" and avoid the arbitrary imposition of artifice upon Shakespeare's works.

From the beginning, new plays have also been an integral part of the Folger's identity. The parallel production of classic plays and contemporary premieres have yielded constructive cross-fertilization of style and approach.

Located two blocks from the United States Capitol, the company provides a unique forum for plays dealing with social issues. Folger premieres in this vein have included Brian Clark's *Whose Life Is It Anyway?,* Tom Cole's *Medal of Honor Rag,* and David Freeman's *Creeps.* In 1976-77, the Folger produced Christopher Sergel's *Black Elk Speaks,* based on the book by John G. Neihardt, which toured nationally in 1977-78 and played at the Kennedy Center in July 1978 as the special benefit performance for "The Longest Walk," sponsored by the Native American Treaties and Rights Organization.

A frontrunner in accessible theatre for the handicapped, the Folger presents sign language-interpreted performances as part of its regularly scheduled programming. Since the inception of the program in 1977, the Folger has acted in cooperation with the National Association of the Handicapped in advising other theatres on developing similar programs.

For the past three seasons, the Folger Theatre Group has played to more than 100 percent capacity houses. The 1979-80 season marks another step in its continuing growth, during which the Folger will present two plays in residence at the Kennedy Center's new Terrace Theatre in addition to the regular five-play schedule at the company's home on Capitol Hill.

Programs and services
Artistic, administrative, and technical/production internships; student performances, programs-in-schools, classes for high school teachers, student and senior citizen ticket discounts, national touring company, post-performance discussions, newsletter, speakers bureau, volunteer auxiliary, interpreted performances for the hearing-impaired.

Productions 1977-78
Teeth 'n' Smiles, book: David Hare; music and
    lyrics: Nick and Tony Bicat
Two Gentlemen of Verona, William
    Shakespeare
Hamlet, William Shakespeare
Mackerel, Israel Horovitz
Richard III, William Shakespeare

Productions 1978-79
Whose Life Is It Anyway?, Brian Clark
The Merry Wives of Windsor, William
    Shakespeare
Richard II, William Shakespeare
Benefit of a Doubt, Edward Clinton
As You Like It, William Shakespeare

Brian Hartigan and friend in
Mackerel. Photo: Joan E. Biren.

Frank Silvera Writers' Workshop

Garland Lee Thompson
Director

Maggie Higgs
Administrative Coordinator

317 West 125th St.
New York, NY 10027
(212) 662-8463

Founded 1973
Garland Lee Thompson

Season
September–June

Schedule
Evenings
Monday
Matinees
Saturday

Facilities
Seating capacity: 125
Stage: flexible

Finances
July 1, 1977–June 30, 1978
$66,000 operating expenses
$ 8,000 earned income
$48,000 unearned income

Audience
Annual attendance: 2,035

AEA Showcase Code

The Frank Silvera Writers' Workshop was founded in 1973 by Garland Lee Thompson and since that time has developed a writer's laboratory presenting more than 90 new playwrights' work each year. The workshop remains a living memorial to Frank Silvera who, prior to his death, was active in the production of black plays and the nurturing of black dramatic artists. His Theatre of Being, based in Los Angeles, provided a model for the Writers' Workshop.

It is the purpose of FSWW to encourage the growth of black and Third World playwrights and to assist them in the development of their craft. Monday and Saturday series of laboratory readings are geared to the needs of each playwright and also provide an opportunity for other writers to benefit from comments and suggestions made during the critique session immediately following each reading.

The Artistic Technical Assistance Collective (ATAC) was formed in 1976-77 to serve as a technicians pool for the workshop, as well as other companies across the nation, drawing on a large pool of lighting and set designers, stage managers and production assistants. It is the hope and aspiration of the ATAC program to create an important new school of communications specialists. The FSWW staged readings, through the writers/directors unit, provide the ATAC apprentices with actual theatrical situations in which to work and practice their skills. Monthly seminars conducted by experts treat various aspects of stage production.

The workshop has additionally sponsored a successful series of playwriting seminars, conducted by Adrienne Kennedy, Richard Wesley, Owen Dodson and Alice Childress, and designed to help playwrights gain new perspectives on their craft and help experienced writers refine their work.

Programs and services
Professional training in technical theatre; playwrights seminars, post-performance discussions, workshop productions and staged readings, guest lecturers, newsletter.

Productions 1977-78
Partake of De Goat Meat, Bhunnie Bernier Molette
Run'ers, Ivey McCray
The Incarnations of Reverend Goode Blacque Dresse, Garland Lee Thompson
the bloodrite, owa

Productions 1978-79
Inacent Black and the Five Brothers, A. Marcus Hemphill
The Royal Road, Sam Shirakawa
No Left Turn, Buriel Clay II
Investments, Ruth Ce. Jones
The Murder of Cyrene Vignette, Malik

Lorey Hayes and Matthew Bernard Johnson in *Inacent Black and the Five Brothers.* Photo: Sunny Bak.

Jack Maret, Suavae Mitchell (rear), Robert Delbert and Doug Handy (front) in *No Left Turn.* Photo: Bert Andrews.

Free Street Theater

Patrick Henry
Artistic Director/Producer

Carrol Hoch
General Manager

59 West Hubbard St.
Chicago, IL 60610
(312) 822-0460

Founded 1969
Patrick Henry, Perry Baer

Season
Year-round

Schedule
Variable

Finances
April 1, 1978–March 31, 1979
$489,000 operating expenses
$131,000 earned income
$350,000 unearned income

Audience
Annual attendance: 150,000

Touring contact
Michael Ross

AEA Actor/Teacher contract

Wilbert Bradley in *Fanfare for the Future*. Photo: David Talbott.

Free Street Theater is the home address for a group of actors, dancers, musicians and technicians working to enliven and enlighten the American community. FST aims to stimulate a more creative society and brings the arts into a more responsible and meaningful relationship with daily life. Toward this end, the Free Street Theater operates the following five programs:

Free Street Theater: The original Free Street program consists of a mobile theatre presenting free outdoor performances in streets, parks, plazas—wherever people congregate. In addition to performance activities, the company offers workshops and seminars designed to give direction, inspiration and encouragement to community-based organizations and artists.

Free Street Too: An ensemble of older people (ages 67 to 80) who advocate the positive contributions older people still can and do make to our total society, the group champions cross-generational communication in performance and workshops.

Theatre for Youth: Two separate production programs—one for elementary school students, one for high school students—run from October through April. A special component of the project is a post-performance workshop program in which performers and audience participate in simulation games exploring the social and ethical questions posed by each production.

Options: This program explores the possible relationships between the performing arts and the handicapped. The goal of the project is to demonstrate how the performing arts can be of benefit to the handicapped individual and facilitate his or her transition from a therapeutic environment to the society at large.

The Stucher Project: FST's unique educational program places creative artists in classrooms, where they function as full-time students for a one-month period. The "Stucher" (part *stu*dent/ part tea*cher*) provides alternative methods of understanding and applying standard classroom concepts.

Programs and services
Artistic, administrative, and technical/production internships; student performances, programs-in-schools, neighborhood residencies, national touring, post-performance discussions, newsletter, souvenir book, free admission to all events.

Productions 1977-78
Rockin' the Cradle, company adaptation of Marc Blitzstein's *The Cradle Will Rock*
Rootabaga Stories, Carey B. Ericson, from Carl Sandburg's stories
Bloody and Bawdy Villains, Patrick Henry and Lewis Marder
Piñata, Patrick Henry and company
New Burlington, Ken Jenkins, from John Baskin's novel
When the Drum Speaks, Patrick Henry; music: Foday Musa Suso
Dummy I, Patrick Henry and company
Storystage
Fanfare for the Future, Patrick Henry and company
The Family of Man, book: Patrick Henry; music and lyrics: Tom Taylor and Joe Godfrey
To Life!, book: Patrick Henry; music and lyrics: Noreen Walker, James Barry and Maxine Feldman
The Third Duckling, Patrick Henry and company
Streetdance, adapt: Patrick Henry and Wilbert Bradley
Musicmini, adapt: John Vitale

Productions 1978-79
Change Places with Me, Patrick Henry and company
The Grimm Gang, adapt: Patrick Henry and company
Nobody, book and lyrics: Patrick Henry; music: Matthew Rose
Tall Tales, Patrick Henry and company
Workaday, Patrick Henry and company
Citisong, Patrick Henry and company
The Family of Man
To Life!
The Third Duckling

Change Places with Me. Photo: Thom O'Connor.

George Street Playhouse

Eric Krebs
Producer

John Herochik
Managing Director

414 George St.
New Brunswick, NJ 08901
(201) 846-2895 (business)
(201) 246-7717 (box office)

Founded 1974
John Herochik, Eric Krebs

Season
October–May

Schedule
Evenings
Tuesday–Sunday
Matinees
Sunday

Facilities
Seating capacity: 260
Stage: thrust

Finances
July 1, 1978–June 30, 1979
$372,000 operating expenses
$187,000 earned expenses
$195,000 unearned income

Audience
Paid capacity: 76%
Subscribers: 2,300
Annual attendance: 65,000

Booked-in events
Solo performances

AEA LORT (D) contract

The George Street Playhouse is committed to the production of a wide mixture of plays, including new scripts, classics and popular contemporary works. During the past several seasons the Playhouse has produced two world premieres per season, including *Paris Was Yesterday* and the new musical *Pettycoat Lane* by Judd Woldin.

One of the great advantages of the Playhouse is its close proximity to New York City, allowing directors to have a great choice of performers for each production. Because of this rich resource, no attempt has been made to assemble a permanent company, although a pool of actors who have worked at George Street does form a kind of unofficial company.

In addition to the mainstage subscription season, George Street has made a policy of creatively serving the surrounding community. Over the past two seasons, the Playhouse has provided support and a base of operations to a full-time children's theatre company, and most recently to Crossroads, the first Equity company in New Jersey to concentrate exclusively on black and Hispanic theatre.

The five-year plan for the Playhouse calls for the continuation of a six-play mainstage series while plans are being completed for a new 500- to 600-seat theatre in central New Jersey.

Programs and services
Administrative and technical/production internships, student performances, programs-in-schools, student and senior citizen ticket discounts, free ticket distribution, post-performance discussions, regional touring of children's and ethnic theatre, newsletter, speakers bureau, volunteer auxiliary, theatre rentals.

Productions 1977-78
The Rainmaker, N. Richard Nash
Steambath, Bruce Jay Friedman
Man and Superman, George Bernard Shaw
Paris Was Yesterday, Paul Shyre, from Janet Flanner's memoirs
Serenading Louie, Lanford Wilson
Arsenic and Old Lace, Joseph Kesselring

Productions 1978-79
The School for Wives, Moliere; adapt: Donald Frame
Long Day's Journey into Night, Eugene O'Neill
Pettycoat Lane, book, music and lyrics: Judd Woldin
Sizwe Bansi Is Dead, Athol Fugard, John Kani and Winston Ntshona
Statements After an Arrest Under the Immorality Act, Athol Fugard
Twelfth Night, William Shakespeare
Dance for Me, Simeon, Joseph Maher

Dana Coen and Jaime Sanchez in *Steambath*. Photo: Suzanne Karp Krebs.

Celeste Holm in *Paris Was Yesterday*. Photo: Suzanne Karp Krebs.

Germinal Stage Denver

Edward R. Baierlein
Artistic and Managing Director

1820 Market St.
Denver, CO 80202
(303) 572-0944

Founded 1974
Edward R. Baierlein,
Sallie Diamond,
Ginger Valone, Jack McKnight

Season
October–May

Schedule
Evenings
Friday–Sunday

Facilities
Seating capacity: 170
Stage: thrust

Finances
Aug. 1, 1978–July 31, 1979
$67,000 operating expenses
$57,000 earned income
$18,000 unearned income

Audience
Paid capacity: 62%
Subscribers: 625
Annual attendance: 12,000

Sallie Diamond and Edward R. Baierlein (rear) in *archy & mehitabel*. Photo: Jim Valone.

Germinal Stage Denver is composed of theatre professionals with the desire to live and work in Denver, Colo. The theatre is located in a converted warehouse in the lower downtown area and is part of a gradual but successful upgrading of a former "skid row" district.

GSD discourages narrow specialization, uses a permanent performance structure a la Copeau, has no children's theatre, offers no classes and "hopes *not* to develop a 'style.'" The theatre is operated as a nonprofit "small business" and takes active steps to avoid institutional goals and an institutional outlook.

GSD's approach to the choice of material is extremely eclectic, ranging from Shaw to Williams to Pinter to de Ghelderode to Handke. It is an actor's theatre, in the sense that most plays are chosen for optimum challenge to the acting company and for the latitude to explore a broad spectrum of performance techniques. For example, a 1976 production of Williams' *In the Bar of a Tokyo Hotel* utilized the lineaments of Noh to enhance the ritual aspects and measured pace of the play.

In five full seasons, GSD has: never missed a scheduled performance, operated on 90 percent earned income, grown from 82 to 170 seats, increased its subscription rolls by 200

percent, and had, in the words of artistic and managing director Edward R. Baierlein, "eight hits, five flops and 14 productions that fell somewhere in between."

Programs and services
Administrative internships, post-performance discussions.

Productions 1977-78
The Great God Brown, Eugene O'Neill
The Friends, Arnold Wesker
Seascape, Edward Albee
The Eagle with Two Heads, Jean Cocteau; trans: Carl Wildman
The Show-Off, George Kelly

Productions 1978-79
The Glass Menagerie, Tennessee Williams
Macbett, Eugene Ionesco; trans: Charles Marowitz
No Man's Land, Harold Pinter
In the Boom Boom Room, David Rabe
The Well of the Saints, John Millington Synge
archy & mehitabel, book: Joe Darion and Mel Brooks, from Don Marquis' stories; music: George Kleinsinger; lyrics: J. Darion

Macbett. Photo: Jim Valone.

GeVa Theatre

Gideon Y. Schein
Artistic Director

Jessica L. Andrews
Managing Director

168 Clinton Ave. South
Rochester, NY 14604
(716) 232-1366 (business)
(716) 232-1363 (box office)

Founded 1972
William and Cynthia Selden

Season
October–April

Schedule
Evenings
Tuesday–Sunday
Matinees
Wednesday, Sunday

Facilities
Seating capacity: 215
Stage: thrust

Finances
July 1, 1978–June 30, 1979
$365,000 operating expenses
$158,000 earned income
$211,000 unearned income

Audience
Paid capacity: 89%
Subscribers: 3,117
Annual attendance: 65,000

Touring contact
Bruce E. Rodgers

AEA LORT (D) contract

Founded in 1972 as the Genesee Valley Arts Foundation, GeVa Theatre is located in the heart of downtown Rochester—a central location allowing it to serve outlying communities, while contributing materially to the revitalization of the inner city.

GeVa was created as a resident repertory company of actors, with the selection of plays dictated by the resources of the acting company. A change in the artistic and administrative leadership of the theatre in 1976-77 led to a change in the production philosophy, which now emphasizes the requirements of each play. While encouraging the frequent return of its theatre artists to maintain a sense of continuity for both the theatre and its audience, the choice of actors, directors and designers now thoroughly reflects the needs of each production, assuring the flexibility in environment and technique required by each play.

As the only professional resident theatre serving the greater Rochester area, GeVa is deeply committed to its community programs which have continued to develop and expand since its inception. At the core is GeVa's evening mainstage subscription series of six plays drawn from both the American and international repertoires. Current emphasis is placed on established plays, although GeVa plans to serve the new playwright as well in forthcoming seasons. In addition, GeVa maintains an active theatre-in-education program. In 1976-77, a National Endowment for the Humanities grant resulted in a touring company project to explore the uses of theatre techniques as teaching instruments. In 1977-78, funding under the Comprehensive Employment and Training Act (CETA) aided in the formation of a separate GeVa on Tour company produced two children's shows aimed at different age groups. With a second CETA grant in 1978-79, GeVa on Tour premiered three original works that played to more than 25,000 children within a 100-mile radius of Rochester. In its Theatre on the Block program, the theatre also gave 50 free public performances, playing to more than 15,000 people. Both grants helped continue the Saturday morning acting workshops at the theatre and expand a touring company program that continues to develop future audiences.

Programs and services
Classes for adults and children; administrative and technical/production internships, student performances, programs-in-schools, study materials, student and senior citizen ticket discounts, voucher program, statewide touring, post-performance discussions, newsletter, speakers bureau, volunteer auxiliary, theatre rentals.

Productions 1977-78
The Front Page, Ben Hecht and Charles MacArthur
Death of a Salesman, Arthur Miller
Scapin, Moliere
The Caretaker, Harold Pinter
A Raisin in the Sun, Lorraine Hansberry
Vanities, Jack Heifner

Productions 1978-79
A Streetcar Named Desire, Tennessee Williams
Diamond Studs, book: Jim Wann; music and lyrics: Bland Simpson and J. Wann
Sizwe Bansi Is Dead, Athol Fugard, John Kani and Winston Ntshona
13 Rue de l'Amour, Georges Feydeau; adapt: Mawby Green and Ed Feilbert
A Moon for the Misbegotten, Eugene O'Neill
The Hostage, Brendan Behan

Anita Birchenall and Edmond Genest in *A Moon for the Misbegotten.* Photo: Carolyn Brown.

Linda Swenson, Lois Hoskin, Lance Davis, Susan Lichtman and Peter Saputo in *The Hostage.* Photo: Carolyn Brown.

Goodman Theatre

Gregory Mosher
Artistic Director

David Mamet
Associate Artistic Director

Janet Wade
Managing Director

200 South Columbus Drive
Chicago, IL 60603
(312) 443-3811 (business)
(312) 443-3800 (box office)

Founded 1925
Art Institute of Chicago

Season
September–June

Schedule
Evenings
Tuesday–Sunday
Matinees
Thursday, Sunday

Facilities
Goodman Theatre
Seating capacity: 683
Stage: proscenium
Latin School
Seating capacity: 300
Stage: thrust
Ruth Page Auditorium
Seating capacity: 200
Stage: proscenium

Finances
July 1, 1978–June 30, 1979
$1,702,000 operating expenses
$1,040,000 earned income
$715,000 unearned income

Audience
Paid capacity: 73%
Subscribers: 15,626
Annual attendance: 128,498

Booked-in events
Music, lectures, special events

AEA LORT (B) and (D) contracts

Brad Sullivan in *Working*. Photo:
Thomas S. England.

Lynn Redgrave (center) in *Saint
Joan*. Photo: Thomas S. England.

The Goodman Theatre was founded in 1925 as a gift to the Art Institute of Chicago from Mr. and Mrs. William O. Goodman as a memorial to their son, Kenneth Sawyer Goodman.

On July 1, 1977, the Chicago Theatre Group was formed to take over from the Art Institute of Chicago the management and financing of professional productions at the Goodman Theatre.

Since 1974, the Goodman has presented several award-winning productions as well as 14 world premieres and five American premieres, including David Mamet's *American Buffalo, A Life in The Theatre* and *Lone Canoe*, scripts by John Guare, Brian Friel, Israel Horovitz, Stephen Schwartz and others. For the first time in Goodman's history, productions traveled to Broadway, the Kennedy Center in Washington, D.C., Philadelphia's Annenberg Center, Princeton's McCarter Theatre Company, the American Shakespeare Theatre in Stratford, Conn., the Westwood Playhouse in Los Angeles and made a statewide tour of Illinois.

The principal programs of the Goodman include the mainstage series, providing a season of six plays, both classics and new scripts, and Goodman 2, a season of experimental work and new scripts primarily utilizing local talent. Both programs are directed by artistic director Gregory Mosher.

A self-contained operation located next to the Art Institute of Chicago, the Goodman auditorium features wood-paneled walls and crystal chandeliers, while the proscenium stage is equipped with a plaster dome cyclorama and an Izenour electronic pre-set lighting system.

Programs and services
Classes for children; artistic, administrative and technical/production internships; student performances, student and senior citizen ticket discounts, free ticket distribution, national touring company, post-performance discussions, workshop productions and staged readings, guest lecturers, speakers bureau, souvenir shop, newsletter, volunteer auxiliary, theatre rentals, theatre tours.

Productions 1977-78
Saint Joan, George Bernard Shaw
The Seagull, Anton Chekhov; trans: Jean-Claude van Itallie
Working, book: Stephen Schwartz, from Studs Terkel's book; music and lyrics: S. Schwartz, et al.
Much Ado About Nothing, William Shakespeare
The Night of the Iguana, Tennessee Williams
Otherwise Engaged, Simon Gray
The Prague Spring, book and lyrics: Lee Kalcheim; music: Joseph G. Raposo
Battering Ram, David Freeman
Annulla Allen: The Autobiography of a Survivor, Emily Mann and Annulla Allen
Hail Scrawdyke! or *Little Malcolm and His Struggle Against the Eunuchs,* David Halliwell

Productions 1978-79
Native Son, Paul Green, from Richard Wright's novel
A Christmas Carol, adapt: Barbara Field
Two-Part Inventions, Richard Howard
Bosoms and Neglect, John Guare
Holiday, Philip Barry
Lone Canoe or *The Explorer,* David Mamet; music and lyrics: Alaric (Rokko) Jans
Emigres, Slawomir Mrozek; trans: Maciej and Teresa Wrone with Robert Holman
Curse of the Starving Class, Sam Shepard
Scenes and Revelations, Elan Garonzik; music: Thom Bishop
The Island, Athol Fugard, John Kani and Winston Ntshona

The Great-American Children's Theatre Company

Teri Solomon Mitze
Executive Producer

Mitchell Hebert
Associate Producer

Box 92123
Milwaukee, WI 53202
(414) 276-4230

Founded 1976
Thomas C. Mitze
Teri Solomon Mitze

Season
October–May

Schedule
Matinees
Monday–Friday
Selected Saturdays and Sundays

Facilities
Pabst Theatre
144 East Wells St.
Seating capacity: 1,432
Stage: proscenium
Gimbel's Forum
101 West Wisconsin Ave.
Seating capacity: 550
Stage: arena
Performing Arts Center
929 North Water St.
Seating capacity: 498
Stage: proscenium

Finances
July 1, 1978–June 30, 1979
$190,000 operating expenses
$165,000 earned income
$ 26,000 unearned income

Audience
Paid capacity: 97%
Annual attendance: 175,000

Booked-in events
Children's theatre

The Great-American Children's Theatre Company was founded to provide professional theatre to young audiences in southeastern Wisconsin, presenting large-scale productions at low prices to its audiences.

Its premiere production *The Apple Tree* broke house records at the Milwaukee Performing Arts Center, playing 66 performances to capacity crowds. In 1977, the turn-of-the-century Pabst Theatre was completely renovated by the city of Milwaukee, and the company's production there of *Ali Baba and the 40 Thieves* played to 84,000 people and set a theatre attendance record in Milwaukee. Later the show was televised by regional CBS affiliate stations. *The Doctor in Spite of Himself* in 1978 brought another 66,000 youngsters to the Pabst. Another popular production, an original musical commissioned by the company, was *It Must Be Magic—A Magical Musical*, a 1979 show that incorporated several grand magic illusions.

To augment mainstage productions, the company instituted "A Peek Behind the Scenes," a preparatory in-school program designed to bridge the gap between the classroom and the theatre experience. "A Peek Behind the Scenes" goes to about 500 schools, reaching an annual audience of 100,000.

Additional programs include the presentation of a major professional touring company each fall to give young audiences a chance to view different approaches to children's theatre, and an annual Breakfast Theatre presentation during November and December, a morning program featuring a musical production.

Programs and services
Developmental drama classes for adults and children; programs-in-schools, study materials, educational posters, film series, hospital performances.

Productions 1977-78
Welcome to the Zoo, book: Bill Solly and Donald Ward; music and lyrics: B. Solly
The Doctor in Spite of Himself, Moliere; adapt: Montgomery Davis

Productions 1978-79
Santa and the Magic Weather People, book: Bill Solly and Donald Ward; music and lyrics: B. Solly
It Must Be Magic—A Magical Musical, book: Bill Solly and Donald Ward; music and lyrics: B. Solly

Kent Miller and Charmaine Underheim in *The Doctor in Spite of Himself*. Photo: Bob Smith.

Nancy Youngblot, L.. Mattioli, Peggy Peterson, Divad and Marla Fries in *It Must Be Magic—A Magial Musical*. Photo: Bob Smith.

Great Lakes Shakespeare Festival

Vincent Dowling
Artistic Diector

Mary Bill
General Manager

Lakewood Civic Auditorium
Franklin Blvd. at Bunts Road
Lakewood, OH 44107
(216) 228-1225 (business)
(216) 521-0090 (box office)

Founded 1962
Community members

Season
July–September
Touring
May, October, November

Schedule
Evenings
Tuesday–Sunday
Matinees
Sunday

Facilities
Seating capacity: 989
Stage: modified thrust

Finances
Nov. 1, 1978–Oct. 31, 1979
$512,000 operating expenses
$263,000 earned income
$227,000 unearned income

Audience
Paid capacity: 70%
Subscribers: 3,500
Annual attendance: 75,000

Touring contact
Mary Bill

AEA LORT (B) contract

Vincent Dowling in *Wild Oats*.
Photo: Marianne Pojman.

Since 1962 the Great Lakes Shakespeare Festival has produced more than 90 plays by the world's great dramatists, with an emphasis on Shakespeare. Under Vincent Dowling's artistic direction, the Festival searches continually for an approach to classical drama expressing all the vigor, power, passion and individuality of the American performer with the color and vitality of his speech, while reflecting the dramatist's true feeling for language and character, so that the artists' intuitive grasp of reality is communicated freely to the audience.

In 1978, festival productions won six of eight Cleveland Critics Circle Awards in a season which included an American premiere, *The Nine Days Wonder of Will Kemp.*

The festival is a cultural and educational resource for the entire state of Ohio, annually presenting its major productions to more than 20,000 students. In 1979, GLSF added a spring tour of Ohio and initiated a four-week artists-in-schools residency in three high schools downstate. The third annual fall tour to 12 Ohio cities in 1979 will feature two full Shakespearean productions.

A permanent home for the festival is planned in the Cleveland Lakefront State Park—a theatre to be built by the state of Ohio and leased to GLSF. A local firm of architects, with an international team of consultants, is already working on the project.

Programs and services
Professional training in acting, directing, design, production and administration; classes for nonprofessionals; artistic, administrative and technical/production internships; student performances, programs-in-schools, study materials, student and senior citizen ticket discounts, statewide touring, post-performance discussions, film series, guest lecturers, speakers bureau.

Productions 1978
Polly, John Gay
Two Gentlemen of Verona, William Shakespeare
What Every Woman Knows, J.M. Barrie
The Nine Days Wonder of Will Kemp, Chris Harris and John David
Wild Oats, John O'Keeffe
King John, William Shakespeare

Productions 1979
Twelfth Night, William Shakespeare
Juno and the Paycock, Sean O'Casey
Clarence, Booth Tarkington
Do Me a Favorite, adapt: Vincent Dowling, from William Shakespeare's works
Blithe Spirit, Noel Coward
Othello, William Shakespeare

Donna Emmanuel, Jon Peter Benson and Jack Milo in *Polly*.
Photo: Marianne Pojman.

The Guthrie Theater

Richard Russell Ramos
Interim Artistic Advisor

Donald Schoenbaum
Managing Director

725 Vineland Place
Minneapolis, MN 55403
(612) 377-2824 (business)
(612) 377-2224 (box office)

Founded 1963
Tyrone Guthrie, Oliver Rea,
Peter Zeisler

Season
June–February

Schedule
Evenings
Monday–Saturday
Matinees
Wednesday, Saturday

Facilities
Seating capacity: 1,441
Stage: thrust

Finances
April 1, 1977–March 31, 1978
$3,527,000 operating expenses
$2,673,000 earned income
$1,040,000 unearned income

Audience
Paid capacity: 80%
Subscribers: 18,800
Annual attendance: 590,979

Touring contact
Jeanne Keller

Booked-in events
Theatre, music

AEA LORT (A) contract

Through a fundamentally classical repertoire, the Guthrie Theater's aim is to develop forms of theatrical art that will excite the imagination, mind and conscience of the upper midwest community. Implicit in this goal is the Guthrie's responsibility to serve with integrity and commitment its audiences, the collaborative artists of the theatre profession and the art of drama.

The Guthrie's auditorium contains a 200-degree arc of seats which partly surrounds an asymmetrical thrust stage. This thrust provides an atmosphere of immediacy and excitement, as well as a surprising sense of intimacy in a 1,441-seat house. The actors are part of a resident company and the directors and designers are both resident and guest artists. The supporting technical facilities are among the most complete in the world. Plays are performed in rotating repertory, offering a theatregoer three or four choices in any given week.

The Guthrie's outreach program responds to a variety of community needs. In addition to touring its five-state region with mainstage productions, a number of smaller programs have also toured. Outreach has pursued an imaginative course in educational programming with community classes in all aspects of theatre scheduled year-round, as well as touring exhibits, workshops and a variety of programs custom-designed for special constituencies throughout the region. *Flashbacks,* a program involving the talents of senior citizens, has received national attention.

Student matinees have become an integral part of metropolitan and regional educational planning, with the Guthrie providing printed study materials, as well as staff-led discussions. The Michael Langham Fellowship Program affords an opportunity for gifted young actors to become members of the acting company for a season. Special ticket discounts provide students, senior citizens and other groups with greater opportunities to attend productions. In this way, the Guthrie draws its audiences from an increasingly wide sector of the Twin Cities and surrounding communities.

During the 1977-78 season, Michael Langham served his final year as artistic director of the theatre, while the season produced during 1978-79 was under the artistic direction of Alvin Epstein.

Programs and services
Classes for nonprofessionals; artistic, administrative and technical/production internships; student performances, programs-in-schools, study materials, touring exhibits, student and senior citizen ticket discounts, voucher program, regional touring, post-performance discussions, workshop productions and staged readings, newsletter, magazine, souvenir book, videotape presentations, volunteer group, theatre rentals.

Productions 1977-78
She Stoops to Conquer, Oliver Goldsmith
A Moon for the Misbegotten, Eugene O'Neill
La Ronde, Arthur Schnitzler; adapt: Ken Ruta
Catsplay, Istvan Orkeny; trans: Clara Gyorgyey
The White Devil, John Webster
Design for Living, Noel Coward
A Christmas Carol, adapt: Barbara Field
Pantagleize, Michel de Ghelderode; adapt:
    Barbara Field

Productions 1978-79
The Pretenders, Henrik Ibsen; trans: Michael
    Feingold
Teibele and Her Demon, Isaac Bashevis Singer
    and Eve Friedman
Boy Meets Girl, Sam and Bella Spewack
Bonjour, là, Bonjour, Michel Tremblay; trans:
    John Van Burek and Bill Glassco
Hamlet, William Shakespeare
A Christmas Carol
Marriage, Nikolai Gogol; adapt: Barbara Field
The Beggar's Opera, John Gay

F. Murray Abraham and Laura Esterman in *Teibele and Her Demon.* Photo: Boyd Hagen.

Stephen Lang, Oliver Cliff (below) and Randall Duk Kim in *Hamlet.* Photo: Boyd Hagen.

Hartford Stage Company

Paul Weidner
Producing Director

William Stewart
Managing Director

Irene Lewis
Associate Director

50 Church St.
Hartford, CT 06103
(203) 525-5601 (business)
(203) 527-5151 (box office)

Founded 1964
Jacques Cartier

Season
October–July

Schedule
Evenings
Tuesday–Sunday
Matinees
Wednesday, Sunday

Facilities
John W. Huntington Theatre
Seating capacity: 489
Stage: thrust
The Old Place
65 Kinsley St.
Seating capacity: 225
Stage: thrust

Finances
July 1, 1978–June 30, 1979
$1,274,000 operating expenses
$ 912,000 earned income
$ 323,000 unearned income

Audience
Paid capacity: 95%
Subscribers: 16,243
Annual attendance: 165,000

Touring contact
W. Ludwell Baldwin

Booked-in-events
Theatre, music, ethnic and
children's theatre

AEA LORT (C) contract

Patti LuPone in *Catchpenny Twist*. Photo: Lanny Nagler.

A long-standing commitment to new American plays has been an outstanding characteristic of the Hartford Stage Company. Under the artistic direction of Paul Weidner, Hartford Stage has shown a preference for literate, verbally acute theatre presented in a varied and balanced season. In addition to contemporary American works, classical and foreign works are frequently highlighted, and a continuing interest in black and urban themes has also been emphasized.

Located itself at the hub of a major urban renewal project, the Hartford Stage Company is governed by an active board of directors which determines broad policies, raises funds and engages the producing and managing directors. A production and administrative staff of 45 works on a seasonal or year-round basis; actors are engaged from show to show, with many returning regularly, and designers are employed in much the same way.

Except for rehearsal space and storage, most activites are contained in one facility, a $2.5 million complex designed by noted architect Robert Venturi and opened in the fall of 1977. The new theatre retains the thrust stage and warm ambience of the theatre's earlier quarters, now known as The Old Place and used occasionally for experimental and workshop productions.

A number of Stage Company productions are designed to attract special audiences or take the theatre's work into the community, in particular a touring ensemble featuring topical and documentary material. The company also has an active publications program and was one of the first theatres to publish its own subscriber magazine, *On the Scene*. In the summer months HSC sponsors a youth theatre for Hartford teenagers, in recent years producing such musicals as *West Side Story* and *Two Gentlemen of Verona*. The Stage Company has also reached audiences beyond the Connecticut region with a Broadway engagement of its premiere production of *My Sister, My Sister* by Ray Aranha, and a nationally televised presentation of Edward Albee's *All Over* for the PBS series *Theater in America*.

Programs and services
Professional training for actors, directors, technicians and administrators; classes for nonprofessionals and children; administrative and technical/production internships, youth theatre, special student performances, programs-in-schools, study materials, student and senior citizen ticket discounts, regional touring, post-performance discussions, workshop productions and staged readings, magazine, souvenir book, speakers bureau, volunteer auxiliary, theatre rentals.

Productions 1977-78
All the Way Home, Tad Mosel, from James Agee's novel, *A Death in the Family*
Past Tense, Jack Zeman
A Flea in Her Ear, Georges Feydeau, trans: John Mortimer
Rain, John Colton and Clemence Randolph, from W. Somerset Maugham's story
Holiday, Philip Barry
They'd Come to See Charlie, James Borrelli
Eve, Larry Fineberg
Mackerel, Israel Horovitz
The Black, the Blue and the Gray, adapt: Irene Lewis and Edward Emmanuel

Productions 1978-79
Catchpenny Twist, Stewart Parker; music: Shaun Davey
Boy Meets Girl, Sam and Bella Spewack
Wedding Band, Alice Childress
Galileo, Bertolt Brecht; adapt: Charles Laughton
The Matchmaker, Thornton Wilder
Bonjour, là, Bonjour, Michel Tremblay; trans: John Van Burek and Bill Glassco
Passing By, Martin Sherman
Home of the Brave, adapt: Irene Lewis, Tana Hicken and David O. Petersen

Bernard Frawley, Richard Mathews, David Shaw, Alexander Scourby and Paul C. Thomas in *Galileo*. Photo: Lanny Nagler.

Hartman Theatre Company

Del Tenney
Margot Tenney
Producing Directors

Roger Meeker
Managing Director

Box 521
Stamford, CT 06904
(203) 324-6781 (business)
(203) 323-2131 (box office)
New York direct line:
(212) 581-0177

Founded 1974
Del and Margot Tenney

Season
October–April

Schedule
Evenings
Tuesday–Sunday
Matinees
Saturday, Sunday

Facilities
Stamford Theatre
307 Atlantic St.
Seating capacity: 600
Stage: proscenium
Landmark Square Playhouse
Seating capacity: 110
Stage: flexible

Finances
July 1, 1978–June 30, 1979
$843,000 operating expenses
$423,000 earned income
$353,000 unearned income

Audience
Paid capacity: 77%
Subscribers: 6,290
Annual attendance: 64,327

Booked-in events
Dance, mime, experimental
theatre, music groups,
puppeteers and individual artists

AEA LORT (B) contract

The Hartman Theatre Company, one of five major resident theatres in Connecticut, strives to present a balanced mixture of classics, revivals and new plays to its subscription audience. Producing directors Margot and Del Tenney maintain a special continuing interest in the development of new plays and have presented such works as Milan Stitt's *The Runner Stumbles,* Mark Eichman's *As to the Meaning of Words,* and A. R. Gurney, Jr.'s *The Middle Ages.* However, the Hartman has become best known for its revivals of European and American classics such as Moliere's *Tartuffe* and Philip Barry's *The Animal Kingdom.*

Located in Fairfield County 45 minutes from Broadway, the Hartman serves residents within a 50-mile radius and is uniquely equipped to draw on many of New York's finest theatrical resources. Since its inception, the company has had a growing inpact on the revitalized downtown Stamford area, corporate headquarters for Pitney Bowes, Xerox, Champion International, General Telephone and Electronics, and many others. The Hartman operates in a renovated theatre which was originally a 1927 vaudeville palace, and also in the Landmark Square Playhouse, a modern space which is the site of new play readings, dark-night seminars on aspects of the professional theatre, and which also functions as a base of operations for visiting artists and performers.

The Playhouse is also the home base for the Hartman's professional intern program, which invites 20 qualified students to join the theatre's operation in production, administration, design or acting. Project Interact, run by acting interns, is one of the Hartman's outreach programs designed to provide students attending productions with a greater understanding of theatre through pre-performance workshops, demonstrations and study guides, as well as through post-performance talk-back sessions.

The Hartman is currently engaged in a long-range fund-raising program designed to establish a capital fund upon which HTC may draw at a future date. The theatre also sponsors at least one major fundraising gala per season. Past events have included a "Rudolph Valentino Evening" and a jazz concert featuring Don Elliott and Gerry Mulligan.

Programs and services
Professional and nonprofessional training in acting, directing, design, production and administration; artistic, administrative and technical/production internships, special student performances, programs-in-schools, study materials for teachers and students, student and senior citizen ticket discounts, corporate subscriptions, post-performance discussions, workshop productions/staged readings, subscriber newsletter, cookbook, speakers bureau, volunteer auxiliary, theatre rentals.

Productions 1977-78
The Mousetrap, Agatha Christie
The Miracle Worker, William Gibson
The Middle Ages, A. R. Gurney, Jr.
Othello, William Shakespeare
The Animal Kingdom, Philip Barry
Jerome Kern at the Hartman
The Servant of Two Masters, Carlo Goldoni
Yerma, Federico Garcia Lorca
Ribbons, David F. Eliet
The Maids, Jean Genet
La Ronde, Arthur Schnitzler
The Three Sisters, Anton Chekhov
Mrile, adapt: Elizabeth J. Moyer
Jumping Mouse, book: Larry Arrick; music and
lyrics: Barbara Damashek

Productions 1978-79
Two for the Seesaw, William Gibson
The Diary of Anne Frank, Frances Goodrich
and Albert Hackett
Absurd Person Singular, Alan Ayckbourn
The Auction Tomorrow, Jerry L. Crawford
The Little Foxes, Lillian Hellman
The Fantasticks, book and lyrics: Tom Jones;
music: Harvey Schmidt

Sally Chamberlin and Fritz
Sperberg in *The Mousetrap.*
Photo: Gerry Goodstein.

Ron Randell, Saylor Creswell and
Jacqueline Coslow in *Absurd
Person Singular.* Photo: Gerry
Goodstein.

Hawaii Public Theater

Eugene Lion
Artistic Director

Patricia Herman
Associate Director

State Foundation on
  Culture and the Arts
250 South King St., Room 310
Honolulu, HI 96817
(808) 941-8660

Founded 1976
Jean Comer
Kenneth A. Kanter

Season
Year-round

Finances
Oct. 1, 1977–Sept. 30, 1978
$359,000 operating expenses
$ 4,000 earned income
$355,000 unearned income

Touring contact
Eugene Lion

AEA Guest Artist contract

Valerie Charles and Patricia
Herman in *The Maids*. Photo: Bill
Soares.

In an increasingly impersonal and technological world, access to the live performing arts is more than a right, it is a necessity. Hawaii Public Theater, formerly the Hawaii Theatre Festival, is dedicated, as an artistic and educational resource, to developing theatre artists and audiences through the agency of a professional repertory theatre serving statewide cultural needs.

Situated at the "Crossroads of the Pacific," Hawaii Public Theater is committed to presenting the best in contemporary and classical plays expressive of a multicultural heritage, which reach not only the traditional theatregoer but also the uninitiated, the geographically and physically isolated, the handicapped and the disadvantaged.

As a catalyst for new theatre, particularly as a company celebrating a regional identity, special emphasis is placed upon commissioning new works by island writers and upon the training and employment of island artists, actors and technicians. Humanism and craftsmanship determine the Public Theater's artistic choices and operating procedures.

Over the last four years, the Public Theater has staged 22 productions free of charge, reaching an audience of over 85,000. Five of the productions were premieres of new plays and original adaptations, seven were presented outdoors, and thirteen were touring productions performed at more than 90 community centers, libraries, hospitals, senior centers, parks, playgrounds, elementary and high schools, junior colleges, office buildings and religious centers.

The Public Theater also co-sponsored, co-produced and assisted 48 other productions presented by 11 local performing groups, reaching an additional quarter-million people.

Furthering its commitment to resident artists, the Public Theater has commissioned new plays by 13 island writers.

Programs and services
Professional training in acting and production, programs-in-schools, free ticket distribution, statewide touring, post-performance discussions, workshop productions and staged readings, children's theatre.

Productions 1977-79
The Fools!, Alexander Ostrovsky; adapt: Eugene Lion
Pictures in the Hallway, Sean O'Casey; adapt: Paul Shyre
Marat/Sade, Peter Weiss; adapt: Adrian Mitchell
The Maids, Jean Genet; adapt: Ellen Boggs, Jo Lechay and Eugene Lion

Jo Diotalevi, Benji Lum, Valerie
Charles and Dick Fair in *Marat/
Sade*. Photo: Bill Soares.

Hippodrome Theatre Workshop

Gregory Hausch
Kerry McKenney
Mary Hausch
Marshall New
Artistic Directors

Bruce Cornwell
Producing Director

1540 Northwest 53rd Ave.
Gainesville, FL 32601
(904) 373-5968 (business)
(904) 375-4477 (box office)

Founded 1973
Bruce Cornwell, Gregory Hausch,
Mary Hausch, Kerry McKenney,
Marshall New

Season
July–June

Schedule
Evenings
Tuesday–Saturday

Facilities
Seating capacity: 287
Stage: flexible

Finances
July 1, 1978–June 30, 1979
$229,000 operating expenses
$138,000 earned income
$ 71,000 unearned income

Audience
Paid capacity: 85%
Subscribers: 3,000
Annual attendance: 50,000

Touring contact
Bruce Cornwell

Booked-in events
Theatre, dance

AEA Guest Artist contract

The Hippodrome Theatre Workshop was founded in 1973 to provide a center for creative and daring productions in an atmosphere of artistic freedom and professional discipline. Since then, the company has discovered a supportive audience eager to experience the innovative staging techniques, immediacy of interpretation and strong visual impact that make Hippodrome events unique. Remarkably, audience subscription has increased 800 percent over the past three years.

The Hippodrome, presently housed in a renovated warehouse, is preparing to move to an historically distinguished neo-classical structure which architecturally anchors the downtown district of Gainesville, Fla. The 1979-80 season has expanded to include eight major productions as well as Second Stage productions. The Hippodrome's artistic and managerial direction evolves collaboratively from its five co-founders. Actors and technical personnel are hired on a per-production basis to supplement the full-time staff of 10.

The Hippodrome is committed to contemporary works, but includes in its repertoire classical works adapted with a contemporary point of view. Past seasons have seen the Southeast premieres of *Equus, The Duck Variations, Vanities, Streamers, Otherwise Engaged, Gemini* and *The Passion of Dracula*. By initiating a program to assist talented playwrights in developing new works, the Hippodrome has created the world premieres of *Cabrona* by Cynthia Buchanan, *Lord Alfred's Lover* by Eric Bentley and the first stage adaptation of *They Shoot Horses, Don't They?* from the novel and screenplay.

As part of its outreach program, the Hippodrome sponsors playwright residencies and tours its major productions. *Equus* recently toured the state's major metropolitan areas and *The Duck Variations* traveled to statewide retirement centers. The Hippodrome's Theatre-in-Education component offers performing arts workshops, intern, and artists-in-schools programs. A visual arts program continues to sponsor the creation of theatre posters that utilize original images by internationally recognized artists.

Programs and services
Professional acting training, classes for nonprofessionals and children; artistic administrative, and technical/production internships; student performances, programs-in-schools, study materials, teacher consulting service, student and senior citizen ticket discounts, charitable benefits, statewide touring, workshop productions and staged readings, newsletter, souvenir book, speakers bureau, volunteer auxiliary, theatre rentals, playwright residencies, art exhibits.

Productions 1977-78
Soap, Allan Albert
Equus, Peter Shaffer
The Tempest, William Shakespeare; adapt:
    Gregory Hausch
Steambath, Bruce Jay Friedman
Streamers, David Rabe
Otherwise Engaged, Simon Gray
Gemini, Albert Innaurato

Productions 1978-79
*The Last Meeting of the Knights of the White
    Magnolia,* Preston Jones
The Passion of Dracula, adapt: Bob Hall and
    David Richmond
Cabrona, Cynthia Buchanan
A Christmas Carol, adapt: Gregory Hausch
The Island, Athol Fugard, John Kani and
    Winston Ntshona
*Statements After an Arrest Under the
    Immorality Act,* Athol Fugard
Lord Alfred's Lover, Eric Bentley
The Norman Conquests, Alan Ayckbourn
    Table Manners
    Living Together
    Round and Round the Garden
They Shoot Horses, Don't They?, Marshall
    New, from Horace McCoy's novel and
    James Poe's screenplay

Graham Gilbert and Mark Sexton
in *Equus.* Photo: Gary Wolfson.

Leigh Montayne, Bruce Cornwell,
Daniel Jesse, Rick Schneider and
Craig Hartley in *The Tempest.*
Photo: Gary Wolfson.

Honolulu Theatre for Youth

Kathleen Collins
Artistic Director

Jane Campbell
Managing Director

Box 3257
Honolulu, HI 96801
(808) 521-3487

Founded 1955
Nancy Corbett

Season
July–May

Facilities
Kaimuki High School Theatre
Seating capacity: 677
Stage: proscenium
Leeward Community College Theatre
Seating capacity: 632
Stage: proscenium
McCoy Pavilion
Seating capacity: 600
Stage: arena

Finances
June 1, 1978–May 31, 1979
$414,000 operating expenses
$109,000 earned income
$320,000 unearned income

Audience
Paid capacity: 80%
Subscribers: 267
Annual attendance: 125,000

Touring contact
Jane Campbell

Thom Kam in *Tales of the Pacific*.
Photo: Hunter Johnson.

Honolulu Theatre for Youth celebrates and reflects its home community. Founded 25 years ago, HTY has grown with Hawaii into a multifaceted theatre appealing to an audience diverse in age and ethnic background. HTY was unique in the nation when, in 1959, it arranged for public school students to attend plays during school hours and thus established theatre education as part of the Hawaii school curriculum. HTY plays attract ever-widening community attention. Audiences at public performances today are half adult, while special school performances of the same plays are seen by 70 percent of Hawaii's public school enrollment.

The HTY feels a responsibility to keep alive the traditions of western theatre while developing original works that speak to the unique mix of cultures embraced by modern Hawaii. Therefore, a season might include Washington Irving's *The Legend of Sleepy Hollow,* Christopher Marlowe's *Doctor Faustus,* and one of the four Wallace Chappell plays based on Pacific legends (the latest, *Folktales of the Philippines,* played to 29,000 people statewide in 1978-79). HTY travels throughout the state every year on a tour underwritten by the Hawaii state legislature, the State Foundation on Culture and the Arts and, for two years, by the National Endowment for the Arts theatre touring program.

With an annual audience of 125,000, HTY is Hawaii's largest theatre. The Comprehensive Employment and Training Act (CETA) has made possible an acting company and training program, and HTY has subsequently transferred CETA artists onto its own payroll. The HTY company is recognized for a unique style of audience involvement growing out of "story theatre" techniques. A one-to-one education program takes actors out of the theatre and into school and community groups.

HTY is guided by a community board of trustees. A strong emphasis in the 25th year (1979-80) is the development of funding sources in the business and foundation communities. The HTY operates without a permanent theatre home, working and producing in state-owned theatres with the cooperation of the state educational system.

Programs and services
Professional training in acting, design, production and administration; student performances, programs-in-schools, study materials, student and senior citizen ticket discounts, free ticket distribution, statewide touring, newsletter, speakers bureau, volunteer auxiliary.

Productions 1977-78
Scapino, adapt: Frank Dunlop and Jim Dale, from Moliere
Tales of the Pacific, Wallace Chappell
The Legend of Sleepy Hollow, Fred Gaines, from Washington Irving's story
Momotaro and Other Japanese Folktales, Wallace Chappell
Sleeping Beauty, adapt: Brian Way
Storytellers, adapt: Brian Way

Productions 1978-79
Folktales of the Philippines, Wallace Chappell
The Phantom Tollbooth, Susan Nanus, from Norton Juster's novel
Horseopera, Kermit Love
The Time Machine, Thomas E. Fuller, from H.G. Wells' novel
Jack and the Beanstalk, adapt: Robert Rafferty

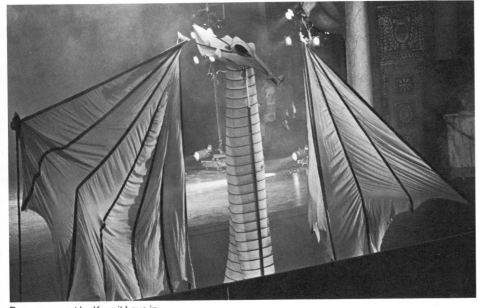

Dragon puppet by Kermit Love in *Horseopera*. Photo: Diane Chong.

Horse Cave Theatre

Warren Hammack
Artistic Director

Julie Beckett
Business Director

Box 215
Horse Cave, KY 42749
(502) 786-1200 (business)
(502) 786-2177 (box office)

Founded 1977

Season
June–September

Schedule
Evenings
Tuesday–Sunday
Matinees
Wednesday, Saturday

Facilities
107-109 Main St.
Seating capacity: 355
Stage: thrust

Finances
Oct. 1, 1977–Sept. 30, 1978
$156,000 operating expenses
$ 61,000 earned income
$ 55,000 unearned income

Audience
Paid capacity: 34%
Subscribers: 938
Annual attendance: 12,100

Booked-in events
Theatre

AEA LORT (D) contract

Horse Cave Theatre opened its doors in June 1977 with a repertory season of three plays. Located in the small town of Horse Cave, Ky., adjacent to Mammoth Cave and at the heart of the state's spectacular cave country, the theatre was founded as a nonprofit corporation in 1975 by a board of directors including local citizens and businessmen. They had in mind two objectives: to provide quality professional theatre to the citizens of South Central Kentucky by presenting works from the best of the world's theatrical heritage and to facilitate the cultural growth of the region by making the creative experience accessible to the larger community.

Artistic director Warren Hammack, hired in the spring of 1977, gathers a company of actors and technicians from across the country each May. Together they work toward a common end, striving to maintain artistic standards and professional polish. The ensemble spirit is fundamental.

The theatre is housed in the renovated Thomas Opera House on Main Street in Horse Cave. Dallas architect David Gibson created a thrust performance space, unique in its stage/audience relationship, boasting remarkable acoustics.

The season, which opens in June and runs through mid-September, consists of plays chosen for their individual merit as well as for the way they blend with other season offerings. Performances are given in rolling repertory, a scheduling concept particularly suited to the many visitors who pass through Kentucky's cave country during the summer months.

The second and third seasons have seen tremendous growth for Horse Cave Theatre. Attendance has nearly doubled, and new educational and outreach programs have been introduced. The 1979 season introduces a fourth play to the customary three, in keeping with the company's original pledge to make theatre available to increasing audiences in southern Kentucky.

Kim Robillard and Terrence Markovich in *Bus Stop*. Photo: Jimmie Lowe.

Programs and services
Classes for children; artistic, administrative and technical/production internships; student performances, study materials, student and senior citizen ticket discounts, workshop productions and staged readings, speakers bureau, volunteer auxiliary, theatre rentals.

Productions 1978
Tartuffe, Moliere; trans: Richard Wilbur
The Odd Couple, Neil Simon
Bus Stop, William Inge

Productions 1979
The Importance of Being Earnest, Oscar Wilde
Wait Until Dark, Frederick Knott
They Knew What They Wanted, Sidney Howard
Of Mice and Men, John Steinbeck

Morris Brown and Terrence Markovich in *Tartuffe*. Photo: Jimmie Lowe.

The Hudson Guild Theatre

David Kerry Heefner
Producing Director

Judson Barteaux
Managing Director

441 West 26th St.
New York, NY 10001
(212) 760-9836 (business)
(212) 760-9847 (box office)

Founded 1922
John Lovejoy Elliot

Season
September–June

Schedule
Evenings
Wednesday–Saturday
Matinees
Saturday, Sunday

Facilities
Arthur Strasser Theatre
Seating capacity: 138
Stage: proscenium

Finances
July 1, 1978–June 30, 1979
$187,000 operating expenses
$124,000 earned income
$ 75,000 unearned income

Audience
Paid capacity: 94%
Subscribers: 2,050
Annual attendance: 23,910

Booked-in events
Children's theatre

AEA letter of agreement

Peg Murray and Shirley Knight in
A Lovely Sunday for Creve Coeur.
Photo: Martha Swope.

Since 1977, the Hudson Guild Theatre has devoted itself exclusively to the production of new plays. HGT provides an environment in which playwrights, actors, directors and designers can develop new works free from the hit-or-miss pressure of the commercial theatre. HGT insists on the right to fail.

Five plays are produced each year in a subscription season. Some have been first plays by previously unknown writers, such as Ernest Thompson's *On Golden Pond.* Others have been new pieces by established authors, such as Tennessee Williams' *A Lovely Sunday for Creve Coeur.* If there is a unifying trait among the works chosen for production, it is that they are realistic plays about human relationships. They are plays for actors.

Each play is rehearsed intensively for four weeks, usually with the playwright in residence the entire time. Rehearsal is followed by a five-week limited run. The plays continue to undergo constant revision and perfecting while in performance. Critics are only invited when the playwright, director and actors feel that the piece is ready.

The success of HGT'S effort has been notable. Two shows from the 1977-78 season moved on to Broadway: *Da,* which won four Antoinette Perry ("Tony") Awards as well as several other citations, and *My Mother Was a Fortune-Teller,* which underwent further revision and a subsequent resident theatre production (Studio Arena Theatre) before returning to New York a year later. The 1978-79 season's *On Golden Pond* also went to Broadway. Perhaps a more important measure of success is that HGT has become a place where actors love to work. Productions at HGT feature both new talent and such veterans as Tammy Grimes, Barnard Hughes, Shirley Knight and Frances Sternhagen. The combination serves as a further catalyst to HGT's efforts to develop new plays to their fullest potential.

Craig Anderson, the company's producing director, was succeeded by David Kerry Heefner at the start of the 1979-80 season.

Programs and services
Classes for nonprofessionals and children; administrative and technical/production internships, free ticket distribution, voucher program, children's theatre.

Productions 1977-78
Treats, Christopher Hampton
The Dodge Boys, George Sibbald
Molly, Simon Gray
Da, Hugh Leonard
My Mother Was a Fortune-Teller, book: Phyllis Newman and Arthur Laurents; music and lyrics: various

Productions 1978-79
On Golden Pond, Ernest Thompson
Winning Isn't Everything, Lee Kalcheim
A Lovely Sunday for Creve Coeur, Tennessee Williams
Ride a Cock Horse, David Mercer
Devour the Snow, Abe Polsky

Ronn Carroll, Tom Aldredge and Frances Sternhagen in *On Golden Pond.* Photo: Martha Swope.

Impossible Ragtime Theatre

Ted Story
Artistic Director/Producer

Laurice Firenze
Executive Director

Cynthia Crane
Producer

120 West 28th St.
New York, NY 10001
(212) 243-7494 (business)
(212) 929-8003 (box office)

Founded 1974
Ted Story, George Ferencz,
Cynthia Crane, Pam Mitchell

Season
October–June

Schedule
Evenings
Thursday–Saturday, Monday
Matinees
Sunday

Facilities
Stage I
Seating capacity: 100
Stage: flexible
Stage II
Seating capacity: 70
Stage: thrust

Finances
July 1, 1978–June 30, 1979
$66,000 operating expenses
$33,000 earned income
$36,000 unearned income

Audience
Paid capacity: 62%
Subscribers: 309
Annual attendance: 11,000

AEA Showcase Code

Impossible Ragtime Theatre, situated in the heart of New York's wholesale flower district, is a director's theatre, maintaining a primary interest in the stage director's creative role in a theatrical community accustomed to playwrights' theatres and performers' theatres. As with all such groups, the sharing of experience and insight is viewed as the means to artistic growth. Therefore, IRT has a joint mission: to provide outstanding theatre for its audiences while at the same time advancing the art and craft of directing.

Under the artistic direction of founder Ted Story, IRT has explored a wide range of material. A typically eclectic season will run the gamut from Agatha Christie to Bertolt Brecht, with a special emphasis on new scripts. Directorial interest weighs heavily in making specific play choices.

As a director's forum, IRT has spent several exciting and fruitful seasons developing a workable approach to the special problems of creative communication among professional directors. In 1979-80, directors from the New York area will be invited to a series of colloquia in order to exchange ideas and concepts of directing. The intended result is a better understanding of the relationship of the director to the total theatrical experience and to other artists. In addition, a highly successful series of new play readings, specifically aimed at the problems of director/playwright collaboration, will be expanded to include directors from outside the company.

Programs and services
Administrative and technical/production internships, free ticket distribution, post-performance discussions, workshop productions and staged readings, new play readings, newsletter, volunteer auxiliary, voucher program, theatre rentals.

Productions 1977-78
Play Strindberg, Friedrich Dürrenmatt; trans: James Kirkup
Women I Have Known, M. Tulis Sessions
Spider's Web, Agatha Christie
Clash by Night, Clifford Odets
Rusty and Rico and Lena and Louie, Leonard Melfi
The Member of the Wedding, Carson McCullers
Where's the Beer, Fritz?, music and lyrics: Dan Schreier and Michael Roth
The Problem, A.R. Gurney, Jr.
Dreams of Flight, Brian Richard Mori
Birdbath, Leonard Melfi
Master Class and *Old Blues,* Jonathan Levy
The Ride Across Lake Constance, Peter Handke; trans: Michael Roloff
The Bedroom, M.H. Appleman

Productions 1978-79
Peril at End House, Arnold Ridley, from Agatha Christie's novel
The Unicorn in Captivity, Mel Arrighi
Windfall Apples, Roma Greth
Brand, Henrik Ibsen; trans: Michael Meyer
Suicide in B Flat, Sam Shepard
Three Men on a Horse, John Cecil Holm and George Abbott
Wed-Lock:
  Trifles, Susan Glaspell
  The Color of Heat, Saul Zachary
Illegal Use of Hands, Michael Zettler
Victoria's Closet, Laurence Carr
The Glass of Water, Eugene Scribe; trans: DeWitt Bodeen
Take Death to Lunch, book and lyrics: Thomas L. Faitos and Amielle Zemach; music: T.L. Faitos

Stephen Mellor, Earl Miller, Brian Hartigan, Thomas O'Rourke and Ann Crumb in *Suicide in B Flat.* Photo: Michael Zettler.

Cecilia Riddett, Mary Skinner and Stephen Mellor in *Victoria's Closet.* Photo: Michael Zettler.

The Independent Eye

Conrad Bishop
Artistic Director

Linda Bishop
Administrative Director

115 North Arch St.
Lancaster, PA 17603
(717) 393-9088

Founded 1974
Conrad and Linda Bishop

Season
August–June

Schedule
Evenings
Friday–Sunday

Facilities
J. F. Steinman Theatre
725 Hamilton Road
Seating capacity: 200
Stage: thrust

Finances
July 1, 1978–June 30, 1979
$64,000 operating expenses
$48,000 earned income
$12,000 unearned income

Audience
Annual attendance: 18,747

Touring contact
Linda Bishop

Macbeth. Photo: Conrad Bishop.

The Independent Eye is a national touring ensemble using popular entertainment forms to examine deeply felt and commonly shared experience. Founded in 1974, the company has presented more than 1,000 performances and workshops in 30 states for colleges, theatres and festivals, churches, conferences, high schools, social agencies and community groups of all kinds. Performance locations have ranged from Off-Off Broadway to Jerusalem to the sanctuary of a south Georgia church.

The Eye's approach is comic in the broad sense, focusing on human incongruities and incorporating the radical mood-swings common to real experience. A broad range of styles has been used to fuse communication with entertainment: Gothic horror melodrama in *Goners,* contemporary cabaret in *Sunshine Blues* and *Black Dog,* fragmentary naturalism in *Dessie* and a mask/puppet/actor synthesis in *Macbeth.* In each piece, the performers' personal stake in the content and the clarity of audience perception are primary.

In 1977, the Eye moved its base of operations from Chicago to Lancaster, Pa., expanded its full-time ensemble to seven members, and began far-reaching local development, while continuing to tour nationally. Work is now centered on four interlocked projects: Theatre for Human Values, a repertory of plays and workshops related to social needs and concerns that touch a broad range of social agencies and community coalitions; Arts Outreach, a touring program embracing the seven-county rural area surrounding Lancaster; the Mask/Mannekin Laboratory employs mask and puppetry techniques as a means of expanding the ensemble's storytelling capabilities; and the Lancaster Project, involving production of the Eye's first full subscription season in 1979-80 and leading toward a permanent local theatre and arts center.

Programs and services
Improvisational workshops for nonprofessionals, programs-in-schools, teaching residencies, student and senior citizen ticket discounts, international touring, newsletter, radio projects.

Productions 1977-78
Black Dog, Conrad Bishop
I Wanna Go Home, Conrad Bishop
Dessie, Conrad and Linda Bishop
Sunshine Blues, Conrad Bishop

Productions 1978-79
Macbeth, William Shakespeare
Who's There?, Conrad Bishop
Black Dog
Dessie
Sunshine Blues

Linda Bishop, Joseph Uher and
Camilla Schade in *Macbeth.*
Photo: Conrad Bishop.

Indiana Repertory Theatre

Edward Stern
Artistic Director

Benjamin Mordecai
Producing Director

411 East Michigan St.
Indianapolis, IN 46204
(317) 635-5277 (business)
(317) 635-5252 (box office)

Founded 1972
Gregory Poggi,
Benjamin Mordecai,
Edward Stern

Season
October–April

Schedule
Evenings
Tuesday–Saturday
Matinees
Saturday, Sunday

Facilities
Athenaeum Theatre
Seating capacity: 396
Stage: proscenium

Finances
July 1, 1978–June 30, 1979
$689,000 operating expenses
$314,000 earned income
$221,000 unearned income

Audience
Paid capacity: 94%
Subscribers: 6,712
Annual attendance: 55,705

Touring contact
Geneva Jordan

Booked-in events
Dance, theatre

AEA LORT (C) contract

Indiana's only professional regional theatre, Indiana Repertory Theatre strives to present quality productions in Indianapolis and serves the entire state through touring productions, presentations and workshops.

Under the artistic direction of Edward Stern, the theatre produces a varied season of classics, established contemporary works and original scripts. By casting on a per-production basis while allowing for numerous returning actors, IRT combines a fluid acting company with an ensemble base.

During the past two seasons, the theatre has expanded its off-night series. While including such attractions as Emlyn Williams' *Dylan Thomas Growing Up* and *Dear Liar* with Katharine Houghton and Ken Jenkins, the series has developed works from within the state. The 1979 Indiana Playwrights' Festival included staged readings of five new scripts by Indiana writers.

IRT has also recently expanded its community service program. In addition to its annual public school touring show, which is seen by approximately 15,000 students, other IRT activities include: the touring of a mainstage production to communities and colleges, numerous workshops in public schools and community theatres, a ticket distribution program making regular performances available to the disadvantaged, as well as small-cast productions for churches, hospitals and senior citizen centers, full-day teacher workshops, and an intern program for recent college graduates.

IRT is presently renovating the Indiana Theatre, a former movie palace, as its new home. To be completed in the fall of 1980, the refurbished building will contain three performing spaces— a 600-seat house for its mainstage productions, a 250-seat house for its second play series and a 100-seat flexible space for its off-night programs. The complex will also include three rehearsal rooms, administrative space and expanded shop and storage areas.

Programs and services

Classes for nonprofessionals and children; artistic, administrative and technical/production internships; student performances, programs-in-schools, teacher workshops, study materials, student and senior citizen ticket discounts, free ticket distribution, statewide touring, workshop productions and staged readings, newsletter, speakers bureau, volunteer auxiliary, theatre rentals.

Productions 1977-78
The Philadelphia Story, Philip Barry
The Birthday Party, Harold Pinter
The Country Girl, Clifford Odets
Vanities, Jack Heifner
The Seagull, Anton Chekhov; trans: Jean-Claude van Itallie
How the Other Half Loves, Alan Ayckbourn

Productions 1978-79
13 Rue de l'Amour, Georges Feydeau; adapt: Mawby Green and El Feilbert
Sizwe Bansi Is Dead, Athol Fugard, John Kani and Winston Ntshona
A Delicate Balance, Edward Albee
The Importance of Being Earnest, Oscar Wilde
Ten Little Indians, Agatha Christie
The Goodbye People, Herb Gardner

Phillip Piro, Bernard Kates and Linda Atkinson in *The Goodbye People*. Photo: S. Eugene Carpenter.

Patrick Tovatt, Katharine Houghton and Ken Jenkins in *13 Rue de l'Amour*. Photo: S. Eugene Carpenter.

INTAR
International Arts Relations

Max Ferrá
Artistic Director

Frank Hibrandt
General Manager

Box 788
Times Square Station
New York, NY 10036
(212) 695-6134

Founded 1966
Max Ferrá, Leonor Datil,
Elsa and Frank Robles

Season
October–June

Schedule
Evenings
Thursday–Saturday
Matinees
Sunday

Facilities
420 West 42nd St.
Seating capacity: 107
Stage: proscenium
508 West 53rd St.
Seating capacity: 110
Stage: proscenium

Finances
July 1, 1977–June 30, 1978
$96,200 operating expenses
$ 6,100 earned income
$76,100 unearned income

Audience
Paid capacity: 75%
Annual attendance: 15,000

Booked-in events
Theatre

Cliff Seidman in *Eyes on the Harem*. Photo: Rafael Llerena.

INTAR (International Arts Relations) believes that the future of Hispanic theatre in the United States depends upon the development of local playwrights and of new plays which reflect the variety and complexity of the Hispanic experience in this country. This "new" Hispanic theatre, as it speaks to the needs and experiences of Spanish-American communities, is a necessary element for massive audience development. It is also through the development of this new repertoire that Hispanic theatre, as other immigrant and ethnic theatres before it, will have an impact upon the American theatre as a whole.

This commitment to developing a new Hispanic theatre is exemplified by INTAR's frequent production in recent seasons of new works, by the resources the theatre has allocated to new playwrights and by the funding INTAR has received for the commissioning, development and production of new works. Although INTAR's priority is to produce original works, an attempt is also made to provide a bridge between the Hispanic community and the community at large by the bilingual production of works from the classical, modern Spanish and Spanish-American repertoires.

INTAR's move in January 1978 to the new "Theatre Row" on 42nd Street has strengthened its programs by providing a better location for its mainstage. The new headquarters has also improved communication with other Off-Off Broadway theatres and supplied additional space for setting up workshops and for the theatre's gallery, which provides exhibition space to Hispanic artists.

Programs and services
Professional training in acting, directing, design, production and administration; artistic and technical/production internships, student and senior citizen ticket discounts, free ticket distribution, voucher program, workshop productions and staged readings, guest lecturers, poetry readings, art exhibits.

Productions 1977-78
Lolita en el Jardin, Maria Irene Fornes; music: Richard Weinstock
Hablemos a Calzon Quitado, Guillermo Gentile; music: Jean Alain
Carmencita, book and lyrics: Manuel Martin, Jr.; music: Georges Bizet and Tania Leon

Productions 1978-79
La Gran Decision, Miguel Mihura; adapt: Max Ferrá and Osvaldo Pradere
Eyes on the Harem, Maria Irene Fornes
Latinos, book: Lynne Alvarez, Manual Martin, Jr., and Omar Torres; music: Eddie Ruperto and O. Torres; lyrics: M. Martin, Frank Rivera and O. Torres

Manuel Yesckas, Tony Diaz and Juan Canas in *La Gran Decision.*
Photo: Rafael Llerena.

Interart Theatre

Margot Lewitin
Artistic Director/Coordinator

Abigail Franklin
Managing Director

549 West 52nd St.
New York, NY 10019
(212) 246-1050 (business)
(212) 279-4200 (box office)

Founded 1970
Marjorie De Fazio,
Margot Lewitin,
Alice Rubinstein,
Jane Chambers

Season
October–June

Schedule
Evenings
Thursday–Sunday
Matinees
Sunday

Facilities
Seating capacity: 40-90
Stage: flexible

Finances
July 1, 1978–June 30, 1979
$120,000 operating expenses
$ 22,000 earned income
$ 61,000 unearned income

Audience
Paid capacity: 64%
Annual attendance: 14,123

AEA letter of agreement

To understand the intent and direction of the Interart Theatre, one must view it within the context of its parent organization, the Women's Interart Center, Inc. The Center is a nonprofit, multi-arts organization which brings to the audience, through public presentations, the breadth and quality of work by contemporary women artists in varying disciplines. At the same time, the center provides space and facilities for artists to explore different media, through training and workshops, including film, video, theatre and writing.

The concept of "interart"—the interactive process that occurs by working in proximity to other art forms and sharing and exchanging ideas and responses—is intrinsic to the total organization. The dedication to interart as a way of approaching the creative process, of growing and expanding one's talent and vision, becomes a sharing experience with the audience as well.

The Interart Theatre is committed to staging new plays and making clear the interactive nature of the theatrical experience. All mainstage productions are fully mounted with the design elements realized as completely as possible.

The Interart Theatre does not identify itself as a "feminist" theatre. Artists tend to work from their own lives, bringing their personal views to bear upon the world through the craft of theatre. Because historically most established artists have been men, a male sensibility has been primarily communicated. By bringing the work primarily of women to the public, the Interart Theatre opens up new perspectives to its audience. It provides a way of viewing the world that is drawn from the life experience of its artists, enabling the audience to share in the discovery of a female sensibility.

The first production, in a newly constructed space, opened in 1973, two years after the center itself was formed. Among the 37 productions mounted by the Interart Theatre have been *The Price of Genius* by Betty Neustat, *The Daughters Cycle Trilogy* by the Women's Experimental Theatre, *Acrobatics* by Joyce Aaron and Luna Tarlor, *Crab Quadrille* and *Olympic Park* by Myrna Lamb, *Cross Country* by Susan Miller, and Shakespeare's *Antony and Cleopatra*, directed by Estelle Parsons.

Programs and services
Technical/production internships; apprenticeships in directing, design and production; free ticket distribution, post-performance discussions, film series, poetry readings, seminars.

Productions 1977-78
Becca, Wendy Kesselman
Where Memories Are Magic and Dreams Invented, Susan Nanus
Hey, Rube, Janet McReynolds
Sister/Sister, company developed
Magic and Lions, music and lyrics company developed from Ernestine Walker's prose-poetry
The Price of Genius, Betty Neustat

Productions 1978-79
The Price of Genius
Sister/Sister
Daughters, company developed
Olympic Park, Myrna Lamb
Sunday, Michel Deutsch; trans: Francoise Kourilsky and Lynne Greenblatt
Antony and Cleopatra, William Shakespeare

Becca. Photo: Laura W. Pettibone.

Kay Medford and Sylvia Gassell in *Where Memories Are Magic and Dreams Invented.* Photo: Laura W. Pettibone.

Intiman Theatre Company

Margaret Booker
Artistic Director

Simon Siegl
General Manager

Box 4246
Seattle, WA 98104
(206) 624-4541 (business)
(206) 447-4651 (box office)

Founded 1972
Margaret Booker

Season
June–October

Schedule
Evenings
Tuesday–Sunday
Matinees
Saturday

Facilities
2nd Stage Theatre
1419 Eighth Ave.
Seating capacity: 342
Stage: thrust

Finances
Jan. 1, 1978–Dec. 31, 1979
$307,000 operating expenses
$190,000 earned income
$ 65,000 unearned income

Audience
Paid capacity: 84%
Subscribers: 4,228
Annual attendance: 44,750

Touring contact
Simon Siegl

AEA LORT (C) contract

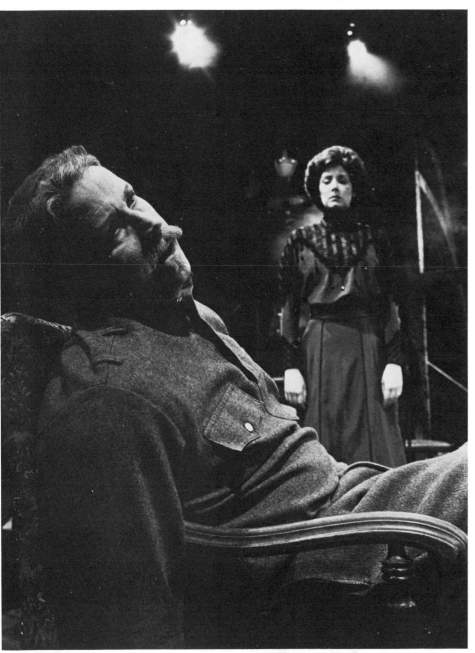

Ted D'Arms and Jean Smart in
The Dance of Death. Photo: Chris
Bennion.

Named after August Strindberg's intimate theatre in Stockholm, the Intiman Theatre Company was founded by artistic director Margaret Booker in 1972 and is now one of four nonprofit professional theatres in Seattle.

Intiman is committed to the development of the resident theatre artist and, to that end, employs a resident company of actors and technicians for a season of five plays. Guest directors and designers are engaged in order to give the company diverse artistic viewpoints and enrich the season's work.

ITC draws its seasons largely from classics, with emphasis placed on a finely tuned ensemble, well-defined style, and faithfulness to the playwrights' original intentions. The company's design aesthetic supports both the play text and the actor as a living artist.

Intiman believes that an optimum relationship between actor and audience is vital to create a satisfactory theatre experience. Intiman presently performs in a rented facility which places the actor in close proximity to the audience. Architectural and feasibility studies for a new 500-seat theatre in Seattle's historic Pike Place Public Market are underway to provide a permanent home for the company.

Programs and services
Artistic, administrative and technical internships; programs-in-schools, student and senior citizen ticket discounts, free ticket distribution, founding member of Seattle's half-price ticket booth; statewide touring for young people, post-performance discussions, workshop productions and staged readings; guest lecturers, subscriber newsletter, volunteer auxiliary, rental of scene shop, annual "Christmas Sampler" presentation of songs and readings available to retirement homes, churches, libraries, etc.

Productions 1978
Henry IV, Luigi Pirandello; adapt: John Reich
The Way of the World, William Congreve
The Three Sisters, Anton Chekhov; trans:
    Randell Jarrell
The Country Girl, Clifford Odets
The Dance of Death, August Strindberg; trans:
    Walter Johnson

Productions 1979
The Loves of Cass McGuire, Brian Friel
Tartuffe, Moliere; trans: Richard Wilbur
Medea, Euripides; trans: Robinson Jeffers
Heartbreak House, George Bernard Shaw
Design for Living, Noel Coward

The Invisible Theatre

Collective Leadership
Contact: Susan Claassen

1400 North First Ave.
Tucson, AZ 85719
(602) 882-9721

Founded 1971
Dennis Hackin

Season
September–July

Schedule
Evenings
Wednesday–Sunday

Facilities
Seating capacity: 80
Stage: flexible

Finances
July 1, 1978–June 30, 1979
$85,000 operating expenses
$45,000 earned income
$44,000 unearned income

Audience
Paid capacity: 75%
Annual attendance: 17,383

Touring contact
Sandra Schemske

Booked-in events
All types

AEA Guest Artist contract

The Invisible Theatre is unique among the Southwest's resident theatres in its emphasis on producing new plays, its educational and outreach program and its Shakespeare Under the Stars summer festival. Founded in 1971, the Invisible Theatre takes its name, an anagram for "I believe in th' arts," from the invisible energy that must flow between performer and audience in creating the magic of theatre.

The Invisible Theatre staff is a collective of artists; the company's approaches to productions are as varied and individual as the plays themselves. The ensemble adapts and incorporates many approaches in relation to the demands of the play and the concept of the director.

The theatre building is a renovated laundry that houses administrative offices, workshop space and performance facility. The performance space seats 80 and allows for flexible staging, essential to the company's innovative techniques. The space also provides an intimate setting for other arts groups.

The educational and outreach program emphasizes the creative potential in all people. Through the Children's Workshop, young people view a presentation and then participate in a workshop that encourages their own creative processes. The workshop also aids teachers to use theatre as a viable teaching method.

Shakespeare Under the Stars is the only southwestern outdoor Shakespeare festival. Located in downtown Tucson, the company attracts more than 5,000 spectators for six weeks each summer.

Through mainstage productions, seminars, educational projects, outreach performances, complimentary tickets and Shakespeare, the Invisible Theatre continues to challenge itself to better serve the community and state in which it makes its home.

Programs and services

Classes for nonprofessionals and children; student performances, programs-in-schools, study materials, student and senior citizen ticket discounts, free ticket distribution, regional touring, post-performance discussions, workshop performances and staged readings, poetry readings, children's theatre, speakers bureau, volunteer auxiliary, theatre rentals.

Productions 1977-78

Hippolytus, Euripides; adapt: Spence Porter
Exhibition, Janet Neipris
Bridge at the Bel Harbour, Janet Neipris
Magical Tales, company developed
Careless, book: Bob Campbell and Scott Carter; music: Merle Reagle; lyrics: Harry S. Robins
Much Ado About Nothing, William Shakespeare
Macbeth, William Shakespeare

Productions 1978-79

Oats, book: Scott Carter and Glenn Young; music and lyrics: George Hawke
Flying Horses, Janet Neipris
Clown Dance, Joan Van Dyke
Arthur, Jim Peck
As You Like It, William Shakespeare
Antony and Cleopatra, William Shakespeare

Molly McKasson and Roger Owen in *Hippolytus.* Photo: Tim Fuller.

Roger Owen and Alex Christopolous in *Macbeth.* Photo: Tim Fuller.

The Iron Clad Agreement

Julia R. Swoyer
Producer/Director

6351 Phillips Ave.
Pittsburgh, PA 15217
(412) 731-2445

Founded 1976
Julia R. Swoyer, K. Wilson Hutton

Season
Year-round

Finances
Sept. 1, 1978–Aug. 31, 1979
$100,000 operating expenses
$ 32,000 earned income
$ 69,000 unearned income

Audience
Annual attendance: 25,000

Touring contact
Julia R. Swoyer

K. Wilson Hutton and Nancy Friedman in *Ford.* Photo: Dan Hankison.

The Iron Clad Agreement is a traveling repertory company, emphasizing the most portable element of theatre—the performer, whose challenge it is to create a theatrical environment in any space in order to be available to the widest range of people. Touring works based on characters and events from America's industrial revolution, Iron Clad has performed in an enormous variety of spaces and circumstances, having by choice no performance space of its own.

The Iron Clad Agreement is seminal theatre, having created 15 original works in its short, three-year existence. Scripts and songs are written specifically for or by the company in the unique Iron Clad style, which lies somewhere between vaudeville and documentary drama. The first year's major effort, *The Gilded Age of Invention Cycle,* portrayed the folk heroes of the 19th century—the inventor/industrialists—in unblinkingly factual fashion, using material drawn from primary research. This past year has seen the development of other new works: *Dynamite* (a labor history play), *Andrew Carnegie* and *The Amazing American Idea Factory.*

Iron Clad is a regional performance company, creating art from an industrial environment and giving it back to the people who inspired it. Two separate adaptations of *Out of This Furnace,* Thomas Bell's novel of immigrant Slovak steelworkers in the Pittsburgh mills, have toured union halls, mill towns and colleges with the most recent version being showcased in New York City.

During 1979-80, Iron Clad will continue its variety of performances in major Eastern cities, in small Pennsylvania towns and occasionally at festivals abroad. New works will include: *Thomas A. Edison; Father K,* the story of a labor activist-priest; *My Dear Sisters,* a look at the Grimke sisters' work in the civil rights/women's rights movements; a yet untitled work about the Heinz family and the history of food processing; and a 13-part labor history series for radio.

Programs and services
Classes for nonprofessionals and children, artistic and administrative internships, programs-in-schools, national touring, post-performance discussions, workshop productions and staged readings.

Productions 1977-78
The Gilded Age of Invention Cycle:
    The Prologue Play, company developed
    Edison, book: Elan Garonzik and company;
    music and lyrics: Robert C. Nesius
    Westinghouse, book: Julia R. Swoyer and
    K. Wilson Hutton; music and lyrics:
    Linda Austern and James R. Krut
    Ford, book: Scott T. Cummings and
    company;
    music and lyrics: Robert C. Nesius
    Barnum, Chris Blaetz; music: Linda Austern
    Burbank, book: Charles V. Peters; music
    and lyrics: Robert C. Nesius
    Eastman, Lawrence Myers; music: Linda
    Austern
    Out of This Furnace, Part I, book: Julia R.
    Swoyer, from Thomas Bell's novel; music
    and lyrics: Robert C. Nesius

Productions 1978-79
Gov't Owned Apples, I. Schtok; adapt: David
    Visser and Charles V. Peters; music and
    lyrics: Robert C. Nesius
Dynamite, company developed
Andrew Carnegie, Steve Mackes and company
The Amazing American Idea Factory, company
    developed
Out of This Furnace, Part II, book: Andy Wolk,
    from Thomas Bell's novel; music and lyrics:
    Robert C. Nesius

K. Wilson Hutton, M.M. Melozzi, Christopher Josephs and James R. Krut in *The Amazing American Idea Factory.* Photo: Dan Hankison.

Jean Cocteau Repertory

Eve Adamson
Artistic Director

P. Carson Wiley
Managing Director

Coral S. Potter
Administrator

330 Broadway
New York, NY 10012
(212) 677-0060

Founded 1971
Eve Adamson

Season
August–June

Schedule
Evenings
Thursday–Sunday
Matinees
Sunday

Facilities
Bouwerie Lane Theatre
Seating capacity: 140
Stage: proscenium

Finances
July 1, 1978–June 30, 1979
$84,000 operating expenses
$52,000 earned income
$28,000 unearned income

Audience
Paid capacity: 63%
Subscribers: 950
Annual attendance: 21,000

Jean Cocteau Repertory, one of the few rotating repertory companies in America, presents unusual classics, both old and new, or plays seen more often in the pages of anthologies than on the stage. Whether the work is a masterpiece, once frequently revived but not recently produced in this country, such as Philip Massinger's *A New Way to Pay Old Debts;* a "closet" drama by a writer famous in another field, as in the case of *The Cenci* by Percy Bysshe Shelley; or a forgotten work by a well-known playwright, like *Vera* by Oscar Wilde, the Cocteau focuses on making the audience's experience strong and immediate. Physical production values are purposely minimal, with the emphasis placed on the relationships among the play, the actors and the audience.

All plays in the repertoire are performed by members of a resident acting company, some of whom have been with the Cocteau since its inception. It is the Cocteau's goal to create an American acting ensemble as highly trained, sensitized and flexible as some of the great European companies. Toward this end, the resident acting ensemble, in addition to its rigorous rehearsal and performance schedule, participates in weekly workshops in acting, dance, speech, mime and stage dueling. The Cocteau also has an active apprenticeship program, whereby serious and dedicated theatre students may participate with the resident ensemble in workshops and productions.

In addition to its regular repertory schedule, the Cocteau presents a special matinee series of innovative productions of better-known classics for school groups. These performances take place at the theatre during school hours and are followed by discussions among teachers, students, cast and director.

Founded in 1971 by Eve Adamson in a storefront on Manhattan's lower east side, the Cocteau has occupied the historic Bouwerie Lane Theatre for the past three seasons. The company is strongly involved in the promotion of New York's Bowery area as a revitalized arts community.

Programs and services
Administrative and technical/production internships, student performances, student and senior citizen ticket discounts, free ticket distribution, voucher program, post-performance discussions, newsletter, souvenir book.

Productions 1977-78
The Caretaker, Harold Pinter
A New Way to Pay Old Debts, Philip Massinger
Hamlet, William Shakespeare
The Cocktail Party, T.S. Eliot
Love's Comedy, Henrik Ibsen
No Exit, Jean-Paul Sartre
Volpone, Ben Jonson
'Tis Pity She's a Whore, John Ford

Productions 1978-79
Volpone
A Mad World, My Masters, Thomas Middleton
The Scarecrow, Percy MacKaye
Hamlet, William Shakespeare
Exit the King, Eugene Ionesco
The Cid, Pierre Corneille
As You Like It, William Shakespeare
In the Bar of a Tokyo Hotel, Tennessee Williams
The Changeling, Thomas Middleton and William Rowley

Barbara Schofield and Coral S. Potter in *The Cocktail Party.* Photo: Gerry Goodstein.

Coral S. Potter and Michele Farr in *Volpone.* Photo: Gerry Goodstein.

Julian Theatre

Richard Reineccius
General Director

Brenda Berlin Reineccius
Associate Director

953 DeHaro St.
San Francisco, CA 94107
(415) 647-5525 (business)
(415) 647-8098 (box office)

Founded 1965
Douglas Giebel,
Richard Reineccius,
Brenda Berlin Reineccius

Season
September–June

Schedule
Evenings
Thursday–Sunday
Matinees
Saturday, Sunday

Facilities
Potrero Hill Neighborhood House
Seating capacity: 160
Stage: flexible

Finances
July 1, 1978–June 30, 1979
$111,000 operating expenses
$ 42,000 earned income
$ 58,000 unearned income

Audience
Paid capacity: 67%
Subscribers: 208
Annual attendance: 14,500

Booked-in-events
Experimental, ethnic and
children's dance and theatre

Cyril Clayton, Laura Basch and David Parr in *The Hypochondriacs*. Photo: Allen Nomura.

The Julian Theatre, in continuous operation since its first production in a small church hall in 1965, is considered one of the San Francisco Bay Area's most daring and innovative small professional theatres. The company converted a gymnasium for performances from 1966 until 1968, when it moved to its present space, the landmark Potrero Hill Neighborhood House overlooking San Francisco Bay, just five minutes from downtown.

While the group has won praise for novel approaches to the classics, it has in recent years put its greatest emphasis on new plays by American writers of all races, and has produced more premieres of plays by West Coast writers than any other California theatre company. Five Bay Area playwrights were engaged in short-term residencies during 1979, completing a new play while working with a director and dramaturg of their choice or approval, then given a workshop production leading to an eventual full production of the play.

Other new plays are chosen for their political or social relevance or emphasis on women as protagonists, such as the past season's *The Biko Inquest, Medal of Honor Rag* and *Hothouse,* and earlier years' *Daddies* and *A Very Gentle Person.*

A third emphasis in choosing new plays is the introduction of important foreign writers to America. Julian has commissioned translations of *Documents from Hell* and *The Hypochondriacs,* and *El Presidente,* adapted for the stage from Carlos Asturias' book, is currently being translated for a Julian production in 1980.

The Julian has toured extensively, with everything from bilingual poetry and mixed media performances in branch libraries and community centers, to fully mounted productions in colleges, arts centers and prisons. It is now preparing its second statewide tour, with Pinter's *Landscape* and a new California play, under the sponsorship of the California Arts Council.

Programs and services
Professional training in acting, directing and production; classes for nonprofessionals and children; artistic, administrative, and technical/ production internships; student performances, programs-in-schools, study materials, student and senior citizen ticket discounts, free ticket distribution, voucher program, regional touring, post-performance discussions, workshop productions and staged readings, guest lecturers, poetry readings, newsletter, script publication, theatre rentals.

Productions 1977-78
The Plough and the Stars, Sean O'Casey
In the Jungle of Cities, Bertolt Brecht
Medal of Honor Rag, Tom Cole
Goethe: Ein Fragment, Michael McClure
New Roots: An Off-Off Broadway Anthology,
     Kay Carney
The Display of Melissa Harding, Hans
     Steinkellner
A Midsummer Night's Dream, William
     Shakespeare
Productions 1978-79
Philadelphia, Here I Come!, Brian Friel
The Hypochondriacs, Botho Strauss; trans:
     Robert Goss
Merry Christmas, Earthling!, company
     developed
No Man's Land, Harold Pinter
Hothouse, Megan Terry
The Biko Inquest, Norman Fenton and Jon Blair
Sam, Sally Netzel

Peter Emmons and David Parr in *Goethe: Ein Fragment*. Photo: Allen Nomura.

Karamu House

Mike Malone
Performing Arts Director

Lois P. McGuire
Executive Director

2355 East 89th St.
Cleveland, OH 44106
(216) 795-7070

Founded 1924
Russell and
Rowena Woodham Jelliffe

Season
October–July

Schedule
Evenings
Thursday–Sunday
Matinees
Variable

Facilities
Arena Theatre
Seating capacity: 100
Stage: arena
Proscenium Theatre
Seating capacity: 233
Stage: proscenium
Lower Auditorium
Seating capacity: 200
Stage: arena

Finances
Jan. 1, 1978–Dec. 31, 1978
$126,000 operating expenses
$ 41,000 earned income
$ 85,000 unearned income

Audience
Paid capacity: 60%
Subscribers: 400
Annual attendance: 24,500

Touring contact
Mittie I. Jordan

Booked-in-events
Dance, music

Karamu House is a metropolitan center for the performing and visual arts, and holds the distinction of being the oldest center for black arts in the country.

"Karamu," a Swahili word meaning "center of the village" or "place of enjoyment for all," became one of the few institutions in the United States which trained black artists and provided a place where they could perform. Many manuscripts and performances by now famous artists premiered on the Karamu stages, including most of the dramatic works of poet/playwright Langston Hughes.

Today, Karamu continues its tradition through extensive programming in all phases of dance, music, theatre and the visual arts. Some of the area's most capable artists and teachers established and maintained the high standards of excellence which gave Karamu a national, and indeed, international reputation. More than 3,000 students participated in the 1978 Cultural Arts and Education Division workshops.

Under Mike Malone's direction, Karamu's Performing Arts Division continues to honor its commitment to the community by providing entertaining, socially relevant and educationally valuable productions, some of which would not ordinarily be presented on other area stages. As the 1980s approach, Karamu has begun to focus on the program for which it is best known, the performing arts, and will move into the next decade with a professional performing arts unit.

Two 1978-79 productions adapted, directed and choreographed by Malone have received national attention. *Langston,* a "choreodrama" from the works of Langston Hughes, was performed by the touring company at New York's Lincoln Center as part of Black Theatre Arts Festival USA. *Singin' and Shoutin',* the company's updated musical version of Marc Connelly's *The Green Pastures,* was scheduled for a summer 1979 production at the Kennedy Center in Washington, DC.

In May 1979, Karamu was named one of six recipients of a Kennedy Center grant to commission a playwright to produce an original work. The play selected from this project was slated to open the 1979-80 season.

Programs and services
Classes for nonprofessionals and children; artistic, administrative and tecnical/production internships; student performances, programs-in-schools, study materials, student and senior citizen ticket discounts, free ticket distribution, national touring, post-performance discussions,

Don't Bother Me, I Can't Cope.
Photo: Cheryl Reed.

workshop productions and staged readings, guest lecturers, poetry readings, children's theatre, newsletter, volunteer auxiliary.

Productions 1977-78
The Imaginary Invalid, Moliere; adapt: Lucia
  Colombi
Livin' Fat, Judi Ann Mason
Don't Bother Me, I Can't Cope, music and lyrics:
  Micki Grant
Eden, Steve Carter
The Island, Athol Fugard, John Kani and
  Winston Ntshona
The Life and Times of Stag-o-Lee, book: Mike
  Malone; music and lyrics: H.Q. Thompson
The Brownsville Raid, Charles Fuller

Productions 1978-79
Langston, Mike Malone, from Langston
  Hughes' works; music, H.Q. Thompson
A Rose by Any Other Name, Morna Murphy
Singin' and Shoutin', book: Mike Malone, from
  Marc Connelly's play *The Green Pastures;*
  music and lyrics: H.Q. Thompson
The Mighty Gents, Richard Wesley
Happy Birthday, Daddy, Judi Ann Mason
Medea, adapt: Lucia Colombi, from Countee
  Cullen's adaptation of Euripides' play
Walk Together, Children, music and lyrics
  adapt: Vinie Burrows

Grace Wilson, Marsha Taylor, Regenia Williams and Reggie Scott in rehearsal for *Singin' and Shoutin'* with director Mike Malone (rear). Photo: Niles Wheeler.

Lion Theatre Company

Gene Nye
Artistic Director

Eleanor Meglio
Producing Director

Brad High
Administrative Coordinator

422 West 42nd St.
New York, NY 10036
(212) 736-7930 (business)
(212) 279-4200 (box office)

Founded 1974
Gene Nye
Garland Wright

Season
September–June

Schedule
Evenings
Wednesday–Sunday
Matinees
Saturday, Sunday

Facilities
Seating capacity: 100
State: proscenium

Finances
July 1, 1978–June 30, 1979
$113,000 operating expenses
$ 37,000 earned income
$ 72,000 unearned income

Audience
Paid capacity: 46%
Subscribers: 350
Annual attendance: 6,699

Booked-in events
Theatre

AEA letter of agreement

Music-Hall Sidelights. Photo:
Gregory Grove

K: Impressions of Kafka's. The
Trial. Photo: Gregory Grove.

Lion Theatre Company was founded in a
Connecticut cabin during a blizzard in 1974.
The first two years were summer seasons,
followed by a full season of operation in 1976.
Lion Theatre Company is a collaborative of
theatre artists believing in the concepts of
ensemble and continuity as the keys to fine
theatre. Lion has a resident company of
approximately 35 actors, eight designers, three
directors, two playwrights, a composer, a
choreographer, several technicians and an
administrative staff, all of whom have continued
to work and grow with Lion over the years.
Company members' continuing association with
each other has led to a greater understanding
and appreciation of each artist's problems and
needs, resulting in improved performance. It is,
to some extent, a modified European idea of
repertory; the feeling of home base is ever
present to the members of the company, with
the freedom to come and go as necessary.

Representative productions by the company
include *The Tempest, Gammer Gurton's
Needle, Vanities, Peg o' My Heart, Visions of
Kerouac, K: Impressions of Kafka's* The Trial,
and *The Death and Life of Jesse James.*

Lion is proud of its significant role in the
economic and cultural recovery of New York's
West 42nd Street. Before the now famous
"Theatre Row" was even dreamed of, Lion was
already on the block and its presence in the run-
down section of the city has helped to lead the
way to new development and revitalization.

Programs and services
Free ticket distribution, voucher program,
workshop productions and staged readings,
theatre rentals.

Productions 1977-78
K: Impressions of Kafka's The Trial, company
developed
The Death and Life of Jesse James, Len Jenkin
Mary Rose, J.M. Barrie

Productions 1978-79
Music-Hall Sidelights: A Theatrical Scrapbook,
book and lyrics: Jack Heifner, from Colette's
L' envers du music-hall; music: John
McKinney
The Three Sisters, Anton Chekhov; trans:
Sharon Carnicke
Duel: A Romantic Opera, book, music and
lyrics: Randal Wilson

Living Stage

Robert Alexander
Artistic Director

Thomas C. Fichandler
Executive Director

Arena Stage
Sixth and Maine Ave., SW
Washington, DC 20024
(202) 554-9066

Founded 1966
Robert Alexander

Season
July–June

Finances
July 1, 1978–June 30, 1979
$247,000 operating expenses
$ 50,000 earned income
$197,000 unearned income

Audience
Annual attendance: 10,000

Touring contact
Robert Alexander

AEA LORT (B) contract

For more than 13 years, Living Stage, the community outreach company of Arena Stage, has drawn its material directory from its audiences the world over, making those onlookers both participants and artistic collaborators in the performance process.

The small, multiracial company of improvisational actors and musicians has specialized in using theatre to help "forgotten" or "different" people—the handicapped, the poor, the incarcerated, the young, the old, the helpless—discover their own creative powers. Through an artistic dialogue between the actors and audience, the performance pieces explore the shape and meaning of common experiences and simultaneously celebrate individual discovery.

Audience collaborators have ranged from deaf Arizona youngsters (who took part in 1979 performance/workshops conducted in Phoenix and Tucson) to inmates of the Lorton, Va., Reformatory and the D.C. Women's Detention Center. Living Stage disseminates its philosophy and methodology on how to help disabled children and adults arouse their own creative energies. Locally, workshops are conducted regularly for handicapped children and staff in the D.C. metropolitan area and Fairfax, Va. On a national level, Living Stage visits colleges, universities and resident theatres.

Since 1972, the troupe has continued to develop "rituals," sequences of movement and sound that reveal the deeper feelings and subtleties of behavior of improvised characters. A "language" of nonverbal sounds grew out of this discipline, creating a wide range of expressive possibilities. Both "rituals" and "language" have become vital components of the company's on-the-spot improvisations and their repertoire of theatre pieces having fixed themes and characters.

Programs and services

Professional, nonprofessional and children's acting training, student performance/workshops, programs-in-schools, improvisational workshops for all ages, prison performance/workshops, national touring, support group, newsletter.

Productions 1977-79

All performances are improvisations created by the Living Stage company.

Actor Oran Sandel and musical director Mark Novak create a sculpture with inmates of the Lorton, Va., Reformatory on the theme of freedom. Photo: Tess Steinkolk.

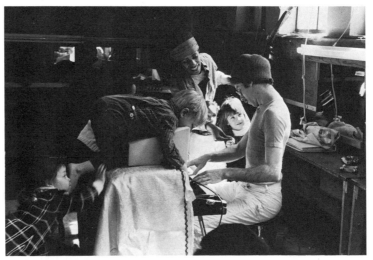

Musical director Mark Novak and actress Rebecca Rice create characters along with 4- and 5-year-olds. Photo: Tess Steinkolk.

Long Wharf Theatre

Arvin Brown
Artistic Director

M. Edgar Rosenblum
Executive Director

222 Sargent Drive
New Haven, CT 06511
(203) 787-4284 (business)
(203) 787-4282 (box office)

Founded 1965
Jon Jory
Harlan Kleiman

Season
October–June

Schedule
Evenings
Tuesday–Sunday
Matinees
Wednesday, Saturday, Sunday

Facilities
Mainstage
Seating capacity: 484
Stage: thrust
Stage II
Seating capacity: 199
Stage: flexible

Finances
July 1, 1978–June 30, 1979
$1,382,000 operating expenses
$ 852,000 earned income
$ 527,000 unearned income

Audience
Paid capacity: 95%
Subscribers: 14,188
Annual attendance: 132,774

Booked-in events
Dance, music, theatre

AEA LORT (B) and (D) contracts

Andra Akers in *Biography*. Photo: William L. Smith.

Maria Tucci and Josef Sommer in *Spokesong*. Photo: William B. Carter.

Now in its 15th season, Long Wharf Theatre continues its emphasis on new and established, home-grown and foreign works that explore human relationships and suit the company's long-standing reputation as an actor's theatre. The intimacy of LWT's two performance spaces—the mainstage that showcases major productions and the two-year-old Stage II, created to highlight works-in-progress and host other theatrical troupes—has greatly enhanced actor/audience involvement.

Many of the world's leading theatrical craftsmen have brought their skills to the unique environment of New Haven. LWT's fortunate location, with its proximity to New York yet its total independence of big city commercial pressures, has allowed accessibility to leading theatre artists. Long Wharf's national and international reputation has resulted in large part from nearby New York's dual position as the world's theatrical and media center.

For all its success at home, much of Long Wharf's renown comes from the extended life its productions have experienced on Broadway and television. Moving to Broadway, virtually intact, such productions as *Spokesong, The Gin Game, Streamers, The Shadow Box, The National Health, The Changing Room,* the 1975 revival of *Ah, Wilderness!, Sizwe Bansi Is Dead* and *The Island* quite naturally have shed luster on their source. Millions of television viewers nationwide have seen the PBS *Theater in America* presentations of *The Widowing of Mrs. Holroyd, Forget-Me-Not Lane* and *Ah, Wilderness!,* while regional audiences have watched two children's theatre productions for Connecticut Public Television, *Doors of Mystery* and *Kaleidoscope.*

The distinguished awards and public acclaim arising from such transfers are rewarding but, to the exasperation of many an ardent young playwright or actor, a Broadway run is far from LWT's first priority. That a play turns out well in New Haven and moves to New York is gratifying, but the potential of transfer does not enter into script selection or casting.

Long Wharf could support a facility twice its current size, perhaps a season twice as full as it now presents. But the LWT philosophy demands concentration on the best possible presentation of the single play in progress. A continuity of leadership underlies and reinforces that guideline—an artistic director and a chairman of the board who have been part of LWT since its inception, and an executive director of only slightly shorter tenure. For Long Wharf, internal growth comes before external expansion.

Programs and services
Administrative and technical/production internships, student performances, study materials, student and senior citizen ticket discounts, free ticket distribution, post-performance discussions, workshop productions and staged readings, newsletter, speakers bureau, volunteer auxiliary, theatre rentals.

Productions 1977-78
Hobson's Choice, Harold Brighouse
The Lunch Girls, Leigh Curran
The Recruiting Officer, George Farquhar
Spokesong, Stewart Parker; music: Jimmy Kennedy
S.S. Glencairn: The Sea Plays, Eugene O'Neill
Bound East for Cardiff
In the Zone
The Long Voyage Home
The Moon of the Caribees
The Philadelphia Story, Philip Barry
Two Brothers, Conrad Bromberg
Macbeth, William Shakespeare

Productions 1978-79
Journey's End, R.C. Sherriff
I Sent a Letter to My Love, Bernice Rubens
Summerfolk, Maxim Gorky; trans: Edward Gilbert and John Tillinger
Biography, S.N. Behrman
Rosmersholm, Henrik Ibsen; trans: Allen Fletcher
Hillbilly Women, book: Elizabeth Stearns; music and lyrics: Clint Ballard, Jr.
Privates on Parade, Peter Nichols; music: Denis King

Looking Glass Theatre

Peter R. Miller
Artistic Director

Ralph J. Stalter, Jr.
Producing Director

The Casino, Roger Williams Park
Providence, RI 02907
(401) 781-1567

Founded 1965
Elaine Ostroff
Arthur Torg

Season
October–June

Finances
July 1, 1978–June 30, 1979
$108,000 operating expenses
$ 52,000 earned income
$ 57,000 unearned income

Audience
Annual attendance: 60,000

Touring contact
Maryanne LaVena

Though searching in earnest for a permanent home, Looking Glass Theatre continues to go where the children are to provide its unique theatrical experiences—as far from its Rhode Island base as Puerto Rico, Chicago and Portland, Maine.

Under the direction of Peter R. Miller, the newly appointed artistic director, LGT addresses the needs of children by providing an atmosphere in which learning can be enjoyable and rewarding, while at the same time creating an environment for discovery in which children can explore their own fears and feelings—affording them the opportunity to invest themselves physically, verbally and emphathetically in the dramatic action.

A Comprehensive Employment and Training Act (CETA) grant provided for the creation of the SPY-Glass Troupe, a four-member ensemble which brings supportive, growth-provoking experiences to children with special needs—physical, developmental or emotional. The troupe works directly with staff and teachers at cooperating institutions to design a specific program for the particular institution, for the particular special children. Workshop sessions are also held in communities to develop a greater awareness of issues surrounding the handicapped, and to allow adults to address different aspects of theatre arts-in-education projects for the handicapped child.

The Pre-School Program employs two creative dramatics specialists in day-care centers and other agencies serving pre-school children. This project also includes workshops with teachers to allow for experimentation with new educational methods that can provide added support to the regular curriculum.

Programs and services
Classes for nonprofessionals and children; artistic, administrative and technical/production internships; programs-in-schools, national touring, post-performance discussions, script publication, speakers bureau.

Productions 1977-78
Inside Doctor Specks, book and lyrics: Rob Anderson; music: Gerald Shapiro
Hatshepsut, Daughter of the Nile, Amy Leonard

Productions 1978-79
The Great Baloney Hoax, Jack Carroll and company
White Wampum: A Legend of the Iroquois, Richard Cameron and Donna Gamage

Alice in the American Wonderland. Photo: Johanne Killeen.

Ron Stetson in *Ijupak.* Photo: Johanne Killeen.

Loretto-Hilton Repertory Theatre

David Frank
Producing Director

Thomas Warner
Administrative Director

Box 28030
St. Louis, MO 63119
(314) 968-7340 (business)
(314) 968-4925 (box office)

Founded 1966
Webster College

Season
September–April

Schedule
Evenings
Tuesday–Sunday
Matinees
Wednesday, Saturday, Sunday

Facilities
130 Edgar Road
Loretto-Hilton Center
Seating capacity: 500-900
Stage: thrust
Studio Theatre
Seating capacity: 140
Stage: flexible

Finances
July 1, 1978–June 30, 1979
$1,222,000 operating expenses
$ 684,000 earned income
$ 510,000 unearned income

Audience
Paid capacity: 83%
Subscribers: 16,600
Annual attendance: 156,580

Touring contact
Maude Essen

Booked-in events
Theatre

AEA LORT (B) contract

Margen Shaw and Margaret Winn
in *Old Times*. Photo:
Michael Eastman.

The Loretto-Hilton Repertory Theatre defines its primary task as serving the community of St. Louis. Its mainstage is dedicated to producing artistically ambitious work that is meaningful to a large and varied audience. The theatre also offers a variety of touring services through its Imaginary Theatre Company, which has developed distinctive and original programs for schools and other institutions.

In 1978, the theatre initiated an additional three-play season in a smaller space known as the Studio Theatre. The emphasis in the studio is placed on fully produced, small-cast contemporary works, with a growing interest in new plays.

The Loretto-Hilton is committed to a nucleus of resident actors, supplemented by guest artists. One of the theatre's highest priorities is maintaining an environment that is pleasant, supportive and rewarding for the artist and craftsman, and which fosters a dedication to the theatre and its audience. Thus, the achievements of the company can be greater than the accomplishments of any one individual.

Although the productions of the past seven years encompass a great variety of plays, the emphasis has been on American works, especialy those with large casts. Because of its resident company and its relationship with Webster College, which provides the theatre with trained and talented apprentices, the theatre is capable of producing more large-cast productions than most regional theatres are able to undertake.

The Loretto-Hilton Theatre is dedicated to making first-rate professional theatre an important element in the lives of as many people in its community as possible. The theatre is the only one of its kind and size in a metropolitan area of 2.5 million people. It has been in operation as an independent corporation for just eight years, during which time its subscription audience has increased from 3,000 to more than 16,000.

Programs and services
Classes for children; student performances, programs-in-schools, study materials, student and senior citizen ticket discounts, regional touring, post-performance discussions, restaurant, children's theatre, newsletter, speakers bureau, volunteer auxiliary.

Productions 1977-78
Macbeth, William Shakespeare
Lu Ann Hampton Laverty Oberlander,
        Preston Jones
The Devil's Disciple, George Bernard Shaw
The Runner Stumbles, Milan Stitt
Canterbury Tales, book: Martin Starkie and
        Nevill Coghill; music: Richard Hill and John
        Hawkins; lyrics: N. Coghill
Ashes, David Rudkin

Productions 1978-79
The Iceman Cometh, Eugene O'Neill
Father's Day, Oliver Hailey
A Penny for a Song, John Whiting
The Three Sisters, Anton Chekhov
Frankenstein, Victor Gialanella, from Mary
        Shelley's novel
Curse of the Starving Class, Sam Shepard
Old Times, Harold Pinter
By Grand Central Station I Sat Down and Wept,
        Geoffrey Sherman and Adrienne Burgess

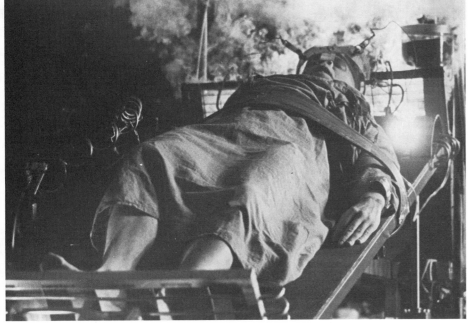

Keith Jochim in *Frankenstein*.
Photo: Michael Eastman.

Los Angeles Actors' Theatre

William Bushnell, Jr.
Producing Director

Joseph B. Sax
Executive Director

1089 North Oxford Ave.
Los Angeles, CA 90029
(213) 464-5603 (business)
(213) 464-5500 (box office)

Founded 1975
Ralph Waite

Season
October–September

Schedule
Evenings
Thursday–Sunday
Matinees
Selected Saturdays, Sundays

Facilities
Mainstage
Seating capacity: 99-181
Stage: flexible
First Stage
Seating capacity: 49
Stage: flexible

Finances
May 1, 1978–April 30, 1979
$365,000 operating expenses
$297,000 earned income
$ 67,000 unearned income

Audience
Paid capacity: 75%
Annual attendance: 35,000

*AEA HAT contract and
99-seat waiver*

Los Angeles Actors' Theatre is a multicultural, bilingual theatre dedicated to the production of original plays and the innovative exploration of established plays. LAAT performs in English and Spanish (the 1979-80 season will include a signed-English production of *The Trojan Women*) in two theatres. At the heart of LAAT's artistic philosophy is a dedication to original material that reflects contemporary life. The company aims to present that work with excellence, beauty and power at the lowest possible cost to Los Angeles' diverse audience.

In addition to an active production schedule, LAAT offers workshops run by highly experienced professionals, and currently include a one-act workshop culminating in an annual festival of the best work, an invitational workshop for advanced playwrights which also culminates in a festival and possible inclusion in the major season, a Third World actors workshop for black, Asian-American, Hispanic performers; the Teatro de la Unidad (an intense workshop in Spanish and English preparatory to the formation of an ensemble which will present an alternative season in English and Spanish), plus several other workshops of shorter duration.

LAAT is currently planning a move to a new three-theatre complex in downtown Los Angeles in the fall of 1980. The new theatre will include a 400-seat mainstage and two 99-seat experimental theatres, an outdoor park performing area, three rehearsal/workshop spaces, complete production facilities and offices to accommodate the company's expanded program.

Programs and services
Professional training in acting, playwriting, production and administration; classes for nonprofessionals; artistic, administrative and technical/production internships, student performances, ticket discounts for students, senior citizens and the unemployed; post-performance discussions, workshop productions and staged readings, guest lecturers, poetry readings.

Productions 1977-78
Waiting for Godot, Samuel Beckett
A Midnight Moon at the Greasy Spoon, Miguel Piñero
The Sistuhs, Saundra Sharp
My Sister, My Sister, Ray Aranha
Voices, Susan Griffin
Playwrights' Workshop Festival of One-Acts, various
Perfume, James Kennedy
Krapp's Last Tape, Samuel Beckett
On the Harmfulness of Tobacco, Anton Chekhov; adapt: Dianne Lewis Hall, Philip Baker Hall and Patrick Tovatt

Productions 1978-79
Skaters, Ted Pezzulo
The Venus of Menschen Falls, Richard Jordan
A Vision of Anne Sexton, Henry Hoffman, from Sexton's works
Trilogy Blue, J. Paul Porter
  Mississippi Jade
  Augie Abrams
  Saint George
The Guntower, Miguel Piñero
Medal of Honor Rag, Tom Cole
Every Good Boy Does Fine, Joseph Hindy
The Schoolteacher and *The Orgy,* Enrique Bueneventura
Playwrights' Workshop Festival of One-Acts, various
Statements After an Arrest Under the Immorality Act, Athol Fugard
The Bacchae, Euripides
Cronica de un Secuestro, Mario Diament
Sizwe Bansi Is Dead and *The Island,* Athol Fugard, John Kani and Winston Ntshona
Old Times, Harold Pinter
The Tricycle (El Triciclo), Fernando Arrabal
Sunday, Joseph Scott Kierland
Playwrights' Workshop Festival of One-Acts, various

Tanya L. Boyd and Diane Dixon in *My Sister, My Sister*. Photo: Craig Dietz.

Danny Glover and Carl Lumbly in *The Island*. Photo: Gay Ann Fitenhoff.

Lovelace Theatre Company

Margo Lovelace
Producer/Director

Thomas Pechar
General Manager

5888½ Ellsworth Ave.
Pittsburgh, PA 15232
(412) 361-4835

Founded 1964
Margo Lovelace

Season
October–July

Facilities
Matinees
Saturday, Sunday

Facilities
*Carnegie Institute Museum of Art
Theatre*
4400 Forbes Ave.
Seating capacity: 188
Stage: proscenium

Finances
Oct. 1, 1978–Sept. 30, 1979
$124,000 operating expenses
$ 63,000 earned income
$ 61,000 unearned income

Audience
Paid capacity: 96%
Subscribers: 1,650
Annual attendance: 75,000

Touring contact
Lori Berger

Fred Michael, "Iola" and David
Early in *The Puppet Proposition.*
Photo: Leonard Schugar.

The Lovelace Theatre Company originated as a traditional touring marionette troupe but has evolved over the past 15 years into a resident professional theatre creating performance pieces with puppets of any and all kinds. Under the artistic direction of Margo Lovelace, the company searches out dramatic literature that lends itself to the unique capacities of puppets and masks. The question always asked about a new production is, "Why produce this play with puppets?" The puppeteers, directors and designers all share the belief that puppets have a special performance potential, different from, but just as appropriate as, the "human" theatre.

Since 1976, Lovelace has presented its performance seasons at the Carnegie Museum of Art in Pittsburgh. From the start, the theatre's priority at the museum has been the development, maintenance and growth of the region's family audience. Artistic and administrative commitment to a program to provide regularly scheduled and ongoing theatre for young people, attending *with* their parents, has resulted in the theatre's establishment as a well-known cultural resource. Besides the resident subscription season, touring activities take Lovelace productions to sponsors throughout Pennsylvania, the mid-Atlantic states and the

Midwest. A recent three-week performance residency at the Smithsonian Institution in Washington, D.C., was a virtual sellout.

Because Lovelace Theatre Company is most interested in how a puppet performs in the context of a play, the company rarely ties itself to a particular puppet form. Thus, a production might mix life-size figures with hand puppets, juxtapose an ancient Javanese rod puppet against a background of contemporary jazz, or bring a masked actor onto the stage with a westernized *bunraku* figure. In both the adult work and the children's productions, in classics or new works, American audiences experience the historically rich tradition of the puppet theatre, with the emphasis on *theatre.*

Programs and services
Student performances, programs-in-schools, internships, study materials, teacher workshops, student and senior citizen ticket discounts, national touring, post-performance discussions, guest lecturers, newsletter.

Productions 1977-78
Beauty and the Beast, company developed
Carnival of the Seventh Moon, Margo Lovelace
The Reluctant Dragon, company developed
    from Kenneth Grahame's novel

Productions 1978-79
The Brave Little Tailor, adapt: David Visser
Hansel and Gretel, adapt: M. Lovelace
Winnie the Pooh, David Visser, from A.A.
    Milne's stories

The Brave Little Tailor. Photo:
Leonard Schugar.

The Magic Theatre

John Lion
General Director

Rossi Snipper
Administrative Director

Building 314, Fort Mason
San Francisco, CA 94123
(415) 441-8001 (business)
(415) 885-9928 (box office)

Founded 1967
John Lion

Season
October–July

Schedule
Evenings
Thursday–Sunday

Facilities
Magic Theatre Northside
Seating capacity: 99
Stage: thrust
Magic Theatre Southside
Seating capacity: 99
Stage: flexible

Finances
July 1, 1978–June 30, 1979
$250,000 operating expenses
$ 63,000 earned income
$156,000 unearned income

Audience
Paid capacity: 75%
Subscribers: 496
Annual attendance: 16,260

AEA 99-seat waiver

Through 12 years and almost 100 productions, San Francisco's Magic Theatre has established a solid reputation as one of the country's leading producers of contemporary theatre. The theatre began in Berkeley in 1968 as an outgrowth of a University of California project on alternate expression in theatre led by Jon Kott. Under the direction of founder and general director John Lion, the theatre dedicates itself to the development of new plays and playwrights with an emphasis on the contributions of American authors. With the added services of dramaturg Martin Esslin, the Magic Theatre strengthens its involvement of the playwright's intentions in the total creative process. Author, director and actors are moved toward new forms of theatrical expression through the encouragement of ensemble experimentation and the exploration of different forms of presentation.

In July 1978, the Magic produced the world premiere of the Pulitzer Prize-winning play *Buried Child* by Sam Shepard, who had been a playwright-in-residence for four years. During the last 12 years, the theatre has had more than 30 resident playwrights and has premiered original material by such authors and collaborators as Shepard, Michael McClure, Nicholas Kazan, Joseph Chaikin, Israel Horovitz, John Robinson, Susan Yankowitz, Martin Epstein, Jock Reynolds, Alan Finneran, Wolfgang Bauer, Jeff Wanshel and others. Many plays produced at the Magic have gone on to further productions elsewhere at such companies as the New York Shakespeare Festival, the Mark Taper Forum, the American Conservatory Theatre, the Royal Court, Arena Stage, the Manhattan Theatre Club and others. The Magic's close association with playwrights has also led to the publication of many plays premiered by the Magic Theatre by such houses as Delacorte, Avon, New Directions, Urizen, West Coast Plays and others.

Future plans for the Magic Theatre include the creation of a new space for staged readings and renovation of one of the two 99-seat theatres to accommodate an audience of 200. All plans aim to keep the new work of the American playwright at the core of the Magic Theatre's operation.

Programs and services
Professional acting training, student and senior citizen ticket discounts, voucher program, residencies for playwrights, newsletter.

Productions 1977-78
Wolves, John Robinson
The Wild Goose, Jeff Wanshel
Minnie Mouse and the Tap-Dancing Buddha, Michael McClure
Home on the Range, Jon Phillip Palmer
Shakespeare the Sadist, Wolfgang Bauer; trans: Renata and Martin Esslin
Buried Child, Sam Shepard

Productions 1978-79
Uncommon Women and Others, Wendy Wasserstein
Two O'Clock Feeding, Madeline Puccioni
The Red Snake, Michael McClure
Sightlines, Mark Eisman
Magnetic Kisses, Wolfgang Bauer; trans: Renata and Martin Esslin
The Autobiography of a Pearl Diver, Martin Epstein
The Barbeque, John Robinson
Suicide in B Flat, Sam Shepard

Peter Coyote and Linda Hoy in *Autobiography of a Pearl Diver.* Photo: James Armstrong.

Buried Child. Photo: Ron Blanchette.

Manhattan Theatre Club

Lynne Meadow
Artistic Director

Barry Grove
Managing Director

321 East 73rd St.
New York, NY 10021
(212) 288-2500 (business)
(212) 472-0600 (box office)

Founded 1970
A. E. Jeffcoat,
Peregrine Whittlesey,
Margaret Kennedy,
Victor Germack, Joseph Tandet

Season
October–June

Schedule
Evenings
Tuesday–Sunday
Matinees
Saturday, Sunday

Facilities
DownStage
Seating capacity: 155
Stage: proscenium
UpStage
Seating capacity: 100
Stage: thrust
Cabaret
Seating capacity: 75
Stage: cabaret

Finances
Oct. 1, 1978–Sept. 30, 1979
$875,000 operating expenses
$538,000 earned income
$346,000 unearned income

Audience
Paid capacity: 90%
Subscribers: 4,825
Annual attendance: 50,000

*AEA Off Broadway contract
and Showcase Code*

Helen Burns in *Catsplay*. Photo:
Gerry Goodstein.

Armelia McQueen, Ken Page,
Irene Cara, Andre de Shields and
Nell Carter in *Ain't Misbehavin'*.
Photo: Gerry Goodstein.

The Manhattan Theatre Club was founded in 1970 by a group of private citizens as an alternative to the commercial theatre. Under the leadership of Lynne Meadow and Barry Grove, MTC has grown from a showcase theatre to a major performing arts center, serving an audience of more than 50,000 people.

In the 1972-73 season, newly appointed artistic director Meadow presented a prolific program of more than 65 events. The program has been developed and refined over the course of seven years to constitute the DownStage Series of five fully produced American and international plays, the UpStage Series of works-in-progress, a cabaret series, a literature series and a program of readings.

The thrust of MTC's artistic policy is toward the development of new theatre works. In choosing work for production, emphasis is placed on finding an "urgent voice" rather than a flawless form. Plays are sought that express compelling personal statements and that can illuminate some aspect of our lives and society.

Highlights of MTC's first seven seasons include *Artichoke* by Joanna Glass, *Losing Time* by John Hopkins, *The Rear Column* by Simon Gray, *Ashes* by David Rudkin, *Catsplay* by Istvan Orkeny, *Ain't Misbehavin'*, *The Blood Knot* by Athol Fugard, *Sea Marks* by Gardner McKay, *Life Class* by David Storey and *The Last Street Play* by Richard Wesley.

Although many of MTC's productions have moved on to extended runs on and off Broadway, MTC primarily provides a professional forum for a variety of material, regardless of its commercial potential. Many new plays at MTC, unsuited for a commercial life in New York, become part of a regional repertoire and have benefited from multiple productions at such companies as the Goodman Theatre, Arena Stage, the New York Shakespeare Festival and the Mark Taper Forum.

Programs and services
Administrative and technical/production internships, student and senior citizen ticket discounts, free ticket distribution, post-performance discussions, workshop productions and staged readings, poetry readings, cabaret, souvenir books, volunteer auxiliary, voucher program, theatre rentals.

Productions 1977-78
Chez Nous, Peter Nichols
Play, That Time and *Footfalls*, Samuel Beckett
Statements After an Arrest Under the Immorality Act, Athol Fugard
Scenes from Soweto, Steve Wilmer
Catsplay, Istvan Orkeny; trans: Clara Gyorgyey
Strawberry Fields, Stephen Poliakoff
Wayside Motor Inn, A. R. Gurney, Jr.
Frankie and Annie, Diane Simkin
Red Fox/Second Hangin', Don Baker and Dudley Cocke
Safe House, Nicholas Kazan
Rib Cage, Larry Ketron
By Strouse, music: Charles Strouse; lyrics: Lee Adams and Martin Charnin
A Lady with a Braid, music and lyrics: Dory Previn
Ain't Misbehavin' music and lyrics: Fats Waller, et al.; adapt: Richard Maltby, Jr.
Has Anyone Here Found Love?, Lois Wyse
Jim Wann's Country Cabaret

Productions 1978-79
The Rear Column, Simon Gray
Grand Magic, Eduardo de Filippo; trans: Carlo Ardito
Artichoke, Joanna Glass
Don Juan Comes Back from the War, Odon von Horvath; trans: Christopher Hampton
The Arbor, Brother Jonathan, O.S.F.
Nongogo, Athol Fugard
Beethoven/Karl, David Rush
Stevie, Hugh Whitemore
Losing Time, John Hopkins
Just a Little Bit Less than Normal, Nigel Baldwin
A Lady Needs a Change, music: various; lyrics: Dorothy Fields; adapt: Bill Gile
Dancing in the Dark, music Arthur Schwartz; lyrics: Howard Dietz, et al.; adapt: Mary O'Hagan
Give My Heart an Even Break, music: George Quincy; lyrics: Thayer Burch
Songs from the City Streets, music and lyrics: Jake Holmes
At Home with Margery Cohen
Jim Wann's Country Cabaret

Mark Taper Forum

Gordon Davidson
Artistic Director

William P. Wingate
General Manager

Los Angeles Music Center
135 North Grand Ave.
Los Angeles, CA 90012
(213) 972-7353 (business)
(213) 972-7392 (Taper box office)
(213) 972-7651
(Forum Laboratory box office)
(213) 466-2161
(Aquarius box office)

Founded 1967
Gordon Davidson

Season
July–June

Schedule
Evenings
Tuesday–Sunday
Matinees
Saturday, Sunday

Facilities
Mark Taper Forum
Seating capacity: 742
Stage: thrust
Forum Laboratory
John Anson Ford Cultural Arts
Theatre
2580 Cahuenga Blvd., Hollywood
Seating capacity: 99
Stage: flexible
Aquarius Theatre
6230 Sunset Blvd., Hollywood
Seating capacity: 1,199
Stage: modified thrust

Finances
July 1, 1978–June 30, 1979
$6,960,000 operating expenses
$5,482,000 earned income
$2,401,000 unearned income

Audience
Paid capacity: 77%
Subscribers: 25,500
Annual attendance: 482,875

Booked-in events
Dance, music, theatre

Touring contact
Susan E. Barton

AEA LORT (A), (B)
and C contracts

The Center Theatre Group/Mark Taper Forum, founded in 1967, was an outgrowth of the Theatre Group, a professional company which had been in residence at the University of California/Los Angeles since 1959.

The Taper's artistic program, under the direction of Gordon Davidson , comprises five interrelated parts: the major subscription season, New Theatre for Now, Forum Laboratory projects, Aquarius Theatre events and affiliated community programs. The mainstage season offers a wide range of productions, including classical works, but with an emphasis on presenting new works and plays not previously seen in the United States or on the West Coast.

Pioneering in the development of new plays, playwrights and directors, New Theatre for Now explores unusual dramatic subjects and innovative staging concepts. The 1978-79 NTFN season took the form of the two-month Playworks festival, during which 12 plays were presented at three locations around Los Angeles. Along with several productions developed by the Taper, Playworks also featured Mabou Mines' production of Beckett's *The Lost Ones* and the West Coast premiere of *The Biko Inquest.* The company's commitment to developing new theatre pieces also finds expression through the Forum Laboratory, a program of workshops performed for invited audiences. At the Lab, actors, writers, directors, composers and designers collaborate in creating projects in new modes of dramatic expression, free from critical and box office pressure.

Aquarius Theatre events include transferred Taper mainstage productions that can sustain longer runs, such as *Zoot Suit,* as well as productions specifically designed for performance there. The theatre is also available for lease to commercial producers and other performing arts organizations.

Related community programs include the Improvisational Theatre Project (ITP) and Project DATE (Deaf Audience Theatre Encounter). ITP offers children and adults innovative experiences which call upon them to develop their imagination and creativity. ITP's material, created for the multiracial company by a resident writer and composer, includes improvised stories based on audience suggestions. The troupe tours locally and statewide, giving performances and workshops in schools and at the Taper. The relatively new Project DATE offers special performances of subscription season shows for the hearing-impaired.

Programs and services
Artistic and administrative internships, student performances, programs-in-schools, study materials; ticket discounts to students, senior citizens, church groups, the underprivileged and the incarcerated; free ticket distribution, "Hot Tix" day-of-performance discounts, regional touring, post-performance discussions, workshop productions and staged readings, newsletter, souvenir book, weekly events calendar.

Productions 1977-78
For Colored Girls who have Considered Suicide/When the Rainbow is Enuf, Ntozake Shange
Comedians, Trevor Griffiths
A Christmas Carol, adapt: Doris Baizley
Getting Out, Marsha Norman
Black Angel, Michael Cristofer
Gethsemane Springs, Harvey Perr
The Winter Dancers, David Lan
Zoot Suit, Luis Valdez

Productions 1978-79
Zoot Suit
Dusa, Fish, Stas and Vi, Pam Gems
A Christmas Carol
Terra Nova, Ted Tally
The Tempest, William Shakespeare
Jazz Set, Ron Milner
Kid Twist, Len Jenkin
The Taking Away of Little Willie, Tom Griffin
In Camera, Robert Pinger
A Life in a Day: Lucky Lindy, Dick D. Zigun
Maud Gonne Says No to the Poet, Susan Rivers
The Trouble with Europe, Paul D'Andrea
The Idol Makers, Stephen Davis Parks
The Biko Inquest, Norman Fenton and Jon Blair
Vienna Notes, Richard Nelson
Ormer Locklear, Marc Norman

Edward James Olmos and Daniel Valdez in *Zoot Suit.* Photo: Jay Thompson.

Stephanie Zimbalist, Brent Carver, Anthony Hopkins and (bottom) Michael Bond in *The Tempest.* Photo: Jay Thompson.

McCarter Theatre Company

Nagle Jackson
Artistic Director

Alison Harris
Managing Director

91 University Place
Princeton, NJ 08540
(609) 452-3616 (business)
(609) 921-8700 (box office)

Founded 1972
Daniel Seltzer

Season
October–April

Schedule
Evenings
Tuesday–Sunday
Matinees
Sunday

Facilities
Seating capacity: 1,077
Stage: proscenium

Finances
July 1, 1978–June 30, 1979
$1,846,000 operating expenses
$1,074,000 earned income
$　742,000 unearned income

Audience
Paid capacity: 74%
Subscribers: 11,522
Annual attendance: 158,000

Touring contact
Thomas Holm

Booked-in events
Dance, film, music,
children's theatre

AET LORT (B) contract

Mariette Hartley and Charlie
Fields in *Put Them All Together.*
Photo: Cliff Moore.

Under the new direction of Nagle Jackson, who succeeds Michael Kahn as artistic director, the McCarter Theatre Company aims to establish itself in the fullest sense as a resident ensemble of actors presenting a season of plays for the community it serves. Within the commercial shadow of New York and in close proximity to that city's artistic resources, McCarter is both challenged and benefited by its locale. It draws strength from its unique setting on the campus of one of the world's major educational institutions, Princeton University, and yet remains an independent professional company serving audiences from throughout New Jersey and eastern Pennsylvania. Part of the company tours and provides outreach programs to many community groups.

Presenting six plays a season in the 1,077-seat McCarter Theatre, the ensemble company utilizes actors with great variety and big-stage technique. The stage is a traditional proscenium one in which non-traditional forms are as welcome as are the classics of world theatre. Guest artists from surrounding metropolitan areas of New York and Philadelphia are invited to expand and enrich the experience of both audience and acting company.

McCarter has presented many new works on its mainstage over the past seven years and maintains a regular seasonal program of staged readings of works-in-progress. Jackson has dedicated McCarter to the development of a truly great acting ensemble on the East Coast to match those which have grown in other areas across the country.

Programs and services
Administrative and technical/production internships, student performances, study materials, student ticket discounts, free ticket distribution, statewide touring, post-performance discussions, workshop productions and staged readings, film series, newsletter, speakers bureau, volunteer auxiliary, theatre rentals.

Productions 1977-78
The Confirmation, Howard Ashman
The Utter Glory of Morrissey Hall, book, music
　　and lyrics: Clark Gesner
The Happy Journey to Trenton and Camden,
　　Queens of France and *The Long Christmas*
　　Dinner, Thornton Wilder
The Torch-Bearers, George Kelly
Toys in the Attic, Lillian Hellman
Much Ado About Nothing, William Shakespeare

Productions 1978-79
A Month in the Country, Ivan Turgenev; trans:
　　Ariadne Nicolaeff
The Aspern Papers, Michael Redgrave, from
　　Henry James' novel
No Time for Comedy, S.N. Behrman
Put Them All Together, Anne Commire
Blues in the Night, music and lyrics: various;
　　adapt: Sheldon Epps
Heartbreak House, George Bernard Shaw

Frank Hamilton, Jeanne Ruskin
and John Wardwell in *Heartbreak*
House. Photo: Cliff Moore.

Meadow Brook Theatre

Terence E. Kilburn
Artistic and General Director

Oakland University
Rochester, MI 48063
(313) 377-3310 (business)
(313) 377-3300 (box office)

Founded 1967
Oakland University

Season
September–May

Schedule
Evenings
Tuesday–Sunday
Matinees
Wednesday, selected Saturdays

Facilities
Seating capacity: 608
Stage: proscenium

Finances
July 1, 1978–June 30, 1979
$895,000 operating expenses
$758,000 earned income
$137,000 unearned income

Audience
Paid capacity: 94%
Subscribers: 14,300
Annual attendance: 142,000

Touring contact
Frank Bollinger

AEA LORT (B) contract

Meadow Brook Theatre is located on the campus of Oakland University in Rochester, Mich., 30 miles from Detroit. After its opening in 1966, Meadow Brook's first four seasons were presented under the leadership of John Fernald, former principal of the Royal Academy of Dramatic Art in London. During that time, the groundwork was laid for building an audience in a region where no professional theatre had previously existed.

In 1970, Terence Kilburn assumed the theatre's artistic leadership and introduced a wider and more varied repertoire, including more contemporary and American plays. Since then, MBT has attracted audiences from nearby suburbs as well as Detroit and Flint. Season subscription sales have increased steadily from 8,100 in 1970 to some 14,000.

The acting company has developed into what is best described as a "revolving" resident troupe. Although each season brings several new actors to the theatre, many performers return frequently, creating a strong sense of ensemble. Kilburn directs three productions each season; guest directors are engaged for other productions. MBT maintains an active school program, based on attendance by high school and junior high school students at matinees. Teachers are invited to preview performances, study materials are available for each play, tours of the facilities are arranged, post-play discussions are conducted by cast members, and lectures on the technical aspects of the theatre are given by the staff.

In 1974, Meadow Brook began a statewide touring program. The early tours lasted only 10 days and played a limited number of towns in Michigan. The 1979 tour of Moliere's *The Adventures of Scapin* played 19 towns over a four-week period. 1979 also saw the beginning of a touring project aimed at high school audiences. A specially created program of Shakespearean scenes was presented to 14 high schools and communities over a two-week period. These programs are sponsored by the Michigan Council for the Arts and are expected to continue expansion during the coming seasons. Meadow Brook has also established an internship program in conjunction with Oakland University, whereby selected students are given academic credit for their participation in MBT productions.

Programs and services
Programs-in-schools, study materials, student ticket discounts, statewide touring, children's theatre, post-performance discussions, volunteer auxiliary, theatre rentals.

Productions 1977-78
She Stoops to Conquer, Oliver Goldsmith
Picnic, William Inge
Table Manners, Alan Ayckbourn
The Corn Is Green, Emlyn Williams
The Tempest, William Shakespeare
The Runner Stumbles, Milan Stitt
The Male Animal, James Thurber and Elliott Nugent
Cole, music and lyrics: Cole Porter; adapt: Benny Green and Alan Strachan

Productions 1978-79
The Devil's Disciple, George Bernard Shaw
That Championship Season, Jason Miller
Ring Round the Moon, Jean Anouilh; adapt: Christopher Fry
The Caine Mutiny Court-Martial, Herman Wouk
Blithe Spirit, Noel Coward
The Deadly Game, James Yaffe, from Friedrich Dürrenmatt's novel *Traps*
The Adventures of Scapin, Moliere; adapt: John Ulmer
Berlin to Broadway with Kurt Weill, music: Kurt Weill; lyrics: various; adapt: Gene Lerner

Bella Jarrett, Jane Badler and Melanie Resnick in *Picnic.* Photo: Dick Hunt.

The Caine Mutiny Court-Martial.
Photo: Dick Hunt.

Medicine Show Theatre Ensemble

Barbara Vann
James Barbosa
Artistic Directors

Jon Beaupre
Business Manager

6 West 18th St.
New York, NY 10011
(212) 255-4991

Founded 1970
Barbara Vann
James Barbosa

Season
September–June

Facilities
Newfoundland Theatre
Seating capacity: 75
Stage: flexible

Finances
Aug. 1, 1978–July 31, 1979
$44,000 operating expenses
$22,000 earned income
$13,000 unearned income

Audience
Paid capacity: 75%
Annual attendance: 10,000

Touring contact
Chris Brandt

Booked-in events
New music, jazz, dance,
experimental theatre

Tina Mandas, John C. Gavin,
James Barbosa, Steven Hanafin
and Lynda Rodolitz in *The
Tragedy of Tragedies* or *The Life
and Death of Tom Thumb the
Great*. Photo: Jon Beaupre.

After 10 years in the maelstrom of New York theatre, Medicine Show still has its innocence. It also has a storefront of pleasing proportions, a resilience born of chronic underfunding, and a staunch and supportive audience sharing its belief that comedy is the peaceful man's best weapon.

Last season the company created the jazz-scored tone poem *Shipping Out* and revamped *Frogs* to encompass current events and concerns. These "chamber works" are given shape and dimension by the performers' interplay and musicality. The "carnival epics"—*The Mummers' Play* and Fielding's *The Tragedy of Tragedies* or *The Life and Death of Tom Thumb the Great*—exult in the extravagances of theatre itself, while mocking its pretensions. The works travel well and play around the city parks, office buildings and the country's college campuses. Their deliberate freedom of form calls for communal discipline of technique and purpose.

Continual research extends and sharpens the techniques. Teaching residencies afford opportunities to share and reexamine. A month-long laboratory at Smith College also evolved five embryonic student-created scripts.

At Medicine Show, plans and energy abound for new forays into the American consciousness, armed with a caustic compassion and a belief in the vitality of theatre.

Programs and services
Professional acting training; artistic, administrative and technical internships; training in collaborative theatre techniques, student performances, programs-in-schools, student and senior citizen ticket discounts, voucher program,national touring, post-performance discussions, workshop productions and staged readings, art exhibits, coloring book.

Productions 1977-78
Frogs, book: Carl Morse and company; music: Yenoin Guibbory; lyrics: C. Morse
The Mummers' Play, company developed; music: Donald Johnston
Don Juan in Hell, George Bernard Shaw

Productions 1978-79
Frogs
Shipping Out, book: Stephen Policoff and company; music: Carol Henry; lyrics: S. Policoff and Chris Brandt
The Mummers' Play
The Tragedy of Tragedies, or *The Life and Death of Tom Thumb the Great,* Henry Fielding; music: Carol Henry

Medicine Show Theatre Ensemble concocts comedy—comedy concerned with the impostures, absurdities and affectations of society, regarding them with the cold glare of intelligence and common sense. Medicine Show produces hard-edged fantasies, refusing to call reality "real." The company is a collaborative endeavor—admittedly a risky situation—but the spirit of adventure weighs heavily in choices of material, techniques and colleagues. Artists of unconventional vision join together to create works that are many-dimensioned, libertarian in spirit, both innocent and complex. While some of these works are philosophically dark, they are all imbued with, and occasionally willfully contradicted by the prankishness and sense of joy with which they are performed.

Milwaukee Repertory Theater Company

John Dillon
Artistic Director

Sara A. O'Connor
Managing Director

Performing Arts Center
929 North Water St.
Milwaukee, WI 53202
(414) 273-7121 (business)
(414) 273-7206 (box office)

Founded 1954
Mary John

Season
September–May

Schedule
Evenings
Tuesday–Sunday
Matinees
Wednesday, Sunday

Facilities
Todd Wehr Theater
Seating capacity: 504
Stage: thrust
Pabst Theater
144 East Wells St.
Seating capacity: 1,388
Stage: proscenium
Court Street Theater
315 West Court St.
Seating capacity: 99
Stage: flexible

Finances
July 1, 1978–June 30, 1979
$1,316,000 operating expenses
$ 952,000 earned income
$ 377,000 unearned income

Audience
Paid capacity
Todd Wehr Theater: 95%
Pabst Theater: 95%
Court Street Theater: 82%
Subscribers: 20,252
Total annual attendance: 200,000

Touring contact
Susan Medak

Booked-in events
Theatre

AEA LORT (C) contract

In its 25 consecutive seasons, the Milwaukee Repertory Theater Company has grown into a diversified producing organization supporting a resident performing ensemble in three Milwaukee theatres, extending its reputation through regional tours and regional and national television productions.

The resident ensemble approach to acting was developed by artistic directors Tunc Yalman (1966-71), Nagle Jackson (1971-77) and continues with current artistic director John Dillon. Dillon directs three of the six mainstage plays, with guest directors or members of the company staging the season's remaining plays. Nationally prominent guest designers, who work with resident technicians in the MRT shops, are frequently engaged. The theatre employs more than 70 people full-time during the nine-month season.

In the last five years, MRT has primarily emphasized the development and production of new plays. At least half of the plays presented each year are new. Although MRT screens hundreds of scripts each year, the main source of new plays is within the company. During the 1979-80 season, MRT will retain three full-time playwrights-in-residence as well as several guest playwrights. Thus, commitments to writers are made over an extended period of time and not on a play-by-play basis.

In addition to the mainstage series, MRT operates the Court Street Theater, a 99-seat converted warehouse open for nine weeks each spring, featuring mostly original works. This expanded production capability, combined with a newly instituted staged reading series, virtually assures that all work by resident writers will be presented in one production mode or another.

Concurrent with MRT's growth in play development, the company has also greatly expanded its touring activities. The last five years have seen five major regional tours, including the 1978 back-to-back productions of *Long Day's Journey into Night* and *Ah, Wilderness!* In addition, MRT presents an annual production of *A Christmas Carol* at the 1,388-seat Pabst Theater, a newly restored Milwaukee landmark.

Recent seasons have also marked the company's entrance into the television arena, including two productions aired nationally on PBS—*Wilder, Wilder,* a collection of four short Thornton Wilder plays, and Daniel Stein's drama *The Trial of the Moke* on *Theater in America.*

Programs and services
Administrative and technical/production internships, student performances, programs-in-schools, study materials, student and senior citizen ticket discounts, regional touring, post-performance discussions, workshop productions and staged readings, magazine, script publication, speakers bureau, volunteer auxiliary.

Productions 1977-78
Richard III, William Shakespeare
Long Day's Journey into Night, Eugene O'Neill
Ah, Wilderness!, Eugene O'Neill
Friends, Kobo Abe; trans: Donald Keene
High Time, Frank Cucci
Namesake, Amlin Gray
A Christmas Carol, adapt: Nagle Jackson
Just a Little Bit Less than Normal, Nigel Baldwin
Custer, Robert Ingham
Medal of Honor Rag, Tom Cole

Productions 1978-79
Romeo and Juliet, William Shakespeare
The Freeway, Peter Nichols
Island, book: Peter Link and Brent Nicholson; music and lyrics: P. Link
Fighting Bob, Tom Cole
Merton of the Movies, George S. Kaufman and Marc Connelly
The Taming of the Shrew, William Shakespeare; adapt: Amlin Gray, John Dillon and Jonathan Abarbanel
A Christmas Carol
Hemingway Before the Storm, Ritch Brinkley and Jonathan Abarbanel
Cops, Terry Curtis Fox
The Bear, Anton Chekhov; trans: Earle Edgerton
Grandma Duck Is Dead, Larry Shue
Bo and *How I Got That Story,* Amlin Gray

Pamela Blade, Jaison Walker, Jenny Burton and W. Chad Mitchell in *Island.* Photo: Mark Avery.

Romeo and Juliet. Photo: Mark Avery.

Missouri Repertory Theatre

Patricia McIlrath
Director

5100 Rockhill Road
Kansas City, MO 64110
(816) 276-2701 (business)
(816) 276-2704 (box office)

Founded 1964
University of Missouri/Kansas
City, Patricia McIlrath

Season
July–September
February–March

Schedule
Evenings
Tuesday–Sunday
Matinees
Wednesday, Saturday, Sunday

Facilities
University Playhouse
51st and Holmes Sts.
Seating capacity: 501
Stage: proscenium
Helen F. Spencer Theatre,
University of Missouri Center
for the Performing Arts
4949 Cherry St.
Opened July 1979
Seating capacity: 733
Stage: flexible

Finances
Oct. 1, 1977–Sept. 30, 1978
$411,000 operating expenses
$182,000 earned income
$289,000 unearned income

Audience
Paid capacity: 82%
Subscribers: 3,817
Annual attendance: 72,000

AEA LORT (B) contract

John Cothran, Jr., Buck Gibbs
and Jim Armstrong in *Purlie
Victorious.*

Missouri Repertory Theatre, now in its 16th season with an expanded company and budget, has just opened its new permanent home. The Helen F. Spencer Theatre, in Kansas City's $11.4 million Center for the Performing Arts housing theatre, music and dance, is the result of unusually close university-community collaboration. Unusual among the country's resident theatres for its close interaction with the University of Missouri/Kansas City professional theatre training program, MRT is a professional company of independent corporate status. The theatre maintains a resident ensemble company and engages six to eight guest directors during the eight-play season. Noted designers and technicians are also employed. Classic, contemporary and new plays have been MRT's hallmark, with experimentation attempted in all productions.

Unusual, too, are the expanding services, audiences and itinerary of Missouri Vanguard Theatre, MRT's touring wing, now in its 12th year of serving Missouri and a four-state Midwest area. MVT offers two plays in repertory, in-school programs for secondary and elementary school children, and acting and technical workshops. The Vanguard ensemble, largely duplicating the resident MRT company, now travels between eight and 12 weeks throughout Missouri and the four-state area, following the resident season in Kansas City, affording many artists more than 32 weeks of employment.

The year 1979 saw the inauguration of a second stage—MRT II—in a small space in the center, seating approximately 100. The focus of this second space is on new or recent American plays. Interns and residents from the University's MFA programs produce the new plays for ever-increasing audiences. Staging is simple; the intent is to create a forum for young American playwrights as a supplement to the traditional new play production as a part of the regular season.

Programs and services
Professional training in acting, directing, design and production; classes for nonprofessionals and children; artistic and technical/production internships, programs-in-schools, study materials, student and senior citizen ticket discounts, regional touring, pre-performance discussions, newsletter.

Productions 1977-78
The Misanthrope, Moliere
Old Times, Harold Pinter
The Morning Star, Henry C. Haskell
Mary Stuart, Friedrich Schiller; adapt:
    John Reich and Jean Stock Goldston
The Hostage, Brendan Behan
Purlie Victorious, Ossie Davis
The Imaginary Invalid, Moliere; trans:
    John Reich
All My Sons, Arthur Miller

Productions 1978-79
Julius Caesar, William Shakespeare
Light Up the Sky, Moss Hart
The Shadow Box, Michael Cristofer
The Seagull, Anton Chekhov; trans:
    Jean-Claude van Itallie
Rashomon, Fay and Michael Kanin
The Happy Hunter, Georges Feydeau;
    adapt: Barnett Shaw
Bus Stop, William Inge
The Little Foxes, Lillian Hellman

Sally Longan, Margaret
Heffernan, Judy Goldman, Mary
Kay Moran and James Armstrong
in *Morning Star.*

Music-Theatre Performing Group/ Lenox Arts Center

Lyn Austin
Cameron Thompson
Producing Directors

18 East 68th St.
New York, NY 10021
(212) 371-9610

Citizens Hall
Stockbridge, MA 01262
(413) 298-9463

Founded 1970
Lyn Austin

Season
New York
January–May
Stockbridge
June–August

Facilities
Citizens Hall
Seating capacity: 100
Stage: flexible

Finances
July 1, 1978–June 30, 1979
$178,000 operating expenses
$ 17,000 earned income
$164,000 unearned income

Audience
Annual attendance: 17,500

Touring contact
Lyn Austin

The Music-Theatre Performing Group/Lenox Arts Center, entering its ninth year, is a laboratory for the development of new American music-theatre.

The organization is pioneering the development of a music-theatre fusing experimental theatre techniques with a wide range of musical forms (contemporary, jazz, opera) and dance. The form which has resulted from this fusion has proved itself a dynamic offshoot of the American musical comedy tradition.

The driving force behind all the group's work is the creation of *new* music-theatre productions—as contrasted to organizations which transfer pieces originated elsewhere into their programs.

The productions begin simply with extensive rehearsal periods in order that the writers, composers, directors and performers may put full focus on the work itself and not on technical trappings. The works then proceed to full production for performances on, Off and Off-Off Broadway, throughout the country, in Europe and on television. Nine months is spent in preparation and performance in New York, and three in Stockbridge, Mass., during the summer.

The company has sought to create dynamic, fresh collaborations by bringing together, for example, just the right writer (who up to that point might have been working solely as a poet or novelist), or just the right composer with just the right director (who up to that point might have been solely a choreographer).

The group is training a core of young performing artists skilled in all facets of this field. This core is developing into a new musical theatre repertory company. Its structure focuses on in-depth work with each artist in the belief that this method will develop major writers, composers and directors far more successfully than a kind of "sausage factory" approach to artistic enterprise.

Programs and services
Professional training in acting, directing, design, production and administration; student performances, student ticket discounts, national touring, post-performance discussions, workshop productions and staged readings, guest lecturers, poetry readings, cabaret, newsletter, script publication.

Productions 1977-78
The American Imagination, book and lyrics: Richard Foreman; music: Stanley Silverman
Twelve Dreams, James Lapine
Viva Reviva, book and lyrics: Eve Merriam; music: Amy Rubin
A Natural Death, Richard Howard

Productions 1978-79
The Tennis Game, book and lyrics: George W.S. Trow; music: William Schimmel
Virgil Thompson: A Profile, music: Virgil Thompson; lyrics: various; adapt: Carman Moore
Prairie Avenue, book and lyrics: George W.S. Trow; music: William Schimmel
Redeye, book and lyrics: Timothy S. Mayer; music: Brad Burg
The Old Man, Wallace Shawn

The Tennis Game. Photo: Stephen Paley.

National Black Theatre

Barbara Ann Teer
Executive Producer

Fredrica Teer
Executive Director

9 East 125th St.
New York, NY 10035
(212) 427-5616

Founded 1968
Barbara Ann Teer

Season
November–May

Schedule
Evenings
Friday, Saturday
Matinees
Sunday

Facilities
Seating capacity: 99
Stage: flexible

Finances
Nov. 7, 1977–Oct. 31, 1978
$137,000 operating expenses
$ 31,000 earned income
$ 82,000 unearned income

Audience
Paid capacity: 75%
Subscribers: 357
Annual attendance: 10,245

Touring contact
Keibu Faison

Dwight Collins and Ayodele
Moore in *Wine in the Wilderness.*
Photo: Adeyemi Lythcott.

The National Black Theatre is an institution dedicated to serve people through theatre. The organization provides those people whose lives it touches with an opportunity to participate in a process of mind expansion and transpersonal growth. The institution is organized around the concept of providing an environment for people to reestablish their basic sense of identity and self-acceptance.

NBT's goal is to train people to transcend the limitations of conventional theatre by developing in each person a sense of wholeness and a strong experience of self-esteem and love.

Certainly NBT is a different and innovative theatrical institution. The concepts and images such as "ugly," "rich," "poor," "black" and "white" have very little relevance in the company's work, stemming as they do from basic cultural conditioning which NBT members have labored to overcome. The company regards them as devices of alienation. The special "rewards" which society normally bestows on people who conceptualize in this way are not forthcoming at NBT.

Programs and services
Professional training in acting and administration; classes for nonprofessionals; artistic, administrative and technical/production internships; senior citizen ticket discounts, voucher program, national touring, post-performance discussions, workshop productions and staged readings, newsletter.

Productions 1977-78
Ritual, Barbara Ann Teer, from Kwame Azular's poem; music and lyrics: B.A. Teer and company
Soljourney into Truth, Barbara Ann Teer
Seven Comes Up Seven Comes Down, Lonne Elder III and Adeyemi Lythcott
Wine in the Wilderness, Alice Childress

Productions 1978-79
Softly Comes a Whirlwind Whispering in Your Ear, Barbara Ann Teer
The Owl and the Pussycat, Bill Manhoff
Soljourney into Truth
Ritual

*Softly Comes a Whirlwind
Whispering in Your Ear.* Photo:
Adeyemi Lythcott.

97

National Shakespeare Company

Philip Meister
Artistic Director

Mustafa Kadaster
General Manager

414 West 51st St.
New York, NY 10019
(212) 265-1340

Founded 1963
Philip Meister
Elaine Sulka

Season
October–May

Finances
June 1, 1978–May 31, 1979
$144,000 operating expenses
$222,000 earned income

Audience
Annual attendance: 250,000

Touring contact
Michael Hirsch

Since 1963, the National Shakespeare Company, under the artistic direction of co-founder and producer Philip Meister, has toured to colleges, universities and communities nationwide with productions of classical drama. NSC's purpose is twofold: to bring the beauty and understanding of Shakespeare's plays to people who would not otherwise have the opportunity to experience them, and to give American actors a chance to perform the classics. NSC productions are directed by such notable theatre practitioners as Mario Siletti, John Houseman, Neil Flanagan and Sue Lawless. The company of 12, which tours with full scenery, lighting and costumes, performs its repertoire of classical plays in 125 cities in 35 states to a total audience of more than 250,000 theatregoers. Company members are selected each spring from regional auditions across the country and the NSC Conservatory.

In response to requests from secondary school teachers nationwide, NSC has developed a program of performances geared to students. Such live in-school performances not only enhance the study of Shakespeare's plays but also serve as an aid to teachers of English, history and drama. The 1978-79 Student Matinee Series was presented to more than 25,000 high school students in New York, Pennsylvania, Illinois and Iowa.

In its 17-year existence, NSC has developed a distinct perspective on the problems facing the professional actor today. The result has been the NSC Conservatory, a professional training program designed to prepare all facets of the actor's instrument: body, imagination and intellect. The Conservatory offers a two-year program in New York City and an intensive eight-week summer program at the company's base in the Catskill Mountains.

NSC's offices and Conservatory are located in the Cubiculo performing arts center, which offers theatre, dance and music programs throughout the year.

Programs and services
Professional acting conservatory, artistic internships, programs-in-schools, national touring.

Productions 1977-78
The Winter's Tale, William Shakespeare
Othello, William Shakespeare
As You Like It, William Shakespeare

Productions 1978-79
Hamlet, William Shakespeare
A Midsummer Night's Dream, William Shakespeare

Mary Agen Cox and Ted Holland
in *A Midsummer Night's Dream.*
Photo: Dinah Carlson.

Kivi Harris and Philip Shaw in *A Midsummer Night's Dream.*
Photo: Dinah Carlson.

National Theatre of the Deaf

David Hays
Producing Director

Tom Boyd
Vice President

c/o O'Neill Theater Center
305 Great Neck Road
Waterford, CT 06385
(203) 443-5378

Founded 1967
David Hays

Season
October–April

Finances
July 1, 1978–June 30, 1979
$549,000 operating expenses
$548,000 earned income

Audience
Annual attendance: 250,000

Touring contact
Mack Scism

AEA Guest Artist contract

Phyllis French and Sam Edwards in *Volpone*. Photo: Robert Steinberg.

Using speech, sign language, pantomime and dance, the National Theatre of the Deaf has developed a unique theatrical style and visual language readily comprehended by all audiences. The second professional theatre of the deaf in the world (a Russian theatre was founded in 1911), NTD has been instrumental in establishing similar troupes in Great Britain, Sweden and Australia, and has assisted the formation of community theatres of the deaf in America.

Due to the social impact of NTD's work, the image of the deaf has been elevated in city after city and country after country. Hearing audiences (fully four-fifths of NTD's attendees), seeing the theatre for the first time, are astonished at the artistic skill of the company and at how easily the performances can be followed without knowledge of sign language. Although important and gratifying, these social goals are secondary to the theatre's primary thrust—the creation of a theatre of visual language, capable of holding its own alongside any theatre company in the world.

Each summer, under the auspices of the O'Neill Theater Center, the NTD holds a summer school in Waterford, Conn., to extend and enhance company skills and to begin the training process for future company members. Deaf community members from throughout the world are also trained in various theatrical disciplines. Each September, the company goes into rehearsal for a new production that

will tour the following year. Between national and internatonal tours, the company is divided into smaller units—Little Theatres of the Deaf—which tour to schools with special repertoires for young people.

Since its inception, NTD has completed more than 20 national tours, totalling more than 2,000 performances in 47 states, including two Broadway appearances. More than 100 million Americans have seen the NTD on both commercial and public television. The company has performed in 15 foreign countries in Europe, the Mideast and the South Pacific. The theatre was also awarded a special Antoinette Perry ("Tony") Award for theatrical excellence in 1977.

Programs and services
Professional and nonprofessional training, programs in schools, study materials for teachers and students, educational workshops, international touring, souvenir book.

Productions 1977-78
The Three Musketeers, adapt: Joe Layton and company, from Alexandre Dumas' novel
Sir Gawain and the Green Knight, adapt: Dennis Scott
Aesop's Fables

Productions 1978-79
Quite Early One Morning, Dylan Thomas
Volpone, Ben Jonson
Cautionary Tales, Hilaire Belloc
Sense and Nonsense, Lewis Carroll
The Giving Tree, Shel Silverstein

Quite Early One Morning. Photo: Robert Steinberg.

Nebraska Theatre Caravan

Charles Jones
Executive Director

Carolyn Rutherford
Company Manager

6915 Cass St.
Omaha, NE 68132
(402) 533-4890

Founded 1976
Charles Jones, Nebraska Arts
Council, Omaha Playhouse

Season
September–May

Finances
July 1, 1978–June 30, 1979
$126,000 operating expenses
$ 81,000 earned income
$ 46,000 unearned income

Audience
Annual attendance: 64,212

Touring contact
Carolyn Rutherford

The Nebraska Theatre Caravan is a professional performance and workshop company designed as a special project of the Omaha Community Playhouse and the Nebraska Arts Council. The primary goal of the Caravan is to provide professional theatre and creative workshop opportunities in areas where distance, financial limitations, or lack of appropriate resources has prevented such activities. Each season the Caravan prepares at least four major productions for its Midwest tour, including at least one full musical, a production for children and a production from Shakespeare specially adapted for the Caravan company.

The Caravan has developed a performance style that allows the company to remain efficiently mobile and flexible and to perform in almost any available space when a traditional theatre auditorium is not available.

The Caravan has found great success in providing a zesty, energetic approach to Shakespeare that appeals to both young people and adults. The company is totally committed to providing quality entertainment as well as valuable educational opportunities for all age groups. Its workshops emphasize student involvement with the actor/workshop leader. The Caravan company offers each community artistic flexibility and total community ownership of the residency program.

During the 1979-80 season the Caravan planned to tour a special adaptation of Charles Dickens' *A Christmas Carol* in addition to its regular season.

Programs and services
Classes for nonprofessionals and children, programs-in-schools, study materials, regional touring.

Productions 1977-78
Scapino, adapt: Frank Dunlop and Jim Dale, from Moliere
The Boar's Head Tavern, Mitchell Edmonds
The Mystery of the Boar's Head, Mitchell Edmonds
The Just-So Stories, Aurand Harris, from Rudyard Kipling's stories

Productions 1978-79
Diamond Studs, book: Jim Wann; music and lyrics: Bland Simpson and J. Wann
Twelfth Night, William Shakespeare
The Boar's Head Tavern
Androcles and the Lion, Aurand Harris

Androcles and the Lion. Photo: John McIntyre.

Jim Armstrong, Carl Baer, Virginia Creamer and Jim Boggess in *Twelfth Night.* Photo: John McIntyre.

Negro Ensemble Company

Douglas Turner Ward
Artistic Director

Gerald S. Krone
Managing Director

133 Second Ave.
New York, NY 10003
(212) 677-3939 (business)
(212) 674-3530 (box office)

Founded 1967
Douglas Turner Ward,
Robert Hooks, Gerald S. Krone

Season
September–June

Schedule
Evenings
Tuesday–Sunday
Matinees
Saturday, Sunday

Facilities
St. Marks Playhouse
Seating capacity: 145
Stage: thrust

Finances
July 1, 1978–June 30, 1979
$709,000 operating expenses
$165,000 earned income
$577,000 unearned income

Audience
Paid capacity: 83%
Annual attendance: 45,000

Touring contact
Gerald S. Krone

AEA LORT (D) contract

Graham Brown and Chuck
Patterson in *The Imprisonment of
Obatala*. Photo: Bert Andrews.

The Negro Ensemble Company was founded to provide a continuing forum for the presentation of theatrical material relevant to black life. That fundamental goal is still its raison d'être.

Utilizing a resident company of actors, directors and designers, NEC deals almost exclusively with new plays and since its inception has premiered more than 80 new works. In fact, its productions have provided a major share of the body of contemporary black dramatic literature.

There comes a time in the life of any creative entity when, to justify its continued existence, it must rejuvenate itself; the 1978-79 season at NEC saw the beginning stage of a long-range plan for revitalization and institutionalization.

First, the program's main thrust entails greater emphasis on developmental projects gauged to strengthen production activity, and 22 new plays were given some form of presentation during the 1978-79 season alone.

Second, the administrative and artistic staffs were revamped and infused with new personnel, and the board structure of the corporation was expanded. One of the company's most significant efforts resulted in the establishment of a development unit staffed with full-time professional personnel, who instituted a plan for the expansion of outside support for the company and the stablization of its institutional base.

Though the company once maintained formal classroom training, NEC now offers on-the-job training and intern programs for developing theatre artists, administrators and technicians. It also continues its commitment to the new playwright through an expanded Playwrights' Unit.

At the conclusion of its 1978-79 New York season, the company appeared in a guest residency at the Arena Stage in Washington, D.C. Past years have seen six national and four international tours, and the 1979-80 season includes a tour of the southeastern U.S. The company is also actively exploring possibilities for the joint development of productions with other resident theatres.

Programs and services
Professional training in directing, design, production and administration; artistic, administrative and technical/production internships; student ticket discounts, voucher program, national touring, workshop productions and staged readings, theatre rentals.

Productions 1977-78
The Offering, Gus Edwards
Black Body Blues, Gus Edwards
Twilight Dinner, Lennox Brown

Productions 1978-79
Nevis Mountain Dew, Steve Carter
Daughters of the Mock, Judi Ann Mason
Everyman and *The Imprisonment of Obatala,*
 Obotunde Ijimere
Old Phantoms, Gus Edwards
A Season to Unravel, Alexis DeVeaux

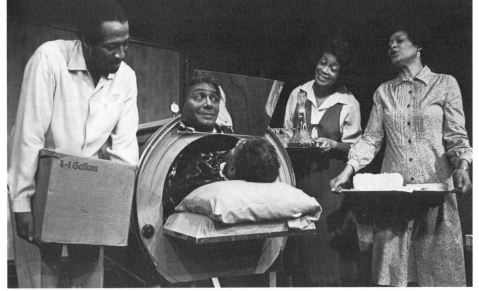

Arthur French, Graham Brown,
Ethel Ayler and Frances Foster in
Nevis Mountain Dew. Photo:
Bert Andrews.

New American Theater

J.R. Sullivan
Artistic Director

Judith B. Rogers
Business/Development Director

117 South Wyman St.
Rockford, IL 61101
(815) 963-9454 (business)
(815) 964-8023 (box office)

Founded 1972
J.R. Sullivan

Season
September–June

Schedule
Evenings
Wednesday–Sunday
Matinees
Saturday

Facilities
118 South Main St.
Seating capacity: 270
Stage: thrust

Finances
June 1, 1978–May 31, 1979
$153,000 operating expenses
$ 95,000 earned income
$ 54,000 unearned income

Audience
Paid capacity: 46%
Subscribers: 1,374
Annual attendance: 20,862

Touring contact
Judith B. Rogers

Booked-in events
Theatre

AEA Guest Artist contract

New American Theater was founded to create a permanent, professional resident company performing a balanced seasonal repertoire. Particular focus, then and now, has been directed to the production of new and provocative works—especially the material of contemporary American dramatists.

Under the artistic direction of founder J.R. Sullivan, NAT has produced seven seasons, attracting new audiences to new plays while rounding out the repertoire with yearly inclusions of classic international works and plays of the American dramatic heritage. Intrinsic to this production policy has been the development of a diverse performance schedule allowing each resident member the fullest opportunity to realize his or her artistic potential.

New American Theater is committed to community involvement and has made itself a resource to Illinois/Wisconsin stateline area academic and community organizations. Principal in this involvement, however, was the establishment of the Young American Theater company. This organization has become a performing unit of Rockford and area high school students studying theatre in workshop sessions with the members of NAT's performing company. In addition to the regular workshop series, YAT performs two full productions each season on the theatre's stage and tours children's productions to stateline area schools and social centers. Another new program is Act/Interact, featuring original touring productions for senior citizens. A black theatre workshop is also offered.

NAT is planning a major relocation of expanded performance and administrative facilities, projected for opening early in 1981. In the meantime, and for the future, the company's goals and intent remain the same: the establishment of a quality regional theatre in this particular Illinois/Wisconsin stateline area, fully staffed with professional administrators and artists presenting seasons of variety and vitality.

Programs and services
Classes for nonprofessionals and children, artistic internships, student performances, programs-in-schools, study materials, student and senior citizen ticket discounts, regional touring, post-performance discussions, newsletter, speakers bureau, volunteer auxiliary.

Productions 1977-78
Winesburg, Ohio, Christopher Sergel, from Sherwood Anderson's novel
Anyone Can Whistle, book: Arthur Laurents; music and lyrics: Stephen Sondheim
Hay Fever, Noel Coward
The Hostage, Brendan Behan
Equus, Peter Shaffer
The Good Doctor, Neil Simon
Firehouse Rites, J.R. Sullivan
Born Yesterday, Garson Kanin

Productions 1978-79
The Belle of Amherst, William Luce
Vanities, Jack Heifner
Picnic, William Inge
Of Mice and Men, John Steinbeck
Two Gentlemen of Verona, book: John Guare and Mel Shapiro, from Shakespeare; music: Galt MacDermot; lyrics: J. Guare
Absurd Person Singular, Alan Ayckbourn
The School for Wives, Moliere; trans: Richard Wilbur
The Shadow Box, Michael Cristofer
The Duck Variations, David Mamet
Dunelawn, (from *Bad Habits*), Terrence McNally
Lovers, Brian Friel
The Last Meeting of the Knights of the White Magnolia, Preston Jones

Roberta Ingrassia and Rod MacDonald in *The Shadow Box*. Photo: David Bishop.

Ann R. O'Donnell, Brooks Gardner and C. Thomas Cunliffe in *The School for Wives*. Photo: Fred Hutcherson.

The New Dramatists

Kathleen Norris
Executive Director

Stephen Harty
Managing Director

424 West 44th St.
New York, NY 10036
(212) 757-6960

Founded 1949
Michaela O'Harra, John Golden,
Moss Hart, Oscar Hammerstein II,
Richard Rodgers,
Howard Lindsay, John Wharton

Season
September–July

Facilities
Theatre
Seating capacity: 100
Stage: modified thrust
Studio
Seating capacity: 40
Stage: arena

Finances
June 1, 1978–May 31, 1979
$109,000 operating expenses
$ 1,500 earned income
$109,000 unearned income

Audience
Annual attendance: 6,000

Joseph Warren, Diane Kagan and
Anne Meacham in *The Corridor*.
Photo: Meryl Joseph.

The New Dramatists was founded in 1949 to encourage and develop playwriting in America. In order to participate in the New Dramatists programs, a playwright applies for membership, submitting two full-length original scripts. These are evaluated by an admissions committee of active members. Once admitted, a playwright is a full participating member for a minimum of three and maximum of seven years.

The New Dramatists offers a range of programs for members, centered on the idea that playwriting is not only an art, but also a craft, and that knowing the basics of this craft is an essential complement to talent. Most members have already achieved a certain level of recognition before joining the New Dramatists, and all have demonstrated professional intent and exceptional promise. In the end, however, education, ambition, talent and dreams are only part of the prerequisite for becoming a

successful playwright. The New Dramatists can provide the second part, giving writers an opportunity to explore the "how" of their craft.

Programs include readings of works-in-progress, craft discussions, production observerships, a members' bulletin, library, loan fund and script analysis panels. The intangible components are more difficult to list: encouragement, support, membership in a community of writers, and perhaps most important–a belief in the goal.

New Dramatists alumni in the 30 years of its existence include such playwights as Robert Anderson, William Inge, Ed Bullins, Richard Foreman and John Guare. Current and alumni members have contributed more than 200 plays to the American theatre.

However, while commercial success for any member is gratifying and welcome, it is not the goal of the New Dramatists. Focused always on producing *playwrights* rather than plays, it is a workshop in the purest sense of the word: a place where work can be done, a climate and opportunity for inspiration, and the means to realize aspiration.

Programs and services

Artistic, administrative, and technical/production internships; free ticket distribution, post-performance discussions, workshop productions and staged readings, guest lecturers, poetry readings, newsletter, script publication, playwrights bulletin, theatre rentals.

Productions 1977-78
Losers, Donald Wollner
The Booth Brothers, Warren Kliewer
The Man Who Drew Circles, Steven Somkin
The Verandah, Clifford Mason
The Sugar Bowl, Stan Taikeff
Avenue B, Jack Gilhooley
Filigree People, Peter Dee
Marvelous Brown, Diane Kagan

Productions 1978-79
Father Dreams, Mary Gallagher
The Ravelle's Comeback, Jack Gilhooley
Flagship, Donald Wollner
Metro Park, Gene Radano
Singles, Robert Lord
The Corridor, Diane Kagan
Mothers and Daughters, John von Hartz
Roosters, Mitchell Yaven
A Cock to Asclepius, Stan Taikeff
Stray Vessels, Mitchell Yaven
Dancin' to Calliope, Jack Gilhooley
The Feathered Serpent, Edward H. Mabley

Andy Bloch, Kathy Danzer and
Tony Diaz in *Roosters*. Photo:
Meryl Joseph.

New Federal Theatre

Woodie King, Jr.
Director

Henry Street Settlement
466 Grand St.
New York, NY 10002
(212) 766-9295 (business)
(212) 766-9334 (box office)

Founded 1970
Woodie King, Jr.

Season
October–June

Facilities
Playhouse
Seating capacity: 350
Stage: proscenium

Finances
June 30, 1977–July 1, 1978
$305,000 operating expenses
$ 60,000 earned income
$175,000 unearned income

Audience
Paid capacity: 100%
Annual attendance: 32,000

Touring contact
Woodie King, Jr.

Booked-in events
Dance, music

AEA Showcase Code

The New Federal Theatre has carved a niche for itself in the theatrical world by bringing minority theatre to the audience for which the theatre was originally designed, Manhattan's lower east side, as well as the greater New York metropolitan area. At the same time, it has brought the work of minority playwrights and actors to national attention and has sponsored productions by various other ethnic theatres. The Henry Street Settlement's Arts for Living Center includes three theatres, rehearsal studios and modern stage equipment, all of which are made available to NFT.

Six to 10 showcase productions are offered each year, as well as several play readings, all designed to give playwrights the opportunity to review and improve a new work before possible production. NFT is currently reevaluating the "showcase" status of its productions and during the 1979-80 season, the company will explore the possibility of extending each production's run to a length of at least four weeks, while developing funding sources to make this possible. For several years, NFT has had a Rockefeller Foundation-supported playwright-in-residence. Two programs run by NFT, the Vocational Workshops Program and the Hispanic Playwright Workshop, have attracted considerable patronage.

Over the past nine years, NFT has produced more than 70 plays, bringing to public attention such dramatists as J.E. Franklin (whose *Black Girl* was filmed with several original cast members from NFT's production), Ron Milner, Ed Pomerantz, Joseph Lizardi and Ntozake Shange. Ed Bullins' *The Taking of Miss Janie* was the first play produced under a trial arrangement between NFT and the New York Shakespeare Festival whereby plays are showcased first at Henry Street and then produced at one of NYSF's theatres. Shange's *For Colored Girls who have Considered Suicide/When The Rainbow is Enuf* was the second, and its success has spread to Broadway and across the country. NFT productions have received *Village Voice* Obie, Drama Desk, Drama Critics Circle and Audelco awards, as well as an Antoinette Perry ("Tony") Award nomination.

Programs and services
Professional training in acting and production; classes for nonprofessionals; senior citizen ticket discounts, voucher program, workshop productions and staged readings, theatre rentals.

Productions 1977-78
Night Song, Patricia Lea
Season's Reasons, Ron Milner
The Block Party, Joseph Lizardi
African Interlude, Martie Evans-Charles
Do Lord Remember Me, James de Jongh
Run'ners, Ivey McCray
Birdland, music and lyrics adapt: Barry Amyer Kaleem; additional music: Elliot Weiss

Productions 1978-79
Hot Dishes!, book, music and lyrics: Maurice Peterson
Black Medea, Ernest Ferlita
Anna Lucasta, Philip Yordan
Take a Giant Step, Louis Peterson
Trouble in Mind, Alice Childress
In Splendid Error, William Branch
A Raisin in the Sun, Lorraine Hansberry
Take It from the Top, music and lyrics: Ruby Dee
Flamingo Flomingo, book, music and lyrics: Lucky Cienfuego
The Glorious Monster in the Bell of the Horn, Larry Neal

Thomas Anderson, Elizabeth Van Dyke, Marcella Lowery, Rony Clanton and Debbie Allen in *Anna Lucasta.* Photo: Bert Andrews.

Do Lord Remember Me.

New Jersey Shakespeare Festival

Paul Barry
Artistic Director/Producer

Edward G. Cimbala
Managing Director

Ellen Barry
Associate Director

Drew University
Madison, NJ 07940
(201) 377-5330 (business)
(201) 377-4487 (box office)

Founded 1963
Paul Barry

Season
June–November

Schedule
Evenings
Tuesday–Sunday

Facilities
Bowne Theatre
Seating capacity: 238
Stage: thrust

Finances
Jan. 1, 1978–Dec. 31, 1978
$230,000 operating expenses
$169,000 earned income
$ 76,000 unearned income

Audience
Paid capacity: 80%
Subscribers: 2,424
Annual attendance: 29,017

Booked-in events
Mime, drama, dance, music

AEA LORT (D) contract

Nicola Sheara and Eric Booth in
Hamlet. Photo: Blair Holley.

The New Jersey Shakespeare Festival began in 1963 with a single play, *The Taming of the Shrew,* offered as part of a 10-play stock season at the Cape May Playhouse. Staging the classics at the Jersey shore seemed madness, but the company enjoyed internal subsidy (alternating commercial and noncommercial fare) to build toward a resident professional company, dedicated to the great plays of the English, Irish and American traditions, performed in rotating repertory. At least two Shakespeare plays were staged each year.

By 1968 NJSF's repertoire grew to three plays during the stock season. Three fall residencies in Boston and two fall tours of New Jersey schools were mounted, along with five summer seasons. In 1970 the first full repertory season was staged and two years later, having had two theatres demolished and recognizing that the resort economy could not provide a year-round constituency, NJSF moved north to Drew University.

After seven Madison seasons, the festival now plays 20-23 weeks of six plays in repertory, with 12 Monday Night Specials (guest attractions of dance, drama, mime and music) as an additional audience lure. The festival has staged 119 productions, including 35

Shakespeare works. It is an actor's theatre, composed of classically trained actors attracted by creative freedom, true repertory structure and a variety of plays, with classical and modern works back-to-back. Innovative productions have included a World War II *Coriolanus,* an 1890s Viennese *Measure for Measure* and a Roman "black Mass" *Titus Andronicus.*

NJSF's intern program attracts hundreds of applicants annually, from which about 80 are selected. Many interns have gone on to join the professional company. Over the past seven years, the number of contributors has increased fivefold. Subscriptions in 1978 increased 55 percent and represented 161 communities, and audiences have been at near-capacity levels with waiting lines for many performances. NJSF has been fortunate in having no accumulated deficit and is conducting a capital fund drive for a new facility.

Programs and services
Professional training in acting, design, production and administration; artistic, administrative and technical/production internships; student performances, programs-in-schools, Audience Symposia series, free ticket distribution, student ticket discounts, corporate coupon books, post-performance discussions, workshop productions and staged readings, children's theatre, Monday Night Specials, subscriber and guild newsletters, speakers bureau, volunteer auxiliary, annual fund-raising art auction.

Productions 1978
Hamlet, William Shakespeare
Love's Labour's Lost, William Shakespeare
Rosencrantz and Guildenstern Are Dead, Tom Stoppard
The Country Girl, Clifford Odets
Arms and the Man, George Bernard Shaw
Who's Afraid of Virginia Woolf?, Edward Albee

Productions 1979
King Lear, William Shakespeare
A Midsummer Night's Dream, William Shakespeare
A Streetcar Named Desire, Tennessee Williams
The Importance of Being Earnest, Oscar Wilde
Travesties, Tom Stoppard
Two for the Seesaw, William Gibson
Luv, Murray Schisgal

Richard Graham, Martha J. Brown and Margery Shaw in *King Lear.*

The New Playwrights' Theatre of Washington

Harry M. Bagdasian
Producing Director

1742 Church St., NW
Washington, DC 20036
(202) 232-1122

Founded 1972
Harry M. Bagdasian

Season
July–June

Schedule
Evenings
Wednesday–Sunday
Matinees
Saturday

Facilities
Seating capacity: 125
Stage: flexible

Finances
July 1, 1978–June 30, 1979
$236,000 operating expenses
$126,000 earned income
$ 89,000 unearned income

Audience
Paid capacity: 64%
Subscribers: 1,157
Annual attendance: 12,350

Under the direction of Harry M. Bagdasian since its inception in June 1972, the New Playwrights' Theatre of Washington (NPTW) has proven itself to be a vital and successful incubator for new plays and playwriting talent. Its founders were, and continue to be, staunch believers that the nation's capital should have a noncommercial theatre devoted exclusively to the creation and production of new plays and musicals by American playwrights and composers.

Good drama cannot be completely created at the typewriter and is best fostered in a noncommercial environment. To this end, the NPTW staff, along with an ever-expanding board of trustees, is working to build a center for such work in Washington, D.C. In addition to its mainstage performance series and works-in-progress reading series, the theatre is developing an ongoing formal training and workshop program, where artists in all theatre-support fields can come together for advanced training and focus their talents in assisting the development of new works.

The first two years of activity found the company operating in a 26-seat basement theatre, producing eight programs of new one-act plays, and slowly gaining the attention of the press and an audience of adventurous theatregoers. For the next two years, the company led a nomadic existence, performing in found spaces and borrowed stages throughout the city. The company finally settled in an old gymnasium in Washington's Dupont Circle area, and NPTW has been working there continuously, year-round, to aid in the development of new plays and musicals.

Now entering its eighth season of work with new playwrights, the company is pleased to see that many of the plays and musicals developed at its small theatre in Washington, D.C., have gone on to be produced on professional stages throughout the country.

Programs and services
Professional training in acting, directing, playwriting and design; ticket discounts for students, senior citizens, the military and the unemployed; free ticket distribution, post-performance discussions, workshop productions and staged readings, guest lecturers, newsletter, speakers bureau, volunteer auxiliary, theatre rentals.

Productions 1977-78
Sweet and Hot: The Songs of Harold Arlen, music and lyrics: Harold Arlen, et al.; adapt: Ken Bloom and Berthe Schuchat
Pinnacle: A Play About Needlepoint and Other Crafts, Mark Stein
Nightmare!, book, music and lyrics: Tim Grundmann
The House of Bedlam, Kenneth Arnold
Hamlet!, William Shakespeare; adapt: John Neville-Andrews
White Horse/Black Horse, Steven Stosny

Productions 1978-79
Out to Lunch, book, music and lyrics: Tim Grundmann
A Whitman Sonata, adapt: Paul Hildebrand, Jr., and Thom Wagner; music: T. Wagner
Splendid Rebels, Ernest Joselovitz
A Christmas Carol, adapt: Harry M. Bagdasian
Breaking the Sweet Glass, Mark Stein
Down One, Barbara Keiler
Eddie's Catchy Tunes, book, music and lyrics: Tim Grundmann

Carmen Vickers, Jan Frederick Shiffman and A. David Johnson in *Hamlet!* Photo: Doc Dougherty.

Agnes Cummings, Jan Frederick Shiffman and Barbara Rappaport in *Eddie's Catchy Tunes.* Photo: Doc Dougherty.

New York Shakespeare Festival

Joseph Papp
Producer

Robert Kamlot
General Manager

Public Theater
425 Lafayette St.
New York, NY 10003
(212) 598-7100 (business)
(212) 598-7150 (Public box office)
(212) 535-5630
(Delacorte box office)

Founded 1954
Joseph Papp

Season
Year-round

Schedule
Evenings
Tuesday–Sunday
Matinees
Saturday, Sunday

Facilities
Newman Theater
Seating capacity: 299
Stage: proscenium
Anspacher Theater
Seating capacity: 275
Stage: thrust
Martinson Hall/Cabaret Theater
Seating capacity: 191
Stage: flexible
LuEsther Hall
Seating capacity: 135-150
Stage: flexible
Other Stage
Seating capacity: 75-108
Stage: flexible
Old Prop Shop
Seating capacity: 55-93
Stage: flexible
Little Theater (Cinema)
Seating capacity: 96

Delacorte Theater, Central Park
Seating capacity: 1,936
Stage: thrust
Mobile Theater
Seating capacity: 1,500
Stage: flexible

Finances
July 1, 1978–June 30, 1979
$7,432,000 operating expenses
$5,764,000 earned income
$1,669,000 unearned income

Audience
Paid capacity: 76%
Public subscribers: 9,500
Delacorte subscribers: 10,000
Total annual attendance:
  3,109,000

*AEA Showcase Code,
Production, LORT (B) and
Off Broadway contracts*

Christopher Plummer, Barbara eda-Young, Carrie Horner, James Naughton and John Kimbrough in *Drinks Before Dinner*. Photo: Martha Swope.

Roscoe Orman, Sonny Jim Gaines and Gylan Kain in *Julius Caesar*. Photo: Bert Andrews.

Under the leadership of Joseph Papp, the New York Shakespeare Festival has been producing plays for nearly a quarter-century, attracting prominent as well as aspiring theatre talent from across the country.

Each summer, the Festival presents free Shakespeare at the Delacorte Theater in Central Park, as well as admission-free performances on the Mobile Theater, which tours New York City parks and playgrounds. Year-round the Festival operates the Public Theater, a landmark building converted to a seven-theatre complex where more than 20 productions, both new plays and classics, are produced each season. In addition, weekly series for jazz, film and poetry aficionados are featured at the Public.

Many Festival productions which originated either in Central Park or at the Public Theater have found continued life on Broadway, Off Broadway, with national touring companies and on network television. Its plays have also been produced at various theatres throughout the U.S. and abroad. Because of the volume of activity generated each season and the size of its audience and annual budget, the New York Shakespeare Festival is widely regarded as one of the foremost theatrical institutions in the country.

Programs and services

Artistic, administrative and technical/production internships; study materials and research archives (Lincoln Center Library for the Performing Arts), student and senior citizen ticket discounts, free ticket distribution, local touring company and national touring of mainstage productions, post-performance discussions, workshop productions and staged readings, film series, guest lecturers, poetry readings, voucher program, cabaret, newsletter, weekly events calendar, playwrights workshop, cooperative programs with other Off Broadway theatres.

Productions 1977-78

The Threepenny Opera, book and lyrics: Bertolt Brecht; trans: Ralph Manheim and John Willett; music: Kurt Weill
Agamemnon, Aeschylus; adapt: Andrei Serban and Elizabeth Swados; music: E. Swados

Unfinished Women Cry in No Man's Land While a Bird Dies in a Gilded Cage, book and lyrics: Aishah Rahman; music: Jackie McLean
Miss Margarida's Way, Roberto Athayde
Landscape of the Body, John Guare
The Misanthrope, Moliere; trans: Richard Wilbur; music: Jobriath Boone, Margaret Pine and Arthur Bienstock
Tales of the Hasidim, Martin Buber; adapt: Paul Sills
The Mandrake, Niccolo Macchiavelli; trans: Wallace Shawn
A Photograph: A Study of Cruelty, Ntozake Shange
The Dybbuk, S. Ansky; trans: Mira Rafalowicz
The Water Engine, David Mamet
A Prayer for My Daughter, Thomas Babe
Museum, Tina Howe
Curse of the Starving Class, Sam Shepard
Runaways, book, music and lyrics: Elizabeth Swados
I'm Getting My Act Together and Taking It on the Road, book and lyrics: Gretchen Cryer; music: Nancy Ford
Man-Wo-Man:
  Michael, Ed Bullins
  Passion Without Reason, Neil Harris

Productions 1978-79

All's Well That Ends Well, William Shakespeare
The Taming of the Shrew, William Shakespeare
An Evening at New Rican Village, music and lyrics adapt: Eduardo Figueroa
Drinks Before Dinner, E. L. Doctorow
The Umbrellas of Cherbourg, book and lyrics: Jacques Demy; trans: Sheldon Harnick and Charles Burr; music: Michel Legrand
Julius Caesar, William Shakespeare
Coriolanus, William Shakespeare
Taken in Marriage, Thomas Babe
Sancocho, book: Ramiro (Ray) Ramirez; music and lyrics: Jimmy Justice and R. Ramirez
Dispatches, music and lyrics: Elizabeth Swados, from Michael Herr's book
Wake Up, It's Time to Go to Bed!, Carson Kievman
The Woods, David Mamet
Happy Days, Samuel Beckett
Spell #7, Ntozake Shange

North Light Repertory Company

Gregory Kandel
Producing Director

Robert Kershaw
General Manager

2300 Green Bay Road
Evanston, IL 60201
(312) 869-7732 (business)
(312) 869-7278 (box office)

Founded 1974
Gregory Kandel

Season
October–May

Schedule
Evenings
Tuesday–Sunday
Matinees
Saturday, Sunday

Facilities
Kingsley Theatre
Seating capacity: 292
Stage: proscenium
Noyes Auditorium
Seating capacity: 200
Stage: proscenium

Finances
July 1, 1978–June 30, 1979
$238,000 operating expenses
$ 99,000 earned income
$127,000 unearned income

Audience
Paid capacity: 66%
Subscribers: 3,950
Annual attendance: 79,215

Touring contact
Gregory Kandel

AEA LORT (D) contract

North Light Repertory Company was founded in 1974 as the Evanston Theatre Company. Among its more significant contributions to Chicago theatre have been its regional premieres of David Mamet's *The Duck Variations,* Tom Stoppard's *Jumpers,* Edward Albee's *Seascape* and Lanford Wilson's *The Mound Builders.*

NLR has been moving quickly toward its goal of presenting new plays by a resident company of actors. The mainstage season now includes five productions of contemporary plays which reflect upon our modern times. In order to provide the mainstage with new works, North Light has instituted a second stage, presently in the form of a New American Plays Festival each spring; a series of monthly readings of works-in-progress; and a year-long residency for playwrights. One of NLR's prime operating tenets is that the author should be a full partner in the production process.

NLR is unusual in that its corporate charter calls for professional productions *and* outreach programming. Among the latter, all specially funded, are creative drama for the elderly; two children's touring companies; touring to high schools; classes for nonprofessionals; Humanities Forum, a series of post-performance discussions; Artists' Perspective, a series of pre-opening lectures; and college level internships.

NLR has recently completed extensive negotiations with the City of Evanston and the local school district and, with their support, will take over an open school for its new facility this fall.

North Light has always been committed to the growth of Chicago's indigenous theatre industry and is one of the founders of the new League of Chicago Theatres (LCT), of which its producing director Gregory Kandel is the first president.

Programs and services
Classes for nonprofessionals and children; administrative and technical/production internships, creative drama for the elderly, study materials, student and senior citizen ticket discounts, voucher program, children's theatre touring, pre-opening and post-performance discussions, workshop productions and staged readings, guest lecturers, newsletter, speakers bureau, volunteer auxiliary, theatre rentals.

Productions 1977-78
The Goodbye People, Herb Gardner
The Mound Builders, Lanford Wilson
Oh, Coward!, music and lyrics: Noel Coward; adapt: Roderick Cook

Productions 1978-79
That Championship Season, Jason Miller
Coming of Age, Frank Cucci
The Horse Latitudes and *The Pokey,* Stephen Black
The Club, music and lyrics adapt: Eve Merriam

Mary Seibel, Judith Ivey and Camilla Hawk in *The Mound Builders.* Photo: Kate Lewis.

The Club. Photo: Lisa Ebright.

Odyssey Theatre Ensemble

Ron Sossi
Artistic Director

Beth Hogan
Administrative Director

12111 Ohio Ave.
Los Angeles, CA 90025
jjw(213) 879-5221 (business)
(213) 826-1626 (box office)

Founded 1968
Ron Sossi

Season
January–December

Schedule
Evenings
Wednesday–Sunday

Facilities
Odyssey 1
Seating capacity: 99
Stage: flexible
Odyssey 2
Seating capacity: 99
Stage: thrust

Finances
July 1, 1978–June 30, 1979
$124,000 operating expenses
$114,000 earned income
$ 10,500 unearned income

Audience
Paid capacity: 78%
Subscribers: 1,160
Annual attendance: 17,000

Touring contact
Ron Sossi

Booked-in events
Dance, music, childen's
and experimental theatre

AEA 99-seat waiver

Franklyn Seales in *Woyzeck*.

Often regarded as a maverick operation in a city dominated by "industry showcase" theatres and more conservative fare, the Odyssey Theatre Ensemble is an experimental theatre company. Firmly dedicated to expanding the boundaries of the medium, radically revitalizing the classics, giving exposure to the best exploratory work from other parts of the world and evolving new theatre works, Odyssey is successfully cultivating a West Coast audience with a taste for the unusual.

Odyssey's 1979 season saw the creation of a vital new work in *The Chicago Conspiracy Trial,* (slated for a New York production and a feature film release), the Off Broadway opening of the Ensemble's controversial *An Evening of Dirty Religious Plays* at the Performing Garage, a California Arts Council–funded statewide tour of Polish playwright Tadeusz Rosewicz's *White Marriage,* the West Coast premiere of Sam Shepard's *Suicide in B Flat* and a unique new production of Brecht's *Baal.* Subscriptions more than tripled and general audience increased by nearly 100 percent.

The year 1980 has been targeted for the conversion of one of Odyssey's 99-seat houses to a 300-seat facility capable of supporting a full-time resident company, preparing the way for the eventual opening of a large-scale, four-theatre complex—an international experimental theatre center.

Programs and services
Professional training in acting, production and administration; artistic, administrative and technical/production internships; student performances, programs-in-schools, student and senior citizen ticket discounts, free ticket distribution, national touring, post-performance discussions, workshop productions and staged readings, guest lecturers, newsletter, speakers bureau, theatre rentals.

Productions 1977-78
An Evening of Dirty Religious Plays:
    Noonday Demons, Peter Barnes
    A Theological Position, Robert Coover
The Threepenny Opera, book and lyrics: Bertolt
    Brecht; trans: Marc Blitzstein; music: Kurt
    Weill
Don Juan, Moliere
Woyzeck, Georg Büchner

Productions 1978-79
The Underpants, Carl Sternheim
The Soft Touch, Neil Cuthbert
White Marriage, Tadeusz Rozewicz
The Chicago Conspiracy Trial, Frank Condon
    and Ron Sossi
Suicide in B Flat, Sam Shepard

Shelly Parsons in *Suicide in B Flat.* Photo: Mitchell Rose.

Old Creamery Theatre Company

Thomas P. Johnson
Artistic Director

Box 160
Garrison, IA 52229
(319) 477-3925 (business)
(319) 477-3165 (box office)

Founded 1971
Thomas P. Johnson

Season
May–October

Schedule
Evenings
Thursday–Sunday
Matinees
Sunday

Facilities
Seating capacity: 265
Stage: thrust

Finances
July 1, 1978–June 30, 1979
$244,000 operating expenses
$134,000 earned income
$121,000 unearned income

Audience
Paid capacity: 60%
Subscribers: 1,000
Annual attendance: 75,000

Touring contact
Thomas P. Johnson

Perhaps the most frequently asked question that any member of the Old Creamery Theatre Company has to answer is, "Why Garrison?" Why would anyone want to start a theatre in a small community in the middle of rural Iowa that is not only far from Broadway, but is quite a ways from almost everything?

When pressed, artistic director Thomas P. Johnson finds it difficult to recall the exact reasons that brought his theatre to Garrison in 1971, though they were largely economic.

"We were young and idealistic and strongly committed to the notion that everyone should have an opportunity to see live theatre on a regular basis, regardless of where he or she lives," says Johnson. "We believed that with a combination of touring and resident theatre we could provide top-quality live theatre to a large number of people in the rural Midwest who otherwise would not be exposed. The problem was that there was no money."

Garrison provided an inexpensive base of operation. There was ample cheap housing, a rehearsal and performance space that could be purchased for very little, and several abandoned buildings that could be used for second-hand building materials. In short, Garrison offered many financial advantages that a city could not.

Eight years later, the original commitment is still there. The difference is the breadth and depth of that commitment. It has doubled and redoubled and is now shared by thousands of people. "We are no longer 10 youngsters with an impossible dream," according to Johnson. "We are the 50 who make up the company; we are the 26,000 who came to the theatre last year; we are the 76,000 school children who watched a performance of our touring show; we are the folks who bring out-of-town visitors to a performance they are proud of; we are the busloads of senior citizens who come to the theatre on Sunday afternoons; we are the season-ticket buyers; we are the contributors; we are the businesses and industries who value our presence; we are the board members, the bankers, the farmers, the clerks, the lawyers, the factory workers, the teachers, the everyday citizens who live and work in Iowa and are glad that there is an Old Creamery Theatre."

Programs and services
Professional training in acting, directing, design, production and administration; classes for nonprofessionals and children; artistic, administrative and technical/production internships; student performances, programs-in-schools, student and senior citizen ticket discounts, free ticket distribution, regional touring, post-performance discussions, children's theatre, newsletter, speakers bureau, volunteer auxiliary.

Productions 1978
The Star-Spangled Girl, Neil Simon
Ten Little Indians, Agatha Christie
A Flea in Her Ear, Georges Feydeau
Death of a Salesman, Arthur Miller
The Matchmaker, Thornton Wilder
Godspell, book: John-Michael Tebelak; music and lyrics: Stephen Schwartz
There's a Girl in My Soup, Terence Frisby
The Comedy Connection, various writers

Productions 1979
Private Lives, Noel Coward
A Streetcar Named Desire, Tennessee Williams
The Lady from Maxim's, Georges Feydeau; adapt: Gene Feist
Not Tonight Dear, I Have a Headache, adapt: Howard Blanning, from Moliere's *The Imaginary Invalid*
Two by Two, book: Peter Stone; music: Richard Rodgers; lyrics: Martin Charnin
Last of the Red Hot Lovers, Neil Simon

Pat O'Brien in *The Miser.*

Stephen Spinella, Lois Renken and Sherry Hoopes in *The Mousetrap.*

Old Globe Theatre

Craig Noel
Producing Director

Robert E. McGlade
General Manager

Box 2171
San Diego, CA 92112
(714) 231-1941 (business)
(714) 239-2255 (box office)

Founded 1937

Season
October– September

Schedule
Evenings
Tuesday–Sunday
Matinees
Saturday (summer only),
Sunday (year-round)

Facilities
Edison Centre for the
Performing Arts
El Prado, Balboa Park
Festival Stage
Seating capacity: 606
Stage: thrust
Spreckels Theatre
Seating capacity: 960
Stage: flexible
Cassius Carter Centre Stage
Seating capacity: 245
Stage: arena

Finances
Oct. 1, 1977–Sept. 30, 1978
$1,560,000 operating expenses
$1,190,000 earned income
$ 151,000 unearned income

Audience
Old Globe Theatre
(destroyed by fire March 1978)
Paid capacity: 64%
Subscribers: 11, 409
Festival Stage
Paid capacity: 97%
Cassius Carter Centre Stage
Paid capacity: 72% summer,
 87% rest of year
Subscribers: 6,185
Total annual attendance: 233,000

Touring contact
Carole Marget

Booked-in events
Dance, music, theatre

AEA LORT (B) contract

Jean-Pierre Stewart and
Katherine McGrath in *A
Midsummer Night's Dream.*
Photo: Bill Reid.

Victor Buono in *The Last of the
Marx Brothers' Writers.* Photo: Bill
Reid.

"Fire" has been the dominant word in the Old Globe Theatre's vocabulary since March 8, 1978. An arsonist set a conflagration outside the stage-left entrance which destroyed the 43-year-old landmark. Alert fire crews saved the production and administrative areas from damage, as well as the adjacent Carter Centre Stage where *Old Times* continued that night on schedule. After a six-day hiatus to arrange for a temporary home, notify patrons, build scenery and props, obtain lighting and sound equipment and emotionally cope with new circumstances, *The Sunshine Boys* continued its run at the Spreckels Theatre in downtown San Diego, where the remainder of the spring season and the five-production 1978-79 season was performed.

At the time of the fire, plans were being formulated for the 29th San Diego National Shakespeare Festival to begin within three months. Immediately following the fire, Richard L. Hay, principal designer of the Oregon Shakespearean Festival, designed a 600-seat thrust stage amphitheatre, constructed in a natural canyon within the Old Globe compound. Exactly 100 days after the fire, the annual summer season opened on the new Festival Stage. Before the ruins had cooled, fund-raising activities began to rebuild the Old Globe Theatre. A $6 million goal to rebuild and remodel the outdated production and administrative areas was established.

Community leadership has played a major role in encouraging the contribution of funds from individuals, organizations, corporations, foundations and governmental agencies. A previously unknown benefactress came forward with a major financial contribution to honor the life and memory of her late husband, Simon Edison. The three-theatre complex—comprising the Old Globe Theatre, the Cassius Carter Centre Stage and the Festival Stage—was named the Edison Centre for the Performing Arts on June 11, 1979. Despite the loss of a much loved and historic theatre, artistic accomplishments continued unabated. The number of productions was undiminished, ancillary theatrical activities thrived and attendance was maintained near levels prior to the fire.

The 1979-80 mainstage subscription series has taken up residence at the California Theatre in downtown San Diego, while the Cassius Carter Centre Stage still maintains its independent three-production season slate.

Programs and services
Classes for children; artistic, administrative and technical/production internships; student performances, programs-in-schools; student, senior citizen and military ticket discounts; statewide touring, workshop productions and staged readings, newsletter, souvenir book, volunteer auxiliary.

Productions 1977-78
The Last of the Marx Brothers' Writers, Louis Phillips
Too True to Be Good, George Bernard Shaw
Sleuth, Anthony Shaffer
The Sunshine Boys, Neil Simon
The Lion in Winter, James Goldman
That Championship Season, Jason Miller
Exit the King, Eugene Ionesco
The Seagull, Anton Chekhov; trans: Stark Young
Old Times, Harold Pinter
Loot, Joe Orton
How the Other Half Loves, Alan Ayckbourn
Henry V, William Shakespeare
A Midsummer Night's Dream, William Shakespeare
The Winter's Tale, William Shakespeare

Productions 1978-79
The Robber Bridegroom, book and lyrics: Alfred Uhry; music: Robert Waldman
Present Laughter, Noel Coward
Toys in the Attic, Lillian Hellman
The Front Page, Ben Hecht and Charles MacArthur
Equus, Peter Shaffer
Otherwise Engaged, Simon Gray
The Enchanted, Jean Giraudoux; trans: Maurice Valency
The Misanthrope, Moliere; trans: Tony Harrison
A Delicate Balance, Edward Albee
The Caretaker, Harold Pinter
Julius Caesar, William Shakespeare
The Comedy of Errors, William Shakespeare
Macbeth, William Shakespeare
The Norman Conquests, Alan Ayckbourn
 Table Manners
 Living Together
 Round and Round the Garden

Omaha Magic Theatre

JoAnn Schmidman
Artistic Director

2309 Hanscom Blvd.
Omaha, NE 68105
(402) 342-2821 (business)
(402) 346-1227 (box office)

Founded 1969
JoAnn Schmidman

Season
September–August

Schedule
Evenings
Friday–Sunday
Matinees
Variable

Facilities
1417 Farnam St.
Seating capacity: 75-100
Stage: flexible

Finances
Sept. 1, 1978–Aug. 31, 1979
$106,000 operating expenses
$ 8,000 earned income
$ 97,000 unearned income

Audience
Paid capacity: 75%
Annual attendance: 8,070

Touring contact
JoAnn Schmidman

Booked-in events
Theatre, film festivals, music

During 1979, Omaha Magic Theatre celebrated its 10th year of bringing ''new'' American musical theatre to the Omaha community and the surrounding four-state area. Since its inception, OMT has been under the artistic direction of JoAnn Schmidman (formerly a member of Joseph Chaikin's Open Theater in New York). Since Schmidman founded the theatre in 1969, more than 50 new musicals in a ''transformational'' style have been produced, and many have toured the country. OMT mounts three or four productions per year, all developed with the playwright, director and composer in residence for the entire developmental process. The theatre serves as a training ground for new composers, designers, directors, actors and writers.

OMT is a ''humanist'' theatre, dedicated to presenting a well-rounded view of contemporary social issues. In recent years, productions that have been developed and premiered at OMT have included a musical about running and jogging *(Running Gag)*, a view of life inside a women's prison *(Babes in the Bighouse)* and the changing American language *(American King's English for Queens)*.

During 1978, in response to the national demand for scripts of original plays, the OMT made available to educators and theatres across the country the complete production package for Megan Terry's *American King's English for Queens*. A second Terry musical, *Babes in the Bighouse*, was published in April 1979. Schmidman's *Running Gag* is scheduled for publication late in 1979.

''Soft sculpture'' set pieces and props are employed for OMT plays to provide quick, easy, lightweight set-ups and strikes for touring. The pieces also facilitate the maintenance of the company's ever-growing repertoire.

The OMT company activities are quite diversified. Touring plays are presented to senior citizens, high school and college students, and in penal institutions. Open community workshops (sessions in acting, movement, story-telling, voice, writing and drawing) are provided, frequently to groups of youths or senior citizens.

The theatre facilities are barrier-free. However, to better serve all handicapped citizens, a sign language interpreter will be added for future productions.

Programs and services
Professional training in acting, directing, production and administration; classes for nonprofessionals and children; artistic, administrative and technical/production internships; student performances, programs-in-schools, study materials; ticket discounts for students, senior citizens and the disadvantaged; free ticket distribution, national touring, post-performance discussions, workshop productions and staged readings, film series, guest lecturers, newsletter, script publication, speakers bureau, theatre rentals, prison and senior citizen institution workshops.

Productions 1977-78
Astral White, book: Mimi Loring; music: Donna Young, Lynn Herrick and Mechelle Keller; lyrics: company developed
American King's English for Queens, book and lyrics: Megan Terry; music: Lynn Herrick and Donna Young
Babes in the Bighouse, book and lyrics: Megan Terry; music: John Sheehan
The Gray Express: A Mystery, book and lyrics: James Larson; music: Nancy Larson
100,001 Horror Stories of the Plains, book and lyrics: Megan Terry and company; music: Nancy Larson
Pro Game, book and lyrics: Megan Terry; music: JoAnn Schmidman
Brazil Fado, book and lyrics: Megan Terry; music: Nancy Larson and company

Productions 1978-79
Astral White
100,001 Horror Stories of the Plains
American King's English for Queens
Running Gag, book: JoAnn Schmidman; music: Marianne de Pury and Lynn Herrick; lyrics: Megan Terry
Goona Goona, book and lyrics: Megan Terry; music: Lynn Herrick

Running Gag. Photo: Mary Easterling.

Astral White. Photo: Megan Terry.

O'Neill Theater Center

George C. White
President

Lloyd Richards
Artistic Director
National Playwrights Conference

1860 Broadway
Suite 601
New York, NY 10023
(212) 246-1485

305 Great Neck Road
Waterford, CT 06385
(203) 443-5378 (business)
(203) 443-1238 (box office)
(212) 925-5032
(New York direct line)

Founded 1964
George C. White

Season
July–August

Facilities
Waterford, CT
Theatre Barn
Seating capacity: 200
Stage: thrust
Amphitheatre
Seating capacity: 300
Stage: thrust
Instant Theatre
Seating capacity: 200
Stage: arena
Barn El
Seating capacity: 200
Stage: flexible

Finances
July 1, 1978–June 30, 1979
$2,481,000 operating expenses
$1,819,000 earned income
$ 888,000 unearned income

Audience
Paid capacity: 37%
Annual attendance: 3,500

AEA LORT (C) contract

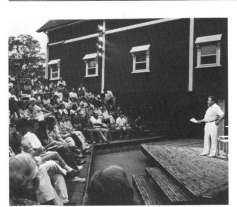

Lloyd Richards greets the audience at the 1979 National Playwrights Conference.

The Eugene O'Neill Theater Center is celebrating its 15th year in 1979 as an umbrella organization supporting and nurturing varied projects in theatre research, development and education. The National Playwrights Conference was the center's first project and has been under the artistic direction of Lloyd Richards 10 years.

NPC was formed at the suggestion of several American playwrights of whom George C. White, the O'Neill's founder and president, asked the question, "What can the American theatre do for you?" The writers wanted a place where they could work with other theatre professionals on the development of new scripts, where they could have the freedom to fail, far from the reach of criticism and the "demands" of an audience. Over the years, NPC has attempted to be that place, encouraging experimentation, exploration and the unembellished creative experience as the basis of all work. In 1976, NPC inaugurated the New Drama for Television Project, designed to give playwrights an opportunity to conceive and develop original material specifically for television. In 15 years, NPC has staged 211 new plays by 155 playwrights.

Concurrent with NPC is the National Critics Institute, a professional workshop, directed by Ernest Schier, which is designed to help critics explore the performing arts and to expand their interpretative writing skills. In 1978, two more O'Neill projects began—the Choreographers Conference and the Composer/Librettist Conference, both under Joseph Krakora's direction and fashioned after NPC.

Another center program is the National Theater Institute, a professional training program for college students under the direction of Lawrence J. Wilker. The O'Neill also sponsors the Creative Arts in Education Program, directed by Joyce Schmidt. The center houses the Monte Cristo Cottage Museum and Library, of which Sally Pavetti is curator, as well as the National and Little Theatres of the Deaf, both under David Hays' artistic direction (see separate listing). The center publishes the *National Playwrights Directory*, edited by Phyllis Kaye.

Programs and services
Professional training for college students; administrative internships, teacher training, newsletter, volunteer auxiliary.

Productions 1978
Threads, Jonathan Bolt
Getting Off, Lee Thomas
Sightlines, Mark Eisman
The Gayden Chronicles, Michael Cook
Texas Dry, John Olive
Put Them All Together, Anne Commire
the bloodrite, owa
No English Spoken, Stephen Davis Parks
All Honorable Men, Michael J. Chepiga
Friends, Crispin Larangeira
China Beach, Brian J. McFadden
Beggar's Choice, Kathleen Betsko
Leela Means to Play, Beverley Simons
Bent, Martin Sherman

Productions 1979
Snow-Pressings, Ray Aranha
She Also Dances, Kenneth Arnold
Pen, Barbara Field
Showdown at the Adobe Motel, Lanny Flaherty
Kernel of Sanity, Kermit Frazier
House of Cards, Theodore Gross
Fob, David Henry Hwang
Whispers, Crispin Larangeira
Terry by Terry, Mark Leib
Wives, Lynda Myles
Skidding into Slow Time, Stephen Davis Parks
Agnes of God, John Pielmeier

Mary-Joan Negro (back to camera), Sheldon Larry, Bob Shontell, Sandra Bertrand and Grayson Hall rehearse the 1978 New Drama for Television production of *Chameleon.* Photo: Jonathan Brandeis.

Ontological-Hysteric Theater

Richard Foreman
Artistic Director

Performing Artservices
463 West St.
New York, NY 10014
(212) 989-4953

Founded 1968
Richard Foreman

Season
December–May

Finances
July 1, 1978–June 30, 1979
$48,400 operating expenses
$41,300 unearned income

Audience
Annual attendance: 750

Touring contact
Performing Artservices

Ontological-Hysteric Theater was founded by Richard Foreman in 1968, and since then it has produced 16 Foreman scripts in the United States and Europe. In addition, Foreman has traveled to various universities and museums across the U.S. to mount productions or produce videotapes of his work using local actors and technicians.

In its early years, the theatre's work was based upon a sort of phenomenological analysis of act, gesture, speech and object. During the last few years, however, the focus of the work has shifted so that the pieces now document with great rapidity in performance the ever-shifting relations between many complicated production and textural elements.

Foreman's works are always created with the company rehearsing in the fully completed set for the entire rehearsal period. From 1974 to 1979, the company maintained its own theatre space. Its unique stage shape (14 feet wide and 80 feet deep) led to a variety of scenic innovations which played a major part in determining the style of performance. The company will seek out different performance spaces for future productions.

Ontological-Hysteric Theater presents one new play each season in New York City and a new European production every two or three years. During the 1978-79 season, the company produced its first feature-length film, *Strong Medicine*, written and directed by Foreman.

The aesthetic roots and concerns of Ontological-Hysteric Theater have often been described as more closely related to 20th-century painting, poetry and music than to existing theatrical traditions. While that is true to a certain extent, Foreman's work continues to notate his own day-by-day efforts to evolve a completely new theatrical grammar, one that reflects the processes and difficulties and "accidents" of the consciousness-at-work.

A book on the theatre's work, *Richard Foreman: Plays and Manifestos*, was published by the New York University Press in 1976. The theatre will present two major new works during the 1979-80 season: *Madness and Tranquility (My Head Was a Sledgehammer)* in New York and *Energy* in Rome, Italy.

Programs and services
Lectures, seminars, international touring.

Productions 1977-79
Blvd. de Paris: I've Got the Shakes, Richard Foreman

Blvd. de Paris: I've Got the Shakes. Photo: Nathaniel Tileston.

Blvd. de Paris: I've Got the Shakes. Photo: Babette Mangolte.

Oregon Shakespearean Festival

Jerry Turner
Producing Director

William W. Patton
General Manager

Box 158
Ashland, OR 97520
(503) 482-2111 (business)
(503) 482-4331 (box office)

Founded 1935
Angus L. Bowmer

Season
February–October

Schedule
Evenings
Tuesday–Sunday
Matinees
Saturday, Sunday (spring, fall)
Tuesday–Sunday (summer)

Facilities
15 South Pioneer St.
Elizabethan Stage
Seating capacity: 1,173
Stage: thrust
Angus L. Bowmer Theatre
Seating capacity: 599
Stage: flexible
Black Swan Theatre
Seating capacity: 138-156
Stage: flexible

Finances
Oct. 1, 1978–Sept. 30, 1979
$2,130,000 operating expenses
$1,704,000 earned income
$ 426,000 unearned income

Audience
Paid capacity
Elizabethan Stage: 103%
Angus L. Bowmer Theatre: 88%
Black Swan Theatre: 95%
Total annual attendance: 252,000

Touring contact
Sally White

AEA Guest Artist contract

Rick Hamilton and Ronald Edmunson Woods in *The Root of the Mandrake.* Photo: Hank Kranzler.

Mother Courage and Her Children. Photo: Hank Kranzler.

The Oregon Shakespearean Festival was founded in 1935 to present the plays of William Shakespeare on the stage roughly equivalent to those of Elizabethan playhouses. Today the Festival operates three theatres in three distinctive modes: the Elizabethan outdoor playhouse, mainly dedicated to Shakespeare and presenting plays in the Elizabethan manner without interruption; the modern Angus L. Bowmer Theatre, which houses classics and modern plays with relatively wide appeal; and the intimate Black Swan, designed for less commercial, more specialized pieces.

The single repertory company which serves all three houses is composed chiefly of young actors and technicians recently graduated from the best of the training schools. At their core is an ensemble of professional actors, directors and designers committed to a yearly season or more of collaborative effort. The thrust of the company is toward creating a collective of young artists dedicated to a wide range of styles and modes and disciplined enough to produce 11 plays in three rotating repertory theatres over an 11-month period.

Ashland is a small town (population 15,000) in rural southern Oregon, but the festival serves an extraordinarily diverse audience spanning many hundreds of miles. The theatre's repertoire is chosen to reflect the diversity. Shakespeare (*all* of Shakespeare, not merely the well-known plays) provides the core, but the festival is also dedicated to British, American and European classics.

Producing director Jerry Turner believes that the festival must also produce plays of contemporary authors with the same dedication and care in production devoted to Shakespeare and the classics. He believes that theatre should be literary but not bookish, classic but not pedantic, popular but not vulgar.

Programs and services
Artistic, administrative and technical/production internships; student performances, programs-in-schools, study materials, college courses in Renaissance Studies, student and senior citizen ticket discounts, post-performance discussions, workshop productions and staged readings, film series, guest lecturers, newsletter, souvenir books, script publication, speakers bureau, volunteer auxiliary, theatre rentals.

Productions 1977-78
Tartuffe, Moliere
Private Lives, Noel Coward
Mother Courage and Her Children, Bertolt Brecht
The Effect of Gamma Rays on Man-in-the-Moon Marigolds, Paul Zindel
The Taming of the Shrew, William Shakespeare
The Tempest, William Shakespeare
Richard III, William Shakespeare
Timon of Athens, William Shakespeare
The Night of the Tribades, Per Olov Enquist; trans: Ross Shideler
Miss Julie, August Strindberg; trans: Jerry Turner

Productions 1978-79
Macbeth, William Shakespeare
The Play's the Thing, Ferenc Molnar; adapt: P. G. Wodehouse
Born Yesterday, Garson Kanin
Who's Happy Now?, Oliver Hailey
The Root of the Mandrake, Niccolo Machiavelli; adapt: Robert Symonds
As You Like It, William Shakespeare
A Midsummer Night's Dream, William Shakespeare
Doctor Faustus, Christopher Marlowe
The Wild Duck, Henrik Ibsen; trans: Jerry Turner
Indulgences in the Louisville Harem, John Orlock

Organic Theater Company

Stuart Gordon
Artistic Director

Rick Obadiah
Managing Director

4520 North Beacon St.
Chicago, IL 60640
(312) 721-3010 (business)
(312) 728-1001 (box office)

Founded 1969
Stuart Gordon

Season
April–January

Schedule
Evenings
Wednesday–Sunday
Matinees
Sunday

Facilities
Leo A. Lerner Theater
Seating capacity: 159
Stage: thrust
*Buckingham Theater
(Opening April 1980)*
Seating capacity: 450
Stage: thrust

Finances
Oct. 1, 1977–Sept. 30, 1978
$193,000 operating expenses
$118,000 earned income
$ 51,000 unearned income

Audience
Paid capacity: 76%
Subscribers: 1,600
Annual attendance: 115,000

Touring contact
Herbert Barrett Management
1860 Broadway
New York, NY 10023
(212) 245-3530

AEA COLT contract

The Organic Theater Company is dedicated to the creation of new plays and original adaptations. The company is composed of theatre professionals who produce theatre that "always attempts to astound and amaze by being totally unpredictable." During the past 10 years, the company has created an assortment of 25 original productions.

The Organic was formed in the fall of 1969 by Stuart Gordon in Madison, Wis. Harassment and attempts to censor the company by the Madison city government convinced Organic to accept Paul Sills' offer to move the troupe to Chicago. With Sills' help the company opened in the Holy Covenant Church in March of 1970 with an original adaptation of George Orwell's *Animal Farm.* Later that year Organic took up residence at the Body Politic in Chicago's Lincoln Avenue area. In 1971 Joseph Papp invited Organic to present its adaptation of Voltaire's *Candide* at the Public Theatre, and in 1973 *Warp,* the world's first science fiction epic play in serial form, was produced on Broadway.

In the fall of 1973, the Organic moved to the Leo A. Lerner Theater at the Uptown Center Hull House. Of the three shows premiered that year, *Bloody Bess* and *The Wonderful Ice Cream Suit* were invited by Amsterdam's Mickery Theatre for a European tour, while the third play, the world premiere of David Mamet's *Sexual Perversity in Chicago,* has since had many productions throughout the world, including an extended Off Broadway run.

In 1975 the company created a two-part adaptation of Mark Twain's *The Adventures of Huckleberry Finn.* The actual book, bubbling over with its original satire, bile and violence, was used as the script. The production successfully toured the United States and Europe.

Organic has adapted many works "from the page to the stage," among them Kurt Vonnegut's *The Sirens of Titan* and Raymond Chandler's *The Little Sister.* The company continues to present works of new American playwrights (as it did in 1976 with the world premiere of Terry Curtis Fox's *Cops)* and to develop new plays such as *Bleacher Bums,* a nine-inning comedy about the diehard Chicago Cubs fans. *Bleacher Bums* has been performed in Philadelphia and New York, was taped for public teleision for broadcast nationally in time for the 1979 World Series, and was invited to the Soviet Union for an engagement in 1980.

In celebration of its 10th anniversary in 1979, Organic instituted its first subscription season and completed financing for its new home, a 450-seat flexible complex scheduled to open in April 1980.

Programs and services
Professional training in acting, directing and administration; artistic, administrative and technical/production internships; student performances, student and senior citizen ticket discounts, international touring, post-performance discussions, workshop productions and staged readings, magazine, theatre rentals.

Productions 1977-78
Bleacher Bums, company developed
The Sirens of Titan, Stuart Gordon and
    company, from Kurt Vonnegut's novel
The Wonderful Ice Cream Suit, Ray Bradbury
Night Feast, Stuart Gordon and company

Productions 1978-79
Campaign, Richard Harris
The Little Sister, Carolyn Purdy-Gordon and
    Stuart Gordon, from Raymond Chandler's
    novel
Jonathan Wild, Lawrence Bommer, from Henry
    Fielding's novel
The Warp Trilogy, Bury St. Edmund and Stuart
    Gordon
    Part I: My Battlefield, My Body
    Part II: Unleashed, Unchained!
    Part III: To Die … Alive!

Meshack Taylor in *Night Feast.*
Photo: Stuart Gordon.

Ian Williams and Dennis Franz in
Bleacher Bums. Photo: Roger
Greenwalt.

Otrabanda Company

John Maynard
Managing Director

Box 2659
New Orleans, LA 70176
(504) 566-7729

Founded 1971
Roger Babb, Diane Brown,
Nelson Camp, David Dawkins,
Graham Paul, Stephen Stern

Season
Year-round

Schedule
Evenings
Thursday–Sunday
Matinees
Sunday

Facilities
Circus Tent
301 Pacific Ave.
Seating capacity: 250
Stage: thrust
Contemporary Arts Center
900 Camp St.
Seating capacity: 200
Stage: flexible

Finances
Jan. 1, 1978–Dec. 31, 1978
$58,000 operating expenses
$29,000 earned income
$25,000 unearned income

Audience
Paid capacity: 60%
Annual attendance: 11,520

Touring contact
Stephen Stern

Louise Smith, Nelson Camp,
Rachelle Bornstein and Graham
Paul in *Glass*. Photo: S. Horowitz.

Originality has always been the keynote of Otrabanda Company's productions. In its more than eight years of existence, almost all of the pieces developed by this New Orleans ensemble have been original and its work with existing texts has been appropriately innovative. Once Otrabanda has created a production, it takes it where people are, be it in a circus tent, a planetarium, a science museum or even the Louisiana Superdome.

Otrabanda's greatest national exposure has come from its annual tour by raft down the Mississippi River. Each summer since 1973, the company members have built a wooden raft in St. Louis and floated 1,100 miles downriver to New Orleans, mooring to offer free circus-tent performances to thousands of people along the way. For many of these people, Otrabanda's shows are the only live theatre they see.

As a direct result of the summer project, Otrabanda settled in New Orleans in 1975. Though principally a touring company, it tries to balance out-of-town residencies with a greater commitment to the city and its region.

Otrabanda's productions draw from a variety of sources: Chinese and Balinese music and dance (the result of a six-month Asian

residency); scientific themes (the company was the first American theatre to receive funding from the National Science Foundation); modern dance techniques; circus and *commedia* styles; Moliere; Brazilian samba rhythms; and the sights, sounds and celebrations of New Orleans. These and other influences will continue to inspire new work from Otrabanda.

Programs and services
Classes for nonprofessionals; student performances, programs-in-schools, student and senior citizen ticket discounts, national touring, post-performance discussions, workshop productions and staged readings, circus tent rentals.

Productions 1977-78
Glass, Mark Dunau and company
Fourth Annual River Raft Revue, company developed
Louisiana Legong, David Dawkins and company

Productions 1978-79
Glass
Louisiana Legong
River Six, company developed
On the Move, company developed
A Christmas Carol, adapt: Roger Babb and Diane Brown

Louisiana Legong. Photo: S.
Horowitz.

PAF Playhouse

Jay Broad
Producer

Joel Warren
General Manager

185 Second St.
Huntington Station, NY 11746
(516) 271-8319 (business)
(516) 271-8282 (box office)

Founded 1966
Clint Marantz

Season
October–June

Schedule
Evenings
Tuesday–Sunday
Matinees
Variable

Facilities
PAF Playhouse
Seating capacity: 527
Stage: thrust
PAF/McDonald's Theatre
Seating capacity: 250
Stage: proscenium

Finances
July 1, 1978–June 30, 1979
$1,136,000 operating expense
$ 725,000 earned income
$ 447,000 unearned income

Audience
Paid capaciy: 83%
Subscribers: 13,000
Annual attendance: 334,000

Touring contact
Lynette Bianchi

AEA LORT (C) contract

PAF Playhouse, the only resident professional theatre on Long Island, now operates two theatres: the newly constructed 527-seat, thrust stage Playhouse and the original, 253-seat proscenium auditorium renamed the PAF/MacDonald's Theatre. The two theatres are adjacent to each other in a converted warehouse facility. Eight plays are projected for 1979-80, six in the Playhouse and two in the Theatre.

In August 1975, Jay Broad became PAF's producer and initiated a policy of staging only new or previously unproduced plays. Since then, PAF has given full professional productions of more than 25 new works, including Jack Heifner's *Vanities,* Albert Innaurato's *Gemini,* Richard Nelson's *The Killing of Yablonski,* George F. Walker's *Gossip* and Olwen Wymark's *Loved.* Three of these productions represent a unique collaboration among nonprofit theatres. *Gemini* was showcased at Playwrights Horizons and moved to PAF after rewriting and recasting, later to the Circle Repertory Company and finally to Broadway. *Vanities* took a similar route, from the Lion Theatre Company to Playwrights Horizons, PAF and the Chelsea Theater Center. *Loved* came to PAF from Syracuse Stage.

The Playhouse does not maintain a resident company but casts each production independently. Since PAF is only an hour's ride from midtown Manhattan, it is able to make full use of New York's pool of actors, directors and designers. Long Island's response to PAF's policy of new works has been extraordinary. Since Broad's appointment, subscriptions have risen steadily from 2,000 to 14,000.

PAF also includes an extensive Arts-in-Education Program with its own residnt Equity company. AIE operates a Theatre for Young People at the PAF/McDonald, presenting mainly new works. PAF's touring company, called Troupe, brings full-scale, participatory theatre productions into Long Island schools. PAF's Chamber Theatre serves these same schools with individual or two-person, class-length presentations. In 1978-79, AIE presented more than 600 performances for nearly 200,000 young people at 176 schools and other public sites. AIE also serves the schools and the Board of Cooperative Educational Services with workshops and demonstrations of creative dramatics in the schools and has done extensive work with the handicapped. Finally, PAF's AIE program operates a Theatre Institute which presents theatre-related courses to both students and adults.

Programs and services

Classes for nonprofessionals and children, administrative and technical/production internships, student performances, programs-in-schools, study materials, student and senior citizen ticket discounts, statewide touring of children's theatre, post-performance discussions, newsletter, volunteer auxiliary.

Productions 1977-78

Events from the Life of Ted Snyder, Jay Broad
Give My Regards to Broadway, Dennis Turner
Down at the Old Bull and Bush, music and lyrics: various; adapt: Dolores Sutton and Roderick Cook
The Killing of Yablonski, Richard Nelson
Hancock's Last Half Hour, Heathcote Williams
Juno's Swans, Elaine Kerr
To Kill a Mockingbird, dramatized from Harper Lee's novel
Razzle Dazzle, Kelly Walters
The Marvelous Adventures of Tyl, Kelly Walters

Productions 1978-79

An Angel Comes to Babylon, Friedrich Dürrenmatt; trans: William McElwee
Slugger, Shelby Buford, Jr.
I Am a Woman, Viveca Lindfors and Paul Austin
Gossip, George F. Walker
Goodnight Grandpa, Walter Landau
Loved, Olwen Wymark
Moby Dick, Richard Harden, from Herman Melville's novel
Gifts, Goats and Gilliflowers, Kelly Patton
Beauty and the Beast, adapt: Bill Thompson

Jack Wrangler, Anne Francine, Dan Desmond and Gerry Bamman in *Gossip.* Photo: Gerry Goodstein.

Deborah Mayo, James Zvanut, Hilary J. Bader, John Rothman and George Carabin in *Beauty and the Beast.* Photo: Gerry Goodstein.

Palisades Theatre Company

Richard Hopkins
Artistic Director

Barbara Seifer
Managing Director

Box 10717
St. Petersburg, FL 33733
(813) 823-1600
Box 40084
Washington, DC 20016
(301) 229-4500

Founded 1974
Richard Hopkins

Schedule
Year-round

Facilities
Paramount Theatre
169 Central Ave.
St. Petersburg, FL 33701
Seating capacity: 200
Stage: thrust

Finances
July 1, 1978–hJune 30, 1979
$199,000 operating expenses
$ 60,000 earned income
$136,000 unearned income

Audience
Annual attendance: 200,000

Touring contact
Angelyn Paige

Gary Thompson in *The Brave Little Tailor*. Photo: David Littel.

Palisades Theatre Company was founded in January 1974 in Washington, D.C., by Richard Hopkins. His vision at that time was to send a traveling band of players into schools, churches, fields and streets to reach that vast part of the American population usually left untouched by theatre.

Today, Palisades operates one touring troupe from its Washington, D.C., base and a second troupe from its newly formed headquarters in St. Petersburg, Fla. Working in cooperation with Eckerd College, both companies tour the eastern seaboard from Connecticut to Florida with special programs for special audiences.

In its five years of touring, Palisades has developed a unique theatrical style, combining mime, puppetry and story theatre in company-developed productions. In the past, the pieces have been collectively created with playwrights and composers in residence.

Palisades is deeply committed to the development of new plays for professionals to perform for children. Recognizing the dearth of quality material for young audiences, Palisades has developed its Children Theatre Lab—an experimental program aimed toward developing new plays, new playwrights and new approaches to theatre for young audiences. Although still in its infancy, the Lab is rapidly proving itself a source of new and daring plays for children.

Palisades is currently renovating its first home in downtown St. Petersburg. In addition to an abundance of children's programming, the intimate facility will nurture contemporary American plays, with an eye toward developing innovative, original works. Its opening is slated for January 1980.

Programs and services
Classes for nonprofessionals, children and the handicapped; artistic, administrative and technical/production internships; programs-in-schools, study materials, national touring, post-performance discussions, workshop productions and staged readings, volunteer auxiliary.

Productions 1977-78
The Brave Little Tailor
The Star-Child, from Oscar Wilde's story
African Tales
The Mime Show
The Taming of the Shrew, William Shakespeare

Productions 1978-79
The Taming of the Shrew
The Brave Little Tailor
African Tales
Snow White
Peter and the Wolf
Holiday Gift
The Mime Show
Aesop in Revue

All productions are adapted or developed by the company.

Doug Hopkins and Patricia Ficke in *Mime Show*. Photo: David Littel.

The Paper Bag Players

Judith Martin
Director

Judith Liss
Administrator

50 Riverside Drive
New York, NY 10024
(212) 362-0431

Founded 1958
Judith Martin, Remy Charlip,
Shirley Kaplan, Sudie Bond,
Daniel Jahn

Season
September–May

Finances
May 1, 1978–April 30, 1979
$266,000 operating expenses
$146,000 earned income
$124,000 unearned income

Audience
Annual attendance: 90,000

Touring contact
Judith Liss

AEA Guest Artist contract

The Paper Bag Players produces original plays for children in a unique style that has brought the company international recognition as innovators in children's theatre. Judith Martin writes, designs and directs all of the shows for the company and Donald Ashwander composes the music. Martin collaborates with Ashwander while sketching ideas with Irving Burton, the company's leading actor, and using the entire cast in rehearsal to develop theatre pieces integrating story, music and dance with the dramatic use of paper props.

Martin's ideas deal with events and experiences that confront both children and adults in contemporary society. Her stories are, in fact, modern-day allegories, which use both extraordinary and commonplace situations. While most of her short plays are humorous, many are lyrical and all are fanciful—a bar of soap tries to persuade a little boy to take a bath; a girl milks a cardboard cow and out comes a carton of milk; a street cleaner falls in love with his trash; a pair of lips escape from a lipstick ad; a family is diverted from their summer vacation by a fruitless search for their dream hamburger. The stories are told in short, cartoonlike scenes, with acting, dancing, singing and sometimes even painting on stage.

The Paper Bag Players is not only a theatre of allegories but very much a musical theatre. Its musicality comes from the inspiration of composer Ashwander. His songs and musical ideas are an essential and basic part of all the Paper Bag plays. He is so much a part of each production that his actual presence playing and performing on the stage seems natural. He has chosen for his instrument the electric harpsichord, which when backed by a Rhythm Master and various small instruments for sound effects, has the volume and variety of a small orchestra.

Paper, cardboard, paints and crayons are, of course, basic elements in the Paper Bag Players' theatre. The props and scenery function in several ways—sometimes as a caricature of the image and sometimes as an abstraction. For example, a jagged piece of cardboard gives the impression of an alligator and a refrigerator box represents a crowded tenement. Costumes or props are drawn and even constructed by the actors on stage as part of the action.

The company has performed in a variety of places, from Lincoln Center and Harlem in New York to rural schools in Kentucky and across the ocean in Israel, Iran, Egypt and London.

Programs and services
Professional administrative training, artistic and administrative internships, student performances, programs-in-schools, study materials, free ticket distribution, international touring, script publication, record albums.

Productions 1977-78
Grandpa
Hot Feet
Everybody, Everybody

Productions 1978-79
Dandelion
Everybody, Everybody

For all productions, Judith Martin authored the book, Donald Ashwander composed the music and Martin and Ashwander collaborated on the lyrics.

Judith Martin and Irving Burton in
Everybody, Everybody.

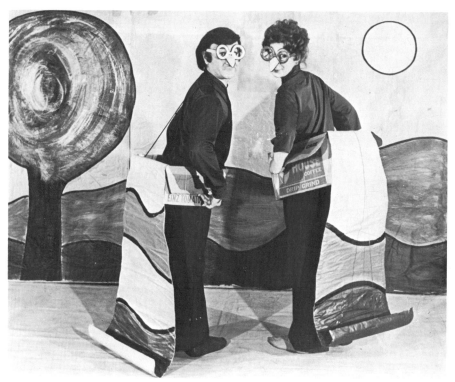

Irving Burton and Judith Martin in
Dandelion.

PART
Performing Arts Repertory Theatre

Jay Harnick
Artistic Director

Charles Hull
Managing Director

131 West 86th St.
New York, NY 10024
(212) 595-7500

Founded 1967
Robert K. Adams, Jay Harnick,
Charles Hull

Season
September–June

Facilities
Town Hall
123 West 43rd St.
Seating capacity: 1,500
Stage: proscenium

Finances
Oct 1, 1977–Sept. 30, 1978
$807,000 operating expenses
$773,000 earned income
$ 36,000 unearned income

Audience
Paid capacity: 75%
Annual attendance: 841,000

Touring contact
Christine Prendergast

Booked-in events
Theatre, dance, opera and puppet
companies

*AEA Theatre for Young
Audiences contract*

Frederic Stone and Deborah
Savadge in *The Unbeatable
Doctor Elizabeth*. Photo: Barry
Kramer.

As the country's largest theatre for young audiences, the Performing Arts Repertory Theatre presented 1,077 performances to more than 900,000 people during the 1977-78 season alone. Of these performances, 897 took place on tour in 32 states and 180 as part of the theatre's resident program.

In its dedication to producing meaningful new works for young people, PART has commissioned established dramatists as well as talented neophytes to create its productions. Since its inception, PART has developed 24 new productions from the collaborations of more than 40 authors, lyricists and composers, among them Saul Levitt, Ossie Davis, Mary Rodgers, Joe Raposo, Alice Childress, Albert Hague, John Morris and John Allen. These works have played to more than 5 million people over the course of 6,842 performances.

Although PART seeks to create a wide range of works, its best-known and most widely performed attractions have been based on historical characters and events. The productions are designed for maximum portability, and the companies also conduct both teacher and student workshops on the many educational tours.

PART's resident series at Manhattan's Town Hall and other area sites presents not only its own productions, but also those of other theatre, dance, opera and puppetry troupes, thus providing the children of the greater New York City area with a well-rounded choice sampling of the performing arts.

Programs and services
Student/teacher performances and workshops, programs-in-schools, study materials, student ticket discounts, national touring, post-performance discussions.

Productions 1977-78
The Unbeatable Doctor Elizabeth, book and
    lyrics: John Allen; music: Joe Raposo
Sara Crewe, the Orphan Princess, book: Mary
    Anderson; music: Shelly Markham; lyrics:
    Carrie Maher
Jim Thorpe, All-American, book and lyrics: Saul
    Levitt; music: Harrison Fisher
Freedom Train, Marvin Gordon
John F. Kennedy: The Road to Camelot, book:
    Daniel Kihoy; music: Donald Siegal; lyrics:
    Robert Joseph
Young Mark Twain, book: John Allen; music:
    Mary Rodgers; lyrics: J. Allen and M.
    Rodgers
Aesop and Other Fables, Marshall Izen
Dinosaurs, Puppets and Picasso, Marshall Izen
Young Tom Edison and the Magic Why, book:
    Robert K. Adams; music and lyrics: Martin
    Kalmanoff

Productions 1978-79
Daniel Boone!, book and lyrics: Ross Yockey;
    music: Gary William Friedman
Young Ben Franklin, book: Allan Cruickshank;
    music: Albert Hague; lyrics: Ray Errol Fox
Jim Thorpe, All-American, book and lyrics: Saul
    Levitt; music: Harrison Fisher
The Unbeatable Doctor Elizabeth, book and
    lyrics: John Allen; music: Joe Raposo
Sara Crewe, the Orphan Princess, book: Mary
    Anderson; music: Shelly Markham; lyrics:
    Carrie Maher
Freedom Train, Marvin Gordon
Aesop and Other Fables, Marshall Izen
Dinosaurs, Puppets and Picasso, Marshall Izen

Daniel Boone! Photo: Joe Griffith.

Performance Community

Byron Schaffer, Jr.
Artistic Director/Producer

Ruth E. Higgins
Producer

Robert W. Snyder
Managing Director

Theatre Building
1225 West Belmont Ave.
Chicago, IL 60657
(312) 929-7367 (business)
(312) 327-5252 (box office)

Founded 1969
Byron Schaffer, Jr.

Season
July–June

Schedule
Evenings
Wednesday–Sunday
Matinees
Sunday

Facilities
North Theatre
Seating capacity: 150
Stage: flexible

Finances
Jan. 1, 1978–Dec. 31, 1978
$130,000 operating expenses
$ 65,000 earned income
$ 69,000 unearned income

Audience
Paid capacity: 63%
Annual attendance: 3,957

Touring contact
Robert W. Snyder

Booked-in events
Dance, music, theatre

The year 1979 marks the 10th anniversary of the Performance Community, formerly known as the Dinglefest Theatre Company. PC is, and has always been, dedicated to three goals: the development of new American plays, the encouragement of young artists and the provision of services to the profession.

This year PC will produce its 21st world premiere; no other theatre in Illinois has exclusively produced original works over so long a period. Each production is fully mounted following six weeks of rehearsal and runs for a guaranteed minimum of six weeks after opening. The playwright is paid and in residence during a least four of the rehearsal weeks; in addition, the playwright's expenses are paid for a return visit to the production during the fifth week of the run. Actors, designers and technicians are salaried for the entire rehearsal-performance period.

The Performance Community has always encouraged the nascent professional. To date our jury has selected 18 visual artists to display their work free-of-charge in our lobby gallery; their work is thereby exposed to a potential audience of 12,000 theatregoers. Of the 51 theatre artists employed by PC for a month or more in 1978, 42 had their first professional experience, and one-half of those have already gone on to find employment with other professional groups.

PC's third objective, services to the profession, is perhaps best represented by its management of Theatre Building, a unique, three-theatre complex which PC founded, designed and renovated. Performance Community utilizes one of the theatres for its own productions and subleases the other theatres at below cost to other nonprofit theatre groups. Presently in residence at Theatre Building are the Travel Light Theatre and Pary Productions, both vigorous, young, independent companies who establish their artistic and managerial objectives as they see fit. PC is presently undertaking a capital drive to purchase Theatre Building, with an eye toward reducing and stabilizing costs for all groups using the facility.

Programs and services
Artistic, administrative and technical/production internships; student and senior citizen ticket discounts, free ticket distribution, voucher program, regional touring, post-performance discussions, art gallery, theatre rentals.

Productions 1977-78
Split the Differents:
  A Distinctive Knock, Colin Stinton
  Touch, Gareth Mann
  Homer, Frank Fetters
Young Bucks, John Kunik
Top Secret, Ken McLean
Tom Swift and His ..., company developed
Vacuum Pact, company developed

Productions 1978-79
Bear, Colin Stinton; music:
  Alaric (Rokko) Jans
The Grab, Maria Katzenbach
Madmen, Steven Stosny
Exit 30, John Kunik
Tom Swift and His ...

John Davenport and Bill Renk in
Exit 30. Photo: Byron Schaffer, Jr.

Teri Brown and Robert Fiddler in
Touch. Photo: Byron Schaffer, Jr.

The Performance Group

Richard Schechner
Executive Director

Deborah Locitzer
General Manager

Joanna Ross
Administrator
The Performing Garage Center

Box 654
Canal Street Station
New York, NY 10013
(212) 966-9796 (business)
(212) 966-3651 (box office)

Founded 1967
Richard Schechner

Season
Year-round

Schedule
Evenings
Tuesday–Sunday

Facilities
The Performing Garage
33-35 Wooster St.
Seating capacity: 150
Stage: flexible
Seating capacity: 75
Stage: flexible
Seating capacity: 150
Stage: flexible

Finances
July 1, 1978–June 30, 1979
$202,000 operating expenses
$137,000 earned income
$ 61,000 unearned income

Audience
Paid capacity: 75%
Annual attendance: 25,200

Touring contact
Joanna Ross

Booked-in events
Experimental theatre,
solo performance artists

John Holms in *Oedipus*. Photo: Clem Fiori.

The Performance Group is a permanent collective in existence for 13 years—one of the oldest experimental theatre companies in America. Through its exploration and redefinition of the roles of language, space, action, performer and audience, TPG has developed the concept of "environmental theatre."

The group's work comprises company-developed pieces *(Commune, Three Places in Rhode Island)*, new American plays *(The Tooth of Crime, Marilyn Project, Cops)*, or the "reconstruction" of classics *(Dionysus in '69, Mother Courage and Her Children, Oedipus)*. Each production generates a new space, a new way of thinking about the audience and a renewed text.

At this time TPG's activites are directed toward three fronts: the work of Richard Schechner; the work of Elizabeth LeCompte and Spalding Gray; and the presenting wing, the Performing Garage Center.

Schechner is currently working on a production of Genet's *The Balcony,* to open in 1980, which will examine the relationships among artistic, sexual and political illusions within a house of illusion, the theatre.

A major artistic development began with TPG in 1975 when Gray and LeCompte began work on *Three Places in Rhode Island.* This trilogy explored non-linear, open narrative form, using the life experiences of Gray as a point of departure. This process is continued in their new production *Point Judith,* scheduled to open in December 1979.

The Performing Garage Center provides a focal point in New York City for the presentation of company-developed experimental theatre work from the United States and Europe, and for companies working in New York without a permanent home. Companies that have appeared include the Organic Theater Company, Theatre X, the Odyssey Theatre Ensemble, Mabou Mines and solo performers Bob Carroll, Stuart Sherman and Paul Zaloom.

Programs and services
Professional acting training, classes for nonprofessionals and children; artistic, administrative and technical/production internships; college residencies, free ticket distribution, international touring, post-performance discussions, workshop productions and staged readings, guest lecturers, script publication.

Productions 1977-78
Oedipus, Seneca; adapt: Ted Hughes
Cops, Terry Curtis Fox
Nayatt School, Elizabeth LeCompte, Spalding
    Gray and company

Productions 1978-79
Three Places in Rhode Island, Elizabeth
    LeCompte, Spalding Gray and company
    Sakonnet Point
    Rumstick Road
    Nayatt School
Cops
Sex and Death to the Age 14, Spalding Gray

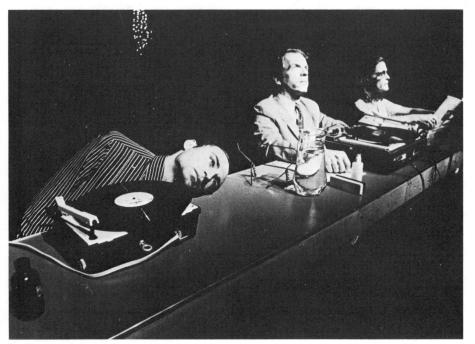

Ron Vawter, Spalding Gray and Joan Jonas in *Nayatt School.* Photo: Bob Van Dantzig.

Periwinkle Productions

Sunna Rasch
Executive Director

Scott Laughead
Artistic Director

Thomas A. Sennett
Business Administrator

262 Broadway
Monticello, NY 12701
(914) 794-1666

Founded 1963
Sunna Rasch

Season
Year-round

Finances
Aug. 1, 1978–July 31, 1979
$117,000 operating expenses
$ 81,000 earned income
$ 25,000 unearned income

Audience
Annual attendance: 100,000

Touring contact
Ingeborg Blythe

*AEA Theatre for Young
Audiences contract*

For 16 years Periwinkle Productions, Inc., one of the oldest Equity children's theatres in the country, has been a pioneer in educational theatre. The company worked in schools before federal funds opened the door for arts in education.

Periwinkle originally sought to bridge theatre and education by developing programs that would expose young audiences to theatre as an entertaining cultural experience, while challenging them intellectually, imaginatively and artistically. Periwinkle's programming began with poetry-theatre and later expanded to include original scripts with themes inspired by the young audiences themselves.

Hooray for Me! is a musical based on one tenager's search for identity. *The Dream Show* by Scott Laughead is about a youngster at the turn of the century who lies to gain recognition. *The Mad Poet Strikes—Again!*, often described as a Periwinkle "classic," is a poetry-theatre show. Programs range from shows for primary to senior high, all committed to professionalism and theatre of the highest order.

This commitment was well rewarded in 1978 when the American Theatre Association awarded Periwinkle the highest honor in the United States in their field: the Jennie Heiden Award for excellence and professionalism.

Periwinkle's work has been featured at many conventions in and out of state. In 1979 Periwinkle had the honor of presenting a performance and workshop at the New York State Humanities and Arts spring conference and was an evening at the state education department's summer Saratoga Arts-in-Education Conference.

In addition to school performance, Periwinkle performs in theatres, parks, civic centers and libraries. Among the leading center which have hosted Periwinkle are the Kennedy Center in Washington, D.C., the Detroit Institute of the Arts, and the Library and Museum of the Performing Arts at New York's Lincoln Center.

Programs and services
Administrative and technical/production internships, student performances, programs-in-schools, study materials, workshops in creative writing and creative dramatics, national touring, post-performance discussions, poetry readings, speaker bureau, volunteer auxiliary, publication of children's writing.

Productions 1977-78
Hooray for Me!, book: Scott Laughead; music and lyrics: Grenaldo Frazier
The Dream Show, Scott Laughead
The Magic Word, Sunna Rasch
The Mad Poet Strikes—Again!, Sunna Rasch
Hey, Hi, Ho for Pooh!, Dennis McGovern
Mask, Mime and Magic, Jack Hill

Productions 1978-79
Hooray for Me!
The Dream Show
The New Magic Word, Sunna Rasch
The Mad Poet Strikes—Again!
Hey, Hi, Ho for Pooh!
As Eye See It, Jack Hill

Steve Tschudy, Helen Hedman, Elli Sugar and Glengo King in *The Mad Poet Strikes—Again!* Photo: Mark Schwanhauser.

Steve Tschudy, Scott Laughead and Sean McKinley in *Hooray for Me!* Photo: Jody Dole.

Philadelphia Drama Guild

Douglas Seale
Artistic Director

Gregory J. Poggi
Managing Director

220 South 16th St.
Philadelphia, PA 19102
(215) 546-6791 (business)
(215) 574-3550 (box office)

Founded 1956
Sidney S. Bloom

Season
October–April

Schedule
Evenings
Tuesday–Sunday
Matinees
Wednesday, Saturday

Facilities
Walnut Street Theatre
825 Walnut St.
Seating capacity: 1,052
Stage: proscenium

Finances
June 1, 1978–May 31, 1979
$904,000 operating expenses
$580,000 earned income
$245,000 unearned income

Audience
Paid capacity: 67%
Subscribers: 16,695
Annual attendance: 107,300

AEA LORT (A) contract

Richard Monette and Domini Blythe in *Saint Joan*. Photo: Peter Lester.

The grass-roots community theatre movement precipitated the birth of the Philadelphia Drama Guild in 1956. Founded by Philadelphians who wished to participate in play production, the company soon settled on a classic repertoire. As local interest and involvement with the company grew, so did the quality of its productions.

In 1971 the company turned professional, operating as a stock company, importing "star" performers and presenting its productions in Philadelphia's historic Walnut Street Theatre.

At the end of the third professional season, the decision was made to abandon the stock system in favor of a resident company. The new company was developed under the artistic direction of Douglas Seale, a veteran of major British, American and Canadian theatre companies. Positive local support for Seale's concept was dramatized by a 50 percent rise in 1975-76 subscriptions.

The avowed goal of the Philadelphia Drama Guild under Seale is simply to produce the finest quality theatre possible. Its mainstage presents a wide range of classics and the best in modern works. An acting company is being developed of sufficient flexibility to ensure the best possible casting, while sustaining the open, harmonious and receptive characteristics of ensemble playing.

Seale describes his company concept as "an artistic ensemble … actors forming a 'pool' of talent that audiences come to know; [actors who] play in three and even four plays a season; who, by appearing regularly, acquire the characteristics of a 'company.'

"This arrangement creates a cohesion, a sense of belonging and the molding of an overall style, as well as a mutual respect between actors, directors and the company organization.

"This very special kind of theatre," Seale concludes, "is possible only with an ongoing resident theatre operating under a consistent artistic policy."

Programs and services
Study materials, student and senior citizen ticket discounts, post-performance discussions, guest lecturers, speakers bureau.

Productions 1977-78
The Show-Off, George Kelly
Travesties, Tom Stoppard
Saint Joan, George Bernard Shaw
Hobson's Choice, Harold Brighouse
Uncle Vanya, Anton Chekhov; trans:
    William Stancil

Productions 1978-79
The Au Pair Man, Hugh Leonard
Arms and the Man, George Bernard Shaw
Private Lives, Noel Coward
The Blood Knot, Athol Fugard
The Night of the Iguana, Tennessee Williams

Donald Ewer, Paxton Whitehead, David Rounds and Edward Atzienza in *Travesties*. Photo: Peter Lester.

Phoenix Theatre

T. Edward Hambleton
Managing Director

Daniel Freudenberger
Artistic Director

1540 Broadway
New York, NY 10036
(212) 730-0787 (business)
(212) 730-0794 (box office)

Founded 1953
T. Edward Hambleton,
Norris Houghton

Season
October–June

Schedule
Evenings
Tuesday–Sunday
Matinees
Saturday, Sunday

Facilities
Marymount Manhattan Theatre
221 East 71st St.
Seating capacity: 249
Stage: proscenium

Finances
July 1, 1978–June 30, 1979
$562,000 operating expenses
$180,000 earned income
$376,000 unearned income

Audience
Paid capacity: 83%
Subscribers: 3,020
Annual attendance: 25,300

AEA Off Broadway contract

The Phoenix Theatre is dedicated to the nurturing and development of new plays and emerging playwrights. Its commitment is reflected in a subscription series of five mainstage productions, a series of staged readings, workshop productions and a program of six specially commissioned plays.

The Phoenix was founded in 1953 as an alternative to Broadway at a time when alternatives did not exist. As theatrical landscapes in New York and the nation have changed, the Phoenix has passed through various incarnations as well, embracing new plays, the classics and a permanent ensemble performing in rotating repertory.

In 1976 artistic director Daniel Freudenberger shifted the Phoenix focus to new plays, balancing new American writing (the core of its work) with dynamic European plays. The Phoenix also collaborates with theatres outside New York to make possible the evolution of such plays as *Getting Out* and *Uncommon Women and Others*. Three Phoenix productions in the last five years have been televised on the PBS *Theater in America* series: *The Rules of the Game, Secret Service* and *Uncommon Women and Others*.

As a producer of new plays, the Phoenix continues to focus the attention of the press on playwrights and their works, and to provide these writers with the enthusiastic support of a growing subscription audience. The theatre is currently in the midst of a major fund-raising campaign to meet the requirements of a $75,000 challenge grant from the National Endowment for the Arts.

During the 1979-80 season, the Phoenix was scheduled to occupy a new developmental theatre space while its subscription productions remained at the Marymount Manhattan Theatre.

Programs and services
Artistic and administrative internships, programs-in-schools, free ticket distribution, student and senior citizen ticket discounts, post-performance discussions, workshop productions and staged readings, newsletter, souvenir book, playwright commissioning program.

Productions 1977-78
Hot Grog, book: Jim Wann; music and lyrics: Bland Simpson and J. Wann
Uncommon Women and Others, Wendy Wasserstein
One Crack Out, David French
The Elusive Angel, Jack Gilhooley
City Sugar, Stephen Poliakoff

Productions 1978-79
Getting Out, Marsha Norman
Later, Corinne Jacker
Says I, Says He, Ron Hutchinson
Big and Little, Botho Strauss; trans: Anne Cattaneo
Chinchilla, Robert David MacDonald

Susan Kingsley and Leo Burmester in *Getting Out*. Photo: Martha Swope.

Uncommon Women and Others.
Photo: Roger Greenwalt.

Pittsburgh Public Theater

Ben Shaktman
General Director

300 Sixth Ave. Building
Suite 1150
Pittsburgh, PA 15222
(412) 765-3400 (business)
(412) 323-1900 (box office)

Founded 1975
Joan Apt, Margaret Rieck,
Ben Shaktman

Season
September–May

Schedule
Evenings
Tuesday–Sunday
Matinees
Thursday, Saturday, Sunday

Facilities
Allegheny Theater
Allegheny Square
Seating capacity: 336
Stage: arena
Edward D. Eddy Theatre
Chatham College
Seating capacity: 285
Stage: proscenium

Finances
July 1, 1978–June 30, 1979
$1,104,000 operating expenses
$ 643,000 earned income
$ 620,000 unearned income

Audience
Paid capacity: 95%
Subscribers: 13,350
Annual attendance: 84,235

AEA LORT (C) contract

Nick Wyman, David Clark and
David Little in *Of Mice and Men*.
Photo: Jack Weinhold and
Nancy Adam.

Joseph Wiseman in *Balyasnikov*.
Photo: Jack Weinhold and
Nancy Adam.

Pittsburgh Public Theater, under the direction of Ben Shaktman, opened in 1975 at the city-owned Allegheny Theater. Offered rent-free, it has been the home of PPT for longer performing seasons each year. The facility's performing space, designed by Peter Wexler, provides a three-tiered scaffolding frame in a flexible 350-seat arena.

In addition to income from subscriptions and single-ticket sales, accounting for approximately 46 percent of the Public Theater's fourth season operating budget, PPT is supported by grants and contributions from 48 corporations, 27 foundations, 2,800 individuals, as well as county, state and federal government agencies.

In its first four seasons, the Public Theater has presented 17 mainstage productions, including plays from the modern and classical repertories. In addition, the Public Theater has produced staged readings, workshop productions and special presentations of new and developing works.

Community educational programs include Open Stage, which introduces live theatre to students from the city schools with both classroom and theatre projects; the Training Program, which offers intense vocational training to inner-city residents, as well as internship and apprentice programs to those interested in professional theatre careers; and Community Arts, which provides lectures, master classes, workshops and tutelage programs to various organizations within the region. Critics, directors and public forums on contemporary problems in today's society have gained wide popularity.

In September 1979, the Public Theater embarked on its first regional tour. In addition to restaging its production of *Vanities*, PPT's three-week tour included a complete range of educational programs during its residencies in eight communities of western Pennsylvania and West Virginia.

Programs and services
Artistic, administrative and technical/production internships; student performances, programs-in-schools, study materials, student and senior citizen ticket discounts, free ticket distribution, post-performance discussions, workshop productions and staged readings, guest lecturers, newsletter, speakers bureau, volunteer auxiliary.

Productions 1977-78
Father's Day, Oliver Hailey
You Never Can Tell, George Bernard Shaw
Balyasnikov, Aleksei Arbuzov; adapt: Ben
   Shaktman
Slow Dance on the Killing Ground, William
   Hanley
Medal of Honor Rag, Tom Cole

Productions 1978-79
The Blood Knot, Athol Fugard
Of Mice and Men, John Steinbeck
The Importance of Being Earnest, Oscar Wilde
Vanities, Jack Heifner
Ashes, David Rudkin
*For Colored Girls who have Considered
   Suicide/When The Rainbow is Enuf*,
   Ntozake Shange

The Play Group

Thomas P. Cooke
Artistic Director

Mark Cantley
Managing Director

1538 Laurel Ave.
Knoxville, TN 37916
(615) 523-7461

Founded 1973

Season
Year-round

Schedule
Evenings
Friday–Sunday

Facilities
Laurel Theatre
Seating capacity: 100
Stage: flexible

Finances
Sept. 1, 1977–Aug. 31, 1978
$53,000 operating expenses
$14,000 earned income
$39,000 unearned income

Audience
Paid capacity: 30%
Annual attendance: 10,000

Touring contact
Mark Cantley

Book-in-events
Dance, music, theatre

After six years on the frontier of contemporary regional theatre, the Play Group continues to explore widely varied theatrical perspectives. Regionally based and community-oriented, the Play Group nonetheless finds much support in touring and consequently has traveled extensively throughout the United States. Although inspired by the tutelage of artistic director Thomas P. Cooke, the Play Group defines its artistic goals through the internal collaboration between the artists in the ensemble. Each individual participates to the extent of his or her ability in all areas of production, administration and development.

The Play Group is dedicated to its grass roots constituency in Knoxville, while at the same time eager to exhibit its work to a wide spectrum of audiences. The resident company is composed of an artistic director, a managing director, a writer-in-residence and seven performers. The company's children's program tours local elementary schools. A community acting ensemble of local actors functions under the direction of a member of the professional ensemble. A women's ensemble of company members travels to area women's centers and participates in a broad range of other feminist activities.

As a participant in the first invitational Experimental Theatre Festival in Ann Arbor, Mich., and as a founding member of Alternate ROOTS (Regional Organization of Theatres South), the Play Group continues to thrive as an important facet of the grass roots resurgence of contemporary theatre in the last decade.

Programs and services
Professional training in acting and administration; classes for nonprofessionals and children; programs-in-schools, study materials, student and senior citizen ticket discounts, national touring, workshop productions and staged readings, poetry readings, theatre rentals.

Productions 1977-78
Hello!, David McIntosh
Tell Me a Story, company devloped
A Doll's House, Henrik Ibsen
Romeo and Juliet, William Shakespeare

Productions 1978-79
Hello!
Tell Me a Story
Lacie, David McIntosh
The Piper Man, book: David McIntosh; music: Mac Pirkle; lyrics: M. Pirkle and D. McIntosh
The Lion in Winter, James Goldman
Myths, company developed

Sheira Freedman and Charles Ragland in *Piper Man.*

Don Jones, Mac Pirkle, Chris Brown and Sheira Freedman in *Hello!*

Players State Theatre

David Robert Kanter
Executive Director

G. David Black
Managing Director

Coconut Grove Playhouse
3500 Main Highway
Coconut Grove, FL 33133
(305) 442-2662 (business)
(305) 442-4000 (box office)

Founded 1977
Thomas Spencer
Gerald Pulver

Season
October–April

Schedule
Evenings
Tuesday–Sunday
Matinees
Wednesday, selected Saturdays
and Sundays

Facilities
Seating capacity: 500
Stage: proscenium

Finances
July 1, 1978–June 30, 1979
$976,000 operating expenses
$535,000 earned income
$450,000 unearned income

Audience
Paid capacity: 60%
Subscribers: 4,600
Annual attendance: 70,000

Touring contact
Alan Yaffe

AEA LORT (C) contract

Clockwise from upper left: Steven Salter, Philip Parker, Robert Murch and Gloria Manon in *The Night of the Iguana.* Photo: Ray Fisher.

Players State Theatre, having completed its second season in Miami's Coconut Grove Playhouse, has watched its audience grow from 38,000 to 50,000 in a competitive entertainment/resort area. In the first two years of the theatre's history, a wide variety of plays was produced. The plays were chosen, cast and directed to prove to the Miami community that the possibility of a quality regional professional theatre existed locally. Whether Shakespeare comedy or tragedy, Tennessee Williams, Alan Ayckbourn or Georges Feydeau, the productions mounted on the Players State Theatre stage were intended to win the praise and support of the community and to be accomplished with style.

Moreover, Players State wanted to tell its new audience that it was not afraid to take a chance, either with a new play or with a forceful, challenging contemporary drama. From the very beginning, in its premiere season, the company offered the controversial drama *Streamers* and, the following year, achieved record box office receipts with another serious play, *The Shadow Box.* Such response has indicated an intelligent, demanding audience for the young company. While there will always be a place for musical and dinner theatre, Players State's place in the Miami community strives to be won through the very best in dramatic literature, classical or contemporary.

Programs and services
Professional training in acting and directing; classes for nonprofessionals and children; administrative and technical/production internships, student performances, programs-in-schools, study materials, student and senior citizen ticket discounts, free ticket distribution, statewide touring, post-performance discussions, newsletter, speakers bureau, volunteer auxiliary, theatre rentals.

Productions 1977-78
Cyrano de Bergerac, Edmond Rostand; trans: Brian Hooker
Violano Virtuoso, Betty Suyker
Othello, William Shakespeare
Streamers, David Rabe
Absurd Person Singular, Alan Ayckbourn
The Drunkard, book and lyrics: Bro Herrod, from William H. Smith's play; music adapted from themes by Barry Manilow

Productions 1978-79
As You Like It, William Shakespeare
The Night of the Iguana, Tennessee Williams
A Flea in Her Ear, Georges Feydeau
The Shadow Box, Michael Cristofer
The Member of the Wedding, Carson McCullers
Irma la Douce, book and lyrics: Alexandre Breffort; adapt: David Heneker, Julian More and Monty Norman; music: Marguerite Monnot

The Shadow Box. Photo: Ray Fisher.

Playhouse on the Square

Jackie Nichols
Artistic Director

Eva Gugenheim
Administrative Director

2121 Madison Ave.
Memphis, TN 38104
(901) 725-0776 (business)
(901) 726-4656 (box office)

Founded 1968
Jackie Nichols

Season
September–June

Schedule
Evenings
Wednesday–Sunday
Matinees
Saturday

Facilities
Playhouse on the Square
2121 Madison Ave.
Seating capacity: 250
Stage: flexible
Circuit Playhouse
1947 Poplar Ave.
Seating capacity: 100
Stage: proscenium
Workshop Theatre
162 North Tucker
Seating capacity: 50
Stage: flexible

Finances
July 1, 1978–June 30, 1979
$212,000 operating expenses
$143,000 earned income
$ 69,000 unearned income

Audience
Paid capacity: 75%
Subscribers: 2,300
Annual attendance: 45,800

With a trio of facilities in regular operation, Playhouse on the Square (the professional arm of Circuit Playhouse, Inc.) entered its 1979-80 season with a new artistic focus. While maintaining a diversified program of quality older plays and challenging new works, the company began placing an emphasis on "follow-up" productions of recent regional, Broadway, and Off Broadway premieres. Too often, playwrights are denied the opportunity of valuable second or third productions due to funding structures which support the novelty of "premiere" productions but fail to provide for crucial subsequent stagings.

A recent $100,000 grant has enabled the Playhouse to establish a major regional theatre of the deaf. Beginning in the fall of 1979, the company will provide a much-needed service to hearing-impaired individuals in the Memphis area, both as participants and spectators. Several environmentally-oriented theatrical events have also helped the Circuit Playhouse make its mark on the community, such as the stagings of *The Hot l Baltimore* in a local hotel lobby, *The Frogs* in an outdoor swimming pool atop a motor inn, *The Rocky Horror Show* in an old movie house, and *Joseph and the Amazing Technicolor Dreamcoat* in a downtown church.

In addition to the year-round Playhouse on the Square, the Circuit Playhouse operation includes a series of new plays, a workshop theatre which trains young actors and directors through work with original material, and a youth theatre that gives free performances before more than 8,000 school children yearly.

Programs and services
Professional acting and administrative training, classes in dance, improvisation, creative writing, and creative dramatics for children, internships, student performances, programs-in-schools, study materials, free ticket distribution, student and senior citizen ticket discounts, separate regional touring company, post-performance discussions, workshop productions and staged readings, newsletter, speakers bureau, volunteer auxiliary, theatre rentals.

Productions 1977-78
Candida, George Bernard Shaw
The School for Wives, Moliere
Of Mice and Men, John Steinbeck
Fallen Angels, Noel Coward
One Flew over the Cuckoo's Nest, Dale Wasserman, from Ken Kesey's novel
Angel Street, Patrick Hamilton
Man of La Mancha, book: Dale Wasserman; music: Mitch Leigh; lyrics: Joe Darion
Twelfth Night, William Shakespeare
Summer and Smoke, Tennessee Williams
The Waltz of the Toreadors, Jean Anouilh; trans: Lucienne Hill
Marat/Sade, Peter Weiss; adapt: Adrian Mitchell

Productions 1978-79
Southern Comfort, music and lyrics: Ronnie B. Baker
The King Is a Fink, book, music and lyrics: Keith Kennedy and George Caldwell, from the syndicated comic strip "The Wizard of Id"
An Evening of Soul, concept: Erma L. Clanton
Diamond Studs, book: Jim Wann; music and lyrics: Bland Simpson and J. Wann
Much Ado About Nothing, William Shakespeare
Light Up the Sky, Moss Hart
Another Part of the Forest, Lillian Hellman
Oliver!, book, music and lyrics: Lionel Bart
The Oldest Living Graduate, Preston Jones
Dames at Sea, book and lyrics: George Haimsohn and Robin Miller; music: Jim Wise
The Rocky Horror Show, book, music and lyrics: Richard O'Brien

Tom Hammond and Jerry Bradley in *The Waltz of the Toreadors.*
Photo: Elbert Greer.

Ridge Johnson, Ned Osterhoff, Stephen Foster and John Carey in *Much Ado About Nothing.*
Photo: Elbert Greer.

Playmakers Repertory Company

Arthur L. Housman
Executive Director

Tom Haas
Artistic Director

Edgar Marston
Managing Director

206 Graham Memorial 052A
University of North Carolina
Chapel Hill, NC 27514
(919) 933-1122 (business)
(919) 933-1121 (box office)

Founded 1976
Arthur L. Housman

Season
October–April

Schedule
Evenings
Tuesday-Sunday
Matinees
Sunday

Facilities
Playmakers Theatre
Seating capacity: 285
Stage: proscenium
Paul Green Theatre
Seating capacity: 505
Stage: thrust

Finances
July 1, 1978–June 30, 1979
$475,000 operating expenses
$136,000 earned income
$339,000 unearned income

Audience
Paid capacity: 83%
Subscribers: 3,386
Annual attendance: 30,453

AEA LORT (D) contract

Elaine Bromka and Michael Medeiras in *A Streetcar Named Desire*. Photo: Lee Howe.

Playmakers Repertory Company is a resident theatre on the campus of the University of North Carolina. Developed from the 58-year tradition of the Carolina Playmakers, PRC's commitment is to create a season of productions that speak with a contemporary voice to the concerns, desires and dreams of Raleigh, Durham and Chapel Hill residents. The playbill is composed of modern American works, selections drawn from the heritage of the American theatre and classics that find a contemporary voice.

Through an association with the Eugene O'Neill Memorial Theater Center's National Playwrights Conference, new American works have been found for the company. PRC continues the commitment to the "Second Step" program initiated by NPC and the Carolina Playmakers, in which the playwright is in residence during the production of the work. Under this program, PRC has presented in recent seasons *Isadora Duncan Sleeps with the Russian Navy, A History of the American Film, Uncommon Women and Others* and *Threads*.

Plays drawn from the repertoire of the American theatre are both familiar and new works, each play chosen for its ability to speak to the concerns of the audience. The recent productions of *Long Day's Journey into Night* and *Cold Storage* suggest the diversity possible within a single season. Currently, PRC is in a four-year program of staging Shakespeare's mature tragic cycle. *Hamlet* and *Macbeth* have been produced, with *Othello* scheduled for the 1979-80 season. The Shakespeare cycle has caused the development of an outreach program to the secondary schools and colleges within the state. Students are reached through a speakers bureau, study guides, post-play discussions and follow-up classroom speakers. Scheduling the Shakespeare play in the same March production period each year has facilitated long-range planning for the school systems and colleges involved.

Working with PRC is the University of North Carolina's Department of Dramatic Arts graduate training program. Master of fine arts degree candidates—actors, directors, designers and playwrights in training—have the PRC company as their model for professional practices and standards. In the third year of graduate training, selected students are invited to apprentice with the company in their area of discipline.

With strong advances in subscription sales and the ability to use the work of the theatre as an educational tool, Playmakers Repertory has come a long way in its four years in becoming a valuable regional resource.

Programs and services
Professional training in acting, directing, design, production and administration; classes for nonprofessionals; student performances, programs-in-schools, study materials, student and senior citizen ticket discounts, free ticket distribution, post-performance discussions, guest lecturers, newsletter, speakers bureau, volunteer auxiliary.

Productions 1977-78
A Streetcar Named Desire, Tennessee Williams
Equus, Peter Shaffer
Play It Again, Sam, Woody Allen
Hamlet, William Shakespeare
Uncommon Women and Others, Wendy Wasserstein
Ah, Wilderness!, Eugene O'Neill
Mr. Roberts, Thomas Heggen and Joshua Logan

Productions 1978-79
Dracula: The Vampire King, adapt: Tom Haas
Threads, Jonathan Bolt
Cold Storage, Ronald Ribman
Long Day's Journey into Night, Eugene O'Neill
Macbeth, William Shakespeare
You Can't Take It with You, George S. Kaufman and Moss Hart

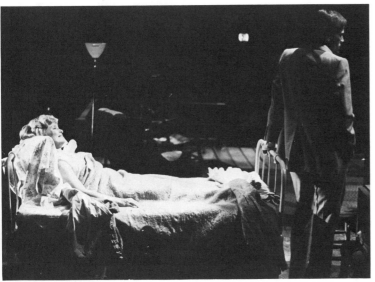

Lenka Peterson and Allan Carlsen in *Threads*. Photo: Michael B. Dixon.

Playwrights Horizons

Robert Moss
Producing Director

Andre Bishop
Artistic Director

Jane Moss
Managing Director

416 West 42nd St.
New York, NY 10036
(212) 564-1235

Box 1832
Flushing, NY 11352
(212) 699-0800 (business)
(212) 699-1660 (box office)

Founded 1971
Robert Moss

Season
September–May

Schedule
Evenings
Manhattan: Thursday–Saturday
Queens: Tuesday–Sunday
Matinees
Manhattan and Queens: Sunday

Facilities
Manhattan Mainstage
Seating capacity: 99
Stage: proscenium
Manhattan Studio Workshop
Seating capacity: 65
Stage: flexible
Queens Festival Theater
Flushing Meadow Park
Seating capacity: 482
Stage: proscenium

Finances
Sept. 1, 1977–Aug. 31, 1978
$495,000 operating expenses
$234,000 earned income
$287,000 unearned income

Audience
Mainstage paid capacity: 82%
Studio paid capacity: 95%
Queens paid capacity: 80%
Queens subscribers: 5,500
Total annual attendance: 46,800

*Manhattan: AEA Showcase Code
Queens: AEA LORT letter of
agreement*

Since its inception nine years ago, Playwrights Horizons has been dedicated to the support and encouragement of new American playwrights. Through readings, workshops and productions, Playwrights Horizons offers writers a professional facility in which to develop their work and refine their talent. Numerous plays have been launched through this developmental process, including *Vanities, Gemini, Kennedy's Children* and *Uncommon Women and Others*. Playwrights Horizons has recently expanded its commitment to also include writers for the musical theatre.

Playwrights Horizons maintains three separate performing spaces, ranging from the intimacy of a workshop environment to the challenge of a large subscription theatre. In its 65-seat Studio Workshop, the company explores the relationship between the script, the actors and the audience. The emphasis is on finding the combination of director and cast which will best illuminate the author's basic intent.

The 99-seat Mainstage serves those playwrights whose work has developed to a point where a fully mounted production is necessary for further growth. Careful consideration is given to production elements and the play is exposed to critical review.

Certain pieces coalesce in these workshop and mainstage productions, warranting a future life. These works are brought to the 482-seat Queens Festival Theater as a basis of the following year's subscription season, complemented by American and European masterworks, chosen specifically to highlight the themes and styles of the new plays.

In pursuing these goals and developing facilities for them, Playwrights Horizons has made a major contribution to both the communities it serves. On West 42nd Street, Playwrights Horizons helped to pioneer the redevelopment efforts that have transformed a block of "porno parlors" into a thriving string of Off Broadway theatres.

In Queens, Playwrights Horizons functions as the borough's only professional theatre. Its student matinee program enables high school students to attend special student matinee performances, offering many adolescents their first experience with live profesional theatre.

Programs and services
Administrative and technical/production internships, student performances, programs-in-schools, study materials, post-performance discussions, workshop productions and staged readings, newsletter, volunteer auxiliary, theatre rentals.

Productions 1977-78
Anything Goes, book: Guy Bolton, P.G. Wodehouse, Howard Lindsay and Russel Crouse; music and lyrics: Cole Porter
Gogol, Len Jenkin
Angel City, Sam Shepard
Back County Crimes, Lanie Robertson
A Christmas Carol, adapt: Christopher Cox
Two Small Bodies, Neal Bell
The Member of the Wedding, Carson McCullers
Three Sons, Richard Lortz
Dial M for Murder, Frederick Knott
Shay, Anne Commire
A Midsummer Night's Dream, William Shakespeare
Hooters, Ted Tally
Awake and Sing!, Clifford Odets
Jungle Coup, Richard Nelson
The Prisoner of Second Avenue, Neil Simon

Productions 1978-79
Oh, What a Lovely War!, music and lyrics adapt: Joan Greenwood and Theatre Workshop
Say Goodnight, Gracie, Ralph Pape
The Eccentricities of a Nightingale, Tennessee Williams
Living at Home, Anthony Giardina
Vienna Notes, Richard Nelson
Breaking and Entering, Neal Bell
In Trousers, music and lyrics: William Finn
Hedda Gabler, Henrik Ibsen; trans: John Osborne
Table Settings, James Lapine
Ladyhouse Blues, Kevin O'Morrison
The Songs of Jonathan Tunick, music: Jonathan Tunick; lyrics: various
The Terrorists, Dallas Murphy, Jr.
Don't Tell Me Everything and Other Musical Arrangements, music: Peter Larson, John Lewis and Josh Rubins; lyrics: J. Rubins
Private Lives, Noel Coward
Sweet Main Street, music and lyrics: Carol Hall, et al.; adapt: Shirley Kaplan
The Show-Off, George Kelly

Mary Testa, Chip Zien and Joanna Green in *In Trousers.* Photo: Susan Cook.

Victor Bevine and David Garrison in *Living at Home.* Photo: Susan Cook.

The Playwrights' Lab

Thomas Dunn
Director

Carolyn Johnson
Coordinator

The Playwrights' Center
2301 East Franklin Ave.
Minneapolis, MN 55406
(612) 332-7481

Founded 1971
Gregg Ahlmquist, Erik Brogger,
Barbara Field, Charles Nolte

Season
September–June

Facilities
Seating capacity: 175
Stage: flexible

Finances
July 1, 1978–June 30, 1979
$112,000 operating expenses
$ 40,000 earned income
$ 72,000 unearned income

Audience
Annual attendance: 6,000

Touring contact
John Olive

Booked-in-events
Music, theatre

AEA Guest Artist contract

The Playwrights' Lab's new
home.

The Playwrights' Lab was founded by four playwrights in 1971, primarily to stage works by Minnesota writers. Four years later it reorganized into a full-service arts organization, emphasizing four main programming areas:

Financial support: The Playwrights' Lab awards fellowship stipends annually to 12 writers, ranging in size from $2,000 to $4,800.

Script development: The Lab accepts unsolicited script submissions, presents staged readings, conducts non-performance workshops as well as "cold" readings for company members and exchanges scripts with other area theatres.

Service: The Lab provides employment, grant and contest information, script referrals and critiques, professional "survival workshop," counseling and script publication.

Education: Classes are offered at the Playwrights' Lab in addition to residencies at local schools, colleges and community centers.

The goal of all Lab programs is the development of good writers and stageworthy scripts. Previously production-oriented, the company in recent years has shifted its focus and now emphasizes the developmental process rather than finished presentation.

Programs and services
Professional training in directing; creative writing classes for nonprofessionals; classes for children, artistic and administrative internships, student performances, programs-in-schools, study materials, free ticket distribution, regional touring, post-performance discussions, workshop productions and staged readings, poetry readings, children's theatre, newsletter, script publication, speakers bureau, theatre rentals.

Productions 1977-78
Small Affections, Kirk Ristau
Hippodrome Murder, Cynthia Hanson
Edges, Frank Pike and David Erickson
Dromenon, Henry Manganiello
Standing on My Knees, John Olive

Productions 1978-79
*Season strictly devoted to staged readings and
non-performance workshops.*

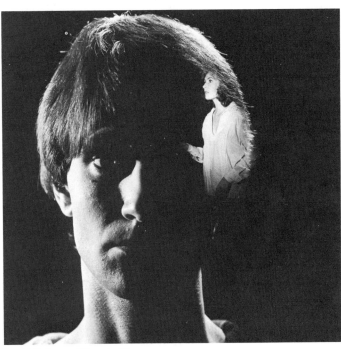

David Potter and Brenda Altman
in *Dromenon.*

Portland Stage Company

Charles Towers
Producing Director

Richard Ostreicher
Managing Director

Box 4876 DTS
Portland, ME 04112
(207) 774-1043 (business)
(207) 774-0465 (box office)

Founded 1974

Season
September–May

Schedule
Evenings
Wednesday–Sunday
Matinees
Saturday, Sunday

Facilities
15 Temple St.
Seating capacity: 151
Stage: thrust

Finances
June 1, 1978–May 31, 1979
$136,000 operating expenses
$ 81,000 earned income
$ 55,000 unearned income

Audience
Paid capacity: 70%
Subscribers: 810
Annual attendance: 17,500

The Portland Stage Company is the only theatre of its kind in Maine: a nonprofit, resident professional theatre offering a winter season of classical, contemporary and new plays. The company was founded with the specific purpose of creating a theatre of quality and substance for the people of southern Maine. Previously, professional theatre was only available in the forms of summer stock "star packages" or a two-hour drive south to Boston.

The growth of the Portland Stage Company has fortunately coincided with the revitalization of the city of Portland, which continues to blend historic preservation and new construction in the development of an attractive and active urban center. PSC has played a major role in establishing Portland as the cultural center for the state, joining the Portland Symphony Orchestra and the Portland Museum of Art in providing a full cultural life for the area. PSC recently completed an intensive two-year institutional development program which included building a new performing space, changing the institution's name (formerly the Profile Theatre), strengthening administrative policy, cutting in half the accumulated debt and tripling subscription sales.

The theatre operates its own 151-seat thrust stage theatre, ideally located in the center of the downtown development district. The size of the performing space has been instrumental in establishing PSC's local reputation as a theatre of intimacy and involvement. The audience/ actor relationship has proved to be a drawing card, and consequently, artistic emphasis is on nuance of character and detail of the stage environment. The usually small-cast productions undergo a full five weeks of rehearsal to achieve these ends. Company members are hired through auditions in Boston and New York, for both full-season and individual show contracts. A selected few actors return each season and over the years a loose ensemble has formed, whose "floating" quality allows both freshness and familiarity.

As the play choices indicate, the theatre's present artistic direction is to produce as wide a variety of quality scripts as possible, maintaining a standard that is distinctive in the area, and thereby developing a richly appreciated theatrical heritage where there has been none. As the audience both grows and deepens, the theatre plans to broaden its artistic policy to include the production of new scripts.

Jeffrey Posson in *Jesse and the Bandit Queen*. Photo: Peter Macomber.

Programs and services
Artistic, administrative and technical/production internships; student performances, programs- in-schools, study materials, adult education class, student and senior citizen ticket discounts, free ticket distribution, statewide touring, preview and post-performance discussions, workshop productions and staged readings, guest lecturers, newsletter, speakers bureau, volunteer auxiliary, theatre rentals.

Productions 1977-78
Who's Afraid of Virginia Woolf?, Edward Albee
Candida, George Bernard Shaw
The School for Wives, Moliere; trans: Richard Wilbur
Waiting for Godot, Samuel Beckett
The Play's the Thing, Ferenc Molnar; adapt: P. G. Wodehouse
Jesse and the Bandit Queen, David Freeman
On the Harmfulness of Tobacco, Swan Song and *The Boor*, Anton Chekhov

Productions 1978-79
The Mandrake, Niccolo Machiavelli
The Runner Stumbles, Milan Stitt
The Importance of Being Earnest, Oscar Wilde
Cat on a Hot Tin Roof, Tennessee Williams
Crime on Goat Island, Ugo Betti
The Stronger, August Strindberg
Play Strindberg, Friedrich Dürrenmatt
Winners (from *Lovers*), Brian Friel

Hamilton Gillet, Bruce Pineau and Time Winters in *The Mandrake*. Photo: Peter Macomber.

The Proposition Workshop

Allan Albert
Artistic Director

Box 745
Radio City Station
New York, NY 10019

Founded 1968
Jeremy Leven
C. Wendell Smith

Season
Year-round

Finances
Oct. 1, 1977–Sept. 30, 1978
$135,000 operating expenses
$115,000 earned income
$ 15,000 unearned income

Audience
Annual attendance: 30,000

Touring contact
Allan Albert

Fyvush Finkel, Marilyn Sokol, Paul Kreppel and Lewis J. Stadlen in *Vagabond Stars.* Photo: Walter H. Scott.

During the past two years, the Proposition Workshop has relocated its home base and sorted its priorities. *The Proposition,* the Workshop's improvisational revue, made the company a landmark in Cambridge, Mass., and one of the principal touring companies in the country. For the past five years, however, the Workshop has turned to creating nonfiction theatre pieces, fusing documentary materials, oral histories and both authentic and original music. These have covered a wide range of historical and contemporary subjects, from whaling to trucking. The shows are similar in style, concept and form and, after originally being produced in Cambridge and Stockbridge, many moved on to New York and national tours.

With the improvisational shows continuing on a more limited basis, the need for a resident base could not be justified; it misdirected the company's energies. In addition, most of the 75-odd actors in the Workshop's history had become New York-based, and since its Off Broadway run (1971-74), the company had also maintained a New York base. A complete move to New York took place in September 1977.

Since that move, the character of its nonfiction work has shaped the format and schedule of the company's year. The pieces take from six months to a year to research and develop, and thus require a project-oriented use of time and space. It is anticipated that two new works will be prepared and/or presented each season; at the moment, pieces are underway on the "Kerouac Fifties" and Coney Island. With each new work, the Workshop hopes to give new shape to an old form, or, ideally, create a new form. In these last respects, the Proposition Workshop is evolving into a theatre not unlike a small choreographer's company in structure and purpose. Although changes have reduced the output and size of the year's work, they reflect the artistic needs of the company and will, in the long run, insure the integrity and quality of the Workshop product.

Programs and services
Professional acting, training, classes for nonprofessionals, programs-in-schools, national touring, post-performance discussions, workshop productions and staged readings, children's theatre, cabaret.

Productions 1977-78
The Proposition, Allan Albert
The Proposition Circus, Allan Albert
A Fable, Jean-Claude van Itallie
Four Years After the Revolution, music and
   lyrics: Richard Peaslee
The Casino, music and lyrics: various; adapt:
   Allan Albert
Soap, music and lyrics: various; adapt: Allan
   Albert

Productions 1978-79
The Proposition
The Proposition Circus
Corral, music and lyrics: various; adapt: Allan
   Albert
Four Years After the Revolution
Night Riders, book: Allan Albert; music: John
   Lewis; lyrics: Josh Rubins
Vagabond Stars, book: Nahma Sandrow and
   Allan Albert; music: Raphael Crystal; lyrics:
   Alan Poul
The Whale Show, music and lyrics: various;
   adapt: Allan Albert

Sonja Amderson in *Four Years After the Revolution.* Photo: Elizabeth Wolynski.

Provisional Theatre

Collective Leadership
Contact: Steven Kent,
Candace Laughlin, Barry Opper

1816½ North Vermont Ave.
Los Angeles, CA 90027
(213) 664-1450

Founded 1972

Season
Year-round

Finances
July 1, 1978–June 30, 1979
$90,000 operating expenses
$40,000 earned income
$48,000 unearned income

Audience
Annual attendance: 20,000

The Provisional Theatre of Los Angeles, with most of its members having worked together for more than 12 years, is one of the oldest touring ensembles in the United States. The ensemble writes and realizes original dramatic pieces about the experience of living and working in a land where loneliness, alienation and cynicism are becoming all too commonplace. Its efforts reflect a belief in discipline and a sense of humor as tools to share in the rediscovery of an authentic American culture. Its members believe that the theatre can be meaningful (as well as entertaining) and that it can reaffirm people's faith in themselves.

The Provisional Theatre believes that theatre is a vital art form and it is committed to taking its work to people who don't call themselves "theatregoers." The 1978-79 season was typical in that it included a summer run in three different Los Angeles locations, residencies with schools and community arts organizations, a California state tour and two national tours with performances and workshops in prisons, senior citizen centers, nursing homes, schools, churches and community centers, as well as theatres.

The group's most recent original work is a good representation of the Provisional Theatre approach. It is called *Inching Through the Everglades or Pie in the Sky and Something on Your Shoe* and is a funny, musical, friendly play about ordinary folks and their struggle to get by—a humorous look at the humanity of people caught in a very inhuman society.

The future work of the Provisional Theatre will continue to revolve around spirit, hope and potential.

Programs and services
Professional training in acting, directing, design, production and administration; classes for nonprofessionals; seminars and workshops in collective management and community organizing; student performances, programs in schools and prisons; ticket discounts for students, senior citizens and the unemployed; free ticket distribution, national touring, post-performance discussions, workshop productions and staged readings, poetry readings, benefit performances, newsletter.

Productions 1977-78
America Piece
Voice of the People, Parts I and II
Songs and Speeches of the People
Inching Through the Everglades, or Pie in the Sky and Something on Your Shoe

Productions 1978-79
Voice of the People, Parts I and II
Songs and Speeches of the People
Inching Through the Everglades, or Pie in the Sky and Something on Your Shoe

All productions are developed by the company.

Larry Hoffman and Candace Laughlin in *Inching Through the Everglades.* Photo: Jay Thompson.

Larry Hoffman, Cricket Parmalee and Candace Laughlin *Inching Through the Everglades.* Photo: Jay Thompson.

Puerto Rican Traveling Theatre Company

Miriam Colón Edgar
Executive Director

Gary S. Levine
Administrator

141 West 94th St.
New York, NY 10025
(212) 749-8474 (business)
(212) 354-1293 (box office)

Founded 1967
Miriam Colón Edgar,
George P. Edgar,
Anibal Otero, Jose Ocasio

Season
January–September

Facilities
304 West 47th St.
Seating capacity: 74
Stage: thrust

Finances
Oct. 1, 1977–Sept. 30, 1978
$178,000 operating expenses
$ 13,000 earned income
$165,000 unearned income

Audience
Paid capacity: 85%
Annual attendance: 35,000

Touring contact
Gary S. Levine

AEA Mini contract

Miriam Colón, Luis Avalos and
Norberto Kerner in *The FM Safe*.
Photo: Ken Howard.

The Puerto Rican Traveling Theatre was founded with the aim of bringing contemporary, relevant, bilingual theatre free of charge to the people of New York. The theatre began as a community-based organization and has maintained its close ties with New York's many neighborhoods while developing its two areas of activity, performance and education.

The permanent theatre, based on 42nd Street's Theatre Row, offers bilingual presentations year-round, spotlighting contemporary dramas by Hispanic and other playwrights. The company's touring unit takes professional productions to community centers, churches, streets and parks throughout the New York metropolitan area.

Three programs execute the company's educational function. The Training Unit gives free bilingual instruction in the performing arts to hundreds of youngsters from low-income families. Sponsored by the U.S. Department of Health, Education and Welfare, the In-School Arts Program offers bilingual, multicultural arts workshops in three junior high schools on Manhattan's upper west side. The company's

Professional Playwrights Unit gives 15 emerging writers the opportunity to read, critique and develop new dramatic works.

In its 12-year history, the theatre has grown from a summer street theatre into a front-runner among professional community-based organizations. Two dramatic developments have underscored this growth. The National Endowment for the Arts has awarded a Challenge Grant to the Puerto Rican Traveling Theatre, the only Hispanic organization in this country so rewarded. New York City has also honored the company's efforts by granting it a long-term lease on a firehouse located in the heart of the Broadway district. The building will be converted into a new 199-seat permanent home for the Puerto Rican Traveling Theatre.

Programs and services
Classes for nonprofessionals and children; administrative internships, student performances, programs-in-schools, student and senior citizen ticket discounts, regional touring, workshop productions and staged readings, poetry readings.

Productions 1978
The FM Safe, Jaime Carrero
Un Jibaro, Ramón Méndez Quinones
La Compañia, Luis Rechani Agrait

Productions 1979
Simpson Street, Edward Gallardo; trans: Tony Diaz and Miriam Colón Edgar
El Macho, Joseph Lizardi; trans: Tony Diaz and J. Lizardi

Maria Norman, Freddy Valle and
Antonia Rey in *Simpson Street*.
Photo: Ken Howard.

The Puppet Workshop

Marc W. Kohler
Executive/Artistic Director

725 Branch Ave.
Providence, RI 02904
(401) 521-4250

Founded 1972
Marc W. Kohler

Season
Year-round

Finances
July 1, 1978–June 30, 1979
$73,000 operating expenses
$32,000 earned income
$39,000 unearned income

Audience
Annual attendance: 50,000

Touring contact
Patricia Bessette

In July 1972, the Puppet Workshop incorporated as a nonprofit theatre with two staff members—the company's director and one musician. The young theatre's goals were quite ambitious for a beginning arts organization. The first was a serious application of puppetry in performances and workshops throughout Rhode Island. Special emphasis was placed upon the value of puppetry as an educational tool. The second goal was to expand the company's operations as a resource center for all working artists—painters, musicians, writers, sculptors and designers.

Each year the Puppet Workshop has seen its goals realized. The company now employs five full-time staff artists and many more who work on a job-to-job basis. The staff consists of a composer/musician, a professional photographer, a costume/set designer and a sculptor, all of whom work with director Marc W. Kohler from a production's concept to its presentation. These same people also operate the company's workshop program.

In addition to more than 300 performances and workshop sessions yearly, activities include a residency at Providence's Meeting Street School for the handicapped, puppetry courses for adults, and special projects for colleges, theatre companies and television.

The puppets and plays produced by the Puppet Workshop are original pieces designed to allow children to actively participate in the event through verbalization, the puppeteers taking their cues from the audience. In this way the company demonstrates that puppets are "alive" with human joys, hopes and fears.

Long-term goals include a more intensive use of puppets with the economically, physically and emotionally handicapped.

Programs and services
Classes for nonprofessionals and children; artistic, administrative and technical/production internships; puppet workshops for adults, lectures on arts management, programs-in-schools, study materials, national touring, post-performance discussions.

Productions 1977-78
The Landing of the Schlunk, company developed
Judy's Dream, company developed
The Story of Esther—A Purim Show, company developed

Productions 1978-79
A Midsummer Night's Dream, William Shakespeare
A Brighter Light, company developed

The Bear's First Christmas in performance at the Rhode Island School of Design Museum. Photo: Rance Price.

A Midsummer Night's Dream. Photo: Rance Price.

Repertorio Español

Rene Buch
Artistic Director

Robert Weber Federico
Associate Artistic Director

Gilberto Zaldivar
Producer

138 East 27th St.
New York, NY 10016
(212) 889-2850

Founded 1969
Gilberto Zaldivar,
Rene Buch, Frances Drucker

Season
Sepember–July

Schedule
Evenings
Friday–Sunday
Matinees
Sundays, selected weekdays

Facilities
Gramercy Arts Theatre
Seating capacity: 180
Stage: proscenium

Finances
Sept. 1, 1978–Aug. 31, 1979
$194,000 operating expenses
$ 70,000 earned income
$124,000 unearned income

Audience
Paid capacity: 55%
Annual attendance: 35,000

Touring contact
Gilberto Zaldivar

Booked-in events
Spanish-language performing
artists and companies

Mirtha Cartaya in *Te Juro Juana que Tengo Ganas.* Photo: Gerry Goodstein.

Although apart from the mainstream of American theatre, Repertorio Español endeavors to achieve the same goals as the major American companies: good theatre.

Dedicated to a theatre of texts, Repertorio Español concentrates on high artistic standards to attract audiences. And because of its standards, the company has become a cultural force offering a sense of identity and cultural esteem to Hispanics.

What began informally in June 1968 has grown into a full-time professional company with a resident facility and a stable company of actors trained in both the classical and modern styles. The diversity of the company with all Spanish-speaking nationalities represented is matched by its repertoire.

Repertorio Español has three unusual features which contribute to its identity: first, all its peformances are in Spanish; second, it is a true rotating repertory company with approximately a dozen productions active each year; and third, the works it stages extend from the great

classics of the Golden Age of Spain to the great new plays of contemporary Latin America. These plays are rarely, if ever, given professional mountings in the USA. A typical weekend series of peformances might include a Lorca tragedy, a venerable classic like *Celestina* and a comedy by Mexico's Carballido, Argentina's Talesnik or Venezuela's Chocron.

This ambitious repertoire is possible due to the artistic decisions of director Rene Buch, designer Robert Weber Federico and a talented company of actors, headed by Cuba's Ofelia González, Ecuador's Alfonso Manosalvas and Puerto Rico's Raul Davila. Together the company has created a style which has distinguished Repertorio Español season after season.

Repertorio Español's service to the Hispanic and academic communities extends beyond its resident theatre through nationwide tours. It also serves as an invaluable audio-visual aid in the study of Spanish literature.

Programs and services
Professional training in acting, student performances, programs-in-schools, study materials, student and senior citizen ticket discounts, national touring, post-performance discussions, theatre rentals.

Productions 1977-78
Te Juro Juana que Tengo Ganas, Emilio Carballido
Bodas de Sangre, Federico Garcia Lorca
Los Japoneses No Esperan, Ricardo Talesnik
Jardín de Otoño, Diana Raznovich
La Celestina, Fernando de Rojas
La Dama Duende, Calderon de la Barca
El Censo, Emilio Carballido
Cien Veces No Debo, Ricardo Talesnik
Los Soles Truncos, Rene Marques
La Fiaca, Ricardo Talesnik

Productions 1978-79
Romeo y Julieta, William Shakespeare; trans: Pablo Neruda
La Revolución, Isaac Chocron
La Moza de Ayacucho, Francisco Cuevas-Cancino
Un Hombre Sincero: Jose Marti, Jose Marti; adapt: Rene Buch
Te Juro Juana que Tengo Ganas
Los Japoneses No Esperan
Jardín de Otoño
La Celestina
La Dama Duende
Bodas de Sangre
Los Soles Truncos
La Fiaca

Romeo y Julieta. Photo: Gerry Goodstein.

Richard Morse Mime Theatre

Richard Morse
Artistic Director

Rasa Lisauskas Allan
Managing Director

224 Waverly Place
New York, NY 10014
(212) 242-0530 (business)
(212) 242-0530 (box office)

Founded 1975
Richard Morse
Rasa Lisauskas

Season
October–April

Schedule
Evenings
Friday–Sunday
Matinees
Saturday, Sunday

Facilities
Seating capacity: 90
Stage: proscenium

Finances
July 1, 1978–June 30, 1979
$90,000 operating expenses
$50,000 earned income
$32,000 unearned income

Audience
Paid capacity: 60%
Subcribers: 50
Annual attendance: 25,000

Touring contact
Gabriel Barre

The Richard Morse Mime Theatre is the only institutional theatre in New York City performing mime on a regular basis. It has been cited for its highly innovative work and is considered a major force in pioneering an original mime tradition in America. Under Richard Morse's artistic direction, the theatre has from its inception departed from traditional mime practices (such as the white face) so often associated with this theatre form.

As a whole, the work draws inspiration from contemporary life, with an emphasis on comedy. Audiences may be "taken" anywhere—from a crowded elevator to a concert hall to a baseball stadium. They may see actors portraying people or objects, such as a flag unfurling in the morning breeze, a building being demolished, a vengeful faucet tormenting a hapless insomniac or even a letter in the process of being read.

While the company is now entering its fifth New York season in its resident theatre, it has also played to enthusiastic audiences across America and abroad on two extended State Department tours to 14 countries. A trip to the Orient is being planned for the 1980-81 season.

The body of work created thus far includes six original full-length productions with casts ranging from two to eight performers, four original children's shows and two programs designed for performance with symphony orchestras.

A distinctive feature of the theatre is its highly developed training program. Classes are offered, both at home and on tour, and the training program is being established as a focal point for actors, directors and teachers exploring the expressive possibilities of their bodies and performance in a wide variety of styles.

Programs and services
Professional training in mime, dance and acting; classes for nonprofessionals and children; student performances, programs-in-schools, master classes and workshops, student and senior citizen ticket discounts, international touring, post-performance discussions, children's theatre, newsletter, theatre rentals, benefit peformances for the handicapped.

Productions 1977-78
The Arts and Leisure Section of The New York Times, Richard Morse
Gifts!, Richard Morse
Tintinnabula, Richard Morse
Pranks, Rasa Lisauskas Allan

Productions 1979-79
Appeal of the Big Apple, Richard Morse
Tintinnabula
The Play of Herod, Noah Greenberg and William Smolden
What the Devil!, Richard Morse, from Igor Stravinsky's *L'Histoire du Soldat*
Inside Up, Rasa Lisauskas Allan
A Chip Off the Old Munk, Rasa Lisauskas Allan

Richard Morse in *Mime and Again!* Photo: Ian Anderson.

Rasa Lisauskas Allan and Richard Morse in *Mime and Again!* Photo: Ian Anderson.

The Ridiculous Theatrical Company

Charles Ludlam
Director

Catherine Smith
Administrative Director

One Sheridan Square
New York, NY 10011
(212) 260-7137

Founded 1967
Charles Ludlam

Season
Year-round

Schedule
Evenings
Tuesday–Sunday
Matinees
Saturday

Facilities
Seating capacity: 200
Stage: thrust

Finances
July 1, 1978–June 30, 1979
$168,000 operating expenses
$ 98,000 earned income
$ 74,000 unearned income

Audience
Paid capacity: 65%
Annual attendance: 25,000

Touring contact
Catherine Smith

Lola Pashalinski and Charles
Ludlam in *Utopia Incorporated*.
Photo: Chris Scott.

The Ridiculous Theatrical Company is a
permanent ensemble of actors which, under the
artistic direction of Charles Ludlam, has
produced and maintained a repertoire of 15
innovative comic dramas over the past 10
years. In addition, they have created and
continue to operate a children's theatre
program which includes *Professor Bedlam's
Educational Punch and Judy Show; Anti-Galaxy
Nebulae,* a science-fiction puppet show; and
The Enchanted Pig, a play combining both
human actors and puppets. Company members
have received a total of six Obie Awards for
acting, design, distinguished achievement and
the puppet theatre.

The company's work over the years has been
primarily concerned with the reevaluation of the
theatrical inventions of comic intent. These
works have been innovative in creating
modernist works of parody, burlesque, travesty
and farce, from the mock-heroic to the wittily
paradoxical. Ludlam has created a body of work
that has given credibility to the genre known as
theatre of the ridiculous. "Ludlamization" has
become a standard critical term to describe a
distinctive comic approach to serious work.

During the 1978-79 season, the company
performed at the Annenburg Festival of the Arts
in Philadelphia and the 99¢ Floating Theatre in
Pittsburgh. At home, they produced two new
plays, *Utopia Incorporated* and *The Enchanted
Pig,* and presented seven works from their
repertoire. The company is presently fund-
raising to continue renovations on its theatre at
One Sheridan Square in Greenwich Village and
preparing for its 1979-80 season, which will
include the first Ludlam adaptation of Charles
Dickens' *A Christmas Carol.*

Programs and services
Senior citizen ticket discounts, free ticket
distribution, voucher program, national touring,
post-performance discussions.

Productions 1977-78
Der Ring Gott Farblonjet
The Ventriloquist's Wife
Camille
Stage Blood
Bluebeard

Productions 1978-79
Anti-Galaxy Nebulae
Stage Blood
The Ventriloquist's Wife
Bluebeard
Corn
Utopia Incorporated
Camille
The Enchanted Pig

All productions are created by Charles Ludlam.

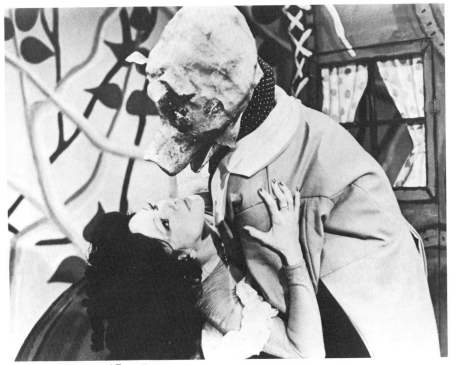

Black-Eyed Susan and Everett
Quinton in *The Enchanted Pig.*

St. Nicholas Theater Company

Steven Schachter
Artistic Director

Peter Schneider
Managing Director

2851 North Halsted St.
Chicago, IL 60657
(312) 975-2320 (business)
(312) 975-2300 (box office)

Founded 1974
David Mamet, Steven Schachter,
William H. Macy, Patricia Cox

Season
September–June

Schedule
Evenings
Tuesday–Sunday
Matinees
Sunday

Facilities
Seating capacity: 174
Stage: thrust

Finances
Aug. 1, 1978–July 31, 1979
$650,000 operating expenses
$400,000 earned income
$325,000 unearned income

Audience
Paid capacity: 85%
Subscribers: 5,500
Annual attendance: 60,000

Touring contact
Tom Thompson

Booked-in events
Music, theatre

AEA LORT letter of argeement

In its five years of existence, the St. Nicholas Theater Company has become one of Chicago's leading centers for the performing arts with a commitment to the development of new plays and playwrights and to the training of theatre artists.

This artistic vision is fulfilled by the St. Nicholas performance programs and the School of the Theater Arts. The performance programs include a five-play mainstage subscription series, the New Work Ensemble Series, the Theater for Young Audiences program and special events.

In the mainstage series, St. Nicholas presents four world or regional premieres and one classic each year for a subscription audience of more than 5,000. In the past four seasons, St. Nicholas has produced 10 world premieres, eight Chicago premieres and four classics.

The New Work Ensemble Series is a five-play program designed to provide new writers, directors, designers and actors the opportunity to collaborate on works-in-progress without commercial pressure. The series also emphasizes the development of a resident ensemble to perform each production. For the 1978-79 season, Theater for Young Audiences was expanded to include tour performances as well as performances at the St. Nicholas Theater.

Special events have played an important part in the development of St. Nicholas' national reputation and audience. Since presenting Lily Tomlin in her week-long sell-out pre-Broadway engagement in 1976, St. Nicholas has welcomed lectures from noted experts in American theatre, such as Robert Lewis, Harold Clurman and John Houseman. The Summer Festival of Special Events presented Donal Donnelly, Geraldine Fitzgerald, Viveca Lindfors, Nacha Guevara, Sarah Miles and the musical revue *Scrambled Feet* over the past two summers.

St. Nicholas School of the Theater Arts began in 1975 with a roster of four classes and 25 students. The school now enrolls 1,500 students annually and offers classes in acting technique, movement, voice, speech, theatre for childen and many special seminars.

Programs and services
Professional training in acting, directing and administration; classes for nonprofessionals and children; artistic, administrative and technical/production internships; student performances, programs-in-schools, study materials, New Work Ensemble Series, student and senior citizen ticket discounts, statewide touring company, post-performance discussions, workshop productions and staged readings, guest lecturers, cabaret, newsletter, volunteer auxiliary, theatre rentals.

Productions 1977-78
Ashes, David Rudkin
The Woods, David Mamet
You Can't Take It with You, George S. Kaufman and Moss Hart
Uncommon Women and Others, Wendy Wasserstein
Barnaby Sweet, Glenn Allen Smith
The Nuclear Family, Mark Frost
Spider, Bobby Joyce Smith
I'd Rather Be It, company developed
The Slow Hours, Bruce Burgun
Marty, Paddy Chayefsky
Great Solo Town, Thomas Babe
The Revenge of the Space Pandas, David Mamet
The Adventures of Captain Marbles and His Acting Squad, Episodes III and IV, William H. Macy and David Kovacs

Productions 1978-79
The 5th of July, Lanford Wilson
Little Eyolf, Henrik Ibsen
All Honorable Men, Michael J. Chepiga
Funeral March for a One-Man Band, book: Ron Whyte; music: Mel Marvin; lyrics: Robert Satuloff
The Curse of an Aching Heart, William Alfred
Understanding Czrbyk, Richard Harris
The Diary of Anne Frank, Frances Goodrich and Albert Hackett
A Dark Night of the Soul, Robert Eisele
The Memoirs of Charlie Pops, Joseph Hart
Fancy's Touch, Bruce Burgun
The Miracle Worker, William Gibson
The Adventures of Captain Marbles and His Acting Squad, Episode V, William H. Macy

Diane Dorsey Fahnstrom and Glenne Headley in *The Diary of Anne Frank.* Photo: Dan Rest.

Don Moffett, Jim Zarlenga, Jody Naymik, Terry Joe and David Puski in *The Memoirs of Charlie Pops.* Photo: Dan Rest.

Seattle Repertory Theatre

John Hirsch
Consulting Artistic Director

Peter Donnelly
Managing Director

Box B
Queen Anne Station
Seattle, WA 98109
(206) 447-4730 (business)
(206) 447-4764 (box office)

Founded 1963

Season
October–May

Schedule
Evenings
Tuesday–Sunday
Matinees
Wednesday, Saturday

Facilities
Seattle Center Playhouse
225 Mercer St.
Seating capacity: 894
Stage: proscenium

Finances
July 1; 1978–June 30, 1979
$1,655,000 operating expenses
$1,294,000 earned income
$ 506,000 unearned income

Audience
Paid capacity: 93%
Subscribers: 23,685
Annual attendance: 229,618

Touring contact
Jeffrey Bentley

*AEA LORT (B) and Young
Audiences contracts*

James Cahill and Megan Cole in
Uncle Vanya. Photo: Greg Gilbert.

Eva LeGallienne and Tim Wilson
in *The Dream Watcher*. Photo:
Greg Gilbert.

At the close of the Seattle World's Fair in 1963, an enthusiastic group of citizens founded the Seattle Repertory Theatre. From a first season's attendance of 67,000, the scope of that enthusiasm has steadily increased to a cumulative total of almost three million theatregoers at the conclusion of SRT's 16th year.

An integral part of the Northwest's cultural lifestyle, the Seattle Repertory Theatre has consistently endeavored to rediscover the imaginative values—both contemporary and traditional—which reflect the vigorous spirit of the people from whom the theatre draws its vitality. Six productions are presented throughout an eight-month season, each running 32 performances from October to May, at the Seattle Center Playhouse. An eclectic playbill is chosen—from Shakespeare, Chekhov and Ibsen, to Stoppard, Nichols and Shaffer. Premiere works are included whenever possible, as well as the most challenging new plays, such as *Equus* or *Catsplay*, from the New York theatre scene. As this volume goes to press, W. Duncan Ross, who has guided SRT's artistic policy for the last nine years, leaves to take up his new post as chairman of the drama division at the University of Southern California. John Hirsch has been named consulting artistic director for the coming season. New directions will certainly play a tangible role in SRT's continued growth, as the new artistic director will be helping to formulate plans for a new all-encompassing theatre complex at the Seattle Center, funded in large part by monies set aside by a two-thirds majority vote of the city's population. The new building is projected to open for the 1981-82 season.

Since 1975, SRT has served its state and region with an innovative, multifaceted program called "Hub-Cities Touring Residency Project." Through this project, a classroom preparation piece is provided, previewing the touring mainstage production; the MOB (Mobile Outreach Bunch) performs a 50-minute revue aimed at junior high school students; and the Rep's mainstage company takes to the road with a full-scale production of a play which has just completed its mainstage run. *Much Ado About Nothing* toured the Northwest in 1978 and *The Glass Menagerie* followed in 1979.

Programs and services
Professional training in production; artistic, administrative and technical/production internships; student performances, programs-in-schools, study materials, performances for the deaf, student and senior citizen ticket discounts, free ticket distribution, regional touring, guest lecturers, children's theatre, newsletter, speakers bureau, volunteer auxiliary, support group, theatre rentals.

Productions 1977-78
The Royal Family, George S. Kaufman and
    Edna Ferber
The Dream Watcher, Barbara Wersba
The National Health, Peter Nichols
Uncle Vanya, Anton Chekhov; trans: David
    Magarshack
Much Ado About Nothing, William Shakespeare
13 Rue de l'Amour, Georges Feydeau; adapt:
    Mawby Green and Ed Feilbert
Discovering Tutankhamun, Phil Shallat

Productions 1978-79
A Penny for a Song, John Whiting
The Master Builder, Henrik Ibsen; trans: Sam
    Engelstad and Jane Alexander
Side by Side by Sondheim, music and lyrics:
    Stephen Sondheim, et al.; adapt: Ned
    Sherrin
The Glass Menagerie, Tennessee Williams
Catsplay, Istvan Orkeny; trans: Clara Gyorgyey
Fallen Angels, Noel Coward
The Energy Show, company developed

Soho Repertory Theatre

Marlene Swartz
Jerry Engelbach
Artistic Directors

19 Mercer Street
New York, NY 10013
(212) 925-2588

Founded 1975
Marlene Swartz
Jerry Engelbach

Season
August–July

Schedule
Evenings
Friday–Sunday
Matinees
Sunday

Facilities
Seating capacity: 85
Stage: thrust

Finances
July 1, 1978–June 30, 1979
$55,000 operating expenses
$38,000 earned income
$13,000 unearned income

Audience
Paid capacity: 70%
Subscribers: 1,026
Annual attendance: 11,722

AEA Showcase Code

Soho Repertory Theatre is located in a 19th-century cast-iron loft building in Manhattan's artistic community South of Houston Street—"Soho." During Soho Rep's first year it produced 13 plays in rotating repertory, including the first New York production in 36 years of Maxwell Anderson's *Key Largo* and the New York premiere of Aristophanes' *Ecclesiazusae* in a new translation for Soho entitled *The Congresswomen.*

Since its beginning five years ago, Soho Rep has presented 65 plays, both classic and modern, and is particularly proud of its premiere productions. Among them have been the New York premieres of Michel de Ghelderode's *Miss Jairus,* Jean Cocteau's *The Knights of the Round Table* (translated by W.H. Auden), Pablo Picasso's *The Four Little Girls* and the world stage premiere of Rod Serling's *Requiem for a Heavyweight.* In 1979 Soho Rep received an award for its one-act play series—a festival of rarely and never-before performed short plays by some of the world's greatest American and European writers.

Soho Rep runs virtually non-stop from August to July, playing a total of five performances of two different plays each weekend. During 1978-79 Soho presented 183 performances of 19 plays. This demanding schedule, unusual for a theatre with Soho Rep's small budget, is a result of Soho's belief that the world's greatest plays should be as convenient to see—and as affordable—as a neighborhood movie.

The commitment of Soho's audience to theatre rather than to individual productions has been a major factor in Soho Rep's growth. Subscriptions have increased nearly 350 percent in four years, giving Soho Rep the largest subscriber audience of an Off-Off Broadway theatre in 1978-79. The acquisition in 1978 of an additional floor for a costume shop and scene shop, additional rehearsal space and expanded office space marks further progress in Soho Rep's development toward a fully paid, permanent company of actors, designers and directors.

Programs and services
Administrative internships, student ticket discounts, free ticket distribution, voucher program, post-performance discussions, newsletter.

Productions 1977-78
The Killing of Sister George, Frank Marcus
The Real Inspector Hound, Tom Stoppard
Misalliance, George Bernard Shaw
The Miser, Moliere; adapt: Moshe Yassur
Peer Gynt, Henrik Ibsen; adapt: Carol Corwen
Mister T, Michael Zettler
The Play's the Thing, Ferenc Molnar; adapt: P.G. Wodehouse
Abelard and Heloise, Ronald Duncan
The Four Little Girls, Pablo Picasso; trans: Roland Penrose
Philadelphia, Here I Come!, Brian Friel
The Magistrate, Arthur Wing Pinero
Soho Theatre of the Air, Carol Corwen
Better Dead, Georges Feydeau; trans: Jude Schanzer and Michael Wells
The Chairs, Eugene Ionesco; trans: Donald M. Allen
Poe in Person, Marilyn Vale, from Edgar Allen Poe's works
Cyrano de Bergerac, Edmond Rostand; trans: Brian Hooker
Traveler Without Luggage, Jean Anouilh; trans: Lucienne Hill

Productions 1978-79
Fallen Angels, Noel Coward
The Servant, Robin Maugham
Richard III, William Shakespeare
Miss Jairus, Michel de Ghelderode; trans: George Hauger
Amphitryon 38, Jean Giraudoux; adapt: S.N. Behrman
Overruled, George Bernard Shaw
The Love of Don Perlimplin and Belisa in the Garden, Federico Garcia Lorca; trans: James Graham-Lujan
Guernica, Fernando Arrabal; trans: Barbara Wright
Only 10 Minutes to Buffalo, Günter Grass; trans: Ralph Manheim
The 12-Pound Look, J.M. Barrie
If You Had Three Husbands, Gertrude Stein; adapt: Randy Knolle
Deathwatch, Jean Genet; trans: Bernard Frechtman
Action, Sam Shepard
Requiem for a Heavyweight, Rod Serling
October 12, 410 B.C., adapt: David Barrett, from Aristophanes; music: Jim Ragland
Dandy Dick, Arthur Wing Pinero
Inadmissible Evidence, John Osborne
The Knights of the Round Table, Jean Cocteau; trans: W.H. Auden

Herbert Rubens, Robert Van den Berg and Steve Parris in *Requiem for a Heavyweight.* Photo: Jerry Engelbach.

Deborah Johnson, Diane Thompson, Lily Knight and Tricia Metz in *The Four Little Girls.* Photo: Jerry Engelbach.

South Coast Repertory

David Emmes
Producing Artistic Director

Martin Benson
Artistic Director

Box 2197
Costa Mesa, CA 92626
(714) 957-2602 (business)
(714) 956-4033 (box office)

Founded 1964
David Emmes
Martin Benson

Season
September–June

Schedule
Evenings
Tuesday–Sunday
Matinees
Saturday, Sunday

Facilities
655 Town Center Drive
Mainstage
Seating capacity: 507
Stage: modified thrust
Second Stage
Seating capacity: 155
Stage: modified thrust

Finances
Sept. 1, 1978–Aug. 31, 1979
$1,307,000 operating expenses
$1,020,000 earned income
$ 233,000 unearned income

Audience
Paid capacity: 90%
Subscribers: 16,826
Annual attendance: 280,000

Touring contact
Ellen Ketchum

AEA LORT (B) contract

John-David Keller, Don Tuche,
DeAnn Mears and Jerome Kilty in
The Learned Ladies. Photo:
Barry Slobin.

South Coast Repertory began in 1964 with a commitment to the general aesthetic of the resident theatre movement—a belief in the artistic development, decentralization and diversification of American theatre, and the intent to serve its regional audience with stimulating and imaginative productions of the best plays in the repertoire of the world theatre.

SCR's balanced playbill includes classical, modern, contemporary, avant-garde and original works. All plays produced reflect the company's respect for and insistence on strong dramatic literature. Of the 124 productions mounted in SCR's 15 seasons, 46 (39 percent) have been world, West Coast or southern California premieres.

SCR maintains a resident company of actors, directors and designers, seeking a certain amount of ensemble and artistic continuity from season to season. The company is augmented each season by artists new to SCR, who bring a fresh perspective to the company, and, on occasion, by special guest artists engaged for specific productions.

The 1978-79 season was SCR's first in its new Fourth Step Theatre complex, a facility which developed from an idea to a fully funded and functioning theatre in less than three years. The 1979-80 season will consist of six productions on the mainstage and five in SCR's new 155-seat Second Stage theatre.

Through its community programs SCR serves Orange County in other ways as well. Its educational theatre program has played to nearly a million elementary, junior and senior high school students during the last five seasons, including approximately 200 touring performances of a commissioned original children's play, *The Energy Show*, in 1978-79. SCR's acting conservatory offers year-round instruction for children, teenagers and adults, and a full-time summer actor training program. Another community program begun in 1977, Creative Dramatics for Seniors, has drawn nationwide attention.

Programs and services
Professional acting training, classes for children; administrative and technical/production internships, student performances, programs-in-schools, student and senior citizen ticket discounts, statewide touring, post-performance discussions, workshop productions and staged readings, guest lecturers, children's theatre, newsletter, souvenir book, souvenir shop, speakers bureau, volunteer auxiliary, creative dramatics workshop for senior citizens.

Productions 1977-78
Private Lives, Noel Coward
*The Last Meeting of the Knights of the White
    Magnolia*, Preston Jones
A Doll's House, Henrik Ibsen
Volpone, Ben Jonson
Comedians, Trevor Griffiths
Otherwise Engaged, Simon Gray
Tomato Surprise, Robin Frederick

Productions 1978-79
The Time of Your Life, William Saroyan
The Contractor, David Storey
The Sorrows of Frederick, Romulus Linney
The Learned Ladies, Moliere; trans:
    Richard Wilbur
Peg o' My Heart, J. Hartley Manners
Spokesong, Stewart Parker; music:
    Jimmy Kennedy
The Energy Show, Robin Frederick

Charles Lanyer, Joan Morris and
John Frederick Jones in
Otherwise Engaged. Photo:
Don Hamilton.

Stage One
The Louisville Children's Theatre

Moses Goldberg
Director

Jenan Dorman
General Manager

2117 Payne St.
Louisville, KY 40206
(502) 895-9486

Founded 1946
Sara Spencer
Ming Dick

Season
September–May

Schedule
Matinees
Monday–Saturday

Facilities
Sara Spencer Campbell Memorial Theatre
Seating capacity: 650
Stage: flexible

Finances
July 1, 1978–June 30, 1979
$124,000 operating expenses
$ 64,000 earned income
$ 66,000 unearned income

Audience
Paid capacity: 56%
Subscribers: 286
Annual attendance: 42,000

Touring contact
Jenan Dorman

Stage One: The Louisville Children's Theatre entered its 34th season in 1979. What began as a Junior League project in 1946 has evolved into an expanding operation serving approximately 50,000 young people this season. The transition to a professional theatre for children began in 1970. The most recent phase in its evolution dates from July 1978, when Moses Goldberg became head of the theatre. With a rapidly growing staff and budget, and a resident company supplemented by guest artists, the theatre is preparing to occupy a new home in the Kentucky Center for the Arts in 1982.

Stage One's productions cover a wide range of materials and styles. The season usually includes at least one new work, often especially commissioned, as well as more traditional scripts for young people. Stage One is particularly known for its unique audience-participation productions developed by Goldberg, which use fairy tales as the framework for improvisationally developed scripts.

Each production is chosen to reflect the divergent needs and interests of children of different ages. Stage One speaks to those needs with plays geared to specific age groups from kindergarten through high school. The youngest children are introduced to theatre through familiar stories presented in intimate productions. As they mature, the plays become more complex, often dealing with modern-day problems facing young people. The season also includes a period or contemporary classic, completing the process which prepares young people to enter the ranks of adult theatregoers.

In addition, Stage One offers Saturday and summer classes for young people, workshops built upon the production experience for teachers and students, and other arts-in-education activities. A regional tour each spring presents three plays in repertory.

Programs and services
Classes for children; artistic, administrative and technical/production internships; student performances, programs-in-schools, study materials, career education workshops, regional touring, volunteer auxiliary, theatre rentals.

Productions 1977-78
Feelings, Bekki Jo Schneider
The Hide and Seek Oydssey of Madeline Gimple, Frank Gagliano
The Little Match Girl, adapt: Bekki Jo Schneider
The Ice Wolf, Joanna Halpert Kraus
Russian Tales, company developed
Aladdin, adapt: Moses Goldberg
Snow White and Rose Red, company developed

Productions 1978-79
Beauty and the Beast, company developed
The Miracle Worker, William Gibson
Holidays at Home, company developed
Cherokee Trails, company developed
The Men's Cottage, Moses Goldberg
Step on a Crack, Susan Zeder
Puss 'n' Boots, company developed

Kirk Davis and John Youngblood in *The Men's Cottage.* Photo: Richard Trigg.

J. Smith and Jill Meyers in *The Miracle Worker.* Photo: Richard Trigg.

Stage South

Gene Lesser
Artistic Director

Francis C. McGovern
General Manager

South Carolina Arts Commission
1800 Gervais St.
Columbia, SC 29201
(803) 758-7928

Founded 1973
Wesley Brustad

Season
October–April

Finances
July 1, 1978–June 30, 1979
$208,000 operating expenses
$ 31,000 earned income
$177,000 unearned income

Audience
Annual attendance: 86,000

Touring contact
Rebecca DesMarais

AEA Guest Artist contract

Ruth McRee in *The Belle of Amherst*. Photo: Pat Crawford.

Darrie Lawrence, Robert Blackburn and Stephen Bordner in *The Subject Was Roses*. Photo: Pat Crawford.

Stage South, the official state theatre of South Carolina, originated in 1973 as a touring program of the South Carolina Arts Commission. With the cooperation of the commission and the consultancy provided through the Foundation for the Extension and Development of the American Professional Theatre (FEDAPT), as well as through support from the federal government, private foundations and the business community, Stage South is in the final stages of development into a full-time resident professional theatre.

With the naming of Gene Lesser to the newly created position of artistic director in 1978, the organization began to define itself as a theatrical resource for the southeastern United States. As the basis for its artistic development, Stage South recognizes the unique social roots of the South that occupy a very special position in the American cultural landscape. There is a common experience in the South which weaves together the threads of a shared historical, social and cultural identity into a fabric of mutually shared sensibilities and traditions. There is a powerful voice in Southern literature that demands to be explored, expressed and understood. Stage South maintains a special attraction and interest in pursuing works with themes and concerns that are of regional significance.

As a true regional theatre, Stage South has three main thrusts. First is an expanded, full season of plays to tour South Carolina and the Southeast. The second major emphasis of the theatre is its Theatre for Youth program. Addressing itself in the past to subjects indigenous to South Carolina, the theatre will now focus attention on Shakespeare and the world classics of literature in a sustained effort to establish a transition from young audiences to adult audiences—an investment in the future.

The third and most innovative of Stage South's efforts is the exploration of a cooperative production unit with South Carolina educational television and public radio. A pilot program is underway for original dramatic adaptations of Southern fiction for television and radio.

Programs and services
Classes for nonprofessionals and children; programs-in-schools, study materials, student and senior citizen ticket discounts, regional touring, post-performance discussions, children's theatre, newsletter, speakers bureau, volunteer auxiliary.

Productions 1977-78
Sea Island Song, book and lyrics: Alice Childress; music: Nathan Woodard
The Subject Was Roses, Frank D. Gilroy

Productions 1978-79
Swamp!, book and lyrics: Dick Goldberg; music: Amy Rubin
Clarence Darrow, David W. Rintels
The Belle of Amherst, William Luce

StageWest

Stephen E. Hays
Producing Director

Robert Rosenbaum
General Manager

1511 Memorial Ave.
West Springfield, MA 01089
(413) 781-4470 (business)
(413) 781-2340 (box office)

Founded 1967
Stephen E. Hays

Season
November–April

Schedule
Evenings
Tuesday–Sunday
Matinees
Variable

Facilities
Seating capacity: 353
Stage: thrust

Finances
July 1, 1978–June 30, 1979
$443,000 operating expenses
$294,000 earned income
$212,000 unearned income

Audience
Paid capacity: 90%
Subscribers: 5,200
Annual attendance: 60,000

AEA LORT (C) contract

StageWest, Massachusetts' oldest resident professional theatre, was founded in November 1967 by Stephen E. Hays, in conjunction with the then newly formed Springfield Theatre Arts Association. From its inception, StageWest has been dedicated to artistic excellence, education and community enrichment programs. The intimate 353-seat theatre and thrust stage are housed on the Eastern States Exposition grounds in West Springfield, Mass.

Springfield, an industrial city, is a cultural melting pot, a context which consistently adds new dimensions and challenges to the theatre experiences at StageWest. Guest directors and an acting company individually selected for each production offer a wide variety of plays and styles including contemporary works, revivals, classics and world premieres.

StageWest has also established itself as an educational resource. Among its many educational programs is its Heritage Matinee Series, which has exposed thousands of school students to professional theatre for the first time. Among the other services are: acting classes for adults and students, a theatre arts workshop for teenagers, career education programs, a speakers bureau and group tours. The internship program brings upper-level university students onto the theatre's administrative and production staffs for concentrated on-the-job training.

StageWest receives wide financial support for its programs beyond ticket sales. In 1978, the Greater Springfield Business Fund for the Arts was successfully initiated to financially support StageWest as well as other cultural institutions in Springfield.

Programs and services

Classes for nonprofessionals and children; artistic, administrative and technical/production internships; student performances, programs-in-schools, student and senior citizen ticket discounts, free ticket distribution, workshop productions and staged readings, children's theatre, speakers bureau, theatre rentals.

Productions 1977-78

The Little Foxes, Lillian Hellman
A Christmas Carol, adapt: Rae Allen and
    Timothy Near
Loot, Joe Orton
Rib Cage, Larry Ketron
The Three Sisters, Anton Chekhov
Vanities, Jack Heifner

Productions 1978-79

A Raisin in the Sun, Lorraine Hansberry
A Christmas Carol
The Mousetrap, Agatha Christie
Good Evening, Peter Cook and Dudley Moore
A View from the Bridge, Arthur Miller
How the Other Half Loves, Alan Ayckbourn

Charles O. Lynch and Michael Moynihan in *A Christmas Carol.* Photo: Alan R. Epstein.

Vasili Bogazianos, John Tormey, Victor Arnold and Margaret Winn in *A View from the Bridge*. Photo: Alan R. Epstein.

The Street Theater

Gray Smith
Executive/Artistic Director

White Plains Armory
35 South Broadway
White Plains, NY 10601
(914) 949-8558

Founded 1970
Gray Smith

Season
Year-round

Finances
June 1, 1978–May 31, 1979
$101,000 operating expenses
$ 2,000 earned income
$ 99,000 unearned income

Audience
Annual attendance: 10,000

Touring contact
Susan Litchfield

Lonnie James and John Willis in
This One's for You. Photo:
Robert F. Rodriguez.

The Street Theater has a nine-year history of taking workshop programs and performances to culturally isolated groups. Founded as the Ossining Street Theater in 1970, it served the black communities and prisons of Westchester County until 1974, with touring activities including colleges, schools, state prisons and Off-Off Broadway. Out of the theatre's Bedford Hills workshop, the company now called "The Family" was developed, later acclaimed for its production of *Short Eyes* by Miguel Piñero. Piñero was first produced by the Street Theater in 1972 at Sing Sing, where he was still an inmate; later the same year the production was seen at the Lincoln Center Street Theatre Festival.

From 1974 to 1976, prison workshop programs were expanded to include 10 New York state correctional facilities, involving 600 inmate participants and 30 productions, half of which were original pieces developed through the workshop process. A number of inmates in these workshops have joined the theatre's staff upon release from prison, as actors and writers. Several of these men were trained to become workshop leaders, going on to conduct workshops in the community and at various prisons.

With an emphasis on performance of original material, the Street Theater now maintains two touring companies: a professional company and a youth company. All actors in the professional company are also workshop leaders, while a youth company serves as a training ground for teenagers with professional potential.

Touring activity includes a wide variety of institutional and community performances throughout Westchester County, including prisons, schools and street locations in 12 communities during the summer. Workshop programs continue to focus on the county's prison population, with a new and extensive program of workshops for potential juvenile offenders.

Programs and services
Professional training in acting and directing; classes for nonprofessionals and children; artistic internships, programs-in-schools, statewide touring, post-performance discussions, poetry readings, prison workshops.

Productions 1977-78
Related Voices
Common Ground

Productions 1978-79
Related Voices
A Play About Us?
This One's for You

All productions are company developed.

Cedric D. Crenshaw, Daryl
Edwards and John Davis in
Related Voices. Photo:
Mary Howard.

Studio Arena Theatre

Neal Du Brock
Executive Producer

Barry Hoffman
Managing Director

710 Main Street
Buffalo, NY 14202
(716) 856-8025 (business)
(716) 856-5650 (box office)

Founded 1965
Neal Du Brock

Season
October–May

Schedule
Evenings
Tuesday–Sunday
Matinees
Thursday, Sunday

Facilities
Seating capacity: 651
Stage: thrust

Finances
June 1, 1978–May 31, 1979
$1,756,000 operating expenses
$1,102,000 earned income
$ 419,000 unearned income

Audience
Paid capacity: 75%
Subscribers: 10,799
Annual attendance: 142,390

Booked-in events
Children's theatre

AEA LORT (B) contract

Serving the 1.5 million population of western New York State, Buffalo's Studio Arena Theatre began its 1979-80 season in a long-awaited new facility designed after its original home, with increased seating capacity and expanded technical capabilities. The largest resident theatre in the state outside of New York City, Studio Arena has presented 120 productions over the past 14 years. A subscription series of seven productions is offered, with play selection balanced between the merits of the script and its potential audience appeal. The Studio Arena season is diversified, encompassing new plays, musicals, contemporary dramas, comedies and classics. Artists are hired from production to production, allowing for maximum flexibility in casting. The proximity of the theatre to New York City allows Studio Arena access to the large number of professional actors, directors, designers and technicians in the New York talent pool.

An intrinsic part of the theatre's artistic thrust is the search for and presentation of new plays. Studio Arena has produced 19 American or world premieres, including Edward Albee's *Box/Mao/Box* (1968), Lanford Wilson's *Lemon Sky* (1970), Howard Sackler's *Semmelweiss* (1977) and the recent Broadway show *The Crucifer of Blood* (1978). Committed to the presentation of quality theatre to its community and region, Studio Arena has consistently attracted some of the country's foremost theatre talent.

Programs and services
Professional training in acting, directing, production and administration; classes for nonprofessionals and children, artistic, administrative technical/production internships, programs-in-schools, study materials, university extension courses, student and senior citizen ticket discounts, free ticket distribution, voucher program, national touring, post-performance discussions, guest lecturers, newsletter, speakers bureau, volunteer auxiliary, theatre rentals.

Productions 1977-78
Sunset, book: Louis LaRusso II; music: Gary William Friedman; lyrics: Will Holt
Semmelweiss, Howard Sackler
Same Time, Next Year, Bernard Slade
The Crucifer of Blood, Paul Giovanni
The Shadow Box, Michael Cristofer
Noel Coward in Two Keys, Noel Coward
Who's Afraid of Virginia Woolf?, Edward Albee

Productions 1978-79
Funny Face, book: Fred Thompson and Paul Gerard Smith; music: George Gershwin; lyrics: Ira Gershwin
For Colored Girls who have Considered Suicide/When The Rainbow is Enuf, Ntozake Shange
A Christmas Carol, adapt: Rae Allen and Timothy Near
Countess Dracula!, Neal Du Brock
The Runner Stumbles, Milan Stitt
Catsplay, Istvan Orkeny; trans: Clara Gyorgyey
The Madwoman of Central Park West, book: Phyllis Newman and Arthur Laurents; music and lyrics: various

Timothy Landfield and Paxton Whitehead in *The Crucifer of Blood.* Photo: Phototech Studios.

James C. Burge, Gwyllum Evans and Betsy Palmer in *Countess Dracula!* Photo: Phototech Studios.

Syracuse Stage

Arthur Storch
Producing Director

James A. Clark
Managing Director

820 East Genesee St.
Syracuse, NY 13210
(315) 423-4008 (business)
(315) 423-3275 (box office)

Founded 1974
Arthur Storch

Season
October–May

Schedule
Evenings
Tuesday–Sunday
Matinees
Variable

Facilities
Seating capacity: 202
Stage: proscenium

Finances
July 1, 1978–June 30, 1979
$851,000 operating expenses
$604,000 earned income
$234,000 unearned income

Audience
Paid capacity: 98%
Subscribers: 6,527
Annual attendance: 61,835

Touring contact
Barbara Beckos

AEA LORT (D) contract

Tom Villard and Lisa Pelikan in
The Butterfingers Angel ....
Photo: Robert Lorenz.

After an inaugural season of three plays in 1974, Syracuse Stage has produced five seasons of six plays each, offered in five-week consecutive runs.

In choosing and producing each season, Syracuse Stage is guided by the complementary principles of artistic balance and excellence. Each season is intended as a harmonious blend of the finest representative comedy and drama from the classical, contemporary, foreign and American repertoires, as well as outstanding new plays from both established playwrights and talented new voices.

Although the theatre does not maintain a resident company for its entire season, performers are often engaged for more than one production. Guest designers and directors are selected individually.

Major support for the theatre comes from city, state and federal sources, as well as local contributors. Significant support is received from Syracuse University, which contributes facilities and a portion of the staff, as well as some operating funds. Syracuse Stage maintains an active association with the university's drama department, serving as a professional resource.

During the past two seasons, public support of the theatre has grown to a point where thousands of people have had to be turned away from the box office. In order to accommodate audience demand, a fund-raising campaign is underway to raise nearly $1 million to renovate an adjacent movie theatre. The opening of the new 500-seat theatre is tentatively scheduled for December 1979.

The theatre has also been expanding its subsidiary programs. An annual statewide tour of a mainstage production was inaugurated during the 1976-77 season and has continued each season. Productions of *Sleuth, Candida* and *The Glass Menagerie* have played in many central New York cities and towns. In order to fulfill its role as an educational resource, the theatre also plans specially designed tours to regional elementary and secondary schools. During the 1978-79 season, Syracuse Stage sponsored a touring production by Theatre in a Trunk, Inc., for more than 60 performances in 35 schools.

Programs and services
Administrative and technical/production internships, student performances, programs-in-schools, study materials, student and senior citizen ticket discounts, free ticket distribution, statewide touring, post-performance discussions, workshop productions and staged readings, guest lecturers, children's theatre, newsletter, souvenir book, speakers bureau, volunteer auxiliary, theatre rentals.

Productions 1977-78
Love Letters on Blue Paper, Arnold Wesker
The End of the Beginning, Sean O'Casey
The Plough and the Stars, Sean O'Casey
Tartuffe, Moliere; trans: Richard Wilbur
That Championship Season, Jason Miller
Candida, George Bernard Shaw
Vanities, Jack Heifner

Productions 1978-79
She Stoops to Conquer, Oliver Goldsmith
The World of Sholom Aleichem, Arnold Perl
*The Butterfingers Angel, Mary and Joseph,
Herod the Nut and the Slaughter of 12
Hit Carols in a Pear Tree,* William Gibson
The Blood Knot, Athol Fugard
Otherwise Engaged, Simon Gray
The Glass Menagerie, Tennessee Williams
Loved, Olwen Wymark

Basil Wallace (standing) and
Thomas Kopache in *The Blood
Knot.* Photo: Robert Lorenz.

Theatre Arts of West Virginia

Ewel Cornett
Producer

John S. Benjamin
Artistic Director

Box 1205
Beckley, WV 25801
(304) 253-8313

Founded 1961

Season
June-September
Touring
October–May

Schedule
Evenings
Summer:
Tuesday–Sunday

Facilities
Cliffside Amphitheatre
Seating capacity: 1,442
Stage: proscenium

Finances
Oct. 1, 1977–Sept. 30, 1978
$440,000 operating expenses
$233,000 earned income
$230,000 unearned income

Audience
Paid capacity: 35%
Subscribers: 621
Annual attendance: 110,129

Touring contacts
Ewel Cornett
John S. Benjamin

AEA Guest Artist contract

Beckley, W. Va., located in the center of America's coal fields, is the home of Theatre Arts of West Virginia, the Mountain State's only resident professional theatre. Conceived in the late 1950s to produce two summer outdoor productions, Theatre Arts expanded in 1972 to a year-round full-time operation with the establishment of its touring wing, Theatre West Virginia.

Theatre West Virginia tours classic and contemporary works 33 weeks a year throughout West Virginia and 11 other states in the Midwest and the Atlantic coastal region. The troupe tours full productions with complete sets, stage, lights, costumes and sound sysem to both public and school audiences. A separate touring unit of professional puppeteers presents full-scale marionette productions designed for children.

Producer Ewel Cornett and artistic director John S. Benjamin direct the theatre's artistic policy firmly toward the highest quality production of the finest theatrical literature to the largest possible audience. Theatre Arts does not believe that the arts are reserved for the elite but rather are a necessity for all.

Perhaps one of the last cultural frontiers, West Virginia continues to prove the viability of Theatre Arts' approach. Audiences have grown steadily over the years to a total annual attendance of more than 110,000, with a 300 percent increase in subscribers for 1978-79. The highest percentage of audiences in West Virginia and surrounding states is composed of blue-collar workers. Free of middle-class artistic prejudices, they are equally as enthusiastic about Shakespeare as they are about a glossy musical, and they enjoy an original work as much as a tried-and-true classic.

In order that quality remains foremost in its vision, Theatre Arts is dedicated to establishing an attractive, creative atmosphere within which its artists can work with freedom and security.

Programs and services
Artistic, administrative and technical/production internships; programs-in-schools, study materials, student and senior citizen ticket discounts, free ticket distribution, regional touring, post-performance discussions, workshop productions and staged readings, guest lecturers, children's theatre, newsletter, souvenir book, speakers bureau, volunteer auxiliary.

Productions 1977-78
Arms and the Man, George Bernard Shaw
The Fantasticks, book and lyrics: Tom Jones; music: Harvey Schmidt
An Evening with Anton Chekhov:
   The Boor
   The Marriage Proposal
   Swan Song
The Firebird, Raymond Masters
Hatfields and McCoys, book and lyrics: Billy Edd Wheeler; music: Ewel Cornett
Honey in the Rock, book and lyrics: Kermit Hunter; music: Ewel Cornett and Jack Kilpatrick

Productions 1978-79
The Importance of Being Earnest, Oscar Wilde
Sleuth, Anthony Shaffer
The Typists and *The Tiger,* Murray Schisgal
Alice Underground, Raymond Masters
Hatfields and McCoys
Honey in the Rock

Don Johnson in *Swan Song.*
Photo: Betty Benjamin.

Don Johnson, Christy Newland, John Hotvedt and John S. Benjamin in *The Fantasticks.*
Photo: Betty Benjamin.

Theatre by the Sea

Jon Kimbell
Producing Director

Drew Souerwine
Managing Director

125 Bow St.
Portsmouth, NH 03801
(603) 431-5846 (business)
(603) 431-6660 (box office)

Founded 1964
Pat and C. Stanley Flower

Season
September-August

Schedule
Evenings
Tuesday–Sunday
Matinees
Wednesday, Saturday, Sunday

Facilities
Ceres Street Theatre
Seating capacity: 274
Stage: thrust
Second Stage
Seating capacity: 98
Stage: thrust
Prescott Park Amphitheatre
Seating capacity: 5,000
Stage: arena

Finances
Sept. 1, 1978–Aug. 31, 1979
$261,000 operating expenses
$180,000 earned income
$ 59,000 unearned income

Audience
Paid capacity: 95%
Subscribers: 2,725
Annual attendance: 127,500

Booked-in events
Music, dance and mime groups,
readings, children's theatre

AEA LORT (D) contract

Ginny Russell (standing),
Stephanie Voss and Tom Celli in
The Runner Stumbles. Photo:
Thomas R. Bloom.

Once called the "theatre that couldn't happen," Theatre by the Sea this year celebrates its 15th season in its tiny waterfront playhouse—and its imminent move into a new, larger facility. A recent *Theatre Crafts* article commented: "By all rights there should not be a theatre in Portsmouth, New Hampshire." The company's growth in four short seasons defies the statement: annual attendance has nearly tripled, season subscriptions have increased by 1,600 percent and the annual budget has grown from $55,000 to $295,000, with a projected budget of more than $500,000 in the new facility for 1979-80.

As the first to settle on the long-derelict Portsmouth waterfront and as an advocate of all local arts, TBS has sparked a major revitalization of the city and a renewed spirit of community. Two of the area's largest arts events are produced by TBS: the annual Ceres Street Fair, which last summer attracted 10,000 visitors and tourists to view the work of 150 artists and craftspeople; and the summer Prescott Park Arts Festival, which drew 150,000 (100,000 of them to TBS musicals).

An outreach program of classes, internship and scholarship programs and presentations to schools and organizations extends TBS' impact far beyond the stage. Moreover, the company has substantially contributed to the area's economic prosperity; over the past 15 years, TBS and its audiences have generated more than $6 million for local coffers. The community has reciprocated by contributing, over eight months, more than $500,000 for the renovation of a nearby 1890 brewery as the new 300-seat home of TBS.

In recent seasons TBS has produced the New England premieres of *Vanities* and *The Shadow Box* and American premieres of *Jubalay* and John Murrell's new translation of *Uncle Vanya.* The move to the new building, which maintains the intimacy and ambience of its smaller theatre, marks the end of one era and the beginning of an exciting new one.

Programs and services
Children's acting training, administrative internships, classes for nonprofessionals, programs-in-schools, student performances, study materials, student, senior citizen, military and group ticket discounts, free ticket distribution, statewide touring, post-performance discussions, workshop productions, staged readings, guest lecturers, poetry readings, mime presentations, restaurant, speakers bureau; subscriber newsletter, support group, volunteer auxiliary.

Productions 1977-78
Sleuth, Anthony Shaffer
Jubalay, Patrick Rose and Merv Campone
My Three Angels, Sam and Bella Spewack
The Sunshine Boys, Neil Simon
The Shadow Box, Michael Christofer
The Glass Menagerie, Tennessee Williams
Oklahoma!, book and lyrics: Oscar
    Hammerstein II; music: Richard Rodgers
Once upon a Mattress, book: Jay Thompson,
    Marshall Barer and Dean Fuller; music:
    Mary Rodgers; lyrics: M. Barer

Productions 1978-79
Relatively Speaking, Alan Ayckbourn
The Runner Stumbles, Milan Stitt
Murder at the Vicarage, Agatha Christie
Uncle Vanya, Chekhov; trans: John Murrell
The Sea Horse, Edward J. Moore
Starting Here, Starting Now, music: David
    Shire; lyrics: Richard Maltby, Jr.
Fiddler on the Roof, book: Joseph Stein; music:
    Jerry Bock; lyrics: Sheldon Harnick
Brigadoon, book and lyrics: Alan Jay Lerner;
    music: Frederick Loewe

Michael Beirne and Janice Fuller
in *The Sea Horse.* Photo: Thomas
R. Bloom.

Theatre Express

William Turner
Artistic Director

Caren Harder
General Manager

4615 Baum Blvd.
Pittsburgh, PA 15213
(412) 621-5477 (business)
(412) 621-5454 (box office)

Founded 1975
Caren Harder, Randell Haynes,
William Turner, Ken Kuta

Season
December–June

Schedule
Evenings
Thursday–Sunday
Matinees
Sunday

Facilities
Seating capacity: 185
Stage: flexible

Finances
Sept. 1, 1978–Aug. 31, 1979
$98,000 operating expenses
$32,000 earned income
$50,000 unearned income

Audience
Paid capacity: 40%
Subscribers: 1,000
Annual attendance: 25,000

Touring contact
Caren Harder

Booked-in events
Theatre, dance, music

Established four years ago by a quartet of Carnegie Mellon University graduates, Theatre Express has developed into a company of artists accomplished in a wide spectrum of theatre disciplines. However, diverse as the talents of its assembled actors, directors and designers may be, Theatre Express retains its commitment to conceptual theatre, specializing in new and unusual plays, musicals and operatic works.

The 1978-79 season marked the transition to a resident operation as Theatre Express, begun principally as a touring troupe, opened its own intimate, 185-seat theatre in a renovated warehouse in Pittsburgh's East End. Thus, the company now bears a twofold responsibility for balancing a program of regional touring with building Pittsburgh's first resident professional experimental theatre.

Theatre Express has developed an eclectic repertoire including new plays and musicals by company members, especially artistic director William Turner, as well as older, avant-garde playwrights (Gertrude Stein and Georg Buchner) and other contemporary voices (Peter Handke, Eugene Ionesco, Sam Shepard and Richard Foreman). The works focus on modern-day problems of identity, morality, media invasion, and others through new forms which re-examine traditional theatrical concepts of character, action and plot.

Programs and services
Classes for nonprofessionals, acting and technical/production internships, programs-in-schools, free ticket distribution, student and senior citizen ticket discounts, regional touring, post-performance discussions, workshop productions and staged readings, newsletter.

Productions 1977-78
The Unlit Corridor, book, music and lyrics:
    William Turner
Son of Arlecchino, Leon Katz
The Marquis de Sade's Justine, adapt:
    Leon Katz
Tuesday, Jewel Walker

Productions 1978-79
The Unlit Corridor
Angel City, Sam Shepard
The Elephant Man, William Turner
Assassins, book, music and lyrics:
    Charles Gilbert, Jr.
Made by Two, book and lyrics: Gertrude Stein;
    music: William Turner
Hotel for Criminals, book and lyrics: Richard
    Foreman; music: Stanley Silverman

Catherine Roberts and Susan Cash in *Made by Two.* Photo: Caren Harder.

Susan Cash, Jed Harris and David Harris in *Hotel for Criminals.* Photo: Caren Harder.

Theater for the New City

George Bartenieff
Crystal Field
Artistic Directors

Sandra Herbst
Office Manager

162 Second Ave.
New York, NY 10003
(212) 254-1109

Founded 1970
George Bartenieff, Crystal Field,
Lawrence Kornfeld, Theo Barnes

Season
July–June

Schedule
Evenings
Thursday–Sunday
Matinees
Variable

Facilities
James Waring Theater
Seating capacity: 130
Stage: flexible
Joe Cino Theater
Seating capacity: 140
Stage: proscenium
Chamber Space
Seating capacity: 48
Stage: flexible

Finances
July 1, 1977–June 30, 1978
$128,000 operating expenses
$ 26,000 earned income
$102,000 unearned income

Audience
Paid capacity: 80%
Annual attendance: 53,000

Touring contact
Sandra Herbst

Booked-in events
Dance, music, theatre

AEA Showcase Code

Rose Wolfe, Mimi Strum, Roberta
Pikser and Maggie Higgs in
Lovely Rita. Photo: Tobias Haller.

Nemeer El Kadi and Crystal Field
in *The Writer's Opera.* Photo:
Charles Marinaro.

Theater for the New City is a unique
experimental, developmental center committed
to community involvement. TNC is dedicated to
the discovery and development of new
American playwrights, as well as the
discovering and nurturing of new experimental
theatre companies. TNC's approach
amalgamates song and dance, live music and
poetry into diverse "total theatre"
experiences. The company annually premieres 10 new plays
by contemporary American playwrights, both
established and unknown. These include full-
length dramas, musicals, operas (often with
original choreography), live music and
multimedia presentations. Great care is taken
by the artistic directors to give the writer,
director and actors the appropriate conditions to
create without undue pressure or interference.

As a developmental center, TNC also presents
many promising new theatre groups from
across the country, as well as from New York.
In this program, TNC has become a home for
the fledgling company to develop as it wishes,
with appropriate performing space and
scheduling and with or without critical exposure.
TNC's Children's Theater program selects only
scripts which involve the children's profound
and innate imaginative abilities.

TNC's Free Summer Street Theater involves a
large interracial cast of 40, including five
musicians, and tours the five-borough area to
bring spectacle and satire to streets and parks
in the city's poorer neighborhoods. Each year,
an original script is developed in the Spring
Street Theater Workshop, where young
apprentices join the regular company and are
trained in juggling, tumbling, clowning and other
performing skills.

In addition, TNC has performed for such special
community events as a Halloween festival, a
local library dedication, fund-raising for a
neighboring church and many others.

Programs and services
Internships, free ticket distribution, regional
touring, poetry readings, children's theatre,
cabaret.

Productions 1977-78
*The Ballad of the Seven Sleeping Brothers in
    China,* Tadeus Micinski
The Time They Turned the Water Off, Crystal
    Field and George Bartenieff
Leona Is a Funny Name, Don Kvares
Face Stool, Henri Gruvman
Winter Sunshine, Arthur Williams
Dry Sherry, John Sherry
Cutups and Cutouts, N. Noble Barrett
Shopping Bag Madonna, Mary Karolly
The Room, Saskia Hegt
The Guillotine, Helen Duberstein
Atonements, Israel Eliraz, from Sholom
    Aleichem's stories; trans: David Zinder
Just Folks, Romulus Linney
Liars, Ron Lampkin
Clara Bow Loves Gary Cooper, Robert Dahdah
    and Mary Boylan
Lives, Edmond Felix
Realism in Our Time, Daryl Chin
Oil!, Neal Tucker
Cancer of Ambition, Richard Levine
Boat Sun Cavern, Arthur Sainer
A Walk in the Moonlight, anonymous
    "Samizdat" play; trans: Algirdas
    Landsbergis
Cosmicomics, Italo Calvino; adapt: Gordon
    Rogoff
The Torrents of Spring, Ivan Turgenev; adapt:
    Donald Sanders
Mirandolina, Carlo Goldoni; adapt: Robert
    Reddy

Productions 1978-79
The King of the Mashed Potatoes, Crystal Field
    and George Bartenieff
Lovely Rita, Thomas Brasch; trans: Viola
    Stephan and Dennis Eichelberger
Buried Child, Sam Shepard
The Fall, Albert Camus; trans: Justin O'Brian
Homebodies, Nicholas Kazan
The Button, Michael McClure
Clara Bow Loves Gary Cooper
Fruit of Zaloom, Paul Zaloom
Hefetz, Hanokh Levin; trans: Rina Elisha
Othello, William Shakespeare
Stewart Sherman's Eighth Spectacle, Stewart
    Sherman
The Writer's Opera, book and lyrics: Rosalyn
    Drexler; music: John Braden
After the Baal-Shem Tov, Arthur Sainer
Metaphysics of a Two-Headed Calf, Stanislaw
    Witkiewicz; trans: Daniel & Eleanor Gerould
Voideville, Gordon Bressac and Ruby Lynn
    Reyner
Up in Seattle, Arthur Williams
Lord Tom Goldsmith, Victor Lipton

Theater of the Open Eye

Jean Erdman
Artistic Director

316 East 88th St.
New York, NY 10028
(212) 534-6363 (business)
(212) 534-6909 (box office)

Founded 1972
Jean Erdman
Joseph Campbell

Season
September–June

Schedule
Evenings
Wednesday–Sunday
Matinees
Saturday, Sunday

Facilities
Seating capacity: 145
Stage: flexible

Finances
July 1, 1978–June 30, 1979
$158,000 operating expenses
$ 95,000 earned income
$ 63,000 unearned income

Audience
Annual attendance: 10,650

Touring contact
Nola Hague

Booked-in events
Dance, theatre

AEA Showcase Code

Theater of the Open Eye has evolved into a permanent association of dancers, actors, musicians and designers whose *raison d'être* is the creation and production of original works of "total theatre." The basis for the theatre's parent organization, the Foundation for the Open Eye, evident in the theatre's repertoire, is a concern for the roots of human thought and feeling as revealed in mythic and poetic images.

Thus, Open Eye productions are inspired by works of poets and visual artists and are staged as a fusion of all the performing arts. The company's production of *Gauguin in Tahiti* told the story of an original spokesman for those spiritual values in life and art that are most endangered by Western civilization, while *Primordial Voices* was a celebration, expressed in the poetry and sacred ritual music, of the arctic existence of the Eskimo. Both productions were brought to life through an interweaving of dramatic scenes, dance, musical motifs, projected light and pictorial effects, justified aesthetically by the multidimensional nature of the images expressed. Most recently the 1978-79 revival of *The Coach with the Six Insides,* based on James Joyce's *Finnegans Wake,* has continued this Open Eye tradition.

Companion projects of Theater of the Open Eye all further this kind of involvement. Children's Theater of the Open Eye presents works in this same interdisciplinary arts style, featuring exciting use of puppetry. The theatre treats its young audiences as imaginative theatregoers who readily respond to the symbolic imagery of folktales from the world's cultures. In another vein, the Foundation offers the seminar series "Realms of the Creative Spirit," which has grown into a year-round presentation of weekend workshops, experimental sessions and lecture-seminars dealing with philosophical, psychological, artistic and mythical subjects. These offerings are complemented by diverse community outreach programs. In order to help support other theatre companies, Theater of the Open Eye has developed a "shelter" program which has, since 1977, provided performing space to six homeless New York ensembles.

One of the theatre's most ambitious recent projects is a New Works Project of staged readings, many of which are developed into full-scale productions.

Programs and services
Classes for children; artistic, administrative and technical/production internships; apprentice program, student performances, programs-in-schools, study materials, student and senior citizen ticket discounts, free ticket distribution, national touring of mainstage productions, regional touring of children's theatre, post-performance discussions, workshop productions and staged readings; seminars in mythology, psychology, anthropology and the creative arts.

Productions 1977-78
Fontana, Valerie Hammer; music: Robert Mahaffay
Raven's Dance, Eric Bass; music: Didi Charney, Robert Mahaffay and Anne Sheedy
The Shining House, Jean Erdman; music: Michael Czajkowski
Moon on Snow, Ken Gaertner; music: Chistopher DeLoach

Productions 1978-79
The Coach with the Six Insides, Jean Erdman, from James Joyce's novel *Finnegans Wake;* music: Teiji Ito
The Masque of Dawn, Eric Bass; music: Bill Buchen and Richard Spendio
George and the Dragon, John Patrick Shanley; music: Tom Shelton
Festival of New Works, month-long staging of 17 theatre pieces at various stages of development from readings through full production

John Proto in *Raven's Dance.*
Photo: Chuck Delaney.

Tom Villard and Shelley Rogers in *Moon on Snow.* Photo: Smitu Kothari.

Theatre X

John Schneider
Sharon Ott
Associate Directors

Colleen Scott
Business Manager

Box 92206
Milwaukee, WI 53202
(414) 278-0555

Founded 1969
Conrad Bishop, Linda Bishop,
Ron Gural

Season
Year-round

Schedule
Evenings
Wednesday–Sunday

Facilities
Water Street Arts Center
1245-47 North Water St.
Seating capacity: 90
Stage: flexible

Finances
Jan. 1, 1978–Dec. 31, 1978
$83,000 operating expenses
$27,000 earned income
$60,000 unearned income

Audience
Paid capacity: 67%
Annual attendance: 10,000

Touring contact
Marc Haupert
Arts Services Associates
Box 92222
Milwaukee, WI 53202

Booked-in events
Mime, experimental and
children's theatre, dance,
poetry readings

Victor DeLorenzo and Tom Gustin
in *A Fierce Longing*. Photo: Sylvia
Plachy.

Deborah Clifton and John Kishline
in *An Interest in Strangers*. Photo:
Bob Van Dantzig.

Theatre X was founded on the belief that the essence of live performance is communication between performer and audience and that, to this end, actors should have the opportunity to contribute substantially to the creation or choice of their material and to its direction and design. Thus, Theatre X has been a home for actor/writers, actor/directors, actor/designers and technicians, and its major work has been the development of exploratory theatre pieces, at the rate of about two a year.

These plays, most of which have toured throughout the United States and in Europe, are remarkably diverse. For example, *The Unnamed* was a minimalist horror show; *Razor Blades* was a revue-style piece about performance and suicide. *A Fierce Longing* was a multimedia epic on the life of Yukio Mishima and *Schmaltz* was a musical comedy. *An Interest in Strangers,* created for the Mickery Theatre in Amsterdam, Holland, combined video and live performance in an analysis of the methods of the news industry. The company's method is to locate the subject matter which best addresses the needs and interests of the theatre's membership at the given time, as well as the form, style and process which best addresses that subject matter, and then to explore those fully. By maintaining its performing base in Milwaukee, in addition to touring, Theatre X fulfills a regional need.

Since 1974, the company's pieces have been scripted by actor/director/playwright John Schneider, a member of Theatre X since its second year. New dimensions have enriched the work since the addition, in 1977, of resident director Sharon Ott and resident composer Mark Van Hecke. Most recently, Theatre X has begun to work selectively with artists from outside the company. Thus, *The Fantod* was written for the company by the Milwaukee Repertory Theater Company's playwright-in-residence Amlin Gray.

Programs and services
Classes for nonprofessionals; student performances, programs-in-schools, student and senior citizen ticket discounts, free ticket distribution, work/ticket exchanges, international touring, post-performance discussions, poetry readings.

Productions 1977-78
And Things That Go Bump in the Night,
 Terrence McNally
The Wreck: A Romance, John Schneider
A Fierce Longing, John Schneider

Productions 1978-79
A Fierce Longing
An Interest in Strangers, John Schneider
Schmaltz, book and lyrics: John Schneider;
 music: Mark Van Hecke
The Fantod: A Victorian Reverie, Amlin Gray

Travel Light Theatre

Michael Cullen
Producer

Sandra Walker
General Manager

The Theatre Building
1225 West Belmont Ave.
Chicago, IL 60657
(312) 281-6060

Founded 1974
Michael Cullen

Season
Year-round

Schedule
Evenings
Wednesday–Sunday

Facilities
Seating capacity: 150
Stage: thrust

Finances
July 1, 1978–June 30, 1979
$145,000 operating expenses
$ 72,000 earned income
$ 61,000 unearned income

Audience
Paid capacity: 41%
Annual attendance: 18,000

Booked-in-events
Music, theatre

AEA COLT contract

Travel Light Theatre was originally founded as a pub theatre troupe, transforming bars, cafes and coffee houses into alternative performing spaces. The concept of bringing theatre to the people, the small playing area, and the constant fight for audience attention made for an adventurous, intense, immediate experience. The company expanded this format with additional troupes that toured Shakespearean productions in the parks, prisons and schools; a children's theatre; and, eventually, dinner theatre productions.

Now in its third season in residence at Chicago's Theatre Building, Travel Light has established itself as a major force in the Off-Loop movement, presenting such fare as *P.S. Your Cat Is Dead, The Rainmaker, Steambath* and *A Hatful of Rain.* The original thrust—new audiences for new theatre together—is still in force. New works, such as *Woody Guthrie; Suburbs of Heaven,* a musical show in a new format; and Vincent Canby's *End of the War* all demonstrate the theatre's commitment.

Travel Light has matured substantially and is now in the midst of its first major subscription drive. In addition, the company has added a "Showcase Series" of works-in-progress and a "Literature as Drama Series," which brings groups of high school students into the theatre to see performances of works they study in class.

Program and services
Professional training in design, production and administration; administrative and technical/production internships, student performances, programs-in-schools, student and senior citizen ticket discounts, voucher program, regional touring, post-performance discussions, workshop productions and staged readings, poetry readings, theatre rentals.

Productions 1977-78
The Dumb Waiter and *The Lover,* Harold Pinter
P.S. Your Cat Is Dead, James Kirkwood
The Rainmaker, N. Richard Nash
Woody Guthrie, Tom Taylor, George Boyd and Michael Diamond

Productions 1978-79
A Hatful of Rain, Michael V. Gazzo
Steambath, Bruce Jay Friedman
Suburbs of Heaven, music and lyrics: Thom Bishop
Woody Guthrie
A Midsummmer Night's Dream, William Shakespeare

Mark Goetzinger and Shelly Carlson in *The Rainmaker.* Photo: Ed Krieger.

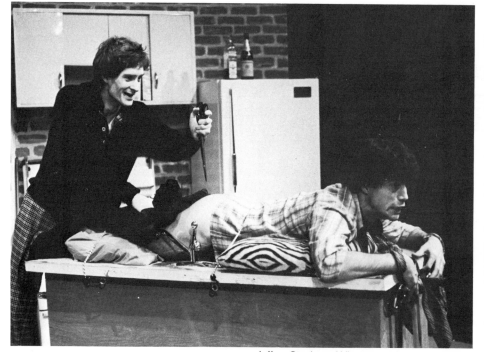

Jeffrey Steele and Vinny Guastaferro in *P.S. Your Cat Is Dead.* Photo: LuAnn Wing.

Trinity Square Repertory Company

Adrian Hall
Artistic Director

E. Timothy Langan
Managing Director

201 Washington St.
Providence, RI 02903
(401) 521-1100 (business)
(401) 351-4242 (box office)

Founded 1964
Adrian Hall

Season
Year-round

Schedule
Evenings
Tuesday–Sunday
Matinees
Wednesday, Saturday, Sunday

Facilities
Upstairs Theatre
Seating capacity: 485
Stage: flexible
Downstairs Playhouse
Seating capacity: 297
Stage: thrust

Finances
July 1, 1978–June 30, 1979
$1,419,000 operating expenses
$ 827,000 earned income
$ 548,000 unearned income

Audience
Paid capacity: 70%
Subscribers: 6,540
Annual attendance: 89,830

Touring contact
E. Timothy Langan

Booked-in events
Dance, music, theatre

AEA LORT (C) contract

Ricardo Wiley, David Kennett and Monique Fowler in *Uncle Tom's Cabin: A History.* Photo: Robert Emerson.

Richard Kneeland and Margot Skinner in *Who's Afraid of Virginia Woolf?* Photo: Jack Spratt.

Trinity Square Repertory Company's staging of classics, contemporary revivals and new works has built the company into a unique American theatrical resource, with a strong, permanent corps of artistic, technical and administrative personnel, as well as a 25-30 member resident acting ensemble. Since 1970 when Trinity Square and artistic director Adrian Hall received the Margo Jones Award, the company's national reputation has increased through the adaptation of original works from the Trinity Square stage to television. Best known are television productions of Hall and Richard Cumming's *Feasting with Panthers* (PBS *Theater in America* series) and *Life Among the Lowly* (also by Hall and Cumming, filmed for the PBS *Visions* series).

Initially founded to serve the Rhode Island community, Trinity Square draws its audience from all over the eastern United States. Project Discovery, which brings high school students to the theatre as part of their curriculum, continues as a major source of new audiences. Originally funded in 1966 by the National Endowment for the Arts and the U.S. Office of Education as part of the Laboratory Theatre Project, the endeavor has become an integral part of area educational systems, with students and schools paying their own admissions, and accounting for increased audiences over the past few seasons.

The launching of a two-year professional training program for theatre practitioners and a three-play summer season were just two significant 1978 achievements for the ever-evolving Trinity Square Repertory Company. Under the direction of Larry Arrick, Trinity Rep Conservatory prepares actors, directors and playwrights for work in the professional theatre. Trinity Summer Rep, a summer season of three attractions, officially makes the company a year-round operation.

Programs and services
Professional conservatory training for actors and directors; artistic, administrative, and technical/production internships; student performances, programs-in-schools, study materials, student and senior citizen ticket discounts, post-performance discussions, workshop productions and staged readings, guest lecturers, newsletter, souvenir book, theatre rentals.

Productions 1977-78
Ethan Frome, Owen and Donald Davis, from Edith Wharton's novel
Rosmersholm, Henrik Ibsen; adapt: Adrian Hall and Richard Cumming
Equus, Peter Shaffer
As You Like It, William Shakespeare
A Christmas Carol, adapt: Adrian Hall and Richard Cumming
The Show-Off, George Kelly
Boesman and Lena, Athol Fugard
Vanities, Jack Heifner
American Buffalo, David Mamet
Seduced, Sam Shepard
The Real Inspector Hound, Tom Stoppard
Whiskey, Terrence McNally

Productions 1978-79
Uncle Tom's Cabin: A History, Adrian Hall and Richard Cumming
A Christmas Carol
Awake and Sing!, Clifford Odets
Death of a Salesman, Arthur Miller
Who's Afraid of Virginia Woolf?, Edward Albee
A Life in the Theatre, David Mamet
Father's Day, Oliver Hailey
The Shadow Box, Michael Cristofer
Jack the Ripper, book and lyrics: Denis DeMarne and Ron Pember; music: R. Pember
Side by Side by Sondheim, music and lyrics: Stephen Sondheim, et al.; adapt: Ned Sherrin
Same Time, Next Year, Bernard Slade
Dial M for Murder, Frederick Knott

Victory Gardens Theater

Dennis Zacek
Artistic Director

Marcelle McVay
Managing Director

3730 North Clark St.
Chicago, IL 60613
(312) 549-1508 (business)
(312) 549-5788 (box office)

Founded 1974

Season
September–June

Schedule
Evenings
Tuesday–Sunday
Matinees
Sunday

Facilities
Mainstage
Seating capacity: 150
Stage: thrust
Studio
Seating capacity: 50
Stage: flexible

Finances
July 1, 1978–June 30, 1979
$244,000 operating expenses
$153,000 earned income
$ 83,000 unearned income

Audience
Mainstage paid capacity: 70%
Studio paid capacity: 80%
Subscribers: 1,200
Total annual attendance: 22,000

Touring contact
Marcelle McVay

AEA COLT contract

Victory Gardens Theater was founded to promote and develop Chicago's theatrical talent—actors, writers, designers and directors—and to provide locally based professional theatre to the Chicago audience. Orginally started by eight Chicago theatre artists, the company was transferred to the sole artistic direction of Dennis Zacek in 1977. Under his supervision, programming at Victory Gardens has expanded to include four major program areas.

On the mainstage, a five-play season is produced including one revival and four premieres. More than half the plays produced at Victory Gardens have been premieres by Chicago authors and the plays are specifically selected for their appeal to Chicago audiences. Zacek has also instituted a policy of producing at least one black play each season.

In the Victory Gardens Studio, a five-play season is produced, consisting of new plays or plays that have a more limited audience. Three of the Studio plays feature students from the Victory Gardens Theater Center, the company's educational arm. Four sections of classes are offered each year in eight-week sessions. Course are geared for the professional and the novice and include classes in basic acting, as well as a very practical course in auditioning. Approximately 150 students are served each session.

Finally, the Readers Theater program presents readings of original script to audiences with discussions afterward. The program allows a playwright to benefit from audience response as well as to hear his script interpreted by experienced actors. Zacek has expanded this program to include 25 scripts per year on alternate Saturday nights. Admission is free. In addition, Victory Gardens is expanding its programming to include touring programs to schools, community groups and other sponsoring organizations in the state.

Programs and services
Professional training in acting, directing, design, production and administration; classes for nonprofessionals; administrative and technical/production internships, student performances, study materials; ticket discounts for students, senior citizens and the handicapped; voucher program, statewide touring, post-performance discussions, workshop productions and staged readings, guest lecturers, restaurant, speakers bureau, volunteer auxiliary, theatre rentals.

Productions 1977-78
June Moon, George S. Kaufman and Ring Lardner
The Cigarette Man, David Blomquist
Colette, Ruth Landis
Ceremonies in Dark Old Men, Lonne Elder III
Heat, William Hauptman
His Satanic Majesty, William J. Norris
Between the Devil and the Deep Blue Sea, music and lyrics: various; adapt: Greg McCaslin
The Night of January 16th, Ayn Rand
This Is My Play Song, music and lyrics: Jackie Taylor

Productions 1978-79
The Homecoming, Harold Pinter
The Transfiguration of Benno Blimpie, Albert Innaurato
Eden, Steve Carter
Peppermints, Mark Larson
Towards the Morning, John Fenn
Dillinger, William J. Norris
Porch, Jeffrey Sweet
Weekends like Other People, David Blomquist
Clowncave, Steven Ivcich
East Liberty, Pa., Allan Bates
Cowboys #2 and *The Unseen Hand,* Sam Shepard

William J. Norris, Laurence Russo and John Ostrander in *The Homecoming.* Photo: Daniel Rest.

Ruth Landis in *Colette.* Photo: Daniel Rest.

Virginia Museum Theatre

Tom Markus
Artistic Director

Baylor Landrum
Administrative Director

Boulevard and Grove Aves.
Richmond, VA 23221
(804) 257-0833 (business)
(804) 257-0831 (box office)

Founded 1955
Virginia Museum of Fine Arts

Season
September–March

Schedule
Evenings
Tuesday–Sunday
Matinees
Wednesday, Saturday

Facilities
Seating capacity: 500
Stage: proscenium

Finances
July 1, 1978–June 30, 1979
$306,000 operating expenses
$251,000 earned income
$ 63,000 unearned income

Audience
Paid capacity: 87%
Subscribers: 8,310
Annual attendance: 61,630

Booked-in-events
Theatre, dance, mime, music, film
and other performing arts

AEA LORT (C) contract

Robert Foley, Sam Tsoutsouvas,
Robert Gerringer (in picture
frame), Margery Murray, and
Warren Kelley in *Volpone*. Photo:
Dennis McWaters.

The Virginia Museum Theatre celebrates its 25th anniversary during the 1979-80 season, and is enjoying the largest subscription audience in its history. Founded in 1955 as a community theatre, VMT became a fully professional company in 1972. Under a succession of eight artistic directors, VMT has served Richmond and Virginia for a quarter of a century.

As a division of the Virginia Museum of Fine Ars, VMT aspires to offer theatre art equal to the gallery art exhibited in the Museum. Its responsibility to serve a diverse audience leads to extremely varied programming. VMT offers a season which is a mix of popular forms, including musicals and new plays. As is appropriate to a museum theatre, a major portion of its fare is composed of classics, given fresh interpretations. *Volpone* was offered in a new adaptation, and this season *Mother Courage and Her Children* is being set in the American Civil War, with music from the period, designs based on the photography of Matthew Brady and a black actress in the title role. VMT believes that the classics speak eloquently to all ages.

In addition to the drama series, VMT offers an International Star Attractions series, presenting dance, mime, and music, both popular and classical; a series of classic and foreign films; and special events such as Irene Worth's *Letter of Love and Affection* and the Hartford Ballet.

VMT places a strong emphasis on educational and community services. In addition to student matinees, there are a public lecture series and the Resident Apprentice Program accredited by many universities, including Virginia Commonwealth University. Community services include the sign-language interpretation of one performance of each production for the hearing-impaired.

VMT believes that theatre is a public celebration and it desires to share that vision and enthusiasm with the largest and most diverse audience it can reach.

Programs and services
Professional training in design, production and administration; classes for nonprofessionals; administrative and technical/production internships, student performances, programs-in-schools, study materials, student ticket discounts, free ticket distribution, statewide touring, post-performance discussions, film series, guest lecturers, restaurant, newsletter, speakers bureau, volunteer auxiliary, theatre rentals, performances for the hearing-impaired.

Productions 1977-78
Vanities, Jack Heifner
Richard III, William Shakespeare
Berlin to Broadway with Kurt Weill, music: Kurt
    Weill; lyrics: various; adapt: Gene Lerner
Let's Get a Divorce, Victorien Sardou and Emile
    de Najac; trans: Brian Kelly
Man and Superman, George Bernard Shaw
Cabaret, book: Joe Masteroff; music: John
    Kander; lyrics: Fred Ebb

Productions 1978-79
Volpone, Ben Jonson; adapt: Robert A. Potter
    and Tom Markus
The Fantasticks, book and lyrics: Tom Jones;
    music: Harvey Schmidt
Dear Liar, Jerome Kilty
Private Lives, Noel Coward

John H. Fields, Nancy Nichols,
Lowell Harris, Warren Kelley and
Jack Axelrod in *The Fantasticks.*
Photo: Dennis McWaters.

Wayside Theatre

James Kirkland
Producing Director

Barbara Swink
General Manager

Box 260
Middletown, VA 22645
(703) 869-1782 (business)
(703) 869-1776 (box office)

Founded 1962
Leo Bernstein

Season
June–December

Schedule
Evenings
Tuesday–Sunday
Matinees
Wednesday, Saturday

Facilities
Seating capacity: 260
Stage: proscenium

Finances
Oct. 1, 1978–Sept. 30, 1979
$208,000 operating expenses
$120,000 earned income
$ 54,000 unearned income

Audience
Paid capacity: 60%
Subscribers: 650
Annual attendance: 49,000

Booked-in events
Children's theatre

Touring contact
Barbara Swink

AEA LORT (D) contract

Wayside Theatre exists in a unique rural area at the northern tip of the Shenandoah Valley, in Middletown, Va., a town with fewer than 600 residents and only four miles of paved roadways.

Since its inception in 1962, Wayside Theatre has traditionally presented a six-to-eight play summer season, drawing its audience mainly from the cities and towns in the Shenandoah Valley, but also from Washington, D.C., and neighboring states.

The 1979 season is Wayside's first as a member of the League of Resident Theatres (LORT), and includes expanded performance and rehearsal schedules. An eight-production schedule features a four-play summer festival, a children's theatre production and a three-play "Fall Great Play Series." After playing at Wayside Theatre, the children's production will tour extensively throughout Virginia for eight weeks.

Wayside Theatre on Tour began in 1974 and produces one new script each season. It provides teachers' guides and in-school workshops for both teachers and students. Last year's ten-week tour of *Virginia Ghost Stories of the Civil War* played to 33,000 school children. Wayside's Great Play Series will begin with productions of *Hamlet, Twelfth Night*, and a revival of last season's *A Christmas Carol*. As an adjunct of Wayside's educational program, each production will play special school matinees.

Under the direction of James Kirkland, Wayside Theatre is committed to the professional production of plays and programs that illuminate social conditions, provide clarity and understanding of past experience, and entertain the imagination with the future possibilities of the human spirit.

Programs and services
Professional training in directing, design, production and administration; classes for nonprofessionals; administrative and technical/production internships, student performances, programs-in-schools, study materials, student ticket discounts, regional touring of children's theatre, post-performance discussions, speakers bureau, volunteer auxiliary.

Productions 1978
Round and Round the Garden, Alan Ayckbourn
Vanities, Jack Heifner
Ring Round the Moon, Jean Anouilh; adapt: Christopher Fry
Charley's Aunt, Brandon Thomas
Volpone, Ben Jonson
Bells Are Ringing, book and lyrics: Betty Comden and Adolph Green; music: Jule Styne
Virginia Ghost Stories of the Civil War, William Stancil
A Christmas Carol, adapt: William Stancil

Productions 1979
Side by Side by Sondheim, music and lyrics: Stephen Sondheim, et al.; adapt: Ned Sherrin
Angel Street, Patrick Hamilton
A Streetcar Named Desire, Tennessee Williams
Harvey, Mary Chase
Shakes and Company!, company developed from William Shakespeare's works
Hamlet, William Shakespeare
A Christmas Carol

Dee Hoty in *Vanities*. Photo: Robert Brooks.

Peter Blaxill, Joan Scorgie and Barbara Sohmers in *Ring Round the Moon*. Photo: Robert Brooks.

The Whole Theatre Company

Olympia Dukakis
Artistic Director

Arnold Mittelman
Producing Director

Sylvia S. Traeger
General Manager

544 Bloomfield Ave.
Montclair, NJ 07042
(201) 744-2933 (business)
(201) 744-2989 (box office)

Founded 1973

Season
October–June

Schedule
Evenings
Wednesday–Sunday
Matinees
Saturday, Sunday

Facilities
Seating capacity: 200
Stage: flexible

Finances
July 1, 1978–June 30, 1979
$409,000 operating expenses
$225,000 earned income
$157,000 unearned income

Audience
Paid capacity: 88%
Subscribers: 3,300
Annual attendance: 26,295

AEA letter of agreement

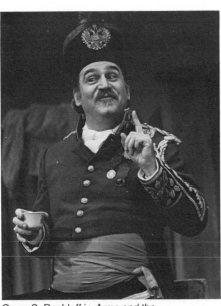

Owen S. Rachleff in *Arms and the Man*. Photo: Raul Rodriguez.

The Whole Theatre Company was founded in 1970 when a group of actors, directors and designers from diverse backgrounds in the commercial and noncommercial theatre began meeting in New York to share ideas about ways of working, both individually and collectively. Three years later, after an intensive period of working together and sharing techniques, the group became an ensemble, settling in Montclair, N.J., with the 94-seat vestibule of the town's First Baptist Church serving as its home.

Now settled since 1978 inside a renovated bank building in the town's business district, WTC continues its multifaceted program of mainstage productions, educational outreach and social service projects which have gained increasing statewide respect and recognition.

The range of playwrights has included Euripides, Moliere, Brecht and Williams, and the company has presented the American premiere of the first English translation of Feydeau's *Before Her Time* as well as an innovative multimedia adaptation of Pirandello's *Six Characters in Search of an Author.*

Subscriptions have grown from 50 in 1973 to the current total of 3,300 from more than 160 different communities. From three original workshops, there are now 25 theatre arts classes serving more than 300 children, teenagers and adults. Regional social service programs encompass an additional 300 students. WTC extends itself toward its audience through courses in schools and colleges, a specially designed communications curriculum for halfway houses and an internship program.

With its new space and growing professional artistic and adminstrative staff, WTC has lately moved into the area of new play development, with its recently instituted New Playwrights Unit and staged readings series geared toward mainstage presentation of locally nurtured plays.

Programs and services
Professional training in acting, design and production; classes for nonprofessionals and children, programs-in-schools, Expressive Arts Program for problem behavior delinquents, student and senior citizen ticket discounts, free ticket distribution, post-performance discussions, workshop productions and staged readings, newsletter, speakers bureau, volunteer auxiliary, theatre rentals.

Productions 1977-78
Mother Courage and Her Children, Bertolt Brecht; trans: Eric Bentley
A Chekhov Christmas:
    The Seduction (from *The Good Doctor),* Neil Simon
    The Marriage Proposal, Anton Chekhov; trans: Theodore Hoffman
    The Brute, Anton Chekhov; trans: Eric Bentley
Father's Day, Oliver Hailey
And Miss Reardon Drinks a Little, Paul Zindel
One Flew over the Cuckoo's Nest, Dale Wasserman, from Ken Kesey's novel

Productions 1978-79
The Trojan Women, Euripides; adapt: Apollo and Olympia Dukakis
The Imaginary Invalid, Moliere; adapt: Miles Malleson
The Homecoming, Harold Pinter
Arms and the Man, George Bernard Shaw
Who's Afraid of Virginia Woolf?, Edward Albee

Maggie Abeckerly and Olympia Dukakis in *The Trojan Women.*

Williamstown Theatre Festival

Nikos Psacharopoulos
Artistic/Executive Director

Gintare Sileika
General Manager

Box 517
Williamstown, MA 01267
(413) 458-8146

Founded 1955
Area residents

Season
June–August

Schedule
Evenings
Tuesday–Saturday
Matinees
Thursday, Saturday

Facilities
Adams Memorial Theatre
Seating capacity: 479
Stage: proscenium
Pine Cobble School
Seating capacity: 120
Stage: thrust
Experimental Theatre
Seating capacity: 150
Stage: flexible

Finances
Dec. 1, 1977–Nov. 30, 1978
$364,000 operating expenses
$257,000 earned income
$108,000 unearned income

Audience
Paid capacity: 96%
Annual attendance: 40,000

Touring contact
Nikos Psacharopoulos

AEA Stock (Y) contract

Celebrating it 25th anniversary season in 1979, the Williamstown Theatre Festival has presented 157 plays ranging from the American masterpieces of Williams, Miller, Wilder and O'Neill to the European classics of Chekhov, Brecht, Moliere, Sheridan, Ibsen, O'Casey, Pirandello, Gorky and Pinter.

Williamtown's second company presents non-Equity experimental productions of the classics, new plays and adaptations. An alternative to the more elaborate mainstage offerings, the company travels to prisons, hospitals, rehabilitation centers and camps in western New England and eastern New York State, providing free theatre to the culturally disenfranchised.

The Festival also sponsors an apprentice workshop, founded 20 years ago to provide comprehensive training in acting, directing and production to gifted students intent on professional careers. Such artists as Santo Loquasto, Austin Pendleton, Christopher Reeve, Jill Clayburgh and Laurie Kennedy went through the program. Staged readings take place in the Festival's experimental theatre space, and the Cabaret program tours late-night musical revues each week to area restaurants. Sunday afternoon entertainment is also presented at the Clark Arts Institute in Williamstown, including such special events as Frank Langella and Blythe Danner in *The Fitzgeralds;* Tammy Grimes in *This Is on Me: Dorothy Parker;* Mildred Dunnock and E.G. Marshall in *Wilder's Women;* and solo performances by Eric Bentley, Geraldine Fitzgerald and Milo O'Shea.

The only summer theatre to have a production presented on the PBS *Theater in America* series (1974's *The Seagull*), the Festival also staged the world premiere of Richard Wilbur's new translation of Moliere's *The Learned Ladies,* and in 1978, the American premiere of Ariadne Nicolaeff's translation of Turgenev's *A Month in the Country.* Over the years Williamstown has been the summer home for some 2,500 artists playing to more than a half-million people.

Programs and services
Professional training in acting, directing and production; artistic, administrative and technical/production internships; classes for nonprofessionals; student performances, programs-in-schools, regional touring of second company, workshop productions and staged readings, cabaret, poetry readings, souvenir book, volunteer auxiliary.

Productions 1978
Idiot's Delight, Robert Sherwood
Design for Living, Noel Coward
The School for Wives, Moliere; trans: Richard Wilbur
The Shadow Box, Michael Cristofer
A Month in the Country, Ivan Turgenev; trans: Ariadne Nicolaeff

Productions 1979
Camino Real, Tennessee Williams
The Matchmaker, Thornton Wilder
The Resistible Rise of Arturo Ui, Bertolt Brecht; trans: George Tabori
Hay Fever, Noel Coward
Charley's Aunt, Brandon Thomas
Children of the Sun, Maxim Gorky; trans: Ariadne Nicolaeff

Richard Kneeland in *Camino Real.* Photo: Marcia Johnston.

Donald Madden in *The Resistible Rise of Arturo Ui.* Photo: Marcia Johnston.

The Wisdom Bridge Theatre

Robert Falls
Artistic Director

Jeffrey Ortmann
Executive Director

1559 West Howard St.
Chicago, IL 60626
(312) 743-6442

Founded 1974
David Beaird

Season
October–May

Schedule
Evenings
Thursday–Sunday
Matinees
Sunday

Facilities
Seating capacity: 150
Stage: thrust

Finances
Aug. 1, 1978–July 31, 1979
$170,000 operating expenses
$ 73,000 earned income
$ 73,000 unearned income

Audience
Paid capacity: 91%
Annual attendance: 12,989

Booked-in events
Mime, revues, experimental
theatre, dance

AEA COLT contract

James Murphy, Janice St. John
and Leland Crooke in *Tartuffe*.
Photo: James C. Clark.

Donald Humbertson in *Carmilla*.
Photo: Jennifer Girard.

Wisdom Bridge Theatre, founded in 1974, is a 150-seat resident company located on Chicago's far north side. During the first few seasons, artistic director David Beaird combined an offbeat aesthetic with tooth-and-nail determination to produce adventurous plays accessible to a general audience.

Following a successful guest-director engagement, Robert Falls was asked to assume artistic directorship in 1977. The 1977-78 award-winning season included two Midwest premieres: *Ladyhouse Blues* and *The Idiots Karamazov*. Ticket sales swelled. Falls opened the 1978-79 season with his first two productions, *The Runner Stumbles* and *Tartuffe;* both shows were received with capacity houses and critical attention. Never before had Wisdom Bridge had to disappoint so many callers with the words, "Sorry, sold out!"

The final production of the 1978-79 season, *Bagtime,* was the theatre's most ambitious effort. An original musical based on the picturesque adventures of a supermarket bag-boy, *Bagtime* is based on the newspaper column and best-selling novel by Bob Greene and Paul Galloway. During its six-week run at Wisdom Bridge, every performance, including previews, was sold out. Due to the tremendous popularity of the piece, the show moved to Chicago's Drury Lane Theatre at Water Tower Place.

In 1979-80, WBT embarked on its first subscription season. Five plays will be presented, among them a new musical based on *The Phantom of the Opera.*

Programs and services
Artistic, administrative and technical/production internships; student and senior citizen ticket discounts, voucher program, post-performance discussions, speakers bureau, volunteer auxiliary, theatre rentals.

Productions 1977-78
Ladyhouse Blues, Kevin O'Morrison
The Idiots Karamazov, Christopher Durang and Albert Innaurato
The Crucible, Arthur Miller
Carmilla, David Campton, from Joseph Sheridan Le Fanu's novella

Productions 1978-79
The Runner Stumbles, Milan Stitt
Tartuffe, Moliere; adapt: Miles Malleson
Comedians, Trevor Griffiths
Bagtime, book: Alan Rosen; music: Louis Rosen; lyrics: Thom Bishop
Suburbs of Heaven, music and lyrics: Thom Bishop

Worcester Foothills Theatre Company

Marc P. Smith
Executive Producer

Box 236
Worcester, MA 01602
(617) 754-3314 (business)
(617) 754-4018 (box office)

Founded 1974
Marc P. Smith

Season
September–May

Schedule
Evenings
Wednesday–Sunday
Matinees
Thursday, Saturday, Sunday

Facilities
6 Chatham St.
Seating capacity: 200
Stage: thrust

Finances
June 1, 1978–May 31, 1979
$206,000 operating expenses
$137,000 earned income
$ 48,000 unearned income

Audience
Paid capacity: 65%
Subscribers: 1,300
Annual attendance: 32,000

It would be difficult now to separate the Worcester Foothills Theatre Company from its audience. From its birth in 1974, Foothills has strived to create a lively dialogue between company and audience. From this dialogue has come the company's creative force and its own artistic vision.

The selections in its eight-play, 32-week season are, therefore, traditional in format and reflect middle-class values, experiences and aspirations. Experimental and new plays are combined with American and European classics. New plays have dealt with such themes as pacifism in World War II, personal rights versus the public good, and the impact of regulatory agencies on the industrial working force. The company has offered regional premieres of such plays as Lawrence Durrell's *An Irish Faustus* and reintroduced audiences to nearly forgotten plays in the American heritage, such as Sidney Howard's *The Silver Cord* and S. N. Behrman's *Dunnigan's Daughter*.

Dialogue is sought on many levels. Company members are encouraged to participate in the life of the community and combine those realities with the artistic vision of the theatre. Thus, company members belong to Rotary, Kiwanis, the PTA, church and synagogue organizations, the adult softball league, etc.

The company is joined to the arts community, the academic world and other cultural organizations by its involvement in committees, study groups and councils. Foothills has become generic to the community in which it lives. It has become part of the community's mainstream; it is linked to all aspects of its historical, social and economic life. This in turn has given a vital audience access to a theatre company which speaks to them personally. The resulting interdependence defines the flavor and the future of the Worcester Foothills Theatre Company.

Programs and services
Professional training in acting, design and production; classes for nonprofessionals and children; artistic, administrative and technical/production internships; student performances, ticket discounts, post-performance discussions, guest lecturers, newsletter.

Productions 1977-78
Dream Girl, Elmer Rice
I Am a Camera, John Van Druten
Tartuffe, Moliere; trans: Miles Malleson
Outward Bound, Sutton Vane
Room Service, John Murray and Allen Boretz
A Moon for the Misbegotten, Eugene O'Neill
An Irish Faustus, Lawrence Durrell
Butterflies Are Free, Leonard Gershe
Time: 1940, Marc P. Smith
Arsenic and Old Lace, Joseph Kesselring

Productions 1978-79
A Thousand Clowns, Herb Gardner
Wait Until Dark, Frederick Knott
The Taming of the Shrew, William Shakespeare
The Rainmaker, N. Richard Nash
The Unexpected Guest, Agatha Christie
The Hasty Heart, John Patrick
The Silver Cord, Sidney Howard
Charley's Aunt, Brandon Thomas
Be a Sport, book: Marc P. Smith; music: Craig
    Simmons; lyrics: James Dempsey and M.P.
    Smith

Mary Stark and Cole Eckhardt in *I Am a Camera*. Photo: Terence Finan.

Yale Repertory Theatre

Lloyd Richards
Artistic Director

Edward A. Martenson
Managing Director

222 York St.
New Haven, CT 06520
(203) 436-1587 (business)
(203) 436-1600 (box office)

Founded 1966
Robert Brustein

Season
September–May

Schedule
Evenings
Monday–Saturday
Matinees
Tuesday, Saturday

Facilities
1120 Chapel St.
Seating capacity: 491
Stage: modified thrust

Finances
July 1, 1977–June 30, 1978
$1,008,000 operating expenses
$ 321,000 earned income
$ 687,000 unearned income

Audience
Paid capacity: 75%
Subscribers: 6,066
Annual attendance: 73,000

Booked-in events
Experimental theatre

AEA LORT (C) contract

John Glover and Carol Kane in
Tales from the Vienna Woods.
Photo: Eugene Cook.

The Yale Repertory Theatre is a professional company affiliated with the Yale School of Drama. Founded in 1966 by the then newly appointed dean, Robert Brustein, it has devoted itself to innovative productions of the classics, to recovering unjustly neglected classics, and to fostering the most daring and exciting new playwriting. Of some 90 productions in 13 seasons, 35 have been world premieres by American playwrights and 13 have been world premieres. Lloyd Richards, who assumed the deanship of the school and directorship of the theatre in the 1979-80 season, intends to extend the YRT's concern to the production of classical plays from the American repertoire.

The Yale School of Drama (founded in 1924 as the graduate department of drama of the School of Fine Arts, and reorganized as a professional school in 1955) serves as the conservatory wing of YRT. The two entities exist in close symbiosis; many YRT members teach at the school, all students train at the theatre, and each year several graduates are offered employment with the company.

YRT offers a subscription series of seven plays, produced in rotating repertory over a 40-week period. Its home is a former Baptist church, which it first occupied in 1971 and completely renovated as a theatre in 1975.

Among its offerings are: a Sunday series of staged readings of new plays; a series of theatre-related films; student matinees of selected repertory offerings; a post-play discussion series; the Yale Cabaret, a late-night weekend cafe featuring comic and satiric sketches, short plays, musical revues and miscellany; and a welter of student productions and workshops, often directed by leading professionals (e.g., Andrei Serban and Lee Breuer) at the School of Drama.

Located at the edge of the Yale campus near downtown New Haven, the YRT serves both the "town-and-gown" communities, and contributes to New Haven's status as the "largest little city" in the American theatre world.

Programs and services
Professional training in acting, directing, design, production and administration; technical/production internships, student performances, programs-in-schools, study materials, student and senior citizen ticket discounts, free ticket distribution, post-performance discussions, workshop productions and staged readings, film series, cabaret, speakers bureau, theatre rentals.

Productions 1977-78
The Ghost Sonata, August Strindberg; trans: Evert Sprinchorn
Reunion and *Dark Pony,* David Mamet
Terra Nova, Ted Tally
Sganarelle: An Evening of Moliere Farces, Moliere; trans: Albert Bermel
Man Is Man, Bertolt Brecht; trans: Steve Gooch
Wings, Arthur Kopit
The Wild Duck, Henrik Ibsen; trans: Michael Meyer

Productions 1978-79
Tales from the Vienna Woods, Odon von Horvath; trans: Chistopher Hampton
'dentity Crisis, Christopher Durang
Guesswork, Robert Auletta
Mahagonny, book and lyrics: Bertolt Brecht; adapt: Keith Hack; music: Kurt Weill
Buried Child, Sam Shepard
The Seagull, Anton Chekhov; trans: Jean-Claude van Itallie
The Bundle, Edward Bond
As You Like It, William Shakespeare

Marianne Owen and Constance Cummings in *Wings.* Photo: Eugene Cook.

Dramatists, Directors and Designers

(a) adaptor
(t) translator
(b) book
(m) music
(l) lyrics
(2) revival

PRODUCTION	DRAMATIST	DIRECTOR	SETS	COSTUMES	LIGHTING
A Contemporary Theatre					
Henry IV, Part I	William Shakespeare	Gregory A. Falls	Shelley Henze Schermer	Sally Richardson	Jody Briggs
The Shadow Box	Michael Cristofer	Robert Loper	Karen Gjelsteen	Sally Richardson	Phil Schermer
Ballymurphy	Michael Neville Stan Keen(m)	Gregory A. Falls	Jerry Williams	Sally Richardson	Paul Bryan
The Sea Horse	Edward J. Moore	M. Burke Walker	Todd Muffatti	Sally Richardson	Al Nelson
Makassar Reef	Alexander Buzo	Bill Ludel	Karen Gjelsteen	Jerry Williams	Phil Schermer
Anything Goes	Guy Bolton (b) P.G. Wodehouse (b) Howard Lindsay (b) Russel Crouse (b) Cole Porter (m,l)	Judith Haskell	Jerry Williams	Jerry Williams	Phil Schermer
A Christmas Carol	Gregory A. Falls (a)	Gregory A. Falls	Shelley Henze Schermer	Sally Richardson	Phil Schermer
The Odyssey	Gregory A. Falls (a) Kurt Beattie (a)	Gregory A. Falls	Shelley Henze Schermer	Sally Richardson	Phil Schermer
The Forgotten Door	Gregory A. Falls (a)	Gregory A. Falls	Shelley Henze Schermer	Sally Richardson	
Man and Superman	George Bernard Shaw	Thomas Gruenewald	Shelley Henze Schermer	Sally Richardson	Jody Briggs
Fanshen	David Hare	Gregory A. Falls	Shelley Henze Schermer	Sally Richardson	Phil Schermer
Otherwise Engaged	Simon Gray	Robert Loper	Scott Weldin	Sally Richardson	Paul Bryan
Holy Ghosts	Romulus Linney	Clayton Corzatte	Carey Wong	Julie James	Jody Briggs
The Water Engine	David Mamet	William West	Karen Gjelsteen	Sally Richardson	Phil Schermer
The Fantasticks	Tom Jones (b,l) Harvey Schmidt (m)	John Kauffman	Shelley Henze Schermer	Sally Richardson	Phil Schermer
Academy Festival Theatre					
Twelfth Night	William Shakespeare	Philip Minor	John Wright Stevens	Laura Crow	John Wright Stevens
After the Season	Corinne Jacker	Marshall W. Mason	John Lee Beatty	Laura Crow	Jennifer Tipton
What the Butler Saw	Joe Orton	Mel Shapiro	Fred Kolouch	Laura Crow	Fred Kolouch
Serenading Louie	Lanford Wilson	Marshall W. Mason	John Lee Beatty	Laura Crow	Dennis Parichy
Charley's Aunt	Brandon Thomas	Christopher Hewett	Bruce H. Monroe	Linda Fisher	Lowell B. Achziger
Morning's at Seven	Paul Osborn	Vivian Matalon	Bruce H. Monroe	Linda Fisher	Marc B. Weiss
Uncle Vanya	Anton Chekhov David Magarshack (t)	George Keathley	Bruce H. Monroe	Linda Fisher	Marc B. Weiss
The Interview	Thom Thomas	Vivian Matalon	Bruce H. Monroe	Linda Fisher	Richard Nelson
Academy Theatre					
Waiting for Godot	Samuel Beckett	Frank Wittow	Dorset Noble	Beverly Bateman	Lorraine Lombard
The Hostage	Brendan Behan	Frank Wittow	Dorset Noble	Dellis Caden	Henry Gaede
The Lady's Not for Burning	Christopher Fry	Frank Wittow	Dorset Noble	Dellis Caden	Henry Gaede
The Blood Knot	Athol Fugard	Frank Wittow	Dorset Noble	Frank Wittow	Henry Gaede
Long Day's Journey into Night	Eugene O'Neill	Frank Wittow	Dorset Noble	Dellis Caden	C. A. Casey
Clerambard	Marcel Ayme	Frank Wittow	Dorset Noble	Dellis Caden	Henry Gaede
Dream Nibbler	John Stephens company	Edward Lee	Dorset Noble	Dellis Caden	Henry Gaede
Batteries Not Included	John Stephens company	Edward Lee	Henry Gaede Dorset Noble		
Crocodile Casserole	company developed	Frank Wittow		Carole Fessenden	

PRODUCTION	DRAMATIST	DIRECTOR	SETS	COSTUMES	LIGHTING
Masks	company developed	Frank Wittow			
Up Close	company developed	Gay Griggs			
Death of a Salesman	Arthur Miller	Mary Nell Santacroce	Michael Stauffer	Michael Stauffer	Michael Stauffer
Tartuffe	Moliere	Leonardo Shapiro	Michael Stauffer	Michael Stauffer	Lauren M. Miller
	Richard Wilbur (t)				
Streamers	David Rabe	Frank Wittow	Michael Stauffer	Michael Stauffer	Lauren M. Miller
Heavenly Shades of Night Are Falling	Jim Peck	Frank Wittow	W. Joseph Stell	Catherine Hiller	Lauren M. Miller
Good Night, Mr. Potato	John Stephens company	John Stephens	John Stephens	Catherine Hiller	
The Wind in the Willows	John Stephens (a) company (a)	John Stephens	Owen Brooks	Catherine Hiller	
The Flexible Fireman	Ethel McFarland Frank Wittow	Frank Wittow	Michael Hickey	Cile Purcell	
Families	company developed	Frank Wittow			

The Acting Company

PRODUCTION	DRAMATIST	DIRECTOR	SETS	COSTUMES	LIGHTING
King Lear	William Shakespeare	John Houseman	Ming Cho Lee	Nancy Potts	David F. Segal
Mother Courage and Her Children	Bertolt Brecht Ralph Manheim (t)	Alan Schneider	Ming Cho Lee	Jeanne Button	David F. Segal
The Duck Variations	David Mamet	Gerald Gutierrez	John Lee Beatty	John David Ridge	David F. Segal
The Other Half	Elinor Jones	Amy Saltz			Skip Rapoport
Chapeau	Alfred Uhry (b,l) Robert Waldman (m)	Gerald Freedman	Santo Loquasto	Santo Loquasto	David F. Segal
Antigone	Jean Anouilh Lewis Galantiere (t)	Alan Schneider	John Jensen	Jeanne Button	David F. Segal
Broadway	George Abbott Philip Dunning	Gerald Gutierrez	John Lee Beatty	John David Ridge	David F. Segal
Romeo and Juliet	William Shakespeare	Nagle Jackson	John Jensen	Jeanne Button	David F. Segal
A Voice of My Own	Elinor Jones Kathrin King Segal (m)	Amy Saltz	Patricia Woodbridge	Jeanne Button	David F. Segal

Actors Theatre of Louisville

PRODUCTION	DRAMATIST	DIRECTOR	SETS	COSTUMES	LIGHTING
Living Together	Alan Ayckbourn	Elizabeth Ives	Paul Owen	Kurt Wilhelm	Paul Owen
Getting Out	Marsha Norman	Jon Jory	Paul Owen	Kurt Wilhelm	Paul Owen
Does Anybody Here Do the Peabody?	Enid Rudd	Charles Kerr	Paul Owen	Kurt Wilhelm	Paul Owen
Andronicus	Jon Jory (b) Jim Wann (m,l)	Jon Jory	Paul Owen	Kurt Wilhelm	Ronald Wallace
The Front Page	Ben Hecht Charles MacArthur	Jon Jory	David Hager	Kurt Wilhelm	Jeff Hill
Lu Ann Hampton Laverty Oberlander	Preston Jones	Patrick Tovatt	Paul Owen	Kurt Wilhelm	Paul Owen
The Mousetrap	Agatha Christie	Elizabeth Ives	Paul Owen	Kurt Wilhelm	Paul Owen
Peg o' My Heart	J. Hartley Manners	Ray Fry	Richard Gould	Kurt Wilhelm	Paul Owen
Daddies	Douglas Gower	Michael Hankins	Paul Owen	Kurt Wilhelm	Michael Hottois
The Bridgehead	Frederick Bailey	Charles Maryan	Paul Owen	Kurt Wilhelm	Michael Hottois

continued

Williamstown Theatre Festival.
Peter Evans, Henry Rinehart,
Elizabeth Council, Yusef Bules,
Blythe Danner, Ellis Rabb and
R. Harris in *A Month in the
Country.*

PRODUCTION	DRAMATIST	DIRECTOR	SETS	COSTUMES	LIGHTING
Sizwe Bansi Is Dead	Athol Fugard John Kani Winston Ntshona	Joe Morton	Michael Hottois	Kurt Wilhelm	Michael Hottois
Third and Oak	Marsha Norman	Jon Jory	Paul Owen	Kurt Wilhelm	Paul Owen
Round and Round the Garden	Alan Ayckbourn	Elizabeth Ives	Richard Gould	Kurt Wilhelm	Paul Owen
A Christmas Carol	Barbara Field (a)	Charles Kerr	Richard Wilcox	Kurt Wilhelm	Paul Owen
An Independent Women	Daniel Stein	Daniel Stein	Paul Owen	Kurt Wilhelm	Paul Owen
The Louisville Zoo	Various	Ray Fry	Paul Owen	Kurt Wilhelm	Paul Owen
The Lion in Winter	James Goldman	Michael Hankins	Paul Owen	Kurt Wilhelm	Paul Owen
Whose Life Is It Anyway?	Brian Clark	Daniel Sullivan	Paul Owen	Kurt Wilhelm	Paul Owen
The Splits	Erika Ritter	Michael Hankins	David Hager	Kurt Wilhelm	Jeff Hill
The Runner Stumbles	Milan Stitt	Peter Bennett	Paul Owen	Kurt Wilhelm	Paul Owen
The Play's the Thing	Ferenc Molnar P.G. Wodehouse (a)	Patrick Henry	Joe Varga	Kurt Wilhelm	Paul Owen
What Every Woman Knows	J.M. Barrie	Ray Fry	David Hager	Kurt Wilhelm	Jeff Hill
Circus Valentine	Marsha Norman	Jon Jory	Paul Owen	Kurt Wilhelm	Paul Owen
Matrimonium	Peter Ekstrom	Ray Fry	Paul Owen	Kurt Wilhelm	Paul Owen
Find Me	Olwen Wymark	Jon Jory	Paul Owen	Kurt Wilhelm	Paul Owen
Crimes of the Heart	Beth Henley	Jon Jory	Paul Owen	Kurt Wilhelm	Paul Owen
Lone Star	James McLure	Stuart White	Paul Owen	Kurt Wilhelm	Paul Owen
Holidays	various	Michael Hankins	Paul Owen	Kurt Wilhelm	Paul Owen
The Gin Game	D.L. Coburn	Richard Russell Ramos	Paul Owen	Kurt Wilhelm	Jeff Hill
The Shadow Box	Michael Cristofer	Michael Hankins	Joe Varga	Kurt Wilhelm	Paul Owens
Gold Dust	Jon Jory (b) Jim Wann (m,l)	Jon Jory	Paul Owen	Kurt Wilhelm	Paul Owen

Actors Theatre of St. Paul

PRODUCTION	DRAMATIST	DIRECTOR	SETS	COSTUMES	LIGHTING
Scenes from American Life	A.R. Gurney, Jr.	Michael Andrew Miner	Dick Leerhoff	Christopher Beesley	Paul Scharfenberger
The Farm	David Storey	Emily Mann	Dick Leerhoff	Christopher Beesley	Susan E. Titus
Down by the Gravois (Under the Anheuser- Busch)	James Nicholson	Michael Andrew Miner	Dick Leerhoff	Christopher Beesley	Paul Scharfenberger
Arms and the Man	George Bernard Shaw	Michael Andrew Miner	Dick Leerhoff	Christopher Beesley	Paul Scharfenberger
The Waltz of the Toreadors	Jean Anouilh Lucienne Hil (t)	Michael Andrew Miner	Dick Leerhoff	Christopher Beesley	Paul Scharfenberger
The Mandrake	Niccolo Machiavelli Camille Gifford (a)	Camille Gifford	Dick Leerhoff	Rita Claire LaDoux	J.M. Bald
Androcles and the Lion	Aurand Harris	Camille Gifford	Dick Leerhoff	Rita Claire LaDoux	J.M. Bald
The Iron Harp	Joseph O'Connor	Michael Andrew Miner	Dick Leerhoff	Christopher Beesley	Paul Scharfenberger
Custer	Robert E. Ingham	George C. White	Dick Leerhoff	Christopher Beesley	Susan E. Titus
U.S.A.	John Dos Passos	Michael Andrew Miner	Michael Andrew Miner	Margaret Churchill	Robert Jorissen
Two for the Seesaw	William Gibson	Michael Andrew Miner	Michael Andrew Miner	Christopher Beesley	Michael Vennerstrom

Alabama Shakespeare Festival

PRODUCTION	DRAMATIST	DIRECTOR	SETS	COSTUMES	LIGHTING
Othello	William Shakespeare	Martin L. Platt	Michael Stauffer	Lynne C. Emmert	Michael Stauffer
The Merchant of Venice	William Shakespeare	Martin L. Platt	Michael Stauffer	Lynne C. Emmert	Michael Stauffer
Private Lives	Noel Coward	Fred Chappell	Michael Stauffer	Lynne C. Emmert	Michael Stauffer
Measure for Measure	William Shakespeare	Martin L. Platt	Michael Stauffer	Lynne C. Emmert	Michael Stauffer

PRODUCTION	DRAMATIST	DIRECTOR	SETS	COSTUMES	LIGHTING
Clarence Darrow	David W. Rintels	Martin L. Platt	Michael Stauffer	Lynne C. Emmert	Roger Foster (1) Lauren Miller (2)
A Lover's Complaint	Martin L. Platt (a)	Martin L. Platt	Michael Stauffer	Lynne C. Emmert	Michael Stauffer
The Taming of the Shrew	William Shakespeare	Martin L. Platt	Michael Stauffer	Lynne C. Emmert	Michael Stauffer
As You Like It	William Shakespeare	Martin L. Platt	Michael Stauffer	Lynne C. Emmert	Michael Stauffer
Macbeth	William Shakespeare	Martin L. Platt	Michael Stauffer	Lynne C. Emmert	Michael Stauffer
The Comedy of Errors	William Shakespeare	Russell Treyz	Michael Stauffer	Lynne C. Emmert	Michael Stauffer
The Country Wife	William Wycherley	Martin L. Platt	Michael Stauffer	Lynne C. Emmert	Michael Stauffer
Oh, William!	Martin L. Platt (a) Various (m,l)	Russell Treyz	Michael Stauffer	Susan Mickey	Lauren Miller
Twelfth Night	William Shakespeare	Martin L. Platt	Michael Stauffer	Lynne C. Emmert	Michael Stauffer

Alaska Repertory Theatre

PRODUCTION	DRAMATIST	DIRECTOR	SETS	COSTUMES	LIGHTING
Sherlock Holmes (and The Curse of the Sign of Four or The Mark of the Timber Toe)	Dennis Rosa (a)	Robert J. Farley	Jamie Greenleaf	Jamie Greenleaf	James Sale
The Fourposter	Jan de Hartog	Clayton Corzatte	Jamie Greenleaf	Jamie Greenleaf	James Sale
The Eccentricities of a Nightingale	Tennessee Williams	Dennis Brite	Jamie Greenleaf	Jamie Greenleaf	James Sale
Diamond Studs	Jim Wann (b,m,l) Bland Simpson (m,l)	Robert J. Farley	Jamie Greenleaf	Jamie Greenleaf	James Sale
A Christmas Carol	Martin L. Platt (a)	Robert J. Farley	Jamie Greenleaf	Nanrose Buchman	James Sale
Terra Nova	Ted Tally	Robert J. Farley	Jamie Greenleaf	Nanrose Buchman	James Sale
The Taming of the Shrew	William Shakespeare	Martin L. Platt	Jamie Greenleaf	Nanrose Buchman	James Sale
Slow Dance on the Killing Ground	William Hanley	Gary D. Anderson	Jamie Greenleaf	Nanrose Buchman	James Sale
Deathtrap	Ira Levin	Robert J. Farley	Jamie Greenleaf	Nanrose Buchman	James Sale

Alliance Theatre Company/Atlanta Children's Theatre

PRODUCTION	DRAMATIST	DIRECTOR	SETS	COSTUMES	LIGHTING
Vanities	Jack Heifner	Fred Chappell	Erik Magnuson	Patricia McMahon	Cassandra Henning
Cole	Cole Porter (m,l) Benny Green (a) Alan Strachan (a)	Fred Chappell	William Schroder	Michael Stauffer	Cassandra Henning
A Christmas Carol	Martin L. Platt (a)	Martin L. Platt	Michael Stauffer	Michael Stauffer	Carol Graebner
Tiger Tail	Tennessee Williams	Harry Rasky	John Wulp	Lynn Pecktal	Carol Graebner
The Diary of Anne Frank	Frances Goodrich Albert Hackett	Fred Chappell	Philipp Jung	Michael Stauffer	Michael Orys Watson
Lu Ann Hampton Laverty Oberlander	Preston Jones	Fred Chappell	Michael Layton	Michael Stauffer	Guy H. Tuttle
The Taming of the Shrew	William Shakespeare	Malcolm Black	Stephen Henrickson	Thom Coates	Jane Reisman
Beauty and the Beast	Bix Doughty (a)	Jim Way	Ruth Ann Doughty	Ruth Ann Doughty	Cassandra Henning
Robin Hood	Sharon O'Brien	Luis Quintin Barroso	Richard Brice	Renee L. Wolfe	Carol Graebner
The Shadow Box	Michael Cristofer	Fred Chappell	W. Joseph Stell	Thom Coates	Carol Graebner
Peter Pan	J.M. Barrie	John Going	Virginia Dancy Elmon Webb	Thom Coates	Michael Stauffer
The Little Foxes	Lillian Hellman	Fred Chappell	Helen Pond Herbert Senn Roger Foster	Thom Coates	W. Joseph Stell

continued

PRODUCTION	DRAMATIST	DIRECTOR	SETS	COSTUMES	LIGHTING
Absurd Person Singular	Alan Ayckbourn	Donald Ewer	Thom Coates	Thom Coates	Michael Stauffer
The Robber Bridegroom	Alfred Uhry (b,l)	Fred Chappell	Michael Stauffer	Thom Coates	Michael Stauffer
	Robert Waldman (m)				
Othello	William Shakespeare	Wallace Chappell	Jonathan Arkin	Thom Coates	Roger Foster
The Halloween Tree	Wallace Chappell (a)	Wallace Chappell	Thom Coates	Thom Coates	Carol Graebner
Tales from the Brothers Grimm	Wallace Chappell (a)	Wallace Chappell	Thom Coates	Thom Coates	Michael Stauffer

AMAS Repertory Theatre

PRODUCTION	DRAMATIST	DIRECTOR	SETS	COSTUMES	LIGHTING
Helen	Lucia Victor (b)	Lucia Victor	Michael Meadows	Bernard Johnson	Paul Sullivan
	Johnny Brandon (m,l)				
Beowulf	Betty Jane Wylie (b,l)	Bernard Johnson	Michael Meadows	Lindsay W. Davis	Paul Sullivan
	Victor Davies (m)				
Come Laugh and Cry with Langston Hughes	Rosetta LeNoire (a)	Voight Kempson	Michael Meadows	Bernard Johnson	Paul Sullivan
Sparrow in Flight	Charles Fuller	Dean Irby	Michael Meadows	Bernard Johnson	Paul Sullivan
	Rosetta LeNoire				
It's So Nice to be Civilized	Micki Grant (b,m,l)	Jeffrey Dunn	Patrick Mann	Bill Baldwin	Paul Sullivan
Suddenly the Music Starts	Johnny Brandon (m,l)	Lucia Victor	Patrick Mann	Virginia Johnson	Paul Sullivan
Boston Boston	William Michael Maher (b)	William Michael Maher	Michael Meadows	Sydney Brooks	Paul Sullivan
	Bill Brohn (m)				
	B. Brohn &				
	W. Maher (l)				

American Conservatory Theatre

PRODUCTION	DRAMATIST	DIRECTOR	SETS	COSTUMES	LIGHTING
Travesties	Tom Stoppard	Nagle Jackson	John Jensen	Robert Morgan	Dirk Epperson
Hotel Paradiso	Georges Feydeau	Tom Moore	Richard Seger	Robert Blackman	Richard Devin
	Maurice Desvallieres				
	Peter Glenville (t)				
Absurd Person Singular	Alan Ayckbourn	Allen Fletcher	Ralph Funicello	Robert Morgan	Dirk Epperson
The National Health	Peter Nichols	Nagle Jackson	Christopher M. Idoine	Elizabeth Covey	F. Mitchell Dana
Julius Caesar	William Shakespeare	Edward Payson Call	Richard Seger	John Conklin	Richard Devin
All the Way Home	Tad Mosel	Edward Hastings	Ralph Funicello	Cathy Edwards	Dirk Epperson
The Master Builder	Henrik Ibsen	Allen Fletcher	Ralph Funicello	Robert Morgan	Richard Devin
	Allen Fletcher (t)				
The Circle	W. Somerset Maugham	Stephen Porter	Robert Blackman	Robert Fletcher	F. Mitchell Dana (1)
					Dirk Epperson (2)
A Christmas Carol	Dennis Powers (a)	Laird Williamson	Robert Blackman	Robert Morgan	F. Mitchell Dana
	Laird Williamson (a)				
Hay Fever	Noel Coward	Nagle Jackson	Ralph Funicello	Robert Morgan	Dirk Epperson
The Visit	Friedrich Dürrenmatt	Laird Williamson	Richard Seger	Robert Blackman	F. Mitchell Dana
	Maurice Valency (a)				
A Month in the Country	Ivan Turgenev	Laird Williamson	Henry May	Robert Blackman	Richard Devin
	Willis Bell (a)				
The Winter's Tale	William Shakespeare	William Ball	Richard Seger	Robert Fletcher	Richard Devin
Ah, Wilderness!	Eugene O'Neill	Allen Fletcher	Ralph Funicello	Robert Morgan	Richard Devin
Heartbreak House	George Bernard Shaw	Allen Fletcher	Ralph Funicello	Robert Blackman	F. Mitchell Dana
The 5th of July	Lanford Wilson	Edward Hastings	Richard Seger	Martha Burke	Dirk Epperson

PRODUCTION	DRAMATIST	DIRECTOR	SETS	COSTUMES	LIGHTING
American Place Theatre					
Cockfight	Elaine Jackson	Woodie King, Jr.	C. Richard Mills	Ruth Morley	Edward M. Greenberg
Passing Game	Steve Tesich	Peter Yates	Kert Lundell	Ruth Morley	Neil Peter Jampolis
Fefu and Her Friends	Maria Irene Fornes	Maria Irene Fornes	Kert Lundell Nancy Tobias	Theo Barnes	Edward M. Greenberg
Conjuring an Event	Richard Nelson	Douglas C. Wager	David Lloyd Gropman	William Ivey Long	Paul Gallo
The Grinding Machine	Annalita Marsili Alexander	Frederick Rolf	Wolfgang Roth	Willa Kim	Edward M. Greenberg
Touching Bottom	Steve Tesich	Robert Brink	Henry Millman	Mimi Maxmen	Craig Evans
Seduced	Sam Shepard	Jack Gelber	Henry Millman	Whitney Blausen	Edward M. Greenberg
Tunnel Fever or The Sheep Is Out	Jonathan Reynolds	Marshall Oglesby	Donato Moreno	Donato Moreno	Dennis Parichy
American Stage Festival					
The Royal Family	George S. Kaufman Edna Ferber	Norman Ayrton	Tony Straiges	David Murin	Arden Fingerhut
The Glass Menagerie	Tennessee Williams	Bill Ludel	William Schroeder	Nanzi Adzima	Dennis J. McHugh
Bandstand	Gary Pearle (a) Nora Peterson (a) Evans Haile (a) Harold DeFelice (a) Susanna Styron (a) various (m,l)	Nora Peterson	John Kasarda	Jess Goldstein	Dennis J. McHugh
A Moon for the Misbegotten	Eugene O'Neill	Stanley Wojewodski, Jr.	Hugh Landwehr	Hilary Sherred	Dennis J. McHugh
Peg o' My Heart	J. Hartley Manners	John Going	Andrew Jackness	Jess Goldstein	Dennis J. McHugh
Dracula	Tom Haas (a)	Harold DeFelice	Hugh Landwehr	David Murin	Dennis J. McHugh
Troupers!	Harold DeFelice (a) various (m,l)	Harold DeFelice	John Kasarda	Carol Oditz	Robby Monk
Of Mice and Men	John Steinbeck	Irene Lewis	John Jensen	John Jensen	Paul Gallo
Tartuffe	Moliere Richard Wilbur (t)	Stanley Wojewodski, Jr.	Hugh Landwehr	Melissa Binder	Annie Wrightson
Artichoke	Joanna Glass	Burke Walker	Adrianne Lobel	Rebecca Carroll	Annie Wrightson
Our Town	Thornton Wilder	Harold DeFelice	Edward Cesaitis	Jess Goldstein	Dennis Parichy
The Hunchback of Notre Dame	Ron Whyte (a)	Edward Cornell	Walter Pickette	Dona Granata	Dennis Parichy
American Pie	Lawrence Smith	Lawrence Smith			
Tall Tales	Lawrence Smith	Lawrence Smith			
American Theatre Company					
The Ruling Class	Peter Barnes	Jerald D. Pope	Richard B. Ellis	Catherine Hillis	Richard B. Ellis
Long Day's Journey into Night	Eugene O'Neill	James E. Runyan	Jerald D. Pope	Catherine Hillis	Ed Taylor
A Christmas Carol	Robert L. Odle (b) Richard Averill (m,l)	Jerald D. Pope	Richard B. Ellis	Catherine Hillis (1) Jo McClelland (2)	Ed Taylor
The Miser	Moliere	Jerald D. Pope	Jerald D. Pope	Catherine Hillis	Harlan R. Wilson III
Lu Ann Hampton Laverty Oberlander	Preston Jones	Jerald D. Pope	Richard B. Ellis	Jo McClelland	Ed Taylor
Vanities	Jack Heifner	Kitty Roberts	Kerry Hauger	Jo McClelland	Kerry Hauger

continued

Hartford Stage Company. George Grizzard and Barbara Baxley in *Past Tense*. Photo: Lanny Nagler.

PRODUCTION	DRAMATIST	DIRECTOR	SETS	COSTUMES	LIGHTING
Dracula	Robert L. Odle (a)	Jerald D. Pope	Richard B. Ellis	Gene Barnhart	Ed Taylor
The Real Inspector Hound	Tom Stoppard	James E. Runyan	Ed Taylor	Jo McClelland	Robert Shafer
The Merry Wives of Windsor	William Shakespeare	Will Huddleston	Ed Taylor	Gene Barnhart	Robert Shafer
Ms. Raccoon's Profession	company (b,l) Richard Averill, et al. (m)	Jerald D. Pope	Robert Shafer	Jo McClelland	Ed Taylor
The Glass Menagerie	Tennessee Williams	James E. Runyan	Richard B. Ellis	Jo McClelland	Ed Taylor

Arena Stage

The National Health	Peter Nichols	David Chambers	Karl Eigsti	Marjorie Slaiman	Hugh Lester
Nightclub Cantata	Elizabeth Swados	Elizabeth Swados	Patricia Woodbridge	Kate Carmel	Cheryl Thacker
Starting Here, Starting Now	David Shire (m) Richard Maltby, Jr. (l)	Richard Maltby, Jr.	Sally Cunningham	Stanley Simmons	John Mulligan
The Caucasian Chalk Circle	Bertolt Brecht John Holstrom (t)	Martin Fried	Santo Loquasto	Santo Loquasto	William Mintzer
A Streetcar Named Desire	Tennessee Williams	Marshall W. Mason	John Lee Beatty	Laura Crow	Hugh Lester
Comedians	Trevor Griffiths	David Chambers	Tony Straiges	Marjorie Slaiman	William Mintzer
Hamlet	William Shakespeare	Liviu Ciulei	Ming Cho Lee	Marjorie Slaiman	Hugh Lester
Gemini	Albert Innaurato	Douglas C. Wager	Christopher Nowak	Rebecca Carroll	William Mintzer
Duck Hunting	Alexander Vampilov Alma H. Law (t)	Zelda Fichandler	Karl Eigsti	Marjorie Slaiman	Hugh Lester
Tales from the Vienna Woods	Odon von Horvath Christopher Hampton (t)	David Chambers	Zack Brown	Marjorie Slaiman	Wiliam Mintzer
The Curse of the Starving Class	Sam Shepard	Douglas C. Wager	Karl Eigsti	Marjorie Slaiman	William Mintzer
The 1940s Radio Hour	Walton Jones	Walton Jones	David Lloyd Gropman	William Ivey Long	Hugh Lester
Ah Wilderness!	Eugene O'Neill	Edward Cornell	Robert Yodice	Marjorie Slaiman	Hugh Lester
Loose Ends	Michael Weller	Alan Schneider	William Ritman	Marjorie Slaiman	Hugh Lester
Don Juan	Moliere Richard Nelson (t)	Liviu Ciulei	Ming Cho Lee	Dunya Ramicova	Hugh Lester
Nevis Mountain Dew	Steve Carter	Horacena J. Taylor	Wynn Thomas	Alvin Perry	Shirley Prendergast
Idiot's Delight	Robert Sherwood	Edward Cornell	Tony Straiges	Marjorie Slaiman	William Mintzer
Tintypes: A Ragtime Revue	Mary Kyte (a) Mel Marvin (a) Gary Pearle (a) various (m,l)	Gary Pearle	Hugh Lester	Jess Goldstein	Roger Milliken

Arizona Theatre Company

Pygmalion	George Bernard Shaw	Sandy Rosenthal	Reagan Cook	Peggy Kellner	Dan T. Willoughby
Slow Dance on the Killing Ground	William Hanley	David Gardiner	Jack Schwanke	Sandra Mourey	Dan T. Willoughby
Equus	Peter Shaffer	Mark Lamos	Reagan Cook	Sandra Mourey	Dan T. Willoughby
Black Comedy	Peter Shaffer	Susan Bay	Reagan Cook	Sandra Mourey	Dan T. Willoughby
The Shadow Box	Michael Cristofer	Sandy Rosenthal	Reagan Cook	Sandra Mourey	Dan T. Willoughby
Rodgers and Hart	Richard Rodgers (m) Lorenz Hart (l) Richard Lewine (a) John Fearnley (a)	Judith Haskell	J. Michael Gillette	Sandra Mourey	Dan T. Willoughby
Cold Storage	Ronald Ribman	Peter Wexler	Reagan Cook	Carolie Jean Tarble	Dan T. Willoughby

PRODUCTION	DRAMATIST	DIRECTOR	SETS	COSTUMES	LIGHTING
A Christmas Carol	Keith Fowler (a)	Clarke Gordon	J. Michael Gillette	Bobbi Culbert	Dan T. Willoughby
Tartuffe	Moliere Richard Wilbur (t)	Israel Hicks	Peggy Kellner	Peggy Kellner	Dan T. Willoughby
The Royal Hunt of the Sun	Peter Shaffer	Sandy Rosenthal	Peter Wexler	Bobbi Culbert	Dan T. Willoughby
Boesman and Lena	Athol Fugard	Israel Hicks	Dan Dryden	Carolie Jean Tarble	Dan T. Willoughby
The Show-Off	George Kelly	Mark Lamos	Bil Mikulewicz	Carolie Jean Tarble Robin R. Willoughby	Dan T. Willoughby

Arkansas Repertory Theatre

Jacques Brel Is Alive and Well and Living in Paris	Jacques Brel (m,l) Eric Blau (a) Mort Shuman (a)	Cliff F. Baker	Byl Harriell	Cliff F. Baker	Byl Harriell
Kennedy's Children	Robert Patrick	Cliff F. Baker	Byl Harriell	Cliff F. Baker	Byl Harriell
Happy Birthday, Wanda June	Kurt Vonnegut	Cliff F. Baker	Byl Harriell	Cliff F. Baker	Byl Harriell
Fitting for Ladies	Georges Feydeau Peter Meyer (t)	Martin L. Platt	Byl Harriell	Martin L. Platt	Byl Harriell
An Evening of Gershwin	George Gershwin (m) Ira Gershwin, et al. (l) Cliff F. Baker (a) Sharon Douglas (a)	Cliff F. Baker	Byl Harriell	Cliff F. Baker	Byl Harriell
The Glass Menagerie	Tennessee Williams	Cliff F. Baker	Byl Harriell	Cliff F. Baker	Byle Harriell
Sweet Charity	Neil Simon (b) Cy Coleman (m) Dorothy Fields (l)	Cliff F. Baker	Byl Harriell	Donia Crafton	Byl Harriell
Celebration	Tom Jones (b,l) Harvey Schmidt (m)	Cliff F. Baker	Byl Harriell	Cliff F. Baker	Byl Harriell
The Boys in the Band	Mart Crowley	Jean Lind	Byl Harriell	Jean Lind	Byl Harriell
Vanities	Jack Heifner	Cliff F. Baker	Byl Harriell	Cyndy Campbell	Byl Harriell
The Runner Stumbles	Milan Stitt	Pat Brown	Guy Couch	Guy Couch	Byl Harriell
Twelfth Night	William Shakespeare	Cliff F. Baker	Arthur Resler	Jean Hendrickson Mary Andreyco	David Eubanks
Who's Afraid of Virginia Woolf?	Edward Albee	Cliff F. Baker	Guy Couch	Cliff F. Baker	Byl Harriell
Lola-Lola	Cliff F. Baker (b) Sharon Douglas (m,l)	Cliff F. Baker	Scot Shapiro	Cliff F. Baker	Scot Shapiro

Asolo State Theater

The Royal Family	George S. Kaufman Edna Ferber	Howard J. Millman	Holmes Easley	Flozanne John	Martin Petlock
Juno and the Paycock	Sean O'Casey	George Keathley	David Emmons	Catherine King	Martin Petlock
She Stoops to Conquer	Oliver Goldsmith	Robert Strane	Holmes Easley	Catherine King	Martin Petlock
The School for Wives	Moliere Eberle Thomas (t)	Thomas Edward West	Robert C. Barnes	Flozanne John	Martin Petlock
Travesties	Tom Stoppard	Bradford Wallace	John Scheffler	Catherine King	Martin Petlock
Richard III	William Shakespeare	Paul Barry	Rick Pike	Rick Pike	Martin Petlock David Malcolm
The Man Who Came to Dinner	George S. Kaufman Moss Hart	Richard G. Fallon	Robert C. Barnes	Catherine King	Jim Rynning Martin Petlock

continued

PRODUCTION	DRAMATIST	DIRECTOR	SETS	COSTUMES	LIGHTING
The Inspector General	Nikolai Gogol Thomas Edward West (t)	Robert Strane	Rick Pike	Catherine King	David Malcolm Martin Petlock
Catsplay	Istvan Orkeny Clara Gyorgyey (t)	Thomas Gruenewald	Bennet Averyt	Catherine King	Martin Petlock
Archy and Friends	company developed (b) John Franceschina (m,l)	Jim Hoskins	Jeff Dean	Sally A. Kos	David Malcolm
Design for Living	Noel Coward	John Ulmer	John Scheffler	Catherine King	Martin Petlock
The Shadow Box	Michael Cristofer	Sandra C. Hastie	John Scheffler	Sally A. Kos	Martin Petlock
Volpone	Ben Jonson	Robert Strane	Howard Bay	Catherine King	Martin Petlock
Let's Get a Divorce	Victorien Sardou Emile de Najac Brian Kelly (t)	Isa Thomas	Bennet Averyt	Catherine King	Martin Petlock John J. Toia
Long Day's Journey into Night	Eugene O'Neill	Bradford Wallace	Bennet Averyt	Diane Berg	Jim Rynning Martin Petlock
A History of the American Film	Christopher Durang (b,l) Mel Marvin (m) John Franceschina (m)	Howard J. Millman Timothy Edward West	David Emmons	Catherine King Sally A. Kos	Martin Petlock
Othello	William Shakespeare	Richard G. Fallon	Sandro LaFerla	Catherine King	Martin Petlock Mark Noble
Stag at Bay	Charles MacArthur Nunnally Johnson	Stephen Rothman	David Emmons	Catherine King	Martin Petlock Edd Kraus
The Cherry Orchard	Anton Chekhov Jean-Claude van Itallie (t)	Mark Epstein	Robert C. Barnes	Carherine King	Martin Petlock Jim Murray
Merlin	company developed (b) John Franceschina (m,l)	Jim Hoskins Max Howard	Jeff Dean	Sally A. Kos	John J. Toia Mark Noble

BAM Theater Company

PRODUCTION	DRAMATIST	DIRECTOR	SETS	COSTUMES	LIGHTING
The Devil's Disciple	George Bernard Shaw	Frank Dunlop	Carl Toms	Carl Toms	F. Mitchell Dana
The Play's the Thing	Ferenc Molnar P. G. Wodehouse (a)	Frank Dunlop	Santo Loquasto	Nancy Potts	F. Mitchell Dana
Julius Caesar	William Shakespeare	Frank Dunlop	Carole Lee Carroll	Dona Granata	F. Mitchell Dana
Waiting for Godot	Samuel Beckett	Walter Asmus	Carol Lee Carroll	Dona Granata	Shirley Prendergast
Gimme Shelter	Barrie Keeffe	Des McAnuff	Stuart Wurtzel	Carol Oditz	Dennis Parichy
On Mount Chimborazo	Tankred Dorst Peter Sander (a)	John Palmer	Christopher Nowak	Nancy Thun	Victor En Yu Tan

Barter Theatre

PRODUCTION	DRAMATIST	DIRECTOR	SETS	COSTUMES	LIGHTING
Two Gentlemen of Verona	William Shakespeare	Ada Brown Mather	Bennet Averyt	Sigrid Insull	Tony Partington
The Mousetrap	Agatha Christie	Dorothy Marie	Bennet Averyt	Sigrid Insull	Tony Partington
Born Yesterday	Garson Kanin	John Olon-Scrymgeour	Parmelee Welles	Sigrid Insull	Sara Ross Morgan
The Corn Is Green	Emlyn Williams	Rex Partington	Parmelee Welles	Sigrid Insull	Sara Ross Morgan
Tartuffe	Moliere	Ada Brown Mather	Parmelee Welles	Sigrid Insull	Sara Ross Morgan
The Apple Tree	Jerry Bock (b,m) Sheldon Harnick (b,l)	John Olon-Scrymgeour	F. Leonard Darby	Carr Garnett	Sara Ross Morgan
Hay Fever	Noel Coward	John Olon-Scrymgeour	Parmelee Welles	Carr Garnett	Tony Partington
The Second Man	S. N. Behrman	Rex Partington	F. Leonard Darby	Carr Garnett	Sara Ross Morgan
How the Other Half Loves	Alan Ayckbourn	Edward Stern	Bennet Averyt	Carr Garnett	Sara Ross Morgan
I Do! I Do!	Tom Jones (b,l) Harvey Schmidt (m)	Owen Phillips	Gregory Buch	Sigrid Insull	Sara Ross Morgan
The Owl and the Pussycat	Bill Manhoff	Dorothy Marie	Gregory Buch	Sigrid Insull	Sara Ross Morgan

PRODUCTION	DRAMATIST	DIRECTOR	SETS	COSTUMES	LIGHTING
Oh, Coward!	Noel Coward	John W. Morrow, Jr.	F. Leonard Darby	Sigrid Insull	Sara Ross Morgan
Vanities	Jack Heifner	Dorothy Marie	Gregory Buch	Carr Garnett	Cindy Limauro
The Wonderful Ones!	Tennessee Williams	Rex Partington		Anne Duff Parker	Cindy Limauro
	Anton Chekhov	Owen Phillips			
A Doll's House	Henrik Ibsen	Rex Partington	Bennet Averyt	Rachel Kurland	Cindy Limauro
Same Time, Next Year	Bernard Slade	Jeff Meredith	Bennet Averyt	Rachel Kurland	Cindy Limauro
Misalliance	George Bernard Shaw	John Going	Bennet Averyt	Rachel Kurland	Cindy Limauro
Dames at Sea	George Haimsohn (b,l)	Voight Kempson	F. Leonard Darby	Georgia Baker	Cindy Limauro
	Robin Miller (b,l)				
	Jim Wise (m)				
Absurd Person Singular	Alan Ayckbourn	Jeff Meredith	F. Leonard Darby	Rachel Kurland	Cindy Limauro
Side by Side by Sondheim	Stephen Sondheim, et al. (m,l)	Larry Alford	F. Leonard Darby	Georgia Baker	Cindy Limauro
	Ned Sherrin (a)				
Luv	Murray Schisgal	Kenneth Robbins	Park Warne	Rachel Kurland	Cindy Limauro
The Fantasticks	Tom Jones (b,l)	Kenneth Robbins	Rex Partington	Judith Dolan	Cindy Limauro
	Harvey Schmidt (m)				
The Public Eye and The Private Ear	Peter Shaffer	Owen Phillips	Rex Partington	Anne Duff Parker	Cindy Limauro

Berkeley Repertory Theatre

A Flea in Her Ear	Georges Feydeau	George Kovach	Ron Pratt	Lesley Skannal	Matthew Cohen
	John Mortimer (t)		Gene Angell		
Rep!	Stanley R. Greenberg	Michael W. Leibert	Jeff Whitman	Lesley Skannal	Matthew Cohen
			Christopher M. Idoine		
Major Barbara	George Bernard Shaw	George Kovach	George Kovach	Marie Anne Chiment	Matthew Cohen
			Tom Odegard		
Mad Oscar	Sheldon Feldner	Peter Donat	Robert Blackman	Marie Anne Chiment	Christopher M. Idoine
The Servant of Two Masters	Carlo Goldoni	Joe Spano	Andrew DeShong	Lesley Skannal	Matthew Cohen
	Joan Liepman (a)				
	Joe Spano (a)				
	Albert Kutchins (a)				
A Moon for the Misbegotten	Eugene O'Neill	Michael W. Leibert	Jeff Whitman	Diana Smith	Matthew Cohen
Wait Until Dark	Frederick Knott	Michael W. Leibert	Ron Pratt	Lesley Skannal	Ken Hein
			Gene Angell		
Arms and the Man	George Bernard Shaw	Maureen O'Reilly	Ron Pratt	Lesley Skannal	Ken Hein
			Gene Angell		
As You Like It	William Shakespeare	George Kovach	John Raymond Freimann	Marie Anne Chiment	Lynn Koolish
They Knew What They Wanted	Sidney Howard	Michael W. Leibert	John Raymond Freimann	Syrell Myers	Lynn Koolish
Misalliance	George Bernard Shaw	George Kovach	John Raymond Freimann	John Raymond Freimann	Lynn Koolish
The Skin of Our Teeth	Thornton Wilder	Michael W. Leibert	Lauren Cory	Merrily Ann Murray	Lynn Koolish
She Stoops to Conquer	Oliver Goldsmith	Maureen O'Reilly	Lauren Cory	Rondi Davis	Lynn Koolish
The Tavern	George M. Cohan	John Raymond Freimann	Noel Uzemack	Warren Travis	Lynn Koolish
He Who Gets Slapped	Leonid Andreyev	Michael W. Leibert	Barbara Sellers	Sarajane Milligan	Lynn Koolish
	Michael W. Leibert (a)				
The Last of the Marx Brothers' Writers	Louis Phillips	Michael W. Leibert	Ron Pratt	Rondi Davis	Lynn Koolish
			Gene Angell		
Room Service	John Murray	John Raymond Freimann	Lauren Cory		Lynn Koolish
	Allen Boretz				

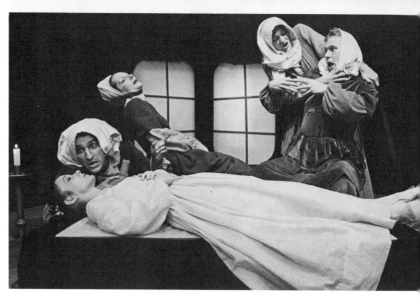

Soho Repertory Theatre. Joan Kelleher, Leo Schaff, Maxine Taylor-Morris, Mark Mikulski and William A. Kilmer in *Miss Jairus*. Photo: Sally Sherwood.

PRODUCTION	DRAMATIST	DIRECTOR	SETS	COSTUMES	LIGHTING
Berkeley Stage Company					
Feedlot	Patrick Meyers	David Ostwald	Jim Curtis	Beverly Schor	Jim Curtis
Womansong	various	Angela Paton	Angela Paton	Angela Paton	Angela Paton
The Sea	Edward Bond	John Vickery	Richard Reynolds	Beverly Schor	Richard Reynolds
The IX John Paul	Rick Foster	John O'Meara	Emery Rogers	Elizabeth Hawk Deborah Gould	Joseph Broido
Three Sons	Richard Lortz	Martin Berman	Richard Mason	Eliza Chugg	Raul Murgatroyd
The Caucasian Chalk Circle	Bertolt Brecht Eric Bentley (t)	Tony Arn	Andrew Doe Tony Arn	Beverly Schor	Jack White
Safe House	Nicholas Kazan	Angela Paton	Angela Paton	Beverly Schor	Suresa Dundes
Earthworms	Albert Innaurato	Robert W. Goldsby	Ariel	Ariel	Toshiro Ogawa
Leading Off and Playing Shortstop	Philip Bosakowski	Tony Arn	Ron Pratt Gene Angell	Beverly Schor	Timothy Lannan
Ashes	David Rudkin	John Vickery Tony Arn	Malcolm Yuill Thornton	Beverly Schor	Timothy Lannan
Artichoke	Joanna Glass	Anne McNaughton	Ron Krempetz	Lani Abbott	Sue Daly
The Dancing Bear Routine	William Harrar	Angela Paton	Mary Gould	Mary Gould	Chuck Ray
Mackerel	Israel Horovitz	Joy Carlin	Lynn Hershman	Lynn Hershman	Peter G. Clark
The Man Who Turned into a Stick	Kobo Abe Donald Keene (t)	Robert W. Goldsby	Ariel	Ariel	Sue Daly
Centralia 1919	Barry Pritchard (b,l) Robert MacDougall (m)	Michael Addison	Donald Cate	Regina Cafe	Donald Cate
Cement	Heiner Muller Helen Fehevary (t) Sue-Ellen Case (t) Marc D. Silberman (t)	Sue-Ellen Case	Ron Pratt Gene Angell	Lani Abbott	Thomas Stocker
The Tennis Game	George W. S. Trow	Robert W. Goldsby	Warren Travis	Warren Travis	Thomas Stocker
Curse of the Starving Class	Sam Shepard	Andrew Doe	Ron Pratt Gene Angell	Lani Abbott	Thomas Stocker
BoarsHead Theater					
Last of the Red Hot Lovers	Neil Simon	Richard Thomsen	Ruth Long	Barbara Thomsen	Ruth Long A. J. Rocchio
Living Together	Alan Ayckbourn	Richard Thomsen	Ruth Long	Barbara Thomsen	Ruth Long A. J. Rocchio
Who's Afraid of Virginia Woolf?	Edward Albee	Arthur Athanason	Ruth Long	Barbara Thomsen	A. J. Rocchio
Private Lives	Noel Coward	Richard Thomsen	Ruth Long	Barbara Thomsen	Robert Palmateer
Equus	Peter Shaffer	John Peakes	Ruth Long	Barbara Thomsen	Ruth Long
Stop the World—I Want to Get Off	Leslie Bricusse (b,m,l) Anthony Newley (b,m,l)	John Peakes	Ruth Long	Barbara Thomsen	A. J. Rocchio
The Runner Stumbles	Milan Stitt	Richard Thomsen	Ruth Long	Barbara Thomsen	Ruth Long
Vanities	Jack Heifner	Barbara Carlisle	Ruth Long	Barbara Thomsen Veronica Smith	A. J. Rocchio
The Sunshine Boys	Neil Simon	Richard Thomsen	Ruth Long	Barbara Thomsen	A. J. Rocchio
Cabaret	Joe Masteroff (b) John Kander (m) Fred Ebb (l)	John Peakes	Ruth Long	Barbara Thomsen	A. J. Rocchio

PRODUCTION	DRAMATIST	DIRECTOR	SETS	COSTUMES	LIGHTING
Fiddler on the Roof	Joseph Stein (b) Jerry Bock (m) Sheldon Harnick (l)	Richard Thomsen	Ruth Long	Sydney Poel	A. J. Rocchio
The Male Animal	James Thurber Elliott Nugent	Richard Thomsen	Ruth Long	Sydney Poel	A. J. Rocchio
The Last Meeting of the Knights of the White Magnolia	Preston Jones	Robert Burpee	Donna Arnink	Barbara Thomsen	Margaret Lee
The Underpants	Carl Sternheim	Richard Thomsen	Donna Arnink	Barbara Thomsen	Margaret Lee
Dandelion Wine	Peter John Bailey (a)	John Peakes	John Peakes	Barbara Thomsen	Margaret Lee
A Life in the Theatre	David Mamet	Barbara Carlisle	Margaret Lee	Barbara Thomsen	Margaret Lee
Uncle Vanya	Anton Chekhov	Richard Thomsen	Ann Gumpper	Barbara Thomsen	Margaret Lee
Steambath	Bruce Jay Friedman	John Peakes	Donna Arnink	Barbara Thomsen	Margaret Lee
Time Steps	Gus Kaikkonen	Richard Thomsen	Kenneth L. Peck	Barbara Thomsen	Margaret Lee
The House of Blue Leaves	John Guare	John Peakes	Donna Arnink	Johanna Lubkowski	Margaret Lee
Harvey	Mary Chase	Richard Thomsen	Donna Arnink	Johanna Lubkowski	Margaret Lee
Man of La Mancha	Dale Wasserman (b) Mitch Leigh (m) Joe Darion (l)	John Peakes	Donna Arnink	Johanna Lubkowski	Margaret Lee
George M!	Michael Stewart (b) John & Fran Pascal (b) George M. Cohan (m,l)	Richard Thomsen	Donna Arnink	Johanna Lubkowski	Margaret Lee
Same Time, Next Year	Bernard Slade	John Peakes	Donna Arnink	Johanna Lubkowski	Margaret Lee

Body Politic Theatre

PRODUCTION	DRAMATIST	DIRECTOR	SETS	COSTUMES	LIGHTING
Lunching	Alan Gross	Mike Nussbaum	Michael W. Merritt	Julie A. Nagel	Michael W. Merritt
Samuel: The First Book of the Kings	company developed	James A. Shiflett David S. Moore	Chip Gore David S. Moore	Sharon Ferguson Phillips	Fill Cadkin
The Baron Must Die	Frank Shiras	Sharon Ferguson Phillips	Nels Anderson	Sharon Ferguson Phillips Peggy Prielozny	Nels Anderson
Let It Play	James Barry John Green Dale McFadden Eric McGill	Dale McFadden	Jamie Smead	Jamie Smead	Jamie Smead
Bingo: Game of the Gods	Virginia Smiley (b) company (b) Melissa Shiflett (m) Karyne G. Pritikin (l)	Sharon Ferguson Phillips	Jamie Smead	Jamie Smead Kim Barrington	Fill Cadkin
Slapstick and Sawdust	T. J. Tatters	T. J. Tatters			J. B. Spector
Red Rover, Red Rover	Oliver Hailey	June Pyskacek	Rick Paul	Cookie Gluck	Gene Wojcik
Angel City	Sam Shepard	Dale McFadden	Thomas Beall	Nanalee Raphael	Robert S. Gold
Spring's Awakening	Frank Wedekind	Joseph Slowik	Nels Anderson	Janet Messmer	Nels Anderson
Statements After an Arrest Under the Immorality Act	Athol Fugard	James D. O'Reilly	James Boley	Bobbie Hodges	John Rodriguez
Scenes from Soweto	Steve Wilmer	James D. O'Reilly	James Boley	Bobbie Hodges	John Rodriguez
Eyes of Wonder	company developed	David S. Moore	David S. Moore	Sharon Ferguson Phillips	Gerald B. Stephens
Hide and Seek	Frank Shiras	Francis X. Kuhn	Esther K. Smith	Esther K. Smith	Esther K. Smith
Dead of Night	John Ostrander	Mary Ellen McGarry	Thomas Beall	Thomas Beall	Thomas Beall
Station J	Richard France	Dale McFadden	Leor Warner	Leor Warner	Leor Warner

PRODUCTION	DRAMATIST	DIRECTOR	SETS	COSTUMES	LIGHTING
The Boston Arts Group					
The Hot l Baltimore	Lanford Wilson	Bart McCarthy	Randy Neale	Virginia Land	Randy Neale
Kansas City K.R.O.W.	Bart McCarthy Arthur Crowley	Bart McCarthy	Arthur Crowley	Virginia Land	
The Dumb Waiter and The Lover	Harold Pinter	Jim Butterfield	Nicholas Linfield	Nicholas Linfield	James Butterfield
Passions, Dreams and Revelations	David Zucker Kate Bentley	David Zucker			Marcie Kirsten
A Martian Trilogy	Bart McCarthy (a)	Bart McCarthy	Ken Lowstetter	Virginia Land	Jude Erwin
The Snark Was a Boojum	Pam Enion (a)	David Zucker	Scott Gray	Pam Enion	
Radio	company developed	Bart McCarthy	Ken Lowstetter	Virginia Land	Bart McCarthy
Macbett	Eugene Ionesco	Bill Miekle	John Chandler	Joann Brandt	Alexander Washington
Yellow Wallpaper	Ann Titolo	James Williams	Rhonda Birnbaum	Ann Titolo	Rhonda Birnbaum
I Can Feel the Air	Lis Adams	Robert Deveau	B. P. Fowler	Ann Marie Clifford	Rhonda Birnbaum
History of Western Civilization	Roger Curtis	Roger Curtis	Roger Curtis	Virginia Land	Jude Erwin
Waiting for Godot	Samuel Beckett	Bart McCarthy	Bart McCarthy	Bart McCarthy	Jude Erwin
Lincoln Log	Bart McCarthy	David Zucker	Bart McCarthy	Virginia Land	
Savages	Christopher Hampton	James J. Perry	Lydia Littlefield	Bart McCarthy	Todd McConchie
Boston Shakespeare Company					
Twelfth Night	William Shakespeare	Bill Cain	Gail Van Voorhis (1) Lauren J. Kurki (2)	Kay Haskell	Patricia Tampone
The Taming of the Shrew	William Shakespeare	Bill Cain	Gail Van Voorhis	Niki Rudisill	Patricia Tampone
Henry IV, Part I	William Shakespeare	Bill Cain	Gail Van Voorhis	Rose Jung	Patricia Tampone
Much Ado About Nothing	William Shakespeare	Janet Buchwald	Gail Van Voorhis	Kay Haskell	Patricia Tampone
Antigone	Jean Anouilh Lewis Galantiere (t)	James Kitendaugh	Gail Van Voorhis	Cheryl Spinaci	Patricia Tampone
As You Like It	William Shakespeare	Bill Cain	Gail Van Voorhis (1) Lauren J. Kurki (2)	Kay Haskell	Patricia Tampone (1) Ned Lyon (2)
Hamlet	William Shakespeare	Bill Cain	Lauren J. Kurki	Kay Haskell	Ned Lyon
The Miser	Moliere Sylvan Barnet (t) Morton Berman (t) William Burto (t)	Tim Ward	Lauren J. Kurki	Elaine Nicholson	Patricia Tampone
Measure for Measure	William Shakespeare	Bill Cain	Lauren J. Kurki	Elaine Nicholson	Patricia Tampone
Two Gentlemen of Verona	William Shakespeare	William Lacey	Lauren J. Kurki	Kay Haskell	Patricia Tampone
Romeo and Juliet	William Shakespeare	Bill Cain	Patricia Tampone	Elaine Nicholson	Patricia Tampone
California Actors Theatre					
Henry IV, Parts I and II	William Shakespeare	James Dunn	Ron Krempetz	Barbara Affonso	Eric Chasanoff
Save Grand Central	William Hamilton	Ed Hastings	Ron Krempetz	Barbara Affonso	Eric Chasanoff
Scapino	Frank Dunlop (a) Jim Dale (a)	James Dunn	Eric Chasanoff	Elaine Saussotte	Eric Chasanoff
The Price	Arthur Miller	G. W. Bailey	Eric Chasanoff	Elaine Saussotte	Eric Chasanoff
You Can't Take It with You	George S. Kaufman Moss Hart	James Dunn	Ron Krempetz	Elaine Saussotte	Eric Chasanoff
Steambath	Bruce Jay Friedman	Harvey Susser	Eric Chasanoff	Elaine Saussotte	Eric Chasanoff
Wild Oats	John O'Keeffe	Douglas Johnson	Eric Chasanoff	Elaine Saussotte	Eric Chasanoff

PRODUCTION	DRAMATIST	DIRECTOR	SETS	COSTUMES	LIGHTING
Plymouth Rock	William Hamilton	Charles Maryan	Atkin Pace	Elaine Saussotte	Jim Sale
The Marriage Proposal and Swan Song	Anton Chekhov Theodore Hoffman (t)	Israel Hicks	Atkin Pace	Elaine Saussotte	Dirk Epperson
The Brute	Anton Chekhov Eric Bentley (t)	Israel Hicks	Atkin Pace	Elaine Saussotte	Dirk Epperson
Bus Stop	William Inge	Charles Maryan	Atkin Pace	Atkin Pace	Dirk Epperson
Playing with Fire	August Strindberg Edwin Bjorkman (t)	Charles Maryan	Atkin Pace	Lana Fritz	Lynn Coolish Barbara Jacoby
The Collection	Harold Pinter	Charles Maryan	Atkin Pace	Lana Fritz	Lynn Coolish Barbara Jacoby
Holiday	Philip Barry	Charles Maryan	Fred Voelpel	Lana Fritz	Carolyn Walker
The Play's the Thing	Ferenc Molnar P. G. Wodehouse (a)	J. Ranelli	Ralph Funicello	Cathleen Edwards	Carolyn Walker
Twelfth Night	William Shakespeare	Charles Maryan	Atkin Pace	Lana Fritz	Richard Moore
Crimes of the Heart	Beth Henley	J. Ranelli	Atkin Pace	Lana Fritz	Barbara Jacoby

The Cambridge Ensemble

The Oresteia	Aeschylus Joann Green (a)	Joann Green	Joann Green	Joann Green	Len Schnabel
Puntila and Matti, His Hired Man	Bertolt Brecht Ralph Manheim (t)	Joann Green	Joann Green	Joann Green	Len Schnabel
A Hell of a Mess	Eugene Ionesco Helen Gary Bishop (t)	Joann Green	Joann Green	Joann Green	Len Schnabel
Tales of Chelm	company developed	Joann Green	Lisa Conley	Joann Green	Joann Green
A Sorrow Beyond Dreams	Peter Handke Ralph Manheim (t)	Joann Green	Joann Green	Joann Green	Len Schnabel
Gulliver's Travels	company developed (a)	Joann Green	Joann Green	Joann Green	Gayle Youngman
The Diary of a Madman	Joann Green (a)	Joann Green	Joann Green	Joann Green	Len Schnabel

Center Stage

The Goodbye People	Herb Gardner	Robert Allan Ackerman	Charles Cosler	Elizabeth Palmer	Charles Cosler
The Rivals	Richard Brinsley Sheridan	Stanley Wojewodski, Jr.	Eldon Elder	Robert Wojewodski	Gilbert Hemsley, Jr.
The Runner Stumbles	Milan Stitt	Stanley Wojewodski, Jr.	Hugh Landwehr	Elizabeth Palmer	Charles Cosler
Ashes	David Rudkin	Stanley Wojewodski, Jr.	Clark Crolius	Dona Granata	Arden Fingerhut
The Night of the Iguana	Tennessee Williams	Edward Berkeley	Peter Harvey	Hilary Rosenfeld	Judy Rasmuson
Blithe Spirit	Noel Coward	Marcia Rodd	Charles Cosler	Robert Wojewodski	Charles Cosler
The Shadow Box	Michael Cristofer	Stanley Wojewodski, Jr.	Andrew Jackness	Robert Wojewodski	Judy Rasmuson
Born Yesterday	Garson Kanin	Steven Robman	Charles Cosler	Dona Granata	Spencer Mosse
A Christmas Carol: Scrooge and Marley	Israel Horovitz (a)	Robert Allan Ackerman	Hugh Landwehr	Robert Wojewodski	Arden Fingerhut
G. R. Point	David Berry	William Devane	Peter Larkin	Laura H. Castro	Neil Peter Jampolis Jane Reisman
You Can't Take It with You	George S. Kaufman Moss Hart	Stanley Wojewodski, Jr.	John Kasarda	Hilary A. Sherred	Bonnie A. Brown
Measure for Measure	William Shakespeare	Stanley Wojewodski, Jr.	Hugh Landwehr	Dona Granata	Arden Fingerhut
Bonjour, là, Bonjour	Michel Tremblay John Van Burek (t) Bill Glassco (t)	Stanley Wojewodski, Jr.	Hugh Landwehr	Robert Wojewodski	Spencer Mosse

Folger Theater Group. John Neville-Andrews and David Cromwell in *Whose Life is it Anyway?* Photo: Joan Marcus.

PRODUCTION	DRAMATIST	DIRECTOR	SETS	COSTUMES	LIGHTING
The Changing Scene					
Mencken	James Crowell	Bob Berkel	Greg Carr	Rae McDowell	Peter Nielson
Day upon Day	Andrea Shepard	Juliet Wittman			Peter Nielson Michael Hetzel
Custer	Robert E. Ingham	Richard Lore	Eric Charles Baldwin	Rae McDowell	Peter Nielson
Batteries Not Included	William Smith company	William Smith	Eric Charles Baldwin		Peter Nielson
Short Plays for a Man on the Moon and The Teachings of John Brown in Florida	Michael Meyers	Michael Meyers	Michael Meyers	Michael Meyers	Peter Nielson
Repast	David Lang	Michael O'Sullivan	Michael O'Sullivan		Peter Nielson
Apparent Discrepancies	Eric Charles Baldwin	Edward Sampson	Eric Charles Baldwin Edward Sampson		Peter Nielson
The Mantis Flies Alone	David Lang	David Lang	Eric Charles Baldwin	Beverly Hainault David Lang Michael O'Sullivan Robbin Sutton	Peter Nielson
The First Interplanetary Voyage of J. Alfred Carnelian	Eric Charles Baldwin	William Smith	Eric Charles Baldwin	Michael O'Sullivan	Peter Nielson
L'Ecole des Veuves	Jean Cocteau	Estelle Mosko	Rod Thompson	Colette Reynders	Peter Nielson
Le Petit Prince	Jacques Ardouin (a)	Barbara Blum	Rod Thompson	Colette Reynders	Peter Nielson
Two Small Bodies	Neal Bell	Bob Berkel	Bob Berkel		Peter Nielson
Coke Dreams and Bride Doll	Teresa Marffie-Evangelista	Teresa Marffie-Evangelista	Russ Stevenson		Peter Nielson
The Man Who Knew John Dillinger	Janet McReynolds	J. H. Crouch	Leonard Latham J. H. Crouch		Peter Nielson
Spit	Bob Breuler	Don Katzman	Peter Nielson		Peter Nielson
Parade of Arms	Don Katzman	Don Katzman	Peter Nielson		Peter Nielson
Chelsea Theater Center					
Rum an Coca Cola	Mustapha Matura	Donald Howarth	Wolfgang Roth	Debra Stein	William Mintzer
Green Pond	Robert Montgomery (b,l) Mel Marvin (m)	David Chambers	Marjorie Kellogg	Marjorie Kellogg	Arden Fingerhut
Old Man Joseph and His Family	Romulus Linney	Robert Kalfin	Carrie F. Robbins	Carrie F. Robbins	Mark DiQuinzio
Biography: A Game	Max Frisch Michael Bullock (t)	Arne Zaslove	Robert Ellsworth	Elizabeth P. Palmer	Robert Graham Small
Strider: The Story of a Horse	Mark Rozovsky (b,m) Uri Riashentsev (l) Steve Brown (a,l) Robert Kalfin (a) S. Vetkin (m) Norman L. Berman (m)	Robert Kalfin Lynne Gannaway	Wolfgang Roth	Andrew Marley	Robby Monk
The Children's Theatre Company					
Aladdin and the Wonderful Lamp	Timothy Mason (a)	Gene Davis Buck	Dahl Delu	Gene Davis Buck	Jon Baker

PRODUCTION	DRAMATIST	DIRECTOR	SETS	COSTUMES	LIGHTING
Thieves' Carnival	Jean Anouilh I. A. Humm (t)	John Clark Donahue	Robert Braun	Gene Davis Buck	Robert Jorrisen
The Little Match Girl	John Clark Donahue (a)	Myron Johnson	Jay Bush Gene Davis Buck	Gene Davis Buck	Jon Baker
Beauty and the Beast	Timothy Mason (a)	John Clark Donahue	Dahl Delu	Gene Davis Buck	Karlis Ozols
A Circle Is the Sun	Frederick Gaines (b,l) John Clark Donahue (b,l)	John Clark Donahue	Donald Pohlman	Gene Davis Buck	Jon Baker
The Pied Piper of Hamelin	Thomas W. Olson (b,l) Richard A. Dworsky (m)	Myron Johnson	Dahl Delu	Dahl Delu	Jon Baker
The Rivals	Richard Brinsley Sheridan	John Clark Donahue	Steven M. Rydberg	Gene Davis Buck	Karlis Ozols
Punch and Judy and the Three Sillies	Timothy Mason (a)	Myron Johnson	Jay Bush	Rae Marie Pekas	Robert Jorrisen
The Legend of Sleepy Hollow	Frederick Gaines (b,l) Roberta Carlson (m)	Bain Boehlke	Paul Maurer	Gene Davis Buck	Jon Baker
Hansel and Gretel	Timothy Mason (a)	Gene Davis Buck	Dahl Delu	Gene Davis Buck	Dahl Delu
A Christmas Carol	Frederick Gaines (a)	Bain Boehlke John Clark Donahue	Jack Barkla Mary Alyce White	Dahl Delu	Robert S. Hutchings, Jr.
The Little Mermaid	Timothy Mason (a)	John Clark Donahue	Dahl Delu	Gene Davis Buck	Robert S. Hutchings, Jr.
Good Morning, Mr. Tillie	John Clark Donahue	John Clark Donahue	Jon Barkla Don Yunker	John Clark Donahue Rae Marie Pekas	Karlis Ozols
Pinocchio	Timothy Mason (a)	Gene Davis Buck	Dahl Delu	Rae Marie Pekas	Robert S. Hutchings, Jr.
The Green Beetle Dance	John Clark Donahue (b,l) Steven M. Rydberg (m)	John Clark Donahue	John Clark Donahue	Gene Davis Buck	Robert S. Hutchings, Jr.
The Sitwells at Sea	Gar Hildenbrand (a)	John Clark Donahue	Steven M. Rydberg	Gene Davis Buck	Karlis Ozols

Cincinnati Playhouse in the Park

PRODUCTION	DRAMATIST	DIRECTOR	SETS	COSTUMES	LIGHTING
The Threepenny Opera	Bertolt Brecht (b,l) Marc Blitzstein (t) Kurt Weill (m)	Michael Murray	Neil Peter Jampolis	Annie Peacock Warner	Neil Peter Jampolis
The Imaginary Invalid	Moliere R. G. Davis (a)	R. G. Davis	Karl Eigsti	Annie Peacock Warner	Neil Peter Jampolis
Benefit of a Doubt	Edward Clinton	Michael Murray	Neil Peter Jampolis	Annie Peacock Warner	Neil Peter Jampolis
Of Mice and Men	John Steinbeck	Robert Brewer	Karl Eigsti	Annie Peacock Warner	Neil Peter Jampolis
The House of Bernarda Alba	Federico Garcia Lorca	Michael Murray	John Lee Beatty	Jennifer von Mayrhauser	Marc B. Weiss
The Royal Family	George S. Kaufman Edna Ferber	John Going	Joseph A. Varga	Caley Summers	Jay Depenbrock
Romeo and Juliet	William Shakespeare	Michael Murray	Paul Shortt	Jennifer von Mayrhauser	Neil Peter Jampolis
Otherwise Engaged	Simon Gray	Edward Berkeley	Neil Peter Jampolis	Ann Firestone	Duke Durfee
Room Service	John Murray Allen Boretz	Michael Murray	Karl Eigsti	Caley Summers	Hugh Lester
Hedda Gabler	Henrik Ibsen	John Going	Marjorie Kellogg	Annie Peacock Warner	Pat Collins
The Buddy System	Jonathan Marc Feldman	Michael Murray	Karl Eigsti	Jennifer von Mayrhauser	Duane Schuler
Man of La Mancha	Dale Wasserman (b) Mitch Leigh (m) Joe Darion (l)	John Going	Neil Peter Jampolis	Caley Summers	Neil Peter Jampolis
Magic to Do	Stephen Schwartz (m,l) Ernie Zulia (a) Frank Bartolucci (a)	Ernie Zulia	Duke Durfee	Ann Firestone	Duke Durfee

PRODUCTION	DRAMATIST	DIRECTOR	SETS	COSTUMES	LIGHTING

Circle in the Square

PRODUCTION	DRAMATIST	DIRECTOR	SETS	COSTUMES	LIGHTING
Tartuffe	Moliere Richard Wilbur (t)	Stephen Porter	Zack Brown	Zack Brown	John McLain
Saint Joan	George Bernard Shaw	John Clark	David Jenkins	Zack Brown	John McLain
13 Rue de l'Amour	Georges Feydeau Mawby Green (a) Ed Feilbert (a)	Basil Langton	Zack Brown	Zack Brown	John McLain
Once in a Lifetime	Moss Hart George S. Kaufman	Tom Moore	Karl Eigsti	Carol Luiken	F. Mitchell Dana
The Inspector General	Nikolai Gogol Betsy Hulick (t)	Liviu Ciulei	Karen Schulz	William Ivey Long	F. Mitchell Dana
Man and Superman	George Bernard Shaw	Stephen Porter	Zack Brown	Zack Brown	F. Mitchell Dana
Spokesong	Stewart Parker Jimmy Kennedy (m)	Kenneth Frankel	Marjorie Kellogg	Bill Walker	John McLain
Loose Ends	Michael Weller	Alan Schneider	Zack Brown	Kristina Watson	David F. Segal

Circle Repertory Company

PRODUCTION	DRAMATIST	DIRECTOR	SETS	COSTUMES	LIGHTING
Feedlot	Patrick Meyers	Terry Schreiber	Hal Tiné	Laura Crow	Dennis Parichy
Ulysses in Traction	Albert Innaurato	Marshall W. Mason	John Lee Beatty	Laura Crow	Dennis Parichy
Lulu	Frank Wedekind	Robert Thirkield	John Lee Beatty	David Murin	Ruth Roberts
Brontosaurus	Lanford Wilson	Daniel Irvine	Nina Friedman	Laura Crow	Gary Seltzer
Cabin 12	John Bishop	Marshall Oglesby	Nina Friedman	Irene Nolan	Gary Seltzer
The 5th of July	Lanford Wilson	Marshall W. Mason	John Lee Beatty	Laura Crow	Marc B. Weiss
Glorious Morning	Patrick Meyers	Terry Schreiber	Hal Tiné	Laura Crow	Dennis Parichy
In the Recovery Lounge	James Farrell	Marshall W. Mason	Tom Lynch	Laura Crow	Dennis Parichy
The Runner Stumbles	Milan Stitt	B. Rodney Marriott	David Potts	Kenneth M. Yount	Dennis Parichy
Winter Signs	John Bishop	Marshall W. Mason	David Potts	Laura Crow	Dennis Parichy
Talley's Folly	Lanford Wilson	Marshall W. Mason	John Lee Beatty	Jennifer von Mayrhauser	Dennis Parichy
Gertrude Stein Gertrude Stein Gertrude Stein	Marty Martin	Milton Moss	Tony Straiges	Garland Riddle	Ruth Roberts
Buried Child	Sam Shepard	Robert Woodruff	David Lloyd Gropman		John P. Dodd

Cleveland Play House

PRODUCTION	DRAMATIST	DIRECTOR	SETS	COSTUMES	LIGHTING
Living Together	Alan Ayckbourn	Paul Lee	Richard Gould	Harriet Cone	Richard Gould
The Learned Ladies	Moliere Richard Wilbur (t)	Ray Walston	Paul Rodgers	Estelle Painter	Paul Rodgers
Round and Round the Garden	Alan Ayckbourn	Paul Lee	Richard Gould	Harriet Cone	Richard Gould
Great Expectations	Paul Lee (a)	Jonathan Bolt	Richard Gould	Estelle Painter	Richard Gould
The Prague Spring	Lee Kalcheim (b,l) Joseph G. Raposo (m)	Larry Tarrant		Harriet Cone	Jack Stewart
The Little Foxes	Lillian Hellman	Evie McElroy	Richard Gould	David Smith	Richard Gould
Knock Knock	Jules Feiffer	Paul Lee		Harriet Cone	
The Romantics	Maxim Gorky William Stancil (t)	Larry Tarrant	Richard Gould	Estelle Painter	Richard Gould
The Club	Eve Merriam (a,m,l)	Terri White	Richard Gould	Estelle Painter	Richard Gould
Night Must Fall	Emlyn Williams	Paul Lee	Richard Gould	Estelle Painter	Richard Gould
The Shadow Box	Michael Cristofer	Larry Tarrant	Richard Gould	Estelle Painter	Richard Gould

Folger Theatre Group. Mikel Lambert, Earle Edgerton, John Hertzler and Paul Collins in *Richard III*. Photo: JEB.

PRODUCTION	DRAMATIST	DIRECTOR	SETS	COSTUMES	LIGHTING
The Importance of Being Earnest	Oscar Wilde	Richard Halverson	David Smith	David Smith	Richard Gould
Gemini	Albert Innaurato	Kenneth Albers	Richard Gould	Estelle Painter	Richard Gould
Equus	Peter Shaffer	Larry Tarrant	Richard Gould	Richard Gould	Richard Gould
Threads	Jonathan Bolt	Jonathan Bolt	Paul Rodgers	Estelle Painter	Paul Rodgers
The Last of the Marx Brothers' Writers	Louis Phillips	Paul Lee	Richard Gould	Estelle Painter	Richard Gould
The Odyssey	Gregory A. Falls (a) Kurt Beattie (a)	Larry Tarrant	Paul Rodgers	Paul Rodgers	Paul Rodgers
Something's Afoot	James McDonald (b,m,l) David Vos (b,m,l) Robert Gerlach (b,m,l)	Judith Haskell	Richard Gould	Estelle Painter	Richard Gould

Cohoes Music Hall

The Glass Menagerie	Tennessee Williams	Louis J. Ambrosio	Michael Anania	Robert Wojewodski	Sid Bennett
Vanities	Jack Heifner	Bill Ludel	Michael Anania	Robert Wojewodski	Toni Goldin
A Moon for the Misbegotten	Eugene O'Neill	Thomas Gruenewald	Michael Anania	Robert Wojewodski	Toni Goldin
The Unexpected Guest	Agatha Christie	Louis J. Ambrosio	Michael Anania	Robert Wojewodski	Toni Goldin
Private Lives	Noel Coward	Harold DeFelice	Michael Anania	Dona Granata	Toni Goldin
Tartuffe	Moliere Richard Wilbur (t)	Thomas Gruenewald	Michael Anania	Nancy Potts Lynda L. Salsbury	Toni Goldin
The Runner Stumbles	Milan Stitt	Louis J. Ambrosio	Michael Anania	Lynda L. Salsbury	Toni Goldiin
Angel Street	Patrick Hamilton	Thomas Gruenewald	Michael Anania	Lynda L. Salsbury	Jane Reisman
Long Day's Journey into Night	Eugene O'Neill	Michael Montel	Michael Anania	Lynda L. Salsbury	Jane Reisman
Oh, Coward!	Noel Coward (m,l) Roderick Cook (a)	Thomas Kahn Gardner	Michael Anania	Lynda L. Salsbury	Jane Reisman
Look Back in Anger	John Osborne	Louis J. Ambrosio	Michael Anania	Lynda L. Salsbury	Jane Reisman

Colonnades Theatre Lab

Moliere in Spite of Himself	Mikhail Bulgakov Michael Lessac (a) Daviid Morgan (a)	Michael Lessac	Robert U. Taylor	Hilary A. Sherred	Randy Becker
Anatomy of an Ensemble	Michael Lessac	Michael Lessac	Randy Becker		Randy Becker
The Ballroom in St. Patrick's Cathedral	Louis Phillips	Michael Lessac	Maura Smolover	Rebecca Kreinen Tere Eglar	Randy Becker

The Cricket Theatre

The Trip Back Down	John Bishop	Louis Salerni	Dick Leehoff	Christopher Beesley	Phillip Billey
Red Rover, Red Rover	Oliver Hailey	Michael Flanagan	Barry Robison	Christopher Beesley	Tom Hamilton
The Club	Eve Merriam (a,m,l)	Nocola Crafts-Foster	Thom Roberts	Christopher Beesley	Tom Hamilton
The Shadow Box	Michael Cristofer	Louis Salerni	Barry Robison	Christopher Beesley	Phillip Billey
Indulgences in the Louisville Harem	John Orlock	Louis Salerni	Thom Roberts	Christopher Beesley	Tom Hamilton
And If That Mockingbird Don't Sing	William Whitehead	Davey Marlin-Jones	Dick Leerhoff	Christopher Beesley	Dick Leerhoff
Streamers	David Rabe	Louis Salerni	Phillip Billey	Christopher Beesley	Phillip Billey

continued

Cincinnati Playhouse. Elizabeth
Moore and Tania Myren in *Romeo
and Juliet*.
Photo: Sandy Underwood.

PRODUCTION	DRAMATIST	DIRECTOR	SETS	COSTUMES	LIGHTING
Mourning Pictures	Honor Moore	Louis Salerni	Phillip Billey	Christopher Beesley	Phillip Billey
Sort of a Love Song	Glenn Allen Smith	Pat Patton	Thom Roberts	Christopher Beesley	Phillip Billey
A Breeze from the Gulf	Mart Crowley	Louis Salerni	Jerry Williams	Christopher Beesley	Phillip Billey
The 5th of July	Lanford Wilson	Peter Thompson	Thom Roberts	Christopher Beesley	Tom Hamilton
Aleola	Gaetan Charlebois	Howard Dallin	Dick Leerhoff	Christopher Beesley	Michael Vennerstrom
The D. B. Cooper Project	John Orlock (b,m,l)	Louis Salerni	Thom Roberts	Christopher Beesley	Phillip Billey
A Life in the Theatre	David Mamet	Louis Salerni	Thom Roberts	Christopher Beesley	Phillip Billey

CSC Repertory

PRODUCTION	DRAMATIST	DIRECTOR	SETS	COSTUMES	LIGHTING
A Midsummer Night's Dream	William Shakespeare	Christopher Martin	Clarke Dunham	Maryanne Powell-Parker	Clarke Dunham
Rosmersholm	Henrik Ibsen Christopher Martin (t)	Christopher Martin	Clarke Dunham	Maryanne Powell-Parker	Clarke Dunham
Serjeant Musgrave's Dance	John Arden	John Shannon	Phillip Graneto	Joseph Bigelow	Phillip Graneto
The Maids	Jean Genet Bernard Frechtman (t)	Christopher Martin	Christopher Martin	Christopher Martin	Christopher Martin
The Running of the Deer	Karen Sunde	Christopher Martin	Christopher Martin	Rachel Kurland	Christopher Martin
The Madwoman of Chaillot	Jean Giraudoux Maurice Valency (a)	Christopher Martin	Christopher Martin	Rachel Kurland	Christopher Martin
Richard II	William Shakespeare	Christopher Martin	Clay Coyle	Terry A. Bennett	Christopher Martin
Henry IV, Part I	William Shakespeare	Christopher Martin	Clay Coyle	Terry A. Bennett	Christopher Martin
Henry IV, Part II	William Shakespeare	Christopher Martin	Clay Coyle	Terry A. Bennett	Christopher Martin
Wild Oats	John O'Keeffe	Christopher Martin Christopher Barns	Clay Coyle	Rachel Kurland	Christopher Martin
The Marquis of Keith	Frank Wedekind Christopher Martin (t)	Christopher Martin	Clay Coyle	Terry A. Bennett	Christopher Martin

Dallas Theater Center

PRODUCTION	DRAMATIST	DIRECTOR	SETS	COSTUMES	LIGHTING
The Imaginary Invalid	Moliere Alec Stockwell (t)	Alert Millaire	Yoichi Aoki	John Henson	Allen Hibbard
Vanities	Jack Heifner	Ryland Merkey	M.G. Johnston	Rayanne Miller	John Henson
The Night of the Iguana	Tennessee Williams	Judith Davis	Cheryl Denson	Cheryl Denson	Randy Moore
Three Men on a Horse	John Cecil Holm George Abbott	Ken Latimer	George Pettit	Rayanne Miller	Sally Netzel
Firekeeper	Mark Medoff	Paul Baker	Virgil Beavers	Virgil Beavers	Randy Moore
The Royal Family	George S. Kaufman Edna Ferber	Ryland Merkey	Peter Wolf	John Henson	Allen Hibbard
Door Play	Sallie Laurie	Mary Sue Jones	Denise Drennan	Rodger M. Wilson	Paul R. Bassett
The Cigarette Man	David Blomquist	Ken Latimer	Linda Blase	Denise Drennan	Bill Wheat
The Night Visit	Roy Hudson	John Logan	Suzanne Chiles	M.G. Johnston	Mark Momberger
Lady Bug, Lady Bug, Fly Away Home	Mary Rohde	Chris Hendrie	James Eddy	Deborah Allen	Roy Hudson
Inside the White Room	Paul R. Bassett	Dick Trousdell	Yoichi Aoki	Shannon Wilson	Michael Scudday
InterWeave		Robyn Flatt John R. Stevens	Rodger M. Wilson	Rodger M. Wilson	Suzanne Chiles
Equepoise	Phil Penningroth (b,l) Howard Quilling (m)	Celeste Varricchio	Suzanne Chiles	Mark Momberger	Michael Scudday

PRODUCTION	DRAMATIST	DIRECTOR	SETS	COSTUMES	LIGHTING
Snow White	company developed (b) Alex Winslow (m,l) Mark Momberger (m,l)	Robyn Flatt John R. Stevens	Steven John Yuhasz	Sandra Howell	James Eddy
The Tiger in Traction	Gifford Wingate (b,l) Robert R. Smith, Jr. (m)	Bryant J. Reynolds	Michael Krueger	Diana Gonzalez	Wayne Lambert
The Adventures of Tom Sawyer	Sam L. Rosen (b,m,l)	Hanna Cusick Wayne Lambert	Sandra Howell	Deborah Linn	Kathy Moberly
A Midsummer Night's Dream	William Shakespeare	Randolph Tallman	Yoichi Aoki	Susan Sleeper	Randy Moore
Lu Ann Hampton Laverty Oberlander, The Last Meeting of the Knights of the White Magnolia and The Oldest Living Graduate	Preston Jones	Paul Baker	Mary Sue Jones	Kathleen Latimer	Linda Blase
The Devil's General	Carl Zuckmayer Ingrid Komar (t)	Harry Buckwitz	John Henson	John Henson	Allen Hibbard
As You Like It	William Shakespeare	Ken Latimer	Virgil Beavers	Kathleen Latimer	Linda Blase
Blood Money	M.G. Johnston (b,l) Jim Abbott (m)	John Logan	Peter Lynch	Cheryl Denson	Robert Duffy
To Kill a Mockingbird	Harper Lee	Robyn Flatt	Virgil Beavers	Virgil Beavers	Randy Bonifay Wayne Lambert
Attic Aphrodite	Sally Netzel	Robert A. Smith	Michael Krueger	Sandra Howell	Randy Bonifay Wayne Lambert
A Disposable Woman	Frederic Hunter	Bryant J. Reynolds	Linda Blase	Charles Hukill	Wayne Lambert
Remember	Preston Jones	Judith Davis	John Holloway	M.G. Johnston	James Eddy
Years in the Making	Glenn Allen Smith	Ken Latimer	Robert Duffy	Sandra Howell	Michael Scudday
Jack and the Beanstalk	Sally Netzel	Beverly Renquist	Charles Hukill	Sally Askins	Katherine Moberly
Heidi	Lucille Miller (a)	Peter Lynch	Jeffrey Kinghorn	Catherine Otey	Rich Waldron
The New Adventures of Raggedy Ann and Andy	company developed	Robyn Flatt John R. Stevens	John Holloway	Paul Robinson	Carol Miles
The Squires and the Golden Kings	Paul Munger (b,l) Maria Figueroa (m)	Hanna Cusick Michael Mullen	Sally Askins	Cliff Smith	Rich Waldron

Dell'Arte

PRODUCTION	DRAMATIST	DIRECTOR	SETS	COSTUMES	LIGHTING
Infancy	Thornton Wilder	Jael Weisman	Alain Schons	Chris Chapman	Alain Schons
The Greenfields	George Courteline Jael Weisman (a)	Jael Weisman	Alain Schons	Michelle Rosenaur	Alain Schons
The Gloaming, Oh My Darling	Megan Terry	Jael Weisman	Alain Schons	Michelle Rosenaur	Alain Schons
Birds of a Feather	Stan Laurel	Jael Weisman	Alain Schons	Michelle Rosenaur	Alain Schons
Bittersweet Blues	Joan Schirle	Jael Weisman	Alain Schons	Joan Schirle	Alain Schons
Save Me a Place at Forest Lawn	Lorees Yerby	Jael Weisman	Alain Schons	Chris Chapman	Alain Schons
The Amazing Zoroasters	Jael Weisman	Jael Weisman	Alain Schons	Chris Chapman	Alain Schons
Cash Valley	Jon' Paul Cook	Jon' Paul Cook	Jon' Paul Cook	Chris Chapman	
Underwater Worlds	Jon' Paul Cook	Jon' Paul Cook	Jon' Paul Cook	Chris Chapman	
Tintypes: A Revue	company developed	Jon' Paul Cook			

PRODUCTION	DRAMATIST	DIRECTOR	SETS	COSTUMES	LIGHTING
Downtown Cabaret Theatre					
All productions are musical revues conceived and written by Claude McNeal, blending popular tunes with new songs by composer Stanley Wietrzychowski and lyricist McNeal.					
The Sixties		Claude McNeal	Ted Drab (1) H. Edward Spires (2)	Mary Miko	Peter Byrne
Lead Ins …		Claude McNeal	Ted Drab	Mary Miko	Peter Byrne
The Fabulous Fifties		Claude McNeal	Ted Drab (1) H. Edward Spires (2)	Mary Miko (1) Joyce Baran (2)	Peter Byrne
The Late Great Billion Dollar Movie		Claude McNeal	H. Edward Spires	Mary Miko	Peter Byrne
The Thirties		Claude McNeal	H. Edward Spires	Mary Miko	Peter Byrne
The Forties—Songs of Love and War		Claude McNeal	H. Edward Spires	Mary Miko	Peter Byrne
The Rise and Fall of the Andrews Sisters		Claude McNeal	Ted Drab	Joyce Baran	Peter Byrne
The Seventies—The Way We Are		Claude McNeal	Ted Drab	Joyce Baran	Peter Byrne
Comedie Cabaret		Claude McNeal	Ted Drab	Joyce Baran	Peter Byrne
East West Players					
Points of Departure	Paul Stephen Lim	Mako	Rae Creevey	Victoria de Kay	Rae Creevey
Bunnyhop	Jeffrey Paul Chan	Mako	Rae Creevey	Victoria de Kay	Rae Creevey
Once upon in America	various	Mako	Rae Creevey	Victoria de Kay	Rae Creevey
O-Men: An American Kabuki	Karen Yamashita	Mako	Rae Creevey	Victoria de Kay	Rae Creevey
Voices in the Shadows	Edward Sakamoto	Mako Alberto Isaac	Rae Creevey		Rae Creevey
The Frogs	Aristophanes Richmond Lattimore (t)	Betty Muramoto Dom Magwili	Rae Creevey	Helen Young	Rae Creevey
Princess Charley	Jim Ploss (b,l) Norman Cohen (b) Roger Perry (m)	Norman Cohen	Woodward Romine	Victoria de Kay	Rae Creevey
The Avocado Kid	Philip Gotanda	Mako Betty Muramoto	Rae Creevey		Rae Creevey
Pacific Overtures	John Weidman (b) Stephen Sondheim (m,l)	Mako	Rae Creevey	Shigeru Yaji	Rae Creevey
El Teatro Campesino					
El Fin del Mundo III	company developed	Daniel Valdez	Roberto Morales	Diane Rodriguez	
Las Cuatros Apariciones de la Virgen de Guadalupe	company developed	Socorro Valdez Cruz	Roberto Morales	Diane Rodriguez	Roberto Morales
La Pastorela	company developed	Luis Valdez	Roberto Morales	Diane Rodriguez	Roberto Morales
La Gran Carpa de los Rasquachis VI	company developed	Socorro Valdez Cruz		Diane Rodriguez	
El Fin del Mundo IV	Luis Valdez	Socorro Valdez Cruz	Roberto Morales	Diane Rodriguez	Yolanda Parra

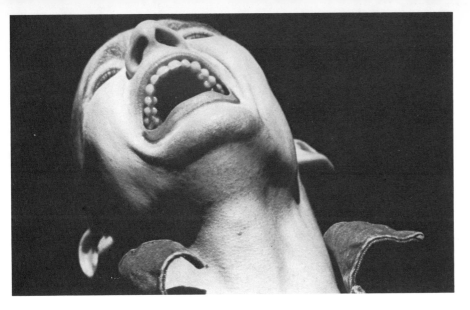

Arena Stage. Andrew Davis in *Comedians.*
Photo: George de Vincent.

PRODUCTION	DRAMATIST	DIRECTOR	SETS	COSTUMES	LIGHTING
The Empty Space Theatre					
Ashes	David Rudkin	Jack Bender	Karen Gjelsteen	Ron Erickson	Scott Hawthorn
The Misanthrope	Moliere Tony Harrison (t)	M. Burke Walker	Karen Gjelsteen	Susan Min	David Butler
Gossip	George F. Walker	Jeffrey Steitzer	Karen Gjelsteen	Ron Erickson	Jeff Robbins
Landscape of the Body	John Guare	Richard A. Edwards	Karen Gjelsteen	Sally Richardson	Phil Schermer
Angel City	Sam Shepard	Glenn Mazen	Karen Gjelsteen	Marian Cottrell	James Royce
Oregon Gothic	Kurt Beattie	M. Burke Walker	Karen Gjelsteen	Marian Cottrell	Cynthia J. Hawkins
The Pulse of New York	John Kauffman company	John Kauffman	David Butler	Julie James	
Illuminatus!, Parts I, II and III	Ken Campbell (a) Chris Langham (a)	Jeffrey Steitzer	Karen Gjelsteen	Sally Richardson	Cynthia J. Hawkins
A Prayer for My Daughter	Thomas Babe	M. Burke Walker	Karen Gjelsteen	Sally Richardson	Phil Schermer
Psychosis Unclassified	Ken Campbell (a)	Kathy Lichter			Donna Grout
Bonjour, là, Bonjour	Michel Tremblay John Van Burek (t) Bill Glassco (t)	Tom Towler	Karen Gjelsteen	Julie James	Phil Schermer
Zastrozzi	George F. Walker	Jeffrey Steitzer	Karen Gjelsteen	Julie James	David Butler
Hooters	Ted Tally	M. Burke Walker	Karen Gjelsteen	Laura Crow	Paul Bryan
Skungpoomery	Ken Campbell	Shaun Austin-Olsen			Paul Bryan
The Voice of the Mountain	John Kauffman company	John Kauffman	Karen Gjelsteen		
Ensemble Studio Theatre					
Reflections of a China Doll	Susan Merson	Barbara Tarbuck	Christopher Nowak	Laura Crowe	Marc B. Weiss
Eulogy for a Small-Time Thief	Miguel Piñero	Jack Gelber	Christopher Nowak	Carol Oditz	Cheryl Thacker
Mama Sang the Blues	Katherine Cortez	Terese Hayden	Fred Kolough	Sigrid Insull	Fred Kolough
Innocent Pleasures	Arthur Giron	Harold Stone	Nancy Tobias	Sigrid Insull	Geoffrey Dunbar
Marathon '78	various	various	Gregory Buch		Geoffrey Dunbar
End of the War	Vincent Canby	David Margulies	David Mitchell	Madeline Cohen	Richard Nelson
Bicycle Boys	Peter Maloney	Ellen Sandler	Christopher Nowak	Madeline Cohen Marcia L. Whitney	Geoffrey Dunbar
Playing Dolls	Susan Nanus	Ellen Sandler	Christopher Nowak	Madeline Cohen Marcia L. Whitney	Geoffrey Dunbar
Buddy Pals	Neil Cuthbert	Jerry Zaks	Christopher Nowak	Madeline Cohen Marcia L. Whitney	Geoffrey Dunbar
The Man with the Flower in His Mouth	Luigi Pirandello	David Shookhoff	Brian Martin	Madeline Cohen	Cal Vornberger
The Old Tune	Robert Pinget Samuel Beckett (a)	David Shookhoff	Brian Martin	Madeline Cohen	Cal Vornberger
Welfare	Marcia Haufrecht	Anthony McKay	Brian Martin	Madeline Cohen	Cal Vornberger
Marathon '79	various	various	Brian Martin Bil Mikulewicz	Charles Schoonmaker Lindsay Davis	Marie-Louise Moretto Sara Schrager
Equinox Theatre					
In the Boom Boom Room	David Rabe	Bruce Bowen	Bill Weatherford	Linda Colvin	Bill Weatherford
Fortune and Men's Eyes	John Herbert	Bruce Bowen	Bruce Bowen	Bruce Bowen	Bruce Bowen
Charlie's Ear	Gary Chason	Gary Chason	Gary Chason	Linda Colvin	Gary Chason

continued

New Jersey Shakespeare
Festival. Geddeth Smith and
Catherine Byers in *Who's Afraid
of Virginia Woolf?*
Photo: Paul Barry.

PRODUCTION	DRAMATIST	DIRECTOR	SETS	COSTUMES	LIGHTING
The Basic Training of Pavlo Hummel	David Rabe	Bruce Bowen	David Sargent	Linda Colvin	David Sargent
Hair	Gerome Ragni (b,l) James Rado (b,l) Galt MacDermot (m)	Doug Holmes	Doug Holmes	Doug Holmes	Doug Holmes
American Buffalo	David Mamet	Bruce Bowen	David Sargent	David Sargent	David Sargent
Denizens	Gary Chason	Gary Chason	Gary Chason	Linda Colvin	Gary Chason
Sexual Perversity in Chicago and The Duck Variations	David Mamet	Bruce Bowen	Bruce Bowen	Bruce Bowen	Chris Eagan
Nightlife	Jeff & Mary Galligan	Jeff & Mary Galligan	David Sargent	Mary Galligan	David Sargent
Sticks and Bones	David Rabe	Bruce Bowen	David Sargent	Bruce Bowen	David Sargent
Solitaire/Double Solitaire	Robert Anderson	Bruce Bowen	Bruce Bowen	Bruce Bowen	Bruce Bowen
The Rocky Horror Show	Richard O'Brien (b,m,l)	Scott Holtzman	David Sargent Tom Dornbusch	Tom Dornbusch	Bruce Bowen
The Idiots Karamazov	Christopher Durang Albert Innaurato	Bruce Bowen	Christ Matthews	Valerie Trevino	Dep Byrkett
The Water Engine and Mr. Happiness	David Mamet	Bruce Bowen	Chris Matthews	Valerie Trevino	Chris Matthews
The Saga of Jean Lafitte	James Clouser	James Clouser	Carsten Petersen	Valerie Trevino	Jeff Salzberg
For Colored Girls who have Considered Suicide/ When The Rainbow is Enuf	Ntozake Shange	Bruce Bowen	Bruce Bowen	L. Keith McGowen	David Sargent
Lenny	Julian Barry	Judy Thomas	Judy Thomas	David Mitchell	Bruce Bowen

The First All Children's Theatre Company

Who's Next?	David Damstra (b,l) Matthew Kaplowitz (m,l)	Meridee Stein Vicky Blumenthal	Kathy Kunkel Denise Weber	Patricia Kraft Cheryl Blalock	Anthony Stein
A Whinny and a Whistle	Cheryl Scammon (b) Mary Steenburgen (b) Matthew Kaplowitz (m,l)	Meridee Stein Olga Holub	Ken Holamon	Ken Holamon	Brian Jayne
Clever Jack and the Magic Beanstalk	Ian Elliot (b) Meridee Stein (b) Judie Thomas (m,l) John Forster (m,l)	Meridee Stein (1) Vicky Blumenthal (1,2)	Kathy Kunkel Denise Weber	Cheryl Blalock	Lee DeWeerdt (2)
The Pushcart Fables	Betsy Shevey (b) Judith Thomashefsky (m,l)	Olga Holub	Alison Ford	Kate McHugh	Paul A. Kowal (1)
Three Tales at a Time	various (b,m,l)	Meridee Stein (1) Vicky Blumenthal (1,2)	Kathy Kunkel Denise Weber	Cheryl Blalock	Anthony Stein
Alice Through the Looking Glass	Susan Dias (b,l) Meridee Stein (b) Philip Namanworth (m)	Meridee Stein Cheryl Scammon	Kathy Kunkel Denise Weber	Patricia Kraft Cheryl Blalock	Lee DeWeerdt
The Incredible Feeling Show	Elizabeth Swados (b,m,l)	Meridee Stein	Mavis Smith	Meridee Stein	Lee DeWeerdt

Florida Studio Theatre

Second Shepherds' Play	Jon Spelman (a)	Jon Spelman	Anne Randolph	Anne Randolph	Anne Randolph
The Promise	Aleksei Arbuzov Ariadne Nicolaeff (t)	Anne Randolph	Tara Buckley	Tara Buckley	Tara Buckley

PRODUCTION	DRAMATIST	DIRECTOR	SETS	COSTUMES	LIGHTING
Extremities	company developed	Jon Spelman	Bob Marietta	Anne Randolph	Anne Randolph
Lunatics and Lovers	Jon Spelman (a)	Joh Spelman	Hariet Haygood	Carol F. Duval	Carol F. Duval
Echoes	N. Richard Nash	Sergei Ponomorov	Sergei Ponomorov	Carol F. Duval	Carol F. Duval
Cabin Fever	Joan Schenkar	Gregory Johnson	Carol F. Duval	Carol F. Duval	Carol F. Duval
When I'm 64 …	Carol F. Duval	Jon Spelman	Carol F. Duval	Carol F. Duval	Carol F. Duval
The Dumb Waiter	Harold Pinter	Robert Miller	Carol F. Duval	Carol F. Duval	Carol F. Duval

Folger Theatre Group

PRODUCTION	DRAMATIST	DIRECTOR	SETS	COSTUMES	LIGHTING
Teeth 'n' Smiles	David Hare (b) Nick & Tony Bicat (m,l)	Jonathan Alper Louis W. Scheeder	David Chapman	Robert Wojewodski	Hugh Lester
Two Gentlemen of Verona	William Shakespeare	Louis W. Scheeder	David Lloyd Gropman	Dona Granata	Elizabeth Toth
Hamlet	William Shakespeare	Jonathan Alper	David Lloyd Gropman	Robert Wojewodski	Paul Gallo
Mackerel	Israel Horovitz	Louis W. Scheeder	David Chapman G. Kerry Comerford	Sheila McLamb	Elizabeth Toth
Richard III	William Shakespeare	Louis W. Scheeder Mikel Lambert	Hugh Lester	Susan Tsu	Hugh Lester
Whose Life Is It Anyway?	Brian Clark	Louis W. Scheeder	Hugh Lester	Jess Goldstein	Hugh Lester
The Merry Wives of Windsor	William Shakespeare	Mikel Lambert	Hugh Lester	Jess Goldstein	Paul Gallo
Richard II	William Shakespeare	Louis W. Scheeder	Scott Johnson	Nancy Thun	Hugh Lester
Benefit of a Doubt	Edward Clinton	Barnet Kellman	Philipp Jung	Tom McAlister	Randy Becker
As You Like It	William Shakespeare	Louis W. Scheeder	Hugh Lester	Hilary A. Sherred	Hugh Lester

Frank Silvera Writers' Workshop

PRODUCTION	DRAMATIST	DIRECTOR	SETS	COSTUMES	LIGHTING
Partake of De Goat Meat	Bhunnie Bernier Molette	Mansoor Nejee-ullah	Joe Gandy Erik Stephenson	Edna Watson	Ernest Baxter
Run'ers	Ivey McCray	Bette Howard	Joe Gandy Erik Stephenson	Edna Watson	Sandra L. Ross
The Incarnations of Reverend Goode Blacque Dresse	Garland Lee Thompson	Dean Irby	Joe Gandy Erik Stephenson	Edna Watson	Sandra L. Ross
the bloodrite	owa	Fred Tyson	Paul Davis	Mary Sevillian	Shahid Abd'allah
Inacent Black and the Five Brothers	A. Marcus Hemphill	Billie Allen	John Harris, Jr.	Leslie V. Day	
The Royal Road	Sam Shirakawa	Stephannie Howard	John Harris, Jr.	Beverly Parks	Gwen Gilliam
No Left Turn	Buriel Clay II	Richard Gant	John Harris, Jr.	Beverly Parks	Sandy Ross
Investments	Ruth Ce. Jones	Helaine Head	John Harris, Jr.	Beverly Parks	Sandy Ross
The Murder of Cyrene Vignette	Malik	Bette Howard	John Harris, Jr.	Karen Perry	Sandy Ross

Free Street Theater

PRODUCTION	DRAMATIST	DIRECTOR	SETS	COSTUMES	LIGHTING
Rockin' the Cradle	Marc Blitzstein (b,m,l) company (a)	Patrick Henry	Patrick Henry	Patrick Henry	Steven B. Parker
Rootabaga Stories	Carey B. Ericson (a)	Carey B. Ericson	Laura Sunkel	Laura Sunkel	
Bloody and Bawdy Villains	Patrick Henry Lewis Marder	Michael Goodwin	Henry Miller	Jessica Hahn	Phil Eickhoff
Piñata	Patrick Henry company	Patrick Henry	Patrick Henry	Margaret Hilligoss	

continued

PRODUCTION	DRAMATIST	DIRECTOR	SETS	COSTUMES	LIGHTING
New Burlington	Ken Jenkins (a)	Patrick Henry	Patrick Henry	Patrick Henry	Steven B. Parker
When the Drum Speaks	Patrick Henry Foday Musa Suso (m)	Patrick Henry	James Boley	Wilbert Bradley	
Dummy I	Patrick Henry company	Patrick Henry	James Boley	Patrick Henry	James Boley
Storystage		Patrick Henry	Henry Miller	Patrick Henry	
Fanfare for the Future	Patrick Henry company	Patrick Henry	James Boley	Patrick Henry	
The Family of Man	Patrick Henry (b) Tom Taylor (m,l) Joe Godfrey (m,l)	Patrick Henry	James Boley	Patrick Henry	
To Life!	Patrick Henry (b) Noreen Walker (m,l) James Barry (m,l) Maxine Feldman (m,l)	Patrick Henry	Patrick Henry	Patrick Henry	
The Third Duckling	Patrick Henry company	Patrick Henry		Patrick Henry	
Streetdance	Patrick Henry (a) Wilbert Bradley (a)	Patrick Henry			
Musicmini	John Vitale (a)	John Vitale			
Change Places with Me	Patrick Henry company	Patrick Henry	Patrick Henry	Patrick Henry	Steven B. Parker
The Grimm Gang	Patrick Henry (a) company (a)	Francis X. Kuhn	Francis X. Kuhn	Patricia Patton	
Nobody	Patrick Henry (b,l) Matthew Rose (m)	Patrick Henry	Patrick Henry	Patrick Henry	Steven B. Parker
Tall Tales	Patrick Henry company	Patrick Henry		Patrick Henry	
Workaday	Patrick Henry company	Patrick Henry		Patrick Henry	Steven B. Parker
Citisong	Patrick Henry company	Patrick Henry	John Aldridge	Patrick Henry	

George Street Playhouse

PRODUCTION	DRAMATIST	DIRECTOR	SETS	COSTUMES	LIGHTING
The Rainmaker	N. Richard Nash	Eric Loeb	Allen Cornell	Sandra Wallace	Daniel Stratman
Steambath	Bruce Jay Friedman	Peter Bennett	Cliff Simon	Sandra Wallace	Daniel Stratman
Man and Superman	George Bernard Shaw	Bob Hall	Allen Cornell	Rachel Kurland	Daniel Stratman
Paris Was Yesterday	Paul Shyre (a)	Paul Shyre	Daniel Proett	Barbara de Portago	Daniel Stratman
Serenading Louie	Lanford Wilson	Terry Schreiber	Hal Tiné	Sandra Wallace	Daniel Stratman Daniel Proett
Arsenic and Old Lace	Joseph Kesselring	Peter Bennett	Daniel Proett	Sandra Wallace	Daniel Stratman
The School for Wives	Moliere Donald Frame (a)	Eric Loeb	Bob Phillips	Jeanetta Oleksa	Daniel Stratman
Long Day's Journey into Night	Eugene O'Neill	Paul Austin	Daniel Proett	Sandra Wallace	Daniel Stratman
Pettycoat Lane	Judd Woldin (b,m,l)	Eric Krebs	Daniel Proett	Vickie McLaughlin	Daniel Stratman
Sizwe Bansi Is Dead	Athol Fugard John Kani Winston Ntshona	Harold Scott	Christopher Nowak	Sandra Wallace	Daniel Stratman
Statements After an Arrest Under the Immorality Act	Athol Fugard	Harold Scott	Christopher Nowak	Sandra Wallace	Daniel Stratman

Intiman Theatre Company.
The Three Sisters.
Photo: Chris Bennion.

PRODUCTION	DRAMATIST	DIRECTOR	SETS	COSTUMES	LIGHTING
Twelfth Night	William Shakespeare	Bob Hall	Bob Hall	Sandra Wallace Bob Hall	Daniel Stratman
Dance for Me, Simeon	Joseph Maher	Isaac Schambelan	Daniel Proett	Sandra Wallace	Daniel Stratman Tom Radcliff
Germinal Stage Denver					
The Great God Brown	Eugene O'Neill	Edward R. Baierlein	Edward R. Baierlein	Donna Evans	Ken Burt
The Friends	Arnold Wesker	Edward R. Baierlein	Paul Caouette		Ken Burt
Seascape	Edward Albee	Ken Burt	Ken Burt	Sallie Diamond	Ken Burt
The Eagle with Two Heads	Jean Cocteau Carl Wildman (t)	Edward R. Baierlein	Edward R. Baierlein	Theresa Holden	Edward R. Baierlein
The Show-Off	George Kelly	Edward R. Baierlein	Paul Caouette	Sarah Campbell	Paul Caouette
The Glass Menagerie	Tennessee Williams	Edward R. Baierlein	Edward R. Baierlein	Sallie Diamond	Edward R. Baierlein
Macbett	Eugene Ionesco Charles Marowitz (t)	Edward R. Baierlein	Edward R. Baierlein	Sarah Campbell	Edward R. Baierlein
No Man's Land	Harold Pinter	Edward R. Baierlein	Edward R. Baierlein	Sallie Diamond	Edward R. Baierlein
In the Boom Boom Room	David Rabe	Edward R. Baierlein	Edward R. Baierlein	Sarah Campbell	Edward R. Baierlein
The Well of the Saints	John Millington Synge	Jim Dexter	Edward R. Baierlein	Deborah Bays	Ken Burt
archy & mehitabel	Mel Brooks (b) Joe Darion (b,l) George Kleinsinger (m)	Edward R. Baierlein	Edward R. Baierlein		Edward R. Baierlein
GeVa Theatre					
The Front Page	Ben Hecht Charles MacArthur	Gideon Y. Schein	Seth Price	Danica Eskind	Seth Price
Death of a Salesman	Arthur Miller	Gideon Y. Schein	Danica Eskind	Danica Eskind	Seth Price
Scapin	Moliere	Nancy Rhodes	Karen Schulz	Danica Eskind	Seth Price
The Caretaker	Harold Pinter	Gideon Y. Schein	Richard M. Isackes	Linda Joan Vigdor	Seth Price
A Raisin in the Sun	Lorraine Hansberry	Woodie King, Jr.	C. Richard Mills	Edna Watson	Seth Price
Vanities	Jack Heifner	Gideon Y. Schein	Seth Price	Linda Joan Vigdor	Seth Price
A Streetcar Named Desire	Tennessee Williams	Gideon Y. Schein	Philipp Jung	Linda Joan Vigdor	Lee Delorme
Diamond Studs	Jim Wann (b,m,l) Bland Simpson (m,l)	Gideon Y. Schein	Philipp Jung	Philipp Jung	Lee Delorme
Sizwe Bansi Is Dead	Athol Fugard John Kani Winston Ntshona	Thomas Bullard	Patricia Woodbridge	Judy Dearing	Lee Delorme
13 Rue de l'Amour	Georges Feydeau Mawby Green (a) Ed Feilbert (a)	Basil Langton	Christopher Nowak	Linda Joan Vigdor	Lee Delorme
A Moon for the Misbegotten	Eugene O'Neill	Richard Russell Ramos	Barry Robison	Barry Robison	Lee Delorme
The Hostage	Brendan Behan	Gideon Y. Schein	Michael Grube	Linda Joan Vigdor	Lee Delorme
Goodman Theatre					
Saint Joan	George Bernard Shaw	John Clark	David Jenkins	James Edmund Brady	F. Mitchell Dana
The Seagull	Anton Chekhov Jean-Claude van Itallie (t)	Gregory Mosher	Joseph Nieminski	Virgil C. Johnson	Pat Collins
Working	Stephen Schwartz (b) various (m,l)	Stephen Schwartz	David Mitchell	Marjorie Slaiman	Pat Collins

continued

Theatre X. Tom Gustin and
Deborah Clifton in *A Fierce
Longing*. Photo: Sylvia Plachy.

PRODUCTION	DRAMATIST	DIRECTOR	SETS	COSTUMES	LIGHTING
Much Ado About Nothing	William Shakespeare	William Woodman	Herbert Senn Helen Pond	Virgil C. Johnson	Stephen Ross
The Night of the Iguana	Tennessee Williams	George Keathley	Joseph Nieminski	Marsha Kowal	Robert Christen
Otherwise Engaged	Simon Gray	William Woodman	Joseph Nieminski	James Edmund Brady	F. Mitchell Dana
The Prague Spring	Lee Kalcheim (b,l) Joseph G. Raposo (m)	Dennis Zacek	Maher Ahmad	Marsha Kowal	Robert Christen
Battering Ram	David Freeman	Gregory Mosher	Maher Ahmad	Christa Scholtz	Robert Shook
Annulla Allen: The Autobiography of a Survivor	Emily Mann Annulla Allen	Emily Mann	Barry Robison	Barry Robison	Philip Eickhoff
Hail Scrawdyke! or *Little Malcolm and His Struggle Against the Eunuchs*	David Halliwell	Michael Maggio	Michael Merritt	Julie Jackson	Robert Christen
Native Son	Paul Green (a)	Gregory Mosher	Joseph Nieminski	Christa Scholtz	Pat Collins
A Christmas Carol	Barbara Field (a)	Tony Mockus	Joseph Nieminski	James Edmund Brady	Robert Christen
Two-Part Inventions	Richard Howard	Michael Feingold	David Lloyd Gropman	Christa Scholtz	Jennifer Tipton
Bosoms and Neglect	John Guare	Mel Shapiro	John Wulp Lynn Pecktal	Willa Kim	Jennifer Tipton
Holiday	Philip Barry	Tony Tanner	Joseph Nieminski	Clifford Capone	Robert Christen
Lone Canoe or *The Explorer*	David Mamet Alaric (Rokko) Jans (m,l)	Gregory Mosher	John Lee Beatty	Christa Scholtz	Pat Collins
Emigres	Slawomir Mrozek Maciej Wrona (t) Teresa Wrona (t) Robert Holman (t)	Gregory Mosher	Maher Ahmad	Jane Morgan Henry	Robert Christen
Curse of the Starving Class	Sam Shepard	Robert Falls	Michael Merritt	Marsha Kowal	Robert Christen
Scenes and Revelations	Elan Garonzik	Betsy Carpenter	James Guenther	Jessica Hahn	Robert Christen
The Island	Athol Fugard John Kani Winston Ntshona	Gregory Mosher	Phil Eickhoff	Phil Eickhoff	Phil Eickhoff

The Great-American Children's Theatre Company

Welcome to the Zoo	Bill Solly (b,m,l) Donald Ward (b)	Montgomery Davis		Rose-Marie Seck	
The Doctor in Spite of Himself	Moliere Montgomery Davis (a)	Montgomery Davis	Al Tucci	Rose-Marie Seck	Joe Tilford
Santa and the Magic Weather People	Bill Solly (b,m,l) Donald Ward (b)	Montgomery Davis		Rose-Marie Seck	
It Must Be Magic— A Magical Musical	Bill Solly (b,m,l) Donald Ward (b)	Montgomery Davis	Al Tucci	Rose-Marie Seck	Carl Schmidt

Great Lakes Shakespeare Festival

Polly	John Gay	Vincent Dowling	John Ezell	Kurt Wilhelm	Richard Coumbs
Two Gentlemen of Verona	William Shakespeare	Daniel Sullivan	John Ezell	Kurt Wilhelm	Richard Coumbs
What Every Woman Knows	J.M. Barrie	Roger Hendricks Simon	John Ezell	Kurt Wilhelm	Richard Coumbs
The Nine Days Wonder of Will Kemp	Chris Harris John David	John David	Louise Belson	Louise Belson	David Percival

PRODUCTION	DRAMATIST	DIRECTOR	SETS	COSTUMES	LIGHTING
Wild Oats	John O'Keeffe	Daniel Sullivan	John Ezell	Kurt Wilhelm	Richard Coumbs
King John	William Shakespeare	Vincent Dowling	John Ezell	Kurt Wilhelm	Richard Coumbs
Twelfth Night	William Shakespeare	Daniel Sullivan	John Ezell	Liz Covey	Carol Sealy
Juno and the Paycock	Sean O'Casey	Vincent Dowling	John Ezell	Liz Covey	Carol Sealy
Clarence	Booth Tarkington	L. Eberle Thomas	John Ezell	Liz Covey	Carol Sealy
Do Me a Favorite	Vincent Dowling (a)	Vincent Dowling	Vincent Dowling	Vincent Dowling	Carol Sealy
Blithe Spirit	Noel Coward	John Reich	John Ezell	Liz Covey	Carol Sealy
Othello	William Shakespeare	Vincent Dowling	John Ezell	Liz Covey	Carol Sealy

The Guthrie Theater

PRODUCTION	DRAMATIST	DIRECTOR	SETS	COSTUMES	LIGHTING
She Stoops to Conquer	Oliver Goldsmith	Michael Langham	Ralph Funicello	Lewis Brown	Duane Schuler
A Moon for the Misbegotten	Eugene O'Neill	Nick Havinga	John Conklin	Lewis Brown	Duane Schuler
La Ronde	Arthur Schnitzler Ken Ruta (t)	Ken Ruta	Ralph Funicello	Lewis Brown	Duane Schuler
Catsplay	Istvan Orkeny Clara Gyorgyey (t)	Stephen Kanee	John Ferguson	Lewis Brown	Duane Schuler
The White Devil	John Webster	Michael Blakemore	Pat Robertson	Annena Stubbs	Duane Schuler
Design for Living	Noel Coward	Michael Langham	Annena Stubbs	Annena Stubbs	Duane Schuler
A Christmas Carol	Barbara Field (a)	Jon Cranney	Jack Barkla	Jack Edwards	Duane Schuler
Pantagleize	Michel de Ghelderode Barbara Field (a)	Stephen Kanee	Jack Barkla	Jack Edwards	Duane Schuler
The Pretenders	Henrik Ibsen Michael Feingold (t)	Alvin Epstein	David Lloyd Gropman	Dunya Ramicova	Duane Schuler
Teibele and Her Demon	Isaac Bashevis Singer Eve Friedman	Stephen Kanee	Desmond Heeley	Desmond Heeley	Duane Schuler
Boy Meets Girl	Sam & Bella Spewack	Peter Mark Schifter	Zack Brown	Zack Brown	Ronald M. Bundt
Bonjour, là, Bonjour	Michel Tremblay John Van Burek (t) Bill Glassco (t)	Steven Robman	Marjorie Kellogg	Jennifer von Mayrhauser	Ronald M. Bundt
Hamlet	William Shakespeare	Stephen Kanee	Jack Barkla	Carrie F. Robbins	Ronald M. Bundt
Marriage	Nikolai Gogol Barbara Field (t)	Anatoly Efros	Valery Leventhal	Valery Leventhal	Ronald M. Bundt
The Beggar's Opera	John Gay	Alvin Epstein	Tony Straiges	Jennifer von Mayrhauser	Duane Schuler

Hartford Stage Company

PRODUCTION	DRAMATIST	DIRECTOR	SETS	COSTUMES	LIGHTING
All the Way Home	Tad Mosel	Paul Weidner	John Conklin	Claire Ferraris	Peter Hunt
Past Tense	Jack Zeman	Paul Weidner	Hugh Landwehr	Claire Ferraris	Judy Rasmuson
A Flea in Her Ear	Georges Feydeau John Mortimer (t)	Norman Ayrton	Marjorie Kellogg	David Murin	Arden Fingerhut
Rain	John Colton Clemence Randolph	Paul Weidner	John Conklin	James Guenther	Steve Woodring
Holiday	Philip Barry	Edward Berkeley	Hugh Landwehr	Claire Ferraris	Beverly Emmons
They'd Come to See Charlie	James Borrelli	Irene Lewis	Hugh Landwehr	Linda Fisher	Arden Fingerhut
Eve	Larry Fineberg	Irene Lewis	Hugh Landwehr	Linda Fisher	Judy Rasmuson
Mackerel	Israel Horovitz	Mark Lamos		Robert Wojewodski	Spencer Mosse
Catchpenny Twist	Stewart Parker	Irene Lewis	Hugh Landwehr	Linda Fisher	Arden Fingerhut

continued

PRODUCTION	DRAMATIST	DIRECTOR	SETS	COSTUMES	LIGHTING
Boy Meets Girl	Sam & Bella Spewack	Bill Ludel	John Falabella	Lowell Detweiler	Arden Fingerhut
Wedding Band	Alice Childress	Paul Weidner	Lowell Detweiler	Claire Ferraris	Steve Woodring
Galileo	Bertolt Brecht	Paul Weidner	John Conklin	John Conklin	Peter Hunt
	Charles Laughton (a)				
The Matchmaker	Thornton Wilder	Daniel Sullivan	John Fallabella	Elizabeth Covey	Judy Rasmuson
Bonjour, là, Bonjour	Michel Tremblay	Paul Weidner	David Lloyd Gropman	Linda Fisher	Paul Gallo
Passing By	Martin Sherman	Ron Lagomarsino	Linda Conaway		Bill Ballou
The Black, the Blue and the Gray	Irene Lewis (a) Edward Emmanuel (a)	Paul Weidner	James Guenther	James Guenther	James Guenther
Home of the Brave	Irene Lewis (a) Tana Hicken (a) David O. Peterson (a)	Ron Lagomarsino	Jay Ferger	Claire Ferraris	

Hartman Theatre Company

PRODUCTION	DRAMATIST	DIRECTOR	SETS	COSTUMES	LIGHTING
The Mousetrap	Agatha Christie	Del Tenney	Roger Meeker	June Stearns	Rick Butler
The Miracle Worker	William Gibson	Tony Giordano	J.D. Ferrara	Gerda Proctor	Roger Meeker
The Middle Ages	A.R. Gurney, Jr.	Melvin Bernhardt	John Lee Beatty	June Stearns	Dennis Parichy
Othello	William Shakespeare	Robert W. Smith	Zack Brown	Annette Beck	Roger Meeker
The Animal Kingdom	Philip Barry	John Going	Hugh Landwehr	Linda Fisher	Jeffrey Schissler
Jerome Kern at the Hartman		William E. Hunt	Ruth Wells	Ruth Wells	Roger Meeker
The Servant of Two Masters	Carlo Goldoni	Larry Arrick	Toni Spadafora	Toni Spadafora	Wendy Chapin
Yerma	Federico Garcia Lorca	Robert S. Eichler	Kathleen Egan	Karen D. Miller	Peggy Peterson
Ribbons	David F. Eliet	Wendy Chapin	Leslie Taylor	Toni Spadafora	Peggy Peterson
The Maids	Jean Genet	Larry Arrick	Stephen Studnicka	Toni Spadafora	Peggy Peterson
La Ronde	Arthur Schnitzler	David F. Eliet	Toni Spadafora	Toni Spadafora	Rheba Rutkowski
The Three Sisters	Anton Chekhov	Wendy Chapin	Rick Butler	Toni Spadafora	Steve Botkin
Mrile	Elizabeth J. Moyer (a)	William Sandwick	Elizabeth J. Moyer	Elizabeth J. Moyer	Steven Hirschberg
Jumping Mouse	Larry Arrick (b) Barbara Damashek (m,l)	Barbara Damashek	Elizabeth J. Moyer	Elizabeth J. Moyer	Peggy Peterson
Two for the Seesaw	William Gibson	Tony Giordano	J.D. Ferrara	Rachel Kurland	John Gisondi
The Diary of Anne Frank	Frances Goodrich Albert Hackett	Gene Frankel	John Falabella	Rachel Kurland	Jeff Davis
Absurd Person Singular	Alan Ayckbourn	Del Tenney	John Wright Stevens	Sarah Nash Gates	Daniel J. Farley
The Auction Tomorrow	Jerry L. Crawford	Del Tenney	James Tilton	Sarah Nash Gates	Rick Butler
The Little Foxes	Lillian Hellman	Tony Giordano	Hugh Landwehr	David Murin	John McLain
The Fantasticks	Tom Jones (b,l) Harvey Schmidt (m)	Joey Patton	J.D. Ferrara	Kathleen Egan	Roger Meeker

Hawaii Public Theater

PRODUCTION	DRAMATIST	DIRECTOR	SETS	COSTUMES	LIGHTING
The Fools!	Alexander Ostrovsky Eugene Lion (a)	Eugene Lion	Bob Maeda Scott Roberts	Katherine James	Richard Kon
Pictures in the Hallway	Sean O'Casey Paul Shyre (a)	Patricia Herman	Patti Coons	Katherine James	Steven Barnes

PRODUCTION	DRAMATIST	DIRECTOR	SETS	COSTUMES	LIGHTING
Marat/Sade	Peter Weiss Adrian Mitchell (a)	Eugene Lion	Richard Mason	Katherine James	Richard Kon
The Maids	Jean Genet Ellen Boggs (a) Jo Lechay (a) Eugene Lion (a)	Eugene Lion	Patti Coons	Katherine James	Richard Kon

Hippodrome Theatre Workshop

Soap	Allan Albert	Marshall New	Marshall New		Kerry McKenney
Equus	Peter Shaffer	Bruce Cornwell	Stuart Sacks	Kerry McKenney Bruce Cornwell	Stuart Sacks
The Tempest	William Shakespeare Gregory Hausch (a)	Gregory Hausch	Gregory Hausch Stuart Sacks	Mary Hausch	Stuart Sacks
Steambath	Bruce Jay Friedman	Bruce Cornwell		Mary Hausch Kerry McKenney	Stuart Sacks
Streamers	David Rabe	Kerry McKenney	Kerry McKenney		Mary Hausch
Otherwise Engaged	Simon Gray	Mary Hausch			Stuart Sacks
Gemini	Albert Innaurato	Bruce Cornwell		Tricia Gerent	Kerry McKenney
The Last Meeting of the Knights of the White Magnolia	Preston Jones	Kerry McKenney		Tricia Gerent	Pam Mara
The Passion of Dracula	Bob Hall (a) David Richmond (a)	Mary Hausch	Dennis Molden	Tricia Gerent	Gregory Hausch
Cabrona	Cynthia Buchanan	Bruce Cornwell	Carlos Asse	Tricia Gerent	Pam Mara
A Christmas Carol	Gregory Hausch (a)	Gregory Hausch		Tricia Gerent	Gregory Hausch
The Island	Athol Fugard John Kani Winston Ntshona	Margaret Bachus		Tricia Gerent	Howard Ramagli, Jr.
Statements After an Arrest Under the Immorality Act	Athol Fugard John Kani Winston Ntshona	Margaret Bachus		Tricia Gerent	Howard Ramagli, Jr.
Lord Alfred's Lover	Eric Bentley	Kerry McKenney	Kerry McKenney	Tricia Gerent	Mary Hausch
Table Manners, Living Together and *Round and Round the Garden*	Alan Ayckbourn	Gregory Hausch		Mary Hausch	
They Shoot Horses, Don't They?	Marshall New (a)	Marshall New	Marshall New	Tricia Gerent	Mary Joye

Honolulu Theatre for Youth

Scapino	Frank Dunlop (a) Jim Dale (a)	Wallace Chappell	Joseph Dodd	Linda Letta	Colin Fraser, Jr.
Tales of the Pacific	Wallace Chappell	Wallace Chappell	Charles Walsh	Linda Letta	Charles Walsh
The Legend of Sleepy Hollow	Fred Gaines (a)	Bain Boehlke	Joseph Dodd	Grace Ligi	Colin Fraser, Jr.
Momotaro and Other Japanese Folktales	Wallace Chappell	Wallace Chappell	Joseph Dodd	Joseph Dodd	Colin Fraser, Jr.
Sleeping Beauty	Brian Way (a)	Wallace Chappell	Joseph Dodd	Grace Ligi	Colin Fraser, Jr.
Storytellers	Brian Way (a)	Jo Diotalevi	Joseph Dodd	Grace Ligi	Colin Fraser, Jr.
Folktales of the Philippines	Wallace Chappell	Wallace Chappell	Joseph Dodd	Joseph Dodd	Colin Fraser, Jr.

continued

Oregon Shakespeare Festival.
JoAnn Johnson Patton, Rex
Rabold and Mary Turner in
MacBeth. Photo: Hank Kranzler.

PRODUCTION	DRAMATIST	DIRECTOR	SETS	COSTUMES	LIGHTING
The Phantom Tollbooth	Susan Nanus (a)	Jo Diotalevi	Joseph Dodd	Grace Ligi	Colin Fraser, Jr.
Horseopera	Kermit Love	Kermit Love	Joseph Dodd	Grace Ligi	Colin Fraser, Jr.
The Time Machine	Thomas E. Fuller (a)	Carole C. Huggins	Joseph Dodd	Joseph Dodd	Colin Fraser, Jr.
Jack and the Beanstalk	Robert Rafferty (a)	David Visser	Joseph Dodd	Grace Ligi	Gerald Kawaoka

Horse Cave Theatre

Tartuffe	Moliere Richard Wilbur (t)	Warren Hammack	John Bos	Susan Cox	John Bos
The Odd Couple	Neil Simon	Warren Hammack	John Bos	Susan Cox	John Bos
Bus Stop	William Inge	Warren Hammack	John Bos	Susan Cox	John Bos
The Importance of Being Earnest	Oscar Wilde	Warren Hammack	John Bos	Linda Roots	James Eddy
Wait Until Dark	Frederick Knott	Warren Hammack	John Bos	Linda Roots	James Eddy
They Knew What They Wanted	Sidney Howard	Warren Hammack	John Bos	Linda Roots	James Eddy
Of Mice and Men	John Steinbeck	Michael Hankins	James Taylor	Linda Roots	James Taylor

The Hudson Guild Theatre

Treats	Christopher Hampton	Michael Montel	Peter Wexler	Donald Brooks	Peter Wexler
The Dodge Boys	George Sibbald	Craig Anderson	Douglas Schmidt	Sandra Nye	John Gleason
Molly	Simon Gray	Stephen Hollis	Philipp Jung	Patricia Adshead	John H. Paull
Da	Hugh Leonard	Melvin Bernhardt	Marjorie Kellogg	Jennifer von Mayrhauser	Arden Fingerhut
My Mother Was a Fortune-Teller	Phyllis Newman (b) Arthur Laurents (b) various (m,l)	Arthur Laurents	Philipp Jung	Bill Kellard	Toni Goldin
On Golden Pond	Ernest Thompson	Craig Anderson	Steven Rubin	Steven Rubin	Craig Miller
Winning Isn't Everything	Lee Kalcheim	George Abbott	Fred Voelpel	Fred Voelpel	Annie Wrightson
A Lovely Sunday for Creve Coeur	Tennessee Williams	Keith Hack	John Conklin	Linda Fisher	Craig Miller
Ride a Cock Horse	David Mercer	Geoffrey Sherman	Philipp Jung	Julie Weiss	Toni Golden
Devour the Snow	Abe Polsky	Terry Schreiber	Steven Rubin	David Murin	Dennis Parichy

Impossible Ragtime Theatre

Play Strindberg	Friedrich Dürrenmatt James Kirkup (t)	Ted Story	Larry Fulton	Margo La Zaro	Gary C. Porto
Women I Have Known	M. Tulis Sessions	Michael T. Gregoric	Larry Fulton		Jo Mayer
Spider's Web	Agatha Christie	Penelope Hirsch	Trueman Kelley	Margo La Zaro	Gary Seltzer
Clash by Night	Clifford Odets	Stephen Zuckerman	Edelmiro Olavarria	Margo La Zaro	Gary Seltzer
Rusty and Rico and Lena and Louie	Leonard Melfi	John Shearin	Tom Warren	Margo La Zaro	Curt Ostermann
The Member of the Wedding	Carson McCullers	Jude Schanzer	Edelmiro Olavarria	Margo La Zaro	Anne L. Peters
Where's the Beer, Fritz?	Daniel M. Schreier (m,l) Michael Roth (m,l)	George Ferencz		Sally J. Lesser Kathleen Smith	John Gisondi
The Problem	A.R. Gurney, Jr.	Penelope Hirsch		Margo La Zaro	Curt Ostermann
Dreams of Flight	Brian Richard Mori	Lawrence Harbison		Margo La Zaro	Curt Ostermann
Birdbath	Leonard Melfi	Alison Mackenzie			Charles S. Bullock

PRODUCTION	DRAMATIST	DIRECTOR	SETS	COSTUMES	LIGHTING
Master Class and *Old Blues*	Jonathan Levy	Ted Weiant	Judy Juracek		Charles S. Bullock
The Ride Across Lake Constance	Peter Handke Michael Roloff (t)	Matthew Maguire			Lisa Grossman
The Bedroom	M.H. Appleman	Anita Khanzadian	Marcie Begleiter	Margo La Zaro	Charles S. Bullock
Peril at End House	Arnold Ridley (a)	Jude Schanzer	Edelmiro Olavarria	James Corry	James Chaleff
The Unicorn in Captivity	Mel Arrighi	Ted Story	James Leonard Joy	Margo La Zaro	Curt Ostermann
Windfall Apples	Roma Greth	Anita Khanzadian	Terry Bennett	Sheryl R. Barenboin	Terry Bennett
Brand	Henrik Ibsen Michael Meyer (t)	Stephen Zuckerman	Stephen Zuckerman	Margo La Zaro	Gary Seltzer
Suicide in B Flat	Sam Shepard	Ted Story	Larry Fulton	Amanda J. Klein	Curt Ostermann
Three Men on a Horse	John Cecil Holm George Abbott	John Pynchon Holms	Tom Warren	Steven L. Birnbaum	Charles S. Bullock
Trifles	Susan Glaspell	Darlene Kaplan	Loy Arcenas	Dolores Gamba	Charles S. Bullock
The Color of Heat	Saul Zachary	Michael Bloom	Loy Arcenas	Dolores Gamba	Charles S. Bullock
Illegal Use of Hands	Michael Zettler	Penelope Hirsch	Larry Fulton	Margo La Zaro	Gary Seltzer
Victoria's Closet	Laurence Carr	Stephen Zuckerman	Raymond C. Recht	Christina Weppner	Richard Winkler
The Glass of Water	Eugene Scribe Dewitt Bodeen (t)	Jon Fraser	Roger Paradiso	Dolores Gamba	Charles S. Bullock
Take Death to Lunch	Thomas L. Faitos (b,l,m) Amielle Zemach (b,l)	Amielle Zemach	Loy Arcenas	Loy Arcenas	Lisa Grossman

The Independent Eye

PRODUCTION	DRAMATIST	DIRECTOR	SETS	COSTUMES	LIGHTING
Black Dog	Conrad Bishop	Conrad Bishop			
I Wanna Go Home	Conrad Bishop	Conrad Bishop			
Dessie	Conrad & Linda Bishop	Conrad Bishop			
Sunshine Blues	Conrad Bishop	Conrad Bishop			
Macbeth	William Shakespeare	Conrad Bishop			Conrad Bishop
Who's There?	Conrad Bishop	Conrad Bishop	Patrick Reed	Ellen Dennis	Kerry Ann Nelson

Indiana Repertory Theatre

PRODUCTION	DRAMATIST	DIRECTOR	SETS	COSTUMES	LIGHTING
The Philadelphia Story	Philip Barry	Edward Stern	John Doepp	Elizabeth Covey	John Doepp Gregg Marriner
The Birthday Party	Harold Pinter	Thomas Gruenewald	David Potts	Arnold S. Levine	Jeff Davis
The Country Girl	Clifford Odets	William Guild	Van Phillips	Arnold S. Levine	Lee Watson
Vanities	Jack Heifner	Charles Kerr	Ursula Belden	Arnold S. Levine	Paul Gallo
The Seagull	Anton Chekhov Jean-Claude van Itallie (t)	Edward Stern	Marjorie Kellogg	Susan Tsu	Arden Fingerhut
How the Other Half Loves	Alan Ayckbourn	Edward Stern	Eric Head	Arnold S. Levine	Geoffrey T. Cunningham
13 Rue de l'Amour	Georges Feydeau Mawby Green (a) Ed Feilbert (a)	Edward Stern	Eric Head	Elizabeth Covey	Jeff Davis
Sizwe Bansi Is Dead	Athol Fugard John Kani Winston Ntshona	Woodie King, Jr.	Ursula Belden	Jess Goldstein	Paul Gallo
A Delicate Balance	Edward Albee	Daniel Sullivan	David Potts	Jess Goldstein	Jeff Davis
The Importance of Being Earnest	Oscar Wilde	John Going	William Schroder	William Schroder	Paul Gallo
Ten Little Indians	Agatha Christie	Thomas Gruenewald	James Leonard Joy	Kenneth M. Yount	Jeff Davis
The Goodbye People	Herb Gardner	Edward Stern	John Doepp	Michael J. Cesario	Geoffrey T. Cunningham

PRODUCTION	DRAMATIST	DIRECTOR	SETS	COSTUMES	LIGHTING
INTAR (International Arts Relations)					
Lolita en el Jardín	Maria Irene Fornes Richard Weinstock (m)	Maria Irene Fornes	Beth Kuhn	Beth Kuhn Margradel Hicks	Joe Ray
Hablemos a Calzon Quitado	Guillermo Gentile Jean Alain (m)	Max Ferrá	John Jackson	Max Ferrá	Gus Pollek
Carmencita	Manuel Martin, Jr. (b,l) Georges Bizet (m) Tania Leon (m)	Manuel Martin, Jr.	Sally Locke	Manuel Yesckas	Jenny Ball
La Gran Decisiòn	Miguel Mihura Max Ferrá (a) Osvaldo Pradere	Max Ferrá	Ken Holamon	Kay Panthaky	John Hickey
Eyes on the Harem Latinos	Maria Irene Fornes Lynne Alvarez (b) Manuel Martin, Jr. (b,l) Omar Torres (b,m,l) Eddie Ruperto (m) Frank Rivera (l)	Maria Irene Fornes Emmanuel Yesckas	Larry Brodsky Lisa Frazza	Frank Krenz Kay Panthaky	Edward M. Greenberg Ronald A. Castleman
Interart Theatre					
Becca	Wendy Kesselman	Barbara Rosoff (1) Gitta Honegger (2)	Lynn Conaway	Jane Stein	Pat Stern
Where Memories Are Magic and Dreams Invented	Susan Nanus	Susan Einhorn	Ursula Belden	Jean Steinlein	Pat Stern
Hey, Rube	Janet McReynolds	Vicki Rue	Barbara Ling	Manzi Adzima	Barbara Ling
Sister/Sister	company developed	Clare Coss Sanda Segal Roberta Sklar		Florence Rutherford (1) Sharon Romanski (2)	Annie Wrightson
Magic and Lions	company developed (m,l)	Glenda Dickerson	Tyrone Mitchell	Ellen Lee	Vantile E. Whitfield (1) Katie Fallon (2)
The Price of Genius	Betty Neustat	Susan Lehman	Christina Weppner	Mary Alice Orito	Pat Stern
Daughters	company developed	Clare Coss Sandra Segal Roberta Sklar		Sharon Romanski	Annie Wrightson
Olympic Park	Myrna Lamb	Georgia Fleenor	Pat Woodbridge	Mary Alice Orito	Paul Sullivan
Sunday	Michel Deutsch Francoise Kourilsky (t) Lynne Greenblatt (t)	Francoise Kourilsky	Beth Kuhn	Sydney Brooks	Beverly Emmons
Antony and Cleopatra	William Shakespeare	Estelle Parsons	Christina Weppner	Mary Alice Orito	Pat Stern
Intiman Theatre					
Henry IV	Luigi Pirandello John Reich (a)	Margaret Booker	Robert A. Dahlstrom	Ron Erickson	James Verdery
The Way of the World	William Congreve	Anthony Cornish	Robert A. Dahlstrom	Nanrose Buchman	Rob Jackson
The Three Sisters	Anton Chekhov Randall Jarrell (t)	Margaret Booker	Carey Wong	Ron Erickson	Richard Devin
The Country Girl	Clifford Odets	Stephen Rosenfield	Pete Davis	Nanrose Buchman	James Verdery

PRODUCTION	DRAMATIST	DIRECTOR	SETS	COSTUMES	LIGHTING
The Dance of Death	August Strindberg Walter Johnson (t)	Margaret Booker	Karen Gjelsteen	Nanrose Buchman	James Verdery
The Loves of Cass McGuire	Brian Friel	Margaret Booker	Michael Miller	Lewis Rampino	James Sale
Tartuffe	Moliere Richard Wilbur (t)	Stephen Rosenfield	Karen Gjelsteen	Rondi Hillstrom Davis	James Sale
Medea	Euripides Robinson Jeffers (a)	Margaret Booker	Robert A. Dahlstrom	Robert A. Dahlstrom	Richard Devin
Heartbreak House	George Bernard Shaw	Anthony Cornish	Robert A. Dahlstrom	Lewis Rampino	James Sale
Design for Living	Noel Coward	Margaret Booker	Karen Gjelsteen	Michael Olich	James Sale

The Invisible Theatre

PRODUCTION	DRAMATIST	DIRECTOR	SETS	COSTUMES	LIGHTING
Hippolytus	Euripides Spence Porter (a)	Susan Claassen	Jack Schwanke	Peter Conway	Russell Stagg
Exhibition	Janet Neipris	Susan Claassen	Liz Schloss		Denny Ballweber
Bridge at the Bel Harbour	Janet Neipris	David Gardiner	Liz Schloss		Denny Ballweber
Magical Tales	company developed				
Careless	Bob Campbell Scott Carter	Page Burkholder	Scott Burkholder		Denny Ballweber
Much Ado About Nothing	William Shakespeare	William Prosser	Reagan Cook	Peter Conway	Denny Ballweber
Macbeth	William Shakespeare	William Prosser	Reagan Cook	Jan Olson	Denny Ballweber
Oats	Scott Carter (b) Glenn Young (b) George Hawke (m,l)	Susan Claassen	Jack Schwanke Dianne Roberts	Deborah McQuire	Gail Reich
Flying Horses	Janet Neipris	Nick Liveratos	Dianne Roberts		Gail Reich
Clown Dance	Joan Van Dyke	Page Burkholder	Susan Claassen		
Arthur	Jim Peck	Susan Claassen	Susan Claassen		Denise Leahy
As You Like It	William Shakespeare	Page Burkholder	Jack Schwanke	Gina Gagliano	James S. Hill
Antony and Cleopatra	William Shakespeare	William Prosser	Jack Schwanke	Jeff Hendry	James S. Hill

The Iron Clad Agreement

PRODUCTION	DRAMATIST	DIRECTOR	SETS	COSTUMES	LIGHTING
The Prologue Play	company developed	Julia R. Swoyer company		Patrice Alexander	
Edison	Elan Garonzik (b) company (b) Robert C. Nesius (m,l)	Julia R. Swoyer company		Patrice Alexander	
Westinghouse	Julia R. Swoyer (b) K. Wilson Hutton (b) Linda Austern (m,l) James R. Krut (m,l)	Julia R. Swoyer company		Patrice Alexander	
Ford	Scott T. Cummings (b) company (b) Robert C. Nesius (m,l)	Julia R. Swoyer company		Patrice Alexander	
Barnum	Chris Blaetz Linda Austern (m)	Julia R. Swoyer company		Patrice Alexander	
Burbank	Charles V. Peters (b) Robert C. Nesius (m,l)	Julia R. Swoyer company		Patrice Alexander	
Eastman	Lawrence Myers Linda Austern (m)	Julia R. Swoyer company		Patrice Alexander	

continued

Actors Theatre of Louisville. Joe Morton in *Andronicus, A Space Fantasy.* Photo: David S. Talbott.

PRODUCTION	DRAMATIST	DIRECTOR	SETS	COSTUMES	LIGHTING
Out of This Furnace, Part I	Julia R. Swoyer (b) Robert C. Nesius (m,l)	Julia R. Swoyer	Jeffrey C. Quinn	Mary Jo Jackson	Jeffrey C. Quinn
Gov't. Owned Apples	I. Schtok David Visser (a) Charles V. Peters (a) Robert C. Nesius (m,l)	Julia R. Swoyer company	Margo Lovelace	Margo Lovelace	
Dynamite	company developed	Julia R. Swoyer company		Patrice Alexander	
Andrew Carnegie	Steve Mackes company	Julia R. Swoyer company		Patrice Alexander	
The Amazing American Idea Factory	company developed	Julia R. Swoyer company		Patrice Alexander	
Out of This Furnace, Part II	Andy Wolk (b) Robert C. Nesius (m,l)	Harold Scott	K. Wilson Hutton	Spangler Cummings	Gregory W. Clepper

Jean Cocteau Repertory

PRODUCTION	DRAMATIST	DIRECTOR	SETS	COSTUMES	LIGHTING
The Caretaker	Harold Pinter	Eve Adamson	James S. Payne	James S. Payne	James S. Payne
A New Way to Pay Old Debts	Philip Massinger	Christopher Martin	Christopher Martin	Christopher Martin	Christopher Martin
Hamlet	William Shakespeare	Eve Adamson	Douglas McKeown	Tina Watson	James S. Payne
The Cocktail Party	T.S. Eliot	Eve Adamson	James S. Payne	James S. Payne	James S. Payne
Love's Comedy	Henrik Ibsen	Martin L.H. Reymert	Douglas McKeown	Charles Elliott James S. Payne	James S. Payne
No Exit	Jean-Paul Sartre	Eve Adamson	James S. Payne	James S. Payne	James S. Payne
Volpone	Ben Jonson	Eve Adamson	James S. Payne	Charles Elliott	James S. Payne
'Tis Pity She's a Whore	John Ford	Eve Adamson	Douglas McKeown	Charles Elliott	James S. Payne
A Mad World, My Masters	Thomas Middleton	Eve Adamson	Charles Elliott	Charles Elliott	James S. Payne
The Scarecrow	Percy MacKaye	Eve Adamson	James Nichols	Charles Elliott	James S. Payne
Exit the King	Eugene Ionesco	Karen Sunde	Tom Keever	Charles Elliott	James S. Payne
The Cid	Pierre Corneille	Martin L.H. Reymert	Martin L.H. Reymert	Charles Elliott	James S. Payne
As You Like It	William Shakespeare	Eve Adamson	Douglas McKeown	Charles Elliott	James S. Payne
In the Bar of a Tokyo Hotel	Tennessee Williams	Eve Adamson	James S. Payne	Charles Elliott Karla Barker	James S. Payne Andy MacCracken
The Changeling	Thomas Middleton William Rowley	Eve Adamson	George Brunner	Charles Elliott	James S. Payne Andy MacCracken

Julian Theatre

PRODUCTION	DRAMATIST	DIRECTOR	SETS	COSTUMES	LIGHTING
The Plough and the Stars	Sean O'Casey	Edward Weingold	Donald Cate	Regina Cate	Donald Cate
In the Jungle of Cities	Bertolt Brecht	Richard Reineccius	Richard Reineccius	Molly Schultz	Jocelyn Bronwyn Reynolds
Medal of Honor Rag	Tom Cole	Brenda Berlin Reineccius	David Overturf Pat Monk	Lyn Meany	Jocelyn Bronwyn Reynolds
Goethe: Ein Fragment	Michael McClure	Richard Reineccius	Donald Cate	Regina Cate	Donald Cate
New Roots: An Off-Off Broadway Anthology	Kay Carney	Kay Carney			
The Display of Melissa Harding	Hans Steinkellner	Edward Weingold	George Gilsbach	Nancy Graham	George Gilsbach
A Midsummer Night's Dream	William Shakespeare	Richard Reineccius	Wendy Westphal Beaupre	Marianella Macchiarini	George Gilsbach

PRODUCTION	DRAMATIST	DIRECTOR	SETS	COSTUMES	LIGHTING
Philadelphia, Here I Come!	Brian Friel	Richard Rekow	Dale Altvater	Lyn Meany	George Gilsbach
The Hypochondriacs	Botho Strauss Robert Goss (t)	Richard Reineccius	James Wright	Richard Battle	George Gilsbach
Merry Christmas, Earthling!	company developed	Alice Truscott David Overturf	David Overturf	Lyn Meany	George Gilsbach
No Man's Land	Harold Pinter	Brenda Berlin Reineccius	John Yarrington	Regina Cate Irene Rosen	George Gilsbach
Hothouse	Megan Terry	Marian Hampton	Bill Eddelman	Irene Rosen	George Gilsbach
The Biko Inquest	Norman Fenton Jon Blair	Richard Reineccius John Doyle	Michael Koppy	Michael Koppy	Jocelyn Bronwyn Reynolds
Sam	Sally Netzel	Robert Struckman	Robert Struckman	George Talbott	Jocelyn Bronwyn Reynolds

Karamu House

The Imaginary Invalid	Moliere Lucia Colombi (a)	Lucia Colombi	Lucia Colombi	Mark Passarell	Lucia Colombi
Livin' Fat	Judi Ann Mason	Margaret Ford-Taylor	Peter B. Harrison	Carol Blanchard	Dennis Moyes
Don't Bother Me, I Can't Cope	Micki Grant (m,l)	Mike Malone	Mark Fitzgibbons	Mark Passarell	Julee Hottois
Eden	Steve Carter	Edmund T. Jenkins	Mark Fitzgibbons	Claudette Colon	James Merrill Stone
The Island	Athol Fugard John Kani Winston Ntshona	Lucia Colombi	Mark Fitzgibbons	Mark Passarell	Peter B. Harrison
The Life and Times of Stag-o-Lee	Mike Malone (b) H. Q. Thompson (m,l)	Mike Malone	Mark Fitzgibbons	Mark Passarell	James Merrill Stone
The Brownsville Raid	Charles Fuller	Glenda Dickerson	Mark Fitzgibbons	Clarrissa Pettijohn	Peter B. Harrison
Langston	Mike Malone (a) H. Q. Thompson (m)	Mike Malone	John Conley	Clarrissa Pettijohn	Dennis Moyes
A Rose by Any Other Name	Morna Murphy	Vanita Vactor	Mark Fitzgibbons	Clarrissa Pettijohn	Peter B. Harrison
Singin' and Shoutin'	Mike Malone (b) H. Q. Thompson (m,l)	Mike Malone	Frank Kiman	Clarrissa Pettijohn	James Merrill Stone
The Mighty Gents	Richard Wesley	J. Herbert Kerr	Frank Kiman	Clarrissa Pettijohn	James Merrill Stone
Happy Birthday, Daddy	Judi Ann Mason	Margaret Ford-Taylor	Frank Kiman	Clarrissa Pettijohn	Michael Stein
Medea	Lucia Colombi (a)	Lucia Colombi	Frank Kiman	Clarrissa Pettijohn	James Merrill Stone
Walk Together, Children	Vinie Burrows (a,m,l)	Vinie Burrows			

Lion Theatre Company

K: Impressions of Kafka's The Trial	company developed	Garland Wright	John Arnone Garland Wright	David James	Garland Wright
The Death and Life of Jesse James	Len Jenkin	Gene Nye	Henry Millman	Robert Wojewodski	Frances Aronson
Mary Rose	J.M. Barrie	Larry Carpenter	Holmes Easley	Sidney Brooks	Frances Aronson
Music Hall Sidelights: A Theatrical Scrapbook	Jack Heifner (b,l) John McKinney (m)	Garland Wright	John Arnone	David James	Frances Aronson
The Three Sisters	Anton Chekhov Sharon Carnicke (t)	Gene Nye	Miguel Romero	Kenneth M. Yount	John Gisondi
Duel: A Romantic Opera	Randal Wilson (b,m,l)	Larry Carpenter	Raymond C. Recht	Kenneth M. Yount	John Gisondi

PRODUCTION	DRAMATIST	DIRECTOR	SETS	COSTUMES	LIGHTING
Living Stage					
All performances are improvisations created by the company.		Robert Alexander			
Long Wharf Theatre					
Hobson's Choice	Harold Brighouse	Arvin Brown	David Jenkins	Bill Walker	Jamie Gallagher
The Lunch Girls	Leigh Curran	Arvin Brown	David Jenkins	Bill Walker	Ronald Wallace
The Recruiting Officer	George Farquhar	Davey Marlin-Jones	John Conklin	John Conklin	Jamie Gallagher
Spokesong	Stewart Parker Jimmy Kennedy (m)	Kenneth Frankel	Marjorie Kellogg	Bill Walker	Ronald Wallace
Bound East for Cardiff In the Zone The Long Voyage Home The Moon of the Caribees	Eugene O'Neill	Edward Payson Call	John Jensen	Linda Fisher	Ronald Wallace
The Philadelphia Story	Philip Barry	Arvin Brown	John Jensen	Bill Walker	Ronald Wallace
Two Brothers	Conrad Bromberg	Arvin Brown	Steven Rubin	Mary Strieff	Ronald Wallace
Macbeth	William Shakespeare	Edward Gilbert	Mark Louis Negin	Mark Louis Negin	Ronald Wallace
Journey's End	R.C. Sherriff	Kenneth Frankel	John Conklin	Carol Oditz	Ronald Wallace
I Sent a Letter to My Love	Bernice Rubens	Arvin Brown	David Jenkins	Bill Walker	Ronald Wallace
Summerfolk	Maxim Gorky Edward Gilbert (t) John Tillinger (t)	Edward Gilbert	Marjorie Kellogg	Bill Walker	Ronald Wallace
Biography	S.N. Behrman	William Francisco	Steven Rubin	Bill Walker	Ronald Wallace
Rosmersholm	Henrik Ibsen Allen Fletcher (t)	Allen Fletcher	John Jensen	Mary Strieff	Jamie Gallagher
Hillbilly Women	Elizabeth Stearns (b) Clint Ballard, Jr. (m,l)	Peter Bennett	John Jensen	Linda Fisher	Ronald Wallace
Privates on Parade	Peter Nichols Denis King (m)	Arvin Brown	David Jenkins	Bill Walker	Ronald Wallace
Looking Glass Theatre					
Inside Doctor Specks	Rob Anderson (b,l) Gerald Shapiro (m)	Bernice Bronson	Karen Carroll	Patricia Hagan	
Hatshepsut, Daughter of the Nile	Amy Leonard	David Novak	Michael Schiener	Patti Booth	
The Great Baloney Hoax	Jack Carroll company	David Novak		April Peters	
White Wampum: Legend of the Iroquois	Richard Cameron Donna Gamage	Richard Cameron	Ed Budz Joe Kopels	Deborah Bertoldi	
Loretto-Hilton Repertory Theatre					
Macbeth	William Shakespeare	David Frank	Grady Larkins	John Carver Sullivan	Glenn Dunn
Lu Ann Hampton Laverty Oberlander	Preston Jones	Davey Marlin-Jones	Heidi Landesman	Carr Garnett	Peter E. Sargent
The Devil's Disciple	George Bernard Shaw	David Frank	John Kavelin	John Carver Sullivan	Glenn Dunn
The Runner Stumbles	Milan Stitt	Norman Gevanthor	Heidi Landesman John Conant	Catherine Reich	Peter E. Sargent

PRODUCTION	DRAMATIST	DIRECTOR	SETS	COSTUMES	LIGHTING
Canterbury Tales	Martin Starkie (b) Nevill Coghill (b,l) Richard Hall (m) John Hawkins (m)	Carl Schurr	John Kavelin	John Carver Sullivan	Peter E. Sargent
Ashes	David Rudkin	Geoffrey Sherman	John Conant	Catherine Reich	David Hitzert
The Iceman Cometh	Eugene O'Neill	Davey Marlin-Jones	Karen Connolly	Carr Garnett	Peter E. Sargent
Father's Day	Oliver Hailey	Leonard Peters	John Carver Sullivan	John Carver Sullivan	Glenn Dunn
A Penny for a Song	John Whiting	David Frank	Paul Wonsek	John Carver Sullivan	Glenn Dunn
The Three Sisters	Anton Chekhov	Geoffrey Sherman	Paul Wonsek	Catherine Reich	Stephen Ross
Frankenstein	Victor Gialanella (a)	Robert Darnell	Grady Larkins Jack Conant	John Carver Sullivan	Peter E. Sargent
Curse of the Starving Class	Sam Shepard	Sheldon Larry	Paul Steinberg	Catherine Reich	Charles Williams
Old Times	Harold Pinter	Davey Marlin-Jones	Tim Jozwick	Sue Larkins	William Frein
By Grand Central Station I Sat Down and Wept	Geoffrey Sherman Adrienne Burgess	Geoffrey Sherman	Paul Wonsek	Catherine Reich	Paul Wonsek

Los Angeles Actors' Theatre

PRODUCTION	DRAMATIST	DIRECTOR	SETS	COSTUMES	LIGHTING
Waiting for Godot	Samuel Beckett	Gwen Arner	Robert W. Zentis	Liza Stewart	Robert W. Zentis
A Midnight Moon at the Greasy Spoon	Miguel Piñero	William Bushnell, Jr.	Jim Tompkins	Eugene Caron	Paulie Jenkins
The Sistuhs	Saundra Sharp	Dick Anthony Williams	Barbara Ling	Dara Marks	Paulie Jenkins
My Sister, My Sister	Ray Aranha	David Downing	Tina Ling Donald Moffat	Dara Marks	Paulie Jenkins
Voices	Susan Griffin	Rae Allen	Dawn Chiang		Barbara Ling
Playwrights' Workshop Festival of One-Acts	various	various			Paulie Jenkins
Perfume	James Kennedy	William Bushnell, Jr. James Kennedy	Paul Appel	Tiny Ossman	Barbara Ling
Krapp's Last Tape	Samuel Beckett	Patrick Tovatt		Ellen Feldman	Linda Tracy
On the Harmfulness of Tobacco	Anton Chekhov Dianne Lewis Hall (a) Philip Baker Hall (a) Patrick Tovatt (a)	Patrick Tovatt		Ellen Feldman	Linda Tracy
Skaters	Ted Pezzulo	Jeremiah Morris	Wendy Milner-Calloway	Tiny Ossman	Paulie Jenkins
The Venus of Menschen Falls	Richard Jordan	Richard Jordan	David L. Snyder	Roberta Weiner	Paulie Jenkins
A Vision of Anne Sexton	Henry Hoffman (a)	Henry Hoffman	Linda Tracy	Susan Tanner	Linda Tracy
Mississippi Jade, Augie Abrams and Saint George	J. Paul Porter	Joe Nunnally	Patrick McFadden		Scott Pinkney
The Guntower	Miguel Piñero	Jonathan Estrin	Tom Weikert	Lisa Wells	Michael Bergfeld
Medal of Honor Rag	Tom Cole	Michael Bloom	Tom Weikert	Lisa Wells	Michael Bergfeld
Every Good Boy Does Fine	Joseph Hindy	David Wheeler	Robert W. Zentis	Barbara Marko	Robert W. Zentis
The Schoolteacher and The Orgy	Enrique Bueneventura	Michael Robelo	Eric Warren	Sara Martin	Paulie Jenkins
Statements After an Arrest Under the Immorality Act	Athol Fugard	Ann Bowen	Keith Hein		Paulie Jenkins
The Bacchae	Euripides	Yurek Bogajewicz	Janos Szablya	Susan Tanner	Paulie Jenkins
Cronica de un Secuestro	Mario Diament	Jaime Jaimes	Jaime Jaimes		Heather Carson

continued

Colonnades Theatre Lab. Berit
Laggerwall and Bill E. Noone in
Moliere in Spite of Himself.
Photo: Diane Gorodnitzki.

PRODUCTION	DRAMATIST	DIRECTOR	SETS	COSTUMES	LIGHTING
Sizwe Bansi Is Dead	Athol Fugard John Kani Winston Ntshona	Ann Bowen	The Matrix Group		Robert Googooian
The Island	Athol Fugard John Kani Winston Ntshona	Robert Woodruff		Rita Yovino	Robert Googooian
Old Times	Harold Pinter	William Bushnell, Jr.	Paulie Jenkins		Paulie Jenkins
The Tricycle (El Triciclo)	Fernando Arrabal	Jaime Jaimes	Paul Appel	Robert Butz	Robert Googooian
Sunday	Joseph Scott Kierland	Dan Mason	Robert W. Zentis	Sylvia Moss	Paulie Jenkins

Lovelace Theatre Company

Beauty and the Beast	company developed	Denise Huot	Margo Lovelace	Margo Lovelace	Denise Huot
Carnival of the Seventh Moon	Margo Lovelace	Margo Lovelace	Margo Lovelace	Margo Lovelace	Penny Holpit Fred Michael
The Reluctant Dragon	company developed	Margaret Raphael		Tim Joswick Tina Haatainen	Fred Michael
The Brave Little Tailor	David Visser	Thomas M. Fontana	Margo Lovelace	Margo Lovelace	Fred Michael
Hansel and Gretel	Margo Lovelace (a)	Richard McElvain	Margo Lovelace	Margo Lovelace	Richard McElvain
Winnie the Pooh	David Visser (a)	Laura Johnson	Margo Lovelace	Margo Lovelace	Laura Johnson

The Magic Theatre

Wolves	John Robinson	Robert Woodruff	Michael Kroschel	Gene De Benedictis	John Chapot
The Wild Goose	Jeff Wanshel	John Lion	Michael Kroschel	Penelope Jones	Robert Gambrill
Minnie Mouse and the Tap- Dancing Buddha	Michael McClure	John Lion	Donald Cate	Regina Cate	John Chapot
Home on the Range	Jon Phillip Palmer	Rena Down	Warren Travis	Warren Travis	Suresa Dundes
Shakespeare the Sadist	Wolfgang Bauer Renata & Martin Esslin (t)	John Lion	John Lion	Allan Purcell	James Orman
Buried Child	Sam Shepard	Robert Woodruff	Michael Kroschel	Skipper Skeoch	John Chapot
Uncommon Women and Others	Wendy Wasserstein	Albert Takazauckas	Michael Kroschel	Skipper Skeoch	Thomas Mourant
Two O'Clock Feeding	Madeline Puccioni	Suresa Dundes	Shevra Tait	Nancy Faw	Patty Ann Farrell
The Red Snake	Michael McClure	John Lion	John Wilson	Niama Weiss	Thomas Mourant
Sightlines	Mark Eisman	John Lion	Ron Madonia	Nancy Faw	Melanie Dane
Magnetic Kisses	Wolfgang Bauer Suresa Dundes (a) John Lion (a)	John Lion	John Wilson	Suresa Dundes	James Orman
The Autobiography of a Pearl Diver	Martin Epstein	Andrew Doe	Michael Kroschel	Suresa Dundes	Ron Madonia
The Barbeque	John Robinson	Theodore Shank	John Amirati	Skipper Skeoch	Thomas Mourant
Suicide in B Flat	Sam Shepard	Robert Woodruff	John Wilson	Skipper Skeoch	John Wilson

Manhattan Theatre Club

Chez Nous	Peter Nichols	Lynne Meadow	John Conklin	Nanzi Adzima	Dennis Parichy
Play, That Time and Footfalls	Samuel Beckett	Alan Schneider	Zack Brown	Zack Brown	Bill Mintzner
Statements After an Arrest Under the Immorality Act	Athol Fugard	Thomas Bullard	David Potts	Judy Dearing	Dennis Parichy

PRODUCTION	DRAMATIST	DIRECTOR	SETS	COSTUMES	LIGHTING
Scenes from Soweto	Steve Wilmer	Thomas Bullard	David Potts	Judy Dearing	Dennis Parichy
Catsplay	Istvan Orkeny	Lynne Meadow	John Lee Beatty	Jennifer von Mayrhauser	Dennis Parichy
	Clara Gyorgyey (t)				
Strawberry Fields	Stephen Poliakoff	Stephen Pascal	Robert Yodice	Judy Dearing	Dennis Parichy
Wayside Motor Inn	A. R. Gurney, Jr.	Tony Giordano	David Potts	Ann Wolff	Jeff Davis
Frankie and Annie	Diane Simkin	Paul Schneider	David Potts	Ann Wolff	Jeff Davis
Red Fox/Second Hangin'	Don Baker	Michael Posnick	David Potts		Curt Osterman
	Dudley Cocke				
Safe House	Nicholas Kazan	Jonathan Alper	David Potts	Flo Rutherford	Bennett Avery
Rib Cage	Larry Ketron	Andy Wolk	David Potts	Linda Fisher	Dennis Parichy
By Strouse	Charles Strouse (m)	Charles Strouse	John Lee Beatty		
	Lee Adams (l)				
	Martin Charnin (l)				
A Lady with a Braid	Dory Previn (m,l)	Caymichael Patton			
Ain't Misbehavin'	Fats Waller, et al. (m,l)	Richard Maltby, Jr.		Pegi Goodman	
	Richard Maltby, Jr. (a)				
Has Anyone Here Found Love?	Lois Wyse	Miriam Fond			
Jim Wann's Country Cabaret		John Haber			
The Rear Column	Simon Gray	James Hammerstein	John Lee Beatty	Judy Dearing	Dennis Parichy
Grand Magic	Eduardo de Filippo	Michael Kahn	Ed Wittstein	Andrew B. Marlay	Dennis Parichy
	Carlo Ardito (t)				
Artichoke	Joanna Glass	Lynne Meadow	Fred Voelpel	Patricia McGourty	Jennifer Tipton
Don Juan Comes Back from the War	Odon von Horvath	Stephen Pascal	Tony Straiges	Jess Goldstein	Dennis Parichy
	Christopher Hampton (t)		Kate Edmunds		
The Arbor	Brother Jonathan, O.S.F.	Kenneth Frankel	Fred Kolouch	Barry Robison	Jamie Gallagher
Nongogo	Athol Fugard	Oz Scott	David Potts	Rachel Kurland	Victor En Yu Tan
Beethoven/Karl	David Rush	Paul Schneider	Barry Robison	Barry Robison	Frances Aronson
Stevie	Hugh Whitemore	Brian Murray	Barry Robison	Barry Robison	Frances Aronson
Losing Time	John Hopkins	Edwin Sherin	Barry Robison	Donna Meyer	Frances Aronson
Just a Little Bit Less than Normal	Nigel Baldwin	Paul Schneider	Barry Robison	Judith Dolan	Tom Schraeder
A Lady Needs a Change	various (m)	Bill Gile		David Toser	
	Dorothy Fields (l)				
	Bill Gile (a)				
Dancing in the Dark	Arthur Schwartz (m)	Christopher Chadman			
	Howard Dietz, et al. (l)				
	Mary O'Hagan (a)				
Give My Heart an Even Break	George Quincy (m)	Jim Kramer			
	Thayer Burch (l)				
Songs from the City Streets	Jake Holmes	Gui Andrisano			
At Home with Margery Cohen		Jose Fernandez			

Mark Taper Forum

PRODUCTION	DRAMATIST	DIRECTOR	SETS	COSTUMES	LIGHTING
For Colored Girls who have Considered Suicide/ When The Rainbow is Enuf	Ntozake Shange	Oz Scott	Ming Cho Lee	Judy Dearing	Marilyn Rennagel

continued

PRODUCTION	DRAMATIST	DIRECTOR	SETS	COSTUMES	LIGHTING
Comedians	Trevor Griffiths	Edward Parone	Peter J. Hall	Peter J. Hall	Martin Aronstein
A Christmas Carol	Doris Baizley (a)	John Dennis	Charles Berliner	Charles Berliner	Pamela Cooper
Getting Out	Marsha Norman	Gordon Davidson	Edward Burbridge	Peter J. Hall	John Gleason
Black Angel	Michael Cristofer	Gordon Davidson	Sally Jacobs	Sally Jacobs	Tharon Musser
Gethsemane Springs	Harvey Perr	John Sullivan	Sally Jacobs	Julie Weiss	Dawn Chiang
The Winter Dancers	David Lan	Kenneth Brecher	Ralph Funicello	Julie Weiss	Pamela Cooper
Zoot Suit	Luis Valdez	Luis Valdez	Roberto J. Morales (1,2) Thomas A. Walsh (2)	Peter J. Hall	Dawn Chiang
Dusa, Fish, Stas and Vi	Pam Gems	Edward Parone	Ralph Funicello	Peter J. Hall	Marilyn Rennagel
Terra Nova	Ted Tally	Gordon Davidson	Peter Wexler	Peter Berggren	Tharon Musser
The Tempest	William Shakespeare	John Hirsch	Ming Cho Lee	Carrie F. Robbins	David F. Segal
Jazz Set	Ron Milner	Bill Duke	Gerry Hariton Vicki Baral	Ingrid Thomas	Pamela Cooper
Kid Twist	Len Jenkin	David Schweizer	Christina Haatainen	Anna Belle Kaufman	Barbara Ling
The Taking Away of Little Willie	Tom Griffin	Wallace Chappell	Scott Johnson	Cheryl Dee Odom	Lee Hausman
In Camera	Robert Pinger	Gordon Hunt	Michael Drew Devine	Carol Brolaski	Michael Drew Devine
A Life in a Day: Lucky Lindy	Dick D. Zigun	Richard Gershman	John Kavelin	Brad R. Loman	Skip Rapoport
Maud Gonne Says No to the Poet	Susan Rivers	Lee Shallat	John Kavelin	Brad R. Loman	Skip Rapoport
The Trouble with Europe	Paul D'Andrea	John Dennis	Warren Travis	Warren Travis	Pamela Cooper
The Idol Makers	Stephen Davis Parks	David Schweizer	Barbara Ling	Louise Hayter	Tom Ruzika
The Biko Inquest	Norman Fenton Jon Blair	Ann Bowen	John Kavelin	Brad R. Loman	John DeSantis
Vienna Notes	Richard Nelson	Gwen Arner	Heidi Landesman	Heidi Landesman	Barbara Ling
Ormer Locklear	Marc Norman	Marc Norman	Thomas A. Walsh	Margaretrose	Karen M. Katz

McCarter Theatre Company

PRODUCTION	DRAMATIST	DIRECTOR	SETS	COSTUMES	LIGHTING
The Confirmation	Howard Ashman	Kenneth Frankel	Marjorie Kellogg	Jennifer von Mayrhauser	Marc B. Weiss
The Utter Glory of Morrissey Hall	Clark Gesner (b,m,l)	Nagle Jackson	Howard Bay	Howard Bay	David Graden
The Happy Journey to Trenton and Camden, Queens of France and The Long Christmas Dinner	Thornton Wilder	Michael Kahn	Raymond C. Recht	Jane Greenwood	Richard Nelson
The Torch-Bearers	George Kelly	Michael Kahn	Ed Wittstein	Jane Greenwood	John McLain
Toys in the Attic	Lillian Hellman	Pat Hingle	Christopher Nowak	Robert Wojewodski	John McLain
Much Ado About Nothing	William Shakespeare	William Woodman	Herbert Senn Helen Pond	Virgil C. Johnson	Richard Nelson
A Month in the Country	Ivan Turgenev Ariadne Nicolaeff (t)	Michael Kahn	Lawrence King Michael H. Yeargan	Jane Greenwood	John McLain
The Aspern Papers	Michael Redgrave (a)	Frith Banbury	Ed Wittstein	Andrew Marlay	John McLain
No Time for Comedy	S. N. Behrman	Gerald Gutierrez	John Lee Beatty	John Lee Beatty	John McLain
Put Them All Together	Anne Commire	Michael Kahn	Lawrence King Michael H. Yeargan	Jane Greenwood	John McLain
Blues in the Night	various (m,l) Sheldon Epps (a)	Sheldon Epps	John Shaffner	Jeanette Oleksa	John McLain
Heartbreak House	George Bernard Shaw	Vivian Matalon	William Ritman	Andrew Marlay	Richard Nelson

Los Angeles Actors' Theatre.
Rudy Ramos and Henry Sanders
in *The Guntower*.
Photo: Len Udis.

PRODUCTION	DRAMATIST	DIRECTOR	SETS	COSTUMES	LIGHTING
Meadow Brook Theatre					
She Stoops to Conquer	Oliver Goldsmith	John Ulmer	Peter-William Hicks	Mary L. Bonnell	Nancy Thompson
Picnic	William Inge	Terence Kilburn	Donald Beckman	Mary L. Bonnell	Frederick Fonner
Table Manners	Alan Ayckbourn	John Ulmer	Larry A. Reed	Mary L. Bonnell	Frederick Fonner
The Corn Is Green	Emlyn Williams	Charles Nolte	C. Lance Brockman	Mary L. Bonnell	Jean A. Móntgomery
The Tempest	William Shakespeare	Terence Kilburn	Peter-William Hicks	Mary L. Bonnell	Larry A. Reed
The Runner Stumbles	Milan Stitt	Charles Nolte	Donald Beckman	Mary L. Bonnell	Nancy Thompson
The Male Animal	James Thurber Elliott Nugent	Terence Kilburn	Douglas Wright	Mary L. Bonnell	Frederick Fonner
Cole	Cole Porter (m,l) Benny Green (a) Alan Strachan (a)	John Sharpe	Peter-William Hicks	Mary L. Bonnell	Peter-William Hicks
The Devil's Disciple	George Bernard Shaw	Terence Kilburn	Peter-William Hicks	Mary L. Bonnell	Frederick Fonner
That Championship Season	Jason Miller	John Ulmer	Douglas Wright	Mary L. Bonnell	Scott Brown
Ring Round the Moon	Jean Anouilh Christopher Fry (a)	Terence Kilburn	Donald Beckman	Mary L. Bonnell	Frederick Fonner
The Caine Mutiny Court-Martial	Herman Wouk	Charles Nolte	Douglas Wright	Mary L. Bonnell	Richard Henson
Blithe Spirit	Noel Coward	Terence Kilburn	Peter-William Hicks	Mary L. Bonnell	Frederick Fonner
The Deadly Game	James Yaffe (a)	Charles Nolte	Peter-William Hicks	Mary L. Bonnell	Jean A. Montgomery
The Adventures of Scapin	Moliere John Ulmer (a)	John Ulmer	Douglas Wright	Mary L. Bonnell	Frederick Fonner
Berlin to Broadway with Kurt Weill	Kurt Weill (m) various (l) Gene Lerner (a)	John Ulmer	Peter-William Hicks	Mary L. Bonnell	Benjamin Levenberg
Medicine Show Theatre Ensemble					
Frogs	Carl Morse (b,l) company (b) Yenoin Guibbory (m)	James Barbosa		Patricia McGourty	
The Mummers' Play	company (a) Donald Johnston (m)	Barbara Vann			
Don Juan in Hell	George Bernard Shaw		Antoni Miralda	Antoni Miralda	Barbara Kopit
Shipping Out	Stephen Policoff (b,l) company (b) Carol Henry (m) Chris Brandt (l)	Tina Mandas	R. Patrick Sullivan	Patricia McGourty	
The Tragedy of Tragedies or The Life and Death of Tom Thumb the Great	Henry Fielding Carol Henry (m)	Barbara Vann	Joel Handorff	Joel Handorff	
Milwaukee Repertory Theater Company					
Richard III	William Shakespeare	John Dillon	David Chapman	Randy Barcelo	Arden Fingerhut
Long Day's Journey into Night	Eugene O'Neill	Irene Lewis	R.H. Graham	Susan Tsu	Arden Fingerhut
Ah, Wilderness!	Eugene O'Neill	Irene Lewis	R.H. Graham	Susan Tsu	Arden Fingerhut

continued

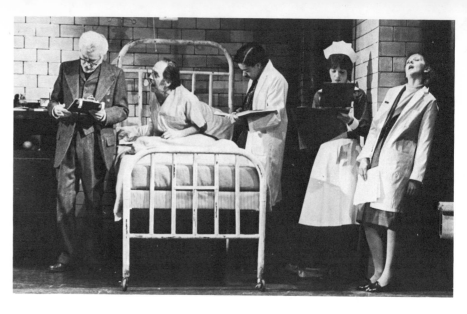

PRODUCTION	DRAMATIST	DIRECTOR	SETS	COSTUMES	LIGHTING
Friends	Kobo Abe Donald Keene (t)	John Dillon	Grady Larkins	Carol Oditz	R.H. Graham
High Time	Frank Cucci	Kenneth Frankel	Fred Kolouch	Rosemary Ingham	Joseph Tilford
Namesake	Amlin Gray	John Dillon	Stuart Wurtzel	Susan Tsu	Spencer Mosse
A Christmas Carol	Nagle Jackson (a)	Norman Berman	Christopher Idoine	Elizabeth Covey	Richard Winkler
Just a Little Bit Less than Normal	Nigel Baldwin	Barry Boys	Joseph Tilford	Marc L. Longlois	Joseph Tilford
Custer	Robert E. Ingham	Sanford Robbins	Valerie Kuehn	Rosemary Ingham	Dennis J. McHugh
Medal of Honor Rag	Tom Cole	Sharon Ott	Elizabeth Mahrt	Barbara Murray	Joseph Tilford
Romeo and Juliet	William Shakespeare	John Dillon	David Jenkins	Susan Tsu	Arden Fingerhut
The Freeway	Peter Nichols	Geoffrey Sherman	Scott Johnson	Pat McGourty	Scott Johnson
Island	Peter Link (b,m,l) Brent Nicholson (b)	Peter Link	Maura Smolover	Maura Smolover	Spencer Mosse
Fighting Bob	Tom Cole	John Dillon	David Emmons	Susan Tsu	Arden Fingerhut
Merton of the Movies	George S. Kaufman Marc Connelly	Bill Ludel	John Lee Beatty	Nanzi Adzima	Spencer Mosse
The Taming of the Shrew	William Shakespeare Amlin Gray (a) John Dillon (a) Jonathan Abarbanel (a)	John Dillon	Marjorie Kellogg	Susan Tsu	Arden Fingerhut
Hemingway Before the Storm	Ritch Brinkley Jonathan Abarbanel	Rod Pilloud	Tim Thomas	Barbara Nieft	Curtis Dretsch
Cops	Terry Curtis Fox	Rod Pilloud	Curtis Dretsch	Kate Bergh	Curtis Dretsch
The Bear	Anton Chekhov Earle Edgerton (t)	Jack McLaughlin-Gray	Valerie Kuehn	Colleen Muscha	Susan McAtee
Grandma Duck Is Dead	Larry Shue	Daniel Mooney	Valerie Kuehn	Marcia Cohen	Susan McAtee
Bo and *How I Got That Story*	Amlin Gray	Sharon Ott	Laura Maurer	Mary Gibson	Ross Hamilton

Missouri Repertory Theatre

PRODUCTION	DRAMATIST	DIRECTOR	SETS	COSTUMES	LIGHTING
The Misanthrope	Moliere	Cyril Ritchard	James Leonard Joy	Vincent Scassellati	Joseph Appelt
Old Times	Harold Pinter	James Assad	Frederic James	Barbara Medlicott	Curt Ostermann
The Morning Star	Henry C. Haskell	Harold Scott	James Leonard Joy	Judith Dolan	Joseph Appelt
Mary Stuart	Friedrich Schiller John Reich (a) Jean Stock Goldstone (a)	John Reich	John Ezell	Vincent Scassellati	Curt Ostermann
The Hostage	Brendan Behan	Francis J. Cullinan	James Leonard Joy	Barbara Medlicott	Joseph Appelt
Purlie Victorious	Ossie Davis	Robert L. Smith	Max Beatty	Judith Dolan	James Shehan
The Imaginary Invalid	Moliere John Reich (t)	John Reich	Baker S. Smith	Vincent Scassellati	Joseph Appelt
All My Sons	Arthur Miller	James Assad	Jack Montgomery	Vincent Scassellati	Michael Scott
Julius Caesar	William Shakespeare	Michael Langham	James Leonard Joy	Vincent Scassellati	Joseph Appelt
Light Up the Sky	Moss Hart	Francis J. Cullinan	James Leonard Joy	Baker S. Smith	Joseph Appelt
The Shadow Box	Michael Cristofer	James Assad	Jack Montgomery	Judith Dolan	Joseph Appelt
The Sea Gull	Anton Chekhov Jean-Claude van Itallie (t)	Boris Tumarin	Daniel Thomas Field	Judith Dolan	Delbert L. Unruh
Rashomon	Fay & Michael Kanin	Andrew Tsubaki	Barry Bengsten	Baker S. Smith	Michael Scott
The Happy Hunter	Georges Feydeau Barnett Shaw (a)	John Reich	John Ezell	Vincent Scassellati	Delbert L. Unruh
Bus Stop	William Inge	Vincent Dowling	Carolyn Leslie Ross	Baker S. Smith	Joseph Appelt
The Little Foxes	Lillian Hellman	Frances J. Cullinan	Carolyn Leslie Ross	Vincent Scassellati	Joseph Appelt

PRODUCTION	DRAMATIST	DIRECTOR	SETS	COSTUMES	LIGHTING
Music-Theatre Performing Group/Lenox Arts Center					
The American Imagination	Richard Foreman (b,l) Stanley Silverman (m)	Richard Foreman	Richard Foreman	Whitney Blausen	Heidi Landesman
Twelve Dreams	James Lapine	James Lapine	James Lapine	Heidi Landesman	Heidi Landesman
Viva Reviva	Eve Merriam (b,l) Amy Rubin (m)	Graciela Daniele	Kate Carmel	Kate Carmel	Cheryl Thacker
A Natural Death	Richard Howard	Michael Feingold	Kate Carmel	Kate Carmel	Cheryl Thacker
The Tennis Game	George W. S. Trow (b,l) William Schimmel (m)	Timothy S. Mayer	Timothy S. Mayer	Lizbeth Fulleman	Lenny Cowles
Virgil Thompson: A Profile	Virgil Thompson (m) various (l) Carman Moore (a)	Carman Moore	Patrick Ryan	Patrick Ryan	Patrick Ryan
Prairie Avenue	George W. S. Trow (b,l) William Schimmel (m)	Timothy S. Mayer	Timothy S. Mayer Lenny Cowles	Whitney Blausen Walker Hicklin	Lenny Cowles
Redeye	Timothy S. Mayer (b,l) Brad Burg (m)	Timothy S. Mayer	Timothy S. Mayer	Lizbeth Fulleman	Lenny Cowles
The Old Man	Wallace Shawn	Timothy S. Mayer	Patrick Ryan	Patrick Ryan	Patrick Ryan
National Black Theatre					
Ritual	Barbara Ann Teer (a,m,l) company (m,l)	Zuri McKie	Nabii Faison	Barbara Jones (l) Royce Morgan (2)	Zuri McKie (l) Marvin Watkins (2)
Soljourney into Truth	Barbara Ann Teer	Barbara Ann Teer	Barbara Ann Teer	Larry LaGaspi Judy Dearing	Omowale Harewood
Seven Comes Up Seven Comes Down	Lonne Elder III Adeyemi Lythcott	Adayemi Lythcott	Paul Davis	Pat Vaughn	Shirley Pendergast
Wine in the Wilderness	Alice Childress	Adayemi Lythcott	Paul Davis	Pat Vaughn	Shirley Pendergast
Softly Comes a Whirlwind Whispering in Your Ear	Barbara Ann Teer	Barbara Ann Teer	Vantile E. Whitfield (aka Motojicho)	Vantile E. Whitfield (aka Motojicho)	Vantile E. Whitfield (aka Motojicho)
The Owl and the Pussycat	Bill Manhoff	Barbara Ann Teer	L. Siuzi Henry (aka Cuz)	Olaitan Callender Royce Morgan	Amy Wilkins
National Shakespeare Company					
The Winter's Tale	William Shakespeare	Mario Siletti	Terry Bennett	Sharon Hollinger	Terry Bennett
Othello	William Shakespeare	Philip Meister	Terry Bennett	Sharon Hollinger	Terry Bennett
As You Like It	William Shakespeare	Sue Lawless	Terry Bennett	Sharon Hollinger	Terry Bennett
Hamlet	William Shakespeare	Mario Siletti	Terry Bennett	Sharon Hollinger	Terry Bennett
A Midsummer Night's Dream	William Shakespeare	Philip Meister	Terry Bennett	Sharon Hollinger	Terry Bennett
National Theatre of the Deaf					
The Three Musketeers	Joe Layton (a) company (a)	Joe Layton	David Hays	Fred Voelpel	David Hays
Sir Gawain and the Green Knights	Dennis Scott (a)	Mack Scism	David Hays	Fred Voelpel	David Hays
Aesop's Fables	Aesop	Mack Scism Linda Bove	David Hays	Fred Voelpel	David Hays
Quite Early One Morning	Dylan Thomas	Dennis Scott	David Hays	Fred Voelpel	David Hays
Volpone	Ben Jonson	Don Redlich	David Hays	Fred Voelpel	David Hays
Cautionary Tales	Hilaire Belloc	Mack Scism	David Hays	Fred Voelpel	David Hays
Sense and Nonsense	Lewis Carroll	Linda Bove	David Hays	Fred Voelpel	David Hays
The Giving Tree	Shel Silverstein	Ed Waterstreet	David Hays	Fred Voelpel	David Hays

PRODUCTION	DRAMATIST	DIRECTOR	SETS	COSTUMES	LIGHTING
Nebraska Theatre Caravan					
Scapino	Frank Dunlop (a) Jim Dale (a)	Charles Jones	James Othuse	Carole Wheeldon	James Othuse
The Boar's Head Tavern	Mitchell Edmonds	Charles Jones	James Othuse	Rita Glass	James Othuse
The Mystery of the Boar's Head	Mitchell Edmonds	Charles Jones	James Othuse	Carole Wheeldon	James Othuse
The Just-So Stories	Aurand Harris (a)	Eleanor Jones	James Othuse	Carole Wheeldon	James Othuse
Diamond Studs	Jim Wann (b,m,l) Bland Simpson (m,l)	Charles Jones	James Othuse	Patt Moser	James Othuse
Twelfth Night	William Shakespeare	Bill Kirk	James Othuse	Patt Moser	James Othuse
Androcles and the Lion	Aurand Harris	Eleanor Jones	James Othuse	Kathy Wilson	James Othuse
Negro Ensemble Company					
The Offering	Gus Edwards	Douglas Turner Ward	Raymond C. Recht	Arthur McGee	Paul Gallo
Black Body Blues	Gus Edwards	Douglas Turner Ward	Raymond C. Recht	Arthur McGee	Paul Gallo
Twilight Dinner	Lennox Brown	Douglas Turner Ward	Samuel Gonzales	Steve Carter	James Fauvell
Nevis Mountain Dew	Steve Carter	Horacena J. Taylor	Wynn Thomas	Alvin Perry	Larry Johnson
Daughters of the Mock	Judi Ann Mason	Glenda Dickerson	Wynn Thomas	Alvin Perry	Larry Johnson
Everyman and The Imprisonment of Obatala	Obotunde Ijimere	Dean Irby	Wynn Thomas	Alvin Perry	Larry Johnson
Old Phantoms	Gus Edwards	Horacena J. Taylor	Wynn Thomas	Alvin Perry	Larry Johnson
A Season to Unravel	Alexis DeVeaux	Glenda Dickerson	Wynn Thomas	Alvin Perry	Larry Johnson
New American Theater					
Winesburg, Ohio	Christopher Sergel (a)	J.R. Sullivan	James Wolk	Jon R. Accardo	James Wolk
Anyone Can Whistle	Arthur Laurents (b) Stephen Sondheim (m,l)	J.R. Sullivan	James Wolk	Ellen M. Kozak	James Wolk
Hay Fever	Noel Coward	William C. Martin	James Wolk	Jon R. Accardo	James Wolk
The Hostage	Brendan Behan	J.R. Sullivan	James Wolk	Cathy Susan Pyles	James Wolk
Equus	Peter Shaffer	J.R. Sullivan	James Wolk	Jon R. Accardo	James Wolk
The Good Doctor	Neil Simon	Ricki G. Ravitts	James Wolk	Jon R. Accardo	James Wolk
Firehouse Rites	J.R. Sullivan	J.R. Sullivan	James Wolk	Jon R. Accardo	James Wolk
Born Yesterday	Garson Kanin	B.J. Jones	James Wolk	Jon R. Accardo	James Wolk
The Belle of Amherst	William Luce	J.R. Sullivan	James Wolk	Jon R. Accardo	James Wolk
Vanities	Jack Heifner	J.R. Sullivan	James Wolk	Jon R. Accardo	James Wolk
Picnic	William Inge	J.R. Sullivan	James Wolk	Jon R. Accardo	James Wolk
Of Mice and Men	John Steinbeck	J.R. Sullivan	James Wolk	Jon R. Accardo	James Wolk
Two Gentlemen of Verona	John Guare (b,l) Mel Shapiro (b) Galt MacDermot (m)	J.R. Sullivan	James Wolk	Jon R. Accardo	James Wolk
Absurd Person Singular	Alan Ayckbourn	J.R. Sullivan	James Wolk	Jon R. Accardo	James Wolk
The School for Wives	Moliere Richard Wilbur (t)	B.J. Jones	James Wolk	Jon R. Accardo	James Wolk
The Shadow Box	Michael Cristofer	J.R. Sullivan	James Wolk	Jon R. Accardo	James Wolk
The Duck Variations	David Mamet	J.R. Sullivan	James Wolk	Jon R. Accardo	James Wolk
Dunelawn (from Bad Habits)	Terrence McNally	H. O'Niel Eley	James Wolk	Jon R. Accardo	James Wolk
Lovers	Brian Friel	G. Michael Johnson	James Wolk	Jon R. Accardo	James Wolk
The Last Meeting of the Knights of the White Magnolia	Preston Jones	J.R. Sullivan	James Wolk	Jon R. Accardo	James Wolk

Long Wharf Theatre. Alice Brereton and Emery Battis in *The Philadelphia Story*. Photo: William L. Smith.

PRODUCTION	DRAMATIST	DIRECTOR	SETS	COSTUMES	LIGHTING
The New Dramatists					
Losers	Donald Wollner	Ellen Sandler			
The Booth Brothers	Warren Kliewer	Warren Kliewer			
The Man Who Drew Circles	Steven Somkin	Cliff Goodwin			
The Verandah	Clifford Mason	Clifford Mason			
The Sugar Bowl	Stan Taikeff	Thomas Gruenewald			
Avenue B	Jack Gilhooley	Pamela Singer			
Filigree People	Peter Dee	David Kerry Heefner			
Marvelous Brown	Diane Kagan	Patricia Carmichael			
Father Dreams	Mary Gallagher	Bill Ludel			
The Ravelle's Comeback	Jack Gilhooley				
Flagship	Donald Wollner	Ellen Sandler			
Metro Park	Gene Radano	Bill Partlan			
Singles	Robert Lord	Philip Adelman			
The Corridor	Diane Kagan	Patricia Carmichael			
Mothers and Daughters	John von Hartz	Norman Thomas			
Roosters	Mitchell Yaven	Jeffrey Martin			
A Cock to Asclepius	Stan Taikeff	Merrily Mossman			
Stray Vessels	Mitchell Yaven	Bill Herndon			
Dancin' to Calliope	Jack Gilhooley				
The Feathered Serpent	Edward H. Mabley	Evelyn Pierce			
New Federal Theatre					
Night Song	Patricia Lea	Walter Jones	Joseph Gandy	Judy Dearing	Ernest Baxter
Season's Reasons	Ron Milner	Ron Milner	C. Richard Mills	Anita Ellis	George Greczylo
The Block Party	Joseph Lizardi	Joseph Lizardi	Jose M. Feliciano	Edna Watson	Sandra Ross
African Interlude	Martie Evans-Charles	Shauneille Perry	C. Richard Mills	Judy Dearing	Sandra Ross
Do Lord Remember Me	James de Jongh	Regge Life	C. Richard Mills	Beverly Parks	Sandra Ross
Run'ners	Ivey McCray	Novella Nelson	C. Richard Mills	Ellen Lee	Victor En Yu Tan
Birdland	Barry Amyer Kaleem (a,m,l) Elliot Weiss (m)	Anderson Johnson	Alvin Perry	Karen Perry	Jeff Miller
Hot Dishes!	Maurice Peterson (b,m,l)	Irving Lee	Robert Edmonds	Rene Lavergneau Wia Carpenter	George Greczylo
Black Medea	Ernest Ferlita	Glenda Dickerson	Michael Fish	Ellen Lee	Pat Stern
Anna Lucasta	Philip Yordan	Ernestine M. Johnston	C. Richard Mills	Edna Watson	Shirley Prendergast
Take a Giant Step	Louis Peterson	Oz Scott	C. Richard Mills	Judy Dearing	Victor En Yu Tan
Trouble in Mind	Alice Childress	Shauneille Perry			
In Splendid Error	William Branch	Charles Turner	C. Richard Mills	Judy Dearing	Shirley Prendergast
A Raisin in the Sun	Lorraine Hansberry	Ernie McClintock	C. Richard Mills	Edna Watson	Victor En Yu Tan
Take It from the Top	Ruby Dee (m,l)	Ossie Davis	Michael Fish	Judy Dearing	Shirley Prendergast
Flamingo Flomingo	Lucky Cienfuego (b,m,l)	Erick Santamaria	Robert Edmonds	Joaquin La-Habana	Faith Baum
The Glorious Monster in the Bell of the Horn	Larry Neal	Glenda Dickerson	Robert Edmonds	Ellen Lee	Cathy Perkins
New Jersey Shakespeare Festival					
Hamlet	William Shakespeare	Paul Barry	Don A. Coleman	Jeffrey L. Ullman	Gary C. Porto
Love's Labour's Lost	William Shakespeare	Paul Barry	Don A. Coleman	Jeffrey L. Ullman	Gary C. Porto

continued

Meadow Brook Theatre. *The Adventures of Scapin.* Photo: Dick Hunt.

PRODUCTION	DRAMATIST	DIRECTOR	SETS	COSTUMES	LIGHTING
Rosencrantz and Guildenstern Are Dead	Tom Stoppard	Paul Barry	Don A. Coleman	Jeffrey L. Ullman	Gary C. Porto
The Country Girl	Clifford Odets	Paul Barry	Don A. Coleman	Jeffrey L. Ullman	Gary C. Porto
Arms and the Man	George Bernard Shaw	John Ulmer	Don A. Coleman	Jeffrey L. Ullman	Gary C. Porto
Who's Afraid of Virginia Woolf?	Edward Albee	Paul Barry	Don A. Coleman	Alice S. Hughes	Gary C. Porto
King Lear	William Shakespeare	Paul Barry	Peter B. Harrison	Ann Emonts	Gary C. Porto
A Midsummer Night's Dream	William Shakespeare	Paul Barry	Peter B. Harrison	Ann Emonts	Gary C. Porto
A Streetcar Named Desire	Tennessee Williams	Paul Barry	Peter B. Harrison	Ann Emonts	Gary C. Porto
The Importance of Being Earnest	Oscar Wilde	John Ulmer	Peter B. Harrison	Kathleen Blake	Gary C. Porto
Travesties	Tom Stoppard	Paul Barry	Peter B. Harrison	Kathleen Blake	Gary C. Porto
Two for the Seesaw	William Gibson	Paul Barry	Peter B. Harrison	Alice S. Hughes	Gary C. Porto
Luv	Murray Schisgal	Paul Barry	Peter B. Harrison	Alice S. Hughes	Gary C. Porto

The New Playwrights' Theatre of Washington

PRODUCTION	DRAMATIST	DIRECTOR	SETS	COSTUMES	LIGHTING
Sweet and Hot: The Songs of Harold Arlen	Harold Arlen et al. (m,l) Ken Bloom (a) Berthe Schuchat (a)	Ken Bloom	Russell Metheny	Mary Kay MacGregor	Laurie Metter
Pinnacle: A Play About Needlepoint and Other Crafts	Mark Stein	Harry M. Bagdasian	Russell Metheny	Nancy J. Klingerman	Robert Marietta
Nightmare!	Tim Grundmann (b,m,l)	Ken Bloom	Russell Metheny	Mary Kay MacGregor	Tomm Tomlinson
The House of Bedlam	Kenneth Arnold	Robert Graham Small	Bruce Daniel	Mary Kay MacGregor	Bruce Daniel
Hamlet!	William Shakespeare John Neville-Andrews (a)	Linda Lehman	Bruce Daniel	Karen M. Hummel Candice Newcomb Mary Kay MacGregor	Bruce Daniel
White Horse/Black Horse	Steven Stosny	Alan Donovan	Robert Marietta	Nancy J. Klingerman	Tomm Tomlinson
Out to Lunch	Tim Grundmann (b,m,l)	Ken Bloom	Kit Grover	Richard D. McGee	Tomm Tomlinson
A Whitman Sonata	Paul Hildebrand, Jr. (a) Thom Wagner (a,m)	Paul Hildebrand, Jr.	Russell Metheny	Carol Ingram	Tomm Tomlinson
Splendid Rebels	Ernest Joselovitz	Robert Schulte	Russell Metheny	A. Newbold Richardson	Robert Marietta
A Christmas Carol	Harry M. Bagdasian (a)	Harry M. Bagdasian	Robert Marietta	Nancy K. Daugherty	Greg Wurz
Breaking the Sweet Glass	Mark Stein	Harry M. Bagdasian	Robert Marietta	Nancy K. Daugherty	Greg Wurz
Down One	Barbara Keiler	Alan Donovan	Russell Metheny	Peter Zakutansky	Robert Marietta
Eddie's Catchy Tunes	Tim Grundmann (b,m,l)	Ken Bloom	Russell Metheny	Peter Zakutansky Ingrid Crepeau	Tomm Tomlinson

New York Shakespeare Festival

PRODUCTION	DRAMATIST	DIRECTOR	SETS	COSTUMES	LIGHTING
The Threepenny Opera	Bertolt Brecht (b,l) Ralph Manheim (t) John Willett (t) Kurt Weill (m)	Richard Foreman	Douglas W. Schmidt	Theoni V. Aldredge	Pat Collins
Agamemnon	Aeschylus Andrei Serban (a) Elizabeth Swados (a,m)	Andrei Serban	Douglas W. Schmidt	Santo Loquasto	Jennifer Tipton

PRODUCTION	DRAMATIST	DIRECTOR	SETS	COSTUMES	LIGHTING
Unfinished Women Cry in No Man's Land While a Bird Dies in a Gilded Cage	Aishah Rahman (b,l) Jackie McLean (m)	Bill Duke	Linda Conaway	Judy Dearing	Shirley Prendergast
Miss Margarida's Way	Roberto Athayde	Roberto Athayde	Santo Loquasto	Santo Loquasto	Martin Tudor
Landscape of the Body	John Guare	John Pasquin	Santo Loquasto	Santo Loquasto	Jennifer Tipton
The Misanthrope	Moliere Richard Wilbur (t) Jobriath Boone (m) Margaret Pine (m) Arthur Bienstock (m)	Bill Gile	Bill Stabile	Carrie F. Robbins	Arden Fingerhut
Tales of the Hasidim	Martin Buber Paul Sills (a)	Paul Sills			Victor En Yu Tan
The Mandrake	Niccolo Machiavelli Wallace Shawn (t)	Wilford Leach	Wilford Leach	Patricia McGourty	Victor En Yu Tan
A Photograph: A Study of Cruelty	Ntozake Shange	Oz Scott	David Mitchell	Beverly Parks	Victor En Yu Tan
The Dybbuk	S. Ansky Mira Rafalowicz (t)	Joseph Chaikin	Woods Mackintosh	Mary Brecht	Beverly Emmons
The Water Engine	David Mamet	Steven Schachter	John Lee Beatty	Laura Crow	Dennis Parichy
A Prayer for My Daughter	Thomas Babe	Robert Allan Ackerman	Bil Mikulewicz	Robert Wojewodski	Arden Fingerhut
Museum	Tina Howe	Max Stafford-Clark	Robert Yodice	Patricia McGourty	Jennifer Tipton
Curse of the Starving Class	Sam Shepard	Robert Woodruff	Santo Loquasto	Santo Loquasto	Martin Tudor
Runaways	Elizabeth Swados (b,m,l)	Elizabeth Swados	Douglas W. Schmidt Woods Mackintosh	Hilary M. Rosenfeld	Jennifer Tipton
I'm Getting My Act Together and Taking It on the Road	Gretchen Cryer (b,l) Nancy Ford (m)	Word Baker		Pearl Somner	Martin Tudor
Michael	Ed Bullins	Ed Bullins	Robert Yodice	Alvin Perry	Victor En Yu Tan
Passion Without Reason	Neil Harris	Ernestine M. Johnston	Robert Yodice	Alvin Perry	Victor En Yu Tan
All's Well That Ends Well	William Shakespeare	Wilford Leach	Wilford Leach	Carol Oditz	Jennifer Tipton
The Taming of the Shrew	William Shakespeare	Wilford Leach	Wilford Leach	Patricia McGourty	Jennifer Tipton
An Evening at New Rican Village	Eduardo Figueroa (a,m,l)	Eduardo Figueroa			
Drinks Before Dinner	E.L. Doctorow	Mike Nichols	Tony Walton	Tony Walton	Jennifer Tipton
The Umbrellas of Cherbourg	Jacques Demy (b,l) Sheldon Harnick (t) Charles Burr (t) Michel Legrand (m)	Andrei Serban	Michael Yeargan	Jane Greenwood	Ian Calderon
Julius Caesar	William Shakespeare	Michael Langham			Jennifer Tipton
Coriolanus	William Shakespeare	Michael Langham			Jennifer Tipton
Taken in Marriage	Thomas Babe	Robert Allan Ackerman	Karen Schultz	Robert Wojewodski	Arden Fingerhut
Sancocho	Ramiro (Ray) Ramirez (b,m,l) Jimmy Justice (m)	Miguel Godreau	Frank J. Boros	Frank J. Boros	Nananne Porcher
Dispatches	Elizabeth Swados (a,m,l)	Elizabeth Swados	Patricia Woodbridge	Hilary M. Rosenfeld	Jennifer Tipton
Wake Up, It's Time to Go to Bed!	Carson Kievman	Carson Kievman	Robert Yodice	Robert Yodice	Pat Collins
The Woods	David Mamet	Ulu Grosbard	John Lee Beatty	Robert Wojewodski	Jennifer Tipton
Happy Days	Samuel Beckett	Andrei Serban	Michael Yeargan Larry King	Jane Greenwood	Jennifer Tipton
Spell #7	Ntozake Shange	Oz Scott	Robert Yodice	Grace Williams	Victor En Yu Tan

PRODUCTION	DRAMATIST	DIRECTOR	SETS	COSTUMES	LIGHTING
North Light Repertory Company					
The Goodbye People	Herb Gardner	George Keathley	Maher Ahmad	Christa Scholtz	Maher Ahmad
The Mound Builders	Lanford Wilson	Gregory Kandel	Maher Ahmad	Marsha Kowal	Maher Ahmad
Oh, Coward!	Noel Coward (m,l)	Dennis Zacek	Maher Ahmad	Christa Scholtz	Robert Atkins
	Roderick Cook (a)				
That Championship Season	Jason Miller	George Keathley	Maher Ahmad	Marsha Kowal	Maher Ahmad
Coming of Age	Frank Cucci	Dennis Zacek	Maher Ahmad	Christa Scholtz	Maher Ahmad
The Horse Latitudes and *The Pokey*	Stephen Black	Gregory Kandel	Maher Ahmad	Marsha Kowal	Maher Ahmad
The Club	Eve Merriam (a,m,l)	Michael Maggio	Maher Ahmad	Christa Scholtz	Maher Ahmad
Odyssey Theatre Ensemble					
Noonday Demons	Peter Barnes	Ron Sossi	Rafigh Ghorbanzadeh	Sherry George	Dawn Chiang
A Theological Position	Robert Coover	Ron Sossi	Rafigh Ghorbanzadeh	Sherry George	Dawn Chiang
The Threepenny Opera	Bertolt Brecht (b,l)	Ron Sossi	Keith Hein	Tiny Ossman	Paulie Jenkins
	Marc Blitzstein (t)				
	Kurt Weill (m)				
Don Juan	Moliere	Ann Bowen	Don Smith	Nancy Tunnel	Corey Cooper
Woyzeck	Georg Buchner	Ron Sossi	Lorraine Brown	Saralena Martin	Paulie Jenkins
The Underpants	Carl Sternheim	Frank Condon	Scott Van Houten	Holden and Sares	Brian Gale
The Soft Touch	Neil Cuthbert	Ron Sossi	Keith Hein	Holden and Sares	Penny Hoxter
White Marriage	Tadeusz Rozewicz	Ron Sossi	Keith Gonzales	Cara Benedetti	Paulie Jenkins
The Chicago Conspiracy Trial	Frank Condon	Frank Condon	Leonard Felix	Kim Simons	Ana Oakes
	Ron Sossi				
Suicide in B Flat	Sam Shepard	Ron Sossi	John Wynne	Cara Benedetti	Ana Oakes
			Leonard Felix		
Old Creamery Theatre Company					
The Star-Spangled Girl	Neil Simon	Thomas P. Johnson	Steve Peters	Alecia Krebs	Bill Gorman
Ten Little Indians	Agatha Christie	Frank Sladek, Jr.	Steve Peters	Alecia Krebs	Bill Gorman
A Flea in Her Ear	Georges Feydeau	Thomas P. Johnson	Steve Peters		Jody Schultz
Death of a Salesman	Arthur Miller	Doug Donald	Steve Peters	Carol Wiederrecht	Bill Gorman
The Matchmaker	Thornton Wilder	Frank Sladek, Jr.	Steve Peters		Susan Ruck
Godspell	John-Michael Tebelak (b)	Doug Donald	Thomas P. Johnson		Marquetta Senters
	Stephen Schwartz (m,l)				
There's a Girl in My Soup	Terence Frisby	Madaline Sparks	Doug Anderson	Bobbie Berry	Steven Hansen
The Comedy Connection	Various	Thomas P. Johnson	Thomas P. Johnson	Melissa Harrington	Steven Hansen
Private Lives	Noel Coward	David Schmaltz	David Brune	Pamela Mason-Brune	Steven Hansen
A Streetcar Named Desire	Tennessee Williams	Thomas P. Johnson	David Brune	Kim Anderson	Steven Hansen
				Marquetta Senters	
The Lady from Maxim's	Georges Feydeau	Thomas P. Johnson	Kennon Balster	Carol Fisher	Steven Hansen
	Gene Feist (a)				
Not Tonight Dear, I Have a Headache	Howard Blanning (a)	Thomas P. Johnson	Kennon Balster	Carol Fisher	Steven Hansen
Two by Two	Peter Stone (b)	Thomas P. Johnson	Doug Anderson	Carol Fisher	Steven Hansen
	Richard Rodgers (m)				
	Martin Charnin (l)				
Last of the Red Hot Lovers	Neil Simon	Nancy Youngblut	Nancy Youngblut	Nancy Youngblut	Randy Mauck

PRODUCTION	DRAMATIST	DIRECTOR	SETS	COSTUMES	LIGHTING
Old Globe Theatre					
The Last of the Marx Brothers' Writers	Louis Phillips	Craig Noel	Peggy Kellner	Donna Couchman	Steph Storer
Too True to Be Good	George Bernard Shaw	Mark Lamos	Steve Lavino	Donna Couchman	William Greenspan
Sleuth	Anthony Shaffer	Sandy McCallum	Dan Dryden	Dianne Holly	Amarante L. Lucero
The Sunshine Boys	Neil Simon	Jack Tygett	Peggy Kellner	Donna Couchman	William Greenspan
The Lion in Winter	James Goldman	Ken Ruta	Peggy Kellner	Peggy Kellner	Amarante L. Lucero
That Championship Season	Jason Miller	Arthur Wagner	Steve Lavino	Dianne Holly	Steve Lavino
Exit the King	Eugene Ionesco	Kevin Tighe	Russel Redmond	Dianne Holly	Steve Lavino
The Seagull	Anton Chekhov Stark Young (t)	Craig Noel	Peggy Kellner	Peggy Kellner	Steph Storer
Old Times	Harold Pinter	Jack Bender	Steph Storer	Dianne Holly	Steph Storer
Loot	Joe Orton	Eric Christmas	Margaret Perry	Donna Couchman	Steve Lavino
How the Other Half Loves	Alan Ayckbourn	Wayne Bryan	Steph Storer	Peggy Kellner	Steph Storer
Henry V	William Shakespeare	Eric Christmas Craig Noel	Peggy Kellner	Peggy Kellner	Sean Murphy
A Midsummer Night's Dream	William Shakespeare	Jack O'Brien	Robert Morgan	Robert Morgan	Sean Murphy
The Winter's Tale	William Shakespeare	Peter Donat	Robert Blackman	Robert Blackman	Sean Murphy
The Robber Bridegroom	Alfred Uhry (b,l) Robert Waldman (m)	Jack Tygett	Robert Green	Dianne Holly	Steve Lavino
Present Laughter	Noel Coward	Craig Noel	John David Peters	Donna Couchman	Steph Storer
Toys in the Attic	Lillian Hellman	Craig Noel	Nick Reid	Susan Muick	Steph Storer
The Front Page	Ben Hecht Charles MacArthur	Sandy McCallum	Steve Lavino	Donna Couchman	Steve Lavino
Equus	Peter Shaffer	Neil Flanagan	Steph Storer	Donna Couchman	Steph Storer
Otherwise Engaged	Simon Gray	William Roesch	Steph Storer	Donna Couchman	Steph Storer
The Enchanted	Jean Giraudoux Maurice Valency (t)	Scott Boultin	Steve Lavino	Claremarie Verheyen	Steve Lavino
The Misanthrope	Moliere Tony Harrison (t)	Ken Ruta	Steph Storer	Dianne Holly	Steph Storer
A Delicate Balance	Edward Albee	Martin Gerrish	Mark Donnelly	Dianne Holly	Raymond E. Mondoux
The Caretaker	Harold Pinter	Arthur Wagner	Steph Storer	Dianne Holly	Steph Storer
Julius Caesar	William Shakespeare	Jerome Kilty	Cliff Faulkner	Deborah Dryden	John McLain
The Comedy of Errors	William Shakespeare	Ken Ruta	Cliff Faulkner	Lewis Brown	John McLain
Macbeth	William Shakespeare	Nagle Jackson	Cliff Faulkner	Peggy Kellner	John McLain
Table Manners, Living Together and *Round and Round the Garden*	Alan Ayckbourn	Craig Noel	Mark Donnelly	Peggy Kellner	Steve Lavino
Omaha Magic Theatre					
Astral White	Mimi Loring (b) Donna Young (m) Lynn Herrick (m) company (l)	JoAnn Schmidman	Diane Degan	Wes Bailey Mechelle Keller	Elisa Stacy
American King's English for Queens	Megan Terry (b,l) Lynn Herrick (m) Donna Young (m)	JoAnn Schmidman	Diane Degan	JoAnn Schmidman	Elisa Stacy

continued

Theatre Arts of West Virginia.
Barbara Lockard and Laura
Treacy in *The Importance of
Being Earnest.*
Photo: David S. Talbot.

PRODUCTION	DRAMATIST	DIRECTOR	SETS	COSTUMES	LIGHTING
Babes in the Bighouse	Megan Terry (b,l) John Sheehan (m)	JoAnn Schmidman	Diane Degan	JoAnn Schmidman	Colbert McClellan
The Gray Express: A Mystery	James Larson (b,l) Nancy Larson (m)	JoAnn Schmidman	Diane Degan	JoAnn Schmidman	James Larson
100,001 Horror Stories of the Plains	Megan Terry (b,l) company (b,l) Nancy Larson (m)	JoAnn Schmidman	Diane Degan	Barbara Morrell	Elisa Stacy
Pro Game	Megan Terry (b,l) JoAnn Schmidman (m)	JoAnn Schmidman Judith Katz	Diane Degan	JoAnn Schmidman	James Larson
Brazil Fado	Megan Terry (b,l) Nancy Larson (m) company (m)	Joe Guinan JoAnn Schmidman	Diane Degan	JoAnn Schmidman	James Larson
Running Gag	JoAnn Schmidman (b) Marianne de Pury (m) Lynn Herrick (m) Megan Terry (l)	JoAnn Schmidman	Diane Degan Megan Terry	Elizabeth Scheuerlein	Colbert McClellan
Goona Goona	Megan Terry (b,l) Lynn Herrick (m)	JoAnn Schmidman	Megan Terry Elizabeth Scheuerlein LaDonna Spurgin	Elizabeth Scheuerlein	Colbert McClellan

O'Neill Theater Center

PRODUCTION	DRAMATIST	DIRECTOR	SETS	COSTUMES	LIGHTING
Threads	Jonathan Bolt	John Dillon	1978 Resident Designers: Bil Mikulewicz Fred Voelpel		1978 Resident Designers: Ian Calderon Arden Fingerhut
Getting Off	Lee Thomas	Tony Giordano			
Sightlines	Mark Eisman	Dennis Scott			
The Gayden Chronicles	Michael Cook	John Dillon			
Texas Dry	John Olive	Sheldon Larry			
Put Them All Together	Anne Commire	Robert Allan Ackerman			
the bloodrite	owa	Oz Scott			
No English Spoken	Stephen Davis Parks	John Dillon			
All Honorable Men	Michael J. Chepiga	Dennis Scott			
Friends	Crispin Larangeira	Tony Giordano			
China Beach	Brian J. McFadden	Robert Allan Ackerman			
Beggar's Choice	Kathleen Betsko	Oz Scott			
Leela Means to Play	Beverley Simons	Robert Allan Ackerman			
Bent	Martin Sherman	Dennis Scott			
Snow-Pressings	Ray Aranha	Dennis Scott	1979 Resident Designers: Marjorie Kellogg Harry Lines Fred Voelpel		1979 Resident Designers: Ian Calderon Arden Fingerhut
She Also Dances	Kenneth Arnold	Dennis Scott			
Pen	Barbara Field	Steven Robman			
Showdown at the Adobe Motel	Lanny Flaherty	Sheldon Larry			
Kernel of Sanity	Kermit Frazier	Oz Scott			
House of Cards	Theodore Gross	Oz Scott			
Fob	David Henry Hwang	Robert Allan Ackerman			
Whispers	Crispin Larangeira	Steven Robman			
Terry by Terry	Mark Leib	Tony Giordano			

PRODUCTION	DRAMATIST	DIRECTOR	SETS	COSTUMES	LIGHTING
Wives	Lynda Myles	Robert Allan Ackerman			
Skidding into Slow Time	Stephen Davis Parks	Tony Giordano			
Agnes of God	John Pielmeier	Robert Allan Ackerman			

Ontological-Hysteric Theater

Blvd. de Paris: I've Got the Shakes written, directed & designed by Richard Foreman

Oregon Shakespearean Festival

PRODUCTION	DRAMATIST	DIRECTOR	SETS	COSTUMES	LIGHTING
Tartuffe	Moliere	Sabin Epstein	Richard L. Hay	Merrily Ann Murray	Dirk Epperson
Private Lives	Noel Coward	Dennis Bigelow	William Bloodgood	Jeannie Davidson	Dirk Epperson
Mother Courage and Her Children	Bertolt Brecht	Jerry Turner	Richard L. Hay	Jeannie Davidson	Dirk Epperson
The Effect of Gamma Rays on Man-in-the-Moon Marigolds	Paul Zindel	William Glover	Richard L. Hay	Phyllis A. Corcoran	Robert Peterson
The Taming of the Shrew	William Shakespeare	Judd Parkin	William Bloodgood	Robert Blackman	Dirk Epperson
The Tempest	William Shakespeare	Michael Addison	William Bloodgood	Jeannie Davidson	Dirk Epperson
Richard III	William Shakespeare	Pat Patton	William Bloodgood	Jeannie Davidson	Dirk Epperson
Timon of Athens	William Shakespeare	Jerry Turner	Richard L. Hay	Jeannie Davidson	Dirk Epperson
The Night of the Tribades	Per Olov Enquist Ross Shideler (t)	Jerry Turner	Richard L. Hay	Jeannie Davidson	Robert Peterson
Miss Julie	August Strindberg Jerry Turner (t)	Elizabeth Huddle	Richard L. Hay	Jeannie Davidson	Dirk Epperson
Macbeth	William Shakespeare	Pat Patton	Richard L. Hay	Jeannie Davidson	Dirk Epperson
The Play's the Thing	Ferenc Molnar P.G. Wodehouse (a)	Dennis Bigelow	Richard L. Hay	Deborah Dryden	Dirk Epperson
Born Yesterday	Garson Kanin	James Moll	William Bloodgood	Merrily Ann Murray	Dirk Epperson
Who's Happy Now?	Oliver Hailey	Michael W. Leibert	Richard L. Hay	Jeannie Davidson	Robert Peterson
The Root of the Mandrake	Niccolo Machiavelli Robert Symonds (a)	Judd Parkin	Richard L. Hay	Merrily Ann Murray	Robert Peterson
As You Like It	William Shakespeare	Audrey Stanley	William Bloodgood	Robert Blackman	Dirk Epperson
A Midsummer Night's Dream	William Shakespeare	Dennis Bigelow	William Bloodgood	Jeannie Davidson	Dirk Epperson
Doctor Faustus	Christopher Marlowe	Jerry Turner	Richard L. Hay	Jeannie Davidson	Dirk Epperson
The Wild Duck	Henrik Ibsen Jerry Turner (t)	Jerry Turner	William Bloodgood	Jeannie Davidson	Dirk Epperson
Indulgences in the Louisville Harem	John Orlock	Michael Kevin	Michael Chapman	Toni Lovaglia	Robert Peterson

Organic Theater Company

PRODUCTION	DRAMATIST	DIRECTOR	SETS	COSTUMES	LIGHTING
Bleacher Bums	company developed	Stuart Gordon			Stuart Gordon
The Sirens of Titan	Stuart Gordon company (a)	Stuart Gordon	Jim Maronek	Maggie Bodwell	Jim Maronek
The Wonderful Ice Cream Suit	Ray Bradbury	Stuart Gordon	John Paoletti Mary Griswold	Cookie Gluck	Geoffrey Bushor
Night Feast	Stuart Gordon company	Stuart Gordon	Rick Paul	Cookie Gluck	Stuart Gordon
Campaign	Richard Harris	Stuart Gordon	Dean Taucher	Carolyn Purdy-Gordon	Stuart Gordon

continued

Theater of the Open Eye. Howard Schechter, Jean Erchman and Trueman Kelley in *The Coach with the Six Insides*. Photo: Ken Howard.

PRODUCTION	DRAMATIST	DIRECTOR	SETS	COSTUMES	LIGHTING
The Little Sister	Carolyn Purdy-Gordon (a) Stuart Gordon (a)	Stuart Gordon	Rick Paul	Kaye Nottbusch	David K. H. Elliott
Jonathan Wild	Lawrence Bommer (a)	Stuart Gordon	Rick Paul	Kaye Nottbusch	David K.H. Elliott
Warp I: My Battlefield, My Body!	Stuart Gordon Bury St. Edmund	Stuart Gordon	Rick Paul	Cookie Gluck	
Warp II: Unleashed, Unchained!					
Warp III: To Die … Alive!					

Otrabanda Company

Glass	Mark Dunau company	Roger Babb	Roger Babb John Maynard	Rachelle Bornstein	Roger Babb John Maynard
Fourth Annual River Raft Revue	company developed				
Louisiana Legong	David Dawkins company	David Dawkins company	John Maynard	Rachelle Bornstein Linda Schexnaydre	John Maynard
River Six	company developed	Graham Paul	Graham Paul	Betsy Newman Linda Schexnaydre	
On the Move	company developed	Rachelle Bornstein Suzanne Morgan		Rachelle Bornstein	John Maynard
A Christmas Carol	Roger Babb (a) Diane Brown (a)	Roger Babb	John Maynard	Rachelle Bornstein	John Maynard

PAF Playhouse

Events from the Life of Ted Snyder	Jay Broad	Jay Broad	David Chapman	Carol Oditz	Richard Harden
Give My Regards to Broadway	Dennis Turner	Anthony Stimac	Eldon Elder	Susan Hum Bick	Eldon Elder
Down at the Old Bull and Bush	various (m,l) Dolores Sutton (a) Roderick Cook (a)	Roderick Cook	Herbert Senn Helen Pond	Laura Crow	F. Mitchell Dana
The Killing of Yablonski	Richard Nelson	Peter Mark Schifter	John Arnone	William Ivey Long	Marc B. Weiss
Hancock's Last Half Hour	Heathcote Williams	Jay Broad	William Ivey Long	William Ivey Long	David F. Segal
Juno's Swans	Elaine Kerr	Michael Flanagan	Marc B. Weiss	David Toser	Marc B. Weiss
To Kill a Mockingbird	Harper Lee	Kelly Walters	David Chapman	Carol Oditz	Richard Harden
Razzle Dazzle	Kelly Walters	Kelly Walters	Jimmy Cuomo	Alison Ford	Leslie A. Deweerdt
The Marvelous Adventures of Tyl	Kelly Walters	Kelly Walters	Jimmy Cuomo	Virginia Johnson	Leslie A. Deweerdt
An Angel Comes to Babylon	Fredrich Dürrenmatt William McElwee (t)	Jay Broad	Ursula Belden	A. Christina Giannini	Victor En Yu Tan
Slugger	Shelby Buford, Jr.	Marshall W. Mason	David Potts	Judy Dearing	Dennis Parichy
I Am a Woman	Viveca Lindfors Paul Austin	Paul Austin	Suzanne Benton	Joe Eula	Beverly Emmons
Gossip	George F. Walker	Peter Mark Schifter	Philipp Jung	William Ivey Long	Larry Crimmins
Goodnight Grandpa	Walter Landau	Jay Broad	David Lloyd Gropman	William Ivey Long	David F. Segal
Loved	Olwen Wymark	Arthur Storch	David Chapman	Patricia McGourty	Judy Rasmuson
Moby Dick	Richard Harden (a)	Richard Harden	Patrick Mann	Ursula Belden	Paul Gallo
Gifts, Goats and Gilliflowers	Kelly Patton	Kelly Patton	Charles Cosler	Charles Cosler	Charles Cosler
Beauty and the Beast	Bill Thompson (a)	Bill Thompson	Jack Stewart	Zoe Brown	Toni Goldin

PRODUCTION	DRAMATIST	DIRECTOR	SETS	COSTUMES	LIGHTING
Palisades Theatre Company					
All productions are adapted or developed by the company.					
The Brave Little Tailor		Richard Hopkins (1) David Johnson (2)	David Johnson	Kim Goodrich	
The Star-Child		Richard Hopkins	Jim Carlson	Jim Carlson	
African Tales		Barbara Seifer (1) Henry Fonte (2)	David Johnson	Barbara Seifer (1) David Johnson (2)	
The Mime Show		Richard Hopkins	Fernando Fonseca	Fernando Fonseca	
The Taming of the Shrew	William Shakespeare	Richard Hopkins	David Johnson	David Johnson	
Snow White		Richard Hopkins	David Johnson	David Johnson	
Peter and the Wolf		Jeffrey Rosenstock	David Johnson	David Johnson	
Holiday Gift		Richard Hopkins	David Johnson	David Johnson	
Aesop in Revue		Jeffrey Rosenstock	David Johnson	David Johnson	
The Paper Bag Players					
Grandpa	Judith Martin (b,l) Donald Ashwander (m,l)	Judith Martin	Judith Martin	Judith Martin	George Greczylo
Hot Feet	Judith Martin (b,l) Donald Ashwander (m,l)	Judith Martin	Judith Martin	Judith Martin	George Greczylo
Everybody, Everybody	Judith Martin (b,l) Donald Ashwander (m,l)	Judith Martin	Judith Martin	Judith Martin	George Greczylo
Dandelion	Judith Martin (b,l) Donald Ashwander (m,l)	Judith Martin	Judith Martin	Judith Martin	George Greczylo
PART					
The Unbeatable Doctor Elizabeth	John Allen (b,l) Joe Raposo (m)	Jay Harnick	Hal Tiné	Carol H. Beule	
Sara Crewe, the Orphan Princess	Mary Anderson (b) Shelly Markham (m) Carrie Maher (l)	Deborah Savadge	Richard B. Williams	Carol H. Beule	
Jim Thorpe, All-American	Saul Levitt (b,l) Harrison Fisher (m)	John Henry Davis	Raymond C. Recht	Joyce Aysta	
Freedom Train	Marvin Gordon	Gloria Jones Schultz	Hal Tiné	Ben Benson	
John F. Kennedy: The Road to Camelot	Daniel Kihoy (b) Donald Siegal (m) Robert Joseph (l)	Rick Atwell	Richard B. Williams	Joyce Aysta	
Young Mark Twain	John Allen (b,l) Mary Rodgers (m,l)	Jay Harnick	Jonathan Lawson	Joel Vig	
Aesop and Other Fables	Marshall Izen				
Dinosaurs, Puppets and Picasso	Marshall Izen				
Young Tom Edison and the Magic Why	Robert K. Adams (b) Martin Kalmanoff (m,l)	William Koch	Richard B. Williams	Joyce Aysta	
Daniel Boone!	Ross Yockey (b,l) Gary William Friedman (m)	John Henry Davis	Christopher Thomas	Debra Stein	
Young Ben Franklin	Allan Cruickshank (b) Albert Hague (m) Ray Errol Fox (l)	J. T. Hoyt	Jean Vickery	Debra Stein	

PRODUCTION	DRAMATIST	DIRECTOR	SETS	COSTUMES	LIGHTING
Performance Community					
A Distinctive Knock	Colin Stinton	Thomas M. Doman	Jon Gantt	Teri Brown	Thomas Herman
Touch	Gareth Mann	Thomas M. Doman	Jon Gantt	Teri Brown	Thomas Herman
Homer	Frank Fetters	Thomas M. Doman	Jon Gantt	Teri Brown	Thomas Herman
Young Bucks	John Kunik	Byron Schaffer, Jr.	Byron Schaffer, Jr.	Teri Brown	Mary Fran Loftus
Top Secret	Ken McLean	Betsy Tucker	Jon Gantt	Cathy Norgren	Jon Gantt
Tom Swift and His ...	company developed	Robert Fiddler (1) George H. Gorham (2)			
Vacuum Pact	company developed	Robert Fiddler			
Bear	Colin Stinton Alaric (Rokko) Jans (m)	Byron Schaffer, Jr.	Jon Gantt	Kevin Seligman	Jon Gantt
The Grab	Maria Katzenbach	Ruth E. Higgins	Jon Gantt	Teri Brown	Jon Gantt
Madmen	Steven Stosny	Byron Schaffer, Jr.	Jon Gantt		Jon Gantt
Exit 30	John Kunik	Byron Schaffer, Jr.	Jon Gantt		Jon Gantt
The Performance Group					
Oedipus	Seneca Ted Hughes (a)	Richard Schechner	Jim Clayburgh	Theodora Skipitares	Jim Clayburgh
Cops	Terry Curtis Fox	Richard Schechner	Jim Clayburgh	Sigrid Insull	Jim Clayburgh
Nayatt School	Elizabeth LeCompte Spalding Gray company	Elizabeth LeCompte	Elizabeth LeCompte Bruce Porter		Jim Clayburgh
Sakonnet Point, Rumstick Road and *Nayatt School*	Elizabeth LeCompte Spalding Gray company	Elizabeth LeCompte	Elizabeth LeCompte Jim Clayburgh Bruce Porter		Elizabeth LeCompte Jim Clayburgh
Sex and Death to the Age 14	Spalding Gray				
Periwinkle Productions					
Hooray for Me!	Scott Laughead (b) Grenaldo Frazier (m,l)	Elaine Kanas Sunna Rasch	Jay Sardonia	Judy Perry	Scott Laughead
The Dream Show	Scott Laughead	Scott Laughead (1) Larry Becker (2)	Earl Wertheim Beth Kuhn	Mary Alice Orito	Earl Wertheim
The Magic Word	Sunna Rasch	Scott Laughead	Earl Wertheim	Susan Scherer	Scott Laughead
The Mad Poet Strikes— Again!	Sunna Rasch	Dennis McGovern Sunna Rasch	Sunna Rasch	Judy Perry	Scott Laughead
Hey, Hi, Ho for Pooh!	Dennis McGovern	Dennis McGovern	Gustave Kaitz	Ron Greenberg	Scott Laughead
Mask, Mime and Magic	Jack Hill	Jack Hill	Jack Hill	Jack Hill	Jack Hill
The New Magic Word	Sunna Rasch	Scott Laughead	Brian Hayes	Susan Scherer	Scott Laughead
As Eye See It	Jack Hill	Jack Hill	Jack Hill	Jack Hill	Jack Hill
Philadelphia Drama Guild					
The Show-Off	George Kelly	Michael Montel	John Kasarda	Kristina Watson	Spencer Mosse
Travesties	Tom Stoppard	Douglas Seale	John Kasarda	David Murin	Spencer Mosse
Saint Joan	George Bernard Shaw	Douglas Seale	John Kasarda	Kristina Watson	Spencer Mosse
Hobson's Choice	Harold Brighouse	Brian Murray	John Kasarda	David Murin	Spencer Mosse
Uncle Vanya	Anton Chekhov William Stancil (t)	Douglas Seale	John Kasarda	David Murin	Spencer Mosse
The Au Pair Man	Hugh Leonard	Douglas Seale	John Kasarda	David Murin	Spencer Mosse

PRODUCTION	DRAMATIST	DIRECTOR	SETS	COSTUMES	LIGHTING
Arms and the Man	George Bernard Shaw	Tony van Bridge	John Kasarda	David Murin	Spencer Mosse
Private Lives	Noel Coward	Douglas Seale	John Kasarda	David Murin	Spencer Mosse
The Blood Knot	Athol Fugard	Thomas Bullard	John Kasarda	Liz Bass	Spencer Mosse
The Night of the Iguana	Tennessee Williams	Douglas Seale	John Kasarda	Kristina Watson	Spencer Mosse

Phoenix Theatre

PRODUCTION	DRAMATIST	DIRECTOR	SETS	COSTUMES	LIGHTING
Hot Grog	Jim Wann (b,m,1) Bland Simpson (m,1)	Edward Berkeley	James Tilton	Hilary Rosenfeld	James Tilton
Uncommon Women and Others	Wendy Wasserstein	Seven Robman	James Tilton	Jennifer von Mayrhauser	James Tilton
One Crack Out	David French	Daniel Freudenberger	James Tilton	Julie Weiss	Paul H. Everett
The Elusive Angel	Jack Gilhooley	Steven Robman	James Tilton	Jennifer von Mayrhauser	James Tilton
City Sugar	Sephen Poliakoff	Daniel Freudenberger	James Tilon	Julie Weiss	James Tilton
Getting Out	Marsha Norman	Jon Jory	James Tilton	Kurt Wilhelm	James Tilton
Later	Corinne Jacker	Daniel Freudenberger	James Tilton	Julie Weiss	James Tilton
Says I, Says He	Ron Hutchinson	Steven Robman	David Jenkins	Dona Granata	Spencer Mosse
Big and Little	Botho Strauss	Daniel Freudenerger	James Tilton	Julie Weiss	James Tilton
Chinchilla	Robert David MacDonald	Philip Prowse	Philip Prowse	Philip Prowse	Philip Prowse

Pittsburgh Public Theater

PRODUCTION	DRAMATIST	DIRECTOR	SETS	COSTUMES	LIGHTING
Father's Day	Oliver Hailey	Michael Flanagan	Virginia Dancy Elmon Webb	David Toser	Bennett Averyt
You Never Can Tell	George Bernard Shaw	Jack Going	Virginia Dancy Elmon Webb	David Toser	Bennet Averyt
Balyasnikov	Aleksei Arbuzov Ben Shaktman (a)	Ben Shaktman	Henry Heymann	Henry Heymann	Bennet Averyt
Slow Dance on the Killing Ground	William Hanley	Terry Schreiber	Karl Eigsti	David Toser	Bennett Averyt
Medal of Honor Rag	Tom Cole	Terry Schreiber	Karl Eigsti	David Toser	Bennett Averyt
The Blood Knot	Athol Fugard	Ben Shaktman	Bruce Miller Ben Shaktman	Laura Crow	Bennett Averyt
Of Mice and Men	John Steinbeck	Ben Shaktman	John Jensen	Laura Crow	Bennett Averyt
The Importance of Being Earnest	Oscar Wilde	Ben Shaktman	Cletus Anderson	David Toser	Bennett Averyt
Vanities	Jack Heifner	Terry Schreiber	John Jensen	David Toser	Bennett Averyt
Ashes	David Rudkin	Terry schreiber	John Jensen	David Toser	Bennett Averyt
For Colored Girls who have Considered Suicide/ When The Rainbow is Enuf	Ntozake Shange	Regge Life	Hal Tine	David Toser	Bennett Averyt

The Play Group

PRODUCTION	DRAMATIST	DIRECTOR	SETS	COSTUMES	LIGHTING
Hello!	David McIntosh	Thomas P. Cooke		LeAnn Davis	Michael Baish
Tell Me a Story	company developed				
A Doll's House	Henrik Ibsen	Katharine Pearson			Michael Baish
Romeo and Juliet	William Shakespeare	Chris Brown	Michael Baish		Michael Baish
Lacie	David McIntosh	Katharine Pearson	Jim Leitnaker		Margo Solod
The Piper Man	David McIntosh (b,l) Mac Pirkle (m,l)	Thomas P. Cooke	Thomas P. Cooke	David Chappell Thomas P. Cooke	Jim Houstel
The Lion in Winter	James Goldman	Chris Brown			Michael Baish
Myths	company developed	Katharine Pearson			

continued

PRODUCTION	DRAMATIST	DIRECTOR	SETS	COSTUMES	LIGHTING
Players State Theatre					
Cyrano de Bergerac	Edmond Rostand Brian Hooker (t)	John Ulmer	John Schleffler	Joy A. Breckenridge	James Riley
Violano Virtuoso	Betty Suyker	John Ulmer	John Scheffler	Joy A. Breckenridge	Michael Martin
Othello	William Shakespeare	Michael Montel	James Riley	Joy A. Breckenridge	Kenneth N. Kurtz
Streamers	David Rabe	Michael Montel	Lyle Baskin	Maria Marrero	Lyle Baskin
Absurd Person Singular	Alan Ayckbourn	Michael Montel	Charles Herbst	Joy A. Breckenridge	Charles Herbst
The Drunkard	Bro Herrod (b,l) Barry Manilow (m)	Judith Haskell	Kenneth N. Kurtz	Joy A. Breckenridge	Jeff L. Moore
As You Like It	William Shakespeare	Michael Montel	Kenneth N. Kurtz	Joy A. Breckenridge	Kenneth N. Kurtz
The Night of the Iguana	Tennessee Williams	George Keathley	James Riley	Joy A. Breckenridge	James Riley
A Flea in Her Ear	Georges Feydeau	Sue Lawless	Charles Herbst	Maria Marrero	Michael Gebhardt
The Shadow Box	Michael Cristofer	Joseph Adler	Lyle Baskin	Maria Marrero	Michael Martin
The Member of the Wedding	Carson McCullers	Nafe Katter	Lyle Baskin	Joy A. Breckenridge	Richard Bergman
Irma la Douce	Alexandre Breffort (b,l) David Heneker (a) Julian More (a) Monty Norman (a) Marguerite Monnot (m)	Michael Montel	Kenneth N. Kurtz	Joy A. Breckenridge	Kenneth N. Kurtz David Goodman
Playhouse on the Square					
Candida	Shaw	John Crawford Irvine	Jackie Nichols	Kris Hanley	Stephen Forsyth
The School for Wives	Moliere	John Crawford Irvine	Jackie Nichols	Kris Hanley	Stephen Forsyth
Of Mice and Men	John Steinbeck	Gene Wilkins	Jackie Nichols	Kris Hanley	Stephen Forsyth
Fallen Angels	Noel Coward	Gene Wilkins	Jackie Nichols	Kris Hanley	Stephen Forsyth
One Flew over the Cuckoo's Nest	Dale Wasserman	Phillip Price	Reagan Cook	Susan Noel	Stephen Forsyth
Angel Street	Patrick Hamilton	Gary Gibber	Gary Gibber		Stephen Forsyth
Man of La Mancha	Dale Wasserman (b) Mitch Leigh (m) Joe Darion (l)	Jamie Brown	J. Robin Modereger		J. Robin Modereger
Twelfth Night	Shakespeare	Lester Malizia	Lester Malizia	Alan Armstrong	Stephen Forsyth
Summer and Smoke	Tennessee Williams	Ron Lagomarsino	Henry Swanson	Ginger Travis	Stephen Forsyth
The Waltz of the Toreadors	Jean Anouilh	Thomas Winberry	Thomas Winberry		Stephen Forsyth
Marat/Sade	Peter Weiss	Lester Malizia	J. Robin Modereger		Stephen Forsyth
Southern Comfort	Ronnie B. Baker (m,l)	Ron Lagomarsino	Greg Peeples	Ron Lagomarsino	Stephen Forsyth
The King Is a Fink	Keith Kennedy & George Caldwell (b,m,l)	Gary Gibber	Kathee O'Brien	Douglas Koertge	Gary Fassler
An Evening of Soul	Erma L. Clanton (c)	Erma L. Clanton	Erma L. Clanton	Barbara Cole	Bob Wilson
Diamond Studs	Jim Wann (b) Bland Simpson & J. Wann (m,l)	Lester Malizia	J. Robin Modereger	Rebecca Senske	Stephen Forsyth
Much Ado About Nothing	Shakespeare	Lester Malizia	J. Robin Modereger	Rebecca Senske	Stephen Forsyth
Light Up the Sky	Moss Hart	Phillip Price	Joe Ragey	Rebecca Senske	Stephen Forsyth
Another Part of the Forest	Lillian Hellman	Phillip Price	Joe Ragey	Rebecca Senske	Stephen Forsyth
Oliver!	Lionel Bart (b,m,l)	Lester Malizia	J. Robin Modereger	Rebecca Senske	Stephen Forsyth
The Oldest Living Graduate	Preston Jones	Lester Malizia	Amie Devereaux	Rebecca Senske	Stephen Forsyth

The Cricket Theatre. *The Club.*
Photo: Mike Paul.

PRODUCTION	DRAMATIST	DIRECTOR	SETS	COSTUMES	LIGHTING
Dames at Sea	George Haimsohn & Robin Miller (b,l) Jim Wise (m)	Lester Malizia	J. Robin Modereger	Rebecca Senske	David Crist
The Rocky Horror Show	Richard O'Brien (b,m,l)	Lester Malizia	J. Robin Modereger	Rebecca Senske	Stephen Foster

Playmakers Repertory Company

A Streetcar Named Desire	Tennessee Williams	Bill Ludel	Larry von Werssowetz	Nancy J. Woodfield	Larry von Werssowetz
Equus	Peter Shaffer	Tom Haas	David M. Glenn	David Hearn	David M. Glenn
Play It Again, Sam	Woody Allen	Bill Peters	David J. Lockner	David O. Rogers	David J. Lockner
Hamlet	William Shakespeare	Tom Haas	Steven Rubin	Steven Rubin	Randall J. Bailey
Uncommon Women and Others	Wendy Wasserstein	Mary Gallagher	Larry von Werssowetz	Nancy J. Woodfield	Larry von Werssowetz
Ah, Wilderness!	Eugene O'Neill	Tom Haas	David M. Glenn	Bobbi Owen	David M. Glenn
Mr. Roberts	Thomas Heggen Joshua Logan	Tom Rezzuto	David J. Lockner	Faye Listerman	David J. Lockner
Dracula: The Vampire King	Tom Haas (a)	Tom Haas	David M. Glenn	Bobbi Owen	David M. Glenn
Threads	Jonathan Bolt	Amy Saltz	Patricia Woodbridge	Bobbi Owen	Howell Binkley
Cold Storage	Ronald Ribman	Errol Selsby	Linwood Taylor	Bobbi Owen	Linwood Taylor
Long Day's Journey into Night	Eugene O'Neill	Tom Haas	David M. Glenn	Bobbi Owen	David M. Glenn
Macbeth	William Shakespeare	Tom Haas	Judie Juracek	Judie Juracek	Randall J. Bailey
You Can't Take It with You	George S. Kaufman Moss Hart	Bill Peters	David M. Glenn Bobbi Owen	David M. Glenn Bobbi Owen	David M. Glenn Bobbi Owen

Playwrights Horizons

Anything Goes	Guy Bolton (b) P. G. Wodehouse (b) Howard Lindsay (b) Russel Crouse (b) Cole Porter (m,l)	Larry Carpenter	Christopher Thomas	Kenneth M. Yount	Frances Aronson
Gogol	Ken Jenkin	David Schweizer	Charles Stone	Khorshid Panthaky	Marty Kapell
Angel City	Sam Shepard	Marty Kapell	Charles Stone	Khorshid Panthaky	Marty Kapell
Back County Crimes	Lanie Robertson	Howard DeFelice	Marty Kapell	Khorshid Panthaky	Marty Kapell
A Christmas Carol	Christopher Cox (a)	Christopher Cox	Richard B. Williams	A. Christina Giannini	Pat Stern
Two Small Bodies	Neal Bell	Thomas Babe	Richard Kerry	William Ivey Long	James Chaleff
The Member of the Wedding	Carson McCullers	Philip Himberg	Christopher Thomas	William D. Anderson	Mimi Maxmen
Three Sons	Richard Lortz	Rob O'Rourke	Jimmy Cuomo	Susan Denison	Marilyn Rennagel
Dial M for Murder	Frederick Knott	Robert Moss	Harry Lines	Tricia Blackburn	Todd Lichtenstein
Shay	Anne Commire	Elinor Renfield	Jane Thurn	Michael J. Cesario	Pat Stern
A Midsummer Night's Dream	William Shakespeare	Robert Moss	Richard W. Kerry	Ronald A. Castleman	Toni Goldin
Hooters	Ted Tally	Gary Pearle	Charles McCarry	Elizabeth P. Palmer	Frances Aronson
Awake and Sing!	Clifford Odets	Alfred Gingold	Carl A. Baldasso	Mary Brownlow	Marilyn Rennagel
Jungle Coup	Richard Nelson	Andre Ernotte	Heidi Landesman	William Ivey Long	Paul Gallo
The Prisoner of Second Avenue	Neil Simon	Susan Schulman	D.J. Markley	Patricia Eiben	Ruth Roberts
Oh, What a Lovely War!	Joan Greenwood (a,m,l) Theatre Workshop (a,m,l)	Philip Himberg	Heidi Landesman	A. Christina Giannini	Paul Gallo

continued

American Conservatory Theatre.
The Visit. Photo: William Ganslen.

PRODUCTION	DRAMATIST	DIRECTOR	SETS	COSTUMES	LIGHTING
Say Goodnight, Gracie	Ralph Pape	Austin Pendleton	Douglas E. Ball	Patricia E. Weigleb	Cheryl Thacker
The Eccentricities of a Nightingale	Tennessee Williams	Betsy Shevey	Bob Phillips	Elizabeth P. Palmer	Candice Dunn
Living at Home	Anthony Giardina	Thomas Gruenewald	James Leonard Joy	Kenneth M. Yount	David K. H. Elliott
Vienna Notes	Richard Nelson	Andre Ernotte	Heidi Landesman	William Ivey Long	Paul Gallo
Breaking and Entering	Neal Bell	Barnet Kellman	Bil Mikulewicz	Robert Wojewodski	Annie Wrightson
In Trousers	William Finn (m,l)	William Finn	Donato Moreno	Robert Wojewodski	Annie Wrightson
Hedda Gabler	Henrik Ibsen John Osborne (t)	Philip Himberg	Richard B. Williams	Andrew Marlay	Pat Stern
Table Settings	James Lapine	James Lapine	Richard Goodwin	Robert Wojewodski	Annie Wrightson
Ladyhouse Blues	Kevin O'Morrison	Tony Giordano	Hugh Landwehr	David Murin	Spencer Mosse
The Songs of Jonathan Tunick	Jonathan Tunick (m) various (l)				
The Terrorists	Dallas Murphy, Jr.	Gary Pearle	Judi Juracek	Kenneth M. Yount	Frances Aronson
Don't Tell Me Everything and Other Musical Arrangements	Peter Larson (m) John Lewis (m) Josh Rubins (m,l)	Caymichael Patton	Barry Robison		Annie Wrightson
Private Lives	Noel Coward	Garland Wright	John Arnone	Lindsay W. Davis	Frances Aronson
Sweet Main Street	Carol Hall, et al. (m,l) Shirley Kaplan (a)	Shirley Kaplan	Henry Millman	Genii Charnin	Milton Duke
The Show-Off	George Kelly	Bill Ludel	Bil Mikulewicz	Elizabeth P. Palmer	Annie Wrightson

The Playwrights' Lab

Small Affections	Kirk Ristau	Scott Rubsam	Jim Rust		
Hippodrome Murder	Cynthia Hanson	Emily Mann	Jim Rust		
Edges	Frank Pike David Erickson	J. L. McLure	Jim Rust		
Dromenon	Henry Manganiello	Bob Greep	Jim Rust		
Standing on My Knees	John Olive	Michael Robertson	Jim Rust		

Portland Stage Company

Who's Afraid of Virginia Woolf?	Edward Albee	Susan Dunlop	Matthew Freedman	Susan Dunlop	Charles Towers
Candida	George Bernard Shaw	Frank Goodman	Matthew Freedman	Jeffrey Ullman	Matthew Freedman
The School for Wives	Moliere Richard Wilbur (t)	Charles Towers	Jack Doepp	Jeffrey Ullman	Jack Doepp
Waiting for Godot	Samuel Beckett	Jacqueline Weiss	Matthew Freedman	Jacqueline Weiss	Matthew Freedman
The Play's the Thing	Ferenc Molnar P.G. Wodehouse (a)	Frank Goodman	David Dorwart	Jeffrey Ullman	Matthew Freedman
Jesse and the Bandit Queen	David Freeman	Susan Dunlop	Matthew Freedman	Susan Dunlop	Charles Towers
On the Harmfulness of Tobacco, Swan Song and The Boor	Anton Chekhov	Frank Goodman	Matthew Freedman	Susan Dunlop	Matthew Freedman
The Mandrake	Niccolo Machiavelli	Charles Towers	Sparks Mellon	Mikhail Druhan	Charles Towers
The Runner Stumbles	Milan Stitt	Susan Dunlop	Matthew Freedman	Susan Dunlop	Matthew Freedman
The Importance of Being Earnest	Oscar Wilde	Patricia Riggin	Sparks Mellon	Polly Smith	Allen Saless
Cat on a Hot Tin Roof	Tennessee Williams	Charles Towers	Jack Doepp	Linda Chambers Lee	Charles Towers
Crime on Goat Island	Ugo Betti	Susan Dunlop	Matthew Freedman	Susan Dunlop	Allen Saless

PRODUCTION	DRAMATIST	DIRECTOR	SETS	COSTUMES	LIGHTING
The Stronger	August Strindberg	Susan Dunlop	Matthew Freedman	Susan Dunlop	Allen Saless
Play Strindberg	Friedrich Dürrenmatt	Susan Dunlop	Matthew Freedman	Susan Dunlop	Allen Saless
Winners (from Lovers)	Brian Friel	Susan Dunlop	Matthew Freedman	Susan Dunlop	Allen Saless

The Proposition Workshop

PRODUCTION	DRAMATIST	DIRECTOR	SETS	COSTUMES	LIGHTING
The Proposition	Allan Albert	Allan Albert	David Lloyd Gropman (1) Philipp Jung (2)		Dick Williams
The Proposition Circus	Allan Albert	Allan Albert		Hilary M. Rosenfeld (1) Michael Sharp (2)	
A Fable	Jean-Claude van Itallie	Allan Albert	Karen R. Schulz	Ann Halliday Wallace	Dick Williams
Four Years After the Revolution	Richard Peaslee (m,l)	Allan Albert	Bill Groom	Ann Halliday Wallace (1) Shepard Goldman (2)	Dick Williams
The Casino	various (m,l) Allan Albert (a)	Allan Albert	Cletus Johnson	Cletus Johnson	Dick Williams
Soap	various (m,l) Allan Albert (a)	Allan Albert	Philip & Nancy Bailey	Eloise Lowry	Dick Williams
Corral	various (m,l) Allan Albert (a)	Allan Albert	Woods Mackintosh	Hilary M. Rosenfeld	Dick Williams
Night Riders	Allan Albert (b) John Lewis (m) Josh Rubins (l)	Allan Albert	Bill Groom	Ann Halliday Wallace	Stephen Pollock
Vagabond Stars	Nahma Sandrow (b) Allan Albert (b) Raphael Crystal (m) Alan Poul (l)	Allan Albert	Bill Groom	Carol Oditz	Dick Williams
The Whale Show	various (m,l) Allan Albert (a)	Allan Albert	David Lloyd Gropman Michael Sharp	Hilary M. Rosenfeld	Dick Williams

Provisional Theatre

All productions are company developed, directed and designed.
America Piece
Voice of the People, Parts I
  and II
Songs and Speeches of
  the People
Inching Through the
  Everglades, or Pie in the
  Sky and Something on
  Your Shoe

Puerto Rican Traveling Theatre Company

PRODUCTION	DRAMATIST	DIRECTOR	SETS	COSTUMES	LIGHTING
The FM Safe	Jaime Carrero	Alba Oms	Rob Strohmeier	Maria Ferreira Contessa	Larry Johnson
Un Jíbaro	Ramón Méndez Quinones	Francisco Prado	Julio Biaggi	Maria Ferreira Contessa	Larry Johnson
La Compañia	Luis Rechani Agrait	Francisco Prado	Julio Biaggi	Maria Ferreira Contessa	Larry Johnson
Simpson Street	Edward Gallardo Tony Diaz (t) Miriam Colón Edgar (t)	Miriam Colón Edgar	Carl A. Baldasso	Maria Ferreira Contessa	Larry Johnson
El Macho	Joseph Lizardi Tony Diaz (t)	Harold Scott	Carl A. Baldasso	Maria Ferreira Contessa	Larry Johnson

PRODUCTION	DRAMATIST	DIRECTOR	SETS	COSTUMES	LIGHTING
The Puppet Workshop					
The Landing of the Schlunk	company developed	Marc W. Kohler	Marc W. Kohler Kevin Lima	Marc W. Kohler Kevin Lima	
Judy's Dream	company developed	Marc W. Kohler	Marc W. Kohler Kevin Lima Rance Price	Kevin Lima Lynne Blake	
The Story of Esther— A Purim Show	company developed	Marc W. Kohler	Marc W. Kohler Kevin Lima	Kevin Lima Lynne Blake	
A Midsummer Night's Dream	William Shakespeare	Marc W. Kohler	Marc W. Kohler Kevin Lima	Kevin Lima Jackie Karch	
A Brighter Light	company developed	Marc W. Kohler	Marc W. Kohler Kevin Lima Rance Price	Marc W. Kohler Kevin Lima	
Repertorio Español					
Te Juro Juana que Tengo Ganas	Emilio Carballido	Rene Buch	Robert Weber Federico	Maria Ferreira Contessa	Robert Weber Federico
Bodas de Sangre	Federico Garcia Lorca	Rene Buch	Robert Weber Federico	Maria Ferreira Contessa	Robert Weber Federico
Los Japoneses No Esperan	Ricardo Talesnik	Rene Buch	Robert Weber Federico	Maria Ferreira Contessa	Robert Weber Federico
Jardín de Otoño	Diana Raznovich	Delfor Peralta	Robert Weber Federico	Maria Ferreira Contessa	Robert Weber Federico
La Celestina	Fernando de Rojas	Rene Buch	Robert Weber Federico	Robert Weber Federico	Robert Weber Federico
La Dama Duende	Calderon de la Barca	Rene Buch	Robert Weber Federico	Robert Weber Federico	Robert Weber Federico
El Censo	Emilio Carballido	Delfor Peralta	Robert Weber Federico	Maria Ferreira Contessa	Robert Weber Federico
Cien Veces No Debo	Ricardo Talesnik	Brau Villar	Robert Weber Federico	Maria Ferreira Contessa	Robert Weber Federico
Los Soles Truncos	Rene Marques	Rene Buch	Robert Weber Federico	Maria Ferreira Contessa	Robert Weber Federico
La Fiaca	Ricardo Talesnik	Rene Buch	Robert Weber Federico	Maria Ferreira Contessa	Robert Weber Federico
Romeo y Julieta	William Shakespeare Pablo Neruda (t)	Rene Buch	Robert Weber Federico	Robert Weber Federico	Robert Weber Federico
La Revolucìon	Isaac Chocron	Rene Buch	Robert Weber Federico	Maria Ferreira Contessa	Robert Weber Federico
La Moza de Ayacucho	Francisco Cuevas-Cancino	Rene Buch		Maria Ferreira Contessa	Robert Weber Federico
Un Hombre Sincero: Jose Marti	Jose Marti Rene Buch (a)	Rene Buch			Robert Weber Federico
Richard Morse Mime Theatre					
The Arts and Leisure Section of The New York Times	Richard Morse	Richard Morse		Kristin Sakai	Gabriel Barre
Gifts!	Richard Morse	Richard Morse		Rasa Lisauskas Allan	Gabriel Barre
Tintinnabula	Richard Morse	Richard Morse		Rasa Lisauskas Allan	Gary Seltzer (1) Jim Shelly (2)
Pranks	Rasa Lisauskas Allan	Rasa Lisauskas Allan		Rasa Lisauskas Allan	Gabriel Barre
Appeal of the Big Apple	Richard Morse	Richard Morse		Amelia Peck	Jim Shelly
The Play of Herod	Noah Greenberg William Smolden	Richard Morse	Carl Baldasso	Patricia Adshead	Jim Shelly
What the Devil!	Richard Morse (a)	Richard Morse	Carl Baldasso	Patricia Adshead	Jim Shelly
Inside Up	Rasa Lisauskas Allan	Rasa Lisauskas Allan		Celia Hughes	Jim Shelly
A Chip Off the Old Munk	Rasa Lisauskas Allan	Rasa Lisauskas Allan		Rasa Lisauskas Allan	Jim Shelly

Alaska Repertory Theatre. Eric Uhler, Joe Meek, Miller Lide and James Secrest in *Terra Nova*. Photo: Jim Lavrakas.

PRODUCTION	DRAMATIST	DIRECTOR	SETS	COSTUMES	LIGHTING
The Ridiculous Theatrical Company					
Der Ring Gott Farblonjet	Charles Ludlam	Charles Ludlam	Charles Ludlam	Charles Ludlam	Richard Currie
The Ventriloquist's Wife	Charles Ludlam	Charles Ludlam	Charles Ludlam	Charles Ludlam	
Camille	Charles Ludlam	Charles Ludlam	Bob-Jack Callejo	Mary Brecht	Richard Currie
Stage Blood	Charles Ludlam	Charles Ludlam	Bob-Jack Callejo	Arthur Brady	Richard Currie
Bluebeard	Charles Ludlam	Charles Ludlam	Bob-Jack Callejo	Mary Brecht	Richard Currie
Anti-Galaxy Nebulae	Charles Ludlam	Charles Ludlam			
Corn	Charles Ludlam	Charles Ludlam	Edouardo Franceschi	Company	Richard Currie
Utopia Incorporated	Charles Ludlam	Charles Ludlam	K.K.	K.K.	Charles Ludlam
					Lawrence Eichler
Camille	Charles Ludlam	Charles Ludlam	Bob-Jack Callejo	Mary Brecht	Richard Currie
The Enchanted Pig	Charles Ludlam	Charles Ludlam	Bob-Jack Callejo	Gabrial Berry	Lawrence Eichler
St. Nicholas Theater Company					
Ashes	David Rudkin	Steven Schachter	David Emmons	Stephen English	James Highland
The Woods	David Mamet	David Mamet	Michael Merritt	Stephen English	Robert Christen
You Can't Take It with You	George S. Kaufman Moss Hart	Gerald Gutierrez	David Emmons	Julie Nagel	James Highland
Uncommon Women and Others	Wendy Wasserstein	Mike Nussbaum	Maher Ahmad	Christa Scholtz	Rebecca Binks
Barnaby Sweet	Glenn Alenn Smith	Steven Schachter	Christopher Harris	Jessica Hahn	Tom Herman
The Nuclear Family	Mark Frost	Emily Mann	Barry Robison	Barry Robison	Tom Herman
Spider	Bobby Joyce Smith				
I'd Rather Be It	company developed	Audrey Neenan			
The Slow Hours	Bruce Burgun	Jim Wise	William Arnold	Sandy Kabins	Dan Kobayashi
Marty	Paddy Chayefsky	Steven Schachter	Raynette Smith	Sherry Ravitz	Raynette Smith
Great Solo Town	Thomas Babe	William Esper	William Arnold	Rosalyn Kreiner	Edward Schuenemann
The Revenge of the Space Pandas	David Mamet	Steven Schachter	David Emmons	Julie Nagel	Thomas Herman
The Adventures of Captain Marbles and His Acting Squad, Episodes III and IV	William H. Macy David Kovacs	Catherine M. Goedert	David Emmons	Nanalee Raphael	Thomas Herman
The 5th of July	Lanford Wilson	Steven Schachter	Barry Robison	Barry Robison	Thomas Herman
Little Eyolf	Henrik Ibsen	Steven Schachter	David Emmons	Julie Nagel	Geoffrey Bushor
All Honorable Men	Michael J. Chepiga	Dennis Scott	Peter Winter	Jessica Hahn	Gary Heitz
Funeral March for a One-Man Band	Ron Whyte (b) Mel Marvin (m) Robert Satuloff (l)	Amy Saltz	David Emmons	Thomas McKinley	Michael Philippi
The Curse of an Aching Heart	William Alfred	Gerald Gutierrez	John Lee Beatty	Julie Nagel	Rita Pietraszek
Understanding Czrbyk	Richard Harris	Jim Wise	Michael Philippi	Jerry Kelly	Michael Philippi
The Diary of Anne Frank	Frances Goodrich Albert Hackett	Bruce Burgun	James Boley	Wendy Woodside	Jerry Kelly
A Dark Night of the Soul	Robert Eisele	Cynthia Sherman	Leah Slavensky-Marvel	Rosalyn Kriener	Dan Kobayashi
The Memoirs of Charlie Pops	Joseph Hart	Rob Maxey	Edward Schuenemann	D.R. Edwards	J. Douglas Flahaven
Fancy's Touch	Bruce Burgun	Jim Wise	Michael Tomko	D.R. Edwards	Kathleen M. Daly
The Miracle Worker	William Gibson	Catherine M. Goedert	David Emmons	Jessica Hahn	Kathleen M. Daly

continued

Actors Theatre of St. Paul. Jim
Cada, Steven Pringle, Hugh
Sheppard, David M. Kwiat and
Mari Rovang in *Custer* or
Whoever Heard of Fred Benteen?
Photo: Richie Christy.

PRODUCTION	DRAMATIST	DIRECTOR	SETS	COSTUMES	LIGHTING
The Adventures of Captain Marbles and His Acting Squad, Episode V	William H. Macy	Catherine M. Goedert	David Emmons	Nanalee Raphael	Dan Kobayashi

Seattle Repertory Theatre

The Royal Family	George S. Kaufman Edna Ferber	Daniel Sullivan	Robert Dahlstrom	Lewis D. Rampino	Joe Pacitti
The Dream Watcher	Barbara Wersba	Brian Murray	Ed Wittstein	Lewis D. Pampino	Patricia Collins
The National Health	Peter Nichols	Duncan Ross	Eldon Elder	Lewis D. Rampino	Richard Devin
Uncle Vanya	Anton Chekhov David Magarshack (t)	Duncan Ross	Robert Dahlstrom	Lewis D. Rampino	Joe Pacitti
Much Ado About Nothing	William Shakespeare	Duncan Ross (1) Robert Dahlstrom (2)	Pete Davis	Lewis D. Rampino	Richard Devin
13 Rue de l'Amour	Georges Feydeau Mawby Green (a) Ed Feilbert (a)	Daniel Sullivan	Robert Blackman	Lewis D. Rampino	Richard Devin
Discovering Tutankhamun	Phil Shallat	Lori Larsen			
A Penny for a Song	John Whiting	Ducan Ross	Robert Dahlstrom	Lewis D. Rampino	F. Mitchell Dana
The Master Builder	Henrik Ibsen Sam Engelstad (t) Jane Alexander (t)	Vivian Matalon	Eldon Elder	Elizabeth Covey	Richard Devin
Side by Side by Sondheim	Stephen Sondheim et al. (m,l) Ned Sherrin (a)	Judith Haskell	Robert Dahlstrom	Lewis D. Rampino	Robert Scales
The Glass Menagerie	Tennessee Williams	Daniel Sullivan	Robert Blackman	Elizabth Covey	Richard Devin
Catsplay	Istvan Orkeny Clara Gyorgyey (t)	Duncan Ross	Robert Dahlstrom	Lewis D. Rampino	Jo Mayer
Fallen Angels	Noel Coward	William Glover	James Leonard Joy	Lewis D. Rampino	F. Mitchell Dana
The Energy Show	company developed	John Kauffman	Rachel Keebler	Carol Hanford	

Soho Repertory Theatre

The Killing of Sister George	Frank Marcus	Marlene Swartz	Marlene Swartz	Jeff Novak	Jerry Engelbach
The Real Inspector Hound	Tom Stoppard	Timothy Brennan	Timothy Brennan Paul Moser	Timothy Brennan	Paul Moser
Misalliance	George Bernard Shaw	Trueman Kelley	Mark Haack	Deborah Shaw	Mark Haack
The Miser	Moliere Moshe Yassur (a)	Moshe Yassur	Moshe Yassur Sue Cox	Sue Cox Kirstine Messick	Jerry Englebach
Peer Gynt	Henrik Ibsen Carol Corwen (a)	Carol Corwen	Trueman Kelley	Jeff Novak	Jerry Englebach
Mister T	Michael Zettler	Stephen Zuckerman	Trueman Kelley	Margo La Zaro	Gary Seltzer
The Play's the Thing	Ferenc Molnar P.G. Wodehouse (a)	Jack H. Cunningham	Rebecca Cunningham	Rebecca Cunningham	Howard Becknell
Abelard and Heloise	Ronald Duncan	Trueman Kelley	Trueman Kelley	Sue Cox	Carol Corwen
The Four Little Girls	Pablo Picasso Roland Penrose (t)	Richard Gershman	Rosaria Sinisi	Donato Moreno	D. Schweppe
Philadelphia, Here I Come!	Brian Friel	Ron Daley	Ron Daley	Sue Cox	Preston Yarber
The Magistrate	Arthur Wing Pinero	James Milton	Oakley Hall III	Margo La Zaro	Linnea Tillet Barbara Tulliver

PRODUCTION	DRAMATIST	DIRECTOR	SETS	COSTUMES	LIGHTING
Soho Theatre of the Air	Carol Corwen	Carol Corwen	Mark Haack	Sue Cox	Carol Corwen
Better Dead	Georges Feydeau	Jude Schanzer	Nanette Reynolds	Sue Cox	Carol Corwen
	Jude Schanzer (t)				
	Michael Wells (t)				
The Chairs	Eugene Ionesco	Jon Fraser	Nanette Reynolds	Mary Mola	Carol Corwen
	Donald M. Allen (t)				
Poe in Person	Marilyn Vale (a)	Marilyn Vale	Jerry Engelbach	Marilyn Vale	Chaim Gitter
Cyrano de Bergerac	Edmond Rostand	Jerry Engelbach	Jerry Engelbach	Deborah Friedman	Chaim Gitter
	Brian Hooker (t)			Sue Cox	
Traveler Without Luggage	Jean Anouilh	Marlene Swartz	Eddie Olavarria	Margo La Zaro	Chaim Gitter
	Lucienne Hill (t)				
Fallen Angels	Noel Coward	Trueman Kelley	Mark Haack	Danajean Cicerchi	Chaim Gitter
The Servant	Robin Maugham	Marlene Swartz	Marlene Swartz	Karl Jeff Novak	Chaim Gitter
			Carol Corwen		
Richard III	William Shakespeare	Jerry Engelbach	Jerry Engelbach	Sue Cox	Gerry King
Miss Jairus	Michel de Ghelderode	Carol Corwen	Carol Corwen	Deborah Friedman	Toby Mailman
	George Hauger (t)				
Amphitryon 38	Jean Giraudoux	Jude Schanzer	Loy Arcenas	Richard Hornung	Gerry King
	S. N. Behrman (a)				
Overruled	George Bernard Shaw	Gene Santarelli	Eric Schultz	Leslie Day	Toby Mailman
The Love of Don Perlimplin	Federico Garcia Lorca	Mary Ryder	Eric Schultz	Leslie Day	Toby Mailman
and *Belisa in the Garden*	James Graham-Lujan (t)				
Guernica	Fernando Arrabal	Mitchell Engelmeyer	Eric Schultz	Sue Cox	Toby Mailman
	Barbara Wright (t)				
Only 10 Minutes to Buffalo	Günter Grass	Alison Mackenzie	Eric Schultz	Sue Cox	Toby Mailman
	Ralph Manheim (t)				
The Twelve-Pound Look	J. M. Barrie	Alison Mackenzie	Michael Gallagher	Deborah Friedman	Toby Mailman
If You Had Three	Gertrude Stein	Randy Knolle	Michael Gallagher	Deborah Friedman	Toby Mailman
Husbands	Randy Knolle (a)				
Deathwatch	Jean Genet	Denise Merat	Michael Gallagher	Deborah Friedman	Toby Mailman
	Bernard Frechtman (t)				
Action	Sam Shepard	Chris Silva	Michael Gallagher	Deborah Friedman	Toby Mailman
Requiem for a	Rod Serling	Richard Leighton	Eric Schultz	Michael Casey	Chaim Gitter
Heavyweight					
October 12, 410 B.C.	David Barrett (a)	Alison Mackenzie	Loy Arcenas	Sally J. Lesser	Toby Mailman
	Jim Ragland (m)			Kathleen Smith	
Dandy Dick	Arthur Wing Pinero	Gene Santarelli	Tom Bruno	Deborah Friedman	Toby Mailman
Inadmissible Evidence	John Osborne	Marlene Swartz	Jerry Engelbach	Jeffrey Novak	Gary Seltzer
The Knights of the Round	Jean Cocteau	Jerry Engelbach	Steven Brant	David Bess	Steven Brant
Table	W. H. Auden (t)				

South Coast Repertory

Private Lives	Noel Coward	David Emmes	Michael Devine	Charles Tomlinson	Thomas Ruzika
The Last Meeting of the	Preston Jones	Martin Benson	Cliff Faulkner	Louise Hayter	Dawn Chiang
Knights of the White					
Magnolia					
A Doll's House	Henrik Ibsen	David Emmes	Susan Tuohy	Barbara Cox	Thomas Ruzika
Volpone	Ben Jonson	Daniel Sullivan	Michael Devine	Charles Tomlinson	Dawn Chiang
Comedians	Trevor Griffiths	Martin Benson	Cliff Faulkner	Louise Hayter	Dawn Chiang
Otherwise Engaged	Simon Gray	David Emmes	Cliff Faulkner	Barbara Cox	Dawn Chiang

PRODUCTION	DRAMATIST	DIRECTOR	SETS	COSTUMES	LIGHTING
Tomato Surprise	Robin Frederick	John-David Keller	Cliff Faulkner	Cliff Faulkner	
The Time of Your Life	William Saroyan	Martin Benson	Cliff Faulkner	Louise Hayter	Dawn Chiang
The Contractor	David Storey	Martin Benson	Cliff Faulkner	Dwight Richard Odle	Susan Tuohy
The Sorrows of Frederick	Romulus Linney	David Emmes	Susan Tuohy	Louise Hayter	Dawn Chiang
The Learned Ladies	Moliere Richard Wilbur (t)	Robert Benedetti	Cliff Faulkner	Dwight Richard Odle	Susan Tuohy
Peg o' My Heart	J. Hartley Manners	John-David Keller	Cliff Faulkner	Cliff Faulkner	Dawn Chiang
Spokesong	Stewart Parker Jimmy Kennedy (m)	David Emmes	Michael Devine	Dwight Richard Odle	Thomas Ruzika
The Energy Show	Robin Frederick	John-David Keller	Cliff Faulkner	Dwight Richard Odle	

Stage One: The Louisville Children's Theatre

Feelings	Bekki Jo Schneider	Bekki Jo Schneider	John Campbell	Cathy Campbell	
The Hide and Seek Odyssey of Madeline Gimple	Frank Gagliano	Carolyn Bezenek	John Campbell	John Campbell	John Campbell
The Little Match Girl	Bekki Jo Schneider (a)	Bekki Jo Schneider	John Campbell	Cathy Campbell	
The Ice Wolf	Joanna Halpert Kraus	Marilee Herbert-Slater	John Campbell	Cathy Campbell	John Campbell
Russian Tales	company developed	Bekki Jo Schneider	John Campbell	Cathy Campbell	
Aladdin	Moses Goldberg (a)	Moses Goldberg	John Campbell	Doug Watts	John Campbell
Snow White and Rose Red	company developed	Bekki Jo Schneider	John Campbell	Cathy Campbell	
Beauty and the Beast	company developed	Moses Goldberg	Deanna Drennon	Karen Edwards	
The Miracle Worker	William Gibson	Moses Goldberg	Lindsay Davis	Lindsay Davis	Michael Hottois
Holidays at Home	company developed	Bekki Jo Schneider	Bekki Jo Schneider	Marty Crawley	
Cherokee Trails	company developed	Bekki Jo Schneider	Sarah Frederick	Brenda Wood	
The Men's Cottage	Moses Goldberg	Moses Goldberg	Ken Terrill	Ken Terrill	Moses Goldberg
Step on a Crack	Susan Zeder	Moses Goldberg	Matthew Rosmus	Laura Nodzak	Matthew Rosmus
Puss 'n' Boots	company developed	Moses Goldberg	Deanna Drennon	Doug Watts	

Stage South

Sea Island Song	Alice Childress (b,l) Nathan Woodard (m)	Leonard Peters	Vittorio Cappece	Vittorio Cappece	
The Subject Was Roses	Frank D. Gilroy	Gene Lesser	John A. Olbrych, Jr.	Kristina Watson	John A. Olbrych, Jr.
Swamp!	Dick Goldberg (b,l) Amy Rubin (m)	Elizabeth Keen	Tom Lynch	Judanna Lynn	
Clarence Darrow	David W. Rintels	Gene Lesser	Cathleen Armstrong	John Dunn	Mike Mosley
The Belle of Amherst	William Luce	Gene Lesser	Stephen Judd		Michael Sapp

Stage West

The Little Foxes	Lillian Hellman	Rae Allen	Laurence King	Christina Weppner	Barley Harris
A Christmas Carol	Rae Allen (a) Timothy Near (a)	Timothy Near	Jerry Rojo (1,2) Tom Cariello (2)	Christina Weppner	John Gisondi
Loot	Joe Orton	Peter Mark Schifter	Tom Cariello	Christina Weppner	Barley Harris
Rib Cage	Larry Ketron	Rae Allen	Tom Cariello	Christina Weppner	Barley Harris
The Three Sisters	Anton Chekhov	Rae Allen	Jerry Rojo	Christina Weppner	Barbara Ling
Vanities	Jack Heifner	Larry Carpenter	Christina Weppner	Christina Weppner	John Gisondi
A Raisin in the Sun	Lorraine Hansberry	Harold Scott	Tom Cariello	Sigrid Insull	Robby Monk
The Mousetrap	Agatha Christie	Marc B. Weiss	Bernard J. Vyzga	Sigrid Insull	Leslie Spohn

PRODUCTION	DRAMATIST	DIRECTOR	SETS	COSTUMES	LIGHTING
Good Evening	Peter Cook Dudley Moore	Cash Baxter	Joe Long	Karen Kinsella	Paul J. Horton
A View from the Bridge	Arthur Miller	Davey Marlin-Jones	Marc B. Weiss	Sigrid Insull	Robby Monk
How the Other Half Loves	Alan Ayckbourn	Edward Stern	Bernard J. Vyzga	Karen Kinsella	Paul J. Horton

The Street Theater

All productions are company developed.

Related Voices		Raymond Barry			
Common Ground		Patricia Smith			
A Play About Us?		C. Lester Franklin			
This One's for You		Martin Henderson Patricia Smith			

Studio Arena Theatre

Sunset	Louis LaRusso II (b) Gary W. Friedman (m) Will Holt (l)	Tommy Tune	Douglas W. Schmidt	Joseph G. Aulisi	Jeffrey Schissler
Semmelweiss	Howard Sackler	Edwin Sherin	John Wulp	Ann Roth	Marc B. Weiss
Same Time, Next Year	Bernard Slade	Michael Montel	William Ritman	Diane R. Schaller	Peter Gill
The Crucifer of Blood	Paul Giovanni	Paul Giovanni	Robert P. Van Nutt	Robert P. Van Nutt	Robby Monk
The Shadow Box	Michael Cristofer	Warren Enters	Larry Aumen	Donna Eskew	Peter Gill
Noel Coward in Two Keys	Noel Coward	Richard Barr	Michael Healy	Donna Eskew	Peter Gill
Who's Afraid of Virginia Woolf?	Edward Albee	Richard Barr	Michael Healy	Clifford Capone	Peter Gill
Funny Face	Fred Thompson, Paul G. Smith (b) George Gershwin (m) Ira Gershwin (l)	Neal Du Brock	David Mitchell	Theoni V. Aldredge	Jennifer Tipton
For Colored Girls who have Considered Suicide / When The Rainbow is Enuf	Ntozake Shange	Oz Scott	Ming Cho Lee	Judy Dearing	Jennifer Tipton
A Christmas Carol	Rae Allen (a) Timothy Near (a)	Warren Enters	Christian Thee	Donna Eskew	Peter Gill
Countess Dracula!	Neal Du Brock	Neal Du Brock	Christian Thee	Jane Greenwood	Craig Miller
The Runner Stumbles	Milan Stitt	Warren Enters	John T. Baun	A. Holly Olsen	Peter Gill
Catsplay	Istvan Orkeny Clara Gyorgyey (t)	Stephen Porter	John T. Baun	Suzy Benzinger A. Holly Olsen	Peter Gill
The Madwoman of Central Park West	Phyllis Newman Arthur Laurents (b) various (m,l)	Arthur Laurents	Philipp Jung	Florence Klotz	Ken Billington

Syracuse Stage

Love Letters on Blue Paper	Arnold Wesker	Arthur Storch	Eldon Elder	Lowell Detweiler	Judy Rasmuson
The End of the Beginning	Sean O'Casey	Arthur Storch	Eldon Elder	Lowell Detweiler	Judy Rasmuson
The Plough and the Stars	Sean O'Casey	Peter Maloney	Elmon Webb Virginia Dancy	Linda Fisher	Lee Watson
Tartuffe	Moliere Richard Wilbur (t)	John Going	William Trotman	James Berton Harris	Judy Rasmuson

continued

The Paper Bag Players.
Everybody, Everybody.

PRODUCTION	DRAMATIST	DIRECTOR	SETS	COSTUMES	LIGHTING
That Championship Season	Jason Miller	William Putch	Elmon Webb Virginia Dancy	Liz Bass	James E. Stephens
Candida	George Bernard Shaw	Bill Ludel	William Schroder	Nanzi Adzima	James E. Stephens
Vanities	Jack Heifner	John Going	Neil Peter Jampolis	William Schroder	Neil Peter Jampolis
She Stoops to Conquer	Oliver Goldsmith	John Going	William Schroder	James Berton Harris	Barry Arnold
The World of Sholom Aleichem	Arnold Perl	Steven Kaplan	John Arnone	Nanzi Adzima	Geoffrey T. Cunningham
The Butterfingers Angel...	William Gibson	Arthur Storch	John Doepp	William Schroder	Judy Rasmuson
The Blood Knot	Athol Fugard	Thomas Bullard	John Kasarda	Liz Bass	Spencer Mosse
Otherwise Engaged	Simon Gray	Harold Stone	Virginia Dancy Elmon Webb	Patricia McGourty	James E. Stephens
The Glass Menagerie	Tennessee Williams	Harold Scott	William Schroder	Liz Bass	James E. Stephens
Loved	Olwen Wymark	Arthur Storch	John Arnone	Patricia McGourty	Judy Rasmuson

Theatre Arts of West Virginia

PRODUCTION	DRAMATIST	DIRECTOR	SETS	COSTUMES	LIGHTING
Arms and the Man	George Bernard Shaw	John S. Benjamin	Bernard J. Vyzga	Thomas Hansen	Dale Harris
The Fantasticks	Tom Jones (b,l) Harvey Schmidt (m)	Ewel Cornett John S. Benjamin	Bernard J. Vyzga	Thomas Hansen	Dale Harris
The Boor	Anton Chekhov	Ewel Cornett	Bernard J. Vyzga	Thomas Hansen	Dale Harris
The Marriage Proposal	Anton Chekhov	John S. Benjamin	Bernard J. Vyzga	Thomas Hansen	Dale Harris
Swan Song	Anton Chekhov	John S. Benjamin	Bernard J. Vyzga	Thomas Hansen	Dale Harris
The Firebird	Raymond Masters	John S. Benjamin	Raymond Masters	Raymond Masters	Raymond Masters
Hatfields and McCoys	Billy Edd Wheeler (b,l) Ewel Cornett (m)	John S. Benjamin	Thomas P. Struthers	Cynthia T. Krich	Stephen R. Woodring
Honey in the Rock	Kermit Hunter (b,l) Ewel Cornett (m) Jack Kilpatrick (m)	John S. Benjamin	Thomas P. Struthers	Cynthia T. Krich	Stephen R. Woodring
The Importance of Being Earnest	Oscar Wilde	Ewel Cornett	Vittorio Capecce	Thomas Hansen	Brian Tuck
Sleuth	Anthony Shaffer	John S. Benjamin	Vittorio Capecce	Thomas Hansen	Brian Tuck
The Typists and *The Tiger*	Murray Schisgal	John S. Benjamin	Vittorio Capecce	Thomas Hansen	Brian Tuck
Alice Underground	Raymond Masters	John S. Benjamin Raymond Masters	Raymond Masters	Raymond Masters	John S. Benjamin

Theatre By The Sea

PRODUCTION	DRAMATIST	DIRECTOR	SETS	COSTUMES	LIGHTING
Sleuth	Anthony Shaffer	Miriam Fond	James E. Carroccio	Varel McComb	Daniel Raymond
Jubalay	Patrick Rose Merv Campone	Russell Treyz	John Shaffner	Varel McComb	Ned Hallick
My Three Angels	Sam & Bella Spewack	Alfred Gingold	Leslie E. Rollins	Kathie Iannicelli	Daniel Raymond
The Sunshine Boys	Neil Simon	Thomas Lee Sinclair	Larry Fulton	Kathie Iannicelli	Daniel Raymond
The Glass Menagerie	Tennessee Williams	Russell Treyz	Leslie E. Rollins	Kathie Iannicelli	Daniel Raymond
Oklahoma!	Oscar Hammerstein II (b,l) Richard Rodgers (m)	Russell Treyz	Larry Fulton	Kathie Iannicelli	James Trudeau
Once upon a Mattress	Jay Thompson, Marshall Barer & Dean Fuller (b) Mary Rodgers (m) Marshall Barer (l)	Russell Treyz	Larry Fulton	Kathie Iannicelli	James Trudeau
Relatively Speaking	Alan Ayckbourn	Richard Magavero	Bob Phillips	Kathie Iannicelli	James Trudeau

PRODUCTION	DRAMATIST	DIRECTOR	SETS	COSTUMES	LIGHTING
The Runner Stumbles	Milan Stitt	Thomas R. Bloom	Bob Phillips	Kathie Iannicelli	James Trudeau
Murder at the Vicarage	Agatha Christie Charles Moie & Barbara Toy (a)	Russell Treyz	Bob Phillips	Kathie Iannicelli	James Trudeau
Uncle Vanya	Chekhov John Murrell (t)	Jon Kimbell	Bob Phillips	Kathie Iannicelli	James Trudeau
The Sea Horse	Edward J. Moore	Tom Celli	Bob Phillips	Kathie Iannicelli	James Trudeau
Starting Here, Starting Now	David Shire (m) Richard Maltby, Jr. (l)	John Montgomery	Larry Fulton	Kathie Iannicelli	James Trudeau
Fiddler on the Roof	Joseph Stein (b) Jerry Bock (m) Sheldon Harnick (l)	John Montgomery	Larry Fulton	Kathie Iannicelli	
Brigadoon	Alan Jay Lerner (b,l) Frederick Loewe (m)	John Montgomery	Larry Fulton	Kathie Iannicelli	

Theatre Express

PRODUCTION	DRAMATIST	DIRECTOR	SETS	COSTUMES	LIGHTING
The Unlit Corridor	William Turner (b,m,l)	William Turner	John Hodges William Turner	Lesley Beck	William Turner
Son of Arlecchino	Leon Katz	Word Baker	Word Baker	Caren Harder	Michael Katz
The Marquis de Sade's Justine	Leon Katz (a)	Jed Harris	John Hodges	Lesley Beck	Michael Katz
Tuesday	Jewel Walker	Jewel Walker	Tim Joswick	Heidi Holman Pribram	Tim Joswick
Angel City	Sam Shepard	Jed Harris	Norman Russell	June Fortunato	Norman Russell
The Elephant Man	William Turner	Jed Harris	Norman Russell	William Turner	Norman Russell
Assassins	Charles Gilbert, Jr. (b,m,l)	William Turner	William Turner	William Turner	William Turner
Made by Two	Gertrude Stein (b,l) William Turner (m)	Tom Hearn William Turner	Dan Wallace William Turner	Dan Wallace William Turner	Norman Russell William Turner
Hotel for Criminals	Richard Foreman (b,l) Stanley Silverman (m)	William Turner	Dan Wallace	Dan Wallace	William Turner

Theater for the New City

PRODUCTION	DRAMATIST	DIRECTOR	SETS	COSTUMES	LIGHTING
The Ballad of the Seven Sleeping Brothers in China	Tadeus Micinski	Viola Stephan	Deiter Finke	Dennis Eichelberger	Peter Abode
The Time They Turned the Water Off	Crystal Field George Bartenieff	Crystal Field	Donald Brooks	Edmond Felix	
Leona Is a Funny Name	Don Kvares	Ted Mornel	Brian Evans	Ann Artymowich	Stephen Edelstein
Face Stool	Henri Gruvman	Henri Gruvman	Henri Gruvman	Henri Gruvman	Ann Artymowich
Winter Sunshine	Arthur Williams	Robert Dahdah	Donald Brooks	Joan Durant	Donald Brooks
Dry Sherry	John Sherry	Martin Oltarsh	Stephen Edelstein	I.A. Brown	Barbara A. Schwartz
Cutups and Cutouts	N. Noble Barrett	Robert Stocking	Robert Stocking	Bernice Benolken	Ray McCutcheon
Shopping Bag Madonna	Mary Karolly	Anthony DeVito		Anthony DeVito	Donald Brooks
The Room	Saskia Hegt	Saskia Hegt	Funs Van Woerkum		Peter Fonte
The Guillotine	Helen Duberstein	Steve Reed	Pamela Badyk	Michael Arian	Barbara Tulliver
Atonements	Israel Eliraz (a) David Zinder (t)	Rena Elisha	Mitchell Greenberg	Edmond Felix	Craig Kennedy
Just Folks	Romulus Linney				
Liars	Ron Lampkin	Ken Buckshi	Jane Przybysz	Jane Przybysz	Betty Whiteside
Clara Bow Loves Gary Cooper	Robert Dahdah Mary Boylan	Robert Dahdah	Steve Edelstein	Gene Galvin	Steve Edelstein

continued

PRODUCTION	DRAMATIST	DIRECTOR	SETS	COSTUMES	LIGHTING
Lives	Edmond Felix	Edmond Felix	Edmond Felix	Edmond Felix	Betty Whiteside
Realism in Our Time	Daryl Chin	Daryl Chin	Steve Edelstein	Jane Przybysz	Betty Whiteside
Oil!	Neal Tucker	Seth Allen	Saint-Amant	Saint-Amant	Barbara A. Schwartz
Cancer of Ambition	Richard Levine	Richard Levine	Richard Levine	Richard Levine	
Boat Sun Cavern	Arthur Sainer	Crystal Field	Steve Edelstein	Helyna Kuzman	Steve Edelstein
A Walk in the Moonlight	anonymous Algirdas Landsbergis (t)	Jonas Jurassas	Steve Edelstein	Helyna Kuzman	Nat Cohen
Cosmicomics	Italo Calvino Gordon Rogoff (a)	Gordon Rogoff	Venessa James	Venessa James	Ken Tabachnik
The Torrents of Spring	Ivan Turgenev Donald Sanders (a)	Donald Sanders	Venessa James	Venessa James	Ken Tabachnik
Mirandolina	Carlo Goldoni Robert Reddy (a)	Robert Reddy	Richard Belknap	Robert Reddy	Russel Krum
The King of the Mashed Potatoes	Crystal Field George Bartenieff	Crystal Field	Elaine Weissman Molly Renda	Edmond Felix	
Lovely Rita	Thomas Brasch Viola Stephan (t) Dennis Eichelberger (t)	Viola Stephan	Dieter Finke	Deirdre Hennings	Bob Herman
Buried Child	Sam Shepard	Robert Woodruff	David Gropman	Jess Goldstein	John P. Dodd
The Fall	Albert Camus Justin O'Brian (t)	Daniel Negrin	Beverly Owen	Sally Anne Parsons	Gary Harris
Homebodies	Nicholas Kazan	James Milton	Harold Branwell	James Milton	Bette Johnson
The Button	Michael McClure	James Milton	Harold Branwell	James Milton	Bette Johnson
Fruit of Zaloom	Paul Zaloom	Paul Zaloom	Paul Zaloom	Paul Zaloom	Bette Johnson
Hefetz	Hanokh Levin Rina Elisha (t)	Rina Elisha	Elaine Weissman Molly Renda	Edmond Felix	Tony Golden
Othello	William Shakespeare	Peter Schuman	Amy Trompetter	Peter Schuman	Amy Trompetter
Stewart Sherman's Eighth Spectacle	Stewart Sherman	Stewart Sherman		Stewart Sherman	Stewart Sherman
The Writer's Opera	Rosalyn Drexler (b,l) John Braden (m)	John Vaccaro	Wes Cronk	Bernard Roth	Charles Embry
After the Baal-Shem Tov	Arthur Sainer	Crystal Field	Elaine Weissman Molly Renda	Helyna Kuzman	Steve Edelstein
Metaphysics of a Two-Headed Calf	Stanislaw Witkiewicz Daniel & Eleanor Gerould (t)	Steve Reed	John Slavin	Maura Clifford	Allen Lampel
Voideville	Gordon Bressac Ruby Lynn Reyner	Gordon Bressac	Robby Mazza	Bernard Roth	Russel Krum
Up in Seattle	Arthur Williams	John Herbert McDowell	Donald Brooks	Maura Clifford	Russel Krum
Lord Tom Goldsmith	Victor Lipton	Arthur Sainer	Elaine Weissman Molly Renda	Mary Rindfleisch	Mark Ginsberg

Theater of the Open Eye

PRODUCTION	DRAMATIST	DIRECTOR	SETS	COSTUMES	LIGHTING
Fontana	Valerie Hammer Robert Mahaffay (m)	Valerie Hammer	Bernard Baschet	Valerie Hammer	George Gracey
Raven's Dance	Eric Bass Didi Charney (m) Robert Mahaffay (m) Anne Sheedy (m)	Eric Bass	Wayne Schrengohst	Susan Humbuck	William Morrison
The Shining House	Jean Erdman Michael Czajkowski (m)	Jean Erdman	William Morrison	Deborah Stein	William Morrison

A Contemporary Theatre.
Man and Superman.
Photo: Chris Bennion.

PRODUCTION	DRAMATIST	DIRECTOR	SETS	COSTUMES	LIGHTING
Moon on Snow	Ken Gaertner Christopher DeLoach (m)	Trueman Kelley	Trueman Kelley	Deborah Stein	William Morrison
The Coach with the Six Insides	Jean Erdman (a) Teiji Ito (m)	Jean Erdman	Dan Butt Milton Howarth	Gail Ryan	William Morrison
The Masque of Dawn	Eric Bass Richard Spendio (m) Bill Buchen (m)	Eric Bass	Dennis Valinsky Eric Bass Norman Tempia	Nomi Frederick Norman Tempia	William Morrison
George and the Dragon	John Patrick Shanley Tom Shelton (m)	Erin Blackwell			
Festival of New Works	various	various			

Theatre X

And Things That Go Bump in the Night	Terrence McNally	Sharon Ott	Monica Ehlke		John Kishline
The Wreck: A Romance	John Schneider	Sharon Ott	John Kishline Willem Dafoe		John Schneider
A Fierce Longing	John Schneider	Sharon Ott	John Kishline Monica Ehlke Jerome Fortier	Irene Apalsch Sharon Ott	Robert Sieger
An Interest in Strangers	John Schneider	John Schneider	John Kishline Robert Sieger	Deborah Clifton	Robert Sieger
Schmaltz	John Schneider (b,l) Mark Van Hecke (m)	Sharon Ott John Schneider	Stewart Johnson	Ellen Kozak	John Kishline
The Fantod: A Victorian Reverie	Amlin Gray	Sharon Ott	Stewart Johnson	Ellen Kozak	John Kishline

Travel Light Theatre

The Dumb Waiter and *The Lover*	Harold Pinter	Michael Maggio	Peter Winter	Kaye Nottbusch	Peter Winter
P.S. Your Cat Is Dead	James Kirkwood	Russ Tutterow	Peter Winter	Kaye Nottbusch	Gary Heitz
The Rainmaker	N. Richard Nash	Joe Guastaferro	Peter Winter	Kaye Nottbusch	Gary Heitz
Woody Guthrie	Tom Taylor George Boyd Michael Diamond	George Boyd	John Scavone (1) Bob Doepel (2)	Tom Taylor	Daniel Adams
A Hatful of Rain	Michael V. Gazzo	Joe Guastaferro	Peter Winter	Nanalee Raphael	D.R. Edwards
Steambath	Bruce Jay Friedman	Russ Tutterow	Bob Doepel	Kate Bergh	Gary Heitz
Suburbs of Heaven	Thom Bishop (m,l)	Gail Isaacson	Bob Doepel	Jessica Hahn	Gary Heitz
A Midsummer Night's Dream	William Shakespeare	James D. O'Reilly	Bob Doepel	Pauline Brailsford	Gary Heitz

Trinity Square Repertory Company

Ethan Frome	Owen & Donald Davis	Adrian Hall	Eugene Lee	Ann Morrell	Eugene Lee
Rosmersholm	Henrik Ibsen Adrian Hall (a) Richard Cumming (a)	Adrian Hall	Eugene Lee	Ann Morrell	Sean Kevin Keating
Equus	Peter Shaffer	Larry Arrick	Robert D. Soule	Ann Morrell	John F. Custer
As You Like It	William Shakespeare	Ann McBey Brebner	Robert D. Soule	Ann Morrell	John F. Custer
A Christmas Carol	Adrian Hall (a) Richard Cumming (a)	Adrian Hall	Eugene Lee (1) Robert D. Soule (2)	Betsey Potter Ann Morrell	Sean Kevin Keating (1) John F. Custer (2)

continued

A Contemporary Theatre.
Anything Goes.
Photo: Chris Bennion.

PRODUCTION	DRAMATIST	DIRECTOR	SETS	COSTUMES	LIGHTING
The Show-Off	George Kelly	George Martin	Robert D. Soule	James Berton Harris	John F. Custer
Boesman and Lena	Athol Fugard	Larry Arrick	Robert D. Soule	Ann Morrell	John F. Custer
Vanities	Jack Heifner	William Radka	Robert D. Soule	Ann Morrell	John F. Custer
American Buffalo	David Mamet	George Martin	Robert D. Soule	Ann Morrell	John F. Custer
Seduced	Sam Shepard	Adrian Hall	Eugene Lee	James Berton Harris	Eugene Lee
The Real Inspector Hound	Tom Stoppard	George Martin	David Ward	Mary Aiello Bruce	Mark Rippe
Whiskey	Terrence McNally	Larry Arrick	Robert D. Soule	Mary Aiello Bruce	Mark Rippe
Uncle Tom's Cabin: A History	Adrian Hall Richard Cumming	Adrian Hall	Matthew Jacobs	Vittorio Capecce	Eugene Lee
Awake and Sing!	Clifford Odets	Larry Arrick	Robert D. Soule	Ann Morrell	John F. Custer
Death of a Salesman	Arthur Miller	Larry Arrick	Robert D. Soule	Ann Morrell	John F. Custer
Who's Afraid of Virginia Woolf?	Edward Albee	Larry Arrick	Robert D. Soule	Ann Morrell	John F. Custer
A Life in the Theatre	David Mamet	Larry Arrick	Robert D. Soule	Mary Aiello Bruce	John F. Custer
Father's Day	Oliver Hailey	Timothy Crowe	Robert D. Soule	Annette Rossi	John F. Custer
The Shadow Box	Michael Cristofer	Peter Gerety	Robert D. Soule	Ann Morrell	John F. Custer
Jack the Ripper	Denis DeMarne (b,l) Ron Pember (b,l,m)	Ron Pember	Robert D. Soule	Ann Morrell	John F. Custer
Side by Side by Sondheim	Stephen Sondheim, et al. (m,l) Ned Sherrin (a)	Sharon Jenkins Richard Cumming	Robert D. Soule	Ann Morrell	John F. Custer
Same Time, Next Year	Bernard Slade	George Martin	Robert D. Soule	Ann Morrell	John F. Custer
Dial M for Murder	Frederick Knott	William Radka	Robert D. Soule	Ann Morrell	John F. Custer

Victory Gardens Theater

PRODUCTION	DRAMATIST	DIRECTOR	SETS	COSTUMES	LIGHTING
June Moon	George S. Kaufman Ring Lardner	Dennis Zacek	Tom Beall	Julie Jackson	Robert Shook
The Cigarette Man	David Blomquist	Cecil O'Neal	Rick Paul	Marsha Kowal	Robert Shook
Colette	Ruth Landis	Dennis Zacek	Brad Loman	Brad Loman	Brad Loman
Ceremonies in Dark Old Men	Lonnie Elder III	Dennis Zacek	Maher Ahmad	Marsha Kowal	Robert Shook
Heat	William Hauptman	Mary Jane Osa	Patrick Kerwin	Mary Crowley	Patrick Kerwin
His Satanic Majesty	William J. Norris	Dennis Zacek	Maher Ahmad	Maher Ahmad	Maher Ahmad
Between the Devil and the Deep Blue Sea	various (m,l) Greg McCaslin (a)	Greg McCaslin	Maher Ahmad	Maggie Bodwell	Robert Shook
The Night of January 16th	Ayn Rand	Dennis Zacek		Maggie Bodwell	
This Is My Play Song	Jackie Taylor (m,l)	Dennis Zacek	Maher Ahmad	Maher Ahmad	Maher Ahmad
The Homecoming	Harold Pinter	Dennis Zacek	Maher Ahmad	Marsha Kowal	Robert Shook
The Transfiguration of Benno Blimpie	Albert Innaurato	Dennis Zacek	Joseph S. Sturniolo	Joseph S. Sturniolo	Joseph S. Sturniolo
Eden	Steve Carter	Chuck Smith	Dean Taucher	Kate Bergh	Rebecca Binks
Peppermints	Mark Lawson	Tom Tully	Laura Sunkel	Laura Sunkel	Laura Sunkel
Towards the Morning	John Fenn	Tom Tully	Laura Sunkel	Laura Sunkel	Laura Sunkel
Dillinger	William J. Norris	Dennis Zacek	Dean Taucher	Julie Jackson	Robert Shook
Porch	Jeffrey Sweet	Tom Mula	Tom Beall	Tom Beall	Tom Beall
Weekends like Other People	David Blomquist	Mike Nussbaum	Joseph S. Sturniolo	Kate Bergh	John Rodriguez
Clowncave	Steven Ivcich	Steven Ivcich	David Wesniewski	David Wesniewski	James Roach
East Liberty, Pa.	Allan Bates	Dennis Zacek	Maher Ahmad	Julie Nagel	Robert Shook
Cowboys #2 and *The Unseen Hand*	Sam Shepard	James Roach	Patrick Kerwin	Marsha Kowal	Michael Mortimer

PRODUCTION	DRAMATIST	DIRECTOR	SETS	COSTUMES	LIGHTING
Virginia Museum Theatre					
Vanities	Jack Heifner	William Guild	F. Leonard Darby	C.J. Simpson	James Douglas Bloch
Richard III	William Shakespeare	Martin L. Platt	Richard C. Hankins	Lana Fritz	Richard C. Hankins
Berlin to Broadway with Kurt Weill	Kurt Weill (m) various (l) Gene Lerner (a)	Charles Maryan	Richard C. Hankins	Lana Fritz	James Douglas Bloch
Let's Get a Divorce	Victorien Sardou Emile de Najac Brian Kelly (t)	Tom Markus	Richard C. Hankins	Carol C. Steinke	James Douglas Bloch
Man and Superman	George Bernard Shaw	Tom Markus	Richard C. Hankins	Lana Fritz	James Douglas Bloch
Cabaret	Joe Masteroff (b) John Kander (m) Fred Ebb (l)	L. Bradford Boynton	Richard C. Hankins	Lana Fritz	James Douglas Bloch Richard C. Hankins
Volpone	Ben Jonson Robert A. Potter (a) Tom Markus (a)	Tom Markus	Joseph A. Varga	Lana Fritz	Patricia A. Connors
The Fantasticks	Tom Jones (b,l) Harvey Schmidt (m)	Joey Patton	Joseph A. Varga	Lana Fritz	Patricia A. Connors
Dear Liar	Jerome Kilty	Tom Markus	Joseph A. Varga	Jennifer Van Pernis	Thomas Knapp
Private Lives	Noel Coward	Tom Markus	Joseph A. Varga	Lana Fritz	Curt Senie
Wayside Theatre					
Round and Round the Garden	Alan Ayckbourn	Davey Marlin-Jones	Jack Stewart	Paige Southard	T. Blake Conley
Vanities	Jack Heifner	Davey Marlin-Jones	Jack Stewart	Paige Southard	T. Blake Conley
Ring Round the Moon	Jean Anouilh Christopher Fry (a)	John Ulmer	William Barclay	Paige Southard	T. Blake Conley
Charley's Aunt	Brandon Thomas	James Kirkland	William Barclay	Paige Southard	T. Blake Conley
Volpone	Ben Jonson	Keith Fowler	Jack Stewart	Paige Southard	T. Blake Conley
Bells Are Ringing	Betty Comden (b,l) Adolph Green (b,l) Jule Styne (m)	Harold Herman	Jack Stewart	Paige Southard	T. Blake Conley
Virginia Ghost Stories of the Civil War	William Stancil	James Kirkland	William Barclay	Lynn Sams	
A Christmas Carol	William Stancil (a)	James Kirkland	William Barclay	Richard von Ernst	T. Blake Conley
Side by Side by Sondheim	Stephen Sondheim et al. (m,l) Ned Sherrin (a)	James Kirkland	William Barclay	Richard von Ernst	T. Blake Conley
Angel Street	Patrick Hamilton	John Ulmer	William Barclay	Richard von Ernst	Michael Weferling
A Streetcar Named Desire	Tennessee Williams	Davey Marlin-Jones	William Barclay	Richard von Ernst	T. Blake Conley
Harvey	Mary Chase	James Kirkland	William Barclay	Richard von Ernst	T. Blake Conley
Shakes and Company!	company developed (a)	Tom Herman	Reggie Augustine	Reggie Augustine	
Hamlet	William Shakespeare	James Kirkland	William Barclay	Reggie Augustine	Doug Gruber
A Christmas Carol	William Stancil (a)	James Kirkland		Richard von Ernst	
The Whole Theatre Company					
Mother Courage and Her Children	Bertolt Brecht Eric Bentley (t)	W.T. Martin Arnold Mittelman	Paul Dorphley	Veronica Deisler	Marshall Spiller
The Seduction (from The Good Doctor)	Neil Simon	Arnold Mittelman	Raymond C. Recht	Sigrid Insull	Marshall Spiller

continued

PRODUCTION	DRAMATIST	DIRECTOR	SETS	COSTUMES	LIGHTING
The Marriage Proposal	Anton Chekhov Theodore Hoffman (t)	Arnold Mittelman	Raymond C. Recht	Sigrid Insull	Marshall Spiller
The Brute	Anton Chekhov Eric Bentley (t)	Arnold Mittelman	Raymond C. Recht	Sigrid Insull	Marshall Spiller
Father's Day	Oliver Hailey	Bernard Hiatt	Paul Dorphley	Mary-Margaret Bergamini-Tobias	Marshall Spiller
And Miss Reardon Drinks a Little	Paul Zindel	Bernard Hiatt Louis Zorich	Tony Negron	Sigrid Insull	Marshall Spiller
One Flew over the Cuckoo's Nest	Dale Wasserman	Olympia Dukakis	Tony Negron	Mary-Margaret Bergamini-Tobias	Marshall Spiller
The Trojan Women	Euripides Apollo & Olympia Dukakis (a)	Apollo Dukakis	Paul Dorphley	Sigrid Insull	Marshall Spiller
The Imaginary Invalid	Moliere Miles Malleson (a)	John Henry Davis	Raymond C. Recht	Sigrid Insull	Marshall Spiller
The Homecoming	Harold Pinter	Arnold Mittelman	Paul Dorphley	Sigrid Insull	Marshall Spiller
Arms and the Man	George Bernard Shaw	Olympia Dukakis	Anthony Krivitski	Sigrid Insull	Marshall Spiller
Who's Afraid of Virginia Woolf?	Edward Albee	Arnold Mittelman	Paul Dorphley	Sigrid Insull	Marshall Spiller

Williamstown Theatre Festival

PRODUCTION	DRAMATIST	DIRECTOR	SETS	COSTUMES	LIGHTING
Idiot's Delight	Robert Sherwood	Nikos Psacharopoulos	Andrew Jackness	Dunya Ramicova	Roger Meeker
Design for Living	Noel Coward	Gerald Gutierrez	Franco Colavecchia	David Murin	Mitchell Kurtz
The School for Wives	Moliere Richard Wilbur (t)	Jean-Bernard Bucky	Hugh Landwehr	Donato Moreno	Paul Gallo
The Shadow Box	Michael Cristofer	Richard Chamberlain	Christopher Nowak	Rita B. Watson	Roger Meeker
A Month in the Country	Ivan Turgenev Ariadne Nicolaeff (t)	Nikos Psacharopoulos	John Conklin	Clifford Capone	Jennifer Tipton
Camino Real	Tennessee Williams	Nikos Psacharopoulos	John Conklin	Jess Goldstein	Jennifer Tipton
The Matchmaker	Thornton Wilder	Walton Jones	Tom Lynch	Jess Goldstein	Mitchell Kurtz
The Resistible Rise of Arturo Ui	Bertolt Brecht George Tabori (t)	Peter H. Hunt	John Conklin	Rita Ryack	Peter H. Hunt
Hay Fever	Noel Coward	Tom Moore	Karen Schulz	Rita B. Watson	Roger Meeker
Charley's Aunt	Brandon Thomas	Michael Montel	Tom Lynch	Linda Fisher	Roger Meeker
Children of the Sun	Maxim Gorky Ariadne Nicolaeff (t)	Nikos Psacharopoulos	Hugh Landwehr	Dunya Ramicova	Roger Meeker

The Wisdom Bridge Theatre

PRODUCTION	DRAMATIST	DIRECTOR	SETS	COSTUMES	LIGHTING
Ladyhouse Blues	Kevin O'Morrison	Robert Falls	David Emmons	Julie A. Nagel	Mary M. Badger
The Idiots Karamazov	Christopher Durang Albert Innaurato	Robert Falls	John Yeck III	Tom McKinley	Larry Schoememan
The Crucible	Arthur Miller	Patrick O'Gara	Michael W. Merritt	Julie Jackson	Michael W. Merritt
Carmilla	David Campton (a)	Aubrey Berg	David Emmons	Christa Scholtz	Michael W. Merritt
The Runner Stumbles	Milan Stitt	Robert Falls	Gary Baugh	Julie Jackson	Mary M. Badger
Tartuffe	Moliere Miles Malleson (a)	Michael Maggio Robert Falls	Gary Baugh	Julie Jackson	Rebecca Binks
Comedians	Trevor Griffiths	Judd Parkin	Robert Doepel	Kate Bergh	Tom Herman
Bagtime	Alan Rosen (b) Louis Rosen (m) Thom Bishop (l)	Robert Falls	Michael W. Merritt	Tom McKinley	Robert Shook
Suburbs of Heaven	Thom Bishop (m,l)	Gail Issacson	Gary Baugh	Joyce Winer	Dan McKearnan

PRODUCTION	DRAMATIST	DIRECTOR	SETS	COSTUMES	LIGHTING
Worcester Foothills Theatre Company					
Dream Girl	Elmer Rice	Kricker James	Lindon Rankin	Anna Mae Gravel	Sal Gionesi, Jr.
I Am a Camera	John Van Druten	Tom Panko	Don Ricklin	Katrina Ploof	Sal Gionesi, Jr.
Tartuffe	Moliere Miles Malleson (t)	Kit Lindberg	Don Ricklin	Anna Mae Gravel	Sal Gionesi, Jr.
Outward Bound	Sutton Vane	Jack Magune	Lindon Rankin	Katrina Ploof	Sal Gionesi, Jr.
Room Service	John Murray Allen Boretz	Jack Magune	Don Ricklin	Anna Mae Gravel	Sal Gionesi, Jr.
A Moon for the Misbegotten	Eugene O'Neill	Rose Dresser	Lindon Rankin Don Ricklin	Judy Hutchins	Sal Gionesi, Jr.
An Irish Faustus	Lawrence Durrell	Kit Lindberg	Lindon Rankin Don Ricklin	Anna Mae Gravel	Sal Gionesi, Jr.
Butterflies Are Free	Leonard Gershe	Rose Dresser	Don Ricklin	Anna Mae Gravel	Sal Gionesi, Jr.
Time: 1940	Marc P. Smith	Marc P. Smith	Don Ricklin	Anna Mae Gravel	Sal Gionesi, Jr.
Arsenic and Old Lace	Joseph Kesselring	Andy Fuller	Don Ricklin	Katrina Ploof	Sal Gionesi, Jr.
A Thousand Clowns	Herb Gardner	Jack Magune	Don Ricklin	Valerie Quigley	Sal Gionesi, Jr.
Wait Until Dark	Frederick Knott	Jack Magune	Don Ricklin	Valerie Quigley	Sal Gionesi, Jr.
The Taming of the Shrew	William Shakespeare	Rose Dresser	Lindon Rankin	Diane Lent Holmes	Sal Gionesi, Jr.
The Rainmaker	N. Richard Nash	Rose Dresser	Don Ricklin	Diane Lent Holmes	Sal Gionesi, Jr.
The Unexpected Guest	Agatha Christie	Clifford V. Ammon	Don Ricklin	Diane Lent Holmes	Sal Gionesi, Jr.
The Hasty Heart	John Patrick	Kricker James	Lindon Rankin	Diane Lent Holmes	Sal Gionesi, Jr.
The Silver Cord	Sidney Howard	David Schmalz	Don Ricklin	Diane Lent Holmes	Sal Gionesi, Jr.
Charley's Aunt	Brandon Thomas	Jack Magune	Don Ricklin	Diane Lent Holmes	Sal Gionesi, Jr.
Be a Sport	Marc P. Smith (b,l) Craig Simmons (m) James Dempsey (l)	Marc P. Smith	Lindon Rankin	Diane Lent Holmes	Sal Gionesi, Jr.
Yale Repertory Theatre					
The Ghost Sonata	August Strindberg Evert Sprinchorn (t)	Andrei Serban	Michael H. Yeargan	Dunya Ramicova	Thomas Skelton
Reunion and Dark Pony	David Mamet	Walton Jones	Kate Edmunds	Kate Edmunds	William Conner
Terra Nova	Ted Tally	Travis S. Preston	Jess Goldstein	Jess Goldstein	Robert Jared
Sganarelle: An Evening of Moliere Farces	Moliere Albert Bermel (t)	Andrei Serban	Michael H. Yeargan	Dunya Ramicova	James H. Gage
Man Is Man	Bertolt Brecht Steve Gooch (t)	Ron Daniels	Nancy Thun	Dunya Ramicova	Thomas Skelton
Wings	Arthur Kopit	John Madden	Andrew Jackness	Jeanne Button	Tom Schraeder
The Wild Duck	Henrik Ibsen Michael Meyer (t)	Robert Brustein	Michael H. Yeargan	Jeanne Button	William B. Warfel
Tales from the Vienna Woods	Odon von Horvath Christopher Hampton (t)	Keith Hack	Tony Straiges	Dunya Ramicova	Thomas Skelton
'dentity Crisis	Christopher Durang	Frank Torok	Michael H. Yeargan	Marjorie Graf	Robert Jared
Guesswork	Robert Auletta	Robert Gainer	Michael H. Yeargan	Marjorie Graf	Robert Jared
Mahagonny	Bertolt Brecht (b,l) Keith Hack (a) Kurt Weill (m)	Keith Hack	Michael H. Yeargan	Nan Cibula	William M. Armstrong
Buried Child	Sam Shepard	Adrian Hall	Adrianne Lobel	Judianna Makovsky	William B. Warfel
The Seagull	Anton Chekhov Jean-Claude van Itallie (t)	Robert Brustein	Michael H. Yeargan	Dunya Ramicova	Thomas Skelton
The Bundle	Edward Bond	John Madden	Andrew Jackness	Susan Hilferty	Robert Jared
As You Like It	William Shakespeare	Andrei Belgrader	Tom Lynch	Adrianne Lobel	William M. Armstrong

Programs and Services

	Professional training	Classes for nonprofessionals	Classes for children	Internships	Student performances	Programs-in-schools	Classroom study materials	Student ticket discount	Senior citizen discount	Other discount(s)	Free ticket distribution	Childrens' Productions	Mainstage touring	Separate touring company
A Contemporary Theatre			●	●	●	●		●	●	●	●	●		●
Academy Festival Theatre					●		●	●	●	●				
Academy Theatre	●	●	●	●	●	●	●	●		●	●	●	●	●
The Acting Company				●		●						●		
Actors Theatre of Louisville	●		●	●	●					●		●		●
Actors Theatre of St. Paul				●	●	●	●	●	●	●		●	●	
Alabama Shakespeare Festival	●		●		●		●	●		●				●
Alaska Repertory Theatre	●			●		●	●	●		●		●		
Alliance Theatre/Atlanta Children's Theatre			●	●	●	●	●	●		●	●	●		●
AMAS Repertory Theatre	●	●	●	●	●			●	●		●	●		●
American Conservatory Theatre	●	●	●	●	●	●	●	●	●	●		●		
American Place Theatre	●			●	●		●		●	●				
American Stage Festival	●	●	●	●	●			●	●		●			
American Theatre Company	●	●	●			●		●	●		●	●	●	●
Arena Stage				●	●			●	●		●			●
Arizona Theatre Company		●	●	●	●	●		●	●		●		●	
Arkansas Repertory Theatre		●		●	●	●	●	●				●		
Asolo State Theater	●			●	●	●	●	●			●			●
BAM Theater Company					●	●		●	●	●				
Barter Theatre	●			●	●	●	●	●		●		●	●	●
Berkeley Repertory Theatre				●	●	●		●	●	●	●			
Berkeley Stage Company				●	●	●		●	●	●				
BoarsHead Theater	●			●				●	●	●	●			
Body Politic	●	●	●		●	●		●	●	●	●	●	●	●
The Boston Arts Group	●			●	●	●		●	●	●	●	●	●	
Boston Shakespeare Company				●	●			●	●	●	●			
California Actors Theatre				●	●	●	●	●	●	●		●		●
The Cambridge Ensemble	●	●	●	●	●		●			●	●	●	●	
Center Stage		●	●	●	●	●	●	●			●			●
The Changing Scene	●	●			●	●		●			●		●	
Chelsea Theater Center				●	●	●	●	●	●	●	●			
The Children's Theatre Company		●	●	●	●	●	●	●	●		●	●		
Cincinnati Playhouse in the Park				●	●	●	●	●	●	●		●		

242

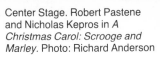

Workshops/Staged readings	Post-performance discussions	Booked-in events	Cabaret	Film series	Lecturers	Poetry readings	Newsletter/Magazine	Script publication	Speakers bureau	Volunteer auxiliary	Programs for the handicapped	Theatre rentals	Other Programs	
	●	●				●				●		●	●	**A Contemporary Theatre**
	●					●		●	●				●	**Academy Festival Theatre**
●	●	●			●			●			●		●	**Academy Theatre**
●	●		●			●		●					●	**The Acting Company**
●	●	●		●		●	●	●	●				●	**Actors Theatre of Louisville**
	●	●				●		●	●				●	**Actors Theatre of St. Paul**
●	●		●	●		●		●	●			●		**Alabama Shakespeare Festival**
	●	●				●		●	●				●	**Alaska Repertory Theatre**
●	●	●			●		●			●		●		**Alliance Theatre/Atlanta Children's Theatre**
														AMAS Repertory Theatre
●	●	●			●		●		●			●	●	**American Conservatory Theatre**
●	●		●				●					●	●	**American Place Theatre**
●	●	●				●		●				●	●	**American Stage Festival**
	●		●		●		●		●	●				**American Theatre Company**
●	●		●			●					●			**Arena Stage**
●	●	●	●		●		●		●	●			●	**Arizona Theatre Company**
●	●					●			●	●		●	●	**Arkansas Repertory Theatre**
●	●					●			●					**Asolo State Theater**
	●					●					●		●	**BAM Theater Company**
●	●			●		●		●	●	●		●		**Barter Theatre**
	●							●	●	●		●		**Berkeley Repertory Theatre**
●	●					●							●	**Berkeley Stage Company**
●	●					●		●					●	**BoarsHead Theater**
	●			●	●						●		●	**Body Politic**
	●	●		●							●			**The Boston Arts Group**
	●					●					●			**Boston Shakespeare Company**
●	●			●		●		●	●		●			**California Actors Theatre**
●	●	●										●		**The Cambridge Ensemble**
	●			●			●	●			●			**Center Stage**
●		●		●		●	●		●					**The Changing Scene**
●	●	●	●		●	●	●		●			●	●	**Chelsea Theater Center**
	●	●					●	●	●	●		●		**The Children's Theatre Company**
●	●	●	●			●		●	●			●		**Cincinnati Playhouse in the Park**

Yale Repertory Theatre. Ford Rainey, Tony Shalhoub and Clarence Felder in *Buried Child*. Photo: Eugene Cook.

	Professional training	Classes for nonprofessionals	Classes for children	Internships	Student performances	Programs-in-schools	Classroom study materials	Student ticket discount	Senior citizen discount	Other discount(s)	Free ticket distribution	Childrens' Productions	Mainstage touring	Separate touring company
Circle in the Square	●		●		●	●	●	●	●	●				
Circle Repertory Company			●	●			●	●	●					
Cleveland Play House	●		●	●	●	●	●	●	●	●	●	●		
Cohoes Music Hall	●		●	●		●		●	●					
Colonnades Theatre Lab	●		●	●			●	●				●		
The Cricket Theatre				●		●		●	●					
CSC Repertory	●			●				●		●				
Dallas Theater Center	●		●	●		●	●	●			●	●		
Dell'Arte	●					●	●	●			●	●		
Downtown Cabaret Theatre				●		●		●	●		●	●		
East West Players	●	●		●		●		●	●		●	●	●	
El Teatro Campesino	●		●			●	●		●		●	●	●	●
The Empty Space Theatre				●			●	●	●	●	●			●
Ensemble Studio Theatre	●			●			●	●						
Equinox Theatre	●	●		●	●	●			●			●		
The First All Children's Theatre Company	●			●	●	●	●		●	●	●	●		
Florida Studio Theatre		●	●	●		●	●	●	●			●		
Folger Theatre Group				●	●	●		●	●					●
The Frank Silvera Writers' Workshop	●	●							●					
Free Street Theater				●	●	●					●	●	●	●
George Street Playhouse				●	●	●		●	●		●	●		
Germinal Stage Denver				●										
GeVa Theatre			●	●	●	●		●	●	●			●	
Goodman Theatre			●	●	●			●	●	●	●		●	
The Great-American Children's Theatre			●			●	●				●			
Great Lakes Shakespeare Festival	●	●		●	●	●	●	●				●		
The Guthrie Theater		●		●	●	●	●	●	●			●	●	
Hartford Stage Company	●	●		●	●	●	●	●			●		●	
Hartman Theatre Company	●	●		●	●	●	●	●	●		●			
Hawaii Public Theater	●				●						●	●	●	
Hippodrome Theatre Workshop	●	●		●	●	●		●	●			●	●	
Honolulu Theatre for Youth	●			●	●	●	●				●	●	●	
Horse Cave Theatre			●	●	●		●	●	●	●				

	Workshops/Staged readings	Post-performance discussions	Booked-in events	Cabaret	Film series	Lecturers	Poetry readings	Newsletter/Magazine	Script publication	Speakers bureau	Volunteer auxiliary	Programs for the handicapped	Theatre rentals	Other Programs
Circle in the Square	●	●					●							●
Circle Repertory Company	●	●	●				●							
Cleveland Play House	●	●	●		●		●			●	●		●	●
Cohoes Music Hall	●	●					●				●		●	
Colonnades Theatre Lab	●					●	●			●			●	●
The Cricket Theatre	●	●					●			●			●	●
CSC Repertory	●	●					●				●		●	
Dallas Theater Center	●	●	●		●	●	●			●				●
Dell' Arte														●
Downtown Cabaret Theatre			●				●			●	●			●
East West Players	●						●		●					
El Teatro Campesino	●			●	●		●	●						
The Empty Space Theatre	●	●			●		●				●			●
Ensemble Studio Theatre	●	●					●							●
Equinox Theatre	●	●			●	●	●			●			●	●
The First All Children's Theatre Company		●					●							●
Florida Studio Theatre		●	●	●		●	●	●	●	●			●	
Folger Theatre Group		●	●				●		●	●	●	●		●
The Frank Silvera Writers' Workshop	●	●			●		●							●
Free Street Theater		●					●							●
George Street Playhouse		●					●		●	●		●		
Germinal Stage Denver		●												
GeVa Theatre		●					●		●	●		●		●
Goodman Theatre	●	●	●			●	●				●		●	●
The Great-American Children's Theatre			●	●										●
Great Lakes Shakespeare Festival		●		●	●				●					
The Guthrie Theater	●	●	●				●			●		●		●
Hartford Stage Company	●	●	●				●		●	●		●		●
Hartman Theatre Company	●	●	●				●		●	●		●		●
Hawaii Public Theater	●	●												●
Hippodrome Theatre Workshop	●		●				●		●	●		●		●
Honolulu Theatre for Youth							●		●	●				
Horse Cave Theatre	●		●						●	●		●		

245

	Professional training	Classes for nonprofessionals	Classes for children	Internships	Student performances	Programs-in-schools	Classroom study materials	Student ticket discount	Senior citizen discount	Other discount(s)	Free ticket distribution	Childrens' Productions	Mainstage touring	Separate touring company
The Hudson Guild Theatre		●	●	●					●	●	●			
Impossible Ragtime Theatre				●					●	●				
The Independent Eye		●				●		●	●			●		
Indiana Repertory Theatre		●	●	●	●	●	●	●	●		●	●		
INTAR (International Arts Relations)	●			●	●			●	●	●	●	●		
Interart Theatre				●					●	●				
Intiman Theatre Company				●	●		●	●	●					●
The Invisible Theatre		●	●	●	●	●	●		●	●		●	●	
The Iron Clad Agreement		●	●	●	●							●		
Jean Cocteau Repertory	●			●	●			●	●	●	●	●		
Julian Theatre	●	●	●	●	●	●	●	●	●			●		
Karamu Performing Arts Theatre		●	●	●	●	●		●	●	●		●	●	
Lion Theatre Company									●	●				
Living Stage/Arena Stage	●	●	●		●	●								●
Long Wharf Theatre			●	●		●	●	●			●		●	
Looking Glass Theatre		●	●	●		●	●							●
Loretto-Hilton Repertory Theatre			●		●	●	●	●			●	●	●	
Los Angeles Actors' Theatre	●	●		●			●	●	●	●				
Lovelace Theatre Company			●	●	●	●	●	●	●	●				●
The Magic Theatre	●						●	●	●					
Manhattan Theatre Club			●					●	●		●			
Mark Taper Forum				●	●	●	●	●	●	●			●	
McCarter Theatre Company			●	●		●	●			●			●	●
Meadow Brook Theatre					●	●	●					●		
Medicine Show Theatre Ensemble	●			●	●	●	●	●			●	●	●	
Milwaukee Repertory Theater Company				●	●	●	●	●	●			●		
Missouri Repertory Theatre	●	●	●	●		●	●	●	●	●	●			●
Music-Theatre Perf. Group/Lenox Arts Center	●				●			●		●		●		
National Black Theatre	●	●		●				●	●	●	●	●	●	
National Shakespeare Company	●			●			●							●
National Theatre of the Deaf	●	●			●	●						●		
Nebraska Theatre Caravan		●	●		●	●						●		
Negro Ensemble Company	●			●			●			●		●		

	Workshops/Staged readings	Post-performance discussions	Booked-in events	Cabaret	Film series	Lecturers	Poetry readings	Newsletter/Magazine	Script publication	Speakers bureau	Volunteer auxiliary	Programs for the handicapped	Theatre rentals	Other Programs
The Hudson Guild Theatre											●			
Impossible Ragtime Theatre	●	●					●			●		●		●
The Independent Eye		●					●						●	
Indiana Repertory Theatre	●						●		●	●		●		
INTAR (International Arts Relations)	●		●		●	●							●	
Interart Theatre		●	●	●		●							●	
Intiman Theatre Company	●	●	●		●		●			●			●	
The Invisible Theatre	●	●	●				●		●	●		●		
The Iron Clad Agreement	●	●												●
Jean Cocteau Repertory		●					●							
Julian Theatre	●	●	●		●	●	●	●				●		
Karamu Performing Arts Theatre	●	●	●		●	●	●			●				
Lion Theatre Company	●		●									●		
Living Stage/Arena Stage							●			●	●		●	
Long Wharf Theatre	●	●	●				●	●		●		●		
Looking Glass Theatre		●						●	●				●	
Loretto-Hilton Repertory Theatre		●	●				●	●	●					
Los Angeles Actors' Theatre	●	●			●	●								
Lovelace Theatre Company		●			●	●	●							
The Magic Theatre														●
Manhattan Theatre Club	●	●		●		●				●		●		●
Mark Taper Forum	●	●	●				●				●			●
McCarter Theatre Company	●	●	●	●			●			●		●		
Meadow Brook Theatre		●								●		●		●
Medicine Show Theatre Ensemble	●	●												●
Milwaukee Repertory Theater Company	●	●	●		●		●		●	●				●
Missouri Repertory Theatre							●						●	
Music-Theatre Perf. Group/Lenox Arts Center	●	●			●	●	●	●						
National Black Theatre	●	●					●							
National Shakespeare Company														
National Theatre of the Deaf													●	
Nebraska Theatre Caravan														
Negro Ensemble Company	●											●		●

Guthrie Theater. Mark Lamos, Michael Gross and Jeff Chandler in *Rosencrantz and Guildenstern are Dead.* 1976-77 season.

	Professional training	Classes for nonprofessionals	Classes for children	Internships	Student performances	Programs-in-schools	Classroom study materials	Student ticket discount	Senior citizen discount	Other discount(s)	Free ticket distribution	Childrens' Productions	Mainstage touring	Separate touring company
New American Theater		●	●	●	●	●	●	●	●	●		●		●
The New Dramatists				●							●			
New Federal Theatre	●	●						●	●					
New Jersey Shakespeare Festival	●			●	●	●		●		●	●			
The New Playwrights' Theatre of Washington	●	●						●	●	●				
New York Shakespeare Festival				●			●	●	●	●		●		●
North Light Repertory Company		●	●	●			●			●		●		●
Odyssey Theatre Ensemble	●			●	●	●		●		●		●		
Old Creamery Theatre Company	●	●	●	●	●			●		●		●	●	●
Old Globe Theatre			●	●	●			●	●	●		●	●	
Omaha Magic Theatre	●	●	●	●	●	●		●		●		●		
O'Neill Theater Center				●										
Ontological-Hysteric Theater												●		
Oregon Shakespearean Festival			●	●	●	●	●	●	●					
Organic Theater Company	●			●	●			●	●	●		●		●
Otrabanda Company		●			●	●		●	●			●		
PAF Playhouse		●	●	●	●	●	●	●			●		●	●
Padisades Theatre Company		●	●	●	●	●	●					●		
The Paper Bag Players	●			●	●	●	●				●	●	●	
PART (Performing Arts Repertory Theatre)					●	●	●	●				●		
Performance Community				●				●	●		●			●
The Performance Group	●	●	●	●							●	●	●	
Periwinkle Productions				●	●	●	●				●	●		
Philadelphia Drama Guild						●	●	●	●	●				
Phoenix Theater				●		●					●			
Pittsburgh Public Theater				●	●	●	●	●	●			●		
The Play Group	●	●	●			●	●	●				●		
Players State Theatre	●	●	●	●	●	●		●			●			●
Playhouse on the Square	●			●	●	●	●	●			●			●
Playmakers Repertory Company	●	●			●	●		●			●			
Playwrights Horizons					●	●	●							
The Playwrights' Lab	●	●	●	●	●	●	●				●	●	●	●
Portland Stage Company			●	●	●	●	●	●	●	●				●

Workshops	Staged readings	Post-performance discussions	Booked-in events	Cabaret	Film series	Lecturers	Poetry readings	Newsletter/Magazine	Script publication	Speakers bureau	Volunteer auxiliary	Programs for the handicapped	Theatre rentals	Other Programs	
	●	●					●		●	●				●	New American Theater
●	●				●	●	●	●				●		●	The New Dramatists
●		●										●			New Federal Theatre
●	●	●					●		●	●				●	New Jersey Shakespeare Festival
●	●	●			●		●		●	●		●		●	The New Playwrights' Theatre of Washington
●	●		●	●	●	●	●					●		●	New York Shakespeare Festival
●	●				●		●		●	●		●		●	North Light Repertory Company
●	●	●			●		●		●			●			Odyssey Theatre Ensemble
	●						●		●	●					Old Creamery Theatre Company
●		●					●			●				●	Old Globe Theatre
●	●	●			●	●	●		●			●		●	Omaha Magic Theatre
							●			●				●	O'Neill Theater Center
														●	Ontological-Hysteric Theater
●	●				●	●	●	●	●	●		●		●	Oregon Shakespearean Festival
●	●						●					●		●	Organic Theater Company
●	●											●			Otrabanda Company
	●						●			●				●	PAF Playhouse
●	●								●	●	●				Palisades Theatre Company
								●						●	The Paper Bag Players
	●	●													PART (Performing Arts Repertory Theatre)
	●	●										●		●	Performance Community
●	●				●			●						●	The Performance Group
●	●					●			●	●				●	Periwinkle Productions
	●				●			●						●	Philadelphia Drama Guild
●	●						●							●	Phoenix Theatre
●	●				●		●		●	●				●	Pittsburgh Public Theater
●		●				●						●		●	The Play Group
	●						●		●	●		●			Players State Theatre
●	●						●		●	●	●	●			Playhouse on the Square
	●				●		●		●	●					Playmakers Repertory Company
●	●						●		●			●			Playwrights Horizons
●	●	●				●		●	●			●		●	The Playwrights' Lab
●	●				●				●	●		●		●	Portland Stage Company

	Professional training	Classes for nonprofessionals	Classes for children	Internships	Student performances	Programs-in-schools	Classroom study materials	Student ticket discount	Senior citizen discount	Other discount(s)	Free ticket distribution	Childrens' Productions	Mainstage touring	Separate touring company
The Proposition Workshop	●	●			●						●	●	●	
Provisional Theatre	●	●		●	●			●	●	●	●		●	
Puerto Rican Traveling Theatre Company		●	●	●	●	●		●	●		●		●	
The Puppet Workshop		●	●	●		●	●						●	
Repertorio Español	●			●	●	●	●	●	●				●	
Richard Morse Mime Theatre	●	●	●		●	●		●	●	●	●	●	●	●
The Ridiculous Theatrical Company							●	●	●	●				●
St. Nicholas Theater Company	●	●	●	●							●		●	
Seattle Repertory Theatre	●			●	●	●	●	●	●	●	●	●	●	●
Soho Repertory Theatre				●				●			●			
South Coast Repertory	●		●	●	●	●	●		●	●		●		●
Stage One: The Louisville Children's Theatre		●	●	●	●	●	●			●			●	
Stage South		●	●			●	●	●	●			●	●	
StageWest		●	●	●	●	●	●	●	●	●	●			
The Street Theater	●	●	●	●		●							●	
Studio Arena Theatre	●	●	●	●		●	●	●	●	●	●		●	
Syracuse Stage				●	●	●	●	●	●	●	●	●		●
Theatre Arts of West Virginia				●		●	●	●			●	●	●	
Theatre by the Sea		●	●	●		●	●	●	●	●			●	
Theatre Express		●		●		●			●		●		●	
Theater for the New City		●				●				●	●	●		●
Theater of the Open Eye			●	●	●	●	●	●		●	●	●	●	●
Theatre X		●				●	●	●	●	●	●		●	
Travel Light Theatre	●			●	●	●		●	●	●	●			●
Trinity Square Repertory Company	●			●	●	●	●	●	●	●				
Victory Gardens Theater	●	●		●			●	●					●	●
Virginia Museum Theatre	●	●		●	●	●		●		●				●
Wayside Theatre	●	●		●	●	●	●	●						●
The Whole Theatre Company	●	●	●			●		●	●	●	●			
Williamstown Theatre Festival	●	●		●						●	●			●
The Wisdom Bridge Theatre				●				●	●	●				
Worcester Foothills Theatre Company	●	●	●	●	●				●					
Yale Repertory Theatre	●			●	●	●	●	●	●	●	●			

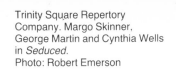

Trinity Square Repertory Company. Margo Skinner, George Martin and Cynthia Wells in *Seduced*.
Photo: Robert Emerson

	Workshops/Staged readings	Post-performance discussions	Booked-in events	Cabaret	Film series	Lecturers	Poetry readings	Newsletter/Magazine	Script publication	Speakers bureau	Volunteer auxiliary	Programs for the handicapped	Theatre rentals	Other Programs
The Proposition Workshop	●	●		●									●	
Provisional Theatre	●	●				●	●						●	●
Puerto Rican Traveling Theatre Company	●					●								
The Puppet Workshop		●												●
Repertorio Español		●	●									●		●
Richard Morse Mime Theatre		●					●			●		●		●
The Ridiculous Theatrical Company		●												
St. Nicholas Theater Company	●	●	●	●		●		●		●		●		
Seattle Repertory Theatre		●	●		●		●	●	●			●		●
Soho Repertory Theatre		●					●							●
South Coast Repertory	●	●				●	●	●	●					●
Stage One: The Louisville Children's Theatre									●			●		●
Stage South		●					●	●	●			●		●
StageWest	●						●					●		
The Street Theater		●				●								●
Studio Arena Theatre		●		●			●	●	●			●		●
Syracuse Stage	●	●		●			●	●	●			●		●
Theatre Arts of West Virginia	●	●	●	●			●	●	●					
Theatre by the Sea	●	●	●	●		●	●	●		●		●		●
Theatre Express	●	●					●							
Theater for the New City			●	●		●								●
Theater of the Open Eye	●	●	●			●								●
Theatre X		●	●			●								
Travel Light Theatre	●	●	●			●						●		
Trinity Square Repertory Company	●	●	●			●	●					●		
Victory Gardens Theater	●	●		●				●	●	●	●	●		●
Virginia Museum Theatre	●	●	●	●	●		●	●	●	●	●	●		●
Wayside Theatre		●						●						
The Whole Theatre Company	●	●	●			●	●	●	●			●		●
Williamstown Theatre Festival	●		●				●		●					●
The Wisdom Bridge Theatre		●	●					●				●		
Worcester Foothills Theatre Company		●		●			●					●		
Yale Repertory Theatre	●	●	●	●	●		●		●			●		●

Theatre on Tour

The following guide is intended for use by sponsoring organizations in locating theatres available for touring in their area. One asterisk (*) indicates that the theatre tours special productions for children; two asterisks indicate dual programming for children and adults. No asterisk indicates general programming for adult audiences. This guide should be used in conjunction with the Regional Index on page 256.

National and International Touring

A Contemporary Theatre*
The Acting Company**
American Conservatory Theatre
Barter Theatre**
The Cambridge Ensemble**
Colonnades Theatre Lab
Dallas Theater Center**
El Teatro Campesino**
The First All Children's Theatre Company*
Florida Studio Theatre**
Folger Theatre Group
Free Street Theater
Goodman Theatre
The Independent Eye
The Iron Clad Agreement**
Karamu House**
Living Stage**
Looking Glass Theatre
Long Wharf Theatre
Lovelace Theatre Company*
Medicine Show Theatre Ensemble**
Music-Theatre Performing Group/Lenox Arts Center**
National Black Theatre**
National Shakespeare Company**
National Theatre of the Deaf**
Negro Ensemble Company
New York Shakespeare Festival
Odyssey Theatre Ensemble
Omaha Magic Theatre**
Ontological-Hysteric Theater
Organic Theater Company
Otrabanda Company**
Palisades Theatre Company**
The Paper Bag Players*
PART (Performing Arts Repertory Theatre)*
The Performance Group
Periwinkle Productions*
The Play Group**
The Proposition Workshop**
Provisional Theatre**
The Puppet Workshop**
Repertorio Español
Richard Morse Mime Theatre**
The Ridiculous Theatrical Company
Studio Arena Theatre
Theatre X**

Statewide and regional touring

Academy Theatre**
A Contemporary Theatre*
The Acting Company**
Actors Theatre of Louisville**
Actors Theatre of St. Paul
Alabama Shakespeare Festival
Alliance Theatre/Atlanta Children's Theatre*
AMAS Repertory Theatre**
American Conservatory Theatre
American Theatre Company**
Arizona Theatre Company
Arkansas Repertory Theatre
Asolo State Theater*
Barter Theatre**
Body Politic**
Boston Arts Group*
California Actors Theatre*
The Cambridge Ensemble**
Center Stage*
The Changing Scene**
Cincinnati Playhouse in the Park
Cleveland Playhouse
Colonnades Theatre Lab
Dallas Theater Center**
Dell'Arte**
East West Players
El Teatro Campesino**
The Empty Space Theatre**
Equinox Theatre
The First All Children's Theatre Company*
Florida Studio Theatre**
Folger Theatre Group
Free Street Theater**
GeVa Theatre**
Goodman Theatre
Great Lakes Shakespeare Festival**
The Guthrie Theater
Hartford Stage Company**
Hawaii Public Theatre**
Hippodrome Theatre Workshop**
Honolulu Theatre for Youth**
The Independent Eye
Indiana Repertory Theatre
Intiman Theatre Company*
The Invisible Theatre**
The Iron Clad Agreement**
Julian Theatre**
Karamu House**
Living Stage**
Looking Glass Theatre*
Loretto-Hilton Theatre**
Lovelace Theatre Company*
Mark Taper Forum**
McCarter Theatre Company**
Meadow Brook Theatre*
Medicine Show Theatre Ensemble**

Milwaukee Repertory Theater Company**
Missouri Repertory Theatre**
Music-Theatre Performing Group/Lenox Arts Center**
National Black Theatre**
National Shakespeare Company**
National Theatre of the Deaf**
Nebraska Theatre Caravan
Negro Ensemble Company
New American Theater**
New York Shakespeare Festival
North Light Repertory Company
Odyssey Theatre Ensemble
Old Creamery Theatre Company**
Old Globe Theatre**
Omaha Magic Theatre**
Ontological-Hysteric Theater
Organic Theater Company
Otrabanda Company**
PAF Playhouse*
Palisades Theatre Company**
The Paper Bag Players*
PART (Performing Arts Repertory Theatre)*
Performance Community
The Performance Group
Periwinkle Productions*
Players State Theatre**
The Play Group**
Playhouse on the Square
The Playwrights' Lab*
Portland Stage Company*
The Proposition Workshop**
Provisional Theatre**
Puerto Rican Traveling Theatre Company
The Puppet Workshop**
Repertorio Español
Richard Morse Mime Theatre**
The Ridiculous Theatrical Company
St. Nicholas Theater Company**
Seattle Repertory Theatre**
South Coast Repertory*
Stage One: The Louisville Children's Theatre*
Stage South**
The Street Theater**
Studio Arena Theatre
Syracuse Stage**
Theatre Arts of West Virginia**
Theatre by the Sea**
Theatre Express
Theater for the New City**
Theater of the Open Eye*
Theatre X
Travel Light Theatre
Victory Gardens Theater
Virginia Museum Theatre**
Wayside Theatre*
Williamstown Theatre Festival**

The Acting Company. Frances
Conroy and Mary Lou Rosato in
*Mother Courage and her
Children.* Photo: Bert Andrews.

Chronology of Resident Theatres

The following list is intended to give an overview of the remarkable growth of the nonprofit professional theatre movement, especially in the last ten years. Years refer to dates of first public performance, or, in a few cases, the company's formal incorporation.

1915
Cleveland Play House

1924
Karamu House

1925
Goodman Theatre

1933
Barter Theatre

1935
Oregon Shakespearean Festival

1937
Old Globe Theatre

1946
Stage One: The Louisville Children's Theatre

1949
The New Dramatists

1950
Arena Stage

1951
Circle in the Square

1953
Phoenix Theatre

1954
Milwaukee Repertory Theater Company
New York Shakespeare Festival

1955
Honolulu Theatre for Youth
Virginia Museum Theatre
Williamstown Theatre Festival

1956
Academy Theatre
Philadelphia Drama Guild

1958
The Paper Bag Players

1959
Dallas Theater Center

1960
Asolo State Theater
Cincinnati Playhouse in the Park

1961
The Children's Theatre Company
Theatre Arts of West Virginia

1962
Great Lakes Shakespeare Festival
Wayside Theatre

1963
Center Stage
The Guthrie Theater
National Shakespeare Company
New Jersey Shakespeare Festival
Periwinkle Productions
Seattle Repertory Theatre

1964
Actors Theatre of Louisville
American Place Theatre
Hartford Stage Company
Lovelace Theatre Company
Missouri Repertory Theatre
O'Neill Theater Center
South Coast Repertory
Theatre by the Sea
Trinity Square Repertory Company

1965
A Contemporary Theatre
American Conservatory Theatre
Chelsea Theater Center
East West Players
El Teatro Campesino
Julian Theatre
Long Wharf Theatre
Looking Glass Theatre
Studio Arena Theatre

1966
Arizona Theatre Company
INTAR (International Arts Relations)
Living Stage/Arena Stage
Loretto-Hilton Repertory Theatre
Meadow Brook Theatre
PAF Playhouse
Yale Repertory Theatre

1967
CSC Repertory
The Magic Theatre
Mark Taper Forum
National Theatre of the Deaf
Negro Ensemble Company
Omaha Magic Theatre
PART (Performing Arts Repertory Theatre)
The Performance Group
Puerto Rican Traveling Theatre Company
The Ridiculous Theatrical Company
StageWest

1968
Atlanta Children's Theatre
Berkeley Repertory Theatre
The Changing Scene
The Hudson Guild Theatre
National Black Theatre
Odyssey Theatre Ensemble
Ontological-Hysteric Theater
Playhouse on the Square
The Proposition Workshop

1969
Alliance Theatre Company
AMAS Repertory Theatre
Body Politic Theatre
Circle Repertory Company
The First All Children's Theatre Company
Free Street Theater
Organic Theater Company
Performance Community
Repertorio Español
Theatre X

1970
American Theatre Company
BoarsHead Theater
Folger Theatre Group
Interart Theatre
Manhattan Theatre Club
Medicine Show Theatre Ensemble
Music-Theatre Performing Group/
    Lenox Arts Center
New Federal Theatre
The Street Theater
Theater for the New City

1971
The Cricket Theatre
Dell'Arte
The Empty Space Theatre
Ensemble Studio Theatre
The Invisible Theatre
Jean Cocteau Repertory
Old Creamery Theatre Company
Otrabanda Company
Playwrights Horizons
The Playwrights' Lab

1972
The Acting Company
Alabama Shakespeare Festival
GeVa Theatre
Indiana Repertory Theatre
Intiman Theatre Company
McCarter Theatre Company
New American Theater
The New Playwrights' Theatre of Washington
Provisional Theatre
The Puppet Workshop
Theater of the Open Eye

1973
The Boston Arts Group
The Cambridge Ensemble
Florida Studio Theatre
The Frank Silvera Writers' Workshop
Hippodrome Theatre Workshop
Palisades Theatre Company
The Play Group
Stage South
The Whole Theatre Company

1974
Berkeley Stage Company
California Actors Theatre
Cohoes Music Hall
George Street Playhouse
Germinal Stage Denver
Hartman Theatre Company
Impossible Ragtime Theatre
The Independent Eye
Lion Theatre Company
North Light Repertory Company
Pittsburgh Public Theater
Portland Stage Company
St. Nicholas Theater Company
Syracuse Stage
Travel Light Theatre
Victory Gardens Theater
The Wisdom Bridge Theatre
Worcester Foothills Theatre Company

1975
American Stage Festival
Boston Arts Group
Boston Shakespeare Company
Downtown Cabaret Theatre
Los Angeles Actors' Theatre
Richard Morse Mime Theatre
Soho Repertory Theatre
Theatre Express

1976
Alaska Repertory Theatre
Arkansas Repertory Theatre
BAM Theater Company
Equinox Theatre
The Great-American Children's Theatre
    Company
Hawaii Public Theater
The Iron Clad Agreement
Nebraska Theatre Caravan
Playmakers Repertory Theatre

1977
Actors Theatre of St. Paul
Horse Cave Theatre
Players State Theatre

Hartman Theatre *Tartuffe*.
Photo: Gerry Goodstein.

Name and Title Index

The following index includes all production titles, dramatists (including adaptors, translators, composers and librettists), artistic directors, administrative directors and theatre founders from pages 3 through 168.

268

The names of several recently-appointed artistic and managing directors were added to certain profiles just before press time; it was unfortunately impossible to include these last minute changes in the body of the index.

Honolulu Theatre for Youth. Bain
Boehlke in *The Legend of Sleepy
Hollow.* Photo: Mazeppa Costa.

About TCG

Theatre Communications Group is the national service organization for the nonprofit professional theatre, established to provide a ~~l forum and communications network for ~~ion and to respond to the needs of ~~heatre and artists for centralized

~~ 1961 under a Ford Foundation ~~CG offers a variety of artistic, ~~nistrative and informational programs and ~~vices assisting noncommercial professional ~~heatre organizations, professional theatre training institutions and individual theatre artists, administrators and technicians.

In addition to its publications, TCG services include a casting service, artist and personnel referral services, annual national auditions, national fellowships in performing arts

management, playwright services, research and management services, subscription consultation, workshops and national conferences.

Along with *Theatre Profiles,* TCG offers a full line of resources in print for theatre professionals, including the monthly feature newsletter *Theatre Communications; Subscribe Now!,* Danny Newman's best-selling handbook outlining the techniques of Dynamic Subscription Promotion; the pocket-sized *Theatre Directory; Information for Playwrights* and the annual *TCG Survey.* For a complete catalog of current offerings, write to the Publications Department, Theatre Communications Group, Inc., 355 Lexington Ave., New York, NY 10017.